PHILIP'S ROAD ATLAS

COMPACT BRITAIN

Skyscan Photolibrary / Alamy

CONTENTS

II **Route planning maps** with key to map pages

VIII **Key to road map symbols**

2 **Road maps at 3.3 miles to 1 inch**

289 **Index** to road maps of Great Britain

www.philips-maps.co.uk

First published in 2006 by Philip's
a division of Octopus Publishing Group Ltd
Carmelite House, 50 Victoria Embankment
London EC4Y 0DZ
An Hachette UK Company
www.hachette.co.uk

Sixth edition 2016
First impression 2016

ISBN 978-1-84907-417-9

Cartography by Philip's
Copyright © 2016 Philip's

The representation in this atlas of any road, drive or track is no evidence of the existence of a right of way.

Information for National Parks, Areas of Outstanding Natural Beauty, National Trails and Country Parks in Wales supplied by the Countryside Council for Wales.

Information for National Parks, Areas of Outstanding Natural Beauty, National Trails and Country Parks in England supplied by Natural England.

Data for Regional Parks, Long Distance Footpaths and Country Parks in Scotland provided by Scottish Natural Heritage.

Gaelic name forms used in the Western Isles provided by Comhairle nan Eilean.

Data for the National Nature Reserves in England provided by Natural England.

Data for the National Nature Reserves in Wales provided by Countryside Council for Wales. Darparwyd data'n ymwneud â Gwarchodfeydd Natur Cenedlaethol Cymru gan Gyngor Cefn Gwlad Cymru.

Information on the location of National Nature Reserves in Scotland was provided by Scottish Natural Heritage.

Data for National Scenic Areas in Scotland provided by the Scottish Executive Office. Crown copyright material is reproduced with the permission of the Controller of HMSO and the Queen's Printer for Scotland. Licence number C02W0003960.

Printed in China

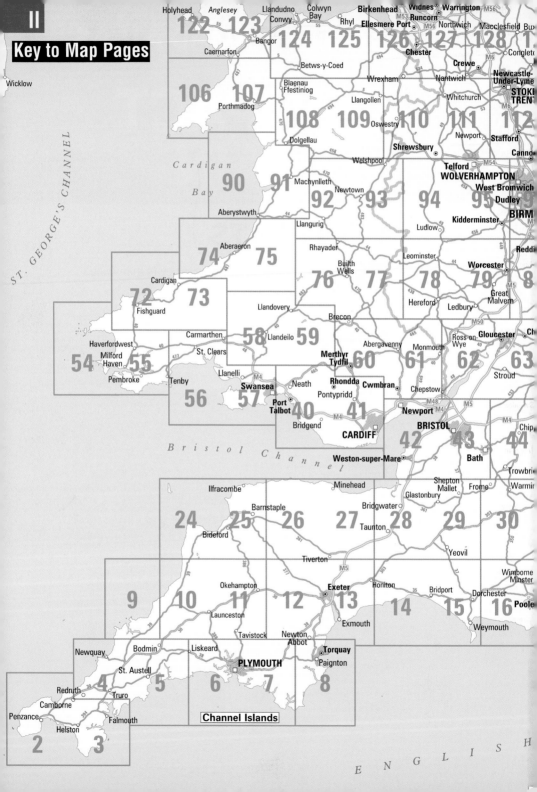

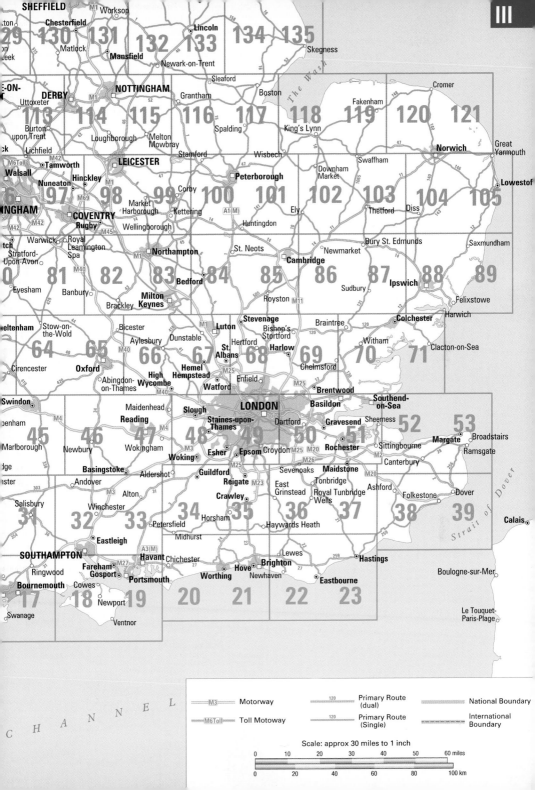

III

SHEFFIELD
Worksop
Chesterfield
Matlock
Lincoln
29 **130** **131** **132** **133** **134** **135**
Mansfield
Newark-on-Trent
Skegness

Sleaford
Grantham
Boston
The Wash
Cromer
Fakenham
E-ON-
DERBY
NOTTINGHAM
Uttoxeter
Burton
upon Trent
Lichfield
113 **114** **115** **116** **117** **118** **119** **120** **121**
Loughborough
Melton
Mowbray
Spalding
King's Lynn
Norwich
Great
Yarmouth
Tamworth
Stamford
Wisbech
Downham
Market
Swaffham
LEICESTER
Walsall
Nuneaton Hinckley
Peterborough
Lowestof
97 **98** **99** **100** **101** **102** **103** **104** **105**
Corby
Market
Harborough
Ely
Thetford
Diss
NGHAM
COVENTRY
Rugby
Kettering
Huntingdon
Bury St. Edmunds
Saxmundham
Wellingborough
Warwick
Royal
Leamington
Spa
Northampton
St. Neots
Newmarket
Cambridge
Ipswich
0 **81** **82** **83** **84** **85** **86** **87** **88** **89**
Stratford-
Upon-Avon
Bedford
Sudbury
Felixstowe
Evesham
Banbury
Milton
Keynes
Royston
Harwich
Brackley
Stow-on-
the-Wold
Bicester
Luton
Stevenage
Bishop's
Stortford
Braintree
Colchester
64 **65** **66** **67** **68** **69** **70** **71**
heltenham
Aylesbury
Dunstable
Hertford
Harlow
Witham
Clacton-on-Sea
Cirencester
Oxford
St.
Albans
Chelmsford
Abingdon-
on-Thames
High
Wycombe
Hemel
Hempstead
Watford
Enfield
Brentwood
Swindon
Maidenhead
Slough
LONDON
Basildon
Southend-
on-Sea
Reading
Staines-upon-
Thames
Dartford
Gravesend
Sheerness
45 **46** **47** **48** **49** **50** **51** **52** **53**
penham
Newbury
Wokingham
Esher
Epsom
Croydon
Rochester
Sittingbourne
Margate
Broadstairs
Marlborough
Woking
Canterbury
Ramsgate
dge
Basingstoke
Aldershot
Guildford
Sevenoaks
Maidstone
nster
Andover
Reigate
East
Grinstead
Tonbridge
Ashford
Salisbury
Alton
Crawley
Royal Tunbridge
Wells
Folkestone
Dover
31 **32** **33** **34** **35** **36** **37** **38** **39**
Winchester
Horsham
Haywards Heath
Hastings
Calais
Eastleigh
Petersfield
Midhurst
Lewes
SOUTHAMPTON
Havant
Chichester
Brighton
Boulogne-sur-Mer
Ringwood
Fareham
Gosport
Hove
Newhaven
Eastbourne
Bournemouth
Cowes
Portsmouth
Worthing
17 **18** **19** **20** **21** **22** **23**
Swanage
Newport
Ventnor
Le Touquet-
Paris-Plage

Strait of Dover

C H A N N E L

M3 — Motorway
M6Toll — Toll Motoway
120 — Primary Route (dual)
120 — Primary Route (Single)
National Boundary
International Boundary

Scale: approx 30 miles to 1 inch

0 10 20 30 40 50 60 miles
0 20 40 60 80 100 km

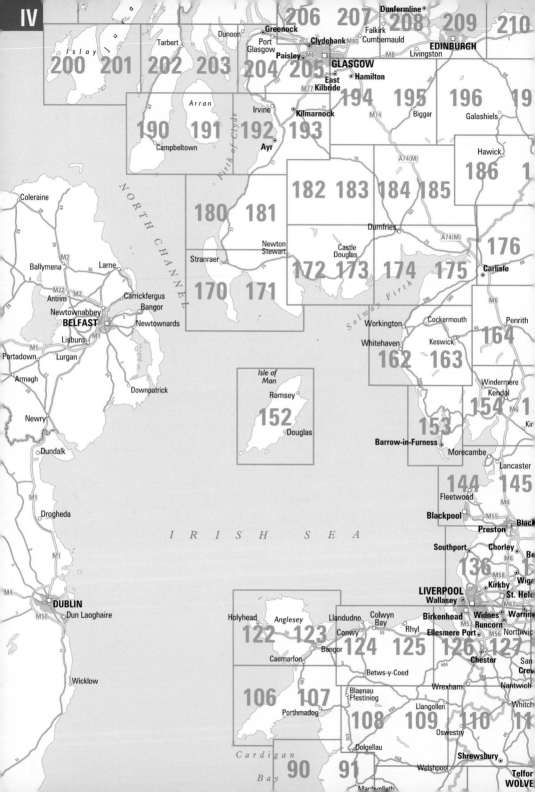

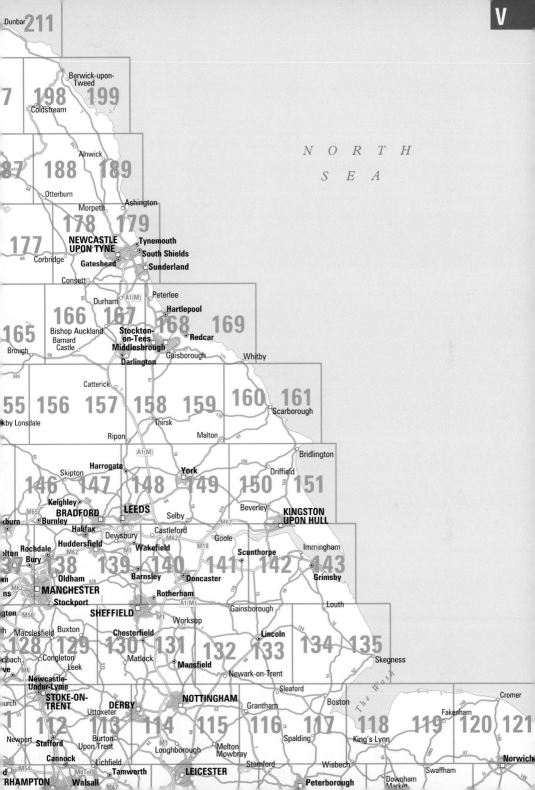

Dunbar **211**

Berwick-upon-Tweed

7 **198** **199**
Coldstream

N O R T H

S E A

Alnwick

187 **188** **189**

Otterburn

Morpeth   Ashington

178 **179**

177 **NEWCASTLE UPON TYNE** Tynemouth
Corbridge   **South Shields**
Gateshead **Sunderland**

Consett

A1(M)   Peterlee

Durham   Hartlepool

166 **167** **168** **169**
Bishop Auckland   **Stockton-on-Tees** Redcar
165 Barnard   **Middlesbrough**
Brough   Castle   **Darlington**   Guisborough   Whitby

Catterick

55 **156** **157** **158** **159** **160** **161**
kby Lonsdale   Scarborough

Thirsk

Ripon   Malton

A1(M)   Bridlington

Harrogate   Driffield

Skipton

146 **147** **148** **149** **150** **151**
Keighley   York   Beverley
BRADFORD **LEEDS**   **KINGSTON**
kburn   Burnley   Halifax   Selby   **UPON HULL**

Rochdale   **Huddersfield** Dewsbury   Castleford   Goole   Immingham
lton   Bury   **Wakefield**
37 **38** **139** **140** **141** **142** **143**
ns   Oldham   **Barnsley** **Doncaster** **Scunthorpe** **Grimsby**

MANCHESTER
Stockport   Rotherham   Louth

Macclesfield   Buxton   **SHEFFIELD** Worksop   Gainsborough

128 **129** **130** **131** **132** **133** **134** **135**
bach   Congleton   **Chesterfield** Lincoln   Skegness
ve   Leek   Matlock   **Mansfield**
Newcastle-   Newark-on-Trent
Under-Lyme   Sleaford

STOKE-ON-   **NOTTINGHAM**   Boston   Cromer
TRENT   **DERBY**   Grantham   Fakenham
1   Uttoxeter
112 **113** **114** **115** **116** **117** **118** **119** **120** **121**
Newport   **Stafford** Burton   Spalding   King's Lynn
Upon Trent   Melton
Cannock   Loughborough   Mowbray   Wisbech   Swaffham   Norwich
Lichfield   Stamford   Downham
d   **Tamworth** **LEICESTER**   Market
RHAMPTON **Walsall**   **Peterborough**

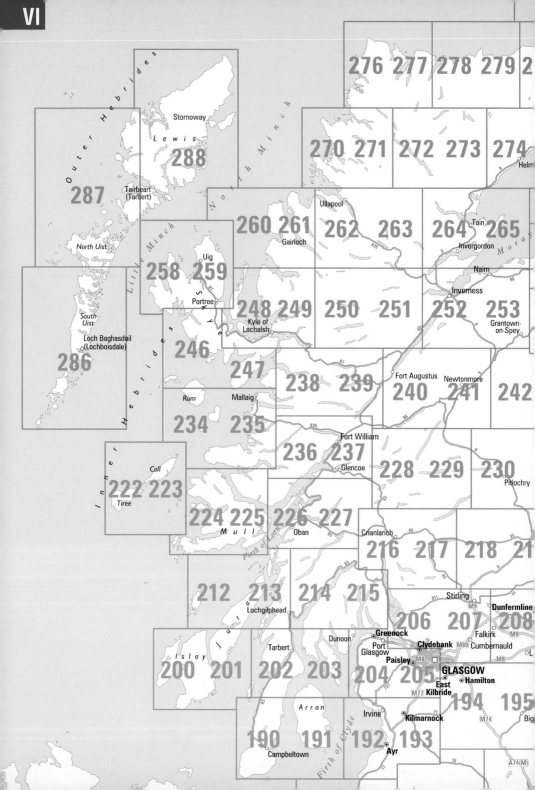

Pentland Firth

Thurso

80 **281**

Wick

275

sdale

Firth

266 **267**
Elgin

Keith

268 **269**
Fraserburgh

Peterhead

254 **255** **256** **257**
Ellon

Inverurie

243 **244** **245**
Aberdeen

Stonehaven

231 **232** **233**
Brechin
Forfar
Montrose

Dundee

Perth
9 **220** **221**
St. Andrews

Kirkcaldy

Firth of Forth

209 **210** **211**
EDINBURGH
vingston
Dunbar

Berwick-upon-
Tweed

196 **197** **198** **199**
Galashiels
Coldstream
gar

Hawick
Alnwick

186 **187** **188** **189**

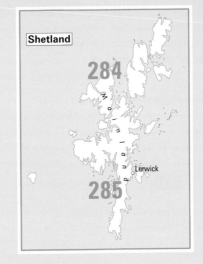

Shetland

284

Mainland

Lerwick

285

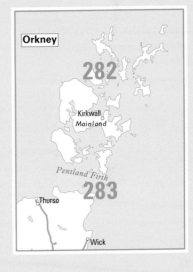

Orkney

282

Kirkwall
Mainland

Pentland Firth

283
Thurso

Wick

*NORTH
SEA*

Road map symbols

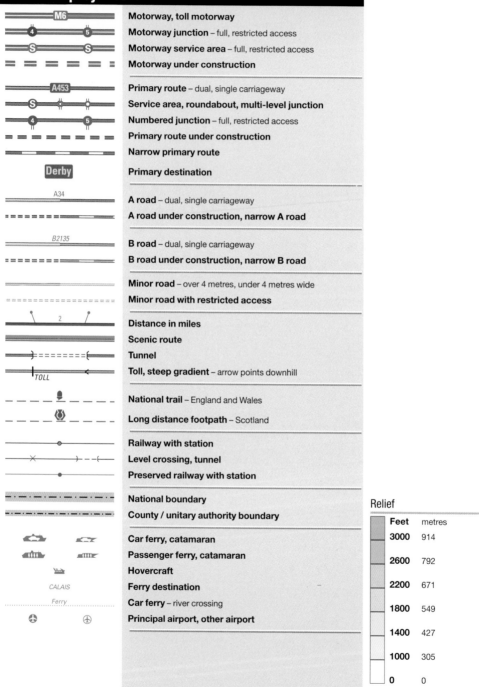

	Motorway, toll motorway
	Motorway junction – full, restricted access
	Motorway service area – full, restricted access
	Motorway under construction
	Primary route – dual, single carriageway
	Service area, roundabout, multi-level junction
	Numbered junction – full, restricted access
	Primary route under construction
	Narrow primary route
	Primary destination
	A road – dual, single carriageway
	A road under construction, narrow A road
	B road – dual, single carriageway
	B road under construction, narrow B road
	Minor road – over 4 metres, under 4 metres wide
	Minor road with restricted access
	Distance in miles
	Scenic route
	Tunnel
	Toll, steep gradient – arrow points downhill
	National trail – England and Wales
	Long distance footpath – Scotland
	Railway with station
	Level crossing, tunnel
	Preserved railway with station
	National boundary
	County / unitary authority boundary
	Car ferry, catamaran
	Passenger ferry, catamaran
	Hovercraft
	Ferry destination
	Car ferry – river crossing
	Principal airport, other airport

Relief

Feet	metres
3000	914
2600	792
2200	671
1800	549
1400	427
1000	305
0	0

Road map symbols

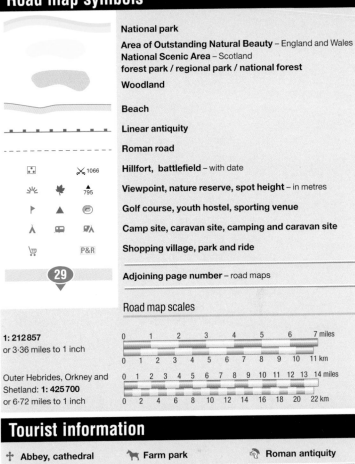

National park

Area of Outstanding Natural Beauty – England and Wales
National Scenic Area – Scotland
forest park / regional park / national forest

Woodland

Beach

Linear antiquity

Roman road

Hillfort, battlefield – with date

Viewpoint, nature reserve, spot height – in metres

Golf course, youth hostel, sporting venue

Camp site, caravan site, camping and caravan site

Shopping village, park and ride

Adjoining page number – road maps

Road map scales

1: 212857
or 3·36 miles to 1 inch

0	1	2	3	4	5	6	7 miles

0	1	2	3	4	5	6	7	8	9	10	11 km

Outer Hebrides, Orkney and
Shetland: **1: 425700**
or 6·72 miles to 1 inch

0	1	2	3	4	5	6	7	8	9	10	11	12	13	14 miles

0	2	4	6	8	10	12	14	16	18	20	22 km

Tourist information

✝ Abbey, cathedral or priory

🗿 Ancient monument

🐟 Aquarium

📷 Art gallery

🦅 Bird collection or aviary

🏰 Castle

⛪ Church

Country park
🏕 England and Wales
🏕 Scotland

🐎 Farm park

❀ Garden

⛵ Historic ship

🏠 House

🏡 House and garden

▨ Motor racing circuit

🏛 Museum

🅿 Picnic area

🚂 Preserved railway

🏇 Race course

🐎 Roman antiquity

🦌 Safari park

🎡 Theme park

Tourist information
ℹ centre open all year
ℹ open seasonally

🐘 Zoo

✦ Other place of interest

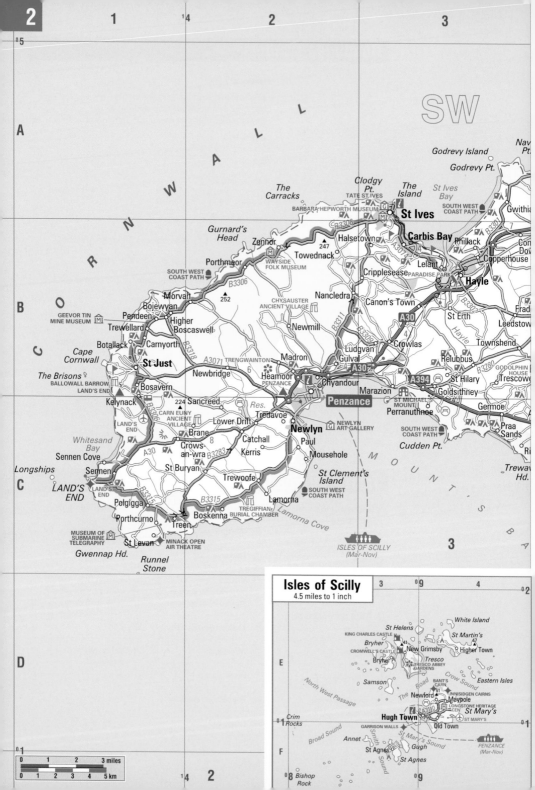

2

SW

CORNWALL

Navax Pt.

Godrevy Island
Godrevy Pt.

St Ives Bay

The Carracks

Clodgy Pt.
TATE ST IVES
The Island

BARBARA HEPWORTH MUSEUM

St Ives
SOUTH WEST COAST PATH
Gwithia

Gurnard's Head

Zennor

Halsetown

Carbis Bay
Rhillack

Con Dov

247

Towednack

A3071
Lelant

Cripplesease
PARADISE PARK

Copperhouse

Porthmeor

WAYSIDE FOLK MUSEUM

Hayle

B3306

Morvah

252

CHYSAUSTER ANCIENT VILLAGE

Nancledra

Canon's Town

St Erth

Leedstow

Frad

Bojewyan

Newmill

GEEVOR TIN MINE MUSEUM

Pendeen

Higher Boscaswell

Ludgvan

Crowlas

Townshend

Trewellard

B3311

Relubbus

GODOLPHIN HOUSE

Carnyorth

Gulval

St Hilary

Trescobe

Botallack

Madron

A30

Goldsithney

Cape Cornwall

TRENGWAINTON

6

St Just

Newbridge

Heamoor
PENZANCE

Chyandour

Marazion

ST MICHAEL'S MOUNT

Perranuthnoe

Germoe

The Brisons

BALLOWALL BARROW
LAND'S END

Bosavern

Penzance

NEWLYN ART GALLERY

SOUTH WEST COAST PATH

Cudden Pt.

Praa Sands

Kelynack

224

Sancreed

Res.

Tredavoe

Newlyn

Ri

Trewa Hd.

Whitesand Bay

CARN EUNY ANCIENT VILLAGE

Lower Drift

Brane

Paul

LAND'S END

A30

8

Catchall

Kerris

Mousehole

M O U N T ' S   B A

Longships

Sennen Cove

Crows-an-wra

B3283

St Buryan

Trewoofe

St Clement's Island

SOUTH WEST COAST PATH

Sennen

LAND'S END

LAND'S END

Polgigga

B3315

Lamorna

B3315

Porthcurno

Boskenna

TREGIFFIAN BURIAL CHAMBER

Lamorna Cove

ISLES OF SCILLY
(Mar-Nov)

3

MUSEUM OF SUBMARINE TELEGRAPHY

Treen

St Levan

MINACK OPEN AIR THEATRE

Gwennap Hd.

Runnel Stone

Isles of Scilly
4.5 miles to 1 inch

White Island

St Helens

KING CHARLES CASTLE

Bryher

New Grimsby

St Martin's

Higher Town

CROMWELL'S CASTLE

Bryher

Tresco
TRESCO ABBEY GARDENS

Crow Sound

North West Passage

Samson

BANTS CARN

INNISIDGEN CAIRNS

Eastern Isles

The Road

Newford

Maypole

LONGSTONE HERITAGE CEN

St Mary's

Crim Rocks

Broad Sound

Hugh Town

GARRISON WALLS

Old Town

ST MARY'S

St Mary's Sound

PENZANCE
(Mar-Nov)

Annet

St Agnes

Smith Sound

Gugh

St Agnes

Bishop Rock

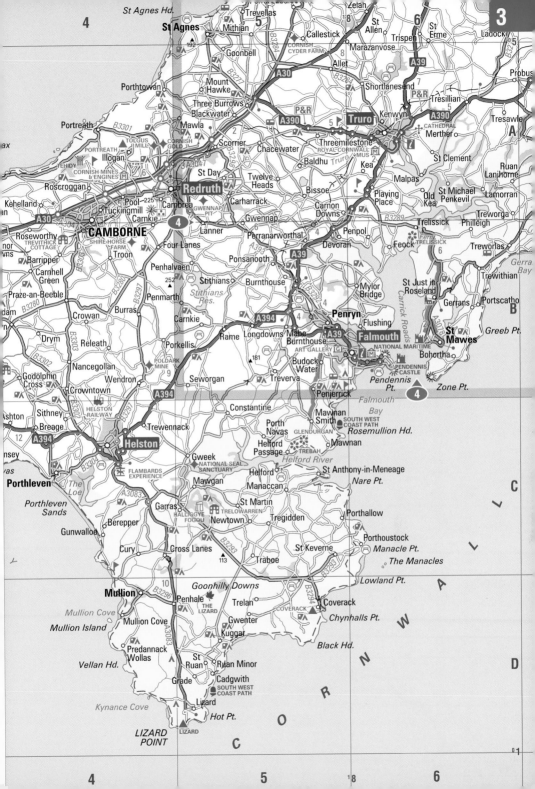

8 A38 1 A8

NEWTON ABBOT

West Ogwell 12 2

Wolborough

SHALDON WILDLIFE TRUST

Combeinteignhead 3 H WEST COAST PATH

SO Stokeinteignhead 13

3 0 4

East Ogwell PRICKLY BALL FARM DECOY PLANT WORLD

BABBACOMBE BAY

0 7 0 7

Woodland Denbury Abbotskerswell Coffinswell

Kingskerswell Maidencombe

Watcombe

A

Forder Grn. Torbryan Ipplepen North Whilborough Barton

MODEL VILLAGE Babbacombe

Landscove BUCKFAST BUTTERFLIES & DARTMOOR OTTER SANCTUARY Broadhempston Compton COMPTON CASTLE Shiphay

Torquay KENT'S CAVERN PREHISTORIC CAVES

WELL FARM & LIFE CENTRE Staverton A380 Cockington TORRE TORRE ABBEY Wellswood Hope's Nose

Dartington Littlehempston DARTINGTON HALL Marldon OLDWAY MANSION Hollicombe LIVING COASTS

A385 DARTINGTON CIDER PRESS CENTRE Shinner's Bridge SOUTH DEVON RAILWAY BERRY POMEROY CASTLE Blagdon T o r b a y

Rattery Cott CASTLE Totnes Berry Pomeroy KIRKHAM Paignton DARTMOUTH STEAM RAILWAY

Tigley A385 Collaton St Mary ZOO TORBAY

7 Belsford TOR BAY

Harberton Ashprington Stoke Gabriel Goodrington

GOLDEN HIND Brixham Berry Head

combe Cornworthy Galmpton Churston Ferrers BERRY HEAD St Mary's Bay

Harbertonford Tuckenhay GREENWAY BERRY HEAD

B Crabadon Washbourne Dittisham RIVER DART Sharkham Pt.

SX SY

Halwell Allaleigh Capton Hillhead

Moreleigh A3122 WOODLANDS LEISURE PARK Dartmouth NEWCOMEN ENGINE HOUSE

Woodford Blackawton A3122 Kingswear Scabbacombe Hd.

Millcombe BAYARDS COVE FORT Warfleet COLETON FISHACRE

dleigh 6 Bowden DARTMOUTH CASTLE Mew Stone

East Allington Stoke Fleming

Goveton Strete Blackpool

C Harleston Sherford Slapton 9 SOUTH WEST COAST PATH

ingsbridge Frittiscombe SLAPTON LEY

Frogmore 7 Chillington Stokenham START BAY

Kernborough Torcross

South Pool Beeson

Beesands

7 Kellaton

East Portlemouth Hallsands

South Allington

START POINT

D East Prawle Lannacombe Bay

Prawle Pt.

S O U T H   D E V O N

PECKS M AND A

0 3 0 3

0   1   2   3 miles
0   1   2   3   4   5 km

2   2 9   3   3 0   4

1	2	3	4

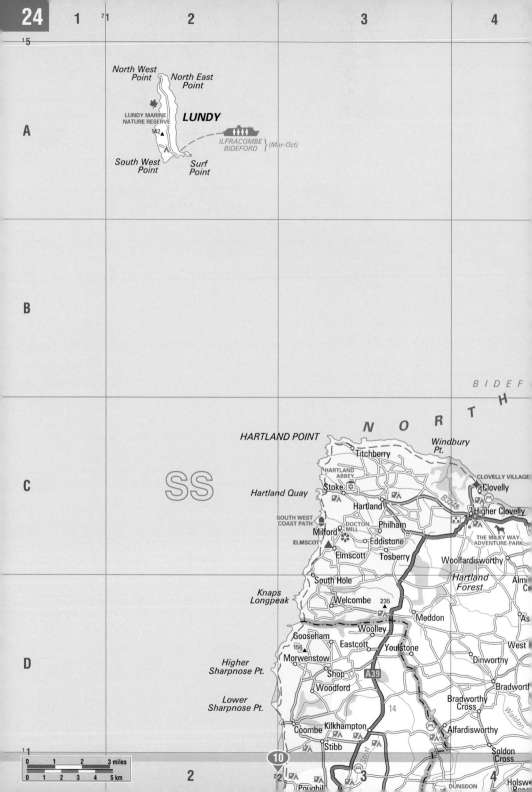

A

North West Point
North East Point

LUNDY MARINE NATURE RESERVE

LUNDY

142

ILFRACOMBE
BIDEFORD } *(Mar-Oct)*

South West Point

Surf Point

B

BIDEF

N O R T H

C

HARTLAND POINT

Windbury Pt.

Titchberry

HARTLAND ABBEY

CLOVELLY VILLAGE

Clovelly

SS

Hartland Quay

Stoke

Hartland

B3248

Higher Clovelly

SOUTH WEST COAST PATH

Milford

DOCTON MILL

Philham

THE MILKY WAY ADVENTURE PARK

ELMSCOTT

Eddistone

Woolfardisworthy

Elmscott

Tosberry

Hartland Forest

Almi C

South Hole

Knaps Longpeak

Welcombe

235

Meddon

As

D

Gooseham

Woolley

West

156

Eastcott

Youlstone

Higher Sharpnose Pt.

Morwenstow

Dinworthy

Shop

A39

Bradworth

Woodford

Bradworthy Cross

Lower Sharpnose Pt.

14

Coombe

Kilkhampton

Alfardisworthy

Stibb

Soldon Cross

10

2

3

4

DUNSDON

Poughill

0   1   2   3 miles
0 1 2 3 4 5 km

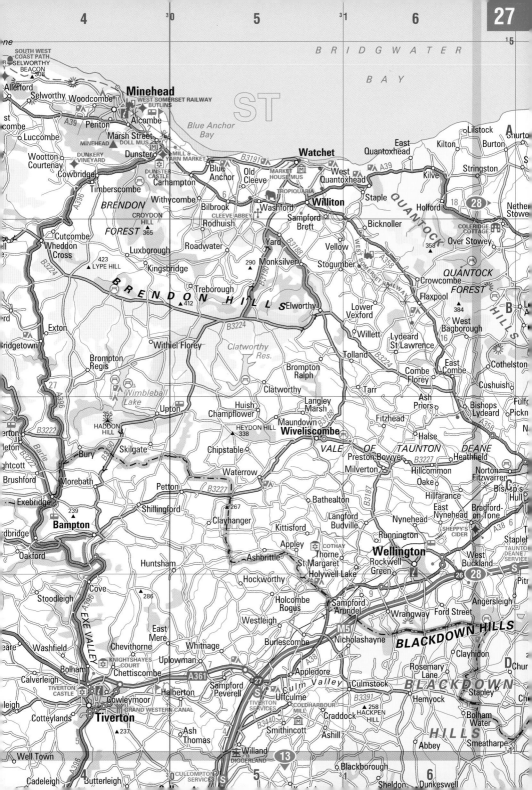

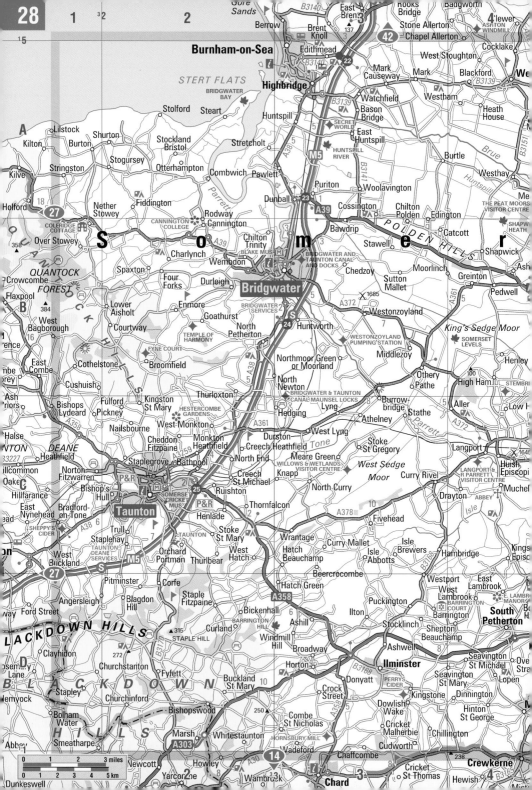

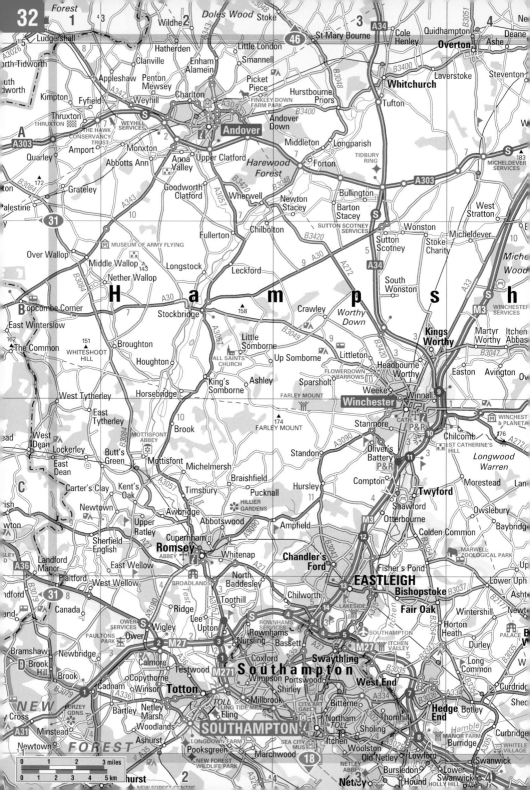

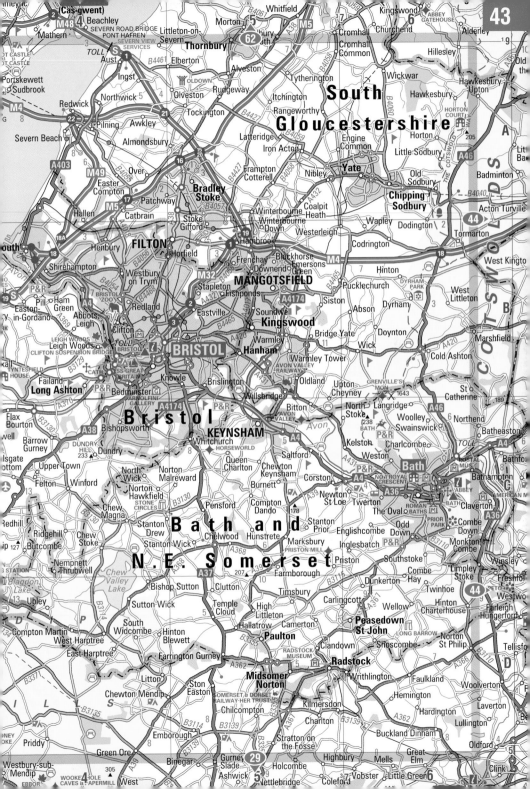

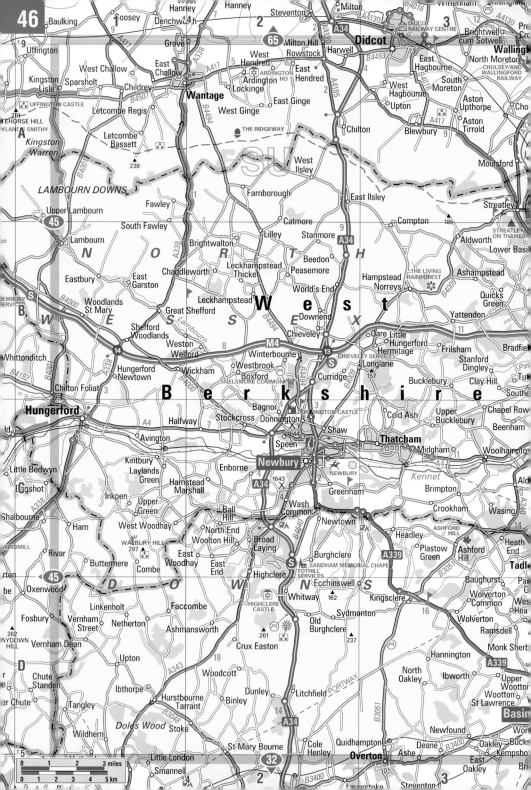

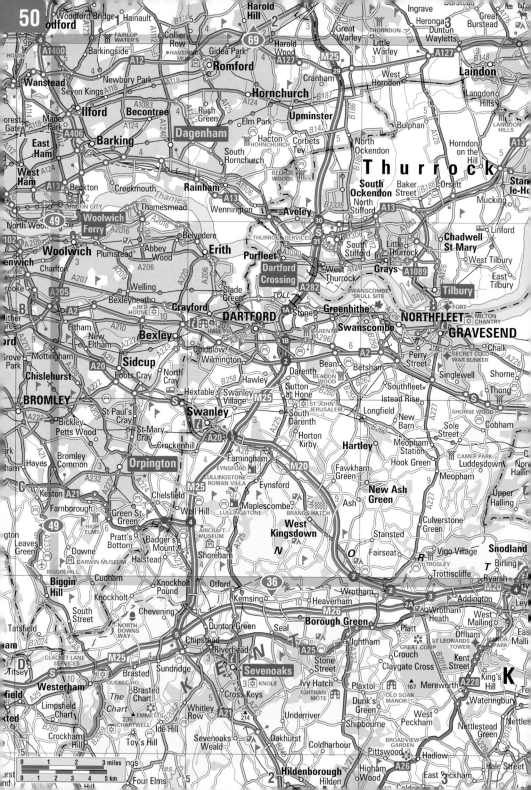

TR

A

B

C

D

Turner Contemporary
THE SHELL GROTTO
Margate
MARGATE
Cliftonville
Foreness Pt.
Kingsgate
Westgate on Sea
B2052
NORTH
FORELAND
Northdown
LIGHTHOUSE
RECULVER
RECULVER TOWERS
AND ROMAN FORT
Minnis Bay
St Peter's
Birchington
QUEX HOUSE
Isle of Thanet
A255
BROADSTAIRS
Reculver
SPITFIRE AND
HURRICANE MEM.
Northwood
BLEAK HOUSE
Hillborough
DICKENS HOUSE MUSEUM
St Nicholas
at Wade
A28
Acol
Northwood
B2050
Newington
Dumpton
A299
B2190
Manston
A256
A299
WINDMILL
omfield
Boyden
Gate
Sarre
A253
Way
Cliffsend
Ramsgate
MARITIME MUSEUM
Hoath
Chislet
Monkton
Minster
15
PEGWELL
BAY
Pegwell
Upstreet
Stour
SANDWICH &
PEGWELL BAY
West Stourmouth
East Stourmouth
A256
ST. AUGUSTINE'S
CROSS
Pegwell
Bay
Grove
STODMARSH
Westmarsh
5
RICHBOROUGH
CASTLE
Preston
Ware
Sandwich
Bay
Stodmarsh
Elmstone
Hoaden
A28
AMPHITHEATRE
Great Stonar
hambreux
WINGHAM
WILDLIFE
PARK
A257
Ickham
Sandwich
Littlebourne
11
Wingham
Guilton
Ash
Marshborough
TOLL
ROYAL ST. GEORGE'S
Bramling
Staple
Woodnesborough
Stone Cross
Worth
ourne
Goodnestone
Gore
A258
Ham
Finglesham
Adisham
GOODNESTONE PARK
Eastry
MARITIME AND
LOCAL HISTORY MUSEUM
Aylesham
Chillenden
Knowlton
Bettesshanger
Sholden
Northbourne
DEAL
Nonington
Easole Street
DEAL CASTLE
Snowdown
Tilmanstone
THE
DOWNS
Womenswold
Elvington
Great
Mongeham
Walmer
WALMER CASTLE
AND GARDENS
Barfrestone
EAST KENT
RLY
39
15
Woolage
Green
Eythorne
East
West
Sutton
Studdal
Ringwould
Kingsdown

A299
A28

71

4
5
6
4
6

19

6
4
6

1   ¹6   2   3   4

A

²3

PEMBROKESHIRE COAST
ARFORDIR PENFRO

Ynysduellyn

Penclegyr   Porthgain   Tre
Abereiddy   Llanrhian
Croes-goch

ST. DAVID'S HEAD
PENMAEN DEWI

Tretio   Treffynno
Trefeddydd-fawr   Carnhedryn   Treglemais
181   ST DAVID'S
Whitesand Bay   Rhodiad
Porth-mawr   Caerfarchell
BISHOP'S PALACE   Rhosson   Whitchurch   Middle Mill

B

Ramsey Sound

Ramsey
Island
Ynys Dewi
RAMSEY ISLAND

CATHEDRAL   **St David's**
(Tyddewi)   Nine   Solva
Wells

S T.   B R I D E S

B A Y

PEMBROKES
COAST
LLWYBR ARFO
PE
BRO

B A E   S A I N   F F R A I D

C

SM

Broad

Little H

Talbenny

Tower Point
Trwyn Tŵr   St Bride's

GRASSHOLM
ISLAND

NATIONAL
NATURE RESERVE   Wooltack Point
79   Trwyn Wooltack

Skomer
Island
Ynys Skomer   SKOMER
ISLAND   Marloes   Hasgua

Broad Sound   MARLOES
SANDS

Gateholm
Island
Ynys Gateholm   St
Ishmael's   San

D

P
E
M

Skokholm
Island
Ynys Skokholm

Dale   MILFOR
ABERDAU

71

B
R
O
K
E

St Ann's Hd.
Pentir St. Ann

Sheep
Island
Ynys y Defaid

²0

S
H
I
R
E

ROSSLARE

E

P
A
R
F
O
R
D
I
R

P E N F

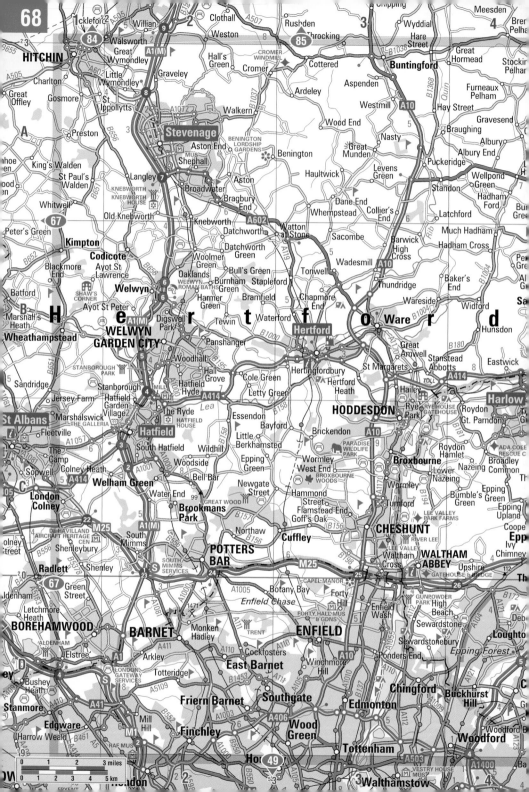

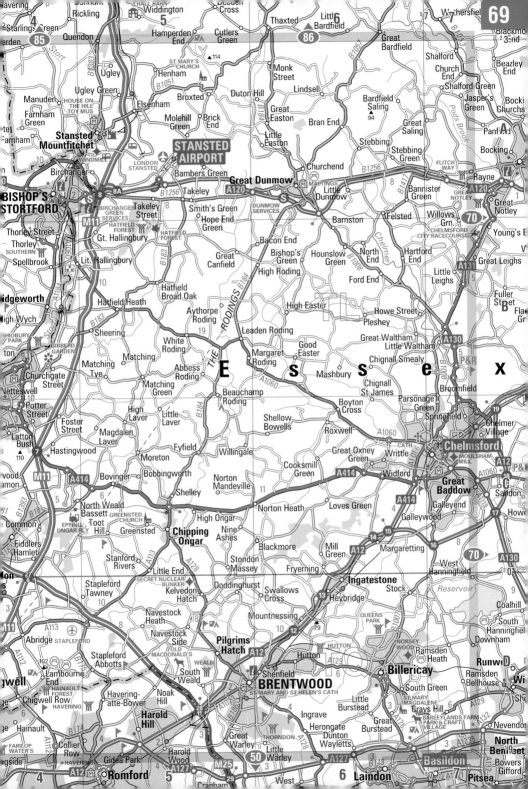

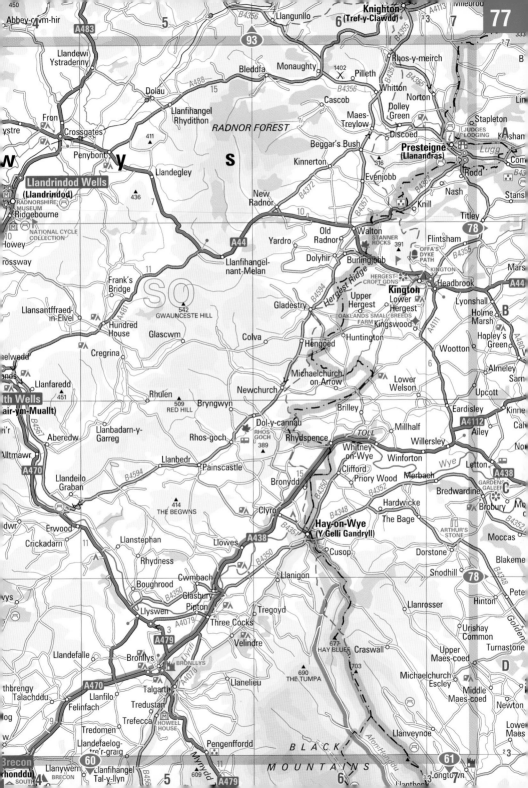

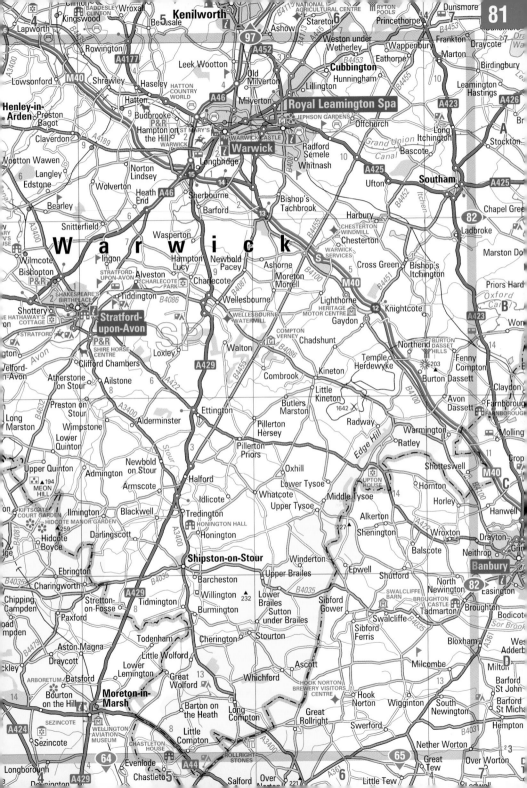

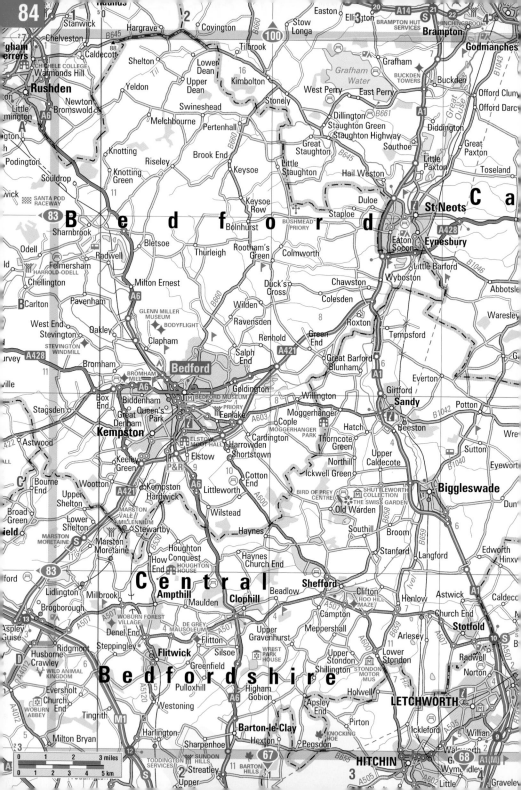

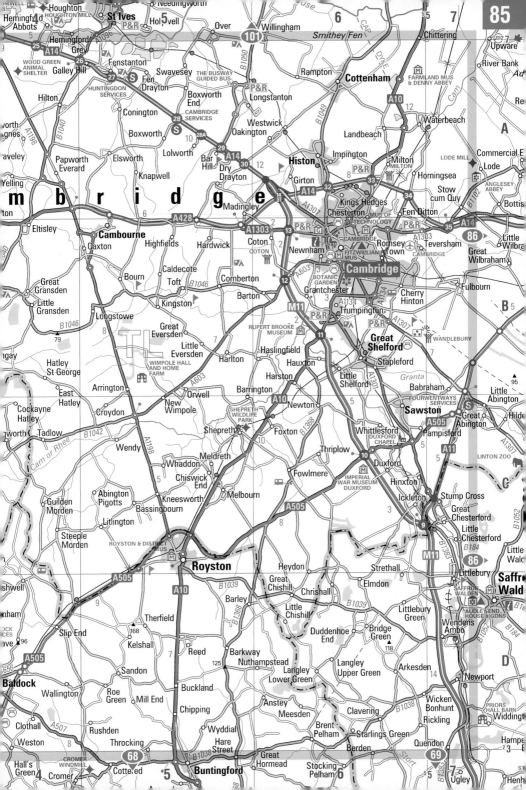

1   2⁴   2   3   4

³2

107

SH

Tal-y-bont

Plas-canol

Llanaber   Caerde

Cutiau

Barmouth
(Abermaw)
RNLI LIFEBOAT MUSEUM

Arthog   Ynysg

A   BARMOUTH BAY   *The Bar*

FAIRBOURNE
STEAM RAILWAY

BAE BERMO   Fairbourne

Friog

20

SNOWD
NATIO
PAR

Llwyngwril

Llangelynin

Rhoslefain   Llanegryn   Peniarth

Llanfendigaid   309

Tonfanau   Bryncrug   Pandy

B   Rhyd-yr-onen
TALYLLYN RAILWAY

Tywyn

Caethle

³0

C A R D I G A N   279

Aberdovey   A493

C   *Aberdovey Bar*   DYFI
Bae Aberdyfi

B A Y   B4353   F

Ynyslas   Llancynfelyn

B A E   BORTH

Borth

Upper Borth   Tal-y-

Dôl-y-Bon

C E R E D I G I O N   Llandre
Pen-y-garn

D   **SN**   Bow
Street

ARTS CENTRE   Plas Gog
NATIONAL
LIBRARY   Clarach   A4159
CLIFF RAILWAY   148   Comins
Capel

Aberystwyth   Coch

Llanbadarn Fawr   A44
P&R
CASTLE
Trefechan   Southgate   Glanrafon
Penparcau   Moriah
Rhydyfelin   Capel

²8

0   1   2   3 miles
0   1   2   3   4   5 km

74

2   ²5   3

4   A470   5   A494   6   9   7 Aber Rhiwlec

ARAN FAWDDWY

Pont y Pennant

2

Nannau

Llanelltyd

108

Bont Newydd

Cywarch

Llanymawddwy

Hen Gerrig

Pen-y-bryn

B4416

Brithdir

513

ntddu   TOLL

CYMER ABBEY

Y Gribin

Bryn Sion

TIR RHIWIOG

Moel y Lly

Penmaenpool   PENMAENPOOL CENTRE

A470

Abergwynant

11

Afon Cerist

A470

Aber Cowarch

545

109

Rhydwen

Dolgellau

Minllyn

A458

KINGS

Dinas-Mawddwy

Cwm-Cewydd

WAUN-OER

MEIRION MILL

Mallwyd

670

Ffridd Goch

893 CADAIR IDRIS

Mynydd Ceiswyn

Mynydd Dolgoed

Aberangell

523

CADER IDRIS

Minffordd

Dyfi Forest

A470

IA

15

Cwm-Llinau

Tal-y-llyn

A487

Corris Uchaf

Aberllefenni

Clegyrnant

Llanfihangel-y-pennant

Cwmderwe

Neinthirio

CASTELL Y BERE

KING ARTHUR'S LABYRINTH & CRAFT CENTRE

Corris

Dol-fôr

Pentre-Celyn

B

Pandy

6

Abergynolwyn

CORRIS RAILWAY AND MUSEUM

Cemmaes

B4405

Esgairgeiliog

Waun

Llanbrynmair

Pantperthog

Plas Llwyngwern

Cemmaes Road

Dolfach

633 TARRENHENDRE

CENTRE FOR ALTERNATIVE TECHNOLOGY

B4404

Llanwrin

6

Commins Coch

Tafolwern

A470

PARC

Pen-y-bont

A489

Abercegir

Llan

Talerddig

CENEDLAETHOL

SENEDD-DY GWAIN GLYNDWR

Machynlleth

Darowen

Bont-Dolgadfan

13

ERYRI

Pennal A493

Penegoes

Tal-y-wern

Cwrt

DOVEY DYFYN

FELIN CREWI WATER MILL

B4518

Forge

Derwenlas

Melinbyrhedyn

Glaspwll

Pant-glâs

468 MOELFRE

Pennant

15

Glandyfi

Aberhosan

P   o   w   y   s

YNYS HIR RESERVE

Eglwys Fach

DYFI FURNACE

Glaslyn

Dylife

92

C

582

GLYNDWR'S WAY

Tre'r-ddôl

521 MOEL-Y-LLYN

Staylittle

18

Llawr-y-glyn

Tre-Taliesin

Source of R. Severn Blaen Hafren

Bont-goch

Nant-y-Moch Reservoir

Llyn Clywedog

482 FAN HILL

Va

Salem

506

PLYNLIMON PUMLUMON FAWR

741

B4518

Pen-bont Rhydybeddau

752

Source of R. Wye Blaen Gwy

yn-coch an

Hafren Forest

Tan Hinon

Old Hall

Glan-y-r D

Llanidloes

Capel Bangor

Dollwen

Goginan

SILVER MOUNTAIN EXPERIENCE

13

Glynbrochan

A470

Dyffryn Castell

564

Pant Mawr

Cwmbelan

VALE OF RHEIDOL RAILWAY

Cwmbrwyno

Ponterwyd

Llanifyny

A44

Llangurig

4

Aberffrwd

75

Ystumtuen

REIDOL HYDRO ELECTRIC STATION

Ysbytycynfyn

92

A470

7

Afon Rheidol

COED RHEIDOL

A4120

6

9

2

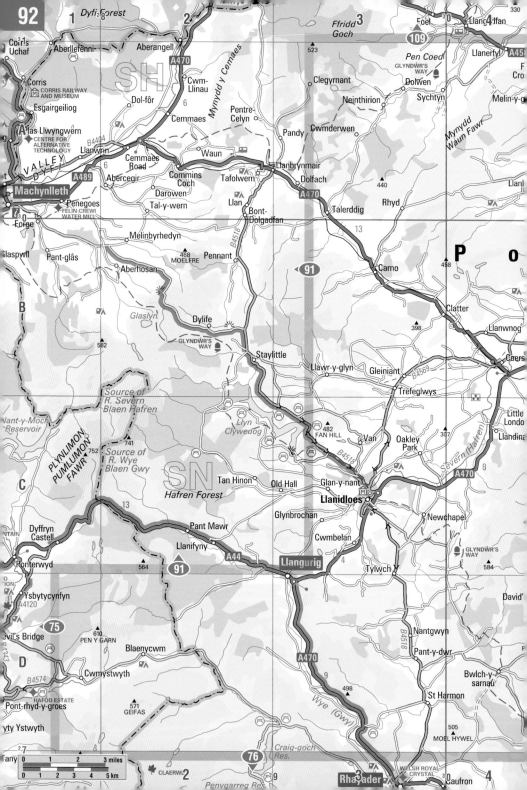

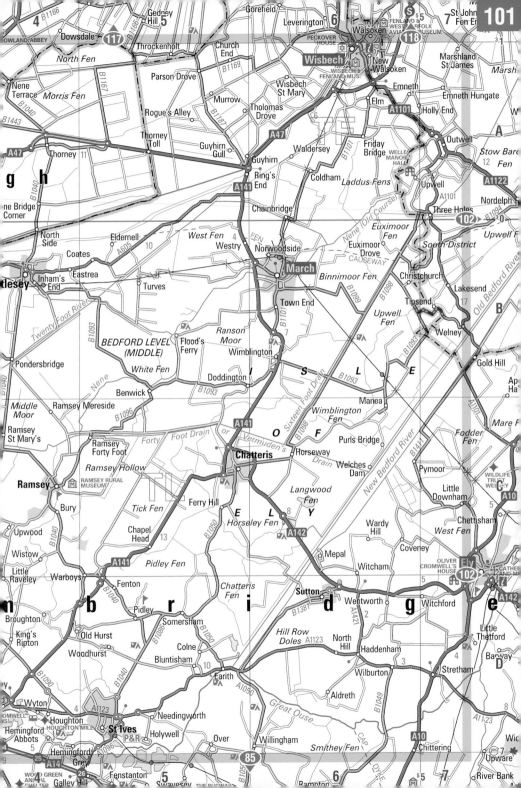

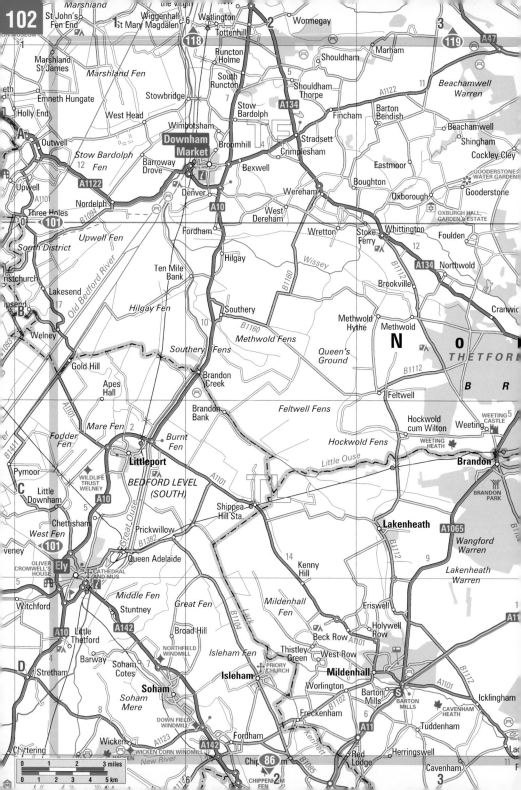

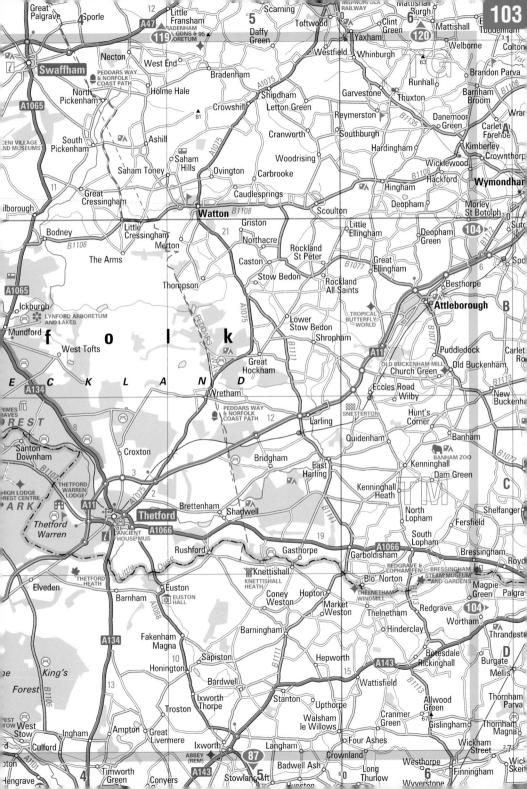

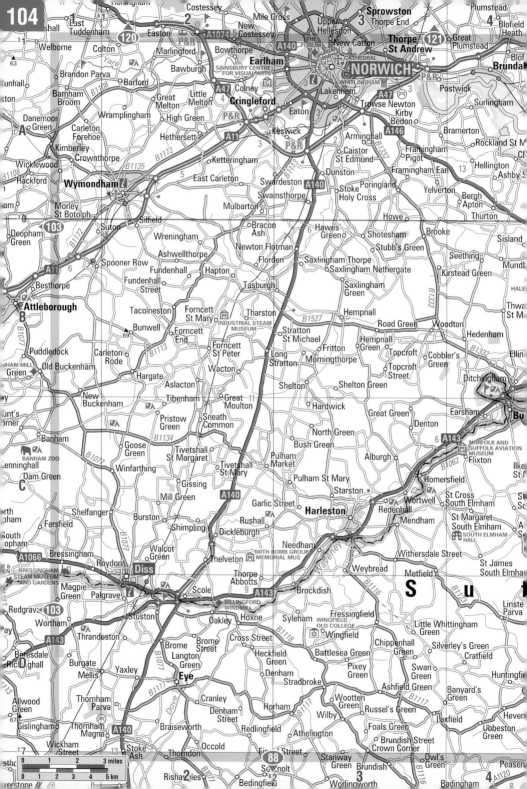

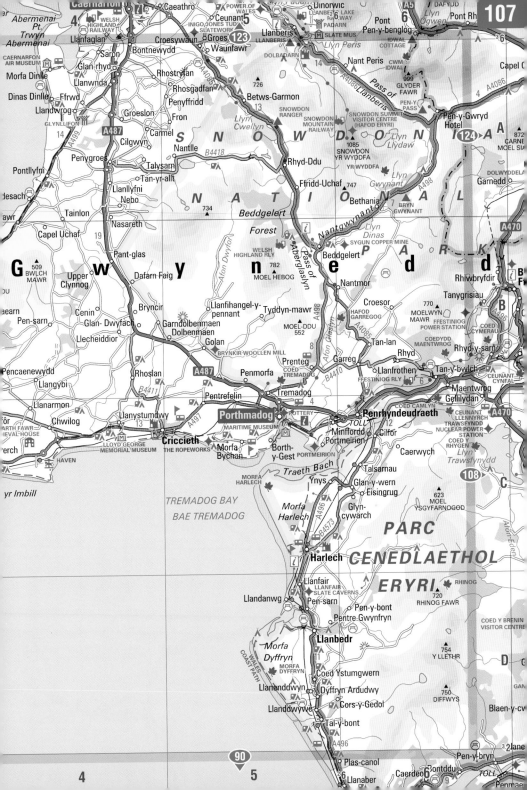

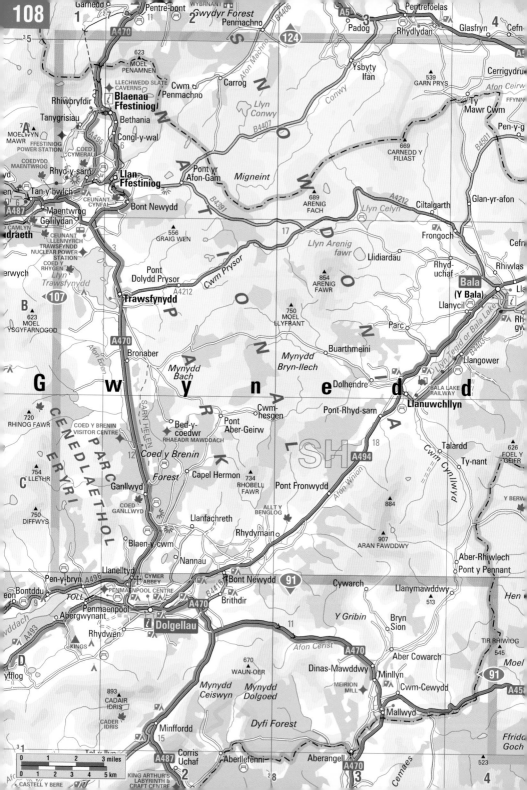

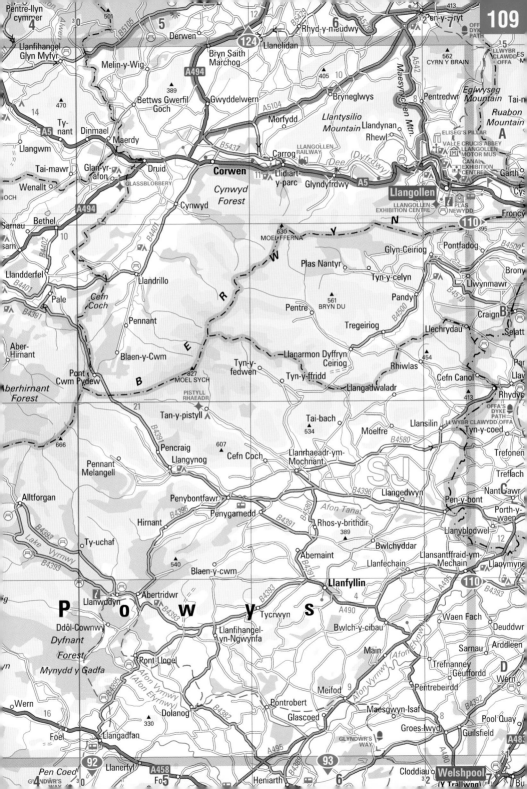

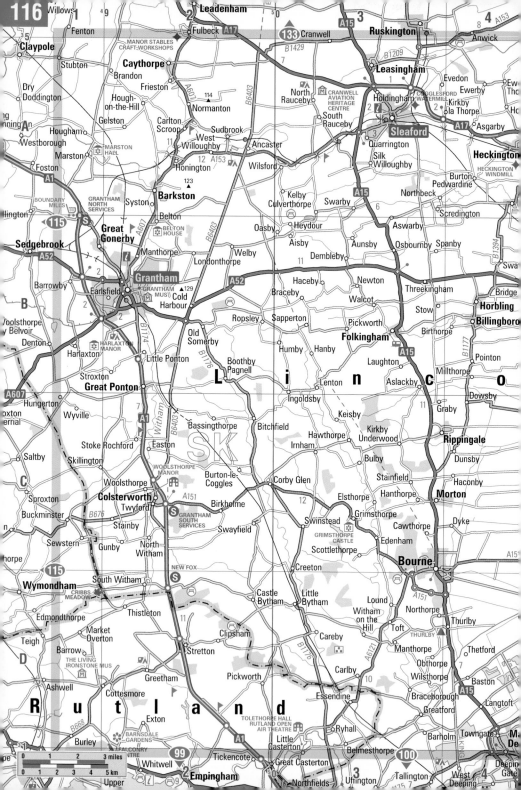

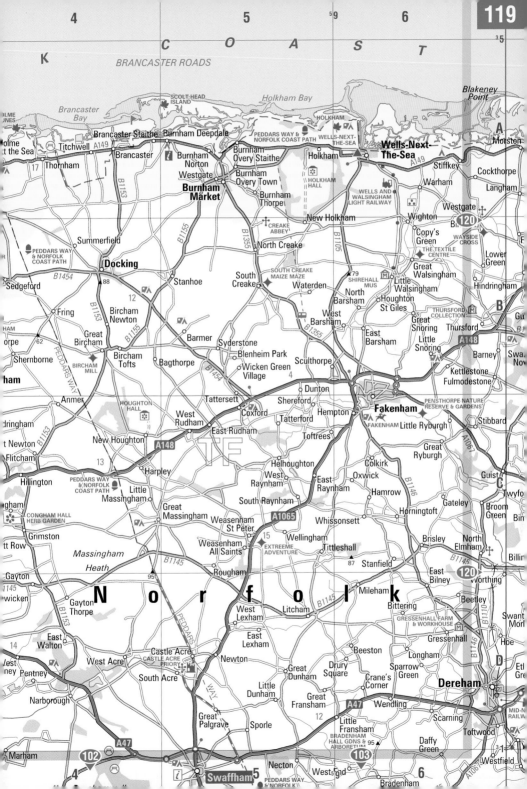

3 5

A

erstrand

Sidestrand
Trimingham

E AST

Southrepps   Gimingham   **Mundesley**

STOW WINDMILL

Lower
Street   Trunch   Paston

B1145   B1159

Knapton   Bacton

Bradfield   Broomholm   Keswick
Edingthorpe   Walcott
Swafield

ORTS
DOM

Edingthorpe   Witton Bridge   Happisburgh
Green
Ridlington
Spa   Crostwight   Whimpwell Green
Valsham   Common

B   TG

Happisburgh   Eccles on Sea
ningham   Common
A149   EAST RUSTON   Hempstead
OLD VICARAGE
GARDEN
estwick   Bengate   Honing   Lessingham   Ingham   Sea Palling
6   Corner
ton   Worstead   East   WAXHAM   Waxham
Ruston   Ingham   GREAT-BARN
B1150   Dilham   Stalham   **NORFOLK**
k   Sloley   Smallburgh   Stalham
Green
Scottow   Hickling   **COAST**
s   MUSEUM OF   Sutton   Hickling
ttle   THE BROADS   Green
utbois   Pennygate   Barton Turf   Hickling Heath   Horsey   WINTERTON
Tunstead   ANT BROADS   Wood   DUNES
Sco   A1151   AND MARSHES   Street   Catfield   HORSEY
Ruston   WROXHAM   Neatishead   Hickling WINDMILL
BARNS   4   Barton   Broad   MARTHAM   East
Coltishall   Ashmanhaugh   RA BOAT TRIP   Broad   HICKLING   BROAD   Somerton
B1354   Irstead   Sharp   BROAD   West   Winterton-on-Sea
Threehammer   Street   Potter   Somerton
ad   Belaugh   **Hoveton**   Common   Heigham   Martham
enham   **Wroxham**   **THE**   Bastwick
Upper   Lower Street   8   Ludham   **Hemsby**   **Newport**
HILLSIDE ANIMAL   Street   A1062   LUDHAM
SANCTUARY   Horning   Upper Street   MARSHES   Repps   Rollesby   Scratby
Crostwick   Wroxham   Thurne   B1152   Ormesby   California
orth   8   Broad   **BROADS**   St Michael
ackheath   Woodbastwick   Ranworth   A149   Filby   Ormesby   D
A115   Salhouse   BURE MARSHES   Clippesby   Broad   11   St Margaret
rowston   New   Panxworth   FAIRHAVEN   Billockby   A1064   CAISTER ROMAN
Rackheath   WOODLAND &   South Walsham   Burgh St   TOWN
horpe End   Little   WATER GARDEN   12   Margaret   Filby   Mautby   West   **Caister-on**
Thorpe   Plumstead   Hemblington   THE   Thrigby   THRIGBY HALL   Caister   **-Sea**
St Andrew   Blofield   North   CANDLEMAKER'S   WILDLIFE GARDENS   West   YARMOUTH
Great   Heath   Burlingham   **Acle**   WORKSHOP   Runham   End   3 1
Plumstead   A47   Stokesby   GREAT YARMOUTH
WICH   Blofield   8   Lingwood   **105**   Damgate   Bure   GREAT DENES
Brundall   5   Beighton   Tunstall   6   A47   5   Runham   **Great**

1   2   2   3

A

The Skerries
Ynysoedd y
Moelrhoniaid

Wilfa
Head
Pen Wilfa
Cemaes
Bay
Bae
Cemlyn Bay   Cemaes
Bae Cemlyn
WYLFA POWER STATION
AND OBSERVATION TOWER
Cemaes
Tregele
Llanba

Carmel Head
Pen Carmel

Llanfairynghornwy

Llanfechell
17

Isle

Church Bay
Porth Swtan

Rhydwyn

Llanfflewyn

Llanrhyddlad
Rh

Carre

DUBLIN
DUN LAOGHAIRE
(Apr–Sept)

HOLYHEAD BAY
BAE
CAERGYBI

Llanfaethlu

A5025

Llanbabo

A

Res

DUBLIN

Llanddeusant

LLYNON
WINDMILL

Angl

North Stack   BREAKWATER

Llantwrog

Elim

Llaner

HOLYHEAD MOUNTAIN   220
Goferydd

Llaingoch

Holyhead
(Caergybi)

Llanfachraeth

Llantrisant

Carmel

South Stack
ELLINS TOWER RSPB RESERVE
PENRHOS FEILW
STANDING STONES

Kingsland

A5   4

Pen-llyn
Res.

Llech

Penrhosfeilw

ANGLESEY

Newlands
Park

Llanynghenedl

(Sir Yn

Penrhyn Mawr

6

Valley

Bodedern

Trefor

B4545

Trearddur

A55

A5

Glan-traeth

Four Mile
Bridge

Caergeiliog

3

A55

2

4

Bryngwran

Gwalch

A5

Holy Island
Ynys Gybi

Llanfihangel
yn Nhowyn

3

5

Rhoscolyn

Llanfairyneubwll

Capel-
gwyn

A4080

Ddrydwy

Cymyran
Bay
Bae Cymyran

4

Llanfaelog

Bryn Du

Pencarnisiog

Se

C

Rhosneigr

WALES COAST
PATH

Bethe

Llangwyfan-isaf

Llangadwaladr

Aberffraw

Hermon

Bodorgan

NEWBOROUGH WARREN
AND YNYS LLANDDWYN

D

Malltraeth Bay
Bae Malltraeth

Llanddwyn I
Ynys Llanddwyn

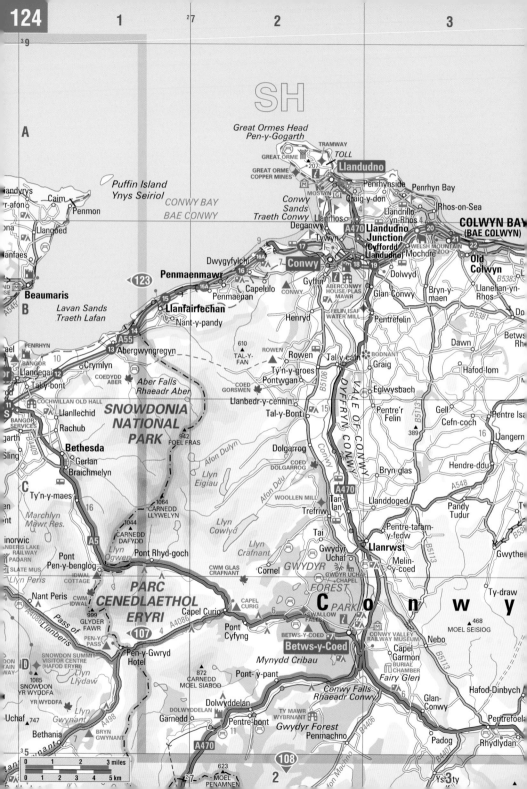

1   7   2   3

9

A

SH

Great Ormes Head
Pen-y-Gogarth

TRAMWAY

GREAT ORME

TOLL

GREAT ORME
COPPER MINES

207

Llandudno

Penrhynside

Penrhyn Bay

CONWY BAY
BAE CONWY

Conwy
Sands
Traeth Conwy

MOSTYN

Craig-y-don

Llandrillo-
yn-Rhos

Rhos-on-Sea

COLWYN BAY
(BAE COLWYN)

Puffin Island
Ynys Seiriol

Caim

Penmon

andyrys

-afon

Llangoed

anfaes

Beaumaris

Penmaenmawr

Deganwy

Llanrhos

Tywyn

A470

Conwy

Llandudno
Junction
(Cyffordd
Llandudno)

20

22

Old
Colwyn

Mochdre

Dolwyd

Dawn

WELSH MOUNTAIN
ZOO

B5383

Llanelian-yn-
Rhos

123

15A

Llanfairfechan

Penmaenan

Capelulo

17

Gyffin

18

19

CONWY

ABERCONWY
HOUSE/PLAS
MAWR

Glan-Conwy

Bryn-y-
maen

B5381

Do

Betws
Rh

Dwygyfylchi

16A

16

15

B

Lavan Sands
Traeth Lafan

A55

14

Abergwyngregyn

Nant-y-pandy

Henryd

FELIN ISAF
WATER MILL

Pentrefelin

13

PENRHYN

BANGOR

Llandegai

12

Crymlyn

Talybont

COEDYDD
ABER

Aber Falls
Rhaeadr Aber

COED
GORSWEN

610
TAL-Y-
FAN

ROWEN

Rowen

Ty'n-y-groes

Pontwgan

Llanbedr-y-cennin

Tal-y-cafn

BODNANT

Graig

Pentre'r
Felin

Eglwysbach

Gell

Cefn-coch

Hafod-lom

16

Llangern

Pentre Isa

10

COCHWILLAN OLD HALL

S

BANGOR
SERVICES

garth

B4409

Sling

Llanllechid

Rachub

Bethesda

Gerlan

Braichmelyn

SNOWDONIA
NATIONAL
PARK

942
FOEL FRAS

Afon Dulyn

Dolgarrog

COED
DOLGARROG

Tal-y-Bont

VALE OF CONWY
DYFFRYN CONWY

389

B5113

B5383

A548

Hendre-ddu

C

Ty'n-y-maes

16

1064
CARNEDD
LLYWELYN

1044

CARNEDD
DAFYDD

Llyn
Eigiau

Llyn
Cowlyd

Afon Ddu

WOOLLEN MILL

Bryn-glas

Conwy

Tan-
lan

A470

Llanddoged

A548

Pandy
Tudur

Gwythe

Marchlyn
Mawr Res.

inorwic

SLATE MUS

A5

Pont
Pen-y-benglog

IDWAL
COTTAGE

Llyn
Ogwen

Pont Rhyd-goch

CWM GLAS
CRAFNANT

Llyn
Crafnant

Cornel

GWYDYR

GWYDYR UCHA
CHAPEL

Gwydyr
Uchaf

Llanrwst

Melin-
y-coed

B5113

Pentre-tafarn-
y-fedw

Ty-draw

468
MOEL SEISIOG

Llyn Peris

Llyn

PARC
CENEDLAETHOL
ERYRI

999
GLYDER
FAWR

107

A4086

Capel Curig

Capel
Curig

6

FOREST

C o n

w y

Nebo

Capel
Garmon

BURIAL
CHAMBER

PARK

SWALLOW
FALLS

CONWY VALLEY
RAILWAY MUSEUM

B5113

Hafod-Dinbych

D

Pass of
Llanberis

SNOWDON SUMMIT
VISITOR CENTRE
(HAFOD ERYRI)

1085
SNOWDON
YR WYDDFA

PEN-Y-
PASS

Pen-y-Gwryd
Hotel

Pont
Cyfyng

A4086

Mynydd Cribau

Betws-y-Coed

Fairy Glen

Glan-
Conwy

Pentrefoela

Uchaf

747

Llyn
Llydaw

Bethania

Llyn
Gwynant

BRYN
GWYNANT

A498

872
CARNEDD
MOEL SIABOD

Pont-y-pant

DOLWYDDELAN

Garnedd

11

Pentre-bont

TY MAWR
WYBRNANT

Gwydyr Forest

Penmachno

Conwy Falls
Rhaeadr Conwy

6

Hafod-Dinbych

Padog

Rhydlydan

5

0   1   2   3 miles
0 1 2 3 4 5 km

27

623
MOEL
PENAMNEN

108

2

3 ty

Ys

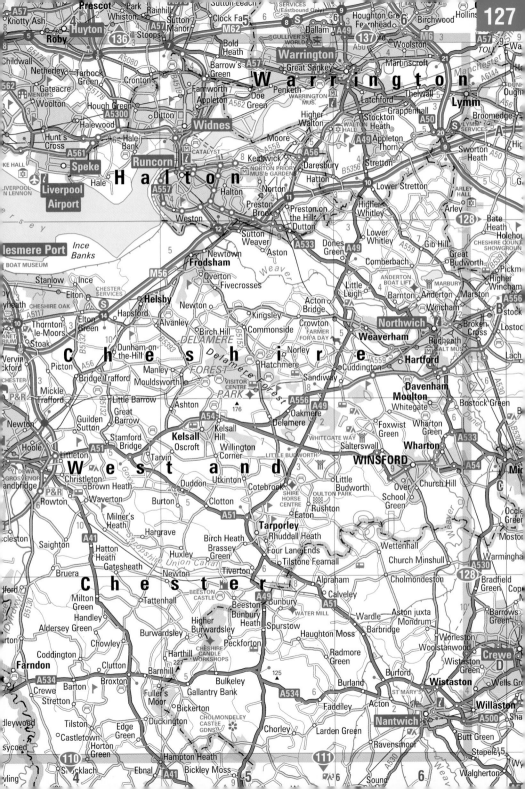

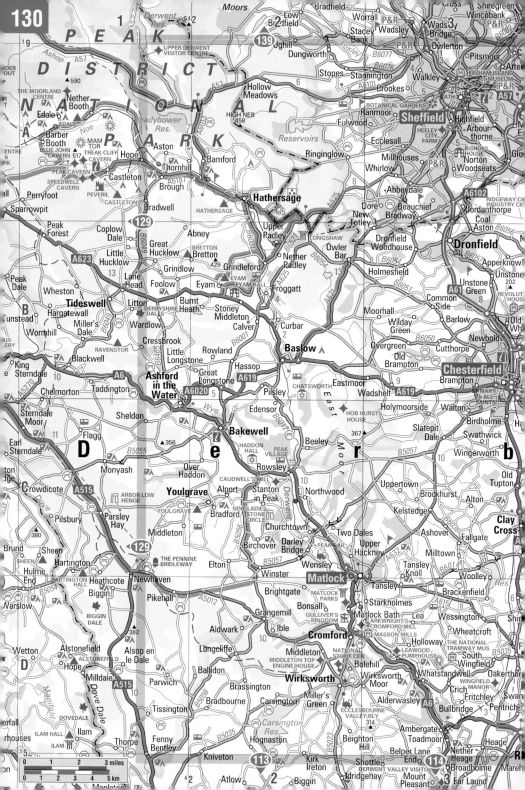

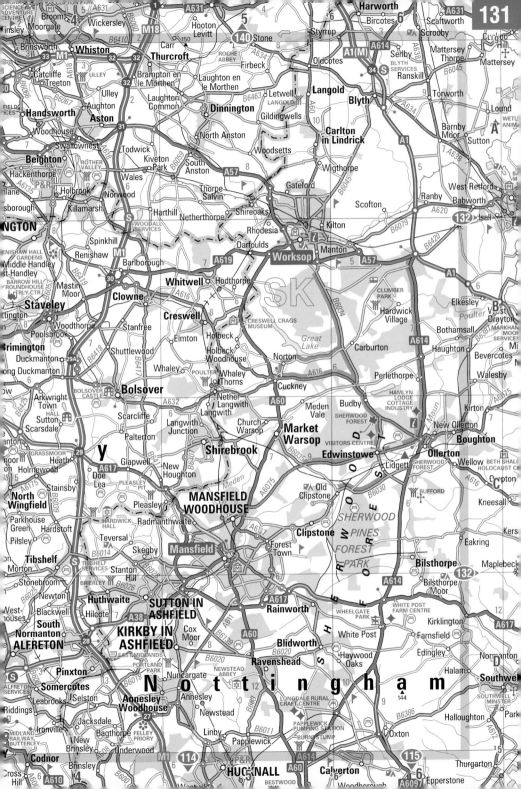

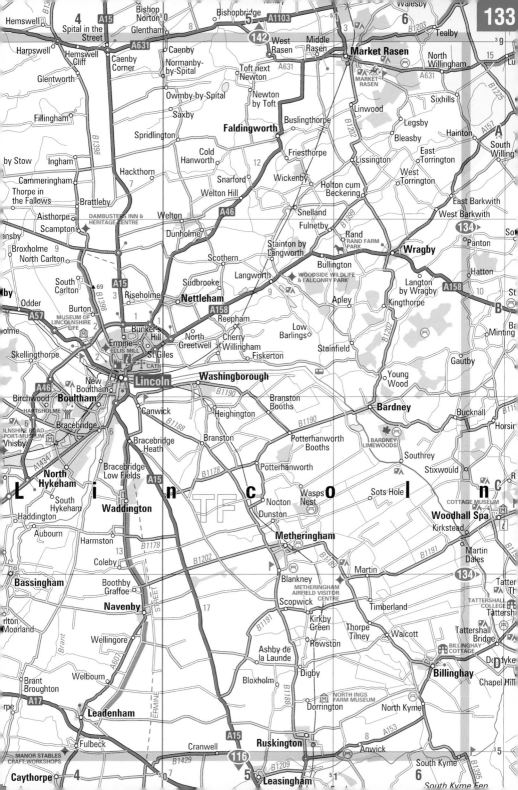

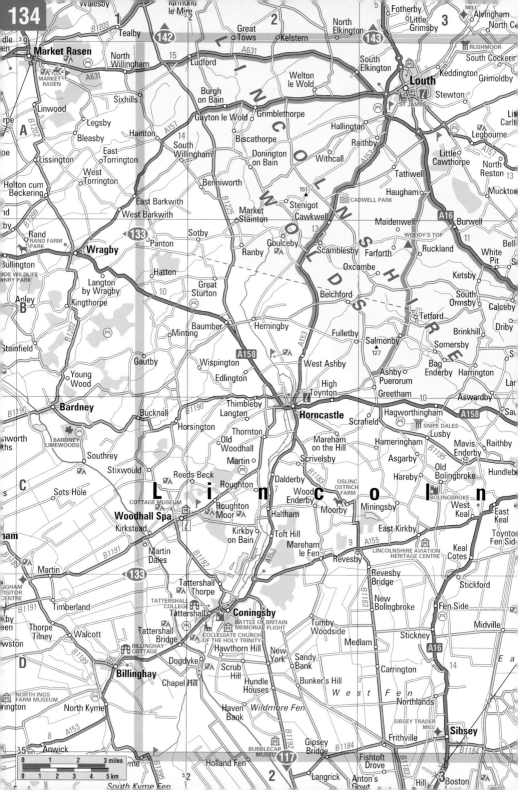

Saltfleetby
St Clements
Saltfleetby
All Saints
Saltfleetby
St Peter
Theddlethorpe
St Helen
Theddlethorpe
All Saints
SALTFLEETBY
THEDDLETHORPE
SEAL SANCTUARY
& NATURE CENTRE
Meers
Bridge
Mablethorpe
Great
Carlton
South
eston
Gayton
le Marsh
Trusthorpe
Strubby
Withern
Thorpe
Sutton
on Sea
Tothill
uthorpe
Maltby
le Marsh
Sandilands
Woodthorpe
Beesby
CLAYTHORPE WATER MILL
AND WILDFOWL GARDENS
Saleby
Hannah
Aby
Markby
Asserby
South
oresby
ALFORD
WINDMILL
Bilsby
Huttoft
Haugh
ALFORD
MANOR HOUSE
Rigsby
Alford
Farlesthorpe
Anderby
ON YOUR MARQUES
Mumby
Authorpe
Row
Well
Cumberworth
Helsey
**Chapel
St Leonards**
Ulceby
Bonthorpe
Hogsthorpe
Claxby
Willoughby
Sloothby
Skendleby
HARDY'S ANIMAL FARM
Partney
Addlethorpe
Ingoldmells
Scremby
Welton
le Marsh
FANTASY ISLAND
Spilsby
Candlesby
Ashby by
Partney
GUNBY HALL
Orby
Orby Marsh
Winthorpe
FUNCOAST WORLD
NORTHCOTE HEAVY
HORSE CENTRE
Great
Steeping
Bratoft
**Burgh
le Marsh**
Seathorne
Halton
Holegate
Irby in
the Marsh
NATURELAND SEAL
SANCTUARY
Toynton
St Peter
Firsby
BURGH LE
MARSH WINDMILL
THE VILLAGE
CHURCH
FARM
Skegness
THE LIFEBOAT
STATION
Little
Steeping
Thorpe
St Peter
Croft
Thorpe
Culvert
New
Leake
Thorpe
Fendykes
**Wainfleet
All Saints**
Seacroft
Croft Marsh
Eastville
Wainfleet Bank
MAGDALEN
MUSEUM
Wainfleet St Mary
GIBRALTAR POINT
e Bank
Wainfleet Tofts
Friskney
Eaudike
Wainfleet
Sand
Friskney
New
Leake
Wrangle
Bank
Friskney
Tofts
Eastville
Friskney Flats
e Commonside
Wrangle Lowgate
Old
Leake
Wrangle
Hurn's End
Leverton Outgate

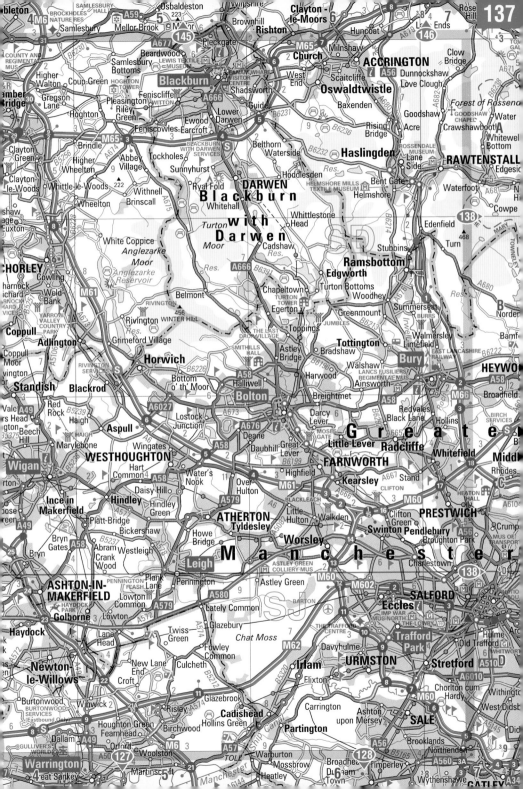

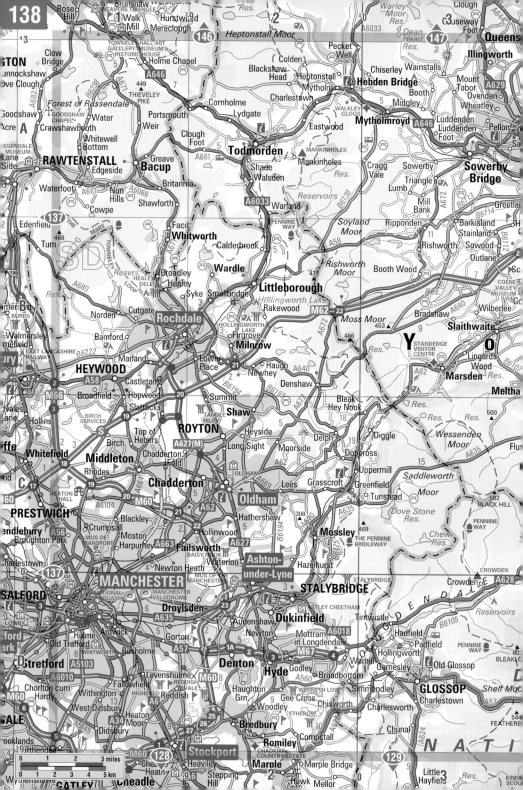

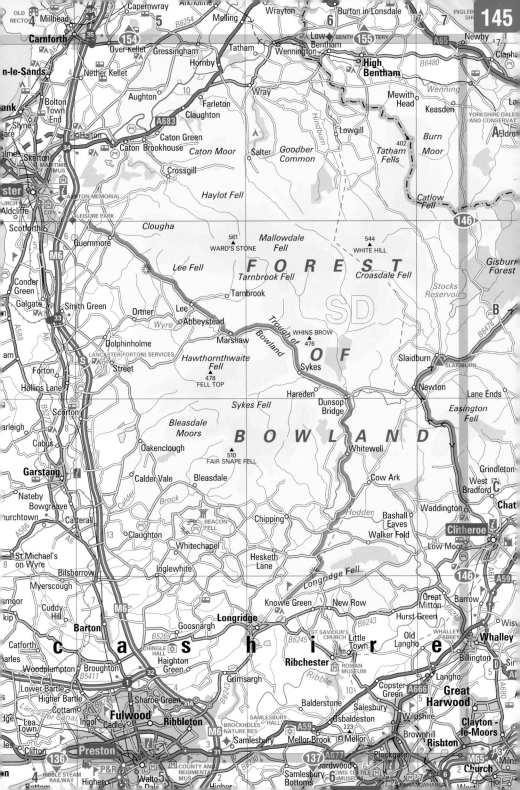

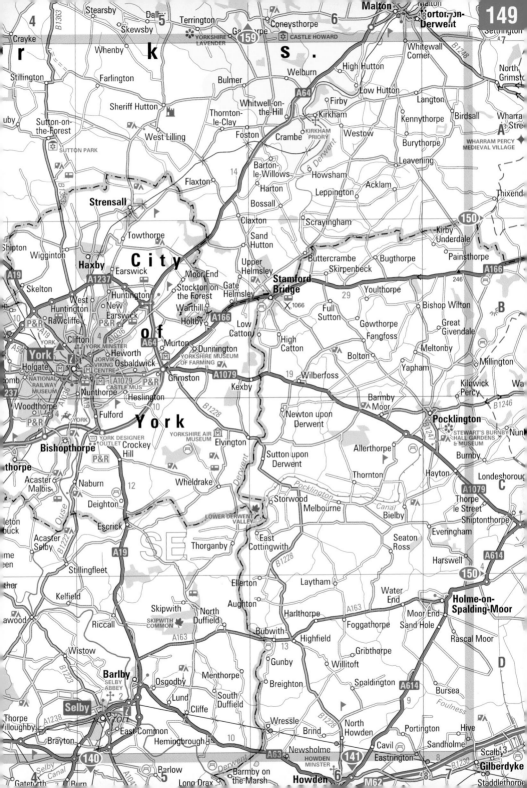

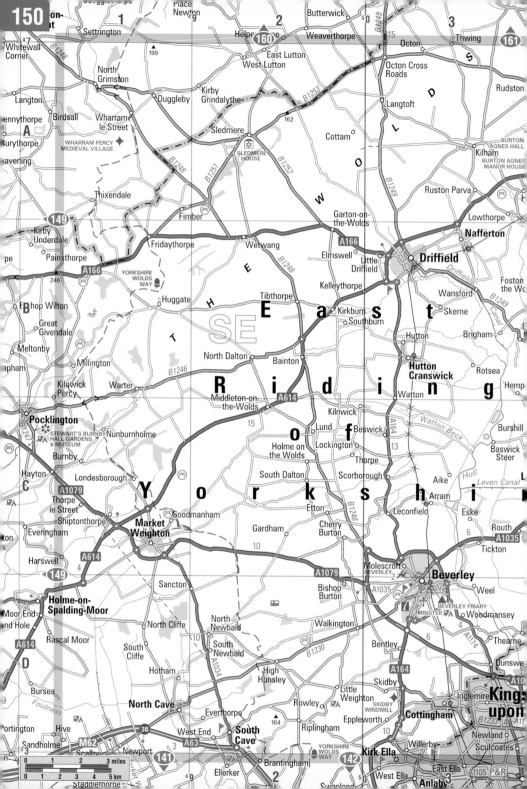

4   A165   5   FLAMBOROUGH₅3   6

Grindale   A165   B1229
Flamborough   161   B1259   FLAMBOROUGH HEAD

Boynton   B1255

SEWERBY HALL AND GARDENS
PRIORY   Sewerby
BAYLE MUSEUM   BONDVILLE MODEL VILLAGE
Bridlington   OLD PENNY MEMORIES
Bessingby   West Hill
Carnaby   Hilderthorpe
Haisthorpe   A614   P&R   **A**
olme
Burton Agnes   BRIDLINGTON BIRDS OF PREY
& ANIMAL PARK   *BRIDLINGTON BAY*

Fraisthorpe

Gransmoor   Barmston
eat Kelk   Lissett   14   **B**
Gembling   A165   Ulrome   TA
16   SKIPSEA CASTLE   Skipsea
B1249   Beeford   Skipsea Brough
rth   Dunnington   B1242
dingham
Bewholme   Atwick

North Cliff
Hornsea   **C**
Hornsea Mere   HORNSEA MUSEUM
Brandesburton   Hornsea Bridge
Seaton   FREEPORT HORNSEA   B1244   Rolston
e   Catwick   Sigglesthorne   Goxhill
Little   Mappleton
Hatfield
A165   B1243   Rise   Great Hatfield   Great Cowden
g Riston
Arnold   Withernwick
aux   New   B1242
Skirlaugh   Ellerby   Aldbrough
Marton   West   East Newton
Newton   **D**
Old   17
Ellerby   Flinton   BURTON CONSTABLE
13   Coniston   HALL   Garton
Swine   Grimston
Thirtleby   Sproatley   Humbleton   Fitling   Hilston
Bransholme   Ganstead
Sutton   B1238   B1240   Lelley   Owstwick   Tunstall
on Hull   Bilton   Elstronwick   North End
ll   Sutton Ings   B1239   Preston   Burton   Roos
Stoneferry   Summergangs   West   Pidsea   143   Waxholme
A165   WILBERFORCE   End   142   Owt orne
HOUSE   Salt nd   B1362   Rimswell
Marfleet   A1033   **Hedon**   5   2   6   **Withernsea**
STREETLIFE

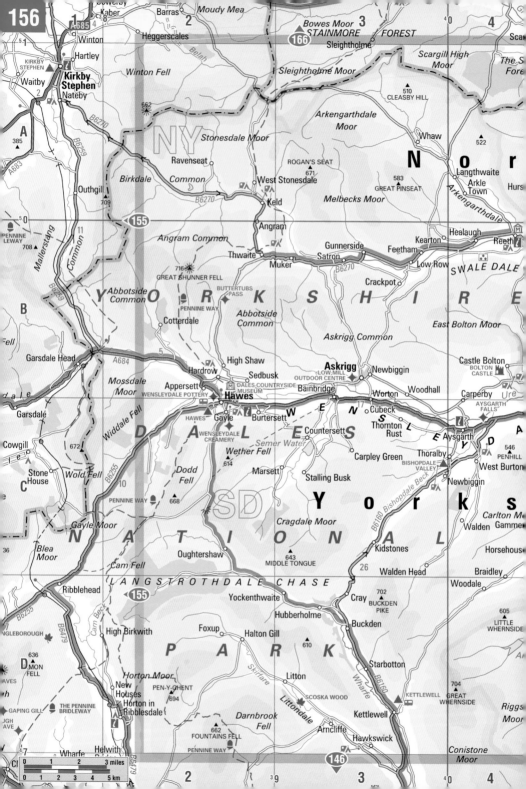

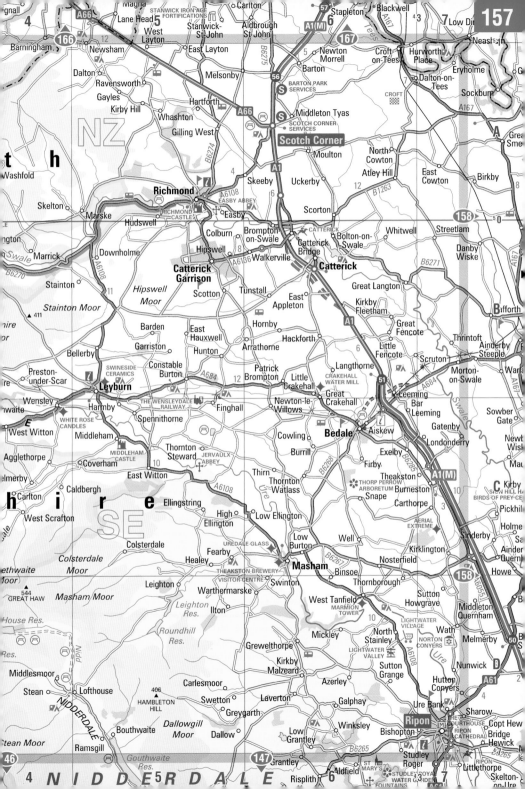

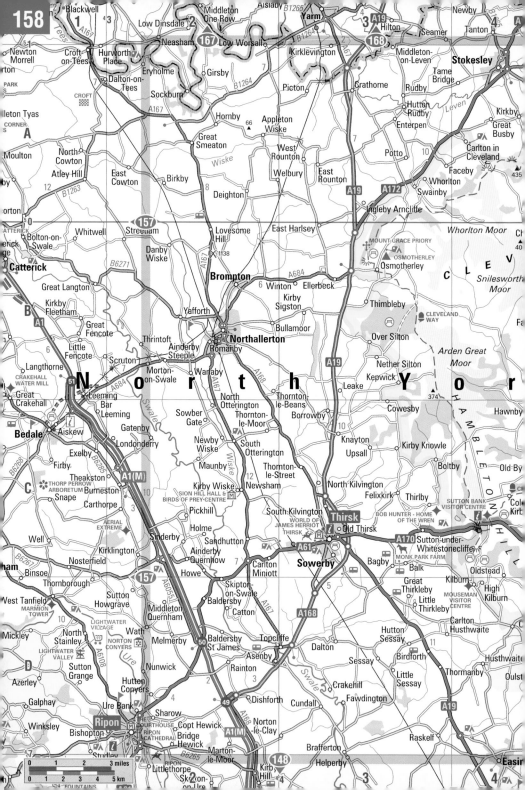

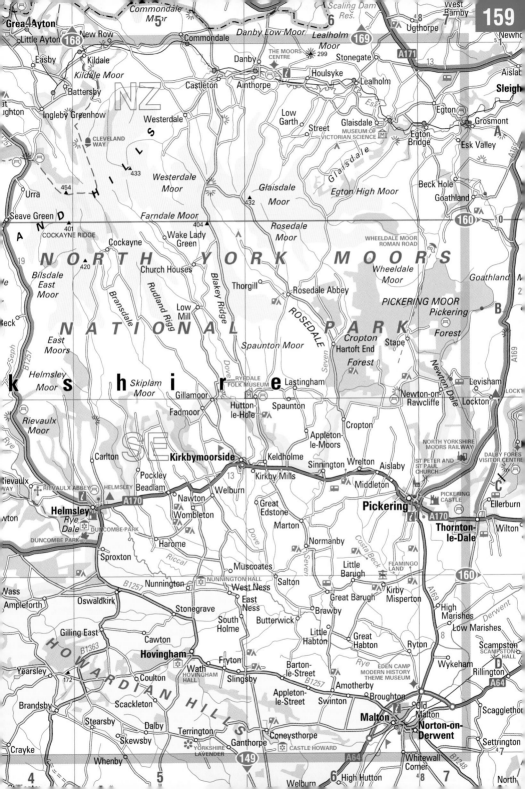

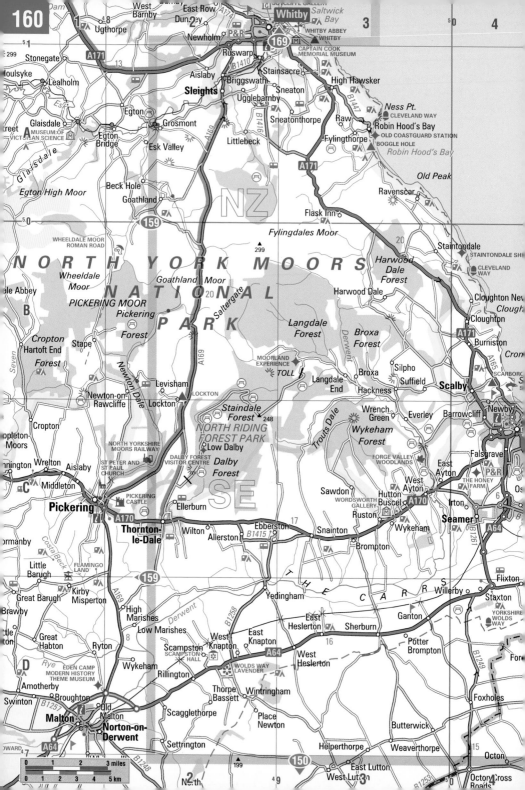

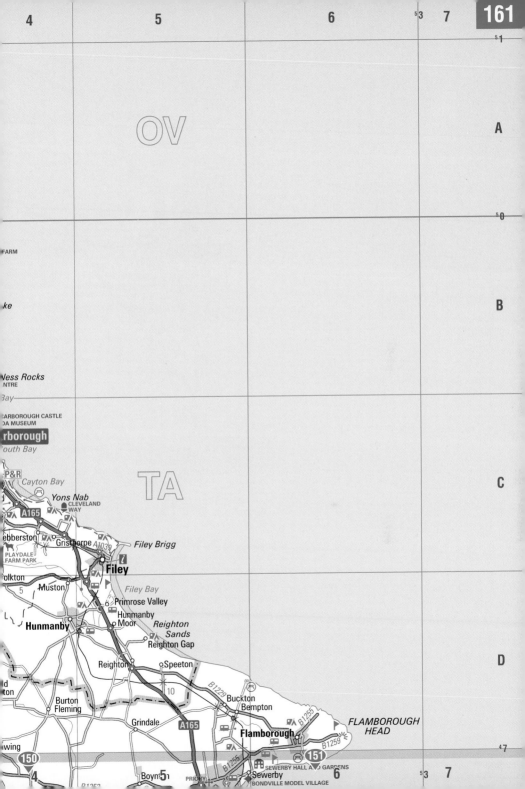

5 1

A

5 0

B

FARM

ke

Ness Rocks
NTRE

Bay

ARBOROUGH CASTLE
A MUSEUM

rborough
outh Bay

OV

TA

C

P&R
Cayton Bay
Yons Nab
CLEVELAND
WAY
A165
ebberston
Grist horpe A1039 Filey Brigg
PLAYDALE
FARM PARK
Filey
olkton
Muston Filey Bay
5
Primrose Valley
Hunmanby
Moor
Hunmanby Reighton
Sands
Reighton Gap

D

Reighton Speeton
B1229
10
Buckton
Burton Bempton
Fleming
B1255
Grindale A165 FLAMBOROUGH
HEAD
Flamborough
B1259
150 151
4 7
B1255
wing
4 6 5 3 7
Boyn 5
SEWERBY HALL AND GARDENS
PRIORY Sewerby
B1253 BONDVILLE MODEL VILLAGE

Allonby Bay

173 174

54 9 30 3

Crosscanonby
Allerby
Crosby

MARYPORT
MARITIME
MUSEUM
Maryport
Dearham

A

Flimby
Dovenby
Standingstone
6 Broughton
Moor
A596
Siddic
Camerton
Great
Broughton
Little
Broug

Derwent

North Side
Seaton
Great
Clifton
Bridgefoot
Greysout

Workington
HELENA
THOMPSON MUS
Stainburn
A595
Little Clifton
Eaglesfie

Westfield
3 A596
Deanscales

Mossbay
4 Winscales
Dean

B

NX

Harrington
High
Harrington
Branthwaite

Distington
Ullock

4 Pica

Lowca
247
Asby

Moresby
Arlecdon
15

Parton
Moresby
Parks
WALK MILL
Rowrah
HIGH LEYS
Kirkland

Bransty
THE RUM STORY
B5294
Frizington

Whitehaven
HAIG COLLIERY
MINING MUSEUM
5
Hensingham
**Cleator
Moor**
Ennerdale
Bridge

Saltom Bay
Mirehouse
5
Moor
Row
Wath Brow

C

ST
BEES HEAD
Sandwith
A595
Cleator
LONGLANDS LAKE

Rottington

Wilton

St Bees
Egremont

Coulderton
Thornhill
Haile
Middletown
6
Nethertown
Beckermet
8
Calder

Braystones
322

D

High
Sellafield
SELLAFIELD
VISITORS CENTRE
Calder Bridge
A595

Calder Hall
Welling

Gosforth

Seascale

50
153
3 Holmrook

0 1 2 3 miles
0 1 2 3 4 5 km
9 2 30 3 Drigg

A

B

NZ

C

MINIATURE
RAILWAY
**Saltburn-
by-the-Sea**
CHRIS BIRKBECK
INTERNATIONAL RALLY
SCHOOL
166
Brotton   Skinningrove
Carlin
How   Boulby
Loftus   A174
North   Kilton   Easington   **Staithes**
Skelton   Thorpe   Port Mulgrave
Lingdale   Hinderwell
ck   Margrove   Stanghow   Liverton   Roxby   Runswick   Runswick Bay
d   Park   Newton   Bay   Kettleness
9   Moorsholm   Mulgrave   Goldsborough
d   A171   B1366   Ellerby   14
Res.   Scaling   B1266   A174   Lythe   Sandsend
ale   Scaling Dam   Mickleby   East   **Sandsend** Wyke
Res.   West   Barnby   East Row   SUTCLIFFE GALLERY
Commondale   Danby Low Moor   Lealholm   Barnby   Dunsley   **Whitby**
     Moor   Ugthorpe   Newholm   P&R
159   299   Stonegate   **160**   Ruswarp
Danby   Housyke   13   Aislaby   B1410   Stai 9 acre
     A171   Briggswath   High Hawsker

THE DRACULA
EXPERIENCE
Saltwick
Bay

WHITBY ABBEY
WHITBY

CAPTAIN COOK
MEMORIAL MUSEUM

D

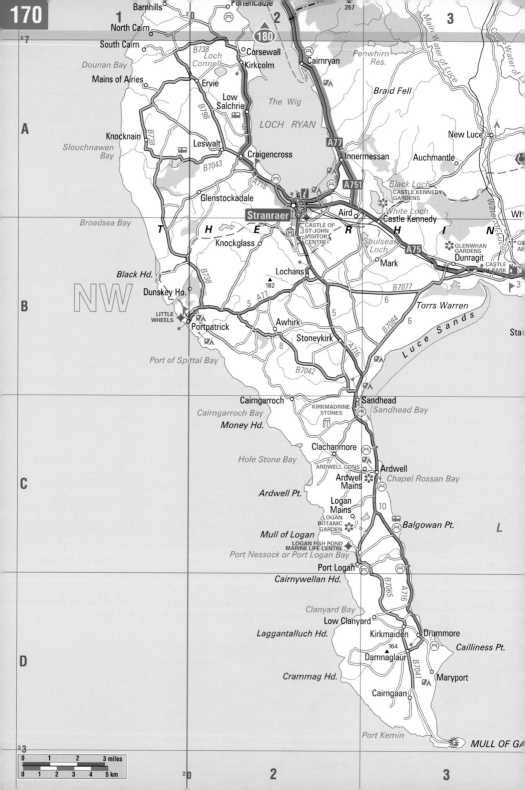

1   **2**   **3**

Barnhills
North Cairn
Portencalzie
257

South Cairn
180
Corsewall
Cairnryan
Penwhirn Res.

Dounan Bay
Loch Connell
Kirkcolm

Mains of Airies
B738
Ervie
Braid Fell

B7798
Low Salchrie
The Wig

A
Knocknain
Leswalt
LOCH RYAN
New Luce

Slouchnawen Bay
B7043
Craigencross
A77
Innermessan
Auchmantle

A718
A751
Black Loch
CASTLE KENNEDY GARDENS

Broadsea Bay
Glenstockadale
White Loch

T H E
Stranraer
Aird
Castle Kennedy

Knockglass
CASTLE OF ST-JOHN VISITOR CENTRE
R
Mark
A75
H
GLENWHAN GARDENS
I
N
Dunragit

NW
Black Hd.
B738
Lochans
182
A77
Soulseat Loch
B7077
6
Torrs Warren
CASTLE OF PARK

B
Dunskey Ho.
LITTLE WHEELS
5
5
Luce Sands
Sta

Portpatrick
Awhirk
B7084
6

8
Stoneykirk
A716

Port of Spittal Bay
B7042

Cairngarroch
Sandhead
Sandhead Bay

Cairngarroch Bay
KIRKMADRINE STONES

Money Hd.

Clachanmore

Hole Stone Bay
ARDWELL GDNS
Ardwell
Chapel Rossan Bay

C
Ardwell Pt.
Ardwell Mains
10
Balgowan Pt.
L

Logan Mains
LOGAN BOTANIC GARDEN

Mull of Logan
LOGAN FISH POND MARINE LIFE CENTRE

Port Nessock or Port Logan Bay
Port Logan

Cairnywellan Hd.
B7065
A716

Clanyard Bay
Low Clanyard

Laggantalluch Hd.
Kirkmaiden
Drummore
Cailliness Pt.

164
Damnaglaur

D
Crammag Hd.
B7041
Maryport

Cairngaan

Port Kemin
MULL OF GA

0   1   2   3 miles
0 1 2 3 4 5 km

2   **3**

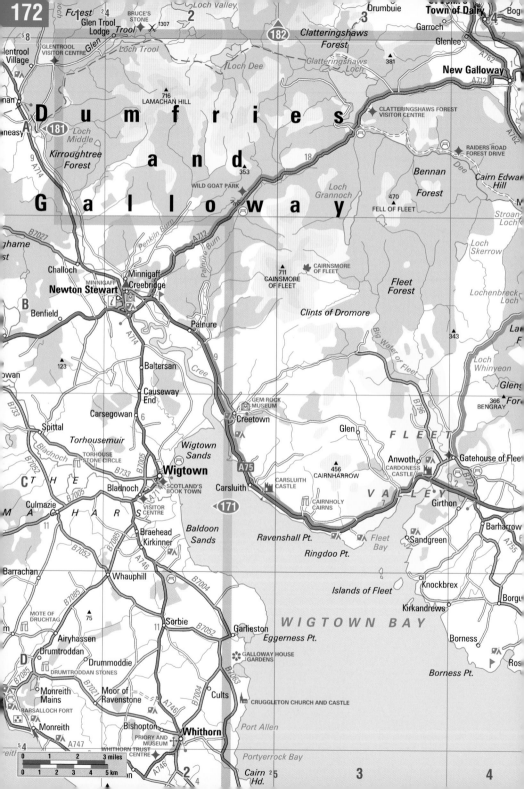

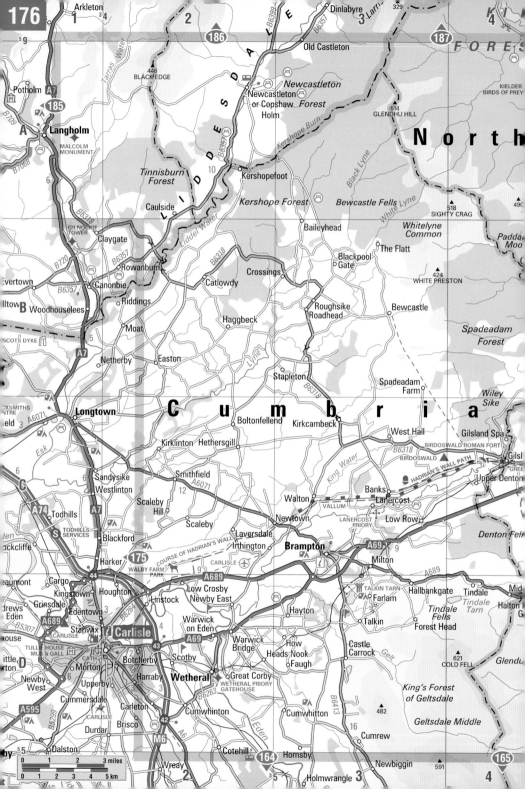

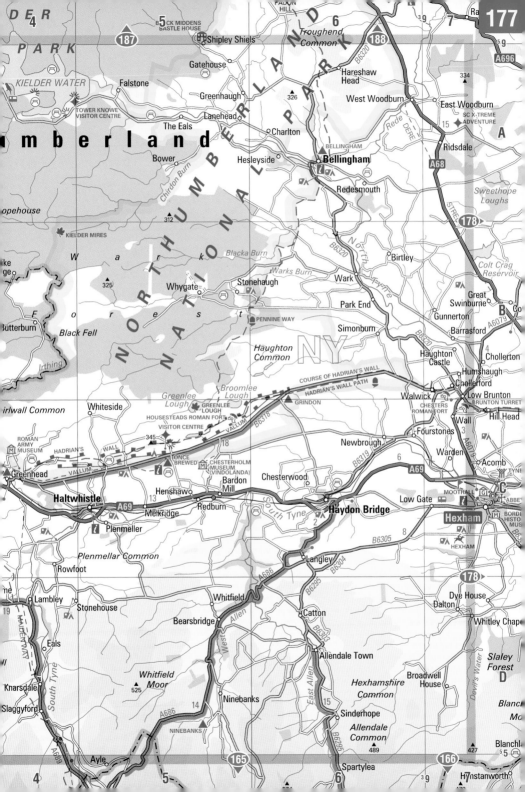

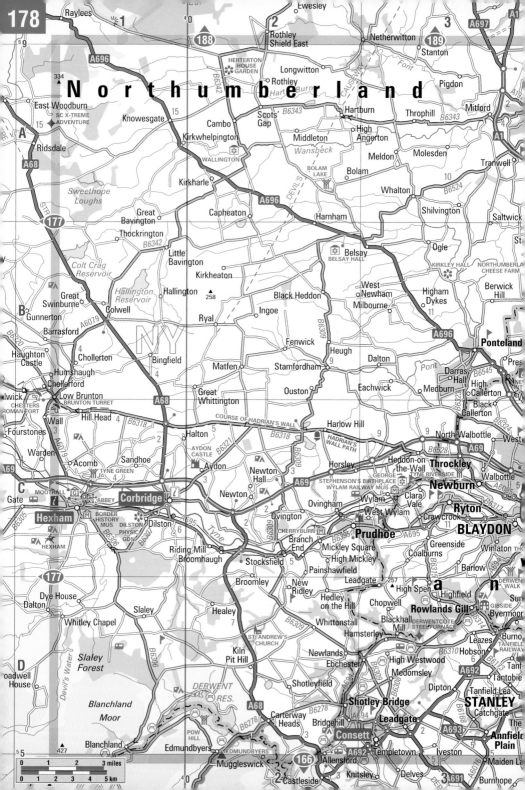

5   4   6

THE SANCTUARY WILDLIFE CENTRE
Ulgham
Linton
Ellington
Lynemouth
COLLIERY MUSEUM
189
Beacon Pt.
Woodhorn
QUEEN ELIZABETH II
A189
A197
NORTHUMBRIA CRAFT CENTRE
Longhirst
on
Pegswood
Ashington
WANSBECK
Hirst
North Seaton
Newbiggin-by-the-Sea
Bothal
Morpeth
A196
Stakeford
A1068
West Sleekburn
Cambois
Guide Post
Scotland Gate
Choppington
Hepscott
East Sleekburn
Clifton
Bedlington Station
Cowpen
BLYTH
Nedderton
Bedlington
B1331
BEDLINGTON
A193
A189
Bebside
Newsham
A1061
A192
East Hartford
New Delaval
B1329
PLESSEY WOODS
Shankhouse
ton
5
Blyth
A1172
New Hartley
Seaton
Seaton Sluice
SEATON DELAVAL HALL
Nelson Village
A1068
Cramlington
Southfield
East Cramlington
Seaton Delaval
Hartley
ST MARY'S LIGHTHOUSE
St Mary's or Bait I.
renkley
A19
Seghill
Holywell
Dinnington
Seaton Burn
Dudley
A190
A192
B1325
A193
Earsdon
Brunswick Village
Wide Open
Burradon
3 Backworth
A1148
WHITLEY BAY
Hazlerigg
A1056
Camperdown
Monkseaton
i
T
P&R
y
Killingworth
Shiremoor
n
e
Marden
Cullercoats
NZ
ONAL
A1
Longbenton
A191
STEPHENSON RAILWAY MUSEUM
BLUE REEF AQUARIUM TYNEMOUTH
CASTLE & PRIORY
AMSTERDAM
Kenton
ngton
nkfoot
A189
A19
THE RISING SUN
North Shields
Tynemouth
ARBEIA ROMAN FORT AND MUSEUM
Gosforth
A191
A1058
Willington
ROYAL QUAYS
Kenton
Jesmond
WALLSEND
South Shields
SOUTH SHIELDS MUSEUM
d
EWCASTLE PON TYNE
Heaton
Tyne Tunnel
TOLL
Westoe
THE LEAS AND MARSDEN ROCK
Marsden Bay
tswood
695
NEWCASTLE DISCOVERY
METROLAND
Byker
Jarrow
BEDE'S WORLD
ST PAUL'S MONASTERY
Harton
Marsden
Dunston
Walker
SEGEDUNUM FORT
84
SOUTER LIGHTHOUSE
ckham
Gateshead
INTERNATIONAL STADIUM
NEWCASTLE KEEP
Hebburn
A1300
2
Whitburn Colliery
Bensham
SHIPLEY ART GAL
B1426
Tyne
Pelaw
Hedworth
Boldon Colliery
Whiteleas Cleadon
Whitburn
ckham
A692
i
Felling
A194
A19
A184
A1018
d
A1
Carr Hill
W
e
a
r
Boldon
A183
Street Gate
Low Fell
A194(M)
Usworth
Downhill
FULWELL WINDMILL
Fulwell
Roker
Chowdene
Hylton Castle
Southwick
Marley Hill
Lamesley
Springwell
A1290
Castletown
South Hylton
Monkwearmouth
NATIONAL GLASS CENTRE
ST PETER'S CHURCH
ANGEL OF THE NORTH
Blackfell
STATION MUS
Pallion
SUNDERLAND MINSTER
Kibblesworth
65
A1231
WASHINGTON
High Barnes
i
Sunderland
Birtley
WASHINGTON SERVICES
S
Lambton
THE WILDFOWL & WETLANDS TRUST
Pennywell
Hendon
Urpeth
Ouston
64
PENSHAW MON
Perkinsville
Barley Mow
Fatfield
A183
East Herrington
New Silksworth
A1018
D
Beamish
Pelton
A693
Rickleton
Penshaw
A690
Burdon
Tunstall
Ryhope
West Pelton
63
Shiney Row
A182
New Herrington
Doxford Park
A19
RYHOPE ENGINES MUS
Grange Villa
B6313
Bournmoor
Newbottle
B286
5
craghead
CHESTER-LE-STREET
Wear
A183
Fence Houses
Seaton
B1404
Northlea
SEAHAM
Edmondsley
THE ANKERS HOUSE
B1284
Chester Moor
Great Lumley
A1(M)
Colliery Row
167
HOUGHTON-LE-SPRING
A1052
West Lea
B1287
Waldridge
B6532
5
4
6
5
4
6

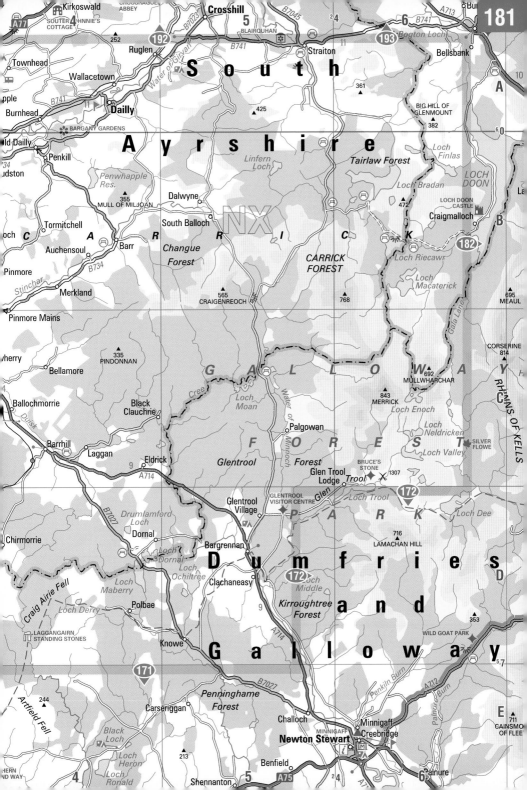

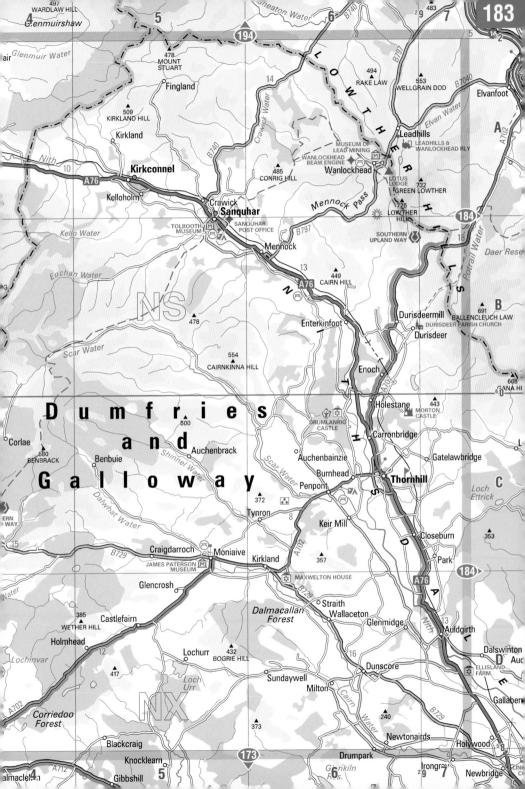

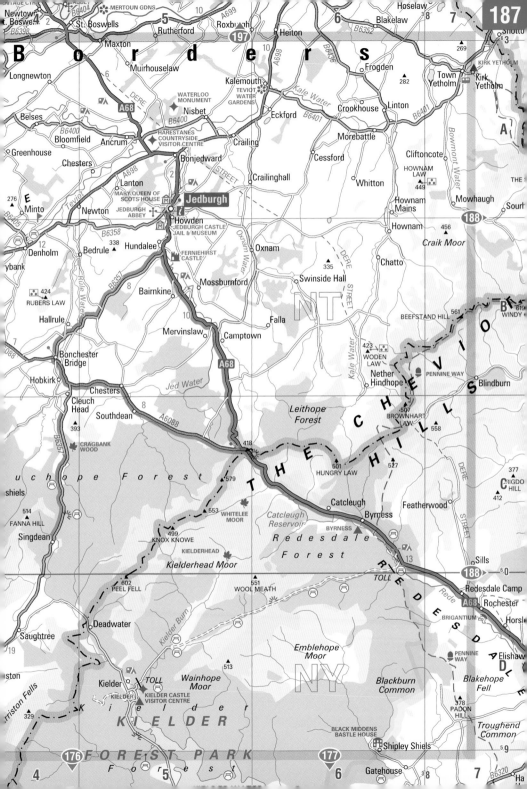

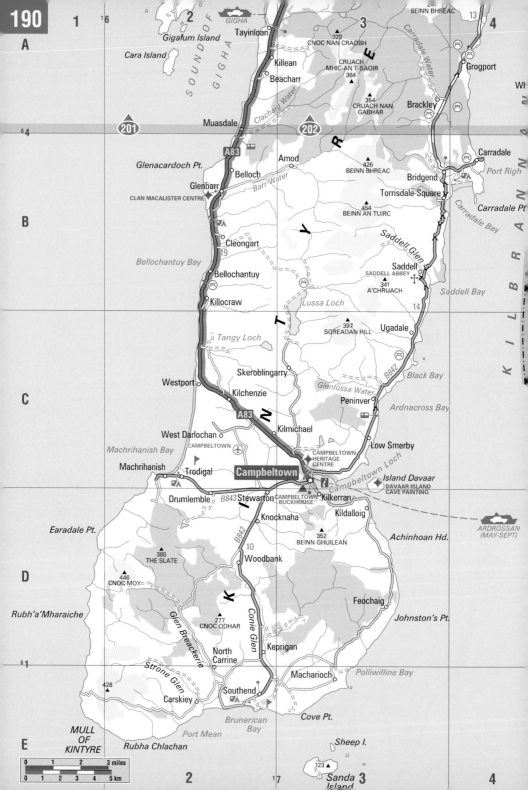

ISLE OF ARRAN

NORTH ARRAN

A841

MEALL NAN DAMH
573
570
Thundergay
Loch Tanna
859
798
Pirnmill
721
Imachar
BEINN BHARRÁIN
CIR MHÒR
BEINN TARSUINN
825
874
GOAT FELL

ISLE OF ARRAN

202
203

NORTH SANNOX FARM PARK
Sannox
Sannox Bay
Corrie

ARDROSSAN

Dougarie
Glen Iorsa
228
BRODICK
BRODICK CASTLE
Brodick Bay
ISLE OF ARRAN HERITAGE MUSEUM
Brodick
Strathwhillan

Auchagallon
Glenloig
A'CHRUACH
512

192

Tormore
MACHRIE MOOR STANDING STONES
503
Clauchlands Pt.

Machrie Bay
Balmichael
Blairbeg
Margnaheglish
KING'S CAVE
Lamlash
Lamlash Bay
Cordon

Torbeg
Shiskine
Holy Island
314

madoon Pt.
Kingscross Pt.
Blackwaterfoot
Kilpatrick
KILPATRICK DUN
458
TIGHVEIN
Auchencairn
Kingscross
Drumadoon Bay
Knockenkelly
Whiting Bay

Glenree
North Kiscadale
Whiting Bay
South Kiscadale
Largymore

Brown Hd.
CARN BAN
Corriecravie
GLENASHDALE FALLS
Largybeg

Sliddery
Lagg
Levencorroch
Dippin
Dippin Head

TORRYLINN CAIRN
Kilmory
Bennan
Kildonan
Bennan Hd.
Sound of Pladda

Pladda

NR
NS
192

180

4 5 6 7
A B C D E

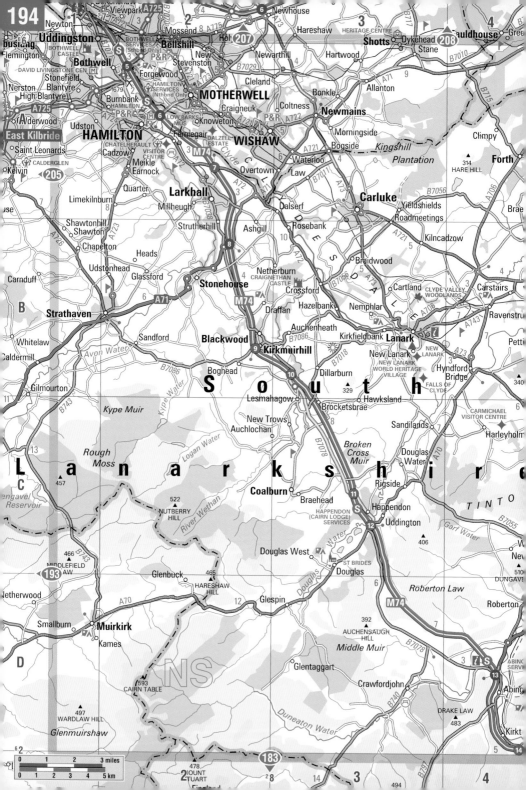

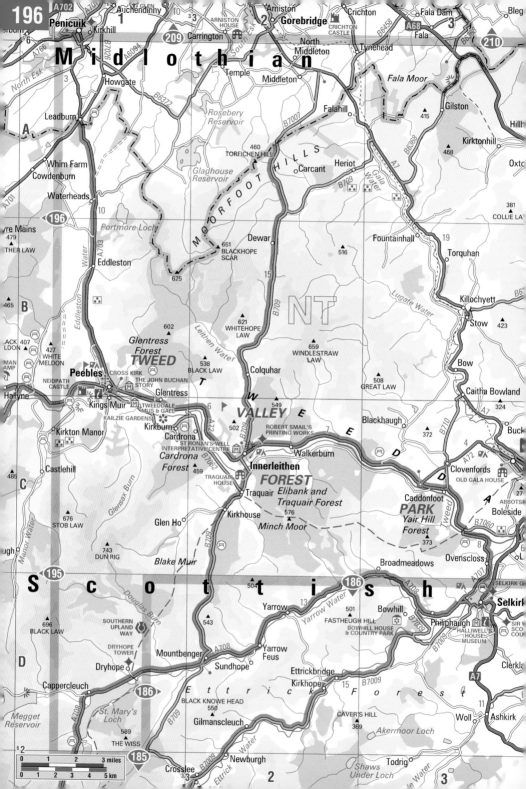

1 ²1 2 3

⁶8

A

Rubha Bholsa

212

Nave Island

Ardnave Pt.

Gortantaoid

Bu
BUNN

316

Carraig Bhan

Ardnave

Killinallan

An Clachan

Sanaigmore

Leckgruinart

Loch Gruinart

Braigo

Loch Gruinart Nature
Reserve Visitors Centre

Loch
Finlaggan

Loch Cam

Ballinaby

Carnduncan

B8018

Aoradh

B8017

Craigens

Loch

Ballygrant

B

Saligo Bay

I S L A Y

Sorn

8

K

Loch
Gorm

Coul Pt.

Coull

Sunderland

B8018

Blackrock

A847

Redhouses

Daill

Coul Pt.

Kilchoman

Conisby

Bridgend

Machir Bay

Kilchiaran

Bruichladdich

Bowmore

Kilchiaran Bay

Islay Life
Museum

BOWMORE
ROUND
CHURCH

A846

Mulindry

RHINNS

ISLAY

Kilennan

Tormisdale

232

Port
Charlotte

15

OF

Lossit

Laggan

Duich

BE

Lossit Pt.

Nerabus

Laggan
Pt.

Laggan

C

Rubha na Faing

ISLAY

A847

13

B8016

Portnahaven

LAGGAN

Port Wemyss

BAY

Glenegedale

BEINN

Orsay

Rinns Pt.

ISLAY

Port Alsaig

Rubha Mór

Kintra

Leorin

D

Cornabus

Imeraval

A846

Lagav

Dùn Mór Ghil

Lower Cragabus

Port Ellen

Laph

THE OA

152

LAPHROAIG
DISTILLERY

Lower
Killeyan

Risabus

Texa

AMERICAN MONUMENT
Mull of Oa

Inerval

202

Rubha nan Leacan

⁶4

0   1   2   3 miles
0 1 2 3 4 5 km

²1 2 3

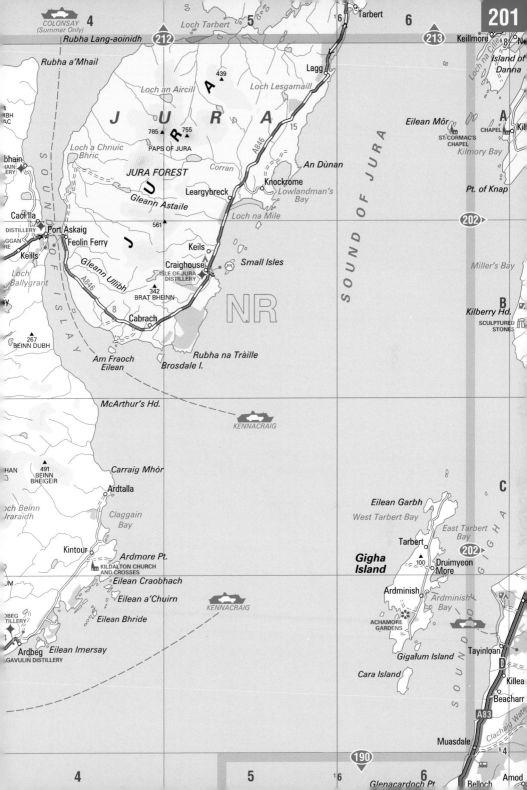

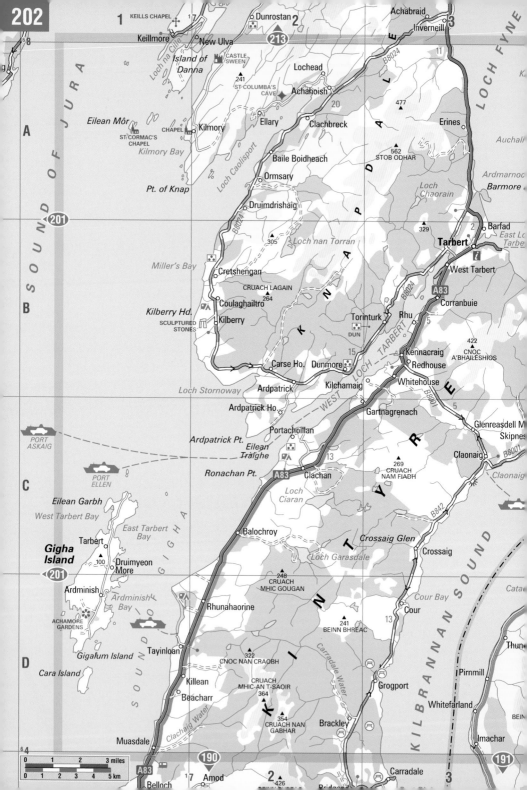

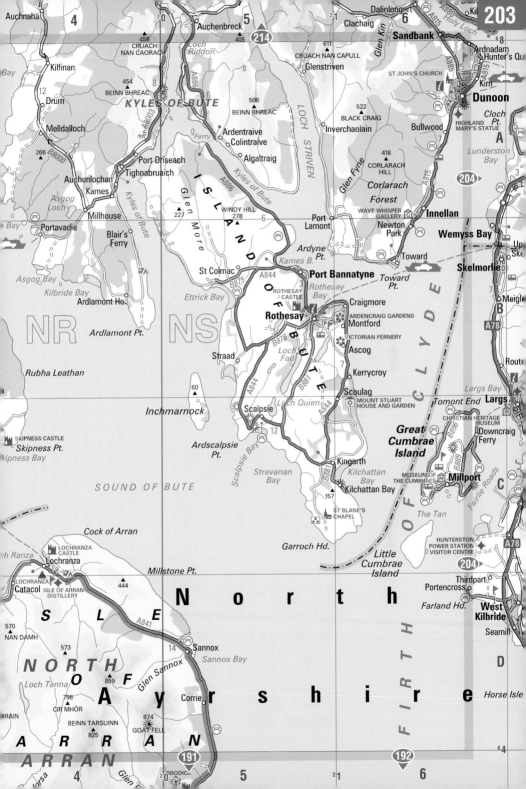

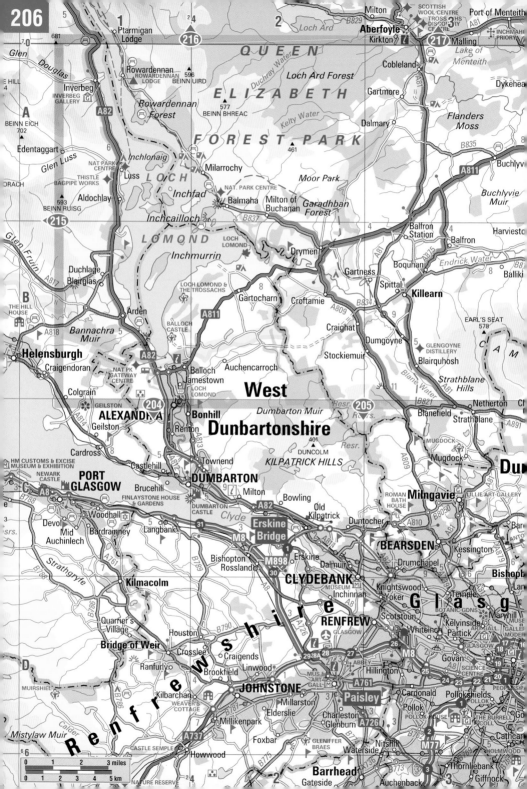

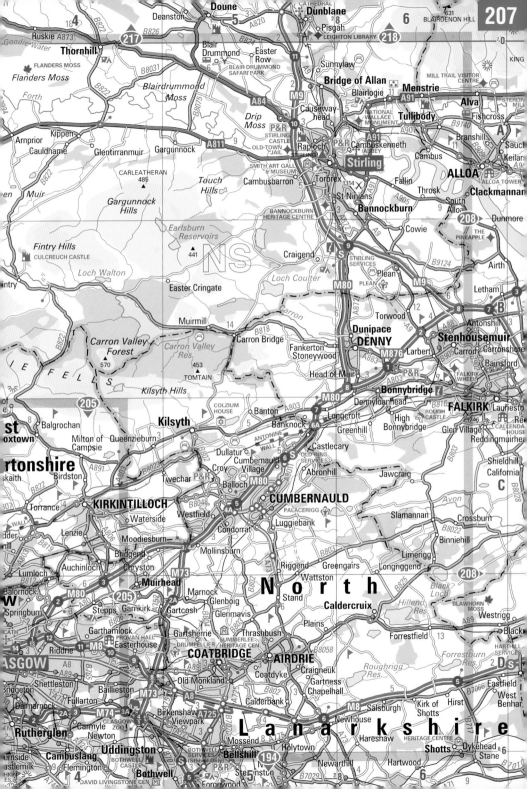

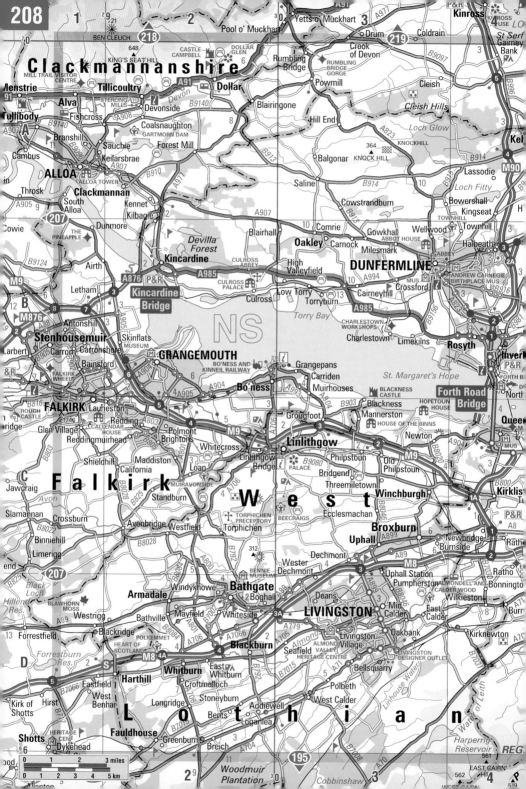

Largo Bay

1 A917 **5** St Monan's Windmill

ST MONAN'S WINDMILL

St Monans 2 221 **3**

Ardross

ST MONAN'S CHURCH

Ruddons Pt.

Earlsferry Elie

Sauchar Pt.

Chapel
Ness

ISLE OF MAY

Isle of May

A

FIRTH OF FORTH

209

B

Fidra

Craigleith

Bass Rock

Eyebroughy

SCOTTISH SEABIRD CENTRE
MUSEUM

**North
Berwick**

TANTALLON CASTLE

DIRLETON CASTLE
& GARDENS

MUIRFIELD

Dirleton 187

Auldhame

Gullane Bay

9

Scoughall

Gullane A198 Kingston Whitekirk

West
Fenton B1345 Fenton
Barns B1347

St. Baldred's Cradle

Aberlady Bay

Aberlady

MYRETON
MOTOR MUSEUM

Drem

B1377

Tyne
Mouth

JOHN MUIR

JOHN
BIRTH

Craigielaw

THE CHESTERS
FORT

East
Fortune

MUSEUM
OF FLIGHT

Peffer Burn

Tyninghame

A198

Belhaven **Dunb**

Gosford Bay

GOSFORD
HOUSE

Ballencrieff

B1347

Preston

B1407 West Barns

i

Spittal

A6137

Athelstaneford

East Linton

PRESTON MILL &
PHANTASSIE DOOCOT

**Cockenzie
and
Port Seton**

B1377

A198 5

HOPETOUN MON ▲ 181

A199

Biel Water

1296 ✕

1650 ✕

**Me
Pink**

Longniddry

JANE WELSH
CARLYLE MUSEUM

HAILES
CASTLE

A1

Traprain

Pitcox

Spott

SETON
COLLEGIATE
CHURCH

1745

B6063

Huntington

Elvingston

ST MARY'S COLLEGIATE CH

Tyne

B6370

Tranent

A1

A199

Gladsmuir 8

Haddington

Luggate
Burn

Stenton

Halls

Macmerry

Penston

A6093

Papple

E a s t

Garvald

D

New Winton

New
Town 10

Samuelston

B6368 B6369 B6370

Bolton

Dunbar Common

397
BRANSLY HILL

Ormiston

209

Carfrae

L o t h i a n

398 ▲

Bothwell Water

Pencaitland

B6355

Danskine

Spartleton Edge

GLENKINCHIE
DISTILLERY

East Saltoun

West Saltoun

Gifford

B6355

Whiteadder
Reservoir

Peastonbank

Gilchriston 12

Quarryford

Longyester

D Peason
Panhead

A68

Long Newton

LAMMERMUIR HILLS

Humbie

Fala
Dam

Stobshiel

Blegbie

527 ▲
LAMMER LAW

535 ▲
MEIKLE SAYS LAW

379 ✕
CRANSHAWS
HILL

Hopes
Reservoir

Whiteadder
Water

Fala

B6457

0   1   2   3 miles

0   1   2   3   4   5 km

196

197

5 **2** **3**

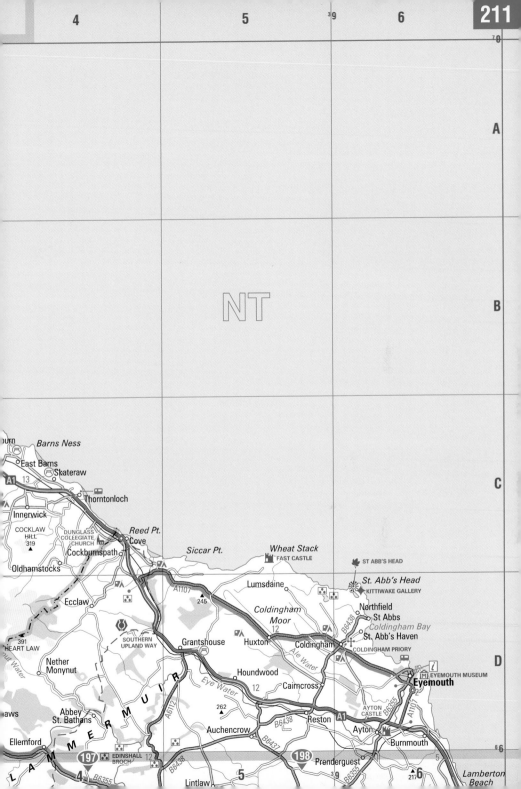

Tiraghoil Bunessa.4 Lee

Loch Assapol

R O S S   O F   M U L L

376 CRUACHAN MIN

376

Carsaig

Carsaig Bay

Rubha Dubh

224

225

Ardalanish Uisken Scoor
Ardchiavaig

125

CARSAIG ARCHES

Malcolm's Pt.

Rubha nam Braithrean

Eilean a'Chalmain

Rubh Ardalanish

A

NM

OBAN

B

7 0

Rubh'a'Geadha

Kiloran Bay Balnahard

KILORAN GARDENS

Kiloran

Kilchattan

COLONSAY

Scalasaig 136

C

NR

Glende

Corpach Bay

Loch Staosnaig

Garvard Rubha Dubh

BBINN 4

453
RAINBERG MOR

Shian Bay

Shian

Dubh Eilean PRIORY

Oronsay

Loch Righ Môr

Eilean nan Ron

318

D

Rubh'an t-Sàilein

PORT ASKAIG
(Summer Only)

Loch Tarbert

6 8

0 1 2 3 miles
0 1 2 3 4 5 km

200

Rubha Bholsa

Rubha a'Mhail

Rubha Lang-aoinidh

201

439

Lagg

Lagg

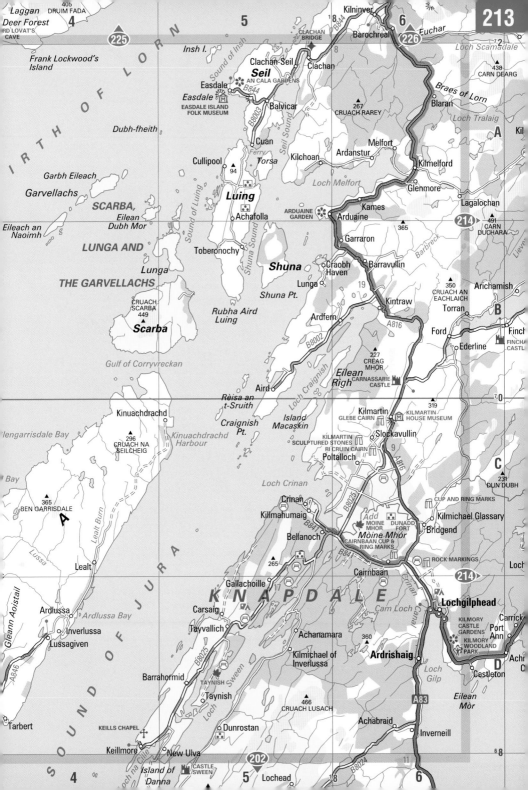

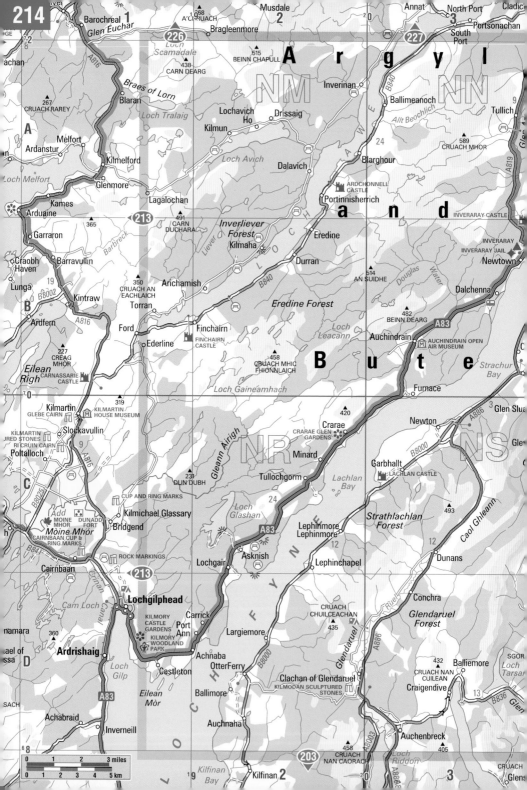

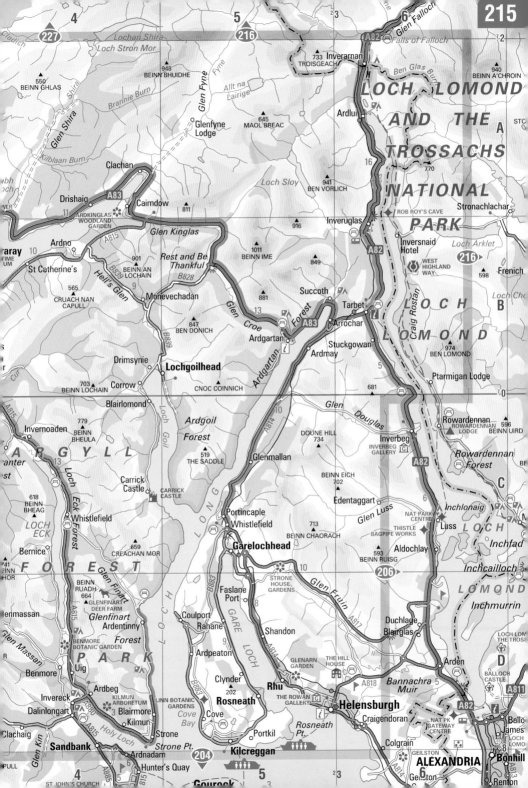

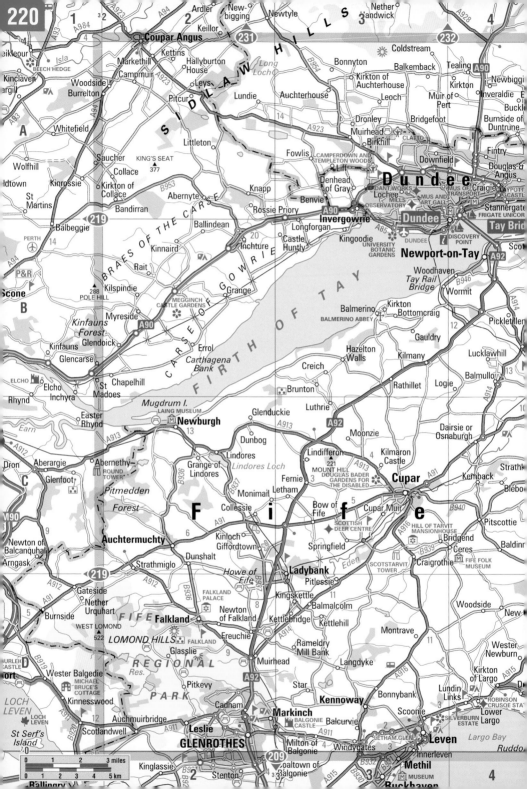

Arbroath

SIGNAL TOWER MUSEUM

The Deil's Heid

Hayshead
Cliffburn
ARBROATH ABBEY

Carmyllie
Denhead
of Arbilot
Arbirlot
Elliot

Hayhillock
Kirkton
of Monikie
Balmirmer
Salmond's Muir
Muirdrum

Monikie
MONIKIE
Craigton
CARLUNGIE
SOUTERRAIN
Newbigging
BARRY MILL
East Haven
Panbride

Wellbank
Drumsturdy
Kellas
SOUTERRAIN
ARDESTIE
Barry
Mains of
Ardestie
CARNOUSTIE
Carnoustie

aldovie
West
Ferry
Barnhill
BROUGHTY CASTLE
MUSEUM
Monifieth
Barry Links
Buddon Ness

A

Tayport
TENTSMUIR

Tentsmuir
Forest

NO

B

euchars
LEUCHARS NORMAN CHURCH
Eden Mouth

ardbridge
EDEN ESTUARY CENTRE
ST ANDREWS BAY

ST ANDREWS
ST ANDREWS AQUARIUM
BRITISH GOLF MUS
St Andrews
Newpark
CATH & ST RULE'S TOWER
Brownhills
Buddo Ness
Babbet Ness

Balone
CRAIGTOUN
ST ANDREWS
BOTANIC GARDEN
Boarhills
Denhead
Prior
Muir
Kingsbarns
Cambo Ness
CAMBO GARDENS
Carr Brigs

Cameron
Res.
Stravithie
Tullybothy Craigs
Craighead

eat Inn
Radernie
Dunino
Balcomie
Fife Ness

C

Lathones
Kingsmuir
Lochty
SCOTLAND'S
SECRET BUNKER
CRAIL TOLBOOTH
Crail
CRAIL MUSEUM AND
HERITAGE CENTRE
West Ness

Largoward
Carnbee
Pitcorthie
Pitkierie
KELLIE CASTLE
AND GARDEN
Kilrenny
FIFE COASTAL
PATH

Colinsburgh
Arncroach
Anstruther Easter
SCOTTISH FISHERIES MUSEUM
Pittenweem
Anstruther Wester

Abercrombie
Kilconquhar
ST FILLAN'S CAVE
ST MONAN'S WINDMILL
St Monans
Ardross
ST MONAN'S
CHURCH
Isle of May
ISLE OF MAY

D

arlsferry
Elie
Sauchar Pt.
Chapel
Ness

286

⁷7

A

NL   **NM**

B

Feall Bay

CASTLEBAY
(Summer only)

Calgary Pt.

Gunna

Crossap Bay

T I R E E

Vaul Bay   Salum   Caolas

Vaul   *Rubha Dubh*

Balephetrish Bay   B8069

Ruaig

Hough Skerries   B8068

Balevullin   *Gott Bay*

R. Chraiginis   Kenovay   *Soa*

C

Kilkenneth   Scarinish   B8065

B8068   Moss   TIREE   Heanish

Middleton   Heylipol   *Rubha Traigh an Duin*

Port Mor   B8065   Crossapol

Barrapol   *Hynish Bay*

Loch a'Phuill   B8067

Rinn Thorbhais   Balephuil   Balemartine

B8066   Mannal

▲141

Balephuil Bay   Hynish

Port Snoig

D

⁷3

0   1   2   3 miles
0   1   2   3   4   5 km

Sanna Point

Sanna Bay

Sanr

Portuairk

Point of
Ardnamurchan
ARDNAMURCHAN LIGHTHOUSE

Achosr

B800

A

Cairns of Coll

234

Rubha Mor

Eilean Mor

Sorisdale

Bousd

An Acairseid

Orms

Ormsaig

Cliad Bay

Arnabost

Gallanach

B8072

Grishipoll

B8071

Loch
Cliad

Ardmore
Bay

lyhaugh

104

73

C O L L

OBAN

Quinish Pt.

Glengor
Castle

Bay

M i s h n i s h

B

Arinagour

B8070

Loch Eatharna

Caliach Pt.

Rubha
an Aird

Sunipol

M o r n i s h

Q u i n i s h

MULL
THEATRE

B

Totronald

Acha

Eilean
Ornsay

Penmore
Mill

Dervaig

Ac

Breachacha
Castle

Friesland

Calgary Bay

Calgary

THE OLD BYRE
HERITAGE CEN

Soa

Loch Breachacha

Treshnish Pt.

Ensay

342
CARN MOR

Achna

Haunn

B8073

Rubh a'Chaoil

224

Burg

Kilninian

Achleck

23

Fanmore

390

C

Treshnish Isles

Fladda

Ballygown

EAS FORS
WATERFALL

Eilean Dioghlum

L O C H   T U A T H

Lunga

Gometra

Bearnus

313

Laggan
Bay

U l v a

Ulva House

Bac Mor

Little
Colonsay

INCH KENNETH
CHAPEL

Inch
Kenneth

D

Staffa

STAFFA

B

FINGAL'S CAVE

MACKINNON'S CAVE

Erisgeir

519

BEIN 3 NA S

1
3
2
234
3

A

COLL
Gallanach
nab
B8072
B8071
B8070
73
Arinagour
Loch Cliad
Loch Eatharna
Eilean Ornsay
riesland
TIREE

OBAN

Ardmore Bay
Ardmore Pt.
Bloody

Quinish Pt.
Glengorm Castle
MULL MUSEUM

Rubha an Aird
Quinish
Mishnish
Tobermory
'S AIRDE-BEINN
292
7

Caliach Pt.
Sunipol
Mornish
Penmore Mill
MULL THEATRE
Dervaig
Achnadrish
SPE

Calgary
THE OLD BYRE HERITAGE CENTRE

Calgary Bay

B

Treshnish Pt.
Ensay
342 CARN MOR
Achnacraig

Haunn
Loch Frisa

Rubh a'Chaoil
B8073
Burg
Kilninian
Bellart

223
Achleck
23
Fanmore
390

Treshnish Isles
Fladda
Ballygown

Eilean Dioghlum
LOCH TUATH
EAS FORS WATERFALL
424 BEINN NA DRISE

Lunga
Gometra
Bearnus
313
Lagganulva

Laggan Bay
Oskamull

Ulva
Ulva House
Killi

Sound of Ulva

C

Bac Mor
LOCH NA KEAL

Little Colonsay
Eorsa

INCH KENNETH CHAPEL
ISLE OF

Staffa
STAFFA
Inch Kenneth
17
De

FINGAL'S CAVE
Balnahard

Erisgeir
MACKINNON'S CAVE
561

519
BEINN NA SREINE

Glen Seilisdeir
ARDMEANACH

THE BURG
Kilfin Bay

D

MACLEAN'S CROSS
Eilean Annraidh
Rubha nan Cearc
LOCH SCRIDAIN

IONA ABBEY AND CATHEDRAL
100
Kintra
Torran

IONA HERITAGE CENTRE
ST COLUMBA EXHIBITION & WELCOME CENTRE
Loch na Lathaich

Iona
Baile Mor
Eorabus
BR

Stac an Aoineadh
Aridhglas
A849
18

Sound of Iona
Fionnphort
Lee

Fidden
Tiraghoil
376 CRUACHAN MIN

Erraid
Bunessan
Loch Assapol

212
ROSS OF MULL

2
Ardalanish
Uisken
Scoor
3
Ardchiavaig

0   1   2   3 miles
0   1   2   3   4   5 km

Jean's Nose
Ardslignish
Eilean
Mor
Oronsay
Auliston Pt.

Glenborrodale
BEN LAGA
Laga
B8007
235
Carna
169

Glencripesdale
Glencripesdale
516
MEALL AN
DAMHAIN

Camuschoirk
Liddesdale
A884
18
B8043
Loch Uisge

TOBERMORY
Calve I.
TOBERMORY
DISTILLERY
Upper
Druimfin

Drimnin
Bonnavoulin
Rhemore
451
BEINN BHUIDHE

571
BEINN IADAIN
Loch Teacuis
M O R V E R N
Gleann Dubh
582
BEINN NAM
BEATHRACH

Loch Uisge
A
Beach

AROS
more

Ardnacross
Killundine

550
STITHEAN NA
RAPLAICH
Loch Arienas

Acharn
Gleann Geal
Claggan

739
BEINN MHEADH

S O U N D
Fiunary
Savary

Larachbeg
KINLOCHALINE
CASTLE
Achranich
Rannoch
ARDTORNISH
GARDENS

437
BEINN A'
CHAISIL

10
NM
O F
Aros Mains
Rubha Mor

Lochaline
226

Loch Tearnait

Loch nan
Clach

Salen
2
Killiechronan
Gruline
B8035
073
Kellan

M U L L
Pennygown
Killbeg
412

Fishnish
Bay
Corrynachenchy
A849
Forsa

Ardtornish
Pt.
ARDTORNISH
CASTLE
GLAIS BHEINN
479

AN
SLEAGHACH
513

Eigna

Camas
Gorm

Knock

I S L A N D
Loch Bà
591
BEINN
A'GHRAIG

O F

Garmony

Scallastle
Bay
Scallastle
Java
Craignure
Bay

Inninmore
Bay
Garbh Shlios

Rubha an
Ridire
Bernera I.

OBAN

Achin

Kil

A KEAL
MULL
B8035
966
BEN MORE

M U L L
704
CORRA-BHEINN
Glen Cannel
Glen More

Coladoir

761
BEINN TALAIDH
Lussa
766
DUN DÀ
GHAOITHE

Craignure

Lochdon

Duart
Bay
Duart Pt.
DUART
CASTLE

Eilean
Musdile
C

Loch Don
Grass Pt.

Kerrera
Ba

more
se
Aird of
inloch
Pennycross

Loch
Fuaron
BEN BUIE
717
698
CREACH BEINN

17
A849
226
Strathcoil

Loch
Airdeglais

248

Ardmore

Bach I.

Rubha
Seanach
D

503
BEINN NA CROISE
Lochbuie
Kinlochspelve
Barachandroman

Croggan
Rubha nan
Sailthean

Loch
Spelve

376
Carsaig
Leidle

405
DRUIM FADA
Laggan
Deer Forest
Rubha
Dubh
LORD LOVAT'S
CAVE
Loch Uisg

Loch Buie

F I R T H   O F   L O R N

CLACHAN
BRIDGE
2
B844

SAIG ARCHES
212
4
Frank Lockwood's
Island
5
213
Insh I.
Sound of Insh
6
Clachan-Seil
Seil
Clachan

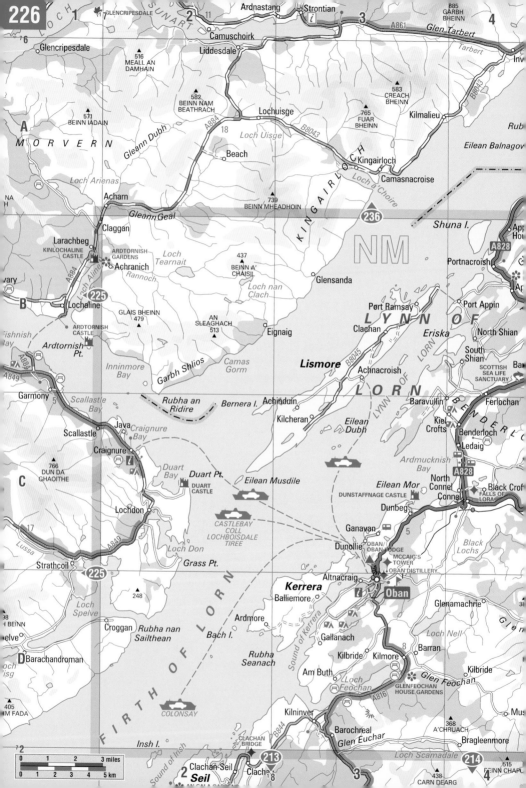

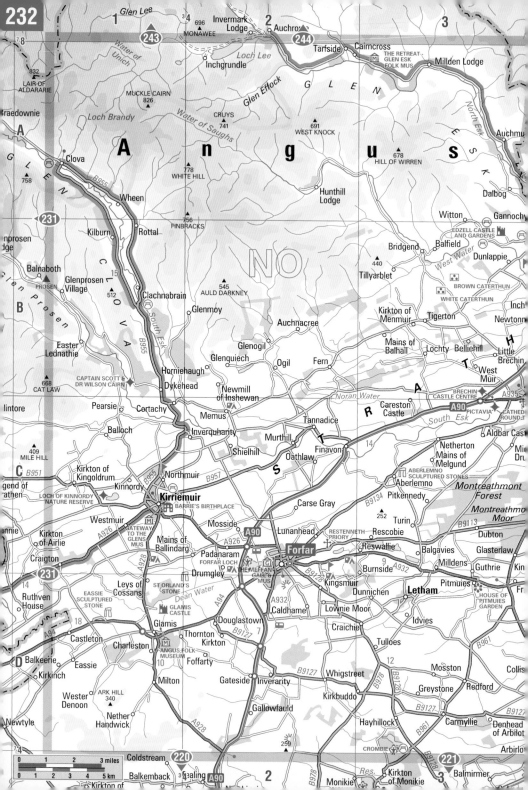

THE SMALL ISLES

Guirdil Bay

388

246

CANNA

Kinloch Glen

Rubha na Roinne

A'Bhrideanach

Kinloch

Loch Scresort

Schooner Pt.

571
ORVAL

R Ù M

Rùm

KINLOCH
CASTLE

Rubha Port
na Caranean

A

Harris

Glen Harris

Rubha Sgorr
an t-Snidhe

812
ASKIVAL

781
AINSHVAL

SOUND OF RÙM

Rubha nam
Meirleach

Bay of Laig

Cleada

Rubha an
Fhasaidh

Eigg

B

393
AN SGURR

Galm

Ki

E

Eilean nan Each

SOUND OF EIGG

137

Port Mor

Muck

C

Sanna Point

223

Sanna Bay

Sanna

Portuairk

Achnaha

Cairns of Coll

Point of
Ardnamurchan
ARDNAMURCHAN LIGHTHOUSE

Achosnich

223

D

Rubha Mor

Eilean Mor

Bousd

Sorisdale

An Acairseid

Ormsaigmore

Kilc

B8007

Ormsaigbeg

Kilchoan
Bay

COLL

rnab

B8072

Gallanach

B8071

0   1   2   3 miles
0 1 2 3 4 5 km

Ardmore Bay

Ardmore Pt.

Blood

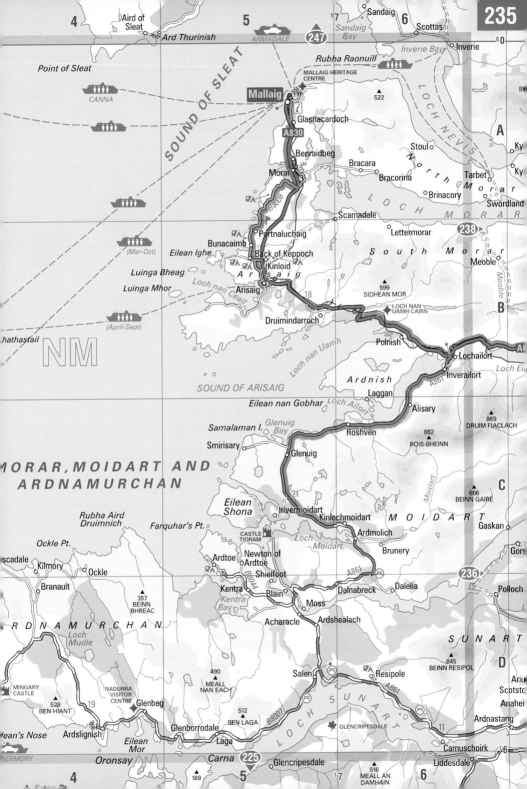

4   5   7   6   8

Sandaig
Scottas
Inverie
Aird of
Sleat
Ard Thurinish
ARMADALE
247
Sandaig
Bay
Inverie Bay
Rubha Raonuill
MALLAIG HERITAGE
CENTRE
Point of Sleat
LOCH NEVIS
522
A
CANNA
Mallaig
A830
Glasnacardoch
Stoul
Ky
Ky
Bepraidbeg
Bracara
Tarbet
Morar
Bracorina
Swordland
Brinacory
North Morar
B8008
Scamadale
LOCH MORAR
Lettermorar
238
Portnaluchaig
South Morar
Meoble
Bunacaimb
Eilean Ighe
Back of Keppoch
Kinloid
599
SIDHEAN MOR
B
Luinga Bheag
Arisaig
Arisaig
18
LOCH NAN
UAMH CAIRN
Luinga Mhor
Loch nan Ceall
Druimindarroch
Polnish
Lochailort
hathastail
Loch nan Uamh
Inverailort
Loch Ei
A
NM
Ardnish
A861
SOUND OF ARISAIG
Laggan
Eilean nan Gobhar
Loch Ailort
Alisary
869
DRUIM FIACLACH
Samalaman I.
Glenuig
Bay
Roshven
882
ROIS-BHEINN
Smirisary
Glenuig
C
MORAR, MOIDART AND
ARDNAMURCHAN
21
666
BEINN GAIRE
Eilean
Shona
Invermoidart
Kinlochmoidart
M O I D A R T
Gaskan
Rubha Aird
Druimnich
Farquhar's Pt.
CASTLE
TIORAM
Loch
Moidart
Ardmolich
Brunery
Ockle Pt.
Ardtoe
Newton of
Ardtoe
A861
236
Gors
scadale
Kilmory
Ockle
Branault
B8044
Shielfoot
Dalnabreck
Dalelia
Polloch
Kentra
Blain
Moss
357
BEINN
BHREAC
Kentra
Bay
Acharacle
Ardshealach
S U N A R T
RDNAMURCHAN
Loch
Mudle
Salen
Resipole
845
BEINN RESIPOL
D
490
MEALL
NAN EACH
A861
Ariu
Scotsto
Anahei
Ardnastang
MINGARY
CASTLE
NADURRA VISITOR
CENTRE
Glenbeg
512
BEN LAGA
LOCH SUNART
11
528
BEN HIANT
19
B8007
GLENCRIPESDALE
ean's Nose
Ardslignish
Glenborrodale
Laga
Camuschoirk
Eilean
Mor
Oronsay
Carna
225
Glencripesdale
516
MEALL AN
DAMHAIN
Liddesdale
BERMORY
4   5   7   6

169

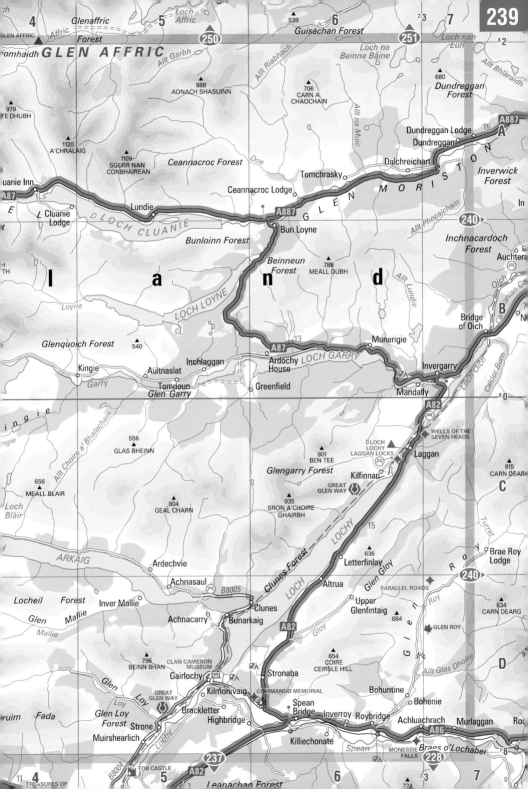

GLEN AFFRIC

Glenaffric Forest
Guisachan Forest

AONACH SHASUINN 888

706 CARN A CHAOCHAIN

680 Dundreggan Forest

Dundreggan Lodge
Dundreggan

A887

15

A

Loch na Beinne Bàine

Loch nan Eun

Allt Bhlaraidh

1120 A'CHRALAIG
979

1109 SGURR NAN CONBHAIREAN

Ceannacroc Forest

Doe

Allt Riabhach

Allt na Muic

Dalchreichart

Tomchrasky

GLEN MORISTON

Inverwick Forest

In

Cluanie Inn
A87

L Cluanie Lodge

Lundie

DLOCH CLUANIE

Ceannacroc Lodge

A887

Bun Loyne

240

Inchnacardoch Forest

Auchtera

Allt Phocaichain

Oich

I   a   n   d

Beinneun Forest
788 MEALL DUBH

B

Bridge of Oich

N

Loyne

LOCH LOYNE

Allt Lundie

Caledonian Ca

Glenquoich Forest
540

Kingie

Aultnaslat

Garry

Inchlaggan

Ardochy House

Munerigie

LOCH GARRY

13

A87

Invergarry

Loch Oich

Calder Burn

7

ingie

ingie

Tomdoun
Glen Garry

Greenfield

Mandally

A82

Wells of the Seven Heads

8

0

MEALL BLAIR 656

GLAS BHEINN 556

804 GEAL CHARN

Glengarry Forest

935 SRON A'CHOIRE GHAIRBH

901 BEN TEE

Loch Lochy
Laggan Locks

Kilfinnan

GREAT GLEN WAY

Laggan

815 CARN DEAR

C

Loch Blàir

ARKAIG

Ardechvie

Achnasaul

B8005

Clunes Forest

LOCH LOCHY

636

Letterfinlay

Glen Gloy

Parallel Roads

834 CARN DEARG

Brae Roy Lodge

240

Glen Roy

9

Locheil Forest

Inver Mallie

Glen   Mallie

Mallie

Clunes
Bunarkaig

Altrua

15

Upper Glenfintaig
684

Glen Roy
GLEN ROY

D

796 BEINN BHAN

Achnacarry

CLAN CAMERON MUSEUM

654 COIRE CEIRSLE HILL

Bohuntine

Bohenie

ruim   Fada

Gairlochy

Stronaba

COMMANDO MEMORIAL

Achluachrach

Murlaggan

Rou

Glen   Loy

GREAT GLEN WAY

Kilmonivaig

Glen Loy Forest

Strone

Brackletter

Highbridge

Spean Bridge

Inverroy

Roybridge

A86

Muirshearlich

Lochy

Killiechonate

Spean

MONESSIE FALLS

Braes o'Lochaber

228

TREASURES OF

B8004

TOR CASTLE

A82

237

11   4

Leanachan Forest

5

6

7

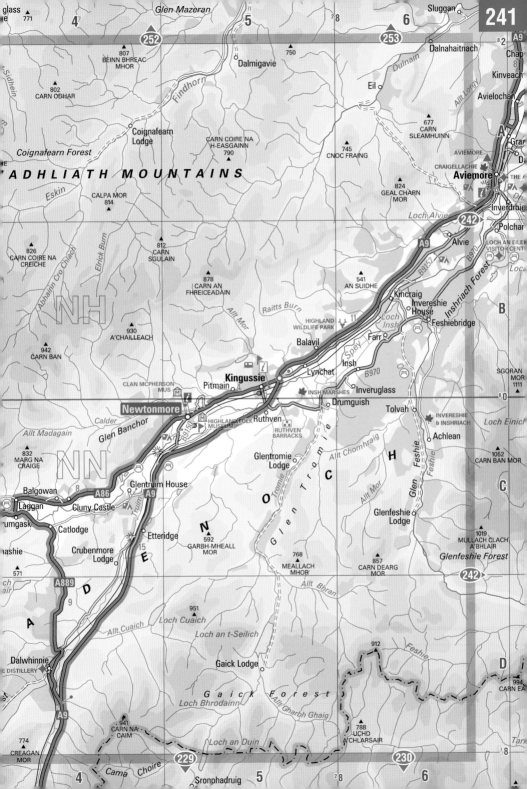

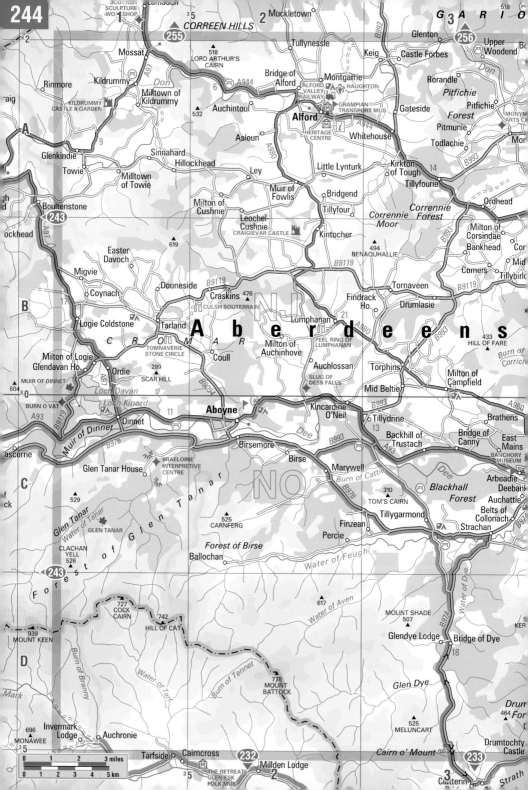

**488
ABHAL BHEAG**

1 Loch
Varkasaig
Balmore
Ose
3

ISLA

2
B885 10

3 Heatherfield
417
258 A863 Glenmore **259**
Mugeary

Bracadale
Loch
Duagrich
A87
9 Conc

Harlosh I.
Tarner I. Ullinish
Struan Coillore
Up

Loch Bracadale
Portnalong
439
ROINEVAL
BR.

Wiay
Idrigill Point
Loch
Harport
Glen Varragill

A
MACLEOD'S
MAIDENS
Fiskavaig
12
Crossal

Rubha
nan Clach
Fernilea
Drynoch
Carbost
A863

ARNAVAL
369
TALISKER
DISTILLERY
Drynoch

Gleann Oraid
Merkadale
Sligachan
Hotel

Talisker Bay
Talisker

Eynort
Glen Brittle
Forest
SGURR NAN
GILLEAN
964

B
NG
445
BEINN BHREAC
Eynort
Grula
459
SGURR
A'GHREADAIDH
973
THE CU

M
I
N
G
I
S

Loch Eynort
GLENBRITTLE
CUILLIN HILLS
Glen Sligac

Glenbrittle House
Bualintur
992
SGURR
ALASDAIR
924
SGURR
NAN EAG
Loch
Coruisk

Loch Brittle
Rubh an Dunain
Soay Sound
Soay

C
Mol-chlach
B

PRINCE

Canna
Garrisdale
Pt.
A'Chill
Rubha Shamhnan Insir

D
Canna Harbour
MALLAIG
(Fri and Sat)

Sanday
Sound of Canna
Kilmory
Kilmory Glen

Guirdil
Bay
Kinloch Glen
Rubha na Roinne

A'Bhrideanach
388
Kinloch
Loch Scresort
Rubha Port
na Caranean

0 1 2 3 miles
0 1 2 3 4 5 km
234
3
571
ORVAL
R **2** Ù
M
KINLOCH
CASTLE
3

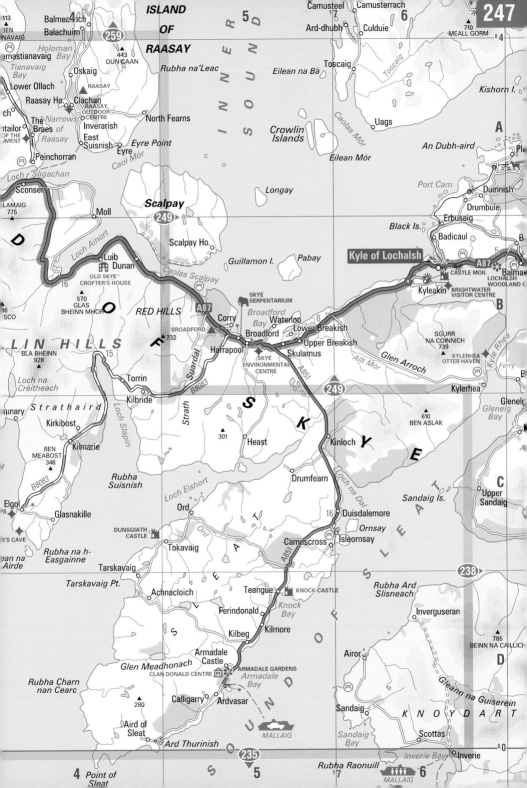

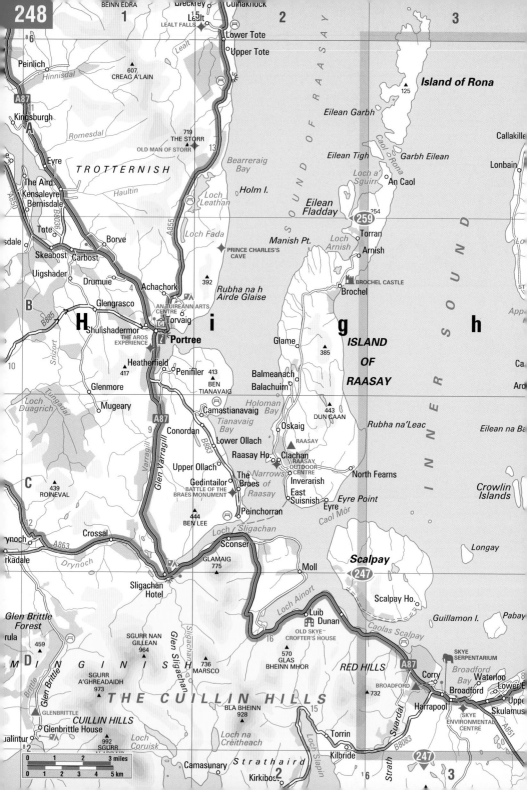

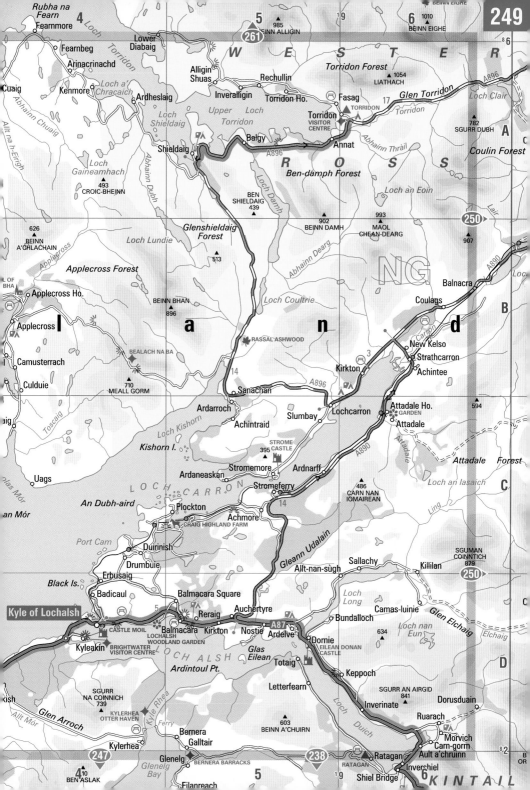

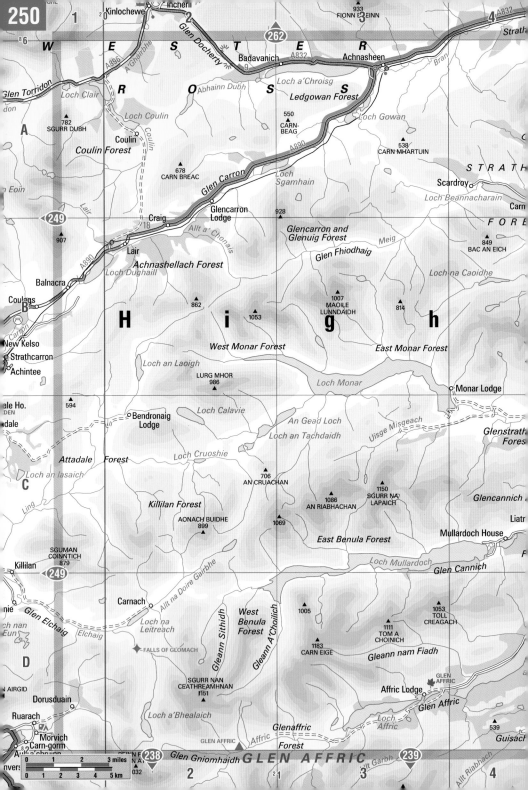

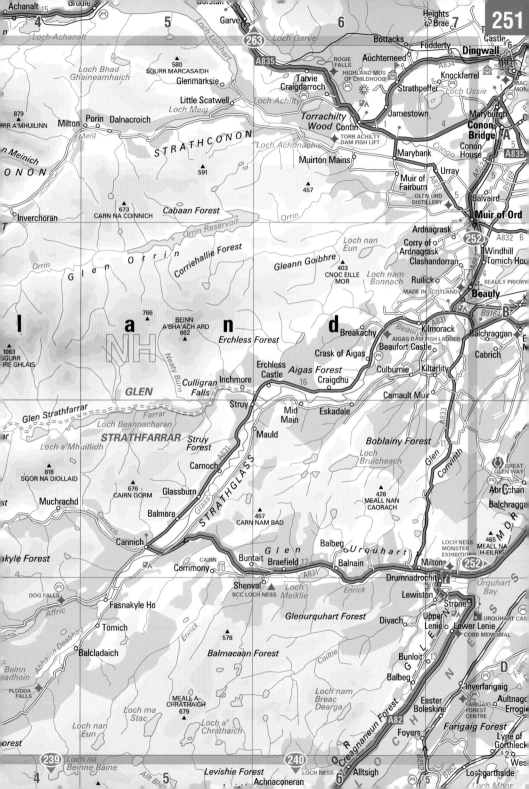

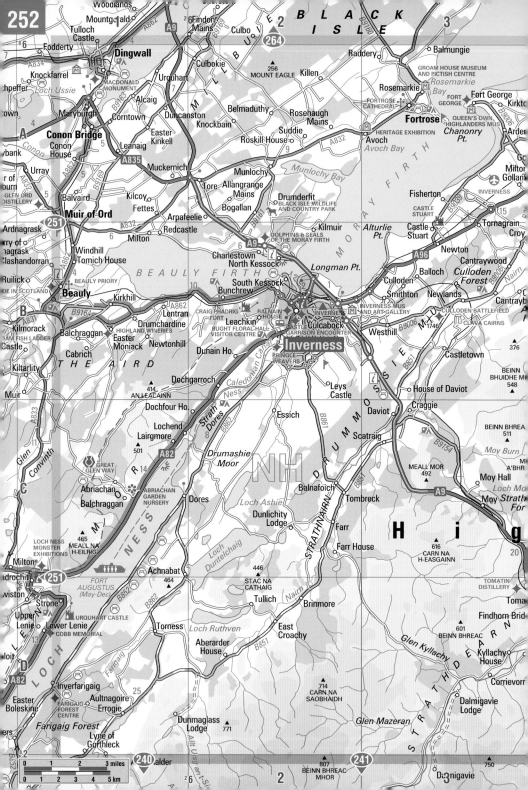

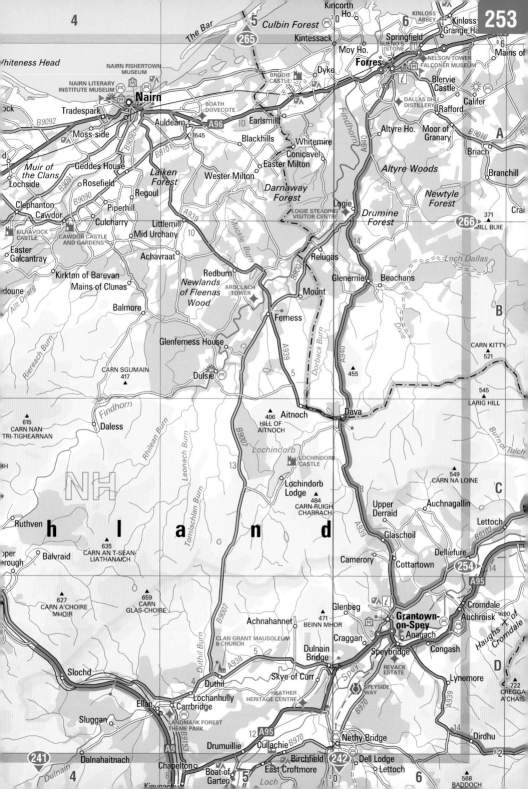

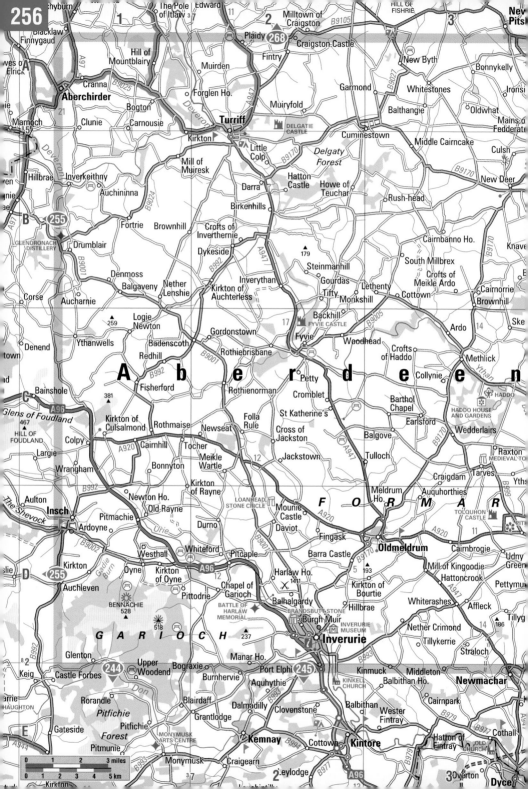

1 2 2 3

A

Fladda-chùain

Rubha H

TARBERT

Lub
Score

LOCHMADDY

Hungladder
Bornesketaig
Kilmuir
FLORA MACDONALD'S
MEMORIAL

K
B

287

Totscore

L

Waternish Point

Kilbride Point

B

Ascrib
Islands

Ru Chorachan

Uig Bay

A855

A87

Idrigill

LOCH

W
A
T
E
R
N
I
S
H

BEN
GEARY
284

Geary

SNIZORT

Ard Beag

TRUMPAN CHURCH
Trumpan

Knockbreck
Gillen

ISLA

Lyndale Pt.

Ardmore Pt.

Lower
Halistra

Upper Halistra

Greshornish
Pt.

Hallin

A87

C

Dunvegan Head

Mingay

Isay

Stein

Lusta

Greshornish

Lyndale Ho.

OF

Treaslane
Suladale

L
O
C
H

D
U
N
V
E
G
A
N

Loch
Bay

B886

Bay River

Loch Greshornish

Loch Snizort

Flashader

Galtrigill

Claigan

Edinbane

Borreraig
BORRERAIG PARK
MUSEUM

Uig

327
BEINN
BHREAC

Blackhill

An Ceannaich

Husabost

DUNVEGAN
CASTLE

SKYE

Lower Milovaig

Feriniquarrie

Glen Bernisda

Oisgill Bay

Upper
Milovaig

Glasphein

Totaig

A850

Loch Pooltiel

Lephin

B884

COLBOST FOLK
MUSEUM

GIANT ANGUS
MACASKILL MUSEUM

CRUACHAN BEINN
A'CHEARCAILL
266

LIGHTHOUSE

Holmisdale

Colbost

Dunvegan

Kilmuir

Neist
Point

Skinidin

Lonmore

Moonen
Bay

Glen Dale

HEALABHAL
MHOR
468

Roskhill

D

Ramasaig

Roag

Vatten

Loch Connan

Hoe Rape

Macleod's
Tables

Orbost

Harlosh

Loch
Varkasaig

Loch Caroy

Ose

Ose

Loch B885

A863

488
HEALABHAL BHEAG

Balmore

Hamara

Hoe Point

246

Bracadale

0   1   2   3 miles
0 1 2 3 4 5 km

Geodha Mor

2

Harlosh I.

A863

10

4 **5** **6** **8**

260
261

Eilean Trodda*y*

Rubha na h-Aiseig

A

Balmacqueen
Kilmaluag
20
SEUM OF
AND LIFE

Eilean
Flodigarry
Flodigarry

MEALL NA
SUIRAMACH
543

Digg
Glashvin
THE QUIRAING
Brogaig
Stenscholl
TROTTERNISH
Staffin
Staffin I.
Staffin Bay

NG

Kilt Rock
KILT ROCK & MEALT FALLS

B

466
BIOD BUIDHE

Elishader
Maligar
Valtos
Loch Mealt
A855

Marishader
Garros
Rubha nam
Brathairean

Balnaknock
611
BEINN EDRA
Breckrey
Culnaknock

g
Conon
Lealt
LEALT FALLS

S
O
U
N
D

O
F

R
A
A
S
A
Y

Lower Tote
Upper Tote

Hinnisdal
N **D**

607
CREAG A'LAIN

Island of Rona
125

C

ourgh
Romesdal

719
THE STORR
OLD MAN OF STORR
13

Bearrreraig
Bay

Eilean Garbh

Callakille
Lonbain

Eilean Tigh
Garbh Eilean

Eyre
TROTTERNISH
Haultin

Holm I.

Caol Rona

An Caol
Loch a'
Sguirr

Aird
saleyre
rnisdale
Tote
Borve
Loch
Leathan

Eilean
Fladday

249
Torran

Loch nan
Eun

Skeabost
Carbost
Loch Fada

PRINCE CHARLES'S
CAVE

Manish Pt.
Loch
Arnish
Arnish

CHAPEL
ST MAELRUB

Jigshader
Drumuie
4
392

Rubha na h
Airde Glaise

BROCHEL CASTLE
Brochel

D

Achachork
AN TUIREANN ARTS
CENTRE
Torvaig

Glengrasco
Shulishadermor
THE AROS
EXPERIENCE
Portree

Glame

ISLAND

I
N
N
E
R

S
O
U
N
D

Applecross
Bay

Heatherfield
417
Penifiler
413
BEN
TIANAVAIG

Balmeanach
Balachuirn
385

OF

RAASAY

Camusteel
Ard-dhubh
8

Glenmore
Mugeary
4
A87
B883

Camastianavaig
Tianavaig

Holoman
Bay
248

5
Uskaig

DUN CAAN
443
6

Eilean na Bà
Toscai

Snizort
Tungadal
grich

1   5   2   3

Garbh
Eilean

Eilean Mhuire

Eilean an Tighe

Na h-Eileanan Mòra
(Shiant Islands)

A

288

288

B

NG

259

Eilean Trodday

Rubha
Hunish

Rubha na h-Aiseig

259

C DUN LM
CASTLE

20   Balmacqueen

Duntulm   Kilmaluag

MUSEUM OF
ISLAND·LIFE

Eilean
Flodigarry

Flodigarry

MEALL NA
SUIRAMACH
543

Staffin I.

Kilvaxter

Balgown   Digg
Glashvin   Staffin
Bay
Brogaig

THE QUIRAING

Stenscholl   Staffin

Linicro

TROTTERNISH   Kilt Rock
KILT ROCK & MEALT FALLS

466
BIOD BUIDHE

Elishader

D   Maligar   Loch Mealt

Uig   Marishader   Valtos

UIG   Garros   Rubha nam
Brathairean

Balnaknock   611
BEINN EDRA   Breckrey   Culnaknock   Island of Rona

Earlish   Lealt
LEALT FALLS

8 6   Lower Tote

0   1   2   3 miles
0 1 2 3 4 5 km   Upper Tote

607   5   2   3

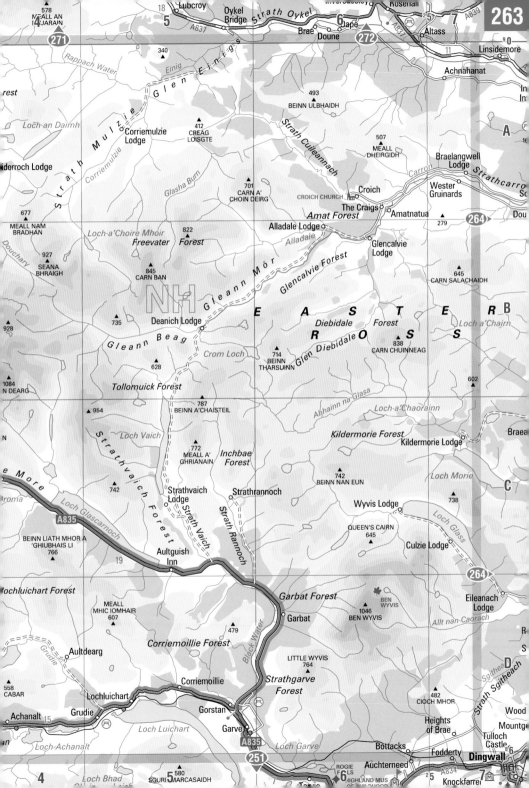

Backies

DUNROBIN CASTLE
MUSEUM & GARDENS

Golspie

A9

5 274 **6**

30 90

NH NJ A

xton

LOCH
FLEET

Littleferry

ourpenny

Embo

Embo Street

dy

WITCHES STONE
OLD POST OFFICE
VISITOR CENTRE

rnoch

LOCH FIRTH

Tarbat Ness
TARBAT NESS LIGHTHOUSE

*Whiteness
Sands*

Wilkhaven

TARBAT DISCOVERY
CENTRE

Bindal
Portmahomack

B

Rockfield

us's

Inver
Arboll

Balnagall
Lochslin

Tarrel

*Loch
Eye*

B9165

Geanies House

Rhynie
Fearn Station

Fearn

9165

Hill of Fearn

Fearn

FEARN
ABBEY

Hilton of Cadboll

Loans of Tullich

Balintore

C

SHANDWICK STONE
Shandwick

B9175

Ankerville

Chapelhill

Pitcalnie

Port an Righ

Nigg

203

unt Canisp

King's Cave

abruaich

266

g Ferry

Castlecraig

RTY
HOUSE

Burghead

Sutors of Cromarty

r's Birthplace
& MUSEUM

BURGHEAD BAY

M O R A Y

Findhorn

Lower
Hempriggs

D

Miltonhill

F I R T H

*Findhorn
Bay*

B9011

NELSON TOWER

KINLOSS
ABBEY

Kinloss

Kincorth
Ho.

Grange Hall

A96

The Bar

Culbin Forest

Kintessack

Springfield

Moy Ho.

SUENO'S
STONE

Mains

253

Forres

Whiteness Head

4

5

BRODIE

Dyke

ALCONER MUSEUM

6

Blervie

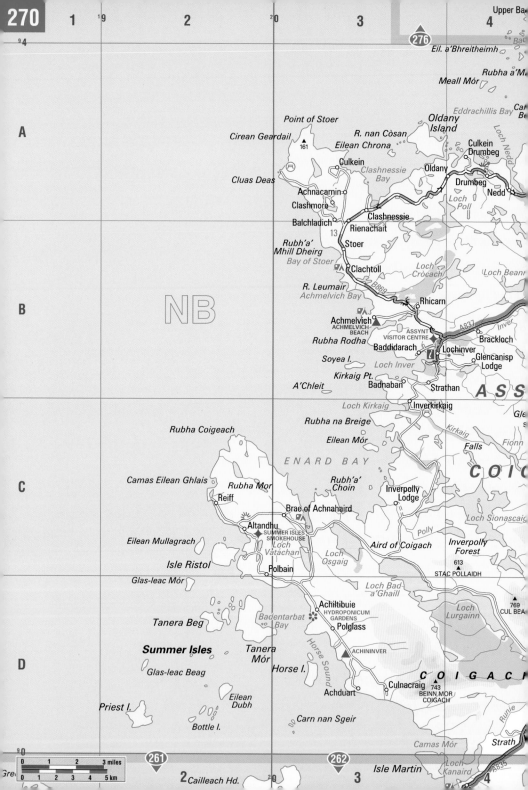

1   21   2   3   4

A

CAPE WRATH

Kearvaig

371
SGRIBHIS-
BHEINN

Geodha Ruadh na Fola

Inshore

Loch
Keisgaig

Bay of Keisgaig

Achie

457
FASHVEN

Geodha Ruadh

Loch Air
na Bein

Am Balg

B

423
BEINN DEARG

Sandwood
Loch

Rubh'an Fhir Léithe

485
CREAG
RIABHACH

Grudi

Loch na
Gáinimh

Strath Shinary

332
GHLAS
BHEINN

Sheigra

Balchrick

A838

Droman

Oldshore Beg

Eilean Roin Mor

Oldshoremore

521
FARRMHEALL

19

Gualin Ho.

Loch Clash

Kinlochbervie

Badcall

B801

Strath Dionar

Bagh Loch an Roin

Achriesgill

CRAN

C

Loch Inchard

9

Achlyness

L. na Claise
Carnaich

Loch Dughaill

Ceathramh Garbh

Dionard

Ardmore Pt.

Rhiconich

GANU MOR
908
Foinaven

Rubha Ruadh

Ardmore

A838

Fanagmore

NORTH-WEST SUTHERLAND

Tarbet

Loch a'Garbh-
bhaid Mór

Loch Diona

Handa Island

Foindle

Loch Laxford

Loch an Easa
Uaine

Loch nam
Brac

Laxford Bridge

Sound of Handa

787
ARKLE

A838

Scourie Bay

D

Lochstack Lodge

Scourie More

Laxford

Scourie

Rubh'Aird an t-Sionnaich

Gorm Loch

Loch Stack

Upper Badcall

Lower Badcall

719
BEN STACK

Eil. a'Bhreitheimh

BEINN AUSKAIRD
386

Strath Stack

0   1   2   3 miles
0 1 2 3 4 5 km

270

Achfary

332

18

Rubha a'Mhecard

A894

Loch
Crocach

R E A Y   F O R E S

271

Lochmore Lodge

Moall Mór

2   3   4

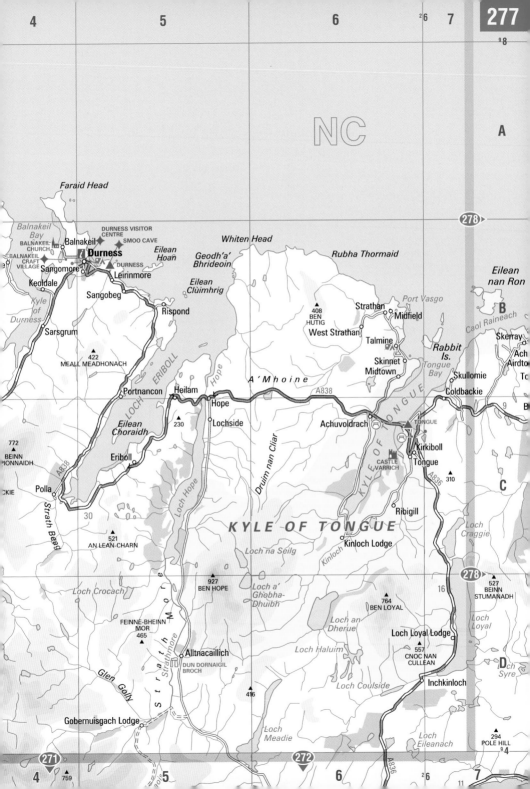

4   5   6   26   7

98

A

NC

Faraid Head

Balnakeil Bay
BALNAKEIL CHURCH
Balnakeil
DURNESS VISITOR CENTRE
SMOO CAVE
BALNAKEIL CRAFT VILLAGE
Sangomore
Durness
DURNESS
Leirinmore
Keoldale
Sangobeg
Sarsgrum
Kyle of Durness
Rispond

Eilean Hoan
Whiten Head

Geodh'a' Bhrideoin
Eilean Clùimhrig

Rubha Thormaid

Eilean nan Ron

B

Caol Raineach

Port Vasgo

408 BEN HUTIG
Strathan
West Strathan
Midfield
Talmine
Skinnet
Midtown

Skerray
Ach Airdto
To

Rabbit Is.
Tongue Bay
Skullomie
Coldbackie

422 MEALL MEADHONACH

LOCH ERIBOLL

A'Mhoine
A838

Portnancon
Heilam
Hope
230
Lochside
Hope

Eilean Choraidh

Eriboll

772 BEINN PIONNAIDH.

KIE

Polla

A838

30

521 AN LEAN-CHARN

Loch Hope

Druim nan Cliar

KYLE OF TONGUE

Achuvoldrach
CASTLE VARRICH
Tongue
Kirkiboll
Tongue

310

C

9

B

Ribigill

Loch Craggie

KYLE OF TONGUE

Kinloch
Kinloch Lodge

Loch na Seilg

Loch Crocach

927 BEN HOPE

Loch a' Ghobha-Dhuibh

Strath More

FEINNE-BHEINN MOR 465

Alltnacaillich
DUN DORNAIGIL BROCH

Glen Golly

416

764 BEN LOYAL

Loch an Dherue

Loch Haluim

Loch Loyal Lodge

557 CNOC NAN CULLEAN

Loch Coulside

Inchkinloch

527 BEINN STUMANADH

16

278

Loch Loyal

D
ch Syre

294 POLE HILL

94

Gobernuisgach Lodge

Loch Meadie

Loch Eileanach

Loch Eileanach

A836

271

759

272

6   26   7

11

4   5   6

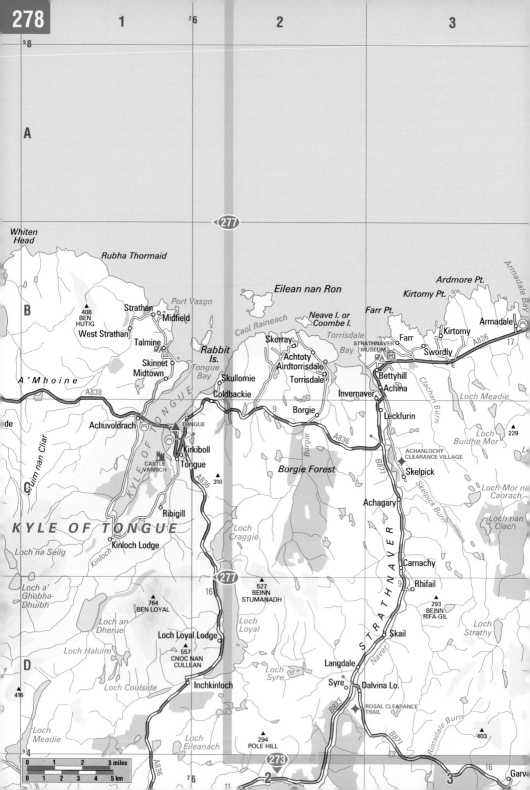

Langaton Point
Nethertown
Red Head
Island of STROMA
53
Mell Head
Uppertown
St John's Pt.
Men of Mey
Boars of Duncansby

ST. MARGARETS HOPE
BURWICK (May-Sept)

Muckle Skerry
Pentland Skerries

283

East Mey
Gills Bay
CASTLE OF MEY
19
Mey
Gills
Barrock
A836
Inkstack
Kirkstyle
Huna
Canisbay
John o' Groats
DUNCANSBY HEAD
Stacks of Duncansby

A
283

Lochend
Brabster
124
Gill Burn
Tofts
Skirza
Skirza Head
Freswick
Freswick Bay
Slickly
Ness Head
Reaster
BUCHOLLY CASTLE
madden
Alterwall
CAITHNESS BROCH CENTRE
Lyth
LYTH ARTS CENTRE
Nybster
Auckengill
Barrock Ho.
Sortat
16
Brough Head
Howe
Keiss
KEISS CASTLE
Mireland

ND

B

Kirk
Loch of Wester
Myrelandhorn
SINCLAIR'S BAY
Killimster
Mains of Watten
B876

Reiss
CASTLE SINCLAIR
CASTLE GIRNIGOE
Noss Head
Winless
60
B874
Sealky Head
Bilbster
Ackergill
Staxigoe
Strath
A882
WICK
WICK HERITAGE MUS
Papigoe
Wick
Broadhaven
Stirkoke Ho.
Milton
Wick Bay
Newton
Old Wick
lipster
Whiterow
CASTLE OF OLD WICK
South Hd.
Gote O'Tram
Tannach
Hempriggs House
Loch Hempriggs
Helman Hd.
141
HILL OF OLICLETT
A99
Gansclet
Thrumster
Loch of Yarrows
Sarclet
212
Sarclet Hd.
Ulbster
17
CAIRN OF GET
Whaligoe
275
HILL O' MANY TANES
4
Bruan
Mid

C

D

4
5
6
35
7

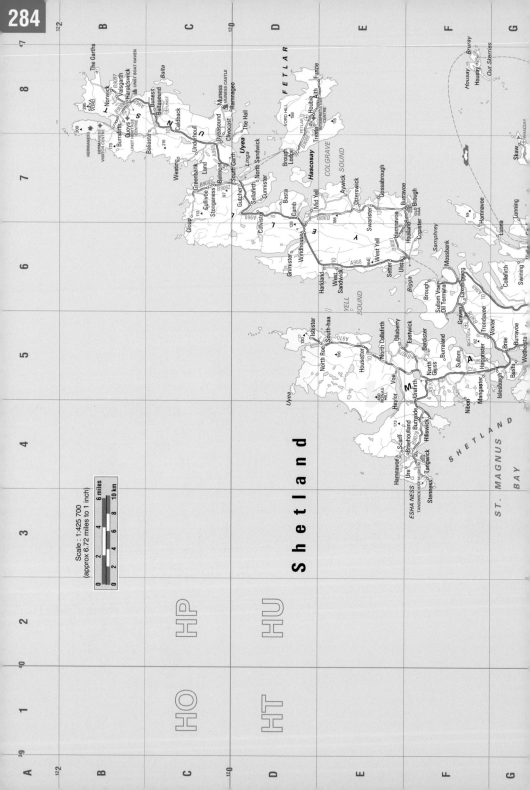

Scale : 1:425 700
(approx 6.72 miles to 1 inch)

0   2   4   6 miles
0 2 4 6 8 10 km

Shetland

FETLAR

SHETLAND

ST. MAGNUS BAY

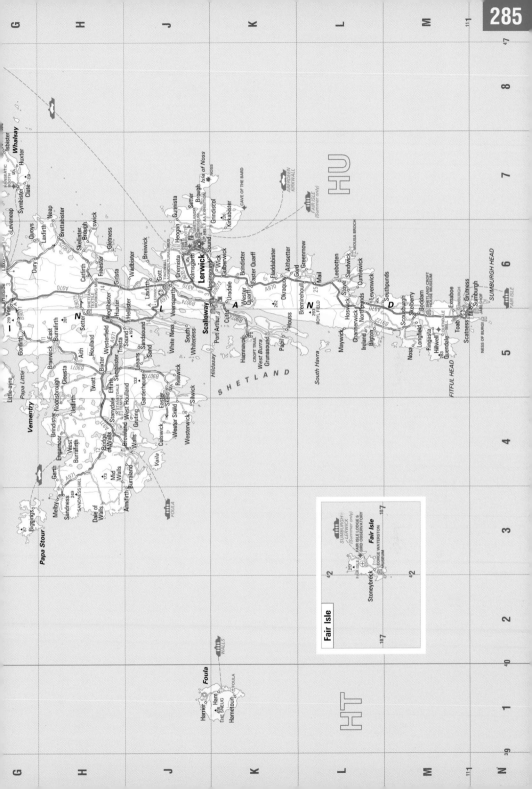

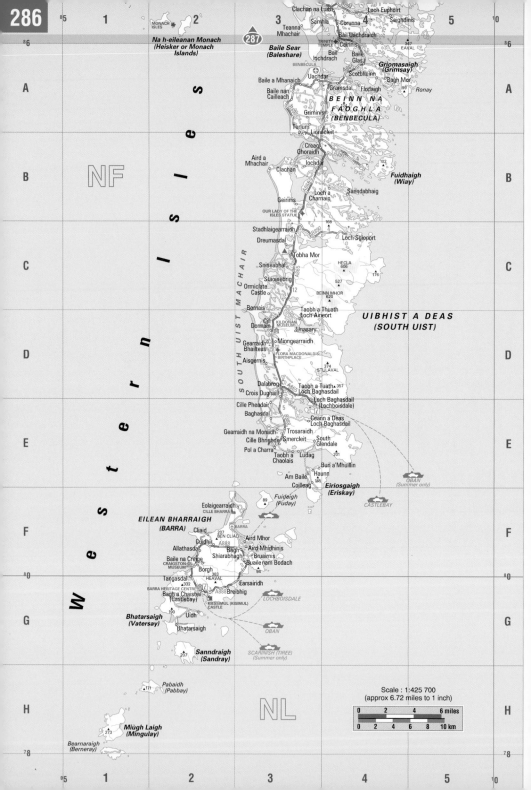

Western Isles

NF

NL

Na h-eileanan Monach
(Heisker or Monach
Islands)

MONACH
ISLES

287

Baile Sear
(Baleshare)

Clachan na Luib
Teanna
Mhachair

Loch Euphoirt
Samhla
Corunna
Saighdinis

Cairinis
Bail Uachdraich

TRINITY
TEMPLE

Bail
Iochdrach

Baile
Glas

Cairinis

EAVAL

Griomasaigh
(Grimsay)

Baile a Mhanaich
Gramsdal
Flodaigh

Bagh Mor

Baile nan
Cailleach
Uachdar
Scotbheinn

Ronay

Geirinis
Forlum
Lionacleit

BEINN NA
FAOGHLA
(BENBECULA)

BENBECULA

Aird a
Mhachair
Clachan

Creag
Ghoraidh
Iochdar

Fuidhaigh
(Wiay)

Geirinis
Sanndabhaig

Loch a
Charnain

OUR LADY OF THE
ISLES STATUE

Stadhlaigearraidh
Dreumasdal

Loch Sgioport

Tobha Mor

HECLA
606

Sniseabhal
Staoinebrig
Ormiclate
Castle
Bornais

BEINN MHOR
620

176

527

UIBHIST A DEAS
(SOUTH UIST)

Cill
Donnain
KILDONAN
MUSEUM
Uhasary

Taobh a Thuath
Loch Aineort

Gearraidh
Bhailteas
Miongearraidh

Aisgernis

FLORA MACDONALD'S
BIRTHPLACE

374
STULAVAL

Dalabrog
Crois Dughaill

Taobh a Tuath
Loch Baghasdail

357

Cille Pheadair
Baghasdail

Loch Baghasdail
(Lochboisdale)

Ceann a Deas
Loch Baghasdail

Gearraidh na Monadh
Cille Bhrighde
Smercleit

Trosaraidh

South
Glendale

OBAN
(Summer only)

Pol a Charra
Taobh a
Chaolais

Ludag
Bun a'Mhuillin

CASTLEBAY

Am Baile
Coilleag

Haunn
185

Eiriosgaigh
(Eriskay)

Fuideigh
(Fuday)

OBAN

Eolaigearraidh
CILLE BHARRA

Barra

EILEAN BHARRAIGH
(BARRA)

Cliaid
Cuidhir

207
BEN CLIAD

Aird Mhor

A888
Aird Mhidhinis

Allathasdal
Bagh
Shiarabhagh

Bruairnis
Buaile nam Bodach

Baile na Creige
CRAIGSTON
MUSEUM

Borgh

Tangasdal
HEAVAL

Earsairidh

332
BARRA HERITAGE CENTRE

A888
Breibhig

Bagh a Chaisteil
(Castlebay)

KIESSIMUL (KISIMUL)
CASTLE

LOCHBOISDALE

Uidh
Bhatarsaigh
(Vatersay)

OBAN

Bhatarsaigh

383

Sanndraigh
(Sandray)

SCARINISH (TIREE)
(Summer only)

207

Pabaidh
(Pabbay)

171

Miùgh Laigh
(Mingulay)

Bearnaraigh
(Berneray)

273

Scale : 1:425 700
(approx 6.72 miles to 1 inch)

0   2   4   6 miles
0 2 4 6 8 10 km

SOUTH UIST MACHAIR

Index to road maps

How to use the index

Example

Thistleton Rutland **116** D2

— grid square
— page number
— county or unitary authority (only shown for duplicate names)

Glos	**Gloucestershire**	Powys	**Powys**
Gtr Man	**Greater Manchester**	Ptsmth	**Portsmouth**
Guern	**Guernsey**	Reading	**Reading**
Gwyn	**Gwynedd**	Redcar	**Redcar and Cleveland**
Halton	**Halton**		
Hants	**Hampshire**	Renfs	**Renfrewshire**
Hereford	**Herefordshire**	Rhondda	**Rhondda Cynon Taff**
Herts	**Hertfordshire**	Rutland	**Rutland**
Highld	**Highland**	S Ayrs	**South Ayrshire**
Hrtlpl	**Hartlepool**	S Glos	**South Gloucestershire**
Hull	**Hull**		
IoM	**Isle of Man**	S Lanark	**South Lanarkshire**
IoW	**Isle of Wight**	S Yorks	**South Yorkshire**
Invclyd	**Inverclyde**	Scilly	**Scilly**
Jersey	**Jersey**	Shetland	**Shetland**
Kent	**Kent**	Shrops	**Shropshire**
Lancs	**Lancashire**	Slough	**Slough**
Leicester	**City of Leicester**	Som	**Somerset**
Leics	**Leicestershire**	Soton	**Southampton**
Lincs	**Lincolnshire**	Staffs	**Staffordshire**
London	**Greater London**	Southend	**Southend-on-Sea**
Luton	**Luton**	Stirling	**Stirling**
M Keynes	**Milton Keynes**	Stockton	**Stockton-on-Tees**
M Tydf	**Merthyr Tydfil**	Stoke	**Stoke-on-Trent**
Mbro	**Middlesbrough**	Suff	**Suffolk**
Medway	**Medway**	Sur	**Surrey**
Mers	**Merseyside**	Swansea	**Swansea**
Midloth	**Midlothian**	Swindon	**Swindon**
Mon	**Monmouthshire**	T&W	**Tyne and Wear**
Moray	**Moray**	Telford	**Telford and Wrekin**
N Ayrs	**North Ayrshire**	Thurrock	**Thurrock**
N Lincs	**North Lincolnshire**	Torbay	**Torbay**
N Lanark	**North Lanarkshire**	Torf	**Torfaen**
N Som	**North Somerset**	V Glam	**The Vale of Glamorgan**
N Yorks	**North Yorkshire**		
NE Lincs	**North East Lincolnshire**	W Berks	**West Berkshire**
		W Dunb	**West Dunbartonshire**
Neath	**Neath Port Talbot**	W Isles	**Western Isles**
Newport	**City and County of Newport**	W Loth	**West Lothian**
		W Mid	**West Midlands**
Norf	**Norfolk**	W Sus	**West Sussex**
Northants	**Northamptonshire**	W Yorks	**West Yorkshire**
Northumb	**Northumberland**	Warks	**Warwickshire**
Nottingham	**City of Nottingham**	Warr	**Warrington**
Notts	**Nottinghamshire**	Wilts	**Wiltshire**
Orkney	**Orkney**	Windsor	**Windsor and Maidenhead**
Oxon	**Oxfordshire**		
Pboro	**Peterborough**	Wokingham	**Wokingham**
Pembs	**Pembrokeshire**	Worcs	**Worcestershire**
Perth	**Perth and Kinross**	Wrex	**Wrexham**
Plym	**Plymouth**	York	**City of York**
Poole	**Poole**		

Abbreviations used in the index

Aberdeen	**Aberdeen City**	Ches W	**Cheshire West and Chester**
Aberds	**Aberdeenshire**		
Ald	**Alderney**	Clack	**Clackmannanshire**
Anglesey	**Isle of Anglesey**	Conwy	**Conwy**
Angus	**Angus**	Corn	**Cornwall**
Argyll	**Argyll and Bute**	Cumb	**Cumbria**
Bath	**Bath and North East Somerset**	Darl	**Darlington**
		Denb	**Denbighshire**
Bedford	**Bedford**	Derby	**City of Derby**
Bl Gwent	**Blaenau Gwent**	Derbys	**Derbyshire**
Blackburn	**Blackburn with Darwen**	Devon	**Devon**
		Dorset	**Dorset**
Blackpool	**Blackpool**	Dumfries	**Dumfries and Galloway**
Bmouth	**Bournemouth**		
Borders	**Scottish Borders**	Dundee	**Dundee City**
Brack	**Bracknell**	Durham	**Durham**
Bridgend	**Bridgend**	E Ayrs	**East Ayrshire**
Brighton	**City of Brighton and Hove**	E Dunb	**East Dunbartonshire**
		E Loth	**East Lothian**
Bristol	**City and County of Bristol**	E Renf	**East Renfrewshire**
		E Sus	**East Sussex**
Bucks	**Buckinghamshire**	E Yorks	**East Riding of Yorkshire**
C Beds	**Central Bedfordshire**		
		Edin	**City of Edinburgh**
Caerph	**Caerphilly**	Essex	**Essex**
Cambs	**Cambridgeshire**	Falk	**Falkirk**
Cardiff	**Cardiff**	Fife	**Fife**
Carms	**Carmarthenshire**	Flint	**Flintshire**
Ceredig	**Ceredigion**	Glasgow	**City of Glasgow**
Ches E	**Cheshire East**		

A

Abbas Combe ... 29 C7
Abberley ... 79 A5
Abberton Essex .. 71 B4
  Worcs. ... 80 B2
Abberwick ... 189 B4
Abbess Roding .. 69 B5
Abbey ... 27 D6
Abbey-cwm-hir .. 93 D4
Abbeydale ... 130 A3
Abbey Dore ... 78 D1
Abbey Field ... 70 A3
Abbey Hulton .. 112 A3
Abbey St.
  Bathans ... 211 D4
Abbeystead ... 145 B5
Abbey Town ... 175 C4
Abbey Village .. 137 A5
Abbey Wood .. 50 B1
Abbots
  Bickington ... 25 D4
Abbots Bromley .113 C4
Abbotsbury ... 15 C5
Abbotsham ... 25 C5
Abbotskerswell .. 8 A2
Abbots Langley.. 67 C5
Abbots Leigh... 43 B4
Abbotsley... 84 B4
Abbots Morton .. 80 B3
Abbots Ripton...100 D4
Abbots Salford .. 80 B3
Abbotswood ... 32 C2
Abbotts Ann ... 32 A2
Abcott ... 94 D1
Abdon ... 94 C3
Aber ... 74 D3
Aberaeron ... 74 B2
Aberaman ... 41 A5
Aberangell ... 91 A6
Aber-Arad ... 73 C6
Aberarder ... 240 D2
Aberarder
  House ... 252 D2
Aberarder
  Lodge ... 240 D3
Aberargie ... 219 C6
Aberarth ... 74 B3
Aberavon ... 40 B2
Aber-banc ... 73 B6
Aberbeeg ... 41 A7
Abercanaid ... 41 A5
Abercarn ... 41 B7
Abercastle ... 55 A4
Abercegir ... 91 B6
Aberchirder ... 268 D1
Aber Cowarch ... 91 A6
Abercraf ... 59 D5
Abercrombie ... 221 D5
Abercych ... 73 B5
Abercynafon ... 60 B2
Abercynon ... 41 B5
Aberdalgie ... 219 B5
Aberdare
  Aberdâr ... 41 A4
Aberdaron ... 106 D1
Aberdeen ... 245 B6
Aberdesach ... 107 A4
Aberdour ... 209 B4
Aberdovey ... 90 C4
Aberdulais ... 40 A2
Aberedw ... 77 C4
Abereiddy ... 54 A3
Abererch ... 106 C3
Aberfan ... 41 A5
Aberfeldy ... 230 D2
Aberffraw ... 122 D3
Aberffrwd ... 75 A5
Aberford ... 148 D3
Aberfoyle ... 217 D5
Abergavenny Y
  Fenni ... 61 B4
Abergele ... 125 B4
Aber-Giâr ... 58 A2
Abergorlech ... 58 B2
Abergwesyn ... 76 B2
Abergwili ... 58 C1

Abergwynant ... 91 A4
Aber-gwynfi ... 40 B3
Abergwyngregyn 123 C6
Abergynolwyn... 91 B4
Aber-Hirnant .. 109 B4
Aberhosan ... 91 C6
Aberkenfig... 40 C3
Aberlady ... 210 B1
Aberlemno ... 232 C3
Aberllefenni ... 91 B5
Abermagwr ... 75 A5
Abermeurig ... 75 C4
Abermule ... 93 B5
Abernaint ... 109 C6
Abernant ... 73 D6
Aber-nant ... 41 A5
Abernethy ... 219 C6
Abernyte ... 220 A2
Aberporth ... 73 A5
Aber-Rhiwlech .. 108 C4
Abersoch ... 106 D3
Abersychan ... 61 C4
Aberthin ... 41 D5
Abertillery
  Abertyleri ... 41 A7
Abertridwr
  Caerph ... 41 C6
  Powys ... 109 D5
Abertysswg ... 60 C3
Aberuthven ... 219 C4
Aber-Village... 60 A3
Aberyscir ... 60 A1
Aberystwyth ... 90 D3
Abhainn Suidhe .287 D5
Abingdon-on-
  Thames ... 65 D5
Abinger Common. 35 B4
Abinger Hammer. 34 B3
Abington ... 194 D4
Abington Pigotts . 85 C5
Ab Kettleby ... 115 C5
Ab Lench ... 80 B3
Ablington Glos... 64 C2
  Wilts. ... 31 A5
Abney ... 130 B1
Aboyne ... 244 C2
Abram ... 137 C5
Abriachan ... 252 C1
Abridge ... 69 D4
Abronhill ... 207 C5
Abson ... 43 B6
Abthorpe ... 82 C3
Abune-the-Hill .. 282 E3
Aby ... 135 B4
Acaster Malbis ..149 C4
Acaster Selby ...149 C4
Accrington ... 137 A6
Acha ... 223 B4
Achabraid ... 213 D6
Achachork ... 259 D4
Achafolla ... 213 A5
Achagary ... 278 C3
Achahoish ... 202 A2
Achalader ... 231 D5
Achallader ... 228 D2
Acha Mor ... 288 E4
Achanalt ... 263 D4
Achandunie ... 264 C2
Ach'an Todhair.. 237 B4
Achany ... 272 D3
Achaphubuil ... 237 B4
Acharacle ... 235 D5
Acharn Highld... 236 D1
  Perth ... 229 D6
Acharole ... 280 C4
Achath ... 245 A4
Achavanich ... 280 D3
Achavraat ... 253 B5
Achddu ... 57 B4
Achduart ... 270 D3
Achentoul ... 274 A2
Achfary ... 271 A5
Achgarve ... 261 A5
Achiemore
  Highld. ... 277 B4
  Highld. ... 279 C4
A'Chill ... 246 D1
Achiltibuie ... 270 D3
Achina ... 278 B3
Achinduich ... 272 D3
Achingills ... 280 B3

Achintee Highld .. 237 B5
  Highld. ... 249 B6
Achintraid ... 249 C5
Achlean ... 241 C6
Achleck ... 224 B3
Achluachrach ...239 D6
Achlyness ... 276 C3
Achmelvich ... 270 B3
Achmore Highld.. 249 C5
  Stirling ... 217 A5
Achnaba Argyll... 214 D2
  Argyll ... 226 C4
Achnabat ... 252 C1
Achnacarnin ... 270 A3
Achnacarry ... 239 C5
Achnacloich
  Argyll ... 227 C4
  Highld. ... 247 D4
Achnaconeran ... 240 A2
Achnacraig ... 224 B3
Achnacroish ... 226 B3
Achnadrish ... 224 A3
Achnafalnich ... 227 D7
Achnagarron... 264 C2
Achnaha ... 234 D3
Achnahanat ... 263 A7
Achnahannet ... 253 D5
Achnairn ... 272 C3
Achnaluachrach 273 D4
Achnasaul ... 239 C5
Achnasheen ... 250 A3
Achosnich ... 234 D3
Achranich ... 226 B2
Achreamie ... 279 B6
Achriabhach ... 237 C5
Achriesgill ... 276 C3
Achrimsdale ... 274 D3
Achtoty ... 278 B2
Achurch ... 100 C2
Achuvoldrach ...277 C6
Achvaich ... 264 A3
Achvarasdal... 279 B5
Ackergill ... 281 C5
Acklam Mbro ...168 D2
  N Yorks. ...149 A6
Ackleton ... 95 B5
Acklington ... 189 C5
Ackton ... 140 A2
Ackworth Moor
  Top ... 140 B2
Acle ... 121 D6
Acock's Green ... 96 C4
Acol ... 53 C5
Acomb Northumb 178 C1
  York ... 149 B4
Aconbury ... 78 D3
Acre ... 137 A6
Acrefair ... 110 A1
Acre Street ... 19 B6
Acton Ches E. ...127 D6
  Dorset ... 16 D3
  London ... 49 A5
  Shrops. ... 93 C7
  Suff ... 87 C4
  Wrex ... 126 D3
Acton
  Beauchamp ... 79 B4
Acton Bridge ... 127 B5
Acton Burnell ... 94 A3
Acton Green ... 79 B4
Acton Pigott ... 94 A3
Acton Round ... 95 B4
Acton Scott ... 94 C2
Acton Trussell ..112 D3
Acton Turville ... 44 A2
Adbaston ... 111 C6
Adber ... 29 C5
Adderley ... 111 A5
Adderstone ... 199 C5
Addiewell ... 208 D2
Addingham ... 147 C4
Addington Bucks.. 66 A2
  Kent ... 37 A4
  London ... 49 C6
Addinston ... 197 A4
Addiscombe ... 49 C6
Addlestone ... 48 C3
Addlethorpe ...135 C5
Adel ... 148 D1
Adeney ... 111 D6
Adfa ... 93 A4

Adforton ... 94 D2
Adisham ... 53 D4
Adlestrop ... 64 A3
Adlingfleet ... 141 A6
Adlington ... 137 B5
Admaston Staffs .112 C4
  Telford ... 111 D5
Admington ... 81 C5
Adstock ... 83 D4
Adstone ... 82 B2
Adversane ... 34 D3
Advie ... 254 C2
Adwalton ... 139 A5
Adwell ... 66 D1
Adwick le
  Street ... 140 C3
Adwick upon
  Dearne ... 140 C2
Adziel ... 269 D4
Ae Village ... 184 D2
Affleck ... 256 D3
Affpuddle ... 16 B2
Affric Lodge ... 250 D3
Afon-wen ... 125 B6
Afton ... 18 C2
Agglethorpe ...157 C4
Agneash ... 152 C4
Aigburth ... 126 A3
Aiginis ... 288 D5
Aike ... 150 C3
Aikerness ... 282 C5
Aikers ... 283 H5
Aiketgate ... 164 A2
Aikton ... 175 C5
Ailey ... 78 C1
Ailstone ... 81 B5
Ailsworth ... 100 B3
Ainderby
  Quernhow ... 158 C2
Ainderby
  Steeple ... 158 B2
Aingers Green ... 71 A5
Ainsdale ... 136 B2
Ainsdale-on-
  Sea ... 136 B2
Ainstable ... 164 A3
Ainsworth ... 137 B6
Ainthorpe ... 159 A6
Aintree ... 136 D2
Aird Argyll ... 213 B5
  Dumfries ... 170 A2
  Highld. ... 261 C4
  W Isles ... 288 D6
Aird a Mhachair 286 B3
Aird a' Mhulaidh 288 F2
Aird Asaig ... 288 G2
Aird Dhail... 288 A5
Airdens ... 264 A2
Aird Mhidhinis .. 286 F3
Aird Mhighe
  W Isles ... 287 F5
  W Isles ... 288 H2
Aird Mhor... 286 F3
Aird of Sleat ... 247 D4
Airdrie ... 207 D5
Airdtorrisdale ... 278 B2
Aird Uig ... 287 A5
Airidh a
  Bhruaich ... 288 F3
Airieland ... 173 C5
Airmyn ... 141 A5
Airntilly ... 219 A5
Airor ... 247 D6
Airth ... 208 B1
Airton ... 146 B3
Airyhassen ... 171 C5
Aisby Lincs ... 116 B3
  Lincs. ... 141 D6
Aisgernis ... 286 D3
Aiskew ... 157 C6
Aislaby N Yorks. ..159 C6
  N Yorks. ... 160 A2
  Stockton ... 168 D2
Aisthorpe ... 133 A4
Aith Orkney ... 282 F3
  Shetland ... 284 D8
  Shetland ... 285 H5
Aithsetter ... 285 K6
Aitkenhead ... 192 E3
Aitnoch ... 253 C5
Akeld ... 188 A2

Akeley ... 83 D4
Akenham ... 88 C2
Albaston ... 11 D5
Albourne ... 21 A5
Albrighton Shrops 95 A6
  Shrops ... 110 D3
Alburgh ... 104 C3
Albury Herts ... 68 A4
  Sur ... 34 B3
Albury End ... 68 A4
Alby Hill ... 120 B3
Alcaig ... 252 A1
Alcaston ... 94 C2
Alcester ... 80 B3
Alciston ... 22 B3
Alcombe Som... 27 A4
  Wilts. ... 44 C2
Alconbury ... 100 D3
Alconbury
  Weston ... 100 D3
Aldbar Castle ... 232 C3
Aldborough Norf 120 B3
  N Yorks. ... 148 A3
Aldbourne ... 45 B6
Aldbrough ... 151 D5
Aldbrough St
  John ... 167 D5
Aldbury ... 67 B4
Aldcliffe ... 145 A4
Aldclune ... 230 B3
Aldeburgh ... 89 B5
Aldenham ... 67 D6
Alderbury ... 31 C5
Aldercar ... 114 A2
Alderford ... 120 D3
Alderholt ... 31 D5
Alderley ... 62 D3
Alderley Edge ... 128 B3
Aldermaston ... 46 C3
Aldermaston
  Wharf ... 47 C4
Alderminster ... 81 C5
Alder's End ... 79 C4
Aldersey Green .127 D4
Aldershot ... 34 A1
Alderton Glos... 80 D3
  Northants. ... 83 C4
  Shrops ... 110 C3
  Suff ... 88 C4
  Wilts. ... 44 A2
Alderwasley ... 130 D3
Aldfield ... 147 A6
Aldford ... 127 D4
Aldham Essex... 70 A3
  Suff ... 87 C6
Aldie ... 264 B3
Aldingbourne ... 20 B2
Aldingham ... 154 D1
Aldington Kent... 38 B2
  Worcs. ... 80 C3
Aldington Frith.. 38 B2
Aldochlay ... 206 A1
Aldreth ... 101 D6
Aldridge ... 96 A3
Aldringham ... 89 A5
Aldsworth ... 64 B2
Aldunie ... 255 D4
Aldwark Derbys .130 D2
  N Yorks. ... 148 A3
Aldwick ... 20 C2
Aldwincle ... 100 C2
Aldworth ... 46 B3
Alexandria ... 206 C1
Alfardisworthy .. 24 D3
Alfington ... 13 B6
Alfold ... 34 C3
Alfold Bars ... 34 C3
Alfold Crossways 34 C3
Alford Aberds ...244 A2
  Lincs. ... 135 B4
  Som ... 29 B6
Alfreton ... 131 D4
Alfrick ... 79 B5
Alfrick Pound ... 79 B5
Alfriston ... 22 B3
Algaltraig ... 203 A5
Algarkirk ... 117 B5
Alhampton ... 29 B6
Aline Lodge ... 288 F2
Alisary ... 235 C6

Alkborough ...141 A6
Alkerton ... 81 C6
Alkham ... 39 A4
Alkington ... 111 B4
Alkmonton ... 113 B5
Alladale Lodge .. 263 B6
Allaleigh ... 8 B2
Allanaquoich ...242 C4
Allangrange
  Mains ... 252 A2
Allanton Borders .198 A2
  N Lanark ... 194 A3
Allathasdal... 286 F2
All Cannings ... 45 C4
Allendale Town .177 D6
Allenheads ... 165 A6
Allensford ... 178 D2
Allens Green ... 69 B4
Allensmore ... 78 D2
Allenton ... 114 B1
Aller ... 28 C4
Allerby ... 162 A3
Allerford ... 27 A4
Allerston ... 160 C2
Allerthorpe ... 149 C6
Allerton Mers... 127 A4
  W Yorks. ... 147 D5
Allerton
  Bywater ... 140 A2
Allerton
  Mauleverer ... 148 B3
Allesley ... 97 C6
Allestree ... 114 B1
Allet ... 4 C2
Allexton ... 99 A5
Allgreave ... 129 C4
Allhallows ... 51 B5
Allhallows-on-
  Sea ... 51 B5
Alligin Shuas ... 249 A5
Allimore Green .102 D2
Allington Lincs... 115 A6
  Wilts. ... 31 B6
  Wilts. ... 45 C4
Allithwaite ... 154 D2
Alloa ... 208 A1
Allonby ... 174 D3
Alloway ... 192 D3
All Saints South
  Elmham ... 104 C4
All Stretton ... 94 B2
Allt ... 57 B5
Alltchaorunn ... 237 D5
Alltforgan ... 109 C4
Alltmawr ... 77 C4
Alltnacaillich... 277 D5
Allt na h-Airbhe 262 A3
Allt-nan-sùgh... 249 D6
Alltsigh ... 240 A2
Alltwalis ... 58 B1
Alltwen ... 40 A2
Alltyblaca... 75 D4
Allwood Green ..103 D6
Almeley ... 78 B1
Almer ... 16 B3
Almholme ... 140 C3
Almington ... 111 B6
Alminstone Cross 24 C4
Almondbank ... 219 B5
Almondbury ...139 B4
Almondsbury... 43 A5
Alne ... 148 A3
Alness ... 264 D2
Alnham ... 188 B2
Alnmouth ... 189 B5
Alnwick ... 189 B4
Alperton ... 49 A4
Alphamstone... 87 D4
Alpheton ... 87 B4
Alphington ... 13 B4
Alport ... 130 C2
Alpraham ... 127 D5
Alresford ... 71 A4
Alrewas ... 113 D5
Alsager ... 128 D2
Alsagers Bank... 112 A2
Alsop en le
  Dale ... 129 D6
Alston Cumb ...165 A5
  Devon. ... 14 A3
Alstone ... 80 D2
Alstonefield ... 129 D6

Alswear 26 C2
Altandhu. 270 C2
Altanduin 274 B2
Altarnun 10 C1
Altass 272 D2
Alterwall. 281 B4
Altham 146 D1
Althorne 70 D3
Althorpe 141 C6
Alticry 171 B4
Altnabreac
  Station 279 D6
Altnacealgach
  Hotel. 271 C5
Altnacraig 226 D3
Altnafeadh 237 D6
Altnaharra 272 A3
Altofts 139 A6
Alton Derbys 130 C3
  Hants 33 B6
  Staffs 113 A4
Alton Pancras . . . 15 A7
Alton Priors 45 C5
Altrincham. 128 A2
Altrua 239 D6
Altskeith 217 D4
Altyre Ho. 253 A6
Alva 208 A1
Alvanley 127 B4
Alvaston 114 B1
Alvechurch 96 D3
Alvecote 97 A5
Alvediston 30 C3
Alveley 95 C5
Alverdiscott 25 C6
Alverstoke 19 B5
Alverstone 19 C4
Alverton 115 A5
Alves 266 C2
Alvescot 64 C3
Alveston S Glos . . . 43 A5
  Warks. 81 B5
Alvie 241 B6
Alvingham 143 D5
Alvington 62 C2
Alwalton 100 B3
Alweston 29 D6
Alwinton 188 C2
Alwoodley 148 C1
Alyth 231 D6
Amatnatua. 263 A6
Am Baile 286 E3
Ambergate. 130 D3
Amber Hill 117 A5
Amberley Glos 63 C4
  W Sus. 20 A3
Amble 189 C5
Amblecote 96 C1
Ambler Thorn . . . 138 A3
Ambleside 154 A2
Ambleston 55 B6
Ambrosden 65 B7
Am Buth 226 D3
Amcotts 141 B6
Amersham. 67 C4
Amesbury. 31 A5
Amington 97 A5
Amisfield 184 D2
Amlwch 123 A4
Amlwch Port 123 A4
Ammanford
  Rhydaman 57 A6
Amod. 190 B3
Amotherby 159 D6
Ampfield 32 C3
Ampleforth 159 D4
Ampney Crucis . . . 63 C6
Ampney St Mary . . 64 C1
Ampney St Peter . 64 C1
Amport 32 A1
Ampthill 84 D2
Ampton 103 D4
Amroth 56 B1
Amulree 218 A3
Anagach 253 D6
Anaheilt 236 C2
Anancaun 262 D2
An Caol 248 A3
Ancaster. 116 A2
Anchor 93 C5
Anchorsholme . . 144 C3
An Cnoc 288 D5

Ancroft 198 B3
Ancrum 187 A5
Anderby 135 B5
Anderson 16 B2
Anderton 127 B6
Andover 32 A2
Andover Down . . 32 A2
Andoversford 63 B6
Andreas 152 B4
Anfield 136 D2
Angersleigh. 28 D1
Angle. 55 D4
An Gleann Ur. . . . 288 D5
Angmering. 20 B3
Angram N Yorks . . 148 C4
  N Yorks 156 B2
Anie 217 C5
Ankerville 265 C4
Anlaby 142 A2
Anmer 119 C4
Annan 175 B4
Annat Argyll 227 D5
  Highld. 249 A5
Anna Valley 32 A2
Annbank. 193 C4
Annesley 131 D5
Annesley
  Woodhouse . . . 131 D4
Annfield Plain. . . 178 D3
Annifirth. 285 H3
Annitsford 179 B4
Annscroft 94 A2
Ansdell 136 A2
Ansford 29 B6
Ansley 97 B5
Anslow 113 C6
Anslow Gate . . . 113 C5
Anstey Herts 85 D6
  Leics. 98 A2
Anstruther
  Easter. 221 D5
Anstruther
  Wester. 221 D5
Ansty Hants. 33 A6
  Warks. 97 C6
  Wilts. 30 C3
  W Sus. 35 D5
Anthill Common. . 33 D5
Anthorn 175 C4
Antingham. 121 B4
An t-Ob
  Leverburgh . . . 287 F5
Anton's Gowt . . . 117 A5
Antonshill 208 B1
Antony 6 B3
Anwick 133 D6
Anwoth 172 C3
Apes Hall 102 B1
Apethorpe 100 B2
Apeton 112 D2
Apley 133 B6
Apperknowle. . . . 130 B3
Apperley. 63 A4
Apperley Bridge 147 D5
Appersett. 156 B2
Appin. 226 B4
Appin House 226 B4
Appleby 142 B1
Appleby-in-
  Westmorland . . 165 C4
Appleby Magna . . 97 A6
Appleby Parva. . . 97 A6
Applecross 249 B4
Applecross Ho. . . 249 B4
Appledore Devon. 25 B5
  Devon. 27 D5
  Kent. 38 C1
Appledore Heath. 38 B1
Appleford. 65 D6
Applegarthtown 185 D4
Appleshaw. 32 A2
Applethwaite. . . . 163 B5
Appleton Halton. 127 A5
  Oxon. 65 C5
Appleton-le-
  Moors. 159 C6
Appleton-le-
  Street. 159 D6
Appleton
  Roebuck 149 C4
Appleton Thorn. 127 A6

Appleton Wiske . 158 A2
Appletreehall . . . 186 B4
Appletreewick . . . 147 A4
Appley. 27 C5
Appley Bridge. . . 136 C4
Apse Heath 19 C4
Apsley End. 84 D3
Apuldram. 20 B1
Aquhythie 245 A4
Arabella 265 C4
Arbeadie. 244 C3
Arbirlot. 233 D4
Arboll 265 B4
Arborfield 47 C5
Arborfield Cross. . 47 C5
Arborfield
  Garrison 47 C5
Arbour-thorne . . 130 A3
Arbroath. 233 D4
Arbuthnott 233 A5
Archiestown 254 B3
Arclid 128 C2
Ardachu 273 D4
Ardalanish 224 E2
Ardanaiseig 227 D5
Ardaneaskan . . . 249 C5
Ardanstur 213 A6
Ardargie House
  Hotel 219 C5
Ardarroch 249 C5
Ardbeg Argyll . . . 201 D4
  Argyll 215 D4
Ardcharnich 262 B3
Ardchiavaig 224 E2
Ardchullarie
  More. 217 C5
Ardchyle 217 B5
Ard-dhubh. 249 B4
Arddleen 110 D1
Ardechvie. 239 C5
Ardeley. 68 A3
Ardelve 249 D5
Arden 206 B1
Ardens Grafton. . . 80 B4
Ardentinny. 215 D4
Ardentraive 203 A5
Ardeonaig 217 A6
Ardersier 252 A3
Ardessie 262 B2
Ardfern 213 B6
Ardgartan. 215 B5
Ardgay 264 A1
Ardgour 237 C4
Ardheslaig. 249 A4
Ardiecow 267 C6
Ardindrean 262 B3
Ardingly 35 D6
Ardington. 46 A2
Ardlair. 255 D6
Ardlamont Ho. . . 203 B4
Ardleigh 71 A4
Ardler 231 D6
Ardley 65 A6
Ardlui. 215 B6
Ardlussa 213 D4
Ardmair. 262 A3
Ardmay 215 B5
Ardminish 202 D1
Ardmolich 235 C6
Ardmore Argyll. . 226 D2
  Highld. 264 B3
  Highld. 276 C3
Ardnacross 225 B4
Ardnadam 203 A6
Ardnagrask 251 B7
Ardnarff 249 C5
Ardnastang 236 C2
Ardnave 200 A2
Ardno 215 B4
Ardoch 219 A5
Ardochy House . . 239 B6
Ardo Ho. 257 D4
Ardoyne 256 D1
Ardpatrick 202 B2
Ardpatrick Ho. . . 202 C2
Ardpeaton 215 D5
Ardrishaig 213 D6
Ardross Fife 221 D5
  Highld. 264 C2
Ardrossan 204 D2
Ardross Castle . . 264 C2

Ardshealach . . . 235 D5
Ardsley 140 C1
Ardslignish 235 D4
Ardtalla. 201 C4
Ardtalnaig 218 A2
Ardtoe. 235 C5
Ardtrostan 217 B6
Arduaine 213 A5
Ardullie. 264 D1
Ardvasar. 247 D5
Ardvorlich 217 B6
Ardwell. 170 C3
Ardwell Mains. . . 170 C3
Ardwick 138 D1
Areley Kings 95 D6
Arford 34 C1
Argoed 41 B6
Argoed Mill 76 A3
Arichamish 214 B2
Arichastlich. . . . 216 A2
Aridhglas 224 D2
Arileod 223 B4
Arinacrinachd. . . 249 A4
Arinagour. 223 B5
Arion 282 F3
Arisaig 235 B5
Ariundle 236 C2
Arkendale 148 A2
Arkesden 85 D6
Arkholme 155 D5
Arkleton 186 D2
Arkle Town 156 A4
Arkley 68 D2
Arksey. 140 C3
Arkwright Town 131 B4
Arle 63 A5
Arlecdon 162 C3
Arlesey 84 D3
Arleston 111 D5
Arley 128 A1
Arlingham 62 B3
Arlington Devon. . 25 A7
  E Sus 22 B3
  Glos 64 C2
Armadale Highld 278 B3
  W Loth 208 D2
Armadale
  Castle. 247 D5
Armathwaite . . . 164 A3
Arminghall. 104 A3
Armitage 113 D4
Armley 148 D1
Armscote 81 C5
Armthorpe 140 C4
Arnabost 223 B5
Arncliffe 156 D3
Arncroach 221 D5
Arne. 16 C3
Arnesby 98 B3
Arngask 219 C6
Arnisdale 238 A2
Arnish 248 B2
Arniston Engine 209 D6
Arnol 288 C4
Arnold E Yorks . . 151 C4
  Notts 114 A3
Arnprior 207 A4
Arnside. 154 D3
Aros Mains. 225 B4
Arowry 110 B3
Arpafeelie 252 A2
Arrad Foot 154 C2
Arram 150 C3
Arrathorne. 157 B6
Arreton 19 C4
Arrington. 85 B5
Arrivain. 216 A2
Arrochar. 215 B5
Arrow 80 B3
Arthington 147 C6
Arthingworth . . . 99 C4
Arthog. 90 A4
Arthrath 257 C4
Arthurstone. . . . 231 D6
Artrochie 257 C5
Arundel 20 B3
Aryhoulan 237 C4
Asby. 162 B3
Ascog 203 B6
Ascot. 48 C2
Ascott 81 D6

Ascott-under-
  Wychwood 64 B4
Asenby 158 D2
Asfordby. 115 D5
Asfordby Hill. . . . 115 D5
Asgarby Lincs. . . 116 A4
  Lincs. 134 C3
Ash Kent 50 C2
  Kent. 53 D4
  Som 29 C4
  Sur 34 A1
Ashampstead . . . 46 B3
Ashbocking 88 B2
Ashbourne 113 A5
Ashbrittle. 27 C5
Ash Bullayne . . . 12 A2
Ashburton 7 A6
Ashbury Devon . . 11 B6
  Oxon. 45 A6
Ashby 141 C7
Ashby by
  Partney 135 C4
Ashby cum
  Fenby 143 C4
Ashby de la
  Launde. 133 D5
Ashby-de-la-
  Zouch 114 D1
Ashby Folville . . . 115 D5
Ashby Magna . . . 98 B2
Ashby Parva 98 C2
Ashby
  Puerorum 134 B3
Ashby St Ledgers 82 A2
Ashby St Mary . . 104 A4
Ashchurch 80 D2
Ashcombe 13 D4
Ashcott 28 B4
Ashdon 86 C1
Ashe 32 A4
Asheldham. 70 C3
Ashen 86 C3
Ashendon 66 B2
Ashfield Carms. . . 58 C3
  Stirling 218 D2
  Suff 88 A3
Ashfield Green . 104 D3
Ashfold
  Crossways. 35 D5
Ashford Devon . . 25 B6
  Hants 31 D5
  Kent. 38 A2
  Sur 48 B3
Ashford Bowdler . 94 D3
Ashford
  Carbonell 94 D3
Ashford Hill 46 C3
Ashford in the
  Water. 130 C1
Ashgill. 194 B2
Ash Green 97 C6
Ashill Devon 27 D5
  Norf 103 A4
  Som 28 D3
Ashingdon 70 D2
Ashington
  Northumb. . . . 179 A4
  Som 29 C5
  W Sus. 21 A4
Ashintully
  Castle. 231 B5
Ashkirk 186 A3
Ashlett 18 A3
Ashleworth 63 A4
Ashley Cambs . . . 86 A2
  Ches E. 128 A2
  Devon. 26 D1
  Dorset 17 A5
  Glos 63 D5
  Hants 17 B6
  Hants 32 B2
  Northants. 99 B4
  Staffs 111 B6
Ashley Green 67 C4
Ashley Heath
  Dorset 17 A5
  Staffs 111 B6
Ash Magna 111 B4
Ashmanhaugh. . 121 C5
Ashmansworth . . 46 D2
Ashmansworthy . 24 D4
Ash Mill 26 C2

Ashmore. 30 D3
Ashorne 81 B6
Ashover 130 C3
Ashow. 97 D6
Ashprington 8 B2
Ash Priors 27 C6
Ashreigney 26 D1
Ash Street 87 C6
Ashtead 35 A4
Ashton Ches W . . 127 C5
  Corn 3 C4
  Hants 33 D4
  Hereford 78 A3
  Invclyd. 204 A2
  Northants. 83 C4
  Northants. . . . 100 C2
Ashton Common . 44 D2
Ashton-In-
  Makerfield . . . 137 D4
Ashton Keynes . . 63 D6
Ashton under
  Hill 80 D2
Ashton-under-
  Lyne 138 D2
Ashton upon
  Mersey. 137 D6
Ashurst Hants. . . . 32 D2
  Kent. 36 C3
  W Sus. 21 A4
Ashurstwood. . . . 36 C3
Ash Vale 34 A1
Ashwater 11 B4
Ashwell Herts. . . . 85 D4
  Rutland. 115 D6
  Som 28 D3
Ashwellthorpe . . 104 B2
Ashwick 29 A6
Ashwicken 119 D4
Ashybank 186 B4
Askam in
  Furness 153 C3
Askern 140 B3
Askerswell 15 B5
Askett 66 C3
Askham Cumb. . . 164 C3
  Notts 132 B2
Askham Bryan . . 149 C4
Askham Richard 148 C4
Asknish. 214 C2
Askrigg 156 B3
Askwith. 147 C5
Aslackby. 116 B3
Aslacton 104 B2
Aslockton 115 B5
Asloun. 244 A2
Aspatria 174 D4
Aspenden. 68 A3
Asperton 117 B5
Aspley Guise 83 D6
Aspley Heath. . . . 83 D6
Aspull 137 C5
Asselby. 141 A5
Asserby 135 B4
Assington. 87 D5
Assynt Ho. 264 D1
Astbury 128 C3
Astcote 82 B3
Asterley 94 A1
Asterton 94 B1
Asthall. 64 B3
Asthall Leigh . . . 64 B4
Astley Shrops . . . 111 D4
  Warks. 97 C6
  Worcs. 79 A5
Astley Abbotts . . 95 B5
Astley Bridge . . . 137 B6
Astley Cross. 79 A6
Astley Green . . . 137 D6
Aston Ches E . . . 111 A5
  Ches W. 127 B5
  Derbys 130 A1
  Hereford 94 D2
  Herts 68 A2
  Oxon. 64 C4
  Shrops 111 C4
  Staffs 111 A6
  S Yorks 131 A4
  Telford 95 A4

Aston continued
W Mid 96 C3
Wokingham 47 A5
Aston Abbotts . . 66 A3
Aston Botterell . . 95 C4
Aston-By-Stone 112 B4
Aston Cantlow . . 80 B4
Aston Clinton . . 66 B3
Aston Crews . . . 62 A2
Aston Cross . . . 80 B2
Aston End 68 A2
Aston Eyre 95 B4
Aston Fields . . . 80 A2
Aston Flamville. . 98 B1
Aston Ingham . . 62 A2
Aston juxta
Mondrum 127 D6
Aston le Walls. . 82 B1
Aston Magna. . . 81 D4
Aston Munslow. . 94 C3
Aston on Clun. . . 94 C1
Aston-on-Trent 114 C2
Aston Rogers . . . 94 A1
Aston Rowant . . 66 D2
Aston Sandford . 66 C2
Aston Somerville 80 D3
Aston Subedge. . 80 C4
Aston Tirrold. . . 46 A3
Aston Upthorpe . 46 A3
Astrop 82 D2
Astwick 84 D4
Astwood M Keynes 83 C6
Worcs. 79 B6
Astwood Bank. . . 80 A3
Aswarby 116 B3
Aswardby 134 B3
Atcham 94 A3
Atch Lench. 80 B3
Athelhampton. . 16 B1
Athelington . . .104 D3
Athelney. 28 C3
Athelstaneford . 210 C2
Atherington . . . 25 C6
Atherstone. . . . 97 B6
Atherstone on
Stour 81 B5
Atherton 137 C5
Atley Hill. 157 A6
Atlow. 113 A6
Attadale 249 C6
Attadale Ho. . . .249 C6
Attenborough . .114 B3
Atterby 142 D1
Attercliffe 130 A3
Attleborough
Norf 103 B6
Warks. 97 B6
Attlebridge . . .120 D3
Atwick 151 B4
Atworth 44 C2
Aubourn 133 C4
Auchagallon . .191 B4
Auchallater . . .243 D4
Aucharnie 256 B1
Auchattie 244 C3
Auchavan 231 B5
Auchbreck 254 D3
Auchenback . . .205 C5
Auchenblae. . . .233 A5
Auchenbrack. . .183 C5
Auchenbreck . .214 D3
Auchencairn
Dumfries 173 C5
Dumfries 184 D2
N Ayrs 191 C6
Auchencrosh. . .180 D3
Auchendinny. . .209 D5
Auchengray. . . .195 A4
Auchenhalrig . .267 C4
Auchenheath. . .194 B3
Auchenlochan. . .203 A4
Auchenmalg . .171 B4
Auchensoul . . .181 B4
Auchentiber . . .204 D3
Auchertyre. . . .249 D5
Auchgourish . . .242 A2
Auchincarroch . .206 B2

Auchindrain. . . .214 B3
Auchindrean . . .262 B3
Auchininna 256 B1
Auchinleck. 193 C5
Auchinloch 205 A6
Auchinroath . . .266 D3
Auchintoul. 244 A2
Auchiries 257 C5
Auchlee 245 C5
Auchleven 256 D1
Auchlochan 194 C3
Auchlossan 244 B2
Auchlunies 245 C5
Auchlyne 217 B5
Auchmacoy 257 C4
Auchmair 255 D4
Auchmantle 170 A3
Auchmillan 193 C5
Auchmithie 233 D4
Auchmuirbridge
. . . . .220 D2
Auchmull 232 A3
Auchnacree 232 B2
Auchnagallin. . .253 C6
Auchnagatt 257 B4
Auchnaha. 214 D2
Auchnashelloch 218 C2
Aucholzie 243 C6
Auchrannie 231 C6
Auchroisk. 253 D6
Auchronie 244 D1
Auchterarder . .218 C4
Auchteraw. 240 B2
Auchterderran . .209 A5
Auchterhouse . .220 A3
Auchtermuchty. .220 C2
Auchterneed . . .251 A6
Auchtertool . . .209 A5
Auchtertyre . . .266 D2
Auchtubh 217 B5
Auckengill 281 B5
Auckley 140 C4
Audenshaw 138 D2
Audlem. 111 A5
Audley. 128 D2
Audley End 87 D4
Auds 268 C1
Aughton E Yorks.149 D6
Lancs 136 C2
Lancs 145 A5
S Yorks. 131 A4
Wilts. 45 D6
Aughton Park. .136 C2
Auldearn 253 A5
Aulden 78 B2
Auldgirth 183 D7
Auldhame 210 B2
Auldhouse 205 C6
Ault a'chruinn. .249 D6
Aultbea. 261 B5
Aultdearg. 263 D4
Aultgrishan . . .261 B4
Aultguish Inn. . .263 C5
Aultibea 274 B4
Aultiphurst. . . .279 B4
Aultmore 267 D5
Aultnagoire . . .252 D1
Aultnamain Inn. .264 B2
Aultnaslat. 239 B5
Aulton 255 D7
Aundorach. 242 A2
Aunsby 116 B3
Auquhorthies . .256 D3
Aust. 43 A4
Austendike 117 C5
Austerfield. . . .141 D4
Austrey 97 A5
Austwick 146 A1
Authorpe 135 A4
Authorpe Row. .135 B5
Avebury 45 C5
Aveley 50 A2
Avening 63 D4
Averham. 132 D2
Aveton Gifford . . 7 C5
Avielochan 242 A2
Aviemore 242 A1
Avington Hants . .32 B4
W Berks. 46 C1
Avoch 252 A3
Avon 17 B5

Avonbridge 208 C2
Avon Dassett. . . .81 C7
Avonmouth 43 B4
Avonwick 7 B6
Awbridge 32 C2
Awhirk 170 B2
Awkley 43 A4
Awliscombe. . . . 13 A6
Awre 62 C3
Awsworth 114 A2
Axbridge 42 D3
Axford Hants. . . .33 A5
Wilts. 45 C6
Axminster 14 B2
Axmouth. 14 B2
Axton 125 A6
Aycliffe 39 A5
Aycliffe. 167 C5
Aydon 178 C2
Aylburton 62 C2
Ayle 165 A5
Aylesbeare. . . . 13 B5
Aylesbury 66 B3
Aylesby 143 C4
Aylesford 37 A5
Aylesham 53 D4
Aylestone 98 A2
Aylmerton 120 B3
Aylsham 120 C3
Ayton 79 D4
Aymestrey 78 A2
Aynho 82 D2
Ayot St Lawrence. 68 B1
Ayot St Peter. . . 68 B2
Ayr 192 C3
Aysgarth 156 C4
Ayside 154 C2
Ayston 99 A5
Aythorpe Roding 69 B5
Ayton 211 D6
Aywick 284 E7
Azerley 157 D6

B

Babbacombe 8 A3
Babbinswood . .110 B2
Babcary 29 C5
Babel. 59 B5
Babell 125 B6
Babraham 85 B7
Babworth 132 A1
Bac. 288 C5
Bachau 123 B4
Backaland 282 D6
Backaskaill 282 B5
Backbarrow . . .154 C2
Backe 56 A2
Backfolds 269 D5
Backford 127 B4
Backford Cross. .126 B3
Backhill Aberds . .256 C2
Aberds 257 C5
Backhill of
Clackriach. . . .257 B4
Backhill of
Fortree. 257 B4
Backhill of
Trustach 244 C3
Backies. 274 D2
Backlass. 280 C4
Back of
Keppoch 235 B5
Back Rogerton .193 C5
Backwell. 42 C3
Backworth 179 B5
Bacon End 69 B6
Baconsthorpe . .120 B3
Bacton Hereford. . 78 D1
Norf 121 B5
Suff 87 A6
Bacton Green . . .87 A6
Bacup 138 A1
Badachro 261 C4
Badanloch
Lodge 273 A5
Badavanich . . .250 A3
Badbea. 45 A5
Badby 82 B2
Badcall 276 C3
Badcaul 262 A2

Baddeley Green .129 D4
Baddesley
Clinton 97 D5
Baddesley Ensor . 97 B5
Baddidarach . . .270 B3
Baddoch. 242 D4
Badenscoth 256 C2
Badenyon 243 A6
Badger 95 B5
Badger's Mount . . 50 C1
Badgeworth. . . . 63 B5
Badgworth 42 D2
Badicaul 249 D4
Badingham 88 A4
Badlesmere. . . . 52 D2
Badlipster 280 D4
Badluarech 262 A1
Badminton. 44 A2
Badnaban. 270 B3
Badninish 264 A3
Badrallach. 262 A2
Badsey 80 C3
Badshot Lea . . . 34 B1
Badsworth 140 B2
Badwell Ash . . . 87 A5
Bagby 158 C3
Bag Enderby . . .134 B3
Bagendon 63 C6
Bagh a Chaisteil
Castlebay 286 G2
Baghasdal 286 E3
Bagh Mor. 286 A4
Bagh
Shiarabhagh. . .286 F3
Bagillt 126 B2
Baginton 97 D6
Baglan 40 B2
Bagley 110 C3
Bagnall 129 D4
Bagnor 46 C2
Bagshot Sur 48 C2
Wilts. 45 C7
Bagthorpe Norf .119 B4
Notts 131 D4
Bagworth 98 A1
Bagwy Llydiart . 61 A6
Bail Àrd
Bhuirgh 288 B5
Baildon 147 D5
Baile 287 F4
Baile Ailein 288 E3
Baile a
Mhanaich . . .286 A3
Baile an Truiseil 288 B4
Bailebeag. 240 A3
Baile Boidheach 202 A2
Baile Glas. 286 A4
Baile Mhartainn 287 G2
Baile Mhic
Phail. 287 G3
Baile Mor Argyll. .224 D1
W Isles 287 H2
Baile na Creige. .286 F2
Baile nan
Cailleach. . . .286 A3
Baile Raghaill . .287 G2
Baileyhead. . . .176 B3
Bailiesward . . .255 C5
Baillieston 205 B6
Bail' lochdrach. .286 A4
Bail Uachdraich 287 H3
Bail' Ur
Tholastaidh. . .288 C6
Bainbridge. . . .156 B3
Bainsford 208 B1
Bainshole. 255 C7
Bainton E Yorks .150 B2
Pboro. 100 A3
Bairnkine 187 B5
Baker's End . . . 68 B3
Baker Street 50 A3
Bakewell 130 C2
Bala Y Bala. . . .108 B4
Balachuirn 248 B2
Balavil 241 B5
Balbeg Highld. . .251 C6
Highld. 251 D6
Balbeggie 219 B6
Balbithan 245 A4
Balbithan Ho. . .245 A5
Balblair Highld. . .264 A1

Balblair continued
Highld. 264 D3
Balby 140 C3
Balchladich 270 A3
Balchraggan
Highld. 252 B1
Highld. 252 C1
Balchrick 276 C2
Balchrystie. . . .221 D4
Balcladaich . . .251 D4
Balcombe. 35 C6
Balcombe Lane. . 35 C6
Balcomie 221 C6
Balcurvie 220 D3
Baldersby 158 D2
Baldersby St
James. 158 D2
Balderstone . . .145 D6
Balderton
Ches W. 126 C3
Notts 132 D3
Baldhu 4 C2
Baldinnie 220 C4
Baldock 84 D4
Baldovie 221 A4
Baldrine 152 C4
Baldslow 23 A5
Baldwin 152 C3
Baldwinholme. . .175 C6
Baldwin's Gate .112 A1
Bale 120 B2
Balearn 269 D5
Balemartine . . .222 C2
Balephuil 222 C2
Balerno 209 D4
Balevullin 222 C2
Balfield 232 B3
Balfour 282 F5
Balfron 206 B3
Balfron Station. .206 B3
Balgaveny 256 B1
Balgavies 232 C3
Balgonar 208 A3
Balgove 256 C3
Balgowan 241 C4
Balgown 258 B3
Balgrochan 205 A6
Balgy 249 A5
Balhaldie 218 D3
Balhalgardy . . .256 D2
Balham 49 B5
Balhary 231 D6
Baliasta 284 C8
Baligill 279 B4
Balintore Angus. .231 C6
Highld. 265 C4
Balintraid 264 C3
Balk 158 C3
Balkeerie 232 D1
Balkemback . . .220 A3
Balkholme 141 A5
Balkissock 180 C3
Ball 110 C2
Ballabeg 152 D2
Ballacannel . . .152 C4
Ballachulish . . .237 D4
Ballajora. 152 B4
Ballaleigh. 152 C3
Ballamodha . . .152 D2
Ballantrae 180 C2
Ballaquine 152 C4
Ballards Gore . . 70 D3
Ballasalla IoM . .152 B3
IoM 152 D2
Ballater 243 C6
Ballaugh. 152 B3
Ballaveare 152 D3
Ballcorach 254 D2
Ballechin 230 C3
Balleigh 264 B3
Ballencrieff . . .210 C1
Ballentoul 230 B2
Ball Haye Green 129 D4
Ball Hill. 46 C2
Ballidon 130 D2
Balliemore
Argyll 214 D3
Argyll 226 D3
Ballikinrain . . .206 B3
Ballimeanoch . .214 A3
Ballimore Argyll. .214 D2
Stirling 217 C5

Ballinaby 200 B3
Ballindean 220 B2
Ballingdon. 87 C4
Ballinger
Common 67 C4
Ballingham 78 D3
Ballingry. 209 A4
Ballinlick 230 D3
Ballinluig 230 C3
Ballintuim 231 C5
Balloch Angus . .232 C1
Highld. 252 B3
N Lanark 207 C5
W Dunb 206 B1
Ballochan. 244 C2
Ballochford . . .255 C4
Ballochmorrie. .181 C4
Balls Cross 34 D2
Balls Green 71 A4
Ballygown 224 B3
Ballygrant 200 B3
Ballyhaugh. . . .223 B4
Balmacara 249 D5
Balmacara
Square. 249 D5
Balmaclellan. . .173 A4
Balmacneil. . . .230 C3
Balmacqueen . .259 A4
Balmae 173 D4
Balmaha. 206 A2
Balmalcolm. . . .220 D3
Balmeanach . . .248 B2
Balmedie 245 A6
Balmer Heath . .110 B3
Balmerino 220 B3
Balmerlawn 18 A2
Balmichael 191 B5
Balmirmer. 221 A5
Balmore Highld. .251 C5
Highld. 253 B4
Highld. 258 D2
Perth 230 C3
Balmule 209 B5
Balmullo 220 B4
Balmungie 252 A3
Balnaboth 231 B7
Balnabruaich. . .264 D3
Balnabruich. . . .275 B5
Balnacoil 274 C2
Balnacra. 250 B1
Balnafoich 252 C2
Balnagall 265 B4
Balnaguard . . .230 C3
Balnahard Argyll .212 C2
Argyll 224 C3
Balnain 251 C6
Balnakeil 277 B4
Balnaknock . . .259 B4
Balnapaling. . . .264 D3
Balne. 140 B3
Balochroy. 202 C2
Balone 221 C4
Balornock 205 B6
Balquharn 219 A5
Balquhidder . . .217 B5
Balsall. 97 D5
Balsall Common .97 D5
Balsall Hth. 96 C3
Balscott 81 C6
Balsham 86 B1
Baltasound 284 C8
Balterley. 128 D2
Baltersan 171 A6
Balthangie 268 D3
Baltonsborough . 29 B5
Balvaird 252 A1
Balvicar 213 A5
Balvraid Highld. .238 A2
Highld. 253 C4
Bamber Bridge. .137 A4
Bambers Green . 69 A5
Bamburgh 199 C5
Bamff 231 C6
Bamford Derbys. .130 A2
Gtr Man 138 B1
Bampton Cumb. .164 D3
Devon. 27 C4
Oxon. 64 C4
Bampton
Grange. 164 D3
Banavie 237 B5
Banbury 82 C1

Bancffosfelen 57 A4
Banchory 244 C3
Banchory-
Devenick 245 B6
Bancycapel 57 A4
Bancyfelin 56 A3
Bancyffordd 73 C7
Bandirran 220 A2
Banff 268 C1
Bangor 123 C5
Bangor-is-y-
coed 110 A2
Banham 103 C6
Bank 18 A1
Bankend 174 B3
Bankglen 182 A4
Bankhead
Aberdeen 245 A5
Aberds 244 B3
Bank Newton . . . 146 B3
Banknock 207 C5
Banks Cumb 176 C3
Lancs 136 A2
Bankshill 185 D4
Bank Street 79 A4
Banningham 120 C4
Banniskirk Ho. . . 280 C3
Bannister Green . . 69 A6
Banstead 35 A5
Bantham 7 C5
Banton 207 C5
Banwell 42 D2
Banyard's Green . . 51 C6
Bapchild 51 C6
Barabhas 288 C4
Barabhas Iarach 288 C4
Barabhas
Uarach 288 B4
Barachandroman
. . . . 225 D5
Barassie 192 B3
Baravullin 226 C3
Barbaraville 264 C3
Barber Booth . . . 129 A6
Barbieston 182 A2
Barbon 155 C5
Barbridge 127 C6
Barbrook 26 A2
Barby 98 D2
Barcaldine 227 B4
Barcheston 81 D5
Barcombe 22 A2
Barcombe Cross . . 22 A2
Barden 157 B5
Bardennoch 182 C3
Barden Scale. . . . 147 B4
Bardfield Saling . . 69 A6
Bardney 133 C6
Bardon 114 D2
Bardon Mill 177 C5
Bardowie 205 A5
Bardrainney. 204 A3
Bardsea 154 D2
Bardsey 148 C2
Bardwell 103 D5
Bare 145 A4
Barfad 202 B3
Barford Norf 104 A2
Warks. 81 A5
Barford St John . . 82 D1
Barford St Martin. 31 B4
Barford St
Michael 82 D1
Barfrestone 53 D4
Bargoed Bargod . . 41 B6
Bargrennan 181 D5
Barham Cambs . . 100 D3
Kent 53 D4
Suff 88 B2
Barharrow 172 C4
Barhill 173 B6
Bar Hill 85 A5
Barholm 116 D3
Barkby 98 A3
Barkestone-le-
Vale 115 B5
Barkham. 47 C5
Barking London . . 50 A1
Suff 87 B6

Barkingside 50 A1
Barking Tye 87 B6
Barkisland 138 B3
Barkston Lincs . . 116 A2
N Yorks. 148 D3
Barkway 85 D5
Barlaston 112 B2
Barlavington 20 A2
Barlborough 131 B4
Barlby 149 D5
Barlestone 98 A1
Barley Herts 85 D5
Lancs 146 C2
Barley Mow 179 D4
Barleythorpe 99 A5
Barling 51 A6
Barlow Derbys . . 130 B3
N Yorks. 140 A4
T&W 178 C3
Barmby Moor . . . 149 C6
Barmby on the
Marsh. 141 A4
Barmer 119 B5
Barmoor Castle . 198 C3
Barmoor Lane
End 198 C4
Barmouth
Abermaw 90 A4
Barmpton 167 D6
Barmston 151 B4
Barnack 100 A2
Barnacle 97 C6
Barnard Castle . 166 D3
Barnard Gate. . . . 65 B5
Barnardiston 86 C3
Barnbarroch . . . 173 C6
Barnburgh 140 C2
Barnby 105 C5
Barnby Dun 140 C4
Barnby in the
Willows 132 D3
Barnby Moor . . . 131 A6
Barnes Street . . . 36 B4
Barnet 68 D2
Barnetby le
Wold. 142 C2
Barney 120 B1
Barnham Suff . . . 103 D4
W Sus. 20 B2
Barnham
Broom 104 A1
Barnhead 233 C4
Barnhill Ches W . 127 D4
Dundee. 221 A4
Moray. 266 D2
Barnhills. 180 D1
Barningham
Durham 166 D3
Suff 103 D5
Barnoldby le
Beck 143 C4
Barnoldswick . . 146 C2
Barns Green 35 D4
Barnsley Glos . . . 64 C1
S Yorks. 139 C6
Barnstaple 25 B6
Barnston Essex . . 69 B6
Mers. 126 A2
Barnstone 115 B5
Barnt Green. 96 D3
Barnton Ches W . 127 B6
Edin 209 C4
Barnwell All
Saints. 100 C2
Barnwell St
Andrew 100 C2
Barnwood 63 B4
Barochreal. 226 D3
Barons Cross . . . 78 B2
Barr 181 B4
Barra Castle . . . 256 D2
Barrachan 171 C5
Barrack 256 B3
Barraglom 288 D2
Barrahormid . . . 213 D5
Barran 226 D3
Barrapol 222 C2
Barras Aberds . . 245 D5
Cumb 165 D6
Barrasford 177 B7
Barravullin. 213 B6
Barregarrow . . . 152 C3

Barrhead 205 C4
Barrhill 181 C4
Barrington Cambs 85 C5
Som 28 D3
Barripper 3 B4
Barrmill 204 C3
Barrock. 281 A4
Barrock Ho. 281 B4
Barrow Lancs . . . 146 D1
Rutland. 116 D1
Suff 86 A3
Barroway Drove 102 A1
Barrowburn 188 B1
Barrowby 116 B1
Barrowcliff 160 C4
Barrowden. 99 A6
Barrowford 146 D2
Barrow Green . . . 51 C6
Barrow Gurney . . 43 C4
Barrow Haven . . 142 A2
Barrow-in-
Furness 153 D3
Barrow Island . . 153 D2
Barrow Nook . . . 136 C3
Barrows Green
Ches E 128 D1
Cumb 154 C4
Barrow's Green . 127 A5
Barrow Street . . . 30 B2
Barrow upon
Humber 142 A2
Barrow upon
Soar 114 D3
Barrow upon
Trent. 114 C1
Barry 221 A5
Barry Y Barri . . . 41 E6
Barry Island 41 E6
Barsby. 115 D4
Barsham 105 C4
Barston 97 D5
Bartestree 78 C3
Barthol Chapel . 256 C3
Barthomley 128 D2
Bartley 32 D2
Bartley Green . . . 96 C3
Bartlow 86 C1
Barton Cambs . . . 85 B6
Ches W 127 D4
Glos 64 A2
Lancs 136 C2
Lancs 145 D5
N Yorks. 157 A6
Oxon. 65 C6
Torbay 8 A3
Warks. 80 B4
Barton Bendish . 102 A3
Barton Hartshorn 82 D3
Barton in Fabis . 114 B3
Barton in the
Beans 97 A6
Barton-le-Clay . . 84 D2
Barton-le-
Street 159 D6
Barton-le-
Willows 149 A6
Barton Mills. . . . 102 D3
Barton on Sea . . 17 B6
Barton on the
Heath 81 D5
Barton St David . 29 B5
Barton Seagrave . 99 D5
Barton Stacey . . . 32 A3
Barton Turf 121 C5
Barton-under-
Needwood. . . . 113 D5
Barton-upon-
Humber 142 A2
Barton
Waterside 142 A2
Barugh 139 C6
Barway 102 D1
Barwell 98 B1
Barwick Herts . . 68 B3
Som 29 D5
Barwick in
Elmet 148 D2
Baschurch 110 C3
Bascote. 81 A7
Basford Green . . 129 D4
Bashall Eaves . . 145 C6
Bashley 17 B6

Basildon 51 A4
Basingstoke. 47 D4
Baslow 130 B2
Bason Bridge 28 A3
Bassaleg 42 A1
Bassenthwaite . . 163 A5
Bassett 32 D3
Bassingbourn . . . 85 C5
Bassingfield 115 B4
Bassingham. . . . 133 C4
Bassingthorpe . . 116 C2
Basta 284 D7
Baston 116 D4
Bastwick 121 D6
Baswick Steer. . . 150 C3
Batchworth
Heath 67 D5
Batcombe Dorset. . 15 A6
Som 29 B6
Bate Heath 128 B1
Batford 67 B6
Bath 43 C6
Bathampton 44 C1
Bathealton 27 C5
Batheaston 44 C1
Bathford 44 C1
Bathgate. 208 D2
Bathley 132 D2
Bathpool Corn . . . 10 D3
Som 28 C2
Bathville 208 D2
Batley 139 A5
Batsford 81 D4
Battersby 159 A4
Battersea 49 B5
Battisborough
Cross 7 C4
Battisford 87 B6
Battisford Tye . . . 87 B6
Battle E Sus. 23 A5
Powys 76 D4
Battledown 63 A5
Battlefield 111 D4
Battlesbridge . . . 70 D1
Battlesden 67 A4
Battlesea Green . 104 D3
Battleton 27 B4
Battram 98 A1
Battramsley. 18 B2
Baughton 80 C1
Baughurst 46 D3
Baulking. 64 D4
Baumber 134 B2
Baunton 63 C6
Baverstock. 31 B4
Bawburgh 104 A2
Bawdeswell 120 C2
Bawdrip 28 B3
Bawdsey 88 C4
Bawtry 141 D4
Baxenden 137 A6
Baxterley 97 B5
Baybridge 32 C3
Baycliff 154 D1
Baydon 45 B6
Bayford Herts . . 68 C3
Som 30 C1
Bayles 165 A5
Baylham 88 B2
Baynard's Green . 65 A6
Bayston Hill 94 A2
Baythorn End . . . 86 C3
Bayton. 95 D4
Beach 236 D1
Beachampton . . . 83 D4
Beachamwell . . . 102 A3
Beachans 253 D6
Beacharr 202 D1
Beachborough . . 38 B3
Beachley 62 D1
Beacon 14 A1
Beacon End 70 A3
Beacon Hill 34 C1
Beacon's Bottom 66 D2
Beaconsfield . . . 67 E4
Beacrabhaic . . . 288 H2
Beadlam 159 C5
Beadlow 84 D3
Beadnell 189 A5
Beaford 25 D6
Beal Northumb . . 199 B4
N Yorks. 140 A3

Beamhurst 113 B4
Beaminster 15 A4
Beamish 179 D4
Beamsley 147 B4
Bean 50 B2
Beanacre 44 C3
Beanley. 188 B3
Beaquoy 282 E4
Bear Cross 17 B4
Beardwood 137 A5
Beare Green 35 B4
Bearley 81 A4
Bearnus 224 B2
Bearpark 167 A5
Bearsbridge. 177 D5
Bearsden 205 A5
Bearsted. 37 A5
Bearstone 111 B6
Bearwood
Hereford 78 B1
Poole 17 B4
W Mid 96 C3
Beattock 184 B3
Beauchamp
Roding 69 B5
Beauchief. 130 A3
Beaufort 60 B3
Beaufort Castle . 251 B7
Beaulieu. 18 A2
Beauly 252 B1
Beaumaris 123 C6
Beaumont Cumb 175 C6
Essex 71 A5
Beaumont Hill . . 167 D5
Beausale 97 D5
Beauworth 33 C4
Beaworthy 11 B5
Beazley End 70 A1
Bebington 126 A3
Bebside 179 A4
Beccles 105 B5
Becconsall 136 A3
Beckbury 95 A5
Beckenham 49 C6
Beckermet 162 D3
Beckfoot Cumb. . . 163 D4
Cumb 174 D3
Beck Foot 155 B5
Beckford 80 D2
Beckhampton . . . 45 C4
Beck Hole 159 A7
Beckingham
Lincs. 132 D3
Notts 141 E5
Beckington 44 D2
Beckley E Sus . . . 37 D6
Hants 17 B6
Oxon. 65 B6
Beck Row 102 D2
Beck Side 153 B3
Beckton 50 A1
Beckwithshaw . . 147 B6
Becontree 50 A1
Bedale 157 C6
Bedburn 166 B4
Bedchester 30 D2
Beddau 41 C5
Beddgelert 107 B5
Beddingham 22 B2
Beddington 49 C6
Bedfield 88 A3
Bedford 84 B2
Bedham 34 D3
Bedhampton 19 A6
Bedingfield 88 A2
Bedlam 147 A6
Bedlington 179 A4
Bedlington
Station 179 A4
Bedlinog 41 A5
Bedminster 43 B4
Bedmond 67 C5
Bednall 112 D3
Bedrule 187 B5
Bedstone 94 D1
Bedwas 41 C6
Bedworth 97 C6
Bedworth Heath . 97 C6
Bed-y-coedwr . . 108 C2
Beeby 98 A3
Beech Hants 33 B5
Staffs 112 B2

Beech Hill
Gtr Man 137 C4
W Berks. 47 C4
Beechingstoke . . 45 D4
Beedon 46 B2
Beeford 151 B4
Beeley 130 C2
Beelsby 143 C4
Beenham 46 C3
Beeny 10 B2
Beer. 14 C2
Beercrocombe . . . 28 C3
Beer Hackett 29 D6
Beesands 8 C2
Beesby 135 A4
Beeson 8 C2
Beeston C Beds . . 84 C3
Ches W 127 D5
Norf 119 D6
Notts 114 B3
W Yorks 148 D1
Beeston Regis. . . 120 A3
Beeswing 173 B6
Beetham 154 D3
Beetley 119 D6
Begbroke 65 B5
Begelly 55 D7
Beggar's Bush . . . 77 A6
Beguildy 93 D5
Beighton Norf . . 105 A4
S Yorks. 131 A4
Beighton Hill . . . 130 D2
Beith 204 C3
Bekesbourne 52 D3
Belaugh 121 D4
Belbroughton . . . 96 D2
Belchamp Otten . 87 C4
Belchamp St
Paul 86 C3
Belchamp Walter 87 C4
Belchford 134 B2
Belford 199 C5
Belhaven 210 C3
Belhelvie 245 A6
Belhinnie 255 D5
Bellabeg 243 A6
Bellamore 181 C4
Bellanoch 213 C5
Bellaty 231 C6
Bell Bar 68 C2
Bell Busk 146 B3
Belleau 135 B4
Bellehiglash 254 C2
Bell End 96 D2
Bellerby 157 B5
Bellever 12 D1
Belliehill. 232 B3
Bellingdon 67 C4
Bellingham 177 A6
Belloch 190 B2
Bellochantuy . . . 190 B2
Bell o' th' Hill . . 111 A4
Bellsbank 182 B2
Bellshill N Lanark 207 D5
Northumb. 199 C5
Bellspool 195 C6
Bellsquarry 208 D3
Bells Yew Green . 36 C4
Belmaduthy 252 A2
Belmesthorpe . . 116 D3
Belmont
Blackburn. . . . 137 B5
London 49 C5
S Ayrs. 192 C3
Shetland. 284 C7
Belnacraig 243 A6
Belowda 5 A4
Belper 114 A1
Belper Lane
End 114 A1
Belsay 178 B3
Belses 187 A4
Belsford 7 B6
Belstead 88 C2
Belston 192 C3
Belstone 11 B6
Belthorn 137 A6
Beltinge 52 C3
Beltoft 141 C6

Belton Leics.....114 C2
Lincs..........116 B2
N Lincs.........141 C5
Norf.........105 A5
Belton in Rutland 99 A5
Beltring.......37 B4
Belts of
Collonach.....244 C3
Belvedere.......50 B1
Belvoir.......115 B6
Bembridge.....19 C5
Bemersyde.....197 C4
Bemerton.......31 B5
Bempton.......161 D5
Benacre.......105 C6
Ben Alder
Lodge.......229 A4
Ben Armine
Lodge.......273 C5
Benbuie.......183 C5
Ben Casgro...288 E5
Benderloch.....226 C4
Bendronaig
Lodge.......250 C2
Benenden.......37 C6
Benfield.......171 A5
Bengate.......121 C5
Bengeworth.....80 C3
Benhall Green....89 A4
Benhall Street.....89 A4
Benholm.......233 B6
Beningbrough...148 B4
Benington Herts..68 A2
Lincs..........117 A6
Benllech.......123 B5
Benmore Argyll..215 C4
Stirling.......216 B4
Benmore Lodge.271 C6
Bennacott....10 B3
Bennan.......191 C5
Benniworth....134 A2
Benover.......37 B5
Bensham.......179 C4
Benslie.......204 D3
Benson.......65 D7
Bent.......233 A4
Bent Gate.......137 A6
Benthall
Northumb.....189 A5
Shrops.......95 A4
Bentham.......63 B5
Benthoul.......245 B5
Bentlawnt.......94 A1
Bentley E Yorks...150 D3
Hants.........33 A6
Suff.........88 D2
S Yorks.......140 C3
Warks.......97 B5
Worcs.......80 A2
Bentley Heath....97 D4
Benton.......26 B1
Bentpath.......185 C6
Bents.......208 D2
Bentworth.......33 A5
Benvie.......220 A3
Benwick.......101 B5
Beoley.......80 A3
Beoraidbeg...235 A5
Bepton.......20 A1
Berden.......69 A4
Bere Alston....6 A3
Bere Ferrers....6 A3
Berepper....3 C4
Bere Regis.....16 B2
Bergh Apton...104 A4
Berinsfield.....65 D6
Berkeley.......62 D2
Berkhamsted....67 C4
Berkley.......30 A2
Berkswell.......97 D5
Bermondsey....49 B6
Bernera.......249 D5
Bernice.......215 C4
Bernisdale....259 C4
Berrick Salome..65 D7
Berriedale....275 B5
Berrier.......164 C1
Berriew.......93 A5

Berrington
Northumb.......198 B4
Shrops.........94 A3
Berrow.......42 D2
Berrow Green....79 B5
Berry Down
Cross.......25 A6
Berry Hill Glos...62 B1
Pembs.......72 B3
Berryhillock....267 C6
Berrynarbor....25 A6
Berry Pomeroy....8 A2
Bersham.......110 A2
Berstane.......282 F5
Berwick.......22 B3
Berwick Bassett..45 B4
Berwick Hill....178 B3
Berwick St
James.......31 B4
Berwick St John..30 C3
Berwick St
Leonard.......30 B3
Berwick-upon-
Tweed.......198 A3
Bescar.......136 B2
Besford.......80 C2
Bessacarr.......140 C4
Bessels Leigh....65 C5
Bessingby.......151 A4
Bessingham....120 B3
Bestbeech Hill...36 C4
Besthorpe Norf..103 B6
Notts.........132 C3
Bestwood.......114 A3
Bestwood
Village.......114 A3
Beswick.......150 C3
Betchworth....35 B5
Bethania Ceredig..75 B4
Gwyn.......107 A6
Gwyn.......108 A2
Bethel Anglesey..122 C3
Gwyn.......109 B4
Gwyn.......123 D5
Bethersden....38 C1
Bethesda Gwyn..123 D6
Pembs.......55 C6
Bethlehem.......58 C3
Bethnal Green....49 A6
Betley.......111 A6
Betsham.......50 B3
Betteshanger....53 D5
Bettiscombe....14 B3
Bettisfield.....110 B3
Betton Shrops...93 A7
Shrops.......111 B5
Bettws Bridgend..40 C4
Mon.........61 B4
Newport.......61 D4
Bettws Cedewain 93 B5
Bettws Gwerfil
Goch.......109 A5
Bettws Ifan....73 B6
Bettws Newydd..61 C5
Bettws-y-crwyn..93 C6
Bettyhill.......278 B3
Betws.......57 A6
Betws Bledrws..75 C4
Betws-Garmon..107 A5
Betws-y-Coed..124 D2
Betws-yn-Rhos..125 B4
Beulah Ceredig..73 B5
Powys.......76 B3
Bevendean....21 B6
Bevercotes....132 B1
Beverley.......150 D3
Beverston.......63 D4
Bevington.......62 D2
Bewaldeth....163 A5
Bewcastle.......176 B3
Bewdley.......95 D5
Bewerley.......147 A5
Bewholme.......151 B4
Bexhill.......23 B5
Bexley.......50 B1
Bexleyheath....50 B1
Bexwell.......102 A2
Beyton.......87 A3
Bhaltos.......287 A5
Bhatarsaigh...286 G2
Bibury.......64 C2
Bicester.......65 A6

Bickenhall.......28 D2
Bickenhill.......97 C4
Bicker.......117 B5
Bickershaw....137 C5
Bickerstaffe...136 C3
Bickerton Ches E 127 D5
N Yorks.......148 B3
Bickington Devon.12 D2
Devon.......25 B6
Bickleigh Devon...7 A4
Devon.......13 A4
Bickleton.......25 B6
Bickley.......49 C7
Bickley Moss....111 A4
Bicknacre.......70 C1
Bicknoller.......27 B6
Bicknor.......37 A6
Bickton.......31 D5
Bicton Shrops....93 C6
Shrops.......110 D3
Bidborough....36 B3
Biddenden....37 C6
Biddenham....84 C2
Biddestone....44 B2
Biddisham....42 D2
Biddlesden....82 C3
Biddlestone....188 C2
Biddulph.......128 D3
Biddulph Moor..129 D4
Bideford.......25 C5
Bidford-on-Avon.80 B4
Bidston.......136 D1
Bielby.......149 C6
Bieldside.......245 B5
Bierley IoW....18 D4
W Yorks.......147 D5
Bierton.......66 B3
Bigbury.......7 C5
Bigbury on Sea....7 C5
Bigby.......142 C2
Biggar Cumb....153 D2
S Lanark.......195 C5
Biggin Derbys...113 A6
Derbys.......129 C6
N Yorks.......148 D4
Bigfrith.......158 D3
Biggings.......285 G3
Biggin Hill....36 A2
Biggleswade....84 C3
Bighouse.......279 B4
Bighton.......33 B5
Bignor.......20 A2
Big Sand.......261 C4
Bigton.......285 L5
Bilberry....5 A5
Bilborough....114 A3
Bilbrook.......27 A5
Bilbrough.......148 C4
Bilbster.......281 C4
Bildershaw....167 C5
Bildeston.......87 C5
Billericay.......69 D6
Billesdon.......99 A4
Billesley.......80 B4
Billingborough..116 B4
Billinge.......136 C4
Billingford.......120 C2
Billingham.......168 C2
Billinghay.......133 D6
Billingley.......140 C2
Billingshurst....34 D3
Billingsley....95 C5
Billington C Beds.67 A4
Lancs.......145 D7
Billockby.......121 D6
Billy Row.......167 B4
Bilsborrow....145 D5
Bilsby.......135 B4
Bilsham.......20 B2
Bilsington.......38 B2
Bilson Green....62 B2
Bilsthorpe.......131 C6
Bilsthorpe
Moor.......131 D6
Bilston Midloth..209 D5
W Mid.......96 B2
Bilstone.......97 A6
Bilting.......38 A2
Bilton E Yorks...151 D4
Bilton in Ainsty..148 C3
Bimbister.......282 F4

Binbrook.......143 D4
Binchester
Blocks.......167 B5
Bincombe.......15 C6
Bindal.......265 B5
Binegar.......29 A6
Binfield.......47 B6
Binfield Hth.......47 B5
Bingham.......115 B5
Bingley.......147 D5
Bings Heath....111 D4
Binham.......120 B1
Binley Hants....46 D2
W Mid.......97 D6
Binley Woods....97 D6
Binniehill.......207 C6
Binsoe.......157 D6
Binstead.......19 B4
Binsted.......33 A6
Binton.......80 B4
Bintree.......120 C2
Binweston.......93 A7
Birch Essex....70 B3
Gtr Man.......138 C1
Bircham
Newton.......119 B4
Bircham Tofts...119 B4
Birchanger.......69 A5
Birchencliffe....139 B4
Bircher.......78 A2
Birch Green....70 B3
Birchgrove Cardiff 41 D6
Swansea.......40 B2
Birch Heath....127 C5
Birch Hill....127 B5
Birchington....53 C4
Birchmoor.......97 A5
Birchover.......130 C2
Birch Vale....129 A5
Birchwood Lincs 133 C4
Warr.......137 D5
Bircotes.......140 D4
Birdbrook.......86 C3
Birdforth.......158 D3
Birdham.......20 C1
Birdholme.......130 C3
Birdingbury....82 A1
Birdip.......63 B5
Birdsall.......149 A7
Birds Edge....139 C5
Birdsgreen.......95 C5
Birdsmoor Gate..14 A3
Birdston.......205 A6
Birdwell.......139 C6
Birdwood.......62 B3
Birgham.......198 C1
Birkby.......158 A2
Birkdale.......136 B2
Birkenhead....126 A3
Birkenhills.......256 B2
Birkenshaw
N Lanark.......207 D4
W Yorks.......139 A5
Birkhall.......243 C6
Birkhill Angus...220 A3
Borders.......185 A5
Birkholme.......116 C2
Birkin.......140 A3
Birley.......78 B2
Birling Kent....50 C3
Northumb.......189 C5
Birling Gap....22 C3
Birlingham....80 C2
Birmingham....96 C3
Birnam.......230 D4
Birse.......244 C2
Birsemore.......244 C2
Birstall Leics...98 A2
W Yorks.......139 A5
Birstwith.......147 B6
Birthorpe.......116 B4
Birtley Hereford..78 A1
Northumb.......177 B6
T&W.......179 D4
Birts Street....79 D5
Bisbrooke.......99 B5
Biscathorpe...134 A2
Biscot.......67 A5
Bisham.......47 A6
Bishampton....80 B2
Bish Mill.......26 C2

Bishop
Auckland.......167 C5
Bishopbridge...142 D2
Bishop Burton..150 D2
Bishop
Middleham....167 B6
Bishopmill.......266 C3
Bishop
Monkton.......148 A2
Bishop Norton..142 D1
Bishopsbourne..52 D3
Bishops
Cannings.......44 C4
Bishop's Castle..93 C7
Bishop's Caundle 29 D6
Bishop's Cleeve..63 A5
Bishops Frome...79 C4
Bishop's Green...69 B6
Bishop's Hull....28 C2
Bishop's
Itchington....81 B6
Bishops Lydeard..27 C6
Bishops Nympton 26 C2
Bishop's Offley..112 C1
Bishop'S
Stortford.......69 A4
Bishop's Sutton..33 B5
Bishop's
Tachbrook....81 A6
Bishops Tawton..25 B6
Bishopsteignton..13 D4
Bishopstoke....32 D3
Bishopston.......57 D5
Bishopstone
Bucks.......66 B3
E Sus.......22 B2
Hereford.......78 C2
Swindon.......45 A6
Wilts.......31 C4
Bishopstrow....30 A2
Bishop Sutton...43 D4
Bishop's
Waltham.......33 D4
Bishopswood....28 D2
Bishop's Wood...95 A6
Bishopsworth...43 C4
Bishop
Thornton.......147 A6
Bishopthorpe...149 C4
Bishopton Darl..167 C6
Dumfries.......171 C6
N Yorks.......157 D7
Renfs.......205 A4
Warks.......81 B4
Bishop Wilton..149 B6
Bishton.......42 A2
Bisley Glos....63 C5
Sur.......34 A2
Bispham.......144 C3
Bispham Green..136 B3
Bissoe.......4 C2
Bisterne Close....17 A6
Bitchfield.......116 C2
Bittadon.......25 A6
Bittaford.......7 B5
Bittering.......119 D6
Bitterley.......94 D3
Bitterne.......32 D3
Bitteswell.......98 C2
Bitton.......43 C5
Bix.......47 A5
Bixter.......285 H5
Blaby.......98 B2
Blackacre.......184 C3
Blackadder
West.......198 A2
Blackawton.......8 B2
Blackborough
End.......118 D3
Black Bourton...64 C3
Blackboys.......36 D3
Blackbrook
Derbys.......114 A1
Mers.......136 D4
Staffs.......111 B6
Blackburn
Aberds.......245 A5
Aberds.......255 C6
Blackburn.......137 A5
W Loth.......208 D2

Black Callerton..178 C3
Black Clauchrie.181 C4
Black Corries
Lodge.......228 C1
Blackcraig.......183 D5
Black Crofts....226 C4
Blackden Heath..128 B2
Blackdog.......245 A6
Black Dog....12 A3
Blackfell.......179 D4
Blackfield.......18 A3
Blackford Cumb..175 B6
Perth.......218 D3
Som.......28 A4
Som.......29 C6
Blackfordby.......114 D1
Blackgang.......18 D3
Blackhall
Colliery.......168 B2
Blackhall Mill...178 D3
Blackhall Rocks.168 B2
Blackham.......36 C2
Blackhaugh.......196 C3
Blackheath Essex .71 A4
Suff.......105 D5
Sur.......34 B3
W Mid.......96 C2
Black Heddon...178 B2
Blackhill Aberds..257 B5
Aberds.......269 D5
Highld.......258 C3
Blackhills Highld.253 A5
Moray.......266 D3
Blackhorse.......43 B5
Blackland.......44 C4
Black Lane....137 C6
Blacklaw.......268 D1
Blackley.......138 C1
Blacklunans....231 B5
Black Marsh....94 B1
Blackmill.......40 C4
Blackmoor.......33 B6
Blackmoor Gate..26 A1
Blackmore.......69 C6
Blackmore End
Essex.......86 D3
Herts.......67 B6
Black Mount....228 D1
Blackness.......208 C3
Blacknest.......33 A6
Black Notley....70 A1
Blacko.......146 C2
Black Pill....57 C6
Blackpool
Blackpool.......144 D3
Devon.......8 C2
Pembs.......55 C6
Blackpool Gate..176 B3
Blackridge.......208 D1
Blackrock Argyll..200 B3
Mon.......60 B4
Blackrod.......137 B5
Blackshaw.......174 B3
Blackshaw
Head.......138 A2
Blacksmith's
Green.......88 A2
Blackstone.......21 A5
Black Tar....55 D5
Blackthorn.......65 B7
Blackthorpe....87 A5
Blacktoft.......141 A6
Blacktop.......245 B5
Black Torrington.11 A5
Blacktown.......42 A1
Blackwall Tunnel 49 A6
Hants.......34 A1
IoW.......18 C4
Blackwaterfoot..191 C5
Blackwell Darl..167 D5
Derbys.......129 B6
Derbys.......131 C4
Warks.......81 C5
Worcs.......96 D2
W Sus.......36 C1
Blackwood.......194 B2
Blackwood Coed
Duon.......41 B6
Blackwood Hill..129 D4
Blacon.......126 C3
Bladnoch.......171 B6

Bladon 65 B5
Blaenannerch 73 B5
Blaenau
  Ffestiniog 108 A2
Blaenavon 61 C4
Blaencelyn. 73 A6
Blaendyryn 59 B6
Blaenffos 73 C4
Blaengarw 40 B4
Blaengwrach 59 E5
Blaen-gwynfi 40 B3
Blaenpennal 75 B5
Blaenplwyf. 75 A4
Blaenporth. 73 B5
Blaenrhondda . . . 40 A4
Blaen-waun 73 D5
Blaen-y-coed . . . 73 D6
Blaenycwm 92 D2
Blaen-y-Cwm
  Denb. 109 B5
  Gwyn 108 C2
  Powys 109 C5
Blagdon N Som. . . 43 D4
  Torbay 8 A2
Blagdon Hill 28 D2
Blagill 165 A5
Blaguegate 136 C3
Blaich 237 B4
Blain 235 D5
Blaina 60 C4
Blair Atholl 230 B2
Blairbeg 191 B6
Blairdaff 244 A3
Blair
  Drummond . . . 207 A5
Blairglas 206 B1
Blairgowrie 231 D5
Blairhall 208 B3
Blairingone 208 A2
Blairland 204 D3
Blairlogie 207 A6
Blairmore 215 D4
Blairmore. 215 D4
Blairnamarrow . . 243 A5
Blairquhosh 206 B3
Blair's Ferry 203 B4
Blairskaith 205 A5
Blaisdon 62 B3
Blakebrook 95 D6
Blakedown. 96 D1
Blakelaw 197 C6
Blakeley 95 B6
Blakeley Lane . . . 112 A3
Blakemere 78 C1
Blakeney Glos . . . 62 C2
  Norf 120 A2
Blakenhall
  Ches E 111 A6
  W Mid 96 B2
Blakeshall 95 C6
Blakesley 82 B3
Blanchland 178 D1
Blandford Forum 16 A2
Blandford St
  Mary 16 A2
Bland Hill 147 B6
Blanefield 205 A5
Blankney 133 C5
Blantyre 194 A1
Blar
  a'Chaorainn . . 237 C5
Blaran 214 A4
Blarghour. 214 A2
Blarmachfoldach
  . . . . 237 C4
Blarnalearoch . . 262 A3
Blashford 17 A5
Blaston 99 B5
Blatherwycke . . . 99 B6
Blawith 154 C1
Blaxhall 89 B4
Blaxton 141 C4
Blaydon 178 C3
Bleadon 42 D2
Bleak Hey Nook . . 138 C3
Blean 52 C3
Bleasby Lincs . . . 133 A6
  Notts 115 A5
Bleasdale 145 C5
Bleatarn 165 D5
Blebocraigs 220 C4
Bleddfa 77 A6

Bledington 64 A3
Bledlow 66 C2
Bledlow Ridge . . . 66 D2
Blegbie 210 D1
Blencarn 165 B4
Blencogo 175 D4
Blendworth 33 D6
Blenheim Park . . 119 B5
Blennerhasset . . 175 D4
Blervie Castle . . 253 A6
Bletchingdon . . . 65 B6
Bletchingley 35 A6
Bletchley
  M Keynes 83 D5
  Shrops 111 B5
Bletherston 55 B6
Bletsoe 84 B2
Blewbury 46 A3
Blickling 120 C3
Blidworth 131 D5
Blindburn 188 B1
Blindcrake 163 A4
Blindley Heath . . 35 B6
Blisland 10 D2
Blissford 31 D5
Bliss Gate 95 D5
Blisworth 83 B4
Blithbury 113 C4
Blitterlees 174 C4
Blockley 81 D4
Blofield 104 A4
Blofield Heath . . 121 D5
Blo' Norton 103 D6
Bloomfield 187 A4
Blore 113 A5
Blount's Green . . 113 B4
Blowick 136 B2
Bloxham 82 D1
Bloxholm 133 D5
Bloxwich 96 A2
Bloxworth 16 B2
Blubberhouses . . 147 B5
Blue Anchor Som . 27 A4
  Swansea 57 C5
Blue Row 71 B4
Blundeston 105 B6
Blunham 84 B3
Blunsdon St
  Andrew 45 A5
Bluntington 96 D1
Bluntisham 101 D5
Blunts 6 A2
Blyborough 142 D1
Blyford 105 D5
Blymhill 112 D2
Blyth Northumb . 179 A5
  Notts 131 A6
Blyth Bridge . . . 195 B6
Blythburgh. 105 D5
Blythe 197 B4
Blythe Bridge . . . 112 A3
Blyton 141 D6
Boarhills 221 C5
Boarhunt 19 A5
Boarshead 36 C3
Boars Head 137 C4
Boars Hill 65 C5
Boarstall 66 B1
Boasley Cross . . . 11 B5
Boath. 264 C1
Boat of Garten . . 242 A2
Bobbing 51 C5
Bobbington 95 B6
Bobbingworth. . . 69 C5
Bocaddon 5 B6
Bochastle 217 D6
Bocking 70 A1
Bocking
  Churchstreet . . 70 A1
Boddam Aberds . 257 B6
  Shetland. 285 M5
Boddington 63 A4
Bodedern 122 B3
Bodelwyddan . . . 125 B5
Bodenham
  Hereford 78 B3
  Wilts. 31 C6
Bodenham Moor . 78 B3
Bodermid 106 D1
Bodewryd 122 A3
Bodfari 125 B5
Bodffordd 123 C4

Bodham 120 A3
Bodiam 37 D5
Bodicote. 82 D1
Bodieve 9 D5
Bodinnick 5 B6
Bodle Street
  Green 23 A4
Bodmin. 5 A5
Bodney 103 B4
Bodorgan 122 D3
Bodsham 38 A3
Boduan 106 C3
Bodymoor Heath . 97 B4
Bogallan. 252 A2
Bogbrae 257 C5
Bogend Borders . 198 B1
  S Ayrs. 192 B3
Boghall 208 D2
Boghead 194 B2
Bognor Regis . . . 20 C2
Bograxie 256 E2
Bogside 194 A3
Bogton 268 D1
Bogue 182 D4
Bohenie 239 D6
Bohortha 4 D3
Bohuntine 239 D6
Boirseam 287 F5
Bojewyan 2 B1
Bolam Durham . . 167 C4
  Northumb. 178 A2
Bolberry 7 D5
Bold Heath 127 A5
Boldon 179 C5
Boldon Colliery . 179 C5
Boldre 18 B2
Boldron 166 D3
Bole 132 A2
Bolehill 130 D2
Boleside 196 C3
Bolham 27 D4
Bolham Water. . . 27 D6
Bolingey 4 B2
Bollington 129 B4
Bollington
  Cross 129 B4
Bolney 35 D5
Bolnhurst 84 B2
Bolshan 233 C4
Bolsover 131 B4
Bolsterstone . . . 139 D5
Bolstone. 78 D3
Boltby 158 C3
Bolter End 66 D2
Bolton Cumb . . . 165 C4
  E Loth. 210 C2
  E Yorks 149 B6
  Gtr Man 137 C6
  Northumb. . . . 189 B4
Bolton Abbey . . . 147 B4
Bolton Bridge . . 147 B4
Bolton-by-
  Bowland 146 C1
Boltonfellend . . . 176 C2
Boltongate 175 D5
Bolton-le-
  Sands 145 A4
Bolton Low
  Houses 175 D5
Bolton-on-
  Swale 157 B6
Bolton Percy . . . 148 C4
Bolton Town
  End 145 A4
Bolton upon
  Dearne 140 C2
Bolventor 10 D2
Bomere Heath . . 110 D3
Bonar Bridge . . . 264 A2
Bonawe 227 C5
Bonby 142 B2
Boncath 73 C5
Bonchester
  Bridge 187 B4
Bonchurch. 19 D4
Bondleigh 12 A1
Bonehill Devon. . 12 D2
  Staffs 97 A4
Bo'ness 208 B2
Bonhill 206 C1

Boningale 95 A6
Bonjedward. . . . 187 A5
Bonkle 194 A3
Bonnavoulin . . . 225 A4
Bonnington Edin 208 D4
  Kent 38 B2
Bonnybank 220 D3
Bonnybridge . . . 207 B6
Bonnykelly 268 D3
Bonnyrigg and
  Lasswade . . . 209 D6
Bonnyton Aberds 256 C1
  Angus. 220 A3
  Angus. 233 C4
Bonsall 130 D2
Bonskeid House 230 B2
Bont. 61 B5
Bontddu 91 A4
Bont-Dolgadfan. 91 B6
Bont-goch. 91 D4
Bonthorpe 135 B4
Bontnewydd
  Ceredig 75 B5
  Gwyn 123 D4
Bont-newydd . . 125 B5
Bont Newydd
  Gwyn 108 A2
  Gwyn 108 C2
Bontuchel 125 D5
Bonvilston 41 D5
Bon-y-maen . . . 57 C6
Booker 66 D3
Boon 197 B4
Boosbeck 169 D4
Boot 163 D4
Booth 138 A3
Boothby
  Graffoe. 133 D4
Boothby Pagnell 116 B2
Boothen 112 A2
Boothferry 141 A5
Boothville 83 A4
Booth Wood . . . 138 B3
Bootle Cumb . . . 153 B2
  Mers. 136 D2
Booton 120 C3
Boot Street 88 C3
Boquhan 206 B3
Boraston 95 D4
Borden Kent . . . 51 C5
  W Sus. 34 D1
Bordley 146 A3
Bordon 33 B7
Bordon Camp . . 33 B6
Boreham Essex . 70 C1
  Wilts. 30 A2
Boreham Street . 23 A1
Borehamwood . . 68 D1
Boreland
  Dumfries 185 C4
  Stirling 217 A5
Borgh W Isles . . 286 F2
  W Isles 287 F4
Borghastan 288 C3
Borgie 278 C2
Borgue Dumfries 172 D4
  Highld. 275 B5
Borley 87 C4
Bornais 286 D3
Bornesketaig. . . 258 A3
Borness 172 D4
Boroughbridge . 148 A2
Borough Green . 36 A4
Borras Head . . . 126 D3
Borreraig 258 C1
Borrobol Lodge . 274 B2
Borrowash 114 B2
Borrowby 158 C3
Borrowdale 163 C5
Borrowfield . . . 245 C5
Borth. 90 C4
Borthwickbrae . 186 B3
Borthwickshiels 186 B3
Borth-y-Gest . . 107 C5
Borve 259 D4
Borve Lodge . . . 287 E5
Borwick 154 D4
Bosavern 2 B1
Bosbury 79 C4
Boscastle 10 B2
Boscombe Bmouth. 17 B5
  Wilts. 31 B6

Boscoppa. 5 B5
Bosham 19 A7
Bosherston 55 E5
Boskenna 2 C2
Bosley 129 C4
Bossall 149 A6
Bossiney 9 C6
Bossingham 38 A3
Bossington 26 A3
Bostock Green . 127 C6
Boston 117 A6
Boston Long
  Hedges. 117 A6
Boston Spa 148 C3
Boston West . . . 117 A5
Boswinger 5 C4
Botallack 2 B1
Botany Bay 68 D2
Botcherby 175 C7
Botcheston 98 A1
Botesdale 103 D6
Bothal 179 A4
Bothamsall 131 B6
Bothel 163 A4
Bothenhampton . 15 B4
Bothwell. 194 A2
Botley Bucks . . . 67 C4
  Hants 32 D4
  Oxon. 65 C5
Botolph Claydon . 66 A2
Botolphs. 21 B4
Bottacks 263 D6
Bottesford Leics 115 B6
  N Lincs. 141 C6
Bottisham 86 A1
Bottlesford 45 D5
Bottom Boat . . . 139 A6
Bottomcraig . . . 220 B3
Bottom House . . 129 D5
Bottom of
  Hutton 136 A3
Bottom o' th'
  Moor. 137 B5
Botusfleming . . . 6 A3
Botwnnog 106 C2
Bough Beech . . . 36 B2
Boughrood 77 D5
Boughspring . . . 62 D1
Boughton Norf. . 102 A2
  Northants. . . . 83 A4
  Notts 131 C6
Boughton Aluph . 38 A2
Boughton Lees . 38 A2
Boughton
  Malherbe. . . . 37 B6
Boughton
  Monchelsea . . 37 A5
Boughton Street . 52 D2
Boulby 169 D5
Boulden 94 C3
Boulmer 189 B5
Boulston 55 C5
Boultenstone . . 243 A7
Boultham 133 C4
Bourn 85 B5
Bourne 116 C3
Bourne End Bucks 48 A1
  C Beds 83 C6
  Herts 67 C5
Bournemouth . . . 17 B4
Bournes Green
  Glos 63 C5
  Southend 51 A6
Bournheath 96 D2
Bournmoor 179 D5
Bournville 96 C3
Bourton Dorset . 30 B1
  N Som 42 C2
  Oxon. 45 A3
  Shrops 94 B3
Bourton on
  Dunsmore . . . 98 D1
Bourton on the
  Hill 81 D4
Bourton-on-the-
  Water 64 A2
Bousd 223 A5
Boustead Hill . . 175 C5
Bouth 154 C2
Bouthwaite . . . 157 D5
Boveney 48 B2
Boverton 41 E4

Bovey Tracey. . . . 12 D3
Bovingdon 67 C5
Bovingdon Green
  Bucks 47 A6
  Herts 67 C5
Bovinger. 69 C5
Bovington Camp .16 C2
Bow Borders . . 196 B3
  Devon. 12 A2
  Orkney 283 H4
Bowbank 166 C2
Bow Brickhill . . . 83 D6
Bowburn. 167 B6
Bowcombe. 18 C3
Bowd 13 B6
Bowden Borders 197 C4
  Devon. 8 C2
Bowden Hill. . . . 44 C3
Bowderdale. . . . 155 A5
Bowdon 128 A2
Bower 177 A5
Bowerchalke . . . 31 C4
Bowerhill. 44 C3
Bower Hinton . . 29 D4
Bowermadden . . 280 B4
Bowers Gifford . 51 A4
Bowershall. 208 A3
Bowertower . . . 280 B4
Bowes. 166 D2
Bowgreave. 145 C4
Bowgreen 128 A2
Bowhill. 186 A3
Bowhouse. 174 B3
Bowland Bridge 154 C3
Bowley 78 B3
Bowlhead Green . 34 C2
Bowling W Dunb. 205 A4
  W Yorks 147 D5
Bowling Bank . . 110 A2
Bowling Green . 79 B6
Bowmanstead . . 154 B2
Bowmore 200 C3
Bowness-on-
  Solway 175 B5
Bowness-on-
  Windermere . 154 B3
Bow of Fife . . . 220 C3
Bowsden 198 B3
Bowside Lodge . 279 B4
Bowston 154 B3
Bow Street 90 D4
Bowthorpe. 104 A2
Box Glos 63 C4
  Wilts. 44 C2
Boxbush 62 B3
Box End 84 C2
Boxford Suff. . . 87 C5
  W Berks 46 B2
Boxgrove 20 B2
Boxley 37 A5
Boxmoor. 67 C5
Boxted Essex . . . 87 D6
  Suff 87 B4
Boxted Cross. . . 87 D6
Boxted Heath . . 87 D6
Boxworth 85 A5
Boxworth End . . 85 A5
Boyden Gate . . . 53 C4
Boylestone 113 B5
Boyndie 268 C1
Boynton 151 A4
Boysack 233 D4
Boyton Corn . . . 10 B4
  Suff 89 C4
  Wilts. 30 B3
Boyton Cross . . 69 C6
Boyton End 86 C3
Bozeat. 83 B6
Braaid 152 D3
Braal Castle. . . 280 B3
Brabling Green . 88 A3
Brabourne 38 A2
Brabourne Lees . 38 A2
Brabster 281 B5
Bracadale. 246 A2
Bracara 235 A6
Braceborough . . 116 D3
Bracebridge . . . 133 C4

Bracebridge
Heath 133 C4
Bracebridge Low
Fields 133 C4
Braceby 116 B3
Bracewell. 146 C2
Brackenfield 130 D3
Brackenthwaite
Cumb 175 D5
N Yorks. 148 B1
Bracklesham 19 B7
Brackletter 239 D5
Brackley Argyll. . .202 D2
Northants. 82 D2
Brackloch 270 B4
Bracknell 47 C6
Braco. 218 D3
Bracobrae 267 D6
Bracon Ash 104 B2
Bracorina. 235 A6
Bradbourne. 130 D2
Bradbury 167 C6
Bradda 152 E1
Bradden 82 C3
Braddock 5 A6
Bradeley. 128 D3
Bradenham Bucks 66 D3
Norf 103 A5
Bradenstoke 44 B4
Bradfield Essex . . .88 D2
Norf 121 B4
W Berks. 47 B4
Bradfield
Combust 87 B4
Bradfield Green .128 D1
Bradfield Heath . .71 A5
Bradfield St
Clare. 87 B5
Bradfield St
George. 87 A5
Bradford Corn . . .10 D2
Derbys 130 C2
Devon. 11 A5
Northumb. 199 C5
W Yorks 147 D5
Bradford Abbas . .29 D5
Bradford Leigh . . .44 C2
Bradford-on-
Avon 44 C2
Bradford-on-
Tone. 28 C1
Bradford Peverell 15 B6
Brading. 19 C5
Bradley Derbys. . .113 A6
Hants 33 A5
NE Lincs 143 C4
Staffs 112 D2
W Mid 96 B2
W Yorks 139 A4
Bradley Green. . . .80 A2
Bradley in the
Moors. 113 A4
Bradley Stoke 43 A5
Bradlow 79 D5
Bradmore Notts . .114 B3
W Mid 96 B1
Bradninch 13 A5
Bradnop. 129 D5
Bradpole 15 B4
Bradshaw
Gtr Man 137 B6
W Yorks 138 B3
Bradstone 11 C4
Bradwall Green .128 C2
Bradway. 130 A4
Bradwell Derbys .129 A6
Essex 70 A2
M Keynes. 83 D5
Norf 105 A6
Staffs 112 A2
Bradwell Grove. . .64 C3
Bradwell on Sea. .71 C4
Bradwell
Waterside 70 C3
Bradworthy 24 D4
Bradworthy
Cross 24 D4
Brae Dumfries. . . .173 A6
Highld. 261 B5

Brae continued
Highld. 272 D2
Shetland. 284 G5
Braeantra. 264 C1
Braedownie. 231 A6
Braefield 251 C6
Braegrum. 219 B5
Braehead
Dumfries 171 B6
Orkney 282 C5
Orkney 283 G6
S Lanark. 194 C3
S Lanark. 195 A4
Braehead of
Lunan 233 C4
Braehoulland 284 F4
Braehungie 275 A5
Braelangwell
Lodge 263 A7
Braemar. 243 C4
Braemore Highld 262 C3
Highld. 275 A4
Brae of
Achnahaird. . . .270 C3
Brae Roy Lodge .240 C1
Braeside. 204 A2
Braes of Enzie. . . .267 D4
Braeswick. 282 D7
Braewick 285 H5
Brafferton Darl . .167 C5
N Yorks. 158 D3
Brafield-on-the-
Green. 83 B5
Bragar. 288 C3
Bragbury End 68 A2
Bragleenmore. . . .226 D4
Braichmelyn 123 D6
Braid 209 D5
Braides 144 B4
Braidley 156 C4
Braidwood. 194 B3
Braigo. 200 B2
Brailsford. 113 A6
Brainshaugh 189 C5
Braintree 70 A1
Braiseworth. 104 D2
Braishfield. 32 C2
Braithwaite
Cumb 163 B5
S Yorks. 140 B4
W Yorks 147 C4
Braithwell 140 D3
Bramber 21 A4
Bramcote Notts . .114 B3
Warks. 97 C7
Bramdean 33 C5
Bramerton 104 A3
Bramfield Herts. . .68 B2
Suff 105 D4
Bramford 88 C2
Bramhall 128 A3
Bramham 148 C3
Bramhope 147 C6
Bramley Hants . . .47 D4
Sur 34 B3
S Yorks. 140 D2
W Yorks 147 D6
Bramling 53 D4
Brampford Speke 13 B4
Brampton Cambs 100 D4
Cumb 165 C4
Cumb 176 C3
Derbys 130 B3
Hereford 78 D2
Lincs. 132 B3
Norf 120 C4
Suff 105 C5
S Yorks. 140 C2
Brampton
Abbotts 62 A2
Brampton Ash. . . .99 C4
Brampton Bryan. .94 D1
Brampton en le
Morthen. 131 A4
Bramshall. 113 B4
Bramshaw 31 D6
Bramshill 47 C5
Bramshott 34 C1
Branault 235 D4
Brancaster 119 A4
Brancaster
Staithe. 119 A4

Brancepeth 167 B5
Branch End 178 C2
Branchill. 266 D1
Branderburgh. . . .266 B3
Brandesburton . .151 C4
Brandeston 88 A3
Brand Green 62 A3
Brandhill 94 D2
Brandis Corner. . . .11 A5
Brandiston. 120 C3
Brandon Durham .167 B5
Lincs. 116 A2
Northumb. 188 B3
Suff 102 C3
Warks. 97 D7
Brandon Bank. . .102 C2
Brandon Creek . .102 B2
Brandon Parva . .104 A1
Brandsby 159 D4
Brandy Wharf . . .142 D2
Brane 2 C2
Bran End 69 A6
Branksome 17 B4
Branksome Park .17 B4
Bransby 132 B3
Branscombe 14 C1
Bransford 79 B5
Bransgore 17 B5
Branshill. 208 A1
Bransholme. 151 D4
Branson's Cross. .96 D3
Branston Leics . . .115 C6
Lincs. 133 C5
Staffs 113 C6
Branstone 19 C4
Bransty 162 C2
Brant
Broughton. 133 D4
Brantham. 88 D2
Branthwaite
Cumb 162 B3
Cumb 163 A5
Brantingham . . .142 A1
Branton
Northumb. 188 B3
S Yorks. 140 C4
Branxholme. 186 B3
Branxholm Park 186 B3
Branxton 198 C2
Brassey Green . . .127 C5
Brassington. 130 D2
Brasted. 36 A2
Brasted Chart 36 A2
Brathens. 244 C3
Bratoft 135 C4
Brattleby 133 A4
Bratton Telford. .111 D5
Wilts. 44 D3
Bratton Clovelly. .11 B5
Bratton Fleming. .26 B1
Bratton Seymour 29 C6
Braughing 68 A3
Braunston. 82 A2
Braunston-in-
Rutland 99 A5
Braunton 25 B5
Brawby 159 D6
Brawl. 279 B4
Brawlbin. 279 C6
Bray. 48 B2
Braybrooke 99 C4
Braye Ald. 7
Brayford 26 B1
Bray Shop 10 D4
Braystones. 162 D3
Braythorn. 147 C6
Brayton. 149 D5
Bray Wick 48 B1
Brazacott 10 B3
Breach 51 C5
Breachacha
Castle 223 B4
Breachwood
Green. 67 A6
Breacleit. 288 D2
Breaden Heath . .110 B3
Breadsall 114 B1
Breadstone 62 C3
Breage 3 C4

Breakachy 251 B6
Bream. 62 C2
Breamore 31 D5
Brean 42 D1
Breanais 287 B4
Brearton. 148 A2
Breascleit. 288 D3
Breaston. 114 B2
Brechfa. 58 B2
Brechin. 232 B3
Breckan 283 G3
Breck of Cruan . .282 F4
Breckrey. 259 B5
Brecon
Aberhonddu 60 A2
Bredbury 138 D2
Brede 23 A6
Bredenbury 79 B4
Bredfield 88 B3
Bredgar 51 C5
Bredicot. 80 B2
Bredon 80 D2
Bredon's Norton .80 D2
Bredwardine 78 C1
Breedon on the
Hill 114 C2
Breibhig W Isles .286 G2
W Isles 288 D5
Breich 208 D2
Breightmet 137 C6
Breighton. 149 D6
Breinton 78 D2
Breinton
Common 78 C2
Breiwick. 285 J6
Bremhill. 44 B3
Bremirehoull. . . .285 L6
Brenchley. 37 B4
Brendon 26 A2
Brenkley. 179 B4
Brent Eleigh 87 C5
Brentford. 49 B4
Brentingby. 115 D5
Brent Knoll 42 D2
Brent Pelham. . . .85 D6
Brentwood. 69 D5
Brenzett 38 C2
Brereton. 113 D4
Brereton Green .128 C2
Brereton Heath. .128 C3
Bressingham. . . .104 C1
Bretby. 113 C6
Bretford 98 D1
Bretforton 80 C3
Bretherdale
Head. 155 A4
Bretherton. 136 A3
Brettabister. 285 H6
Brettenham Norf 103 C5
Suff 87 B5
Bretton Derbys. . .130 B2
Flint 126 C3
Brewer Street. . . .35 A6
Brewlands
Bridge 231 B5
Brewood. 96 A1
Briach 266 D1
Briants Puddle . . .16 B2
Brick End 69 A5
Brickendon 68 C3
Bricket Wood 67 C6
Bricklehampton . .80 C2
Bride. 152 A4
Bridekirk 163 A4
Bridell 73 B4
Bridestowe 11 C6
Brideswell 255 C6
Bridford 12 C3
Bridfordmills. 12 C3
Bridge. 52 D3
Bridge End. 116 B4
Bridgefoot
Angus. 220 A3
Cumb 162 B3
Bridge Green 85 D6
Bridgehampton . .29 C5
Bridge Hewick . .158 D2
Bridgehill. 178 D2
Bridgemary 19 A4
Bridgemont 129 A5
Bridgend Aberds .244 A2

Bridgend continued
Aberds 255 C6
Angus. 232 B3
Argyll 190 B3
Argyll 200 B3
Argyll 214 C1
Cumb 164 D1
Fife. 220 C3
Moray. 255 C4
N Lanark 207 C4
Pembs 73 B4
W Loth 208 C3
Bridgend Pen-y-bont
ar Ogwr 40 D4
Bridgend of
Lintrathen 231 C6
Bridge of Alford 244 A2
Bridge of Allan . .207 A5
Bridge of Avon . .254 C2
Bridge of Awe. . .227 D5
Bridge of Balgie 229 D4
Bridge of Cally . .231 C5
Bridge of Canny 244 C3
Bridge of
Craigisla 231 C6
Bridge of Dee . . .173 C5
Bridge of Don . . .245 A6
Bridge of Dun . . .233 C4
Bridge of Dye . . .244 D3
Bridge of Earn . .219 C6
Bridge of Ericht 229 C4
Bridge of Feugh 245 C4
Bridge of Forss. .279 B6
Bridge of Gairn. .243 C6
Bridge of Gaur . .229 C4
Bridge of
Muchalls 245 C5
Bridge of Oich . .240 B1
Bridge of Orchy 216 A2
Bridge of Waith .282 F3
Bridge of Walls. .285 H4
Bridge of Weir . .204 B3
Bridgerule 10 A3
Bridges 94 B1
Bridge Sollers. . . .78 C2
Bridge Street 87 C4
Bridgeton. 205 B6
Bridgetown Corn. .10 C4
Som 27 B4
Bridge Trafford .127 B4
Bridge Yate 43 B5
Bridgham 103 C5
Bridgnorth. 95 B5
Bridgtown 96 A2
Bridgwater. 28 B3
Bridlington 151 A4
Bridport 15 B4
Bridstow. 62 A1
Brierfield 146 D2
Brierley Glos. 62 B2
Hereford 78 B2
S Yorks. 140 B2
Brierley Hill. 96 C2
Briery Hill. 60 C3
Brigg 142 C2
Briggswath 160 A2
Brigham Cumb . .162 A3
E Yorks. 150 B3
Brighouse 139 A4
Brighstone 18 C3
Brightgate 130 D2
Brighthampton . .65 C4
Brightling. 37 D4
Brightlingsea 71 B4
Brighton Brighton . .21 B6
Corn. 4 B4
Brighton Hill 33 A5
Brightons 208 C2
Brightwalton 46 B2
Brightwell 88 C3
Brightwell
Baldwin 66 D1
Brightwell cum
Sotwell. 65 D6
Brignall. 166 D3
Brig o'Turk 217 D5
Brigsley 143 C4
Brigsteer 154 C3
Brigstock 99 C6
Brill 66 B1
Brilley 77 C6
Brimaston 55 B5

Brimfield 78 A3
Brimington 131 B4
Brimley. 12 C2
Brimpsfield 63 B5
Brimpton 46 C3
Brims. 283 J3
Brimscombe 63 C4
Brimstage 126 A3
Brinacory 235 A6
Brind 149 D6
Brindister
Shetland. 285 H4
Shetland. 285 K6
Brindle 137 A5
Brindley Ford 128 D3
Brineton 112 D2
Bringhurst 99 B5
Brington. 100 D2
Brinian 282 E5
Briningham 120 B2
Brinkhill. 134 B3
Brinkley. 86 B2
Brinklow. 98 D1
Brinkworth 44 A4
Brinmore 252 D2
Brinscall. 137 A5
Brinsea 42 C3
Brinsley 114 A2
Brinsop 78 C2
Brinsworth. 131 A4
Brinton 120 B2
Brisco 175 C7
Brisley 119 C6
Brislington. 43 B5
Bristol 43 B4
Briston 120 B2
Britannia 138 A1
Britford. 31 C5
Brithdir 91 A5
British Legion
Village 37 A5
Briton Ferry. 40 B2
Britwell Salome . .66 D1
Brixham 8 B3
Brixton Devon. 7 B4
London 49 B6
Brixton Deverill . .30 B2
Brixworth 99 D4
Brize Norton 64 C4
Broad Blunsdon .64 D2
Broadbottom. . . .138 D2
Broadbridge 19 A1
Broadbridge
Heath. 35 C4
Broad Campden . .81 D4
Broad Chalke 31 C4
Broadclyst 13 B4
Broadfield
Gtr Man 138 B1
Lancs 136 A4
Pembs 56 B1
W Sus. 35 C5
Broadford 247 B5
Broadford Bridge 34 D1
Broad Green
C Beds 83 C6
Essex 70 A2
Worcs. 79 B5
Broadhaugh 186 C3
Broadhaven. 281 C5
Broad Haven 55 C4
Broadheath 128 A2
Broad Heath 79 A4
Broadhembury . .13 A6
Broadhempston. . .8 A2
Broad Hill. 102 D1
Broad Hinton 45 B5
Broadholme
Derbys 114 A1
Lincs. 132 B3
Broadland Row. . .23 A6
Broadlay. 56 B3
Broad Laying. 46 C2
Bradley Lancs. . . .138 B1
Broadley
Common 68 C4
Broad Marston . . .80 C4
Broadmayne 15 C7
Broadmeadows .196 C3
Broadmere 33 A5
Broadmoor 55 D6

Broadoak 52 C3
Broad Oak Carms. . 58 C2
Cumb 153 A2
Dorset 14 B4
Dorset 30 D1
E Sus 23 A6
E Sus 36 D4
Hereford 61 A6
Mers. 136 D4
Broadrashes 267 D5
Broadsea 269 C4
Broadstairs 53 C5
Broadstone Poole . 17 B4
Shrops 94 C3
Broad Street 37 A6
Broad Street
Green 70 C2
Broad Town. 45 B4
Broadtown Lane. . . 45 B4
Broadwas. 79 B5
Broadwater Herts 68 A2
W Sus. 21 B4
Broadway Carms . 56 B2
Pembs 55 C4
Som 28 D3
Suff 105 D4
Worcs. 80 D3
Broadwell Glos . 62 B1
Glos 64 A3
Oxon. 64 C3
Warks. 82 A1
Broadwell
House 177 D7
Broadwey 15 C6
Broadwindsor . . . 14 A4
Broadwood Kelly 11 A7
Broadwoodwidger
. . . . 11 C5
Brobury 78 C1
Brochel 248 B2
Brochloch 182 C3
Brochroy 227 C5
Brockamin 79 B5
Brockbridge 33 D5
Brockdam 189 A4
Brockdish. 104 D3
Brockenhurst 18 A2
Brocketsbrae 194 C3
Brockford Street . 88 A2
Brockhall 82 A3
Brockham 35 B4
Brockhampton
Glos 63 A6
Hereford 78 D3
Brockholes 139 B4
Brockhurst
Derbys 130 C4
Hants 19 A5
Brocklebank 175 D6
Brocklesby 142 B3
Brockley 42 C3
Brockley Green . . 87 B4
Brockleymoor . . .164 B2
Brockton Shrops . . 94 B3
Shrops 94 B3
Shrops 94 C1
Shrops 95 A5
Telford 111 D6
Brockweir 62 C1
Brockwood 33 C5
Brockworth 63 B4
Brocton 112 D3
Brodick 191 B6
Brodsworth 140 C3
Brogaig. 259 B4
Brogborough 83 D6
Brokenborough . . 44 A3
Broken Cross
Ches E 128 B3
Ches W. 128 B1
Bromborough 126 A3
Brome. 104 D2
Brome Street 104 D2
Bromeswell 88 B4
Bromfield Cumb. .174 D4
Shrops 94 D2
Bromham Bedford . 84 B2
Wilts. 44 C3
Bromley London . . 49 C7
W Mid 96 C2
Bromley
Common 49 C7

Bromley Green . . . 38 B1
Brompton Medway 51 C4
N Yorks. 158 B2
N Yorks. 160 C3
Brompton-on-
Swale 157 B6
Brompton Ralph. . 27 B5
Brompton Regis . . 27 B4
Bromsash. 62 A2
Bromsberrow
Hth. 79 D5
Bromsgrove. 96 D2
Bromyard 79 B4
Bromyard Downs . 79 B4
Bronaber 108 B2
Brongest 73 B6
Bronington 110 B3
Bronllys 77 D5
Bronnant 75 B5
Bronwydd Arms . . 73 D7
Bronydd 77 C6
Bronygarth 110 B1
Brook Carms. 56 B2
Hants 32 C2
Hants 32 D1
IoW 18 C2
Kent 38 A2
Sur 34 B3
Sur 34 C2
Brooke Norf 104 B3
Rutland. 99 A5
Brookenby 143 D4
Brookend 62 D1
Brook End 84 A2
Brookfield 205 B4
Brook Hill. 31 D6
Brookhouse 145 A5
Brookhouse
Green 128 C3
Brookland 38 C1
Brooklands
Dumfries 173 A6
Gtr Man 137 D6
Shrops 111 A4
Brookmans Park . 68 C2
Brooks 93 B5
Brooks Green 35 D4
Brook Street Kent. 36 B3
Kent 38 B1
W Sus. 35 D6
Brookthorpe 63 B4
Brookville 102 B3
Brookwood 34 A2
Broom C Beds. . . .84 C3
S Yorks 140 D2
Warks. 80 B3
Worcs. 96 D2
Broome Norf 105 B4
Shrops 94 C2
Broomedge 128 A2
Broome Park 189 B4
Broomer's
Corner 35 D4
Broomfield
Aberds 257 C4
Essex 69 B7
Kent 37 A6
Kent 52 C3
Som 28 B2
Broomfleet 141 A6
Broom Green 120 C1
Broomhall
Ches E 111 A5
Windsor 48 C2
Broomhaugh. 178 C2
Broomhill Norf. . .102 A2
Northumb. 189 C5
S Yorks. 140 C2
Broom Hill 17 A4
Broomholm 121 B5
Broomley 178 C2
Broompark 167 A5
Broom's Green. . . 79 D5
Broomy Lodge . . . 31 D6
Brora 274 D3
Broseley 95 A4
Brotherhouse
Bar 117 F5
Brotherstone 197 C5
Brothertoft 117 A5
Brotherton 140 A2
Brotton 169 D4

Broubster 279 B6
Brough Cumb 165 D5
Derbys 130 A1
E Yorks 142 A1
Highld. 280 A4
Notts 132 D3
Orkney 282 F4
Shetland. 284 F6
Shetland. 284 F7
Shetland. 284 G2
Shetland. 285 H6
Shetland. 285 J7
Broughall 111 A4
Brough Lodge. . . .284 D7
Brough
Sowerby 165 D5
Broughton
Borders 195 C6
Cambs 101 D4
Flint 126 C3
Hants 32 B2
Lancs 145 D5
M Keynes 83 C5
N Lincs 142 C1
Northants 99 D5
N Yorks 146 B3
N Yorks 159 D6
Orkney 282 C5
Oxon. 81 D7
V Glam 40 D4
Broughton Astley. 98 B2
Broughton Beck 154 C1
Broughton
Common 44 C2
Broughton
Gifford 44 C2
Broughton
Hackett 80 B2
Broughton in
Furness 153 B3
Broughton Mills 153 A3
Broughton
Moor. 162 A3
Broughton Park .138 C1
Broughton Poggs 64 C3
Broughtown 282 C7
Broughty Ferry. . .221 A4
Browhouses 175 B5
Browland 285 H4
Brown Candover . 33 B4
Brown Edge
Lancs 136 B2
Staffs 129 D4
Brown Heath. . . .127 C4
Brownhill Aberds 256 B1
Aberds 256 B3
Blackburn. 145 D6
Shrops 110 C3
Brownhills Fife . .221 C5
W Mid 96 A3
Brownlow. 128 C3
Brownlow
Heath 128 C3
Brownmuir 233 A5
Brown's End 79 D5
Brownshill 63 C4
Brownston 7 B6
Brownyside 189 A4
Broxa. 160 B3
Broxbourne. 68 C3
Broxburn E Loth. .210 C3
W Loth. 208 C3
Broxholme 133 B4
Broxted. 69 A5
Broxton. 127 D4
Broxwood. 78 B1
Broyle Side 22 A2
Brù 288 C4
Bruairnis 286 F3
Bruan 275 A7
Bruar Lodge 230 A2
Brucehill 206 C1
Bruera. 127 C4
Bruern Abbey 64 A3
Bruichladdich . . .200 B2
Bruisyard 88 A4
Brumby. 141 C6
Brund 129 C6
Brundall 104 A4
Brundish. 88 A3
Brundish Street .104 D3
Brunery 235 C6

Brunshaw 146 D2
Brunswick
Village 179 B4
Bruntcliffe 139 A5
Bruntingthorpe . . 98 B3
Brunton Fife 220 B3
Northumb. 189 A5
Wilts. 45 D6
Brushford Devon . 12 A1
Som 27 C4
Bruton. 29 B6
Bryanston. 16 A2
Brydekirk 175 A4
Bryher Scilly 2 E3
Brymbo. 126 D2
Brympton. 29 D5
Bryn Carms 57 B5
Gtr Man 137 C4
Neath 40 B3
Shrops 93 C6
Brynamman 59 D4
Brynberian 72 C4
Brynbryddan 40 B2
Bryncae 41 C4
Bryncethin 40 C4
Bryncir 107 B4
Bryn-coch 40 B2
Bryncroes 106 C2
Bryncrug 90 B4
Bryn Du. 122 C3
Bryneglwys 109 A6
Brynford. 126 B1
Bryn Gates. 137 C4
Bryn-glas 124 C3
Bryn Golau. 41 C4
Bryngwran 122 C3
Bryngwyn Ceredig . 73 B5
Mon 61 C5
Powys 77 C5
Brynhenllan 72 C3
Brynhoffnant. . . . 73 A6
Brynithel 41 A7
Bryn-Iwan 73 C6
Bryn-mawr 106 C2
Brynmawr 60 B3
Brynmenyn 40 C4
Brynmill 57 C6
Brynna 41 C4
Bryn-nantlech. . .125 C4
Bryn-penarth . . . 93 A5
Brynrefail
Anglesey 123 B4
Gwyn 123 D5
Bryn Rhyd-yr-
Arian. 125 C4
Brynsadler. 41 C5
Bryn Saith
Marchog 125 D5
Brynsiencyn. 123 D4
Bryn Sion 91 A6
Brynteg Anglesey 123 B4
Ceredig 58 A1
Bryn-y-gwenin. . . 61 B5
Bryn-y-maen 124 B3
Bryn-yr-eryr 106 B3
Buaile nam
Bodach. 286 F3
Bualintur 246 B3
Buarthmeini 108 B3
Bubbenhall 97 D6
Bubwith 149 D6
Buccleuch 185 A6
Buchanhaven 257 B6
Buchanty 218 B4
Buchlyvie. 206 A3
Buckabank. 164 A1
Buckden Cambs. . 84 A3
N Yorks. 156 D3
Buckenham 105 A4
Buckerell 13 A6
Buckfast. 7 A6
Buckfastleigh 7 A6
Buckhaven. 209 A6
Buckholm. 196 C3
Buckholt 61 B7
Buckhorn
Weston. 30 C1
Buckhurst Hill. . . 68 D4
Buckie. 267 C5
Buckies. 280 B3
Buckingham. 82 D3
Buckland Bucks . . 66 B3

Buckland continued
Devon. 7 C5
Glos 80 D3
Hants 18 B2
Herts 85 D5
Kent 39 A5
Oxon. 64 D4
Sur 35 A5
Buckland Brewer 25 C5
Buckland
Common 67 C4
Buckland
Dinham 43 D6
Buckland Filleigh 11 A5
Buckland in the
Moor. 12 D2
Buckland
Monachorum . . . 6 A3
Buckland
Newton 15 A6
Buckland St
Mary 28 D2
Bucklebury 46 B3
Bucklegate 117 B6
Bucklerheads 221 A4
Bucklers Hard. . . . 18 B3
Bucklesham. 88 C3
Buckley Bwcle . . .126 C2
Bucklow Hill 128 A2
Buckminster 116 C1
Bucknall Lincs . . .133 C6
Stoke 112 A3
Bucknell Oxon . . . 65 A6
Shrops 94 D1
Buckpool 267 C5
Bucksburn 245 B5
Buck's Cross 24 C4
Bucks Green 34 C3
Buckshaw
Village 137 A4
Bucks Horn Oak . 33 A7
Buckskin 47 D4
Buck's Mills. 25 C4
Buckton E Yorks. .161 D5
Hereford 94 D1
Northumb. 199 C4
Buckworth. 100 D3
Budbrooke. 81 A5
Budby 131 C6
Budd's Titson . . . 10 A3
Bude. 10 A3
Budlake 13 B4
Budle. 199 C5
Budleigh
Salterton 13 C5
Budock Water. . . . 4 D2
Buerton 111 A5
Bugbrooke. 82 B3
Buglawton 128 C3
Bugle. 5 B5
Bugley. 30 A2
Bugthorpe 149 B6
Buildwas 95 A4
Built Road 76 B4
Builth Wells Llanfair-
ym-Muallt. 76 B4
Buirgh. 287 E5
Bulby 116 C3
Bulcote. 115 A4
Buldoo 279 B5
Bulford 31 A5
Bulford Camp . . . 31 A5
Bulkeley 127 D5
Bulkington Warks 97 C6
Wilts. 44 D3
Bulkworthy 25 D4
Bullamoor 158 B2
Bullbridge 130 D3
Bullbrook 48 C1
Bulley 62 B3
Bullgill 162 A3
Bull Hill. 18 B2
Bullionfield 220 A3
Bull's Green. 68 B2
Bullwood 203 A6
Bulmer Essex . . . 87 C4
N Yorks. 149 A5
Bulmer Tye 87 D4
Bulphan 50 A3
Bulverhythe. 23 B5

Bulwark 257 B4
Bulwell 114 A3
Bulwick 99 B6
Bumble's Green . . 68 C4
Bun Abhainn
Eadarra 288 G2
Bunacaimb 235 B5
Bun a'Mhuillin . . 286 E3
Bunarkaig 239 D5
Bunbury 127 D5
Bunbury Heath . .127 D5
Bunchrew 252 B2
Bundalloch 249 D5
Buness 284 C8
Bunessan 224 D2
Bungay 104 C4
Bunkers Hill. 65 B5
Bunker's Hill
Lincs. 133 B4
Lincs. 134 D2
Bunloit 251 D7
Bun Loyne 239 C6
Bunnahabhain . . .201 A4
Bunny 114 C3
Buntait 251 C5
Buntingford. 68 A3
Bunwell 104 B2
Burbage Derbys. .129 B5
Leics. 98 B1
Wilts. 45 C6
Burchett's Green 47 A6
Burcombe 31 B4
Burcot. 65 D6
Burcott 66 A3
Burdon 179 D5
Bures. 87 D5
Bures Green 87 D5
Burford Ches E . .127 D6
Oxon. 64 B3
Shrops 78 A3
Burg 224 B2
Burgar. 282 E4
Burgate Hants . . . 31 D5
Suff 104 D1
Burgess Hill. 21 A6
Burgh 80 B2
Burgh by Sands .175 C6
Burgh Castle 105 A5
Burghclere 46 C2
Burghead 266 C2
Burghfield 47 C4
Burghfield
Common 47 C4
Burghfield Hill . . 47 C4
Burgh Heath 35 A5
Burghill 78 C2
Burgh le Marsh. .135 C5
Burgh Muir 256 D2
Burgh next
Aylsham 120 C4
Burgh on Bain. . .134 A2
Burgh St
Margaret. 121 D6
Burgh St Peter . .105 B5
Burghwallis 140 B3
Burham. 51 C4
Buriton 33 C6
Burland. 127 D6
Burlawn 9 D5
Burleigh 48 C1
Burlescombe. 27 D5
Burleston. 16 B1
Burley Hants 17 A6
Rutland. 116 D1
Y Works 148 D1
Burley Gate 78 C3
Burley in
Wharfedale. 147 C5
Burley Lodge. . . . 17 A6
Burley Street 17 A6
Burlingjobb 77 B6
Burlow. 22 A3
Burlton 110 C3
Burmarsh 38 B2
Burmington 81 D5
Burn 140 A3
Burnaston 113 B6
Burnbank. 194 A2

298 Bur–Cap

Burnby 150 C1
Burncross 139 D6
Burneside 154 B4
Burness 282 C7
Burneston 157 C7
Burnett 43 C5
Burnfoot Borders 186 B3
 Borders 186 B4
 E Ayrs........182 B2
 Perth 219 D4
Burnham Bucks ..48 A2
N Lincs 142 B2
Burnham Deepdale.....119 A5
Burnham Green ..68 B2
Burnham Market........119 A5
Burnham Norton 119 A5
Burnham-on-Crouch......70 D3
Burnham-on-Sea 28 A3
Burnham Overy Staithe......119 A5
Burnham Overy Town 119 A5
Burnham Thorpe........119 A5
Burnhead Dumfries 183 C6
S Ayrs........181 A4
Burnhervie......245 A4
Burnhill Green ..95 A5
Burnhope......167 A4
Burnhouse.....204 C3
Burniston 160 B4
Burnlee.........139 C4
Burnley........146 D2
Burnley Lane ...146 D2
Burnmouth 211 D6
Burn of Cambus 218 D2
Burnopfield......178 D3
Burnsall 147 A4
Burnside Angus ..232 C2
E Ayrs........182 A3
Fife.........219 D6
Shetland......284 F4
S Lanark......205 B6
W Loth......208 C3
Burnside of Duntrune......220 A4
Burnswark......175 A4
Burntcommon....34 A3
Burnt Heath.....130 B2
Burnthouse.....4 D2
Burnt Houses...166 C4
Burntisland......209 B5
Burnton......182 B2
Burntwood......96 A3
Burnt Yates......147 A6
Burnwynd......208 D4
Burpham Sur 34 A3
W Sus. 20 B3
Burradon Northumb.....188 C2
T&W.......179 B4
Burrafirth......284 B8
Burraland Shetland......284 F5
Shetland......285 J4
Burras........3 B4
Burravoe Shetland......284 F7
Shetland......284 G5
Burray Village.....283 H5
Burrells.......165 D4
Burrelton......220 A2
Burridge Devon ...25 B6
Hants........32 D4
Burrill........157 C6
Burringham.....141 C6
Burrington Devon 26 D1
Hereford......94 D2
N Som 42 D3
Burrough Green..86 B2
Burrough on the Hill.........115 D5
Burrow-bridge... 28 C3

Burrowhill 48 C2
Burry..........57 C4
Burry Green......57 C4
Burry Port Porth
 Tywyn........57 B4
Burscough 136 B3
Burscough Bridge..........136 B3
Bursea.........149 D7
Burshill........150 C3
Bursledon......18 A3
Burslem........112 A2
Burstall.........88 C1
Burstock........14 A4
Burston Norf....104 C2
 Staffs........112 B3
Burstow 35 B6
Burstwick......143 A4
Burtersett.....156 C2
Burtle.........28 A3
Burton Ches W....126 B3
 Ches W.......127 C5
 Dorset 17 B5
 Lincs........133 B4
 Northumb......199 C5
 Pembs 55 D5
 Som 28 A1
 Wilts........44 B2
Burton Agnes....151 A4
Burton Bradstock 15 C4
Burton Dassett ...81 B6
Burton Fleming .161 D4
Burton Green W Mid....97 D5
 Wrex........126 D3
Burton Hastings ..97 B7
Burton-in-Kendal 154 D4
Burton in Lonsdale 155 D5
Burton Joyce......115 A4
Burton Latimer ..99 D6
Burton Lazars ...115 D5
Burton-le-Coggles........116 C2
Burton Leonard .148 A2
Burton on the Wolds.........114 C3
Burton Overy ..98 B3
Burton Pedwardine 116 A4
Burton Pidsea..151 D5
Burton Salmon .140 A2
Burton Stather .141 B6
Burton upon Stather.........141 B6
Burton upon Trent.........113 C6
Burtonwood ...137 D4
Burwardsley ...127 D5
Burwarton 95 C4
Burwash 37 D4
Burwash Common 36 D4
Burwash Weald ..36 D4
Burwell Cambs....86 A1
 Lincs........134 B3
Burwen........123 A4
Burwick 283 J5
Bury Cambs....101 C4
 Gtr Man......137 B7
 Som 27 C4
 W Sus.......20 A3
Bury Green......68 A4
Bury St Edmunds 87 A4
Burythorpe......149 A6
Busby.........205 C5
Buscot.........64 D3
Bush Bank......78 B2
Bushbury........96 A2
Bushby.........98 A3
Bush Crathie...243 C5
Bush End........36 D4
Bushey.........67 D6
Bushey Heath....67 D6
Bush Green....104 C3
Bushley........80 D1
Bushton.........45 B4
Buslingthorpe...133 A5
Busta........284 G5
Butcher's Cross ..36 D3
Butcombe........43 C4
Butetown.........41 D6

Butleigh 29 B5
Butleigh Wootton 29 B5
Butler's Cross....66 C3
Butler's End....97 C5
Butlers Marston ..81 C6
Butley.........89 B4
Butley High Corner.........89 C4
Butterburn.....177 B4
Buttercrambe ..149 B6
Butterknowle ..166 C4
Butterleigh......13 A4
Buttermere Cumb....163 C4
 Wilts.........46 C1
Buttershaw.....139 A4
Butterstone...231 D4
Butterton......129 D5
Butterwick Durham...167 C6
 Lincs........117 A6
 N Yorks......159 D6
 N Yorks......160 D3
Butt Green......127 D6
Buttington.......93 A6
Buttonoak.......95 D5
Buttsash.........18 A3
Butt's Green 32 C2
Buxhall.........87 B6
Buxhall Fen Street.........87 B6
Buxley.........198 A2
Buxted..........36 D2
Buxton Derbys..129 B5
 Norf.........120 C4
Buxworth 129 A5
Bwlch...........60 A3
Bwlchgwyn......126 D2
Bwlch-Llan 75 C4
Bwlchnewydd 73 D6
Bwlchtocyn....106 D3
Bwlch-y-cibau..109 D6
Bwlch-y-ddar ...109 C6
Bwlch-y-fadfa ...74 D3
Bwlch-y-ffridd ..93 B4
Bwlchygroes 73 C5
Bwlch-y-sarnau..92 D4
Byermoor.......178 D3
Byers Green.....167 B5
Byfield.........82 B2
Byfleet 48 C3
Byford..........78 C1
Bygrave........85 D4
Byker.........179 C4
Bylchau........125 C4
Byley.........128 C2
Bynea..........57 C5
Byrness 187 C6
Bythorn........100 D2
Byton...........78 A1
Byworth........34 D2

C

Cabharstadh ...288 E4
Cablea.........218 A4
Cabourne 142 C3
Cabrach Argyll...201 B4
 Moray........255 D4
Cabrich.........252 B1
Cabus.........145 C4
Cackle Street ...36 D2
Cadbury 13 A4
Cadbury Barton ..26 D1
Cadder.........205 A6
Caddington 67 B5
Caddonfoot......196 C3
Cadeby Leics ...97 A7
 S Yorks......140 C3
Cadeleigh.......13 A4
Cade Street 36 D4
Cadgwith........3 D5
Cadham.........220 D2
Cadishead......137 D6
Cadle.........57 C6
Cadley Lancs...145 D5
 Wilts.........45 C6
 Wilts.........45 D6
Cadmore End ...66 D2
Cadnam.........32 D1
Cadney.........142 C2

Cadole.........126 C2
Cadoxton........41 E6
Cadoxton-Juxta-Neath........40 B2
Cadshaw........137 B6
Cadzow.........194 A2
Caeathro........123 D4
Caehopkin.......59 D5
Caenby.........133 A5
Caenby Corner ..133 A4
Caerau Bridgend... 40 B3
 Cardiff........41 D6
Caér-bryn.......57 A5
Caerdeon........90 A4
Caerfarchell 54 B3
Caergeiliog 122 C3
Caergwrle.......126 D3
Caerleon Caerllion.....61 D5
Caer Llan........61 C6
Caernarfon.....123 D4
Caerphilly Caerffili....41 C6
Caersws.........92 B4
Caerwedros......73 A6
Caerwent 61 D6
Caerwych.......107 C6
Caerwys.........125 B6
Caethle.........90 C4
Caim...........123 B6
Caio...........58 B3
Cairinis........287 H3
Cairisiadar......287 A5
Cairminis.......287 F5
Cairnbaan.......213 C6
Cairnbanno Ho...256 B3
Cairnborrow 255 B5
Cairnbrogie.....256 D3
Cairnbulg Castle........269 C5
Cairncross Angus...232 A2
 Borders......211 D5
Cairndow.......215 A4
Cairness 269 C5
Cairneyhill 208 B3
Cairnfield Ho...267 C5
Cairngaan 170 D3
Cairngarroch...170 C2
Cairnhill 256 C1
Cairnie Aberds...245 B5
 Aberds.......255 B5
Cairnorrie......256 B3
Cairnpark......245 A5
Cairnton 283 G4
Caister-on-Sea .121 D7
Caistor.........142 C3
Caistor St Edmund.........104 A3
Caistron........188 C2
Caitha Bowland .196 B3
Calais Street....87 D5
Calanais 288 D3
Calbost.........288 F5
Calbourne 18 C3
Calceby.........134 B3
Calcot Row 47 B4
Calcott.........52 C3
Caldback.......284 C8
Caldbeck.......163 A6
Caldbergh 157 C4
Caldecote Cambs..85 B5
 Cambs.......100 C3
 Herts........84 D4
 Northants......82 B3
Caldecott Northants....84 A1
 Oxon.........65 D5
 Rutland.......99 B5
Calderbank......207 D6
Calder Bridge .162 D3
Calderbrook ...138 B2
Caldercruix ...207 D6
Calder Hall.....162 D3
Calder Mains...280 C2
Caldermill 205 D6
Calder Vale ...145 C5
Calderwood.....205 C6
Caldhame.......232 D2
Caldicot.........42 A3
Caldwell Derbys..113 D6

Caldwell continued
 N Yorks......167 D4
Caldy.........126 A2
Caledrhydiau....74 C3
Calfsound......282 D6
Calgary.........224 A2
Califer........266 D1
California Falk...208 C2
 Norf.........121 D7
Calke.........114 C1
Callakille......248 A3
Callaly........188 C3
Callander.......217 D6
Callaughton......95 B4
Callestick........4 B2
Calligarry.......247 D5
Callington........6 A2
Callow.........78 D2
Callow End 79 C6
Callow Hill Wilts ..44 A4
 Worcs........95 D5
Callows Grave....78 A3
Calmore.........32 D2
Calmsden 63 C6
Calne.........44 B4
Calow.........131 B4
Calshot 18 A3
Calstock.........6 A3
Calstone Wellington 44 C4
Calthorpe.......120 B3
Calthwaite......164 A2
Calton N Yorks...146 B3
 Staffs........129 D6
Calveley 127 D5
Calver.........130 B2
Calverhall.......111 B5
Calver Hill 78 C1
Calverleigh......27 D4
Calverley.......147 D6
Calvert.........66 A1
Calverton M Keynes....83 D4
 Notts........115 A4
Calvine.........230 B2
Calvo.........174 C4
Cam...........62 D3
Camas-luinie ..249 D6
Camasnacroise .236 D2
Camastianavaig 247 A4
Camasunary ...247 C4
Camault Muir ..251 B7
Camb.........284 D7
Camber.........38 D1
Camberley.......47 C6
Camberwell......49 B6
Camblesforth ..141 A4
Cambo.........178 A2
Cambois.........179 A5
Camborne.........3 A4
Cambourne.......85 B5
Cambridge Cambs..85 B6
 Glos.........62 C3
Cambridge Town 51 A6
Cambus 207 A6
Cambusavie Farm.........264 A3
Cambusbarron .207 A4
Cambuskenneth 207 A6
Cambuslang ...205 B6
Cambusmore Lodge.........264 A3
Camden 49 A5
Camelford 10 C2
Camelsdale......34 C1
Camerory.......253 C6
Camer's Green ..79 D5
Camerton Bath...43 D5
 Cumb........162 A3
 E Yorks......143 A4
Camghouran ...229 C4
Cammachmore .245 C6
Cammeringham 133 A4
Camore.........264 A3
Campbeltown ..190 C3
Camperdown ..179 B4
Camp Hill 97 B6
Campmuir 220 A2
Campsall 140 B3
Campsey Ash... 88 B4
Campton 84 D3
Camptown.......187 B5

Camrose.........55 B5
Camserney....230 D2
Camster.......281 D4
Camuschoirk...235 D6
Camuscross.....247 C5
Camusnagaul Highld....237 B4
 Highld........262 B2
Camusrory.....238 C2
Camusteel 249 B4
Camusterrach...249 B4
Camusvrachan ..229 D5
Canada.........32 D1
Canadia 23 A5
Canal Side.....141 B4
Candacraig Ho...243 A6
Candlesby 135 C4
Candy Mill ...195 B5
Cane End 47 B4
Canewdon 70 D2
Canford Bottom ..17 A4
Canford Cliffs ...17 C4
Canford Magna....17 B4
Canham's Green .87 A6
Canholes......129 B5
Canisbay.......281 A5
Cann...........30 C2
Cann Common ...30 C2
Cannich.........251 C5
Cannington 28 B2
Cannock.........96 A2
Cannock Wood..112 D4
Canonbie.......175 A6
Canon Bridge ...78 C2
Canon Frome ...79 C4
Canon Pyon 78 C2
Canons Ashby...82 B2
Canonstown 2 B3
Canterbury.......52 D3
Cantley Norf....105 A4
 S Yorks......140 C4
Cantlop.........94 A3
Canton.........41 D6
Cantraybruich...252 B3
Cantraydoune ...252 B3
Cantraywood ...252 B3
Cantsfield 155 D5
Canvey Island ...51 A4
Canwick 133 C4
Canworthy Water.10 B3
Caol.........237 B5
Coolas.........222 C3
Coolas Scalpaigh...288 H3
Coolas Stocinis..288 H2
Caol Ila........201 A4
Capel.........35 B4
Capel Bangor ...91 D4
Capel Betws Lleucu.........75 C5
Capel Carmel ..106 D1
Capel Coch.....123 B4
Capel Curig ...124 D2
Capel Cynon 73 B6
Capel Dewi Carms 58 A1
 Ceredig.......58 A1
 Ceredig.......90 D4
Capel Garmon..124 D3
Capel-gwyn....122 C3
Capel Gwyn ...58 C1
Capel Gwynfe ...59 C4
Capel Hendre ...57 A5
Capel Hermon..108 C2
Capel Isaac.....58 C2
Capel Iwan.....73 C5
Capel le Ferne ..39 B4
Capel Llanilltern .41 C5
Capel Mawr...123 C4
Capel St Andrew .89 C4
Capel Seion.....75 A5
Capel Tygwydd ..73 B5
Capel Uchaf....107 B4
Capel-y-graig...123 D5
Capenhurst ...126 B3
Capernwray ...154 D4
Capheaton.....178 A2
Cappercleuch ...196 D1
Capplegill 185 B4
Capton 8 B2

Caputh 219 A5
Carbis Bay 2 B3
Carbost Highld . . 246 A2
Highld. 259 D4
Carbrook 130 A3
Carbrooke 103 A5
Carburton 131 B6
Carcant. 196 A2
Carcary. 233 C4
Carclaze 5 B5
Car Colston 115 A5
Carcroft 140 B3
Cardenden. 209 A5
Cardeston 110 D2
Cardiff Caerdydd. . 41 D6
Cardigan
  Aberteifi. 73 B4
Cardington
  Bedford 84 C2
  Shrops 94 B3
Cardinham. 5 A6
Cardonald 205 B5
Cardow 254 B2
Cardrona 196 C2
Cardross. 206 C1
Cardurnock 175 C4
Careby 116 D3
Careston Castle .232 C3
Carew 55 D6
Carew Cheriton . 55 D6
Carew Newton . . 55 D6
Carey. 78 D3
Carfrae 210 D2
Cargenbridge . 174 A2
Cargill 219 A6
Cargo 175 C6
Cargreen 6 A3
Carham. 198 C2
Carhampton 27 A5
Carharrack. 4 C2
Carie Perth 217 A6
  Perth 229 C5
Carines 4 B2
Carisbrooke. 18 C3
Cark. 154 D2
Carlabhagh 288 C3
Carland Cross . . . 4 B3
Carlby 116 D3
Carlecotes 139 C4
Carlesmoor 157 D5
Carleton Cumb . .164 C3
  Cumb 176 D2
  Lancs 144 D3
  N Yorks. 146 D3
Carleton
  Forehoe. 104 A1
Carleton Rode. . . 104 B2
Carlin How. 169 D5
Carlisle 175 C7
Carlops. 195 A6
Carlton Bedford . . 83 B6
  Cambs 86 B2
  Leics. 97 A6
  Notts 115 A4
  N Yorks. 140 A4
  N Yorks. 157 C4
  N Yorks. 159 C5
  N Yorks. 167 D4
  Stockton. 167 C6
  Suff 89 A4
  S Yorks. 139 B6
  W Yorks. 139 A6
Carlton Colville .105 C6
Carlton Curlieu . 98 B3
Carlton
  Husthwaite. . .158 D3
Carlton in
  Cleveland 158 A4
Carlton in
  Lindrick. 131 A5
Carlton le
  Moorland 133 D4
Carlton Miniott. . 158 C2
Carlton on
  Trent. 132 C2
Carlton Scroop. . 116 A2
Carluke 194 A3
Carmarthen
  Caerfyrddin. . . 73 D7
Carmel Anglesey . 122 B3
  Carms 57 A5

Carmel continued
  Flint 125 B6
  Gwern 6
  Gwyn 107 A4
Carmont 245 D5
Carmunnock . . . 205 C6
Carmyle 205 B6
Carmyllie 232 D3
Carnaby 151 A4
Carnach Highld. . 250 D2
  Highld. 262 A2
  W Isles 288 H3
Carnachy 278 C3
Càrnais 287 A5
Carnbee 221 D5
Carnbo 219 D5
Carnbrea 3 A4
Carnduff 205 D6
Carnduncan. . . . 200 B2
Carne 4 D4
Carnforth 154 D3
Carn-gorm 249 D6
Carnhedryn 54 B4
Carnhell Green . . 3 B4
Carnkie Corn . . . 3 B4
  Corn. 4 D2
Carno 92 B3
Carnoch Highld . 251 A4
  Highld. 251 C5
Carnock 208 B3
Carnon Downs . . 4 C2
Carnousie 268 D1
Carnoustie. 221 A5
Carnwath 195 B4
Carnyorth. 2 B1
Carperby 156 C4
Carpley Green. . . 156 C3
Carr 140 D3
Carradale 190 B4
Carragraich. . . . 288 H2
Carrbridge. 253 D5
Carrefour Selous
  Jersey 6
Carreglefn 122 B3
Carreg-wen. 73 B5
Carr Hill 179 C4
Carrick Argyll . . 214 D2
  Fife. 220 B4
Carrick Castle . . 215 C4
Carrick Ho. 282 C6
Carriden 208 B3
Carrington
  Gtr Man 137 D6
  Lincs. 134 D3
  Midloth. 209 D6
Carrog Conwy . . 108 A2
  Denb. 109 A6
Carron Falk. . . . 208 B1
  Moray. 254 B3
Carronbridge . . 183 C6
Carron Bridge. . . 207 B5
Carronshore . . . 208 B1
Carrshield 165 A6
Carrutherstown .174 A4
Carrville 167 A6
Carsaig Argyll . . 213 D5
  Argyll 225 D4
Carscreugh 171 B4
Carsegowan . . . 171 B6
Carse Gray. . . . 232 C2
Carse Ho. 202 B2
Carseriggan . . . 171 A5
Carsethorn. . . . 174 C2
Carshalton. 49 C5
Carsington 130 D2
Carskiey 190 E2
Carsluith. 171 B6
Carsphairn. . . . 182 C3
Carstairs 194 B4
Carstairs
  Junction 195 B4
Carswell Marsh . 64 D4
Carter's Clay . . . 32 C2
Carterton 64 C3
Carterway
  Heads 178 D2
Carthew 5 B5
Carthorpe 157 C7
Cartington 188 C3
Cartland 194 B3
Cartmel. 154 D2
Cartmel Fell . . . 154 C3

Carway 57 B4
Cary Fitzpaine. . . 29 C5
Cascob 77 A6
Cashlie 228 D3
Cashmoor 30 D3
Cassey Compton . 63 B6
Cassington. 65 B5
Cassop 167 B6
Castell. 125 C6
Castellau 41 C5
Castell-Howell . . 74 D3
Castell-y-bwch . . 61 D4
Casterton. 155 D5
Castle Acre 119 D5
Castle Ashby . . . 83 B5
Castle Bolton . . 156 B4
Castle Bromwich . 96 C4
Castle Bytham. . .116 D2
Castlebythe 55 B6
Castle
  Caereinion 93 A5
Castle Camps . . . 86 C2
Castle Carrock . 176 D3
Castlecary 207 C5
Castle Cary 29 B6
Castle Combe . . 44 B2
Castlecraig 265 D4
Castle
  Donington. . . .114 C2
Castle Douglas . 173 B5
Castle Eaton . . . 64 D2
Castle Eden . . . 168 B2
Castlefairn. . . . 183 D5
Castle Forbes . . 244 A3
Castleford 140 A2
Castle Frome. . . . 79 C4
Castle Green . . . 48 C2
Castle Gresley. . 113 D6
Castle Heaton . . 198 B3
Castle
  Hedingham. . . . 86 D3
Castlehill
  Borders 195 C7
  Highld. 280 B3
  W Dunb 206 C1
Castle Huntly. . . 220 B3
Castle Kennedy . 170 B3
Castlemaddy. . . 182 D3
Castlemartin. . . . 55 E5
Castlemilk
  Dumfries 174 A4
  Glasgow 205 C6
Castlemorris 55 A5
Castlemorton . . . 79 D5
Castle O'er. . . . 185 C5
Castle
  Pulverbatch . . . 94 A2
Castle Rising . . . 118 C3
Castleside 166 A3
Castle Stuart . . . 252 B3
Castlethorpe . . . 83 C5
Castleton Angus. 232 D1
  Argyll 214 D1
  Derbys 129 A6
  Gtr Man 138 B1
  Newport 42 A1
  N Yorks. 159 A5
Castletown
  Ches W. 127 D4
  Highld. 252 B3
  Highld. 280 B3
  IoM 152 E2
  T&W. 179 C5
Castleweary. . . 186 C3
Castley 147 C6
Caston. 103 B5
Castor 100 B3
Catacol 203 D4
Catbrain 43 A4
Catbrook 61 C7
Catchall 2 C2
Catchems Corner . 97 D5
Catchgate 178 D3
Catcleugh 187 C6
Catcliffe 131 A4
Catcott 28 B3
Caterham 35 A6
Catfield 121 C5
Catfirth. 285 H6
Catford 49 B6
Catforth 145 D4

Cathays. 41 D6
Cathcart 205 B5
Cathedine 60 A3
Catherington. . . . 33 D5
Catherton 95 D4
Catlodge 241 C4
Catlowdy 176 B2
Catmore 46 A2
Caton. 145 A5
Caton Green . . . 145 A5
Catrine 193 C5
Cat's Ash 61 D5
Catsfield 23 A5
Catshill 96 D2
Cattal 148 B3
Cattawade 88 D2
Catterall 145 C4
Catterick 157 B6
Catterick Bridge 157 B6
Catterick
  Garrison 157 B5
Catterlen 164 B2
Catterline 233 A6
Catterton 148 C4
Catthorpe. 98 D2
Cattistock. 15 B5
Catton Northumb .177 D6
  N Yorks. 158 D2
Catwick 151 C4
Catworth 100 D2
Caudlesprings. . 103 A5
Caulcott 65 A6
Cauldcots 233 D4
Cauldhame 207 A4
Cauldmill 186 B4
Cauldon 113 A4
Caulkerbush . . . 174 C2
Caulside 176 A2
Caunsall 95 C6
Caunton 132 D2
Causewayend . . 195 C5
Causeway End. . 171 A6
Causeway Foot. . 147 D4
Causewayhead . 174 C4
Causeway-head . 207 A5
Causeyend 245 A6
Causey Park
  Bridge 189 D4
Cautley 155 B5
Cavendish 87 C4
Cavendish
  Bridge 114 C2
Cavenham 86 A3
Caversfield 65 A6
Caversham 47 B5
Caverswall 112 A3
Cavil 149 D6
Cawdor 253 B4
Cawkwell 134 B2
Cawood 149 D4
Cawsand 6 B3
Cawston 120 C3
Cawthorne. 139 C5
Cawthorpe 116 C3
Caxton 85 B5
Caynham 94 D3
Caythorpe Lincs . 116 A2
  Notts 115 A4
Cayton. 161 C4
Ceann a Bhaigh .287 H2
Ceann a Deas Loch
  Baghas-
  dail 286 E3
Ceann Shiphoirt 288 F3
Ceann
  Tarabhaigh. . . 288 F3
Cearsiadair 288 E4
Cefn Berain . . . 125 C4
Cefn-brith 125 D4
Cefn Canol 110 B1
Cefn-coch 124 C3
Cefn Coch 109 C6
Cefn-coed-y-
  cymmer 60 C2
Cefn Cribbwr. . . . 40 C3
Cefn Cross 40 C3
Cefn-ddwysarn. . 109 B4
Cefn Einion 93 C6
Cefneithin 57 A5

Cefn-gorwydd . . . 76 C3
Cefn-mawr 110 A1
Cefn-y-bedd . . . 126 D3
Cefn-y-pant 73 D4
Cei-bach 73 A7
Ceint 123 C4
Cellan 75 D5
Cellarhead 112 A3
Cemaes 122 A3
Cemmaes 91 B6
Cemmaes Road . . 91 B6
Cenarth. 73 B5
Cenin. 107 B4
Central 204 A2
Ceos 288 E4
Ceres. 220 C4
Cerne Abbas . . . 15 A6
Cerney Wick 63 D6
Cerrigceinwen . 123 C4
Cerrigydrudion. . 109 A4
Cessford. 187 A6
Ceunant 123 D5
Chaceley 79 D6
Chacewater 4 C2
Chackmore 82 D3
Chacombe 82 C1
Chadderton 138 C2
Chadderton
  Fold 138 C1
Chaddesden . . . 114 B1
Chaddesley
  Corbett 96 D1
Chaddleworth. . . 46 B2
Chadlington. . . . 64 A4
Chadshunt 81 B6
Chad Valley 96 C3
Chadwell 115 C5
Chadwell St Mary. 50 B3
Chadwick End . . . 97 D5
Chadwick
  Green. 136 D4
Chaffcombe. 28 D3
Chagford 12 C2
Chailey 22 A1
Chainbridge . . . 101 A6
Chain Bridge. . . 117 A6
Chainhurst. 37 B5
Chalbury. 17 A4
Chalbury
  Common 17 A4
Chaldon 35 A6
Chaldon Herring
  or. 16 C1
Chale. 18 D3
Chale Green 18 D3
Chalfont
  Common 67 D5
Chalfont St Giles 67 D4
Chalfont St Peter 67 D5
Chalford 63 C4
Chalgrove 66 D1
Chalk 50 B3
Challacombe. . . . 26 A1
Challoch 171 A5
Challock 52 D2
Chalton C Beds. . 67 A5
  Hants 33 D6
Chalvington. 22 B3
Chancery 75 A4
Chandler's Ford . 32 C3
Channel Tunnel . 38 B3
Channerwick. . . 285 L6
Chantry Som. . . . 29 A7
  Suff 88 C2
Chapel 209 A5
Chapel Allerton
  Som 42 D3
  W Yorks 148 D2
Chapel Amble . . . 9 D5
Chapel Brampton 83 A4
Chapel Chorlton 112 B2
Chapel End 97 B6
Chapel-en-le-
  Frith. 129 A5
Chapelgate 117 C7
Chapel Green
  Warks. 82 A1
  Warks. 97 C5
Chapel
  Haddlesey . . . 140 A3
Chapelhall 207 D5
Chapel Head . . . 101 C5

Chapelhill
  Dumfries 184 C3
  Highld. 265 C4
  N Ayrs 204 D2
  Perth 219 A5
  Perth 220 B2
Chapel Hill
  Aberds 257 C5
  Lincs. 134 D2
  Mon 62 D1
  N Yorks. 148 C2
Chapelknowe . . . 175 A6
Chapel Lawn . . . 93 D7
Chapel-le-Dale . 155 D6
Chapel Milton . . 129 A5
Chapel of
  Garioch 256 D2
Chapel Row 46 C3
Chapel St
  Leonards 135 B5
Chapel Stile . . . 154 A2
Chapelton Angus 233 D4
  Devon. 25 C6
  Highld. 242 A2
  S Lanark. 194 B1
Chapeltown
  Blackburn. . . . 137 B6
  Moray. 254 D3
  S Yorks. 139 D6
Chapmanslade . . 30 A2
Chapmans Well . 11 B4
Chapmore End . . 68 B3
Chappel 70 A2
Chard 14 A3
Chardstock 14 A3
Charfield 62 D3
Charford 80 A2
Charing. 38 A1
Charing Cross . . . 31 D5
Charing Heath . . 38 A1
Charingworth . . . 81 D5
Charlbury. 65 B4
Charlcombe. 43 C6
Charlecote 81 B5
Charles 26 B1
Charlesfield. . . . 175 B4
Charleston
  Angus 232 D1
  Renfs 205 B4
Charlestown
  Aberdeen 245 B6
  Corn 5 B5
  Derbys 138 D3
  Dorset 15 D6
  Fife. 208 B3
  Gtr Man 137 C7
  Highld. 252 B2
  Highld. 261 C5
  W Yorks 138 A2
Charlestown of
  Aberlour 254 B3
Charles Tye 87 B6
Charlesworth . . 138 D3
Charleton 7 C6
Charlton Hants. . . 32 A2
  Herts 68 A1
  London 49 B7
  Northants. 82 D2
  Northumb 177 A6
  Som 43 D5
  Telford 111 D4
  Wilts. 30 C3
  Wilts. 44 A3
  Wilts. 45 D5
  Worcs. 80 C3
  W Sus. 20 A1
Charlton Abbots . 63 A6
Charlton Adam . . 29 C5
Charlton-All-
  Saints 31 C5
Charlton Down . . 15 B6
Charlton
  Horethorne. . . . 29 C6
Charlton Kings . . 63 A5
Charlton
  Mackerell 29 C5
Charlton
  Marshall 16 A2

Charlton
  Musgrove 29 C7
Charlton on
  Otmoor 65 B6
Charltons 168 D4
Charlwood 35 B5
Charlynch 28 B2
Charminster 15 B6
Charmouth 14 B3
Charndon 66 A1
Charney Bassett .65 D4
Charnock
  Richard 137 B4
Charsfield 88 B3
Chart Corner 37 A5
Charter Alley 46 D3
Charterhouse 42 D3
Charterville
  Allotments 64 B4
Chartham 52 D3
Chartham Hatch .52 D3
Chartridge 67 C4
Chart Sutton 37 B6
Charvil 47 B5
Charwelton 82 B2
Chasetown 96 A3
Chastleton 64 A3
Chasty 10 A4
Chatburn 146 C1
Chatcull 112 B1
Chatham 51 C4
Chathill 189 A4
Chattenden 51 B4
Chatteris 101 C5
Chattisham 88 C1
Chatto 187 B6
Chatton 188 A3
Chawleigh 26 D2
Chawley 65 C5
Chawston 84 B3
Chawton 33 B6
Cheadle Gtr Man .128 A3
  Staffs 112 A4
Cheadle Heath .128 A3
Cheadle Hulme .128 A3
Cheam 49 C5
Cheapside 34 A3
Chearsley 66 B2
Chebsey 112 C2
Checkendon 47 A4
Checkley Ches E .111 A6
  Hereford 78 D3
  Staffs 112 B4
Chedburgh 86 B3
Cheddar 42 D3
Cheddington 67 B4
Cheddleton 129 D4
Cheddon
  Fitzpaine 28 C2
Chedglow 63 D5
Chedgrave 105 B4
Chedington 15 A4
Chediston 105 D4
Chedworth 63 B6
Chedzoy 28 B3
Cheeklaw 198 A1
Cheeseman's
  Green 38 B2
Cheglinch 25 A6
Cheldon 26 D2
Chelford 128 B3
Chellaston 114 B1
Chell Heath 128 D3
Chellington 83 B6
Chelmarsh 95 C5
Chelmer Village ..70 C1
Chelmondiston ..88 D3
Chelmorton 129 C6
Chelmsford 69 C7
Chelsea 49 B5
Chelsfield 50 C1
Chelsworth 87 C5
Cheltenham 63 A5
Chelveston 84 A1
Chelvey 42 C3
Chelwood 43 C5
Chelwood
  Common 36 D2
Chelwood Gate ...36 D2

Chelworth 63 D5
Chelworth Green .64 D1
Chemistry 111 A4
Chenies 67 D5
Cheny Longville ..94 C2
Chepstow Cas-
  gwent 62 D1
Chequerfield 140 A2
Cherhill 44 B4
Cherington Glos ..63 D5
  Warks 81 D5
Cheriton Devon ..26 A2
  Hants 33 C4
  Kent 38 B3
  Swansea 57 C4
Cheriton Bishop .12 B2
Cheriton
  Fitzpaine 12 A3
Cheriton or
  Stackpole
  Elidor 55 E5
Cherrington 111 C5
Cherrybank 219 B6
Cherry Burton ..150 C2
Cherry Hinton ..85 B6
Cherry Orchard ..79 B6
Cherry
  Willingham 133 B5
Chertsey 48 C3
Cheselbourne ..16 B1
Chesham 67 C4
Chesham Bois ..67 D4
Cheshunt 68 C3
Chesley Hay 96 A2
Chessington 49 C4
Chester 127 C4
Chesterblade ..29 A6
Chesterfield 130 B3
Chester-Le-
  Street 179 D4
Chester Moor ..167 A5
Chesters Borders 187 A5
  Borders 187 B5
Chesterton Cambs 85 A6
  Cambs 100 B3
  Glos 63 C6
  Oxon 65 A6
  Shrops 95 B5
  Staffs 112 A2
  Warks 81 B6
Chesterwood ..177 C6
Chestfield 52 C3
Cheston 7 B5
Cheswardine 111 C6
Cheswick 198 B4
Chetnole 15 A6
Chettiscombe 27 D4
Chettisham 102 C1
Chettle 30 D3
Chetton 95 B4
Chetwode 66 A1
Chetwynd Aston 111 D6
Cheveley 86 A2
Chevening 36 A2
Chevington 86 B3
Chevithorne 27 D4
Chew Magna 43 C4
Chew Stoke 43 C4
Chewton
  Keynsham 43 C5
Chewton Mendip 43 D4
Chicheley 83 C6
Chichester 20 B1
Chickerell 15 C6
Chicklade 30 B3
Chicksgrove 30 B3
Chidden 33 D5
Chiddingfold 34 C2
Chiddingly 22 A3
Chiddingstone ..36 B2
Chiddingstone
  Causeway 36 B3
Chiddingstone
  Hoath 36 B2
Chideock 14 B4
Chidham 19 A6
Chidswell 139 A5
Chieveley 46 B2
Chignall St
  James 69 C6
Chignall Smealy ..69 B6
Chigwell 68 D4

Chigwell Row 69 D4
Chilbolton 32 B2
Chilcomb 32 C4
Chilcombe 15 B5
Chilcompton 43 D5
Chilcote 113 D6
Childer
  Thornton 126 B3
Child Okeford ..30 D2
Childrey 46 A1
Child's Ercall ..111 C5
Childswickham ..80 D3
Childwall 127 A4
Childwick Green ..67 B6
Chilfrome 15 B5
Chilgrove 20 A1
Chilham 52 D2
Chilhampton ..31 B4
Chilla 11 A5
Chillaton 11 C5
Chillenden 53 D4
Chillerton 18 C3
Chillesford 89 B4
Chillingham 188 A3
Chillington Devon ..8 C1
  Som 28 D3
Chilmark 30 B3
Chilson 64 B4
Chilsworthy Corn. .11 D5
  Devon 10 A4
Chilthorne
  Domer 29 D5
Chiltington 22 A1
Chilton Bucks ..66 B1
  Durham 167 C5
  Oxon 46 A2
Chilton Cantelo ..29 C5
Chilton Foliat ..45 B7
Chilton Lane ..167 B6
Chilton Polden ..28 B3
Chilton Street ..86 C3
Chilton Trinity ..28 B2
Chilvers Coton ..97 B6
Chilwell 114 B3
Chilworth Hants ..32 D3
  Sur 34 B3
Chimney 65 C4
Chineham 47 D4
Chingford 68 D3
Chinley 129 A5
Chinley Head ..129 A5
Chinnor 66 C2
Chipnall 111 B6
Chippenhall
  Green 104 D3
Chippenham
  Cambs 86 A2
  Wilts 44 B3
Chipperfield 67 C5
Chipping Herts ..85 D5
  Lancs 145 C6
Chipping
  Campden 81 D4
Chipping Hill ..70 B2
Chipping Norton .64 A4
Chipping Ongar ..69 C5
Chipping
  Sodbury 43 A6
Chipping Warden 82 C1
Chipstable 27 C5
Chipstead Kent ..36 A2
  Sur 35 A5
Chirbury 93 B6
Chirk Y Waun ..110 B1
Chirk Bank 110 B1
Chirmorrie 181 D4
Chirnside 198 A2
Chirnsidebridge 198 A2
Chirton 45 D4
Chisbury 45 C6
Chiselborough ..29 D4
Chiseldon 45 B5
Chiserley 138 A3
Chislehampton ..65 D6
Chislehurst 50 B1
Chislet 53 C4
Chiswell Green ..67 C6
Chiswick 49 B5
Chiswick End ..85 C5
Chisworth 138 D2
Chithurst 34 D1
Chittering 101 D6

Chitterne 30 A3
Chittlehamholt ..26 C1
Chittlehampton ..26 C1
Chittoe 44 C3
Chivenor 25 B6
Chobham 48 C2
Choicelee 197 A6
Cholderton 31 A6
Cholesbury 67 C4
Chollerford 177 B7
Chollerton 178 B1
Cholmondeston .127 C6
Cholsey 46 A3
Cholstrey 78 B2
Chop Gate 159 B4
Choppington 179 A4
Chopwell 178 D3
Chorley Ches E ..127 D5
  Lancs 137 B4
  Shrops 95 C4
  Staffs 113 D4
Chorleywood 67 D5
Chorlton cum
  Hardy 137 D7
Chorlton Lane ..110 A3
Choulton 94 C1
Chowdene 179 D4
Chowley 127 D4
Chrishall 85 D6
Christchurch
  Cambs 101 B6
  Dorset 17 B5
  Glos 62 B1
  Newport 42 A2
Christian Malford. 44 B3
Christleton 127 C4
Christmas
  Common 66 D2
Christon 42 D2
Christon Bank ..189 A5
Christow 12 C3
Chryston 207 C4
Chudleigh 12 D3
Chudleigh
  Knighton 12 D3
Chulmleigh 26 D1
Chunal 138 D3
Churcham 62 B3
Church Aston ..111 D6
Churchbank 93 D7
Church
  Brampton 83 A4
Churchbridge ..96 A2
Church
  Broughton 113 B6
Church
  Crookham 47 D6
Churchdown 63 B4
Church Eaton ..112 D2
Churchend Essex. .69 A6
  Essex 71 D4
  S Glos 62 D3
Church End
  Cambs 100 C4
  Cambs 101 A5
  C Beds 67 A4
  C Beds 84 D1
  C Beds 84 D3
  Essex 69 A7
  Essex 86 C1
  E Yorks 150 B3
  Hants 47 D4
  Lincs 117 B5
  Warks 97 B5
  Warks 97 B5
  Wilts 44 B4
Church Enstone ..65 A4
Church Fenton ..148 D4
Churchfield 96 B3
Churchgate
  Street 69 B4
Church Green
  Devon 14 B1
  Norf 103 B6
Church Gresley .113 D6
Church
  Hanborough ..65 B5
Church Hill 127 C6
Church Houses .159 B5
Churchill Devon ..14 A3
  Devon 25 A6

Churchill continued
  N Som 42 D3
  Oxon 64 A3
  Worcs 80 B2
  Worcs 96 D1
Churchinford ..28 D2
Church Knowle ..16 C3
Church
  Laneham 132 B3
Church Langton ..99 B4
Church Lawford ..98 D1
Church Lawton ..128 D3
Church Leigh ..112 B4
Church Lench ..80 B3
Church
  Mayfield 113 A5
Church
  Minshull 127 C6
Church Norton ..20 C1
Churchover 98 C2
Church Preen ..94 B3
Church
  Pulverbatch ..94 A2
Churchstanton ..28 D1
Church Stoke ..93 B6
Churchstow 7 C6
Church Stowe ..82 B3
Church Street ..51 B4
Church Stretton .94 B2
Church Town
  N Lincs 141 C5
  Sur 35 A6
Church Village ..41 C5
Church Warsop .131 C5
Churnsike
  Lodge 177 B4
Churston Ferrers .8 B3
Churt 34 C1
Churton 127 D4
Churwell 139 A5
Chute Standen ..45 D7
Chwilog 107 C4
Chyandour 2 B2
Cilan Uchaf 106 D2
Cilcain 126 C1
Cilcennin 75 B4
Cilfor 107 C6
Cilfrew 40 A2
Cilfynydd 41 B5
Cilgerran 73 B4
Cilgwyn Carms ..59 C4
  Gwyn 107 A4
  Pembs 72 C3
Ciliau Aeron ..74 C3
Cill Donnain ..286 D3
Cille Bhrighde .286 E3
Cille Pheadair ..286 E3
Cilmery 76 B4
Cilsan 58 C2
Ciltalgarth 108 A3
Cilwendeg 73 C5
Cilybebyll 40 A2
Cilycwm 59 B4
Cimla 40 B2
Cinderford 62 B2
Cippyn 72 B4
Circebost 288 D2
Cirencester 63 C6
Ciribhig 288 C2
City London 49 A6
  Powys 93 C6
City Dulas 123 B4
Clachaig 215 D4
Clachan Argyll ..202 C2
  Argyll 213 A5
  Argyll 215 A4
  Argyll 226 B3
  Highld 248 C2
  W Isles 286 B3
Clachaneasy ..181 D5
Clachanmore ..170 C2
Clachan na Luib 287 H3
Clachan of
  Campsie 205 A6
Clachan of
  Glendaruel ..214 D2
Clachan-Seil ..213 A5

Clachan
  Strachur 214 B3
Clachbreck 202 A2
Clachnabrain ..232 B1
Clachtoll 270 B3
Clackmannan ..208 A2
Clacton-on-Sea. 71 B5
Cladach
  Chireboist ..287 H2
Claddach-
  knockline ..287 H2
Cladich 227 D5
Claggan Highld. ..225 B5
  Highld. 237 B5
Claigan 258 C2
Claines 79 B6
Clandown 43 D5
Clanfield Hants ..33 D5
  Oxon 64 C3
Clanville 32 A2
Claonaig 202 C3
Claonel 272 D3
Clapgate Dorset ..17 A4
  Herts 68 A4
Clapham Bedford. .84 B2
  London 49 B5
  N Yorks 146 A1
  W Sus 20 B3
Clap Hill 38 B2
Clappers 198 A3
Clappersgate ..154 A2
Clapton 14 A4
Clapton-in-
  Gordano 42 B3
Clapton-on-the-
  Hill 64 B2
Clapworthy 26 C1
Clarach 90 D4
Clara Vale 178 C3
Clarbeston 55 B6
Clarbeston Road .55 B6
Clarborough ..132 A2
Clardon 280 B3
Clare 86 C3
Clarebrand 173 B5
Clarencefield ..174 B3
Clarilaw 186 B4
Clark's Green ..35 C4
Clarkston 205 C5
Clashandorran ..251 B7
Clashcoig 264 A2
Clashindarroch. .255 C5
Clashmore
  Highld. 264 B3
  Highld. 270 A3
Clashnessie 270 A3
Clashnoir 254 D3
Clate 285 G7
Clathy 219 C4
Clatt 255 D6
Clatter 92 B3
Clatterford 18 C3
Clatterin Bridge 233 A4
Clatworthy 27 B5
Claughton Lancs .145 A5
  Lancs 145 C5
  Mers. 126 A3
Claverdon 81 A4
Claverham 42 C3
Clavering 85 D6
Claverley 95 B5
Claverton 44 C1
Clawdd-
  newydd 125 D5
Clawthorpe 154 D4
Clawton 11 B4
Claxby Lincs ..135 B4
  Lincs. 142 D3
Claxton Norf. ..104 A4
  N Yorks. 149 A5
Claybokie 242 D3
Claybrooke
  Magna 98 C1
Claybrooke Parva 98 C1
Clay Common ..105 C5
Clay Coton 98 D2
Clay Cross 130 C3
Claydon Oxon ..82 B1
  Suff 88 B2
Claygate
  Dumfries 175 A6
  Kent 37 B5

Claygate continued
Sur 49 C4
Claygate Cross . . 36 A4
Clayhanger Devon 27 C5
  W Mid 96 A3
Clayhidon 27 D6
  Hants 18 A2
Clay Hill 46 B3
Clay Lake 117 C5
Clayock 280 C3
Claypole 115 A6
Clayton Staffs . . 112 A2
  S Yorks 140 C2
  W Sus 21 A5
  W Yorks 147 D5
Clayton Green . 137 A4
Clayton-le-Moors 146 D1
Clayton-le-Woods 137 A4
Clayton West . . . 139 B5
Clayworth 132 A2
Cleadale 234 B3
Cleadon 179 C5
Clearbrook 7 A4
Clearwell 62 C1
Cleasby 167 D5
Cleat 283 J5
Cleatlam 166 D4
Cleator 162 C3
Cleator Moor . . . 162 C3
Clebrig 272 A3
Cleckheaton . . . 139 A4
Cleehill 94 D3
Clee St Margaret . 94 C3
Cleethorpes . . . 143 C5
Cleeton St Mary . 95 D4
Cleeve 42 C3
Cleeve Hill 63 A5
Cleeve Prior 80 C3
Clegyrnant 91 B7
Clehonger 78 D2
Cleish 208 A3
Cleland 194 A3
Clench Common . . 45 C5
Clenchwarton . . . 118 C2
Clent 96 D2
Cleobury Mortimer 95 D4
Cleobury North . . 95 C4
Cleongart 190 B2
Clephanton 253 A4
Clerklands 186 A4
Clestrain 283 G4
Cleuch Head . . . 187 B4
Cleughbrae 174 A3
Clevancy 45 B4
Clevedon 42 B3
Cleveley 65 A4
Cleveleys 144 C3
Cleverton 44 A3
Clevis 40 D3
Clewer 42 D3
Cley next the Sea 120 A2
Cliaid 286 F2
Cliasmol 287 D5
Cliburn 164 C3
Click Mill 282 E4
Cliddesden 33 A5
Cliffburn 233 D4
Cliffe Medway . . . 51 B4
  N Yorks 149 D5
Cliff End 23 A6
Cliffe Woods 51 B4
Clifford Hereford . . 77 C6
  W Yorks 148 C3
Clifford Chambers 81 B4
Clifford's Mesne . 62 A3
Cliffsend 53 C5
Clifton Bristol . . . 43 B4
  C Beds 84 D3
  Cumb 164 C4
  Derbys 113 A5
  Lancs 145 D4
  Northumb 179 A4
  Nottingham . . . 114 B3
  N Yorks 147 C5
  Oxon 82 D1

Clifton continued
Stirling 216 A3
  S Yorks 140 D3
  Worcs 79 C6
  York 149 B4
Clifton Campville 113 D6
Cliftoncote 187 A7
Clifton Green . . . 137 C6
Clifton Hampden . 65 D6
Clifton Reynes . . 83 B6
Clifton upon Dunsmore 98 D2
Clifton upon Teme 79 A5
Cliftonville 53 B5
Climaen gwyn . . 59 E4
Climping 20 B3
Climpy 194 A4
Clink 30 A1
Clint 147 B6
Clint Green 120 D2
Clintmains 197 C5
Cliobh 287 A5
Clippesby 121 D6
Clipsham 116 D2
Clipston 99 C4
Clipstone 131 C6
Clitheroe 146 C1
Cliuthar 288 H2
Clive 111 C4
Clivocast 284 C8
Clixby 142 C3
Clocaenog 125 D5
Clochan 267 C5
Clock Face 136 D4
Clockmill 197 A6
Cloddiau 93 A6
Clodock 61 A5
Clola 257 B5
Clophill 84 D2
Clopton Northants 100 C2
  Suff 88 B3
Clopton Corner . . 88 B3
Clopton Green . . 86 B3
Closeburn 183 C6
Close Clark 152 D2
Closworth 29 D5
Clothall 85 D4
Clotton 127 C5
Clough Foot 138 A2
Cloughton 160 B4
Cloughton Newlands 160 B4
Clousta 285 H5
Clouston 282 F3
Clova Aberds . . . 255 D5
  Angus 232 A1
Clovelly 24 C4
Clove Lodge . . . 166 D2
Clovenfords 196 C3
Clovenstone . . . 245 A4
Clovullin 237 C4
Clow Bridge . . . 137 A7
Clowne 131 B4
Clows Top 95 D5
Cloy 110 A2
Cluanie Inn 239 A4
Cluanie Lodge . . 239 A4
Clun 93 C7
Clunbury 94 C1
Clunderwen 55 C7
Clune 252 D3
Clunes 239 D6
Clungunford 94 D1
Clunie Aberds . . . 268 D1
  Perth 231 D5
Clunton 94 C1
Cluny 209 A5
Cluny Castle . . . 241 C4
Clutton Bath 43 D5
  Ches W 127 D4
Clwt-grugoer . . . 125 C4
Clwt-y-bont 123 D5
Clydach Mon 60 B4
  Swansea 40 A1
Clydach Vale 41 B4
Clydebank 205 A4
Clydey 73 C5
Clyffe Pypard . . . 45 B4
Clynder 215 D5

Clyne 40 A3
Clynelish 274 D2
Clynnog-fawr . . . 107 A4
Clyro 77 C6
Clyst Honiton . . . 13 B4
Clyst Hydon 13 A5
Clyst St George . . 13 C4
Clyst St Lawrence 13 A5
Clyst St Mary . . . 13 B4
Cnoc Amhlaigh . 288 D6
Cnwch-coch 75 A5
Coachford 255 B5
Coad's Green . . . 10 D3
Coal Aston 130 B3
Coalbrookdale . . . 95 A4
Coalbrookvale . . . 60 C3
Coalburn 194 C3
Coalburns 178 C3
Coalcleugh 165 A6
Coaley 62 C3
Coalhall 182 A2
Coalhill 70 D1
Coalpit Heath . . . 43 A5
Coalport 95 A4
Coalsnaughton . . 208 A2
Coaltown of Balgonie 209 A5
Coaltown of Wemyss 209 A6
Coalville 114 D2
Coalway 62 B1
Coat 29 C4
Coatbridge 207 D5
Coatdyke 207 D5
Coate Swindon . . . 45 A5
  Wilts 44 C4
Coates Cambs . . . 101 B5
  Glos 63 C5
  Lancs 146 C2
  Notts 132 A3
  W Sus 20 A2
Coatham 168 C3
Coatham Mundeville 167 C5
Coatsgate 184 B3
Cobbaton 25 C7
Cobbler's Green 104 B3
Coberley 63 B5
Cobham Kent 50 C3
  Sur 48 C4
Cobholm Island . 105 A6
Cobleland 206 A3
Cobnash 78 A2
Coburty 269 C4
Cockayne 159 B5
Cockayne Hatley . 85 C4
Cock Bank 110 A2
Cock Bridge 243 B5
Cockburnspath . . 211 C4
Cock Clarks 70 C2
Cockenzie and Port Seton 209 C7
Cockerham 145 B4
Cockermouth . . . 163 A4
Cockernhoe Green 67 A6
Cockfield Durham . 166 C4
  Suff 87 B5
Cockfosters 68 D2
Cocking 20 A1
Cockington 8 A2
Cocklake 28 A4
Cockley Beck . . . 163 D5
Cockley Cley . . . 102 A3
Cockshutt 110 C3
Cockthorpe 120 A1
Cockwood 13 C4
Cockyard 78 D2
Codda 10 D2
Coddenham 88 B2
Coddington Ches W 127 D4
  Hereford 79 C5
  Notts 132 D2
Codford St Mary . 30 B3
Codford St Peter . 30 B3
Codicote 68 B2
Codmore Hill . . . 34 D3
Codnor 114 A2
Codrington 43 B6

Codsall 95 A6
Codsall Wood . . . 95 A6
Coedely 41 C5
Coedkernew 42 A1
Coed Mawr 123 C5
Coed Morgan . . . 61 B5
Coedpoeth 126 D2
Coed-Talon 126 D2
Coedway 110 D2
Coed-y-bryn 73 B6
Coed-y-paen 61 D5
Coed-yr-ynys . . . 60 A3
Coed Ystumgwern . . . 107 D5
Coelbren 59 D5
Coffinswell 8 A2
Cofton Hackett . . 96 D3
Cogan 41 D6
Cogenhoe 83 A5
Cogges 65 C4
Coggeshall 70 A2
Coggeshall Hamlet 70 A2
Coggins Mill 36 D3
Coignafearn Lodge 241 A4
Coig Peighinnean . . . 288 A6
Coig Peighinnean Bhuirgh 288 B5
Coilacriech 243 C6
Coilantogle 217 D5
Coilleag 286 E3
Coillore 246 A2
Coity 40 C4
Col 288 C5
Colaboll 272 C3
Colan 4 A3
Colaton Raleigh . 13 C5
Colbost 258 D2
Colburn 157 B5
Colby Cumb 165 C4
  IoM 152 D2
  Norf 120 B4
Colchester 71 A4
Colcot 41 E6
Cold Ash 46 C3
Cold Ashby 98 D3
Cold Ashton 43 B6
Cold Aston 64 B2
Coldbackie 277 C7
Coldbeck 155 A6
Coldblow 50 B2
Cold Blow 55 C7
Cold Brayfield . . . 83 B6
Coldean 21 B6
Coldeast 12 D3
Colden 138 A2
Colden Common . 32 C3
Coldfair Green . . 89 A5
Coldham 101 A6
Cold Hanworth . . 133 A5
Coldharbour Glos . 62 C1
  Kent 36 A3
  Sur 35 B4
Cold Harbour . . . 116 B2
Cold Hatton 111 C5
Cold Hesledon . . 168 A2
Cold Higham 82 B3
Coldingham 211 D6
Cold Kirby 158 C5
Cold Newton 99 A4
Cold Northcott . . 10 C3
Cold Norton 70 C2
Cold Overton . . . 115 D6
Coldrain 219 D5
Coldred 39 A4
Coldridge 12 A1
Coldstream Borders 198 C2
  Angus 220 A3
Coldwaltham 20 A3
Coldwells 257 B6
Coldwells Croft . . 255 D6
Coldyeld 94 B1
Cole 29 B6
Colebatch 93 C7
Colebrook 13 A5
Colebrooke 12 B2
Coleby Lincs 133 C4
  N Lincs 141 B6
Coleford Devon . . . 12 A2

Coleford continued
Glos 62 B1
  Som 29 A6
Cole Green 68 B2
Cole Henley 46 D2
Colehill 17 A4
Coleman's Hatch . 36 C2
Colemere 110 B3
Colemore 33 B6
Coleorton 114 D2
Colerne 44 B2
Colesbourne 63 B5
Colesden 84 B3
Coles Green 88 C1
Cole's Green 88 A3
Coleshill Bucks . . . 67 D4
  Oxon 64 D3
  Warks 97 C5
Colestocks 13 A5
Colgate 35 C5
Colgrain 206 B1
Colinsburgh 221 D4
Colinton 209 D5
Colintraive 203 A5
Colkirk 119 C6
Collace 220 A2
Collafirth 284 G6
Collaton St Mary . 8 B2
College Milton . . 205 C6
Collessie 220 C2
Collier Row 69 D5
Collier's End 68 A3
Collier's Green . . 37 C5
Collier Street 37 B5
Colliery Row . . . 167 A6
Collieston 257 D5
Collin 174 A3
Collingbourne Ducis 45 D6
Collingbourne Kingston 45 D6
Collingham Notts . 132 C3
  W Yorks 148 C2
Collington 79 A4
Collingtree 83 B4
Collins Green . . . 137 D4
Colliston 233 D4
Collycroft 97 C6
Collynie 256 C3
Collyweston 100 A1
Colmonell 180 C3
Colmworth 84 B3
Colnabaichin . . . 243 B5
Colnbrook 48 B3
Colne Cambs 101 D5
  Lancs 146 C2
Colne Edge 146 C2
Colne Engaine . . 87 D4
Colney 104 A2
Colney Heath 68 C2
Colney Street 67 C6
Coln Rogers 64 C1
Coln St Aldwyn's . 64 C2
Coln St Dennis . . . 64 B1
Colpy 256 C1
Colquhar 196 B2
Colsterdale 157 C5
Colsterworth . . . 116 C2
Colston Bassett . . 115 B4
Coltfield 266 C2
Colthouse 154 B2
Coltishall 121 D4
Coltness 194 A3
Colton Cumb 154 C2
  Norf 104 A2
  N Yorks 148 C4
  Staffs 113 C4
  W Yorks 148 D2
Col Uarach 288 D5
Colva 77 B6
Colvend 173 C6
Colvister 284 D7
Colwall Green . . . 79 C5
Colwall Stone . . . 79 C5
Colwell 178 B1
Colwich 112 C4
Colwick 115 A4
Colwinston 40 D4
Colworth 20 B2
Colwyn Bay Bae
Colwyn 124 B3

Colyford 14 B2
Colyton 14 B2
Combe Hereford . . 78 A1
  Oxon 65 B5
  W Berks 46 C1
Combe Common . 34 C2
Combe Down 43 C6
Combe Florey . . . 27 B6
Combe Hay 43 D6
Combeinteignhead 13 D4
Combe Martin . . . 25 A6
Combe Moor 78 A1
Combe Raleigh . . 13 A6
Comberbach . . . 127 B6
Comberton Cambs . 85 B5
  Hereford 78 A2
Combe St Nicholas 28 D3
Combpyne 14 B2
Combridge 113 B4
Combrook 81 B6
Combs Derbys . . . 129 B5
  Suff 87 B6
Combs Ford 87 B6
Combwich 28 A2
Comers 244 B3
Comins Coch 90 D4
Commercial End . 86 A1
Commins Capel Betws 75 C5
Commins Coch . . . 91 B6
Commondale . . . 169 D4
Common Edge . . 144 D3
Commonmoor 6 A1
Commonside . . . 127 B5
Common Side . . . 130 B3
Compstall 138 D2
Compton Devon . . . 8 A2
  Hants 32 C3
  Sur 34 B1
  Sur 34 B2
  W Berks 46 B3
  Wilts 45 D5
  W Sus 33 D6
Compton Abbas . 30 D2
Compton Abdale . 63 B6
Compton Bassett . 44 B4
Compton Beauchamp 45 A6
Compton Bishop . 42 D2
Compton Chamberlayne . . 31 C4
Compton Dando . 43 C5
Compton Dundon 29 B4
Compton Martin . 43 D4
Compton Pauncefoot 29 C6
Compton Valence 15 B5
Comrie Fife 208 B3
  Perth 218 B2
Conaglen House 237 C4
Concha 214 D3
Concraigie 231 D5
Conder Green . . . 145 B4
Conderton 80 D2
Condicote 64 A2
Condorrat 207 C5
Condover 94 A2
Coneyhurst 35 D4
Coneysthorpe . . 159 D6
Coneythorpe . . . 148 B2
Coney Weston . . 103 D5
Conford 33 B7
Congash 253 D6
Congdon's Shop . 10 D3
Congerstone 97 A6
Congham 119 C4
Congleton 128 C3
Congl-y-wal 108 A2
Congresbury 42 C3
Congreve 112 D3
Conicavel 253 A5
Coningsby 134 D2
Conington Cambs . 85 A5
  Cambs 100 C3
Conisbrough . . . 140 D3
Conisby 200 B3

Conisholme....143 D6
Coniston Cumb...154 B2
 E Yorks....151 D4
Coniston Cold..146 B3
Conistone.....146 A3
Connah's Quay.126 C2
Connel.......226 C4
Connel Park...182 A4
Connor Downs...2 B3
Conon Bridge..252 A1
Conon House...252 A1
Cononley.....146 C3
Conordan.....247 A4
Consall......112 A3
Consett......178 D3
Constable
  Burton.....157 B5
Constantine....3 C5
Constantine Bay...9 D4
Contin......251 A6
Contlaw.....245 B5
Conwy.......124 B2
Conyer......51 C6
Conyers Green...87 A4
Cooden......23 B5
Cooil.......152 D3
Cookbury....11 A5
Cookham.....48 A1
  Highld.....238 B2
Cookham Dean..47 A6
Cookham Rise...48 A1
Cookhill.....80 B3
Cookley Suff...104 D4
  Worcs.......95 C6
Cookley Green..66 D1
Cookney.....245 C5
Cookridge...147 C6
Cooksbridge...22 A2
Cooksmill Green.69 C6
Coolham.....35 D4
Cooling.....51 B4
Coombe Corn...4 B4
  Corn......24 D3
  Hants.......33 C5
  Wilts.......45 D5
Coombe Bissett.31 C5
Coombe Hill...63 A4
Coombe Keynes.16 C2
Coombes.....21 B4
Coopersale
  Common....69 C4
Cootham.....20 A3
Copdock.....88 C2
Copford Green..70 A3
Copgrove....148 A2
Copister....284 F6
Cople.......84 C3
Copley......166 C3
Coplow Dale...129 B6
Copmanthorpe.149 C4
Coppathorne...10 A3
Coppenhall...112 D3
Coppenhall
  Moss......128 D2
Copperhouse...2 B3
Coppingford...100 C3
Copplestone...12 A2
Coppull.....137 B4
Coppull Moor..137 B4
Copsale.....35 D4
Copster Green.145 D6
Copston Magna.98 C1
Copt Heath..97 D4
Copt Hewick..158 D2
Copthorne
  Shrops.....110 D3
  Sur........35 C6
Copt Oak....114 D2
Copy's Green..119 B6
Copythorne....32 D2
Corbets Tey...50 A2
Corbridge....178 C1
Corby.......99 C5
Corby Glen..116 C2
Cordon.....191 B6
Coreley.....95 D4
Cores End...48 A1
Corfe.......28 D2
Corfe Castle..16 C3
Corfe Mullen..16 B3

Corfton......94 C2
Corgarff....243 B5
Corhampton...33 C5
Corlae......183 C4
Corley......97 C6
Corley Ash...97 C5
Corley Moor...97 C5
Cornaa......152 C4
Cornabus....200 D3
Cornel......124 C2
Corner Row...144 D4
Corney......153 A2
Cornforth....167 B6
Cornhill....267 D6
Cornhill-on-
  Tweed.....198 C2
Cornholme....138 A2
Cornish Hall End.86 D2
Cornquoy....283 H6
Cornsay.....166 A4
Cornsay
  Colliery...167 A4
Corntown Highld.252 A1
  V Glam......40 D4
Cornwell....64 A3
Cornwood.....7 B5
Cornworthy....8 B2
Corpach.....237 B4
Corpusty....120 B3
Corran Highld...237 C4
  Highld.....238 B2
Corranbuie...202 B3
Corrany.....152 C4
Corrie......203 D5
Corrie Common.185 D5
Corriecravie..191 C5
Corriemoillie..263 D5
Corriemulzie
  Lodge......263 A5
Corrievarkie
  Lodge......229 A4
Corrievorrie..252 D3
Corrimony...251 C5
Corringham
  Lincs......141 D6
  Thurrock....51 A4
Corris......91 B5
Corris Uchaf..91 B5
Corrour Shooting
  Lodge......228 B3
Corrow......215 B4
Corry.......247 B5
Corrykinloch.271 B6
Corrymuckloch.218 A3
Corrynachenchy.225 B5
Corry of
  Ardnagrask..251 B7
Corsback....280 A4
Corscombe....15 A5
Corse Aberds..255 B7
  Glos.......62 A3
Corse Lawn...79 D6
Corse of Kinnoir.255 B6
Corsewall...170 A2
Corsham.....44 B2
Corsindae...244 B3
Corsley.....30 A1
Corsley Heath..30 A2
Corsock....173 A5
Corston Bath..43 C5
  Wilts.......44 A3
Corstorphine..209 C4
Cors-y-Gedol..107 D5
Cortachy....232 C1
Corton Suff..105 B6
  Wilts.......30 A3
Corton Denham..29 C6
Coruanan
  Lodge......237 C4
Corunna.....287 H3
Corwen......109 A5
Coryton Devon..11 C5
  Thurrock....51 A4
Cosby.......98 B2
Coseley.....96 B2
Cosgrove....83 C4
Cosham......19 A5
Cosheston....55 D6
Cossall.....114 A2
Cossington Leics.115 D4
  Som........28 A3
Costa.......282 E4

Costessey....120 D3
Costock.....114 C3
Coston......115 C6
Cote........64 C4
Cotebrook...127 C5
Cotehill....176 D2
Cotes Cumb...154 C3
  Leics......114 C3
  Staffs.....112 B2
Cotesbach....98 C2
Cotgrave....115 B4
Cothall.....245 A5
Cotham......115 A5
Cothelstone...28 B1
Cotherstone..166 D3
Cothill......65 D5
Cotleigh....14 A2
Cotmanhay...114 A2
Cotmaton....13 C6
Coton Cambs...85 B6
  Northants....98 D3
  Staffs.....112 B3
  Staffs.....112 C2
Coton Clanford.112 C2
Coton Hill
  Shrops.....110 D3
  Staffs.....112 B3
Coton in the
  Elms......113 D6
Cott.........8 A1
Cottam E Yorks..150 A2
  Lancs......145 D5
  Notts......132 B3
Cottartown...253 C6
Cottenham....85 A6
Cotterdale..156 B2
Cottered.....68 A3
Cotteridge...96 D3
Cotterstock..100 B2
Cottesbrooke..99 D4
Cottesmore...116 D2
Cotteylands..27 D4
Cottingham
  E Yorks....150 D3
  Northants....99 B5
Cottingley..147 D5
Cottisford...82 D2
Cotton Staffs..113 A4
  Suff........87 A6
Cotton End...84 C2
Cottown Aberds.245 A4
  Aberds.....255 D6
  Aberds.....256 B3
Cotwalton....112 B3
Couch's Mill...5 B6
Coughton
  Hereford....62 A1
  Warks.......80 A3
Coulaghailtro.202 B2
Coulags.....249 B6
Coulby Newham.168 D3
Coulderton...162 D2
Coulin......250 A2
Coull Aberds..244 B2
  Argyll.....200 B2
Coulport....215 D5
Coulsdon....35 A5
Coulston....44 D3
Coulter.....195 C5
Coulton.....159 D5
Cound.......94 A3
Coundon Durham.167 C5
  W Mid......97 C6
Coundon
  Grange....167 C5
Countersett..156 C3
Countess....31 A5
Countess Wear..13 C4
Countesthorpe.98 B2
Countisbury...26 A2
County Oak...35 C5
Coupar Angus.231 D6
Coup Green..137 A4
Coupland....198 C3
Cour........202 D3
Court-at-Street.38 B2
Courteenhall..83 B4
Court Henry..58 C2
Courtsend....71 D4
Courtway....28 B2
Cousland....209 D6
Cousley Wood..37 C4

Cove Argyll..215 D5
  Borders....211 C4
  Devon......27 D4
  Hants......34 A1
  Highld.....261 A5
Cove Bay....245 B6
Cove Bottom..105 D5
Covehithe...105 C6
Coven.......96 A2
Coveney....101 C5
Covenham St
  Bartholomew.143 D5
Covenham St
  Mary......143 D5
Coventry....97 D6
Coverack.....3 D5
Coverham....157 C5
Covesea.....266 B2
Covington
  Cambs.....100 D2
  S Lanark...195 C4
Cowan Bridge.155 D5
Cow Ark....145 C6
Cowbeech....22 A4
Cowbit......117 D5
Cowbridge Lincs.117 A6
  Som........27 A4
Cowbridge V Bont-
  Faen.......41 D4
Cowdale....129 B5
Cowden......36 B2
Cowdenbeath.209 A4
Cowdenburn..195 A7
Cowers Lane..113 A7
Cowes.......18 B3
Cowesby....158 C3
Cowfold.....35 D5
Cowgill....155 C6
Cowie Aberds..245 D5
  Stirling....207 B6
Cowley Devon..13 B4
  Glos.......63 B5
  London.....48 A3
  Oxon.......65 C6
Cowleymoor...27 D4
Cowling Lancs.137 B4
  N Yorks....146 C3
  N Yorks....157 C5
Cowlinge....86 B3
Cowpe......138 A1
Cowpen.....179 A4
Cowpen Bewley.168 C2
Cowplain....33 D5
Cowshill....165 A6
Cowslip Green.42 C3
Cowstrandburn.208 A3
Cowthorpe...148 B3
Coxbank....111 A5
Coxbench....114 A1
Cox Common..105 C4
Coxford Norf..119 C5
  Soton......32 D2
Cox Grn......48 B1
Coxheath....37 A5
Coxhill......39 A4
Coxhoe......167 B6
Coxley......29 A5
Cox Moor....131 D5
Coxwold....158 D4
Coychurch....40 D4
Coylton.....193 C4
Coylumbridge.242 A2
Coynach....244 B1
Coynachie...255 C5
Coytrahen....40 C3
Crabadon.....7 B6
Crabbs Cross..80 A3
Crabtree....35 D5
Crackenthorpe.165 C4
Crackington
  Haven......10 B2
Crackley....97 D5
Crackleybank.111 D6
Crackpot....156 B3
Cracoe......146 A3
Craddock....27 D5
Cradhlastadh.287 A5
Cradley.....79 C5
Cradley Heath..96 C2
Crafthole.....6 B2
Craggan.....253 D6

Craggie Highld..252 C3
  Highld.....274 C2
Cragg Vale...138 A3
Craghead...179 D4
Crai........59 C5
Craibstone...267 D5
Craichie....232 D3
Craig Dumfries.173 A4
  Dumfries....173 B4
  Highld.....250 B2
Craiganor
  Lodge......229 C5
Craig Castle..255 D5
Craig-cefn-parc.40 A1
Craigdam....256 C3
Craigdarroch
  Dumfries...183 C5
  Highld.....251 A6
Craigdhu....251 B6
Craigearn...245 A4
Craigellachie.254 B3
Craigencross.170 A2
Craigend Perth..219 B6
  Stirling....207 B5
Craigendive..214 D3
Craigendoran.215 D6
Craigends...205 B4
Craigens Argyll..200 B2
  E Ayrs.....182 A3
Craighat....206 B2
Craighead...221 D6
Craighlaw
  Mains......171 A5
Craighouse..201 B5
Craigie Aberds..245 A6
  Dundee.....220 A4
  Perth......219 B6
  Perth......231 D5
  S Ayrs.....193 B4
Craigiefield..282 F5
Craigielaw...210 C1
Craiglockhart.209 C5
Craigmalloch.182 C2
Craigmaud...268 D3
Craigmillar..209 C5
Craigmore...203 B6
Craignant...110 B1
Craigneuk
  N Lanark....194 A2
  N Lanark....207 D5
Craignure...225 C6
Craigo......233 B4
Craigow....219 D5
Craig Penllyn.41 D4
Craigrothie..220 C3
Craigroy....266 D2
Craigruie...217 B4
Craigston
  Castle.....268 D2
Craigton
  Aberdeen...245 B5
  Angus......221 A5
  Angus......232 C1
  Highld.....252 B2
Craigtown...279 C4
Craig-y-don..124 A2
Craig-y-nos...59 D5
Craik.......185 B6
Crail.......221 D6
Crailing....187 A5
Crailinghall..187 A5
Craiselound.141 D5
Crakehill....158 D3
Crakemarsh...113 B4
Crambe.....149 A6
Cramlington.179 B4
Cramond....209 C4
Cramond
  Bridge.....209 C4
Cranage....128 C2
Cranberry...112 B2
Cranborne....31 D4
Cranbourne...48 B2
Cranbrook Devon..13 B5
  Kent........37 C5
Cranbrook
  Common....37 C5
Crane Moor..139 C6
Crane's Corner.119 D6
Cranfield....83 C6
Cranford....48 B4

Cranford St
  Andrew.....99 D6
Cranford St John.99 D6
Cranham Glos...63 B4
  London......50 A2
Crank.......136 D4
Crank Wood..137 C5
Cranleigh....34 C3
Cranley.....104 D2
Cranmer Green.103 D6
Cranmore....18 C2
Cranna......268 D1
Crannich....225 B4
Crannoch....267 D5
Cranoe......99 B4
Cransford....88 A4
Cranshaws...210 D3
Cranstal....152 A4
Crantock.....4 A2
Cranwell....116 A3
Cranwich....102 B3
Cranworth...103 A5
Craobh Haven.213 B5
Crapstone....7 A4
Crarae......214 C2
Crask Inn...272 B3
Craskins....244 B2
Crask of Aigas.251 B6
Craster.....189 B5
Craswall.....77 D6
Cratfield...104 D4
Crathes.....245 C4
Crathie Aberds..243 C5
  Highld.....240 C3
Crathorne...158 A3
Craven Arms..94 C2
Crawcrook...178 C3
Crawford Lancs.136 C3
  S Lanark...195 D4
Crawfordjohn.194 D3
Crawick....183 A5
Crawley Hants..32 B3
  Oxon.......64 B4
  W Sus......35 C5
Crawley Down..35 C5
Crawleyside..166 A2
Crawshawbooth.137 A7
Crawton.....233 A6
Cray N Yorks..156 D3
  Perth......231 B5
Crayford....50 B2
Crayke......159 D4
Crays Hill...69 D7
Cray's Pond..47 A4
Creacombe...26 D3
Creagan....227 B4
Creag Ghoraidh.286 B3
Creaguaineach
  Lodge......228 B2
Creaksea....70 D3
Creaton.....99 D4
Creca......175 A5
Credenhill...78 C2
Crediton....12 A3
Creebridge..171 A6
Creech
  Heathfield..28 C2
Creech St
  Michael....28 C2
Creed.......4 C4
Creekmouth...50 A1
Creeting Bottoms.88 B2
Creeting St Mary.88 B1
Creeton.....116 C3
Creetown...171 B6
Creggans...214 B3
Cregneash...152 E1
Creg-ny-Baa..152 C3
Cregrina....77 B5
Creich......220 B3
Creigiau.....41 C5
Cremyll......6 B3
Creslow.....66 A3
Cressage....94 A3
Cressbrook..129 B6
Cresselly....55 D6
Cressing....70 A1
Cresswell
  Northumb...189 D5
  Staffs.....112 B3
Cresswell Quay.55 D6
Creswell....131 B5

Cretingham 88 A3
Cretshengan 202 B2
Crewe Ches E . . . 128 D2
 Ches W 127 D4
Crewgreen 110 D2
Crewkerne 14 A4
Crianlarich 216 B3
Cribyn 75 C4
Criccieth 107 C4
Crich 130 D3
Crichie 257 B4
Crichton 209 D6
Crick Mon 61 D6
 Northants 98 D2
Crickadarn 77 C4
Cricket
 Malherbie 28 D3
Cricket St
 Thomas 14 A3
Crickheath 110 C1
Crickhowell 60 B4
Cricklade 64 D2
Cricklewood 49 A5
Cridling Stubbs . 140 A3
Crieff 218 B3
Criggion 110 D1
Crigglestone 139 B6
Crimond 269 C5
Crimonmogate . . 269 C5
Crimplesham . . . 102 A2
Crinan 213 C5
Cringleford 104 A2
Cringles 147 C4
Crinow 56 A1
Cripplesease 2 B3
Cripplestyle 31 D4
Cripp's Corner . . 37 D5
Croasdale 162 C3
Crockenhill 50 C2
Crockernwell . . . 12 B2
Crockerton 30 A2
Crocketford or
 Ninemile Bar . 173 A6
Crockey Hill 149 C5
Crockham Hill . . 36 A2
Crockleford
 Heath 71 A4
Crockness 283 H4
Crock Street . . . 28 D3
Croeserw 40 B3
Croes-goch 54 A4
Croes-lan 73 B6
Croesor 107 B6
Croesyceiliog
 Carms 57 A4
 Torf 61 D5
Croes-y-
 mwyalch 61 D5
Croesywaun . . . 107 A5
Croft Leics 98 B2
 Lincs 135 C5
 Pembs 73 B4
 Warr 137 D5
Croftamie 206 B2
Croftmalloch . . 208 D2
Crofton Wilts . . 45 C6
 W Yorks 140 B1
Croft-on-Tees . 157 A6
Crofts of
 Benachielt . . 275 A5
Crofts of Haddo 256 C3
Crofts of
 Inverthernie . 256 B2
Crofts of Meikle
 Ardo 256 B3
Crofty 57 C5
Croggan 225 D6
Croglin 164 A3
Croich 263 A6
Crois Dughaill . 286 D3
Cromarty 264 D3
Cromblet 256 C2
Cromdale 253 D6
Cromer Herts . . 68 A2
 Norf 120 A4
Cromford 130 D2
Cromhall 62 D2
Cromhall
 Common . . . 43 A5
Cromor 288 E5
Cromra 240 C3
Cromwell . . . 132 C2

Cronberry 193 C6
Crondall 33 A6
Cronk-y-Voddy . 152 C3
Cronton 127 A4
Crook Cumb 154 B3
 Durham 167 B4
Crookedholm . . 193 B4
Crookes 130 A3
Crookham
 Northumb 198 C3
 W Berks 46 C3
Crookham
 Village 47 D5
Crookhaugh . . . 195 D6
Crookhouse . . . 187 A6
Crooklands . . . 154 C4
Crook of Devon 219 D5
Cropredy 82 C1
Cropston 114 D3
Cropthorne . . . 80 C2
Cropton 159 C6
Cropwell Bishop 115 B4
Cropwell Butler 115 B4
Cros 288 A6
Crosbost 288 E4
Crosby Cumb . . 162 A3
 IoM 152 D3
 N Lincs 141 B6
Crosby
 Ravensworth . 165 D4
Crosby Villa . . 162 A3
Croscombe . . . 29 A5
Cross 42 D3
Crossaig 202 C3
Crossal 246 A3
Crossapol 222 C2
Cross Ash 61 B6
Cross-at-Hand . . 37 B5
Crossburn 207 C6
Crossbush 20 B3
Crosscanonby . . 162 A3
Crossdale
 Street 120 B4
Crossens 136 B2
Crossflatts . . . 147 C5
Crossford Fife . 208 B3
 S Lanark 194 B3
Crossgate 117 C5
Crossgatehall . . 209 D6
Crossgates Fife . 208 B3
 Powys 77 A4
Crossgill 145 A5
Cross Green
 Devon 11 C4
 Suff 87 B4
 Suff 87 B5
 Warks 81 B6
Cross Hands . . 57 A5
Cross-hands . . 73 D4
Cross Hands . . 55 C6
Crosshill E Ayrs . 193 C4
 Fife 209 A4
 S Ayrs 192 E3
Cross Hill 114 A2
Crosshouse . . . 192 B3
Cross Houses . . 94 A3
Crossings 176 B3
Cross in Hand
 E Sus 36 D3
 Leics 98 C2
Cross Inn Ceredig. 73 A6
 Ceredig 75 B4
 Rhondda 41 C5
Crosskeys 41 B7
Cross Keys . . . 36 A3
Crosskirk 279 A6
Cross Lane Head 95 B5
Crosslanes . . . 110 D2
Cross Lanes Corn . 3 C4
 N Yorks 148 A4
 Wrex 110 A2
Crosslee Borders 185 A6
 Renfs 205 B4
Crossmichael . . 173 B5
Crossmoor . . . 144 D4
Cross Oak 60 A3
Cross of
 Jackston . . . 256 C2
Cross o' th'
 hands 113 A6

Crossroads
 Aberds 245 C4
 E Ayrs 193 B4
Cross Street . . 104 D2
Cross Trickett's . 17 A4
Crossway Hereford 79 D4
 Mon 61 B6
 Powys 77 B4
Crossway Green . 79 A6
Crossways . . . 16 C1
Crosswell 72 C4
Crosswood . . . 75 A5
Crosthwaite . . . 154 B3
Croston 136 B3
Crostwick 121 D4
Crostwight . . . 121 C5
Crothair 288 D2
Crouch 36 A4
Croucheston . . . 31 C4
Crouch Hill . . . 29 D7
Crouch House
 Green 36 B2
Croughton . . . 82 D2
Crovie 268 C3
Crow 3 B4
Crowan 3 B4
Crowborough . . 36 C3
Crowcombe . . . 27 B6
Crowdecote . . . 129 C6
Crowden 138 D3
Crow Edge . . . 139 C4
Crowell 66 D2
Crowfield
 Northants . . . 82 C3
 Suff 88 B2
Crow Hill 62 A2
Crowhurst E Sus . 23 A5
 Sur 36 B1
Crowhurst Lane
 End 36 B1
Crowland 117 D5
Crowlas 2 B3
Crowle N Lincs . 141 B5
 Worcs 80 B2
Crowmarsh
 Gifford 47 A4
Crown Corner . 104 D3
Crownhill 6 B3
Crownland . . . 103 E6
Crownthorpe . . 104 A1
Crowntown . . . 3 B4
Crows-an-wra . . 2 C1
Crowshill 103 A5
Crowsnest . . . 94 A1
Crowthorne . . . 47 C6
Crowton 127 B5
Croxall 113 D5
Croxby 142 D3
Croxdale 167 B5
Croxden 113 B4
Croxley Green . . 67 D5
Croxton Cambs . . 84 A4
 N Lincs 142 B2
 Norf 103 C4
 Staffs 112 B1
Croxtonbank . . 112 B1
Croxton Kerrial . 115 C6
Croy Highld . . . 252 B3
 N Lanark 207 C5
Croyde 25 B5
Croydon Cambs . 85 C5
 London 49 C6
Crubenmore
 Lodge 241 C4
Cruckmeole . . . 94 A2
Cruckton 110 D3
Cruden Bay . . . 257 C5
Crudgington . . 111 D5
Crudwell 63 D5
Crug 93 D5
Crugmeer 9 D5
Crugybar 58 B3
Crulabhig 288 D2
Crumlin Crymlyn . 41 B7
Crumpsall 138 C1
Crundale Kent . . 38 A2
 Pembs 55 C5
Cruwys
 Morchard . . . 26 D3
Crux Easton . . . 46 D2
Crwbin 57 A4
Crya 283 G4
Cryers Hill . . . 66 D3

Crymlyn 123 C6
Crymych 73 C4
Crynant 40 A2
Crynfryn 75 B4
Cuaig 249 A4
Cuan 213 A5
Cubbington . . . 81 A6
Cubeck 156 C3
Cubert 4 B2
Cubley 139 C5
Cubley Common 113 B5
Cublington Bucks . 66 A3
 Hereford 78 D2
Cuckfield 35 D6
Cucklington . . . 30 C1
Cuckney 131 B5
Cuckoo Hill . . . 141 D5
Cuddesdon . . . 65 C7
Cuddington Bucks. 66 B2
 Ches W 127 B6
Cuddington
 Heath 110 A3
Cuddy Hill . . . 145 D4
Cudham 36 A2
Cudliptown . . . 11 D6
Cudworth Som . . 28 D3
 S Yorks 140 C1
Cuffley 68 C3
Cuiashader . . . 288 B6
Cuidhir 286 F2
Cuidhtinis 287 F5
Culbo 264 D2
Culbokie 252 A2
Culburnie 251 B6
Culcabock 252 B2
Culcairn 264 D2
Culcharry 253 A4
Culcheth 137 D5
Culdrain 255 C6
Culduie 249 B4
Culford 103 D4
Culfordheath . . 103 D4
Culgaith 165 C4
Culham 65 D6
Culkein 270 A3
Culkein
 Drumbeg . . . 270 A4
Culkerton 63 D5
Cullachie 253 D5
Cullen 267 C6
Cullercoats . . . 179 B5
Cullicudden . . . 264 D2
Cullingworth . . 147 D4
Cullipool 213 A5
Cullivoe 284 C7
Culloch 218 C2
Culloden 252 B3
Cullompton . . . 13 A5
Culmaily 265 A4
Culmazie 171 B5
Culmington . . . 94 C2
Culmstock 27 D6
Culnacraig 270 D3
Culnaknock . . . 259 B5
Culpho 88 C3
Culrain 264 A1
Culross 208 B2
Culroy 192 D3
Culsh Aberds . . . 243 C6
 Aberds 256 B3
Culshabbin . . . 171 B5
Culswick 285 J4
Cultercullen . . . 257 D4
Cults Aberdeen . 245 B5
 Aberds 255 C6
 Dumfries 171 C6
Culverstone
 Green 50 C3
Culverthorpe . . 116 A3
Culworth 82 C2
Culzie Lodge . . 263 C7
Cumberland
 Village 207 C5
Cumberworth . . 135 B5
Cuminestown . . 268 D3
Cumlewick . . . 285 L6
Cummersdale . . 175 C6
Cummertrees . . 174 B4
Cummingston . . 266 C2
Cumnock 193 C5
Cumnor 65 C5
Cumrew 176 D3

Cumwhinton . . . 176 D2
Cumwhitton . . . 176 D3
Cundall 158 D3
Cunninghamhead
 . . . . 204 D3
Cunnister 284 D7
Cupar 220 C3
Cupar Muir 220 C3
Cupernham 32 C2
Curbar 130 B2
Curbridge Hants . 32 C4
 Oxon 64 C4
Curdridge 32 C4
Curdworth 97 B4
Curland 28 D2
Curlew Green . . 89 A4
Currarie 180 B3
Curridge 46 B2
Currie 209 D4
Curry Mallet . . . 28 C3
Curry Rivel 28 C3
Curtisden Green . 37 B5
Curtisknowle . . . 7 B6
Cury 3 C4
Cushnie 268 C2
Cushuish 28 B1
Cusop 77 C6
Cutcloy 171 D6
Cutcombe 27 B4
Cutgate 138 B1
Cutiau 90 A4
Cutlers Green . . 86 D1
Cutnall Green . . 80 A1
Cutsdean 80 D3
Cutthorpe 130 B3
Cutts 285 K6
Cuxham 66 D1
Cuxton 51 C4
Cuxwold 142 C3
Cwm Bl Gwent . . 60 C3
 Denb 125 B5
 Swansea 40 B1
Cwmafan 40 B2
Cwmaman 41 B5
Cwmann 75 D4
Cwmavon 61 C4
Cwmbach Carms . 57 B4
 Carms 73 D5
 Powys 76 B4
 Powys 77 D5
Cwmbâch 41 A5
Cwmbelan 92 C3
Cwmbran
 Cwmbrân . . . 61 D4
Cwmbrwyno . . . 91 D5
Cwm-byr 58 B3
Cwmcarn 41 B7
Cwmcarvan . . . 61 C6
Cwm-Cewydd . . 91 A6
Cwm-cou 73 B5
Cwmcych 73 C5
Cwmdare 41 A4
Cwmderwen . . . 92 A3
Cwmdu Carms . . 58 B3
 Powys 60 A3
Cwmduad 73 C6
Cwm-Dulais . . . 57 B6
Cwmdwr 59 B4
Cwmfelin Bridgend 40 C3
 M Tydf 41 A5
Cwmfelin Boeth . 56 A1
Cwm-felin-fach . 41 B6
Cwmfelin
 Mynach 73 D5
Cwmffrwd 57 A4
Cwm Ffrwd-oer . 61 C4
Cwmgiedd 59 D4
Cwmgors 59 D4
Cwmgwili 57 A5
Cwmgwrach . . . 40 A3
Cwm-hesgen . . 108 C2
Cwmhiraeth . . . 73 C6
Cwm-hwnt . . . 59 E6
Cwmifor 58 C3
Cwm Irfon . . . 76 C2
Cwm-Llinau . . . 91 B6
Cwmllynfell . . . 59 D4
Cwm-mawr . . . 57 A5
Cwmorgan . . . 73 C5
Cwm-parc . . . 40 B4

Cwmpengraig . . . 73 C6
Cwm
 Penmachno . . 108 A2
Cwmrhos 60 A3
Cwmsychpant . . 74 D3
Cwmtillery 60 C4
Cwmwysg 59 C5
Cwm-y-glo Carms 57 A5
 Gwyn 123 D5
Cwmyoy 61 A4
Cwmystwyth . . 92 D1
Cwrt 91 B4
Cwrt-newydd . . 74 D3
Cwrt-y-cadno . . 58 A3
Cwrt-y-gollen . . 60 B4
Cyffylliog 125 D5
Cymer 40 B3
Cyncoed 41 C6
Cynghordy . . . 59 B5
Cynheidre 57 B4
Cynwyd 109 A5
Cynwyl Elfed . . 73 D6
Cywarch 91 A6

D

Dacre Cumb . . . 164 C2
 N Yorks 147 A5
Dacre Banks . . . 147 A5
Daddry Shield . 166 B1
Dadford 82 D3
Dadlington 97 B7
Dafarn Faig . . . 107 B4
Dafen 57 B5
Daffy Green . . . 103 A5
Dagenham 50 A1
Daglingworth . . 63 C5
Dagnall 67 B4
Dail Beag 288 C3
Dail bho Dheas . 288 A5
Dail bho Thuath 288 A5
Daill 200 B3
Dailly 181 A4
Dail Mor 288 C3
Dairsie or
 Osnaburgh . . 220 C4
Daisy Hill 137 C5
Dalabrog 286 D3
Dalavich 214 A2
Dalbeattie 173 B6
Dalblair 182 A4
Dalbog 232 A3
Dalbury 113 B6
Dalby IoM 152 D2
 N Yorks 159 D5
Dalchalloch . . . 229 B6
Dalchalm 274 D3
Dalchenna 214 B3
Dalchirach 254 C2
Dalchork 272 C3
Dalchreichart . . 239 A6
Dalchruin 218 C2
Dalderby 134 C2
Dale 54 D4
Dale Abbey . . . 114 B2
Dale Head 164 D2
Dalelia 235 D6
Dale of Walls . . 285 H3
Daless 253 C4
Dalfaber 242 A2
Dalgarven 204 D2
Dalgety Bay . . . 209 B4
Dalginross 218 B2
Dalguise 230 D3
Dalhalvaig 279 C4
Dalham 86 A3
Dalinlongart . . . 215 D4
Dalkeith 209 D6
Dallam 137 D4
Dallas 266 D2
Dalleagles 182 A3
Dallinghoo 88 B3
Dallington E Sus . 23 A4
 Northants 83 A4
Dallow 157 D5
Dalmadilly 245 A4
Dalmally 227 D6

Dalmarnock.....205 B6
Dalmary.......206 A3
Dalmellington..182 B2
Dalmeny.......208 C4
Dalmigavie 241 A5
Dalmigavie
Lodge........252 D2
Dalmore.......264 D2
Dalnabreck ...235 D5
Dalnacardoch
Lodge........229 A6
Dalnacroich...251 A5
Dalnaglar
Castle.......231 B5
Dalnahaitnach .253 D4
Dalnaspidal
Lodge........229 A5
Dalnavaid.....230 B4
Dalnavie......264 C2
Dalnawillan
Lodge........279 D6
Dalness.......237 D5
Dalnessie.....273 C4
Dalqueich 219 D5
Dalreavoch ...273 D5
Dalry.........204 D2
Dalrymple 192 D3
Dalserf.......194 A3
Dalston 175 C6
Dalswinton ...184 D2
Dalton Dumfries..174 A4
Lancs.........136 C3
Northumb......177 D7
Northumb......178 B3
N Yorks.......157 A5
N Yorks.......158 D3
S Yorks.......140 D2
Dalton-in-
Furness......153 C3
Dalton-le-Dale..168 A2
Dalton-on-Tees 157 A6
Dalton Piercy ..168 B2
Dalveich.....217 B6
Dalvina Lo....278 D2
Dalwhinnie ..241 D4
Dalwood......14 A2
Dalwyne......181 B5
Damerham.....31 D5
Damgate......105 A5
Dam Green....103 C6
Damnaglaur ...170 D3
Damside.......195 B6
Dam Side.....144 C4
Danbury.......70 C1
Danby.........159 A6
Danby Wiske...158 B2
Dandaleith....254 B3
Danderhall....209 D6
Danebridge...129 C4
Dane End.....68 A3
Danehill......36 D2
Danemoor
Green........103 A6
Danesford.....95 B5
Daneshill.....47 D4
Dangerous
Corner.......136 B4
Danskine.....210 D2
Darcy Lever...137 C6
Darenth.......50 B2
Daresbury....127 A5
Darfield.....140 C2
Darfoulds....131 B5
Dargate......52 C2
Darite.......6 A1
Darlaston.....96 B2
Darley.......147 B6
Darley Bridge ..130 C2
Darley Head...147 B5
Darlingscott ..81 C5
Darlington...167 D5
Darliston.....111 B4
Darlton......132 B2
Darnall......130 A3
Darnick......197 C4
Darowen......91 B6
Darra.........256 B2
Darracott....25 B5

Darras Hall 178 B3
Darrington.....140 A2
Darsham.......89 A5
Dartford......50 B2
Dartford
Crossing.....50 B2
Dartington....8 A1
Dartmeet.....12 D1
Dartmouth 8 B2
Darton.......139 C6
Darvel.......193 B5
Darwell Hole....23 A4
Darwen.......137 A5
Datchet......48 B2
Datchworth ...68 B2
Datchworth
Green........68 B2
Daubhill......137 C6
Daugh of
Kinermony ..254 B3
Dauntsey.....44 A3
Dava.........253 C6
Davenham 127 B6
Davenport
Green........128 B3
Daventry......82 A2
Davidson's
Mains........209 C5
Davidstow 10 C2
David's Well ...93 D4
Davington 185 B5
Daviot Aberds...256 D2
Highld.......252 C3
Davoch of
Grange.......267 D5
Davyhulme.....137 D6
Dawley.......95 A4
Dawlish......13 D4
Dawlish Warren .13 D4
Dawn.........124 B3
Daws Heath....51 A5
Daw's House...10 C4
Dawsmere 118 B1
Dayhills......112 B3
Daylesford....64 A3
Ddôl-Cownwy..109 D5
Ddrydwy......122 C3
Deadwater....187 D5
Deaf Hill.....167 B6
Deal.........53 D5
Deal Hall.....71 D4
Dean Cumb....162 B3
Devon.......7 A6
Devon.......25 A6
Dorset.......30 D3
Hants.......33 D4
Som.........29 A6
Deanburnhaugh 186 B2
Deane Gtr Man....137 C5
Hants.......46 D3
Deanich Lodge ..263 B5
Deanland.....30 D3
Dean Prior....7 A6
Dean Row.....128 A3
Deans.........208 D3
Deanscales ...162 B3
Deanshanger...83 D4
Deanston....218 D2
Dearham.....162 A3
Debach.......88 B3
Debden Essex...68 D4
Essex.........86 D1
Debden Cross...86 D1
Debenham.....88 A2
Dechmont 208 C3
Deddington...82 D1
Dedham......87 D6
Dedham Heath...87 D6
Deebank.....244 C3
Deene........99 B6
Deenethorpe...99 B6
Deepcar.....139 D5
Deepcut.....34 A2
Deepdale.....155 C6
Deeping Gate ..100 A3
Deeping St
James........100 A3
Deeping St
Nicholas.....117 D5
Deerhill......267 D5
Deerhurst....63 A4
Deerness.....283 G6

Defford.......80 C2
Defynnog 59 C6
Deganwy.....124 B2
Deighton N Yorks 158 A2
W Yorks......139 B4
York.........149 C5
Deiniolen....123 D5
Delabole.....9 C6
Delamere.....127 C5
Delfrigs......257 D4
Delliefure....254 C1
Dell Lodge....242 A3
Delnabo......243 A4
Delnadamph ...243 B5
Delph........138 C2
Delves.......166 A4
Delvine......231 D5
Dembleby.....116 B3
Denaby Main...140 D2
Denbigh Dinbych.125 C5
Denbury.......8 A2
Denby........114 A1
Denby Dale ...139 C5
Denchworth ...65 D4
Dendron......153 C3
Denel End.....84 D2
Denend.......255 C7
Denford......100 D1
Dengie........70 C3
Denham Bucks ..48 A3
Suff.........86 A3
Suff.........104 D2
Denham Street..104 D2
Denhead Aberds .269 D4
Fife.........221 C4
Denhead of
Arbilot......232 D3
Denhead of
Gray.........220 A4
Denholm......187 B4
Denholme 147 D4
Denholme
Clough.......147 D4
Denio........106 C3
Denmead.....33 D5
Denmore.....245 A6
Denmoss......256 B1
Dennington ...88 A3
Denny........207 B6
Dennyloanhead 207 B6
Denny Lodge...18 A2
Denshaw.....138 B2
Denside.....245 C5
Densole......39 A4
Denston......86 B3
Denstone.....113 A5
Dent.........155 C6
Denton Cambs...100 C3
Darl.........167 D5
E Sus.........22 B2
Gtr Man......138 D2
Kent.........39 A4
Lincs........115 B6
Norf.........104 C3
Northants.....83 B5
N Yorks......147 C5
Oxon.........65 C6
Denton's Green..136 D3
Denver........102 A2
Denwick......189 B5
Deopham.....103 A6
Deopham Green 103 B6
Depden........86 B3
Depden Green ..86 B3
Deptford London..49 B6
Wilts.........31 B4
Derby........114 B1
Derbyhaven...152 E2
Dereham.....120 D1
Deri.........41 A6
Derril........10 A4
Derringstone...39 A4
Derrington....112 C2
Derriton.....10 A4
Derryguaig ...224 C3
Derry Hill.....44 B3
Derrythorpe...141 C6
Dersingham...118 B3
Dervaig......224 A3
Derwen.......125 D5
Derwenlas 91 C5

Desborough ...99 C5
Desford......98 A1
Detchant.....199 C4
Detling.......37 A5
Deuddwr.....110 D1
Devauden.....61 D6
Devil's Bridge...75 A6
Devizes.......44 C4
Devol........204 A3
Devonport.....6 B3
Devonside ...208 A2
Devoran......4 D2
Dewar.......196 B2
Dewlish......16 B1
Dewsbury.....139 A5
Dewsbury Moor 139 A5
Dewshall Court..78 D2
Dhoon.......152 C4
Dhoor.......152 B4
Dhowin......152 A4
Dial Post.....21 A4
Dibden.......18 A3
Dibden Purlieu..18 A3
Dickleburgh...104 C2
Didbrook.....80 D3
Didcot.......46 A3
Diddington....84 A3
Diddlebury....94 C3
Didley.......78 D2
Didling......20 A1
Didmarton....44 A2
Didsbury.....138 D1
Didworthy.....7 A5
Digby........133 D5
Digg.........259 B4
Diggle.......138 C3
Digmoor......136 C3
Dihewyd......74 C3
Dilham.......121 C5
Dilhorne......112 A3
Dillarburn....194 B3
Dillington....84 A3
Dilston......178 C1
Dilton Marsh...30 A2
Dilwyn........78 B2
Dinas Carms...73 C5
Dinas.........106 C2
Dinas Cross...72 C3
Dinas Dinlle...107 A4
Dinas-Mawddwy .91 A6
Dinas Powys...41 D6
Dinder........29 A5
Dinedor......78 D3
Dingestow 61 B6
Dingle.......126 A3
Dingleden 37 C6
Dingley......99 C4
Dingwall.....252 A1
Dinlabyre....186 D4
Dinmael......109 A5
Dinmore......78 B2
Dinnet.......244 C1
Dinnington Som..28 D4
S Yorks......131 A5
T&W.........179 B4
Dinorwic.....123 D5
Dinton Bucks...66 B2
Wilts.........31 B4
Dinwoodie
Mains.......185 C4
Dinworthy....24 D4
Dippen.......191 C6
Dippenhall....33 A7
Dipple Moray...266 D4
S Ayrs.......181 A4
Diptford......7 B6
Dipton.......178 D3
Dirdhu........254 D1
Dirleton......210 B2
Dirt Pot.....165 A6
Discoed......77 A6
Diseworth....114 C2
Dishes.......282 E7
Dishforth....158 D2
Disley.......129 A4
Diss.........104 D2
Disserth......76 B4
Distington....162 B3
Ditchampton ..31 B4
Ditcheat......29 B6
Ditchingham ..104 B4
Ditchling....21 A6

Ditherington...111 D4
Dittisham.....8 B2
Ditton Halton..127 A4
Kent.........37 A5
Ditton Green...86 B2
Ditton Priors...95 C4
Divach.......251 D6
Divlyn........59 B4
Dixton Glos....80 D2
Mon.........61 B7
Dobcross.....138 C2
Dobwalls......5 A7
Doccombe 12 C2
Dochfour Ho. ..252 C2
Dochgarroch ..252 B2
Docking......119 B4
Docklow.......78 B3
Dockray......164 C1
Dockroyd....147 D4
Dodburn......186 C3
Doddinghurst ..69 D5
Doddington
Cambs.......101 B5
Kent.........51 D6
Lincs........133 B4
Northumb.....198 C3
Shrops.......95 D4
Doddiscombsleigh
..............12 C3
Dodford Northants 82 A3
Worcs........96 D2
Dodington....43 A6
Dodleston....126 C3
Dods Leigh ...112 B4
Dodworth....139 C6
Doe Green....127 A5
Doe Lea.....131 C4
Dogdyke.....134 D2
Dogmersfield ..47 D5
Dogridge.....45 A4
Dogsthorpe...100 A3
Dog Village...13 B4
Dolanog......109 D5
Dolau Powys....77 A5
Rhondda......41 C4
Dolbenmaen...107 B5
Dolfach......91 B7
Dolfor.......93 C5
Dol-fôr......91 B6
Dolgarrog....124 C2
Dolgellau....91 A5
Dolgran......58 B1
Dolhendre ...108 B3
Doll.........274 D2
Dollar.......208 A2
Dolley Green...77 A6
Dollwen......91 D4
Dolphin......126 B1
Dolphinholme ..145 B5
Dolphinton...195 B6
Dolton.......25 D6
Dolwen Conwy..124 B3
Powys........92 A3
Dolwyd......124 B3
Dolwyddelan..124 D2
Dôl-y-Bont...90 D4
Dol-y-cannau...77 C6
Dolyhir.......77 B6
Doncaster....140 C3
Donhead St
Andrew.......30 C3
Donhead St Mary 30 C3
Donibristle...209 B4
Donington....117 B5
Donington on
Bain........134 A2
Donington South
Ing..........117 B5
Donisthorpe...113 D7
Donkey Town...48 C2
Donnington Glos..64 A2
Hereford......79 D5
Shrops.......94 A3
Telford.......111 D6
W Berks......46 C2
W Sus........20 B1
Donnington
Wood........111 D6
Donyatt......28 D3
Doonfoot.....192 D3
Dorback Lodge .242 A3

Dorchester Dorset..15 B6
Oxon.........65 D6
Dordon.......97 A5
Dore.........130 A3
Dores........252 C1
Dorking......35 B4
Dormansland...36 B2
Dormanstown..168 C3
Dormington....78 C3
Dormston.....80 B2
Dornal.......181 D4
Dorney.......48 B2
Dornie.......249 D5
Dornoch......264 B3
Dornock......175 B5
Dorrery......279 C6
Dorridge......97 D4
Dorrington Lincs 133 D5
Shrops.......94 A2
Dorsington....80 C4
Dorstone......77 C7
Dorton.......66 B1
Dorusduain...250 D1
Dosthill......97 B5
Dottery......15 B4
Doublebois....5 A6
Dougarie.....191 B4
Doughton......63 D4
Douglas IoM....152 D3
S Lanark.....194 C3
Douglas &
Angus.......220 A4
Douglastown...232 D2
Douglas Water ..194 C3
Douglas West...194 C3
Doulting......29 A6
Dounby......282 E3
Doune Highld...272 D2
Stirling......218 D2
Doune Park...268 C2
Douneside....244 B1
Dounie.......264 A1
Dounreay.....279 B5
Dousland......7 A4
Dovaston.....110 C2
Dove Holes...129 B5
Dovenby......162 A3
Dover.........39 A5
Dovercourt...88 D3
Doverdale 79 A6
Doveridge....113 B5
Doversgreen...35 B5
Dowally......230 D4
Dowbridge...144 D4
Dowdeswell....63 B5
Dowlais......60 C2
Dowland......25 D6
Dowlish Wake...28 D3
Down Ampney...64 D2
Downcraig
Ferry........204 C1
Downderry.....6 B2
Downe........50 C1
Downend IoW...18 C4
S Glos.........43 B5
W Berks.......46 B2
Downfield.....220 A3
Downgate.....11 D4
Downham Essex..70 D1
Lancs........146 C1
Northumb.....198 C2
Downham
Market.......102 A2
Down Hatherley..63 A4
Downhead.....29 A6
Downhill Perth..219 A5
T&W.........179 D5
Downholland
Cross........136 C2
Downholme...157 B5
Downies.....245 C6
Downley......66 D3
Down St Mary...12 A2
Downside Som...29 A6
Sur..........35 A4
Down Thomas...7 B4
Downton Hants..17 B6
Wilts........31 C5
Downton on the
Rock........94 D2
Dowsby......116 C4
Dowsdale....117 D5

Dowthwaitehead
............163 B6
Doxey 112 C3
Doxford 189 A4
Doxford Park....179 D5
Doynton 43 B6
Draffan 194 B2
Dragonby 141 B7
Drakeland Corner . 7 B4
Drakemyre......204 C2
Drake's
Broughton.....80 C2
Drakes Cross....96 D3
Drakewalls......11 D5
Draughton
Northants.......99 D4
N Yorks.......147 B4
Drax.............141 A4
Draycote........98 D1
Draycott Derbys..114 B2
Glos...........81 D4
Som...........42 D3
Draycott in the
Clay...........113 C5
Draycott in the
Moors.........112 A3
Drayford........26 D2
Drayton Leics.....99 B5
Lincs.........117 B5
Norf..........120 D3
Oxon...........65 D5
Oxon..........82 C1
Ptsmth.........19 A5
Som...........28 C4
Worcs..........96 D2
Drayton Bassett..97 A4
Drayton
Beauchamp ...67 B4
Drayton Parslow..66 A3
Drayton St
Leonard........65 D6
Drebley........147 B4
Dreemskerry....152 B4
Dreenhill........55 C5
Drefach Carms....57 A5
Carms.........73 C5
Dre-fach Carms....75 D4
Ceredig........73 C6
Dreghorn.......192 B3
Drellingore......39 A4
Drem...........210 C2
Dresden........112 A3
Dreumasdal....286 C3
Drewsteignton...12 B2
Driby...........134 B3
Driffield E Yorks..150 B3
Glos...........63 D6
Drigg...........153 A1
Drighlington....139 A5
Drimnin........225 A4
Drimpton........14 A4
Drimsynie......215 B4
Drinisiadar.....288 H2
Drinkstone......87 A5
Drinkstone
Green..........87 A5
Drishaig........215 A4
Drissaig........214 A2
Drochil.........195 B6
Droitwich......112 C4
Droitwich Spa....80 A1
Droman........276 C2
Dron...........219 C6
Dronfield.......130 B3
Dronfield
Woodhouse ...130 B3
Drongan........182 A2
Dronley.........220 A3
Droxford........33 D5
Droylsden......138 D2
Druid...........109 A5
Druidston.......55 C4
Druimarbin.....237 B4
Druimavuic.....227 B5
Druimdrishaig..202 A2
Druimindarroch 235 B5
Druimyeon
More..........202 C1
Drum Argyll....203 A4
Perth.........219 D5
Drumbeg.......270 A4

Drumblade.....255 B6
Drumblair 256 B1
Drumbuie
Dumfries......182 D3
Highld........249 C4
Drumburgh.....175 C5
Drumburn......174 B2
Drumchapel....205 A5
Drumchardine..252 B1
Drumchork.....261 B5
Drumclog......193 B6
Drumderfit.....252 A2
Drumeldrie.....220 D4
Drumelzier.....195 C6
Drumfearn......247 C5
Drumgask......241 C4
Drumgley......232 C2
Drumguish.....241 C5
Drumin.........254 C2
Drumlasie......244 B3
Drumlemble.....190 D2
Drumligair......245 A6
Drumlithie......245 D4
Drummoddie....171 C5
Drummond......264 D2
Drummore......170 D3
Drummuir......255 B4
Drummuir
Castle.......255 B4
Drumnadrochit..251 D7
Drumnagorrach 267 D6
Drumoak......245 C4
Drumpark......183 D6
Drumphail......171 A4
Drumrash......173 A4
Drumrunie......271 D4
Drums..........257 D4
Drumsallie......236 B3
Drumstinchall...173 C6
Drumsturdy.....221 A4
Drumtochty
Castle.......244 E3
Drumtroddan...171 C5
Drumuie.......259 D4
Drumuillie.....253 D5
Drumvaich.....217 D6
Drumwhindle...257 C4
Drunkendub...233 D4
Drury..........126 C2
Drury Square....119 D6
Drybeck.......165 D4
Drybridge Moray 267 C5
N Ayrs........192 B3
Drybrook........62 B2
Dryburgh......197 C4
Dry Doddington.115 A4
Dry Drayton.....85 A5
Dryhope.......196 D1
Drylaw.........209 C5
Drym.............3 B4
Drymen.........206 B2
Drymuir........257 B4
Drynoch.......246 A3
Dryslwyn........58 C2
Dryton..........94 A3
Dubford........268 C3
Dubton.........232 C3
Duchally......271 C6
Duchlage......206 B1
Duck Corner.....89 C4
Duckington....127 D4
Ducklington.....65 C4
Duckmanton....131 B4
Duck's Cross.....84 B3
Duddenhoe End ..85 D6
Duddingston....209 C5
Duddington.....100 A1
Duddleswell.....36 D2
Duddo.........198 B3
Duddon........127 C5
Duddon Bridge..153 B3
Dudleston......110 B2
Dudleston
Heath.......110 B2
Dudley T&W.....179 B4
W Mid.........96 B2
Dudley Port.....96 B2
Duffield........114 A1
Duffryn Neath....40 B3
Newport.......42 A1
Dufftown......254 C4
Duffus.........266 C2

Dufton...........165 C4
Duggleby.......150 A1
Duirinish.......249 C4
Duisdalemore...247 C6
Duisky.........237 B4
Dukestown......60 B3
Dukinfield......138 D2
Dulas..........123 B4
Dulcote.........29 A5
Dulford.........13 A5
Dull...........230 D2
Dullatur........207 C5
Dullingham......86 B2
Dulnain Bridge..253 D5
Duloe Bedford....84 A3
Corn............6 B1
Dulsie.........253 B5
Dulverton.......27 C4
Dulwich.........49 B6
Dumbarton.....205 A3
Dumbleton.......80 D3
Dumcrieff......185 B4
Dumfries.......174 A2
Dumgoyne.......206 B3
Dummer.........33 A4
Dumpford........34 D1
Dumpton.........53 C5
Dun............233 C4
Dunain Ho......252 B2
Dunalastair....229 C6
Dunan.........247 B4
Dunans........214 C3
Dunball.........28 A3
Dunbar.........210 C3
Dunbeath.......275 B5
Dunbeg........226 C3
Dunblane.......218 D2
Dunbog........220 C2
Duncanston....252 A1
Duncanstone....255 D6
Dun
Charlabhaigh..288 C2
Dunchurch......98 D1
Duncote.........82 B3
Duncow........184 D2
Duncraggan....217 D5
Duncrievie......219 D6
Duncton........20 A2
Dundas Ho.....283 J5
Dundee........220 A4
Dundeugh......182 D3
Dundon.........29 B4
Dundonald.....192 B3
Dundonnell....262 B2
Dundonnell
Hotel.......262 B2
Dundonnell
House.......262 B3
Dundraw.......175 D5
Dundreggan....239 A7
Dundreggan
Lodge.......240 A1
Dundrennan....173 D5
Dundry.........43 C4
Dunecht.......245 B4
Dunfermline....208 B3
Dunfield........64 D2
Dunford Bridge.139 C4
Dungworth.....130 A2
Dunham........132 B3
Dunham-on-the-
Hill........127 B4
Dunhampton....79 A6
Dunham Town...128 A2
Dunholme.....133 B5
Dunino.........221 C5
Dunipace......207 B6
Dunira.........218 B2
Dunkeld........230 D4
Dunkerton......43 D6
Dunkeswell......13 A6
Dunkeswick....148 C2
Dunkirk Kent....52 D2
Norf..........120 C4
Dunk's Green....36 A4
Dunlappie......232 B3
Dunley Hants....46 D2
Worcs.........79 A5
Dunlichity
Lodge.......252 C2
Dunlop.........205 D4

Dunmaglass
Lodge.......252 D1
Dunmore Argyll..202 B2
Falk..........208 B1
Dunnet........280 A4
Dunnichen.....232 D3
Dunninald.....233 C5
Dunning.......219 C5
Dunnington
E Yorks........151 B4
Warks..........80 B3
York.........149 B5
Dunnockshaw...137 A7
Dunollie.......226 C3
Dunoon........203 A6
Dunragit.......170 B3
Dunrostan.....213 D5
Duns...........198 A1
Dunsby.........116 C4
Dunscore.......183 D6
Dunscroft......141 C4
Dunsdale.......168 D4
Dunsden Green...47 B5
Dunsfold........34 C3
Dunsford........12 C3
Dunshalt.......220 C2
Dunshillock....257 B4
Dunskey Ho.....170 B2
Dunsley........169 D6
Dunsmore.......66 C3
Dunsop Bridge..145 B6
Dunstable.......67 A5
Dunstall........113 C5
Dunstall
Common......80 C1
Dunstall Green...86 A3
Dunstan........189 B5
Dunstan Steads..189 A5
Dunster.........27 A4
Duns Tew........65 A5
Dunston Lincs...133 C5
Norf..........104 A3
Staffs........112 D3
T&W..........179 C4
Dunsville......140 C4
Dunswell.......150 D3
Dunsyre........195 B5
Dunterton.......11 D4
Duntisbourne
Abbots........63 C5
Duntisbourne
Leer..........63 C5
Duntisbourne
Rouse.........63 C5
Duntish.........15 A6
Duntocher.....205 A4
Dunton Bucks....66 A3
C Beds.........84 C4
Norf..........119 B5
Dunton Bassett..98 B2
Dunton Green...36 A3
Dunton Wayletts..69 D6
Duntulm........259 A4
Dunure........192 D2
Dunvant.........57 C5
Dunvegan......258 D2
Dunwich.......105 D5
Dunwood.......129 D4
Dupplin Castle..219 C5
Durdar.........175 C7
Durgates........36 C4
Durham........167 A5
Durisdeer......183 B6
Durisdeermill..183 B6
Durkar.........139 B6
Durleigh........28 B2
Durley Hants.....32 C4
Wilts..........45 C6
Durnamuck.....262 A2
Durness.......277 B5
Durno.........256 D2
Duror.........236 D3
Durran Argyll...214 B2
Highld........280 B3
Durrington Wilts..31 A5
W Sus.........21 B4
Dursley.........62 D3
Durston........28 C2
Durweston......16 A2
Dury...........285 G6
Duston.........83 A4
Duthil.........253 D5

Dutlas..........93 D6
Duton Hill......69 A6
Dutson..........10 C4
Dutton.........127 B5
Duxford Cambs....85 C6
Oxon..........65 D4
Dwygyfylchi...124 B2
Dwyran.........123 D4
Dyce..........245 A5
Dye House......178 D1
Dyffryn Bridgend..40 B3
Carms..........73 D6
Pembs.........72 C2
Dyffryn
Ardudwy 107 D5
Dyffryn Castell..91 D5
Dyffryn Ceidrych .59 C4
Dyffryn Cellwen ..59 E5
Dyke Lincs......116 C4
Moray........253 A5
Dykehead Angus .232 B2
N Lanark......207 E6
Stirling.......206 A3
Dykelands......233 B5
Dykends.......231 C6
Dykeside......256 B2
Dykesmains....204 D2
Dylife..........91 C6
Dymchurch......38 C2
Dymock.........79 D5
Dyrham.........43 B6
Dysart........209 A6
Dyserth........125 B5

E

Eachwick 178 D3
Eadar Dha
Fhadhail 287 A5
Eagland Hill....144 C4
Eagle.........132 C3
Eagle Barnsdale 132 C3
Eagle Moor 132 C3
Eaglescliffe....168 D2
Eaglesfield Cumb 162 B3
Dumfries......175 A5
Eaglesham.....205 C5
Eaglethorpe....100 B2
Eairy..........152 D2
Eakley Lanes....83 B5
Eakring........132 C1
Ealand.........141 B6
Ealing..........49 A4
Eals..........177 D4
Eamont Bridge..164 C3
Earby..........146 C3
Earcroft.......137 A5
Eardington......95 B5
Eardisland.....78 B2
Eardisley........77 C7
Eardiston Shrops 110 C3
Worcs.........79 A4
Earith.........101 D5
Earl Barton......83 A5
Earl Sterndale..129 C5
Earlston Borders 197 C4
E Ayrs.......193 B4
Earl Stonham....88 B2
Earlswood Mon....61 D7
Sur...........35 B5
Warks.........96 D4

Eartham 20 B2
Easby N Yorks...157 A5
N Yorks.......159 A4
Easdale........213 A5
Easebourne.....34 D1
Easenhall.......98 D1
Eashing.........34 B2
Easington Bucks..66 B1
Durham.......168 A2
E Yorks.......143 B5
Northumb.....199 C5
Oxon...........66 D1
Oxon...........82 D1
Redcar.......169 D5
Easington
Colliery......168 A2
Easington Lane..167 A6
Easingwold....148 A4
Easole Street....53 D4
Eassie.........232 D1
East Aberthaw ...41 E5
East Adderbury...82 D1
East Allington 7 C6
East Anstey......26 C3
East Appleton..157 B6
East Ardsley...139 A6
East Ashling.....19 A7
East Auchronie..245 B5
East Ayton.....160 C3
East Bank.......60 C4
East Barkwith..133 A6
East Barming....37 A5
East Barnby....169 D6
East Barnet.....68 D2
East Barns.....211 C4
East Barsham..119 B6
East Beckham...120 B3
East Bedfont....48 B3
East Bergholt....87 D6
East Bilney.....119 D6
East Blatchington 22 B2
East Boldre......18 A2
East Brent.......42 D2
East Bridgford..115 A4
East Buckland....26 B1
East Budleigh....13 C5
East Burrafirth..285 H5
East Burton.....16 C2
Eastbury London..67 D5
W Berks........46 B1
East Butsfield..166 A4
East Butterwick.141 C6
Eastby.........147 B4
East Cairnbeg..233 A5
East Calder....208 D3
East Carleton..104 A2
East Carlton
Northants......99 C5
W Yorks......147 C6
East Chaldon....16 C1
East Challow.....46 A1
East Chiltington..21 A6
East Chinnock...29 D4
East Chisenbury..45 D5
Eastchurch......52 B1
East Clandon....34 A3
East Claydon....66 A2
East Clyne.....274 D2
East Coker......29 D5
Eastcombe......63 C4
East Combe......27 B6
East Common...149 D5
East Compton....29 A6
Eastcote London..48 A4
Northants......82 B3
W Mid.........97 D4
Eastcott Corn....24 D3
Wilts..........44 D4
East
Cottingwith...149 C6
Eastcourt Wilts...45 C6
Wilts..........63 D5
East Cowes......18 B4
East Cowick....141 A4
East Cowton....157 A7

East
Cramlington . . . 179 B4
East Cranmore . . 29 A6
East Creech 16 C3
East Croachy . . . 252 D2
East Croftmore . . 242 A4
East Curthwaite .164 A1
East Dean E Sus. . 22 C3
  Hants 31 C6
  W Sus. 20 A2
East Down 25 A7
East Drayton . . . 132 B2
East Ella 142 A2
East End Dorset . . 16 B3
  E Yorks 143 A4
  Hants 18 B2
  Hants 33 C5
  Hants 46 C2
  Herts 69 A4
  Kent 37 C6
  N Som 42 B3
  Oxon. 65 B4
Easter Ardross . 264 C2
Easter Balmoral 243 C5
Easter
  Boleskine 251 D7
Easter Compton . . 43 A4
Easter Cringate . 207 B5
Easter Davoch . .244 B1
Easter Earshaig .184 B3
Easter Fearn . . .264 B2
Easter
  Galcantray . . .253 B4
Eastergate 20 B2
Easterhouse . . . 207 D4
Easter Howgate .209 D5
Easter Howlaws .197 B6
Easter Kinkell . .252 A1
Easter
  Lednathie 232 B1
Easter Milton . . .253 A5
Easter Moniack .252 B1
Eastern Green . . . 97 C5
Easter Ord 245 B5
Easter Quarff . . .285 K6
Easter Rhynd . . .219 C6
Easter Row 207 A5
Easter
  Silverford 268 C2
Easter Skeld . . . 285 J5
Easterton 44 D4
Eastertown 42 D2
Eastertown of
  Auchleuchries .257 C5
Easter Whyntie . .267 C7
East Farleigh 37 A5
East Farndon 99 C4
East Ferry 141 D6
Eastfield
  N Lanark 208 D1
  N Yorks. 160 C4
Eastfield Hall . .189 C5
East Fortune . . . 210 C2
East Garston 46 B1
Eastgate Durham 166 B2
  Norf 120 C3
East Ginge 46 A2
East Goscote . . . 115 D4
East Grafton 45 C6
East Grimstead . . 31 C6
East Grinstead . . 36 C1
East Guldeford . . 38 C1
East Haddon 82 A3
East Hagbourne . 46 A3
East Halton 142 B3
Eastham 126 A3
East Ham 50 A1
Eastham Ferry . .126 A3
Easthampstead . . 47 C6
East Hanney 65 D5
East
  Hanningfield . . 70 C1
East Hardwick . .140 B2
East Harling 103 C5
East Harlsey . . . 158 B3
East Harnham . . . 31 C5
East Harptree . . . 43 D4
East Harting 33 D6

East Hatley 85 B4
East Hauxwell . . 157 B5
East Haven 221 A5
Eastheath 47 C6
East Heckington 117 A4
East
  Hedleyhope . . .167 A4
East Hendred 46 A2
East Herrington .179 D5
East Heslerton . .160 D3
East Hoathly 22 A3
Easthope 94 B3
Easthorpe Essex . 70 A3
  Leics. 115 B6
  Notts 132 D2
East Horrington . . 29 A5
East Horsley 34 A3
East Horton 198 C4
Easthouses 209 D6
East Huntspill . . . 28 A3
East Hyde 67 B6
East Ilkerton 26 A2
East Ilsley 46 A2
Eastington Devon .12 A2
  Glos 62 C3
  Glos 64 B2
East Keal 134 C3
East Kennett 45 C5
East Keswick . . . 148 C2
East Kilbride . . . 205 C6
East Kirkby 134 C3
East Knapton . . .160 D2
East Knighton . . . 16 C2
East Knoyle 30 B2
East Kyloe 199 C4
East Lambrook . . 28 D4
East Lamington .264 C3
East Langdon 39 A5
East Langton 99 B4
East Langwell . . .273 D5
East Lavant 20 B1
East Lavington . . 20 A2
East Layton 157 A5
Eastleach
  Turville 64 C2
East Leake 114 C3
East Learmouth .198 C4
Eastleigh Devon . 25 C5
  Hants 32 D3
East Leigh 12 A1
East Lexham . . . 119 D5
East Lilburn 188 A3
Eastling 51 D6
East Linton 210 C2
East Liss 33 C6
East Looe 6 B1
East Lound 141 D5
East Lulworth . . . 16 C2
East Lutton 150 A2
East Lydford 29 B5
East Mains 244 C3
East Malling 37 A5
East March 220 A4
East Marden 33 D7
East Markham . . 132 B2
  Lincs. 135 D4
East Marton 146 B3
East Meon 33 C5
East Mere 27 D4
East Mersea 71 B4
East Mey 281 A5
East Molesey 49 C4
Eastmoor Derbys 130 B3
  Norf 102 A3
East Morden 16 B3
East Morton 147 C4
East Ness 159 D5
East Newton . . . 151 D5
Eastney 19 B5
Eastnor 79 D5
East Norton 99 A4
East Nynehead . . 27 C6
East Oakley 46 D3
Eastoft 141 B6
East Ogwell 12 D3
Eastoke 19 B6
Easton Cambs. . .100 D3
  Cumb 175 C5
  Cumb 176 B2
  Devon. 12 C2
  Dorset 15 D6
  Hants 32 B4

Easton continued
  Lincs. 116 C2
  Norf 120 D3
  Som 29 A5
  Suff 88 B3
  Wilts. 44 B2
Easton Grey 44 A2
Easton-in-
  Gordano 43 B4
Easton Maudit . . 83 B5
Easton on the
  Hill 100 A2
Easton Royal 45 C6
East Orchard 30 D2
East Ord 198 A3
East Panson 11 B4
East Peckham . . . 37 B4
East Pennard 29 B5
East Perry 84 A3
East Portlemouth . . 7 D6
East Prawle 8 D1
East Preston 20 B3
East Putford 25 D4
East
  Quantoxhead . . 27 A6
East Rainton 167 A6
East Ravendale .143 D4
East Raynham . . 119 C5
Eastrea 101 B4
East Rhidorroch
  Lodge 262 A4
Eastriggs 175 B5
East Rigton 148 C2
Eastrington 141 A5
East Rounton . . .158 A3
East Row 169 D6
East Rudham . . . 119 C5
East Runton 120 A3
East Ruston 121 C5
Eastry 53 D5
East Saltoun 210 D1
East Sleekburn . .179 A4
East Somerton . . 121 D6
East Stockwith . .141 D5
East Stoke Dorset . 16 C2
  Notts 115 A5
East Stour 30 C2
East Stourmouth . 53 C4
East Stowford . . . 26 C1
East Stratton . . . 32 B4
East Studdal 39 A5
East Suisnish . . .248 C2
East Taphouse . . . 5 A6
East-the-Water . . 25 C5
East Thirston . . .189 D4
East Tilbury 50 B3
East Tisted 33 B6
East Torrington .133 A6
East
  Tuddenham . . .120 D2
East Tytherley . . . 32 C1
East Tytherton . . 44 B3
East Village 12 A3
Eastville Bristol . 43 B5
  Lincs. 135 D4
East Wall 94 B3
East Walton 119 D4
Eastwell 115 C5
East Wellow 32 C2
East Wemyss . . .209 A6
East Whitburn . .208 D2
Eastwick Herts. . . 68 B4
  Shetland. 284 F5
East Williamston . 32 D1
East Winch 118 D3
East Winterslow . 31 B6
East Wittering . . . 19 B6
East Witton 157 C5
Eastwood Notts .114 A2
  Southend 51 A5
  W Yorks 138 A3
East Woodburn . .177 A7
East Woodhay . . . 46 C2
East Worldham . . 33 B6
East Worlington . 26 D2
East Worthing . . . 21 B4
Eathorpe 81 A6
Eaton Ches E. . . .128 C3
  Ches W. 127 C5
  Leics. 115 C5
  Norf 104 A3

Eaton continued
  Notts 132 B2
  Oxon. 65 C5
  Shrops 94 C1
  Shrops 94 C3
Eaton Bishop. . . . 78 D2
Eaton Bray 67 A4
Eaton
  Constantine . . . 94 A3
Eaton Green 67 A4
Eaton Hastings . . 64 D3
Eaton on Tern . . .111 C5
Eaton Socon 84 B3
Eavestone 147 A6
Ebberston 160 C2
Ebbesbourne
  Wake 30 C3
Ebbw Vale Glyn
  Ebwy. 60 C3
Ebchester. 178 D3
Ebford 13 C4
Ebley 63 C4
Ebnal 110 A3
Ebrington 81 D4
East
  Quantoxhead . . 27 A6
Ecchinswell 46 D2
Ecclaw 211 D4
Ecclefechan 175 A4
Eccles Borders . .197 B6
  Gtr Man 137 D6
  Kent 51 C4
Ecclesall. 130 A3
Ecclesfield 139 D6
Ecclesgreig 233 B5
Eccleshall 112 C2
Eccleshill 147 D5
Ecclesmachan . .208 C3
Eccles on Sea . . 121 C6
Eccles Road. . . . 103 B6
Eccleston
  Ches W. 127 C4
  Lancs 136 B4
  Mers. 136 D3
Eccleston Park . .136 D3
Eccup 148 C1
Echt. 245 B4
Eckford 187 A6
Eckington
  Derbys 131 B4
  Worcs. 80 C2
Ecton 83 A5
Edale 129 A6
Edburton 21 A5
Edderside 174 D3
Edderton 264 B3
Eddistone 24 C3
Eddleston 196 B1
Edenbridge 36 B2
Edenfield 137 B6
Edenhall 164 B3
Edenham 116 C3
Eden Park 49 C6
Edensor 130 C2
Edentaggart 215 C6
Edenthorpe 140 C4
Edentown 175 C6
Ederline 214 B1
Edern 106 C2
Edgarley 29 B5
Edgbaston 96 C3
Edgcott Bucks . . . 66 A1
  Som 26 B3
Edge 94 A1
Edgebolton 111 C4
Edge End 62 B1
Edgefield 120 B2
Edgefield Street 120 B2
Edge Green 127 D4
Edge Hill. 136 D2
Edgeside 138 A1
Edgeworth 63 C5
Edgmond 111 D6
Edgmond
  Marsh. 111 C6
Edgton 94 C1
Edgware 68 D1
Edgworth 137 B6
Edinample 217 B5
Edinbane 258 C3
Edinburgh 209 C5
Edingale 113 D6
Edingight Ho. . . .267 D6
Edingley 131 D6

Edingthorpe 121 B5
Edingthorpe
  Green 121 B5
Edington Som. . . . 28 B3
  Wilts. 44 D3
Edintore 255 B5
Edith Weston 99 A6
Edithmead 28 A3
Edlesborough . . . 67 B4
Edlingham 189 C4
Edlington 134 B2
Edmondsham . . . 31 D4
Edmondsley. 167 A5
Edmondthorpe . .115 D6
Edmonstone 282 E6
Edmonton 68 D3
Edmundbyers . . .178 D2
Ednam 197 C6
Ednaston 113 A6
Edradynate 230 C2
Edrom 198 A2
Edstaston 111 B4
Edstone 81 A4
Edvin Loach. 79 B4
Edwalton 114 B3
Edwardstone 87 C5
Edwinsford 58 B3
Edwinstowe 131 C6
Edworth 84 C4
Edwyn Ralph . . . 79 B4
Edzell 232 B3
Efail Isaf 41 C5
Efailnewydd. . . .106 C3
Efailwen 72 D4
Efenechtyd 125 D6
Effingham 35 A4
Effirth 285 H5
Efford 12 A3
Egdon 80 B2
Egerton Gtr Man. 137 B6
  Kent 37 B7
Egerton Forstal . . 37 B6
Eggborough 140 A3
Eggbuckland 7 B4
Eggington 67 A4
Egginton 113 C6
Egglescliffe 168 D2
Eggleston 166 C2
Egham 48 B3
Egleton 99 A5
Eglingham 189 B4
Egloshayle 9 D5
Egloskerry 10 C3
Eglwysbach 124 B3
Eglwys-Brewis . . 41 E5
Eglwys Cross. . . 110 A3
Eglwys Fach 91 C4
Eglwyswen 73 C4
Eglwyswrw. 72 C4
Egmanton 132 C2
Egremont Cumb. .162 C3
  Mers. 136 D2
Egton 159 A7
Egton Bridge. . . .159 A7
Eight Ash Green . 70 A3
Eignaig 226 B2
Eil. 241 A6
Eilanreach 238 A2
Eileanach
  Lodge. 264 D1
Eilean Darach . .262 B3
Einacleite. 288 E2
Eisgean. 288 F4
Eisingrug 107 C6
Elan Village 76 A3
Elberton 43 A5
Elburton 7 B4
Elcho 219 B6
Elcombe 45 A5
Eldernell 101 B5
Eldersfield 79 D6
Elderslie 205 B4
Eldon 167 C5
Eldrick 181 C4
Eldroth 146 A1
Eldwick 147 C5
Elfhowe 154 B3
Elford Northumb. 199 C5
  Staffs 113 D5
Elgin 266 C3
Elgol 247 C4
Elham 38 A3

Elie. 221 D4
Elim 122 B3
Eling 32 D2
Elishader 259 B5
Elishaw. 188 D1
Elkesley 132 B1
Elkstone 63 B5
Ellan 253 D4
Elland 139 A4
Ellary 202 A2
Ellastone 113 A5
Ellemford 211 D4
Ellenbrook. 152 D3
Ellenhall 112 C2
Ellen's Green . . . 34 C3
Ellerbeck 158 B3
Ellerburn 160 C2
Ellerby 169 D5
Ellerdine Heath .111 C5
Ellerhayes 13 A4
Elleric 227 B5
Ellerker. 141 A7
Ellerton E Yorks .149 D6
  Shrops 111 C6
Ellesborough. . . . 66 C3
Ellesmere. 110 B3
Ellesmere Port .127 B4
Ellingham Norf . .105 B4
  Northumb. 189 A4
Ellingstring 157 C5
Ellington Cambs. 100 D3
  Northumb. 189 D5
Elliot 221 A6
Ellisfield 33 A5
Ellistown 114 D2
Ellon 257 C4
Ellonby 164 B2
Ellough 105 C5
Elloughton 142 A1
Ellwood 62 C1
Elm 101 A6
Elmbridge 80 A2
Elmdon Essex. . . . 85 D6
  W Mid 97 C4
Elmdon Heath. . . 97 C4
Elmers End 49 C6
Elmesthorpe 98 B1
Elmfield 19 B5
Elm Hill. 30 C2
Elmhurst. 113 D5
Elmley Castle . . . 80 C2
Elmley Lovett . . . 79 A6
Elmore 62 B3
Elmore Back 62 B3
Elm Park 50 A2
Elmscott. 24 C3
Elmsett 87 C6
Elmstead Market . 71 A4
Elmsted 38 A3
Elmstone 53 C4
Elmstone
  Hardwicke. 63 A5
Elmswell E Yorks .150 B2
  Suff 87 A5
Elmton 131 B5
Elphin 271 C5
Elphinstone 209 C6
Elrick. 245 B5
Elrig 171 C5
Elsdon 188 D2
Elsecar 140 C1
Elsenham 69 A5
Elsfield 65 B6
Elsham 142 B2
Elsing 120 D2
Elslack 146 C3
Elson 110 B2
Elsrickle 195 B5
Elstead 34 B2
Elsted 33 D7
Elsthorpe 116 C3
Elstob 167 C6
Elston Notts 115 A5
  Wilts. 31 A4
Elstone 26 D1
Elstow 84 C2
Elstree 68 D1
Elstronwick 151 D5
Elswick 144 D4
Elsworth. 85 A5
Elterwater 154 A2
Eltham 50 B1

Eltisley 85 B4
Elton Cambs 100 B2
  Ches W. 127 B4
  Derbys 130 C2
  Glos 62 B3
  Hereford 94 D2
  Notts 115 B5
  Stockton 168 D2
Elton Green 127 B4
Elvanfoot 184 A2
Elvaston 114 B2
Elveden 103 D4
Elvingston 210 C1
Elvington Kent . . . 53 D4
  York 149 C5
Elwick Hrtlpl 168 B2
  Northumb 199 C5
Elworth 128 C2
Elworthy 27 B5
Ely Cambs 102 C1
  Cardiff 41 D6
Emberton 83 C5
Embleton Cumb . 163 A4
  Northumb 189 A5
Embo 265 A4
Emborough 43 D5
Embo Street 265 A4
Embsay 147 B4
Emersons Green . 43 B5
Emery Down 18 A1
Emley 139 B5
Emmbrook 47 C5
Emmer Green . . . 47 B5
Emmington 66 C2
Emneth 101 A6
Emneth
  Hungate. 101 A7
Empingham 99 A6
Empshott 33 B6
Emstrey 111 D4
Emsworth. 19 A6
Enborne 46 C2
Enchmarsh 94 B3
Enderby 98 B2
Endmoor 154 C4
Endon 129 D4
Endon Bank . . . 129 D4
Enfield 68 D3
Enfield Wash. . . 68 D3
Enford. 45 D5
Engamoor 285 H4
Engine Common . 43 A5
Englefield 47 B4
Englefield Green . 48 B2
Englesea-brook 128 D2
English Bicknor . 62 B1
Englishcombe. . 43 C6
English
  Frankton 110 C3
Enham Alamein . 32 A2
Enmore 28 B2
Ennerdale
  Bridge 162 C3
Enoch 183 B6
Enochdhu. 231 B4
Ensay. 224 B2
Ensbury 17 B4
Ensdon 110 D3
Ensis 25 C6
Enstone 65 A4
Enterkinfoot . . 183 B6
Enterpen 158 A3
Enville. 95 C6
Eolaigearraidh . 286 F3
Eorabus 224 D2
Eòropaidh 288 A6
Epperstone . . . 115 A4
Epping 69 C4
Epping Green
  Essex 68 C4
  Herts 68 C2
Epping Upland . 68 C4
Eppleby 167 D4
Eppleworth . . . 150 D3
Epsom. 49 C5
Epwell. 81 C6
Epworth 141 C5
Epworth
  Turbary 141 C5
Erbistock. 110 A2
Erbusaig 249 D4
Erchless Castle. . 251 B6

Erdington. 96 B4
Eredine. 214 B2
Eriboll. 277 C5
Ericstane 184 A3
Eridge Green. . . 36 C3
Erines 202 A3
Eriswell. 102 D3
Erith 50 B2
Erlestoke 44 D3
Ermine 133 B4
Ermington 7 B5
Erpingham. . . . 120 B3
Errogie 252 D1
Errol 220 B2
Erskine 205 A4
Erskine Bridge . 205 A4
Ervie 170 A2
Erwarton 88 D3
Erwood. 77 C4
Eryholme 157 A7
Eryrys 126 D2
Escomb. 167 C4
Escrick 149 C5
Esgairdawe . . . 58 A3
Esgairgeiliog. . . 91 B5
Esh. 167 A4
Esher. 48 C4
Esholt 147 C5
Eshott 189 D5
Eshton. 146 B3
Esh Winning . . 167 A4
Eskadale. 251 C6
Eskbank 209 D6
Eskdale Green . 163 D4
Eskdalemuir . . 185 C5
Eske. 150 C3
Eskham. 143 D5
Esk Valley . . . 159 A7
Esprick 144 D4
Essendine . . . 116 D3
Essendon 68 C2
Essich 252 C2
Essington . . . 96 A2
Esslemont . . . 257 D4
Eston. 168 D3
Eswick. 285 H6
Etal 198 C3
Etchilhampton . 44 C4
Etchingham. . . 37 D5
Etchinghill Kent. 38 B3
  Staffs 112 B4
Ethie Castle. . 233 D4
Ethie Mains . . 233 D4
Etling Green . . 120 D2
Eton. 48 B2
Eton Wick . . . 48 B2
Etteridge . . . 241 C4
Ettersgill . . . 166 C1
Ettingshall . . . 96 B2
Ettington . . . 81 C5
Etton E Yorks. . 150 C2
  Pboro 100 A3
Ettrick 185 A5
Ettrickbridge . 186 A2
Ettrickhill . . . 185 A5
Etwall 113 B6
Euston 103 D4
Euximoor Drove 101 B6
Euxton 137 B4
Evanstown . . 41 C4
Evanton . . . 264 D2
Evedon . . . 116 A3
Evelix 264 A3
Evenjobb . . . 77 A6
Evenley . . . 82 D2
Evenlode . . . 64 A3
Evenwood . . 167 C4
Evenwood Gate .167 C4
Everbay. . . . 282 E7
Evercreech . . 29 B6
Everdon . . . 82 B2
Everingham . 149 C7
Everleigh . . . 45 D6
Everley . . . 160 C3
Eversholt . . . 84 D1
Evershot . . . 15 A5
Eversley . . . 47 C5
Eversley Cross . 47 C5
Everthorpe. . . 150 D2
Everton C Beds. . 84 B4
  Hants 18 B1
  Mers. 136 D2

Everton continued
  Notts 141 D4
Evertown 175 A6
Evesbatch 79 C4
Evesham. 80 C3
Evington 98 A3
Ewden Village. . 139 D5
Ewell 49 C5
Ewell Minnis . . 39 A4
Ewelme. 66 D1
Ewen 63 D6
Ewenny 40 D4
Ewerby 116 A4
Ewerby Thorpe. 116 A4
Ewes 185 C6
Ewesley 188 D3
Ewhurst 34 B3
Ewhurst Green
  E Sus 37 D5
  Sur 34 C3
Ewloe 126 C3
Ewloe Grn. . . 126 C2
Ewood. . . . 137 A5
Eworthy . . . 11 B5
Ewshot . . . 33 A7
Ewyas Harold . 61 A5
Exbourne . . . 11 A7
Exbury . . . 18 B3
Exebridge. . . 27 C4
Exelby . . . 157 C6
Exeter . . . 13 B4
Exford . . . 26 B3
Exhall . . . 80 B4
Exley Head . . 147 D4
Exminster . . 13 C4
Exmouth . . . 13 C5
Exnaboe . . . 285 M5
Exning . . . 86 A2
Exton Devon . 13 C4
  Hants . . . 33 C5
  Rutland. . . 116 D2
  Som . . . 27 B4
Exwick . . . 13 B4
Eyam . . . 130 B2
Eydon . . . 82 B2
Eye Hereford . 78 A2
  Pboro . . . 100 A4
  Suff . . . 104 D2
Eye Green . . 100 A4
Eyemouth . . 211 D6
Eyeworth . . 85 C4
Eyhorne Street . 37 A6
Eyke. . . 88 B4
Eynesbury . . 84 B3
Eynort . . 246 B2
Eynsford . . 50 C2
Eynsham. . 65 C5
Eype. . . 14 B4
Eyre Highld . 248 C2
  Highld. . . 259 C4
Eythorne. . 39 A4
Eyton Hereford . 78 A2
  Shrops . . 94 C1
  Wrex . . . 110 A2
Eyton upon the
  Weald Moors .111 D5

F

Faccombe . . 46 D1
Faceby . . . 158 A3
Facit . . . 138 B1
Faddiley . . 127 D5
Fadmoor . . 159 C5
Faerdre . . 40 A1
Failand . . 43 B4
Failford . . 193 C4
Failsworth . 138 C1
Fain . . . 262 C3
Fairbourne . . 90 A4
Fairburn . . 140 A2
Fairfield Derbys . 129 B5
  Stockton. . 168 D2
  Worcs. . . 80 C3
  Worcs. . . 96 D2
Fairford . . 64 C2
Fair Green . 118 D3
Fairhaven. . 136 A2
Fair Hill. . 164 B3
Fairlie . . 204 C2
Fairlight . . 23 A6

Fairlight Cove . . 23 A6
Fairmile 13 B5
Fairmilehead. . . 209 D5
Fairoak 111 B6
Fair Oak 32 D3
Fair Oak Green . 47 C4
Fairseat 50 C3
Fairstead Essex . 70 B1
  Norf 118 D3
Fairwarp. . . . 36 D2
Fairy Cottage . 152 C4
Fairy Cross. . . 25 C5
Fakenham . . 119 C6
Fakenham
  Magna . . . 103 D5
Fala 210 D1
Fala Dam . . 210 D1
Falahill . . . 196 A2
Falcon. . . . 79 D4
Faldingworth . 133 A5
Falfield . . . 62 D2
Falkenham . . 88 D3
Falkirk . . . 208 C1
Falkland . . 220 D2
Falla . . . 187 B6
Fallgate . . 130 C3
Fallin . . . 207 A6
Fallowfield. . 138 D1
Fallsidehill. . 197 B5
Falmer . . . 21 B6
Falmouth . . 4 D3
Falsgrave . . 160 C4
Falstone . . 177 A5
Fanagmore . 276 D2
Fangdale Beck . 159 B4
Fangfoss . . 149 B6
Fankerton . . 207 B5
Fanmore . . 224 B3
Fannich Lodge . 262 D4
Fans. . . . 197 B5
Far Bank. . . 140 B4
Far Bletchley. . 83 D5
Farcet . . . 100 B4
Farden . . . 94 D3
Fareham . . 19 A4
Farewell . . 113 D4
Far Forest . . 95 D5
Farforth . . 134 B3
Faringdon . . 64 D3
Farington . . 136 A4
Farlam . . 176 D3
Farlary . . 273 D5
Far Laund. . 114 A1
Farleigh N Som. . 42 C3
  Sur . . . 49 C6
Farleigh
  Hungerford. . 44 D2
Farleigh Wallop . 33 A5
Farlesthorpe . . 135 B4
Farleton Cumb . 154 C4
  Lancs . . . 145 A5
Farley Shrops . 94 A1
  Staffs . . . 113 A4
  Wilts. . . . 31 C6
Farley Green . 34 B3
Farley Hill Luton . 67 A5
  Wokingham . . 47 C5
Farleys End . . 62 B3
Farlington . . 149 A5
Farlow. . . . 95 C4
Farmborough . 43 C5
Farmcote Glos . 63 A6
  Shrops . . . 95 B5
Farmington . . 64 B2
Farmoor . . 65 C5
Farmtown . . 267 D6
Farnborough
  Hants . . . 34 A1
  London . . 50 C1
  Warks. . . 82 C1
  W Berks. . . 46 A2
Farnborough
  Green . . . 34 A1
Farncombe . . 34 B2
Farndish . . 83 A6
Farndon Ches W. . 127 D4
  Notts . . . 132 D2
Farnell . . 233 C4
Farnham Dorset. 30 D3
  Essex . . . 69 A4
Farnham continued

Farnham continued
  Suff 89 A4
  Sur 34 B1
Farnham
  Common . . 48 A2
Farnham Green . 69 A4
Farnham Royal . 48 A2
Farnhill. . . . 147 C4
Farningham. . 50 C2
Farnley N Yorks .147 C6
  W Yorks . . 147 D6
Farnley Tyas . 139 B4
Farnsfield. . 131 D6
Farnworth
  Gtr Man . 137 C6
  Halton . . 127 A5
Farr Highld . 241 B6
  Highld. . . 252 C2
  Highld. . . 278 B3
Farr House . . 252 C2
Farringdon . 13 B5
Farrington
  Gurney . . 43 D5
Far Sawrey. . 154 B2
Farsley . . 147 D6
Farthinghoe . 82 D2
Farthingloe . 39 A4
Farthingstone. 82 B3
Fartown . . 139 B4
Farway . . 14 B1
Fasag. . . 249 A5
Fascadale . . 235 C4
Faslane Port . 215 D5
Fasnacloich . . 227 B5
Fasnakyle Ho . 251 D5
Fassfern . . 237 B4
Fatfield . . 179 D5
Fattahead. . 268 D1
Faugh . . 176 D3
Fauldhouse . 208 D2
Faulkbourne . 70 B1
Faulkland . . 43 D6
Fauls . . 111 B4
Faversham . 52 C2
Favillar . . 254 C3
Fawdington . 158 D3
Fawfieldhead . 129 C5
Fawkham Green . 50 C2
Fawler. . . 65 B4
Fawley Bucks . 47 A5
  Hants . . 18 A3
  W Berks. . 46 A1
Fawley Chapel . 62 A1
Faxfleet . . 141 A6
Faygate. . 35 C5
Fazakerley . 136 D2
Fazeley . . 97 A5
Fearby . . 157 C5
Fearn. . . 265 C4
Fearnan . . 229 D6
Fearnbeg . . 249 A4
Fearnhead . . 137 D5
Fearn Lodge . 264 B2
Fearnmore. . 261 D4
Fearn Station . 265 C4
Featherstone
  Staffs . . 96 A2
  W Yorks . . 140 A2
Featherwood. . 187 C7
Feckenham . 80 A3
Feering . . 70 A2
Feetham . . 156 B3
Feizor . . 146 A1
Felbridge . . 35 C6
Felbrigg . . 120 B4
Felcourt . . 36 B1
Felden. . . 67 C5
Felindre Carms . 58 B3
  Carms . . 58 C2
  Carms . . 59 C4
  Carms . . 73 C6
  Ceredig . . 75 C4
  Powys . . 93 C5
  Powys . . 77 D4
Felindre Farchog 72 C4
Felinfach Ceredig. 75 C4
  Powys . . 77 B4
Felinfoel . . 57 B5
Felingwm isaf . 58 C2
Felingwm uchaf . 58 C2
Felinwynt . . 73 A5

Felixkirk 158 C3
Felixstowe . . . 88 D3
Felixstowe Ferry .88 D4
Felkington . . 198 B3
Felkirk . . . 140 B1
Felling . . . 179 C4
Fell Side . . 163 A6
Felmersham . 84 B1
Felmingham . 120 C4
Felpham . . 20 C2
Felsham . . 87 B5
Felsted . . 69 A6
Feltham . . 48 B4
Felthorpe. . 120 D3
Felton Hereford . 78 C3
  Northumb. . 189 C4
  N Som . . 43 C4
Felton Butler. . 110 D2
Feltwell . . 102 B3
Fenay Bridge. . 139 B4
Fence . . 146 D2
Fence Houses . 179 D5
Fen Ditton . 85 A6
Fen Drayton. . 85 A5
Fen End . . 97 D5
Fengate Norf . 120 C3
  Pboro . . 100 B4
Fenham . . 199 B4
Fenhouses . . 117 A5
Feniscliffe . . 137 A5
Feniscowles . 137 A5
Feniton . . 13 B6
Fenlake. . 84 C2
Fenny Bentley . 130 D1
Fenny Bridges. 13 B6
Fenny Compton . 81 B7
Fenny Drayton . 97 B6
Fenny Stratford . 83 D5
Fenrother. . 189 D4
Fen Side . . 134 D3
Fenstanton . 85 A5
Fenton Cambs. . 101 D5
  Lincs. . . 132 B3
  Lincs. . . 132 D3
  Stoke . . 112 A6
Fenton Barns . 210 B2
Fenton Town . 198 C3
Fenwick E Ayrs. . 205 D4
  Northumb. . 178 B2
  Northumb. . 199 B4
  S Yorks. . 140 B3
Feochaig . . 190 D3
Feock . . 4 D3
Feolin Ferry . 201 B4
Ferindonald. . 247 D5
Feriniquarrie. . 258 C1
Ferlochan . . 226 B4
Fern. . . 232 B2
Ferndale . . 41 B5
Ferndown. . 17 A4
Ferness . . 253 B5
Ferney Green . 154 B3
Fernham. . 64 D3
Fernhill Heath. . 79 B6
Fernhurst. . 34 D1
Fernie . . 220 C3
Ferniegair . . 194 A2
Fernilea . . 246 A2
Fernilee . . 129 B5
Ferrensby. . 148 A2
Ferring . . 20 B3
Ferrybridge . . 140 A2
Ferryden. . 233 C5
Ferryhill
  Aberdeen . 245 B6
  Durham . . 167 B5
Ferry Hill . 101 C5
Ferryhill Station 167 B6
Ferry Point. . 264 B3
Ferryside . . 56 A3
Fersfield. . 103 C6
Fersit. . . 228 A2
Ferwig . . 73 B4
Feshiebridge. . 241 B6
Fetcham . . 35 A4
Fetterangus . 269 D4
Fettercairn. . 233 A4
Fettes . . 252 A1
Fewcott . . 65 A6

Fewston 147 B5
Ffairfach. 58 C3
Ffair-Rhos 75 B6
Ffaldybrenin 58 A3
Ffarmers 58 A3
Ffawyddog 60 B4
Fforest 57 B5
Fforest-fâch 57 C6
Ffostrasol. 73 B6
Ffos-y-ffin. 74 B3
Ffridd-Uchaf. . . .107 A5
Ffrith 126 D2
Ffrwd. 107 A4
Ffynnon ddrain . . .73 D7
Ffynnongroyw. . .125 A6
Ffynnon-oer 75 C4
Fidden. 224 D2
Fiddes 245 D5
Fiddington Glos. . . .80 D2
Som 28 A2
Fiddleford 30 D2
Fiddlers Hamlet . .69 C4
Field 112 B4
Field Broughton 154 C2
Field Dalling 120 B2
Field Head 98 A1
Fifehead
Magdalen 30 D1
Fifehead Neville. .30 D1
Fifield Oxon 64 B3
Wilts. 45 D5
Windsor 48 B2
Fifield Bavant . . .31 C4
Figheldean 31 A5
Filands 44 A3
Filby 121 D6
Filey. 161 C5
Filgrave 83 C5
Filkins 64 C3
Filleigh Devon 26 C1
Devon. 26 D2
Fillingham 133 A4
Fillongley. 97 C5
Filton. 43 B5
Fimber 150 A1
Finavon 232 C2
Finchairn 214 B2
Fincham. 102 A2
Finchampstead. . .47 C5
Finchdean 33 D6
Finchingfield. 86 D2
Finchley 68 D2
Findern. 113 B7
Findhorn 265 D6
Findhorn
Bridge 253 D4
Findochty. 267 C6
Findo Gask. 219 B5
Findon Aberds . . .245 C6
W Sus. 21 B4
Findon Mains . . .264 D2
Findrack Ho. 244 B3
Finedon 99 D6
Fingal Street 88 A3
Fingask. 256 D2
Fingerpost. 95 D5
Fingest 66 D2
Finghall 157 C5
Fingland Cumb. . . .175 C5
Dumfries 183 A5
Finglesham 53 D5
Fingringhoe. 71 A4
Finlarig. 217 A5
Finmere 82 D3
Finnart 229 C4
Finningham 87 A6
Finningley 141 D4
Finnygaud 267 D6
Finsbury 49 A6
Finstall 80 A2
Finsthwaite 154 C3
Finstock 65 B4
Finstown 282 F4
Fintry Aberds 268 D2
Dundee. 220 A4
Stirling 207 B4
Finzean. 244 C3
Fionnphort. 224 D2
Fionnsbhagh. . . .287 F5

Firbeck 131 A5
Firby N Yorks. 149 A6
N Yorks. 157 C6
Firgrove 138 B2
Firsby 135 C4
Firsdown 31 B6
First Coast 261 A6
Fir Tree. 166 B4
Fishbourne IoW . . .19 B4
W Sus. 20 B1
Fishburn. 167 B6
Fishcross 208 A1
Fisherford 256 C1
N Yorks. 160 D4
Suff 104 C4
Fisher Place 163 C6
Fisher's Pond 32 C3
Fisherstreet. 34 C2
Fisherton Highld . .251 A7
S Ayrs. 192 D3
Fishguard
Abergwaun 72 C2
Fishlake 141 B4
Fishleigh Barton . .25 C6
Fishponds 43 B5
Fishpool 62 A2
Fishtoft. 117 A6
Fishtoft Drove. . .117 A6
Fishtown of
Usan 233 C5
Fishwick. 198 A3
Fiskavaig 246 A2
Fiskerton Lincs. . . .133 B5
Notts 132 D2
Fitling 151 D5
Fittleton 31 A5
Fittleworth 20 A3
Fitton End 118 D1
Fitz. 110 D3
Fitzhead 27 C6
Fitzwilliam 140 B2
Fiunary 225 B5
Five Acres 62 B1
Five Ashes 36 D3
Fivecrosses 127 B5
Fivehead 28 C3
Five Oak Green. . .36 B4
Five Oaks Jersey 6
W Sus. 34 D3
Five Roads 57 B4
Flack's Green 70 B1
Flackwell Heath . .48 A1
Fladbury. 80 C2
Fladdabister 285 K6
Flagg. 129 C6
Flamborough 161 D6
Flamstead 67 B5
Flamstead End . . .68 C3
Flansham 20 B2
Flanshaw 139 A6
Flasby 146 B3
Flash 129 C5
Flashader 258 C3
Flask Inn. 160 A3
Flaunden 67 C5
Flawborough. . . .115 A5
Flawith 148 A3
Flax Bourton 43 C4
Flaxby 148 B2
Flaxholme 114 A1
Flaxley 62 B2
Flaxpool 27 B6
Flaxton 149 A5
Fleckney. 98 B3
Flecknoe 82 A2
Fledborough 132 B3
Fleet Hants 19 A4
Hants. 47 D6
Lincs. 117 C6
Fleetham 189 A4
Fleet Hargate . . .117 C6
Fleetlands 19 A4
Fleetville 67 C6
Fleetwood 144 C3
Flemingston 41 D5
Flemington 205 C6
Flempton 87 A4
Fleoideabhagh. . .287 F5
Fletchertown 175 D5
Fletching 36 D2
Flexbury 10 A3
Flexford 34 B2
Flimby 162 A3
Flimwell 37 C5

Flint Y Fflint 126 B2
Flintham. 115 A5
Flint Mountain . .126 B2
Flinton 151 D5
Flintsham. 77 B7
Flitcham. 119 C4
Flitton. 84 D2
Flitwick. 84 D2
Flixborough. 141 B6
Flixborough
Stather. 141 B6
Flixton Gtr Man. . . .137 D6
N Yorks. 160 D4
Suff 104 C4
Flockton. 139 B5
Flodaigh 286 A4
Flodden. 198 C3
Flodigarry 259 A4
Flood's Ferry. . . .101 B5
Flookburgh 154 D2
Florden. 104 B2
Flore 82 A3
Flotterton 188 C2
Flowton. 88 C1
Flush House 139 C4
Flushing Aberds. . .257 B5
Corn 4 D3
Flyford Flavell. . . .80 B2
Foals Green. 104 D3
Fobbing 51 A4
Fochabers 266 D4
Fochriw 60 C3
Fockerby 141 B6
Fodderletter 254 D2
Fodderty. 251 A7
Foel 109 D4
Foel-gastell. 57 A5
Foffarty. 232 D2
Foggathorpe 149 D6
Fogo 197 B6
Fogorig. 198 B1
Foindle 276 D2
Folda. 231 B5
Fole 112 B4
Foleshill 97 C6
Folke 29 D6
Folkestone. 39 B4
Folkingham 116 B3
Folkington 22 B3
Folksworth 100 C3
Folkton. 161 D4
Folla Rule. 256 C2
Follifoot 148 B2
Folly Gate. 11 B6
Fonthill Bishop . . .30 B3
Fonthill Gifford. . .30 B3
Fontmell Magna. .30 D2
Fontwell 20 B2
Foolow 130 B1
Foots Cray 50 B1
Forbestown 243 A6
Force Mills. 154 B2
Forcett 167 D4
Ford Argyll 214 B1
Bucks. 66 C2
Devon. 25 C5
Glos 64 A1
Northumb. 198 C3
Shrops 110 D3
Staffs 129 D5
Wilts. 44 B2
W Sus. 20 B2
Fordcombe 36 B3
Fordell 209 B4
Forden 93 A6
Ford End 69 B6
Forder Grn. 8 A1
Fordham Cambs. . .102 D2
Essex 70 A3
Norf 102 B2
Fordhouses 96 A2
Fordingbridge . . .31 D5
Fordon 160 D4
Fordoun 233 A5
Ford's Green 87 A6
Fordstreet 70 A3
Ford Street 27 D6
Fordwells 64 B4
Fordwich 52 D3
Fordyce 267 C6
Forebridge 112 C3
Foremark 114 C1
Forest 165 B6

Forest Becks 146 B1
Forestburn
Gate 188 D3
Foresterseat 266 D2
Forest Gate 49 A7
Forest Green. 35 B4
Forest Hall 154 A4
Forest Head. 176 D3
Forest Hill 65 C6
Forest Lane
Head. 148 B2
Forest Lodge
Argyll 228 D1
Highld. 242 A3
Perth 230 A3
Forest Mill 208 A2
Forest Row 36 C2
Forestside 33 D6
Forest Town 131 C5
Forfar 232 C2
Forgandenny 219 C5
Forge 91 C5
Forge Side 60 C4
Forgewood 194 A2
Forgie. 267 D4
Forglen Ho. 268 D1
Formby. 136 C2
Forncett End 104 B2
Forncett St
Mary. 104 B2
Forncett St
Peter 104 B2
Forneth. 231 D4
Fornham All
Saints. 87 A4
Fornham St
Martin 87 A4
Forres 253 A6
Forrestfield 207 D6
Forrest Lodge . . .182 D3
Forsbrook 112 A3
Forse. 275 A6
Forse Ho.. . . . . . .275 A6
Forsinain 279 D5
Forsinard 279 D4
Forsinard
Station 279 D4
Forston. 15 B6
Fort Augustus . . .240 B1
Fortevoit 219 C5
Fort George Guern . . .6
Highld. 252 A3
Forth 194 A4
Forthampton. 79 D6
Forth Road
Bridge 208 C4
Fortingall 229 D6
Forton Hants 32 A3
Lancs 145 B4
Shrops 110 D3
Som 14 A3
Staffs 111 C6
Forton Heath. . . .110 D3
Fortrie. 256 B1
Fortrose. 252 A3
Fortuneswell. 15 D6
Fort William 237 B5
Forty Green 67 D4
Forty Hill 68 D3
Forward Green. . . .88 B1
Fosbury 45 D7
Fosdyke 117 B6
Foss 230 C1
Foss Cross 63 C6
Fossebridge 64 B1
Fosterhouses 141 B4
Foster Street. 69 C4
Foston Derbys 113 B5
Lincs. 115 A6
N Yorks. 149 A5
Foston on the
Wolds 151 B4
Fotherby 143 D5
Fotheringhay . . .100 B2
Foubister 283 G6
Foulby. 140 B1
Foulden Borders . .198 A3
Norf 102 B3
Foulis Castle . . .264 D1
Foul Mile 22 A4
Foulridge 146 C2
Foulsham 120 C2

Fountainhall 196 B3
Four Ashes Staffs . .95 C6
Suff 103 D6
Four Crosses
Powys 93 A4
Powys 110 D1
Wrex 126 D2
Four Elms 36 B2
Four Forks 28 B2
Four Gotes. 118 D1
Fourlane Ends. . .130 D3
Four Lane Ends .127 C5
Four Lanes 3 B4
Fourlanes End. . .128 D3
Four Marks 33 B5
Four Mile
Bridge 122 C2
Four Oaks E Sus. . .37 D6
W Mid 96 B4
W Mid 97 C5
Fourpenny 265 A4
Four Roads Carms. .57 B4
IoM 152 E2
Fourstones 177 C6
Four Throws 37 D5
Fovant. 31 C4
Foveran 257 D4
Fowey 5 B6
Fowley
Common 137 D5
Fowlis 220 A3
Fowlis Wester. . .218 B4
Fowlmere. 85 C6
Fownhope 78 D3
Foxbar. 205 B4
Foxcombe Hill. . . .65 C5
Fox Corner. 34 A2
Foxdale. 152 D2
Foxearth. 87 C4
Foxfield 153 B3
Foxham. 44 B3
Foxhole Corn 5 B4
Swansea 57 C6
Foxholes. 160 D4
Foxhunt Green . . .22 A3
Fox Lane 34 A1
Foxley Norf 120 C2
Wilts. 44 A2
Fox Street 71 A4
Foxt 112 A4
Foxton Cambs. 85 C6
Durham 167 C6
Leics. 99 B4
Foxup 156 D2
Foxwist Green. . .127 C6
Foxwood 95 D4
Foy. 62 A1
Foyers. 251 D6
Fraddam 2 B3
Fraddon 4 B4
Fradley 113 D5
Fradswell 112 B3
Fraisthorpe 151 A4
Framfield 36 D2
Framingham
Earl 104 A3
Framingham
Pigot. 104 A3
Framlingham 88 A3
Frampton Dorset . .15 B6
Lincs. 117 B6
Frampton
Cotterell 43 A5
Frampton
Mansell 63 C5
Frampton on
Severn 62 C3
Frampton West
End 117 A5
Framsden. 88 B2
Framwellgate
Moor. 167 A5
Franche 95 D6
Frankby 126 A2
Frankley. 96 C2
Frank's Bridge . . .77 B5
Frankton. 98 D1
Frant 36 C3
Fraserburgh 269 C4
Frating Green 71 A4
Fratton 19 B5
Freathy 6 B3

Freckenham 102 D2
Freckleton 136 A3
Freeby. 115 C6
Freehay 112 A4
Freeland. 65 B5
Freester 285 H6
Freethorpe 105 A5
Freiston 117 A6
Fremington Devon 25 B6
N Yorks. 156 B4
Frenchay 43 B5
Frenchbeer 12 C1
Frenich 216 D4
Frensham 34 B1
Fresgoe 279 B5
Freshfield 136 C1
Freshford. 44 C1
Freshwater 18 C2
Freshwater Bay . .18 C2
Freshwater East. .55 E6
Fressingfield. . . .104 D3
Freston. 88 D2
Freswick. 281 B5
Fretherne. 62 C3
Frettenham 120 D4
Freuchie. 220 D2
Freuchies 231 B6
Freystrop 55 C5
Friar's Gate 36 C2
Friarton 219 B6
Friday Bridge . . .101 A6
Friday Street 22 B4
Fridaythorpe. . . .150 B1
Friern Barnet 68 D2
Friesland 223 B4
Friesthorpe 133 A5
Frieston 116 A2
Frieth 66 D2
Frilford 65 D5
Frilsham 46 B3
Frimley 34 A1
Frimley Green. . . .34 A1
Frindsbury 51 B4
Fring 119 B4
Fringford 65 A7
Frinsted 37 A6
Frinton-on-Sea . .71 A6
Friockheim 232 D3
Friog 90 A4
Frisby on the
Wreake 115 D4
Friskney 135 D4
Friskney
Eaudike. 135 D4
Friskney Tofts. . .135 D4
Friston E Sus. 22 C3
Suff 89 A5
Fritchley. 130 D3
Fritham. 31 D6
Frith Bank 117 A6
Frith Common . . .79 A4
Frithelstock. 25 D5
Frithelstock
Stone 25 D5
Frithville. 134 D3
Frittenden 37 B6
Frittiscombe 8 C2
Fritton Norf. 104 B3
Norf 105 A5
Fritwell 65 A6
Frizinghall 147 D5
Frizington 162 C3
Frocester 62 C3
Frodesley 94 A3
Frodingham 141 B6
Frodsham 127 B5
Frogden 187 A6
Froggatt 130 B2
Froghall 112 A4
Frogmore Devon . . .7 C6
Hants 34 A1
Frognall 117 D4
Frogshail 121 B4
Frolesworth 98 B2
Frome 30 A1
Frome St Quintin 15 A5
Fromes Hill 79 C4
Fron Denb 125 C5
Gwyn 106 C3
Gwyn 107 A5
Powys 77 D4
Powys 93 A4

Fron *continued*
Powys 93 B5
Froncysyllte 110 A1
Frongoch 108 B4
Frostenden 105 C5
Frosterley 166 B3
Frotoft 282 E5
Froxfield 45 C6
Froxfield Green . . 33 C6
Froyle 33 A6
Fryerning 69 C6
Fryton 159 D5
Fulbeck 133 D4
Fulbourn 85 B7
Fulbrook 64 B3
Fulford Som 28 C2
Staffs 112 B3
York 149 C5
Fulham 49 B5
Fulking 21 A5
Fullarton
Glasgow 205 B6
N Ayrs 192 B3
Fuller's Moor . . . 127 D4
Fuller Street 70 B1
Fullerton 32 B2
Fulletby 134 B2
Full Sutton 149 B6
Fullwood 205 C4
Fulmer 48 A2
Fulmodestone . . . 120 B1
Fulnetby 133 B5
Fulstow 143 D5
Fulwell 179 D5
Fulwood Lancs . . . 145 D5
S Yorks 130 A3
Fundenhall 104 B2
Fundenhall Street 104 B2
Funtington 19 A6
Funtley 19 A4
Funtullich 218 B2
Funzie 284 D8
Furley 14 A2
Furnace Argyll . . . 214 B3
Carms 57 B5
Furnace End 97 B5
Furneaux Pelham 68 A4
Furness Vale 129 A5
Furzehill 26 A2
Furze Platt 48 A1
Fyfett 28 D2
Fyfield Essex 69 C5
Glos 64 C3
Hants 32 A1
Oxon 65 D5
Wilts 45 C5
Fylingthorpe 160 A3
Fyvie 256 C2

G

Gabhsann bho Dheas 288 B5
Gabhsann bho Thuath 288 B5
Gablon 264 A3
Gabroc Hill 205 C4
Gaddesby 115 D4
Gadebridge 67 C5
Gaer 60 A3
Gaerllwyd 61 D6
Gaerwen 123 C4
Gagingwell 65 A5
Gaick Lodge 241 D5
Gailey 112 D3
Gainford 167 D4
Gainsborough
Lincs 141 D6
Suff 88 C2
Gainsford End 86 D3
Gairloch 261 C5
Gairlochy 239 D5
Gairney Bank . . . 208 A4
Gairnshiel Lodge 243 B5
Gaisgill 155 A5
Gaitsgill 164 A1
Galashiels 196 C3
Galgate 145 B4
Galhampton 29 C6
Gallaberry 184 D2
Gallachoille 213 D5
Gallanach Argyll . 223 A5
Argyll 226 D3
Gallantry Bank . . 127 D5
Gallatown 209 A5
Galley Common . . 97 B6
Galleyend 69 C7
Galley Hill 85 A5
Galleywood 69 C7
Gallin 229 D4
Gallowfauld 232 D2
Gallows Green . . 113 A4
Galltair 249 D5
Galmisdale 234 B3
Galmpton Devon . . . 7 C5
Torbay 8 B2
Galphay 157 D6
Galston 193 B5
Galtrigill 258 C1
Gamblesby 165 B4
Gamesley 138 D3
Gamlingay 84 B4
Gammersgill 157 C4
Gamston 132 B2
Ganarew 62 B1
Ganavan 226 C3
Gang 6 A2
Ganllwyd 108 C2
Gannochy Angus . 232 A3
Perth 219 B6
Gansclet 281 D5
Ganstead 151 D4
Ganthorpe 159 D5
Ganton 160 D3
Garbat 263 D6
Garbhallt 214 C3
Garboldisham . . . 103 C6
Garden City 126 C3
Gardenstown . . . 268 C2
Garden Village
Wrex 126 D3
W Yorks 148 D3
Garderhouse 285 J5
Gardham 150 C2
Gardin 284 G6
Gare Hill 30 A1
Garelochhead . . . 215 C5
Garford 65 D5
Garforth 148 D3
Gargrave 146 B3
Gargunnock 207 A5
Garlic Street 104 C3
Garlieston 171 C6
Garlinge Green . . . 52 D3
Garlogie 245 B4
Garmond 268 D3
Garmony 225 B5
Garmouth 266 C4
Garnant 58 D3
Garndiffaith 61 C4
Garndolbenmaen 107 B4
Garnedd 124 D2
Garnett Bridge . . 154 B4
Garnfadryn 106 C2
Garnkirk 207 D4
Garnlydan 60 B3
Garnswllt 57 B6
Garn-yr-erw 60 B4
Garrabost 288 D6
Garraron 213 B6
Garras 3 C5
Garreg 107 B6
Garrick 218 C3
Garrigill 165 A5
Garriston 157 B5
Garroch 182 D3
Garrogie Lodge . 240 A3
Garros 259 B4
Garrow 230 D2
Garryhorn 182 C3
Garsdale 155 C6
Garsdale Head . . 155 B6
Garsdon 44 A3
Garshall Green . . 112 B3
Garsington 65 C6
Garstang 145 C4
Garston 127 A4
Garswood 137 D4
Gartcosh 207 D4
Garth Bridgend 40 B3
Garth *continued*
Gwyn 123 C5
Powys 76 C3
Shetland 285 H4
Wrex 110 A1
Garthamlock 205 B6
Garthbrengy 76 D4
Garthdee 245 B6
Gartheli 75 C4
Garthmyl 93 B5
Garthorpe Leics . . 115 C6
N Lincs 141 B6
Garth Row 154 B4
Gartly 255 C6
Gartmore 206 A3
Gartnagrenach . . 202 C2
Gartness
N Lanark 207 D5
Stirling 206 B3
Gartocharn 206 B2
Garton 151 D5
Garton-on-the-Wolds 150 B2
Gartsherrie 207 D5
Gartymore 274 C4
Garvald 210 C2
Garvamore 240 C3
Garvard 212 C1
Garvault Hotel . . 273 A5
Garve 263 D5
Garvestone 103 A6
Garvock Aberds . . 233 A5
Invclyd 204 A2
Garway 61 A6
Garway Hill 61 A6
Gaskan 236 B1
Gastard 44 C2
Gasthorpe 103 C5
Gatcombe 18 C3
Gateacre 127 A4
Gatebeck 154 C4
Gate Burton 132 A3
Gateford 131 A5
Gateforth 140 A3
Gatehead 192 B3
Gate Helmsley . . 149 B5
Gatehouse 177 A5
Gatehouse of Fleet 172 C4
Gatelawbridge . . 183 C7
Gateley 119 C6
Gatenby 158 C2
Gateshead 179 C4
Gatesheath 127 C4
Gateside Aberds . . 244 A3
Angus 232 D2
E Renf 205 C4
Fife 219 D6
N Ayrs 204 C3
Gathurst 136 C4
Gatley 128 A3
Gattonside 197 C4
Gatwick Airport . . 35 B5
Gaufron 76 A3
Gaulby 98 A3
Gauldry 220 B3
Gaunt's Common 17 A4
Gautby 134 B1
Gavinton 197 A6
Gawber 139 C6
Gawcott 82 D3
Gawsworth 128 C3
Gawthorpe 139 A5
Gawthrop 155 C5
Gawthwaite 153 B3
Gaydon 81 B6
Gayfield 282 B5
Gayhurst 83 C5
Gayle 156 C2
Gayles 157 A5
Gay Street 34 D3
Gayton Mers 126 A2
Norf 119 D4
Northants 83 B4
Staffs 112 C3
Gayton le Marsh 135 A4
Gayton le Wold . . 134 A2
Gayton Thorpe . . 119 D4
Gaywood 118 C3
Gazeley 86 A3
Geanies House . . 265 C4
Gearraidh Bhailteas 286 D3
Gearraidh Bhaird 288 E4
Gearraidh na h-Aibhne 288 D3
Gearraidh na Monadh 286 E3
Geary 258 B2
Geddes House . . . 253 A4
Gedding 87 B5
Geddington 99 C5
Gedintailor 247 A4
Gedling 115 A4
Gedney 117 C7
Gedney Broadgate 117 C7
Gedney Drove End 118 C1
Gedney Dyke 117 C7
Gedney Hill 117 D6
Gee Cross 138 D2
Geilston 206 C1
Geirinis 286 B3
Geise 280 B3
Geisiadar 288 D2
Geldeston 105 B4
Gell 124 C3
Gelli Pembs 55 C6
Rhondda 41 B4
Gellideg 60 C2
Gellifor 125 C6
Gelligaer 41 B6
Gellilydan 107 C6
Gellinudd 40 A2
Gellyburn 219 A5
Gellywen 73 D5
Gelston Dumfries 173 C5
Lincs 116 A2
Gembling 151 B4
Gentleshaw 113 D4
Geocrab 288 H2
Georgefield 185 C5
George Green 48 A3
Georgeham 25 B5
George Nympton . 26 C2
Georgetown 60 C3
Gerlan 123 D6
Germansweek 11 B5
Germoe 2 C3
Gerrans 4 D3
Gerrards Cross . . . 48 A3
Gestingthorpe 87 D4
Geuffordd 109 D7
Gibbet Hill 98 C2
Gibbshill 173 A5
Gib Hill 127 B6
Gidea Park 50 A2
Gidleigh 12 C1
Giffnock 205 C5
Gifford 210 D2
Giffordland 204 D2
Giffordtown 220 C2
Giggleswick 146 A2
Gilberdyke 141 A6
Gilchriston 210 D1
Gilcrux 163 A4
Gildersome 139 A5
Gildingwells 131 A5
Gileston 41 E5
Gilfach 41 B6
Gilfach Goch 41 C4
Gilfachrheda 73 A7
Gillamoor 159 C5
Gillar's Green . . . 136 D3
Gillen 258 C2
Gilling East 159 D5
Gillingham Dorset 30 C2
Medway 51 C4
Norf 105 B5
Gilling West 157 A5
Gillock 280 C4
Gillow Heath 128 D3
Gills 281 A5
Gill's Green 37 C5
Gilmanscleuch . . 196 D2
Gilmerton Edin . . . 209 D5
Perth 218 B3
Gilmonby 166 D2
Gilmorton 98 C2
Gilmourton 205 D6
Gilsland 176 C4
Gilsland Spa 176 C4
Gilston Borders . . 196 A3
Herts 68 B4
Gilwern 60 B4
Gimingham 121 B4
Giosla 288 E2
Gipping 87 A6
Gipsey Bridge . . . 117 A5
Girdle Toll 204 D3
Girlsta 285 H6
Girsby 158 A2
Girtford 84 B3
Girthon 172 C4
Girton Cambs 85 A6
Notts 132 C3
Girvan 180 B3
Gisburn 146 C2
Gisleham 105 C6
Gislingham 104 D1
Gissing 104 C2
Gittisham 13 B6
Gladestry 77 B6
Gladsmuir 210 C1
Glais 40 A2
Glaisdale 159 A6
Glame 248 B2
Glamis 232 D1
Glan Adda 123 C5
Glanaman 57 A6
Glan Conwy 124 B3
Glan-Conwy 124 D3
Glandford 120 A2
Glan-Duar 58 A2
Glandwr 73 D4
Glan-Dwyfach . . . 107 B4
Glandy Cross 72 D4
Glandyfi 91 C4
Glan Gors 123 C4
Glangrwyney 60 B4
Glanmule 93 B5
Glanrafon 90 D4
Glanrhyd Gwyn . . . 106 C2
Pembs 72 B4
Glan-rhyd 107 A4
Glanton 188 B3
Glanton Pike 188 B3
Glan-traeth 122 C2
Glanvilles Wootton 15 A6
Glan-y-don 125 B6
Glan-y-nant 92 C3
Glan-yr-afon
Anglesey 123 B6
Gwyn 108 A4
Gwyn 109 A5
Glan-y-wern 107 C6
Glapthorn 100 B2
Glapwell 131 C4
Glas-allt Shiel . . . 243 D5
Glasbury 77 D5
Glaschoil 253 C6
Glascoed Denb . . . 125 B4
Mon 61 C5
Powys 109 D6
Glascorrie 243 C6
Glascote 97 A5
Glascwm 77 B5
Glasdrum 227 B5
Glasfryn 125 D4
Glasgow 205 B5
Glashvin 259 B4
Glasinfryn 123 D5
Glasnacardoch . . 235 A5
Glasnakille 247 C4
Glasphein 258 D1
Glaspwll 91 C5
Glassburn 251 C5
Glasserton 171 D6
Glassford 194 B2
Glasshouse Hill . . . 62 A3
Glasshouses 147 A5
Glasslie 220 D2
Glasson Cumb 175 B5
Lancs 144 B4
Glassonby 164 B3
Glasterlaw 232 C3
Glaston 99 A5
Glastonbury 29 B5
Glatton 100 C3
Glazebrook 137 D5
Glazebury 137 D5
Glazeley 95 C5
Gleadless 130 A3
Gleadsmoss 128 C3
Gleann Tholàstaidh . . . 288 C6
Gleaston 153 C3
Gleiniant 92 B3
Glemsford 87 C4
Glen Dumfries 172 C3
Dumfries 173 A6
Glenamachrie . . . 226 D4
Glen Auldyn 152 B4
Glenbarr 190 B2
Glenbeg Highld . . . 235 D4
Highld 253 D6
Glen Bernisdale . 259 D4
Glenbervie 245 D4
Glenboig 207 D5
Glenborrodale . . 235 D5
Glenbranter 215 C4
Glenbreck 195 D5
Glenbrein Lodge 240 A2
Glenbrittle House 246 B3
Glenbuchat Lodge 243 A6
Glenbuck 194 D2
Glenburn 205 B4
Glencalvie Lodge 263 B6
Glencanisp Lodge 270 B4
Glencaple 174 B2
Glencarron Lodge 250 A2
Glencarse 219 B6
Glencassley Castle 272 D2
Glenceitlein 227 B6
Glencoe 237 D4
Glencraig 209 A4
Glencripesdale . . 225 A5
Glencrosh 183 D5
Glendavan Ho. . . . 244 B1
Glendevon 219 D4
Glendoebeg 240 B2
Glendoe Lodge . . 240 B2
Glendoick 220 B2
Glendoll Lodge . . 231 A6
Glendoune 180 B3
Glenduckie 220 C2
Glendye Lodge . . 244 D3
Gleneagles Hotel 218 C4
Gleneagles House 218 D4
Glenegedale 200 C3
Glenelg 238 A2
Glenernie 253 B6
Glenfarg 219 C6
Glenfarquhar Lodge 245 D4
Glenferness House 253 B5
Glenfeshie Lodge 241 C6
Glenfield 98 A2
Glenfinnan 238 D3
Glenfoot 219 C6
Glenfyne Lodge . 215 A5
Glengap 173 C4
Glengarnock 204 C3
Glengorm Castle 224 A3
Glengrasco 259 D4
Glenhead Farm . . 231 B6
Glen Ho. 196 C1
Glenhoul 182 D4
Glenhurich 236 C2
Glenkerry 185 A5
Glenkiln 173 A6
Glenkindie 244 A1
Glenlatterach . . . 266 D2
Glenlee 182 D4
Glenlichorn 218 C2
Glenlivet 254 D2
Glenlochsie 231 A4
Glenloig 191 B5
Glenluce 171 B4

Glenmallan 215 C5
Glenmarksie 251 A5
Glenmassan 215 D4
Glenmavis 207 D5
Glenmaye 152 D2
Glenmidge 183 D6
Glen Mona 152 C4
Glenmore Argyll 213 A6
Highld 259 D4
Glenmore Lodge 242 B2
Glenmoy 232 B2
Glen Nevis House 237 B5
Glenogil 232 B2
Glen Parva 98 B2
Glenprosen Lodge 231 B6
Glenprosen Village 232 B1
Glenquiech 232 B2
Glenreasdell Mains 202 C3
Glenree 191 C5
Glenridding 164 D1
Glenrossal 272 D2
Glenrothes 220 D2
Glensanda 226 B3
Glensaugh 233 A4
Glenshero Lodge 240 C3
Glen Sluain 214 C3
Glenstockadale 170 A2
Glenstriven 203 A5
Glentaggart 194 D3
Glen Tanar House 244 C1
Glentham 142 D2
Glentirranmuir 207 A4
Glenton 256 D1
Glentress 196 C1
Glentromie Lodge 241 C5
Glen Trool Lodge 181 C6
Glentrool Village 181 D5
Glentruan 152 A4
Glentruim House 241 C4
Glentworth 133 A4
Glenuig 235 C5
Glenurquhart 264 D3
Glen Village 208 C1
Glen Vine 152 D3
Glespin 194 D3
Gletness 285 H6
Glewstone 62 A1
Glinton 100 A3
Glooston 99 B4
Glororum 199 C5
Glossop 138 D3
Gloster Hill 189 C5
Gloucester 63 B4
Gloup 284 C7
Glusburn 147 C4
Glutt Lodge 274 A3
Glutton Bridge 129 C5
Glympton 65 A5
Glynarthen 73 B6
Glynbrochan 92 C3
Glyn-Ceiriog 109 B7
Glyncoch 41 B5
Glyncorrwg 40 B3
Glyn-cywarch 107 C6
Glynde 22 B2
Glyndebourne 22 A2
Glyndyfrdwy 109 A6
Glyn-neath Glynedd 59 E5
Glynogwr 41 C4
Glyntaff 41 C5
Glyntawe 59 D5
Gnosall 112 C2
Gnosall Heath 112 C2
Goadby 99 B4
Goadby Marwood 115 C5
Goatacre 44 B4
Goathill 29 D6
Goathland 160 A2
Goathurst 28 B2
Goat Lees 38 A2
Gobernuisgach Lodge 277 D5
Gobhaig 287 D5
Gobowen 110 B2
Godalming 34 B2
Godley 138 D2
Godmanchester 100 D4
Godmanstone 15 B6
Godmersham 52 D2
Godney 29 A4
Godolphin Cross 3 B4
Godre'r-graig 59 E4
Godshill Hants 31 D5
IoW 18 C4
Godstone 35 A6
Godwinscroft 17 B5
Goetre 61 C5
Goferydd 122 B2
Goff's Oak 68 C3
Gogar 209 C4
Goginan 91 D4
Golan 107 B5
Golant 5 B6
Golberdon 10 D4
Golborne 137 D5
Golcar 139 B4
Goldcliff 42 A2
Golden Cross 22 A3
Golden Green 36 B4
Golden Grove 57 A5
Goldenhill 128 D3
Golden Hill 17 B6
Golden Pot 33 A6
Golden Valley 63 A5
Golders Green 49 A5
Goldhanger 70 C3
Gold Hill 102 B1
Golding 94 A3
Goldington 84 B2
Goldsborough
N Yorks 148 B2
N Yorks 169 D6
Goldsithney 2 B3
Goldsworthy 25 C4
Goldthorpe 140 C2
Gollanfield 253 A4
Golspie 274 D2
Golval 279 B4
Gomeldon 31 B5
Gomersal 139 A5
Gomshall 34 B3
Gonalston 115 A4
Gonfirth 285 G5
Good Easter 69 B6
Gooderstone 102 A3
Goodleigh 25 B7
Goodmanham 150 C1
Goodnestone
Kent 52 C2
Kent 53 D4
Goodrich 62 B1
Goodrington 8 B2
Goodshaw 137 A7
Goodwick Wdig 72 C2
Goodworth Clatford 32 A2
Goole 141 A5
Goonbell 4 C2
Goonhavern 4 B2
Goose Eye 147 C4
Goose Green
Gtr Man 137 C4
Norf 104 C2
W Sus 21 A4
Gooseham 24 D3
Goosey 65 D4
Goosnargh 145 D5
Goostrey 128 B2
Gorcott Hill 80 A3
Gord 285 L6
Gordon 197 B5
Gordonbush 274 D2
Gordonsburgh 267 C5
Gordonstoun 266 C2
Gordonstown
Aberds 256 C2
Aberds 267 D6
Gore 53 D5
Gorebridge 209 D6
Gore Cross 44 D4
Gorefield 117 D7
Gore Pit 70 B2
Gorey Jersey 6
Gorgie 209 C5
Goring 47 A4
Goring-by-Sea 21 B4
Goring Heath 47 B4
Gorleston-on-Sea 105 A6
Gornalwood 96 B2
Gorrachie 268 D2
Gorran Churchtown 5 C4
Gorran Haven 5 C5
Gorrenberry 186 D3
Gors 75 A5
Gorsedd 125 B6
Gorse Hill 45 A5
Gorseinon 57 C5
Gorseness 282 F5
Gorsgoch 74 C3
Gorslas 57 A5
Gorsley 62 A2
Gorstan 263 D5
Gorstanvorran 236 B2
Gorsteyhill 128 D2
Gorsty Hill 113 C5
Gortantaoid 200 A3
Gorton 138 D1
Gosbeck 88 B2
Gosberton 117 B5
Gosberton Clough 117 C4
Gosfield 70 A1
Gosford 78 A3
Gosforth Cumb 162 D3
T&W 179 C4
Gosmore 68 A1
Gosport 19 B5
Gossabrough 284 E7
Gossington 62 C3
Goswick 199 B4
Gotham 114 B3
Gotherington 63 A5
Gott 285 J6
Goudhurst 37 C5
Goulceby 134 B2
Gourdas 256 B2
Gourdon 233 A6
Gourock 204 A2
Govan 205 B5
Govanhill 205 B5
Goveton 7 C6
Govilon 61 B4
Gowanhill 269 C5
Gowdall 140 A4
Gowerton 57 C5
Gowkhall 208 B3
Gowthorpe 149 B6
Goxhill E Yorks 151 C4
N Lincs 142 A3
Goxhill Haven 142 A3
Goytre 40 C2
Grabhair 288 F4
Graby 116 C3
Grade 3 D5
Graffham 20 A2
Grafham Cambs 84 A3
Sur 34 B3
Grafton Hereford 78 D2
N Yorks 148 A3
Oxon 64 C3
Shrops 110 D3
Worcs 78 A3
Grafton Flyford 80 B2
Grafton Regis 83 C4
Grafton Underwood 99 C6
Grafty Green 37 B6
Graianrhyd 126 D2
Graig Conwy 124 B3
Denb 125 B5
Graig-fechan 125 D6
Grain 51 B5
Grainsby 143 D4
Grainthorpe 143 D5
Grampound 4 C4
Grampound Road 4 B4
Gramsdal 286 A4
Granborough 66 A2
Granby 115 B5
Grandborough 82 A1
Grandtully 230 C3
Grange Cumb 163 C5
E Ayrs 193 B4
Medway 51 C4
Mers 126 A2
Perth 220 B2
Grange Crossroads 267 D5
Grange Hall 265 D6
Grange Hill 68 D4
Grangemill 130 D2
Grange Moor 139 B5
Grangemouth 208 B2
Grange of Lindores 220 C2
Grange-over-Sands 154 D3
Grangepans 208 B3
Grangetown
Cardiff 41 D6
Redcar 168 C3
Grange Villa 179 D4
Granish 242 A2
Gransmoor 151 B4
Granston 55 A4
Grantchester 85 B6
Grantham 116 B2
Grantley 147 A6
Grantlodge 245 A4
Granton Dumfries 184 B3
Edin 209 C5
Grantown-on-Spey 253 D6
Grantshouse 211 D5
Grappenhall 127 A6
Grasby 142 C2
Grasmere 154 A2
Grasscroft 138 C2
Grassendale 126 A3
Grassholme 166 C2
Grassington 147 A4
Grassmoor 131 C4
Grassthorpe 132 C2
Grateley 32 A1
Gratwich 112 B4
Graveley Cambs 84 A4
Herts 68 A2
Gravelly Hill 96 B4
Gravels 94 A1
Graven 284 F6
Graveney 52 C2
Gravesend Herts 68 A4
Kent 50 B3
Grayingham 142 D1
Grayrigg 155 B4
Grays 50 B3
Grayshott 34 C1
Grayswood 34 C2
Graythorp 168 C3
Grazeley 47 C4
Greasbrough 140 D2
Greasby 126 A2
Great Abington 86 C1
Great Addington 99 D6
Great Alne 80 B4
Great Altcar 136 C2
Great Amwell 68 B3
Great Asby 165 D4
Great Ashfield 87 A5
Great Ayton 168 D3
Great Baddow 70 C1
Great Bardfield 86 D2
Great Barford 84 B3
Great Barr 96 B3
Great Barrington 64 B3
Great Barrow 127 C4
Great Barton 87 A4
Great Barugh 159 D6
Great Bavington 178 A1
Great Bealings 88 C3
Great Bedwyn 45 C6
Great Bentley 71 A5
Great Billing 83 A5
Great Bircham 119 B4
Great Blakenham 88 B2
Great Blencow 164 B2
Great Bolas 111 C5
Great Bookham 35 A4
Great Bourton 82 C1
Great Bowden 99 C4
Great Bradley 86 B2
Great Braxted 70 B2
Great Bricett 87 B6
Great Brickhill 83 D6
Great Bridgeford 112 C2
Great Brington 82 A3
Great Bromley 71 A4
Great Broughton
Cumb 162 A3
N Yorks 158 A4
Great Budworth 127 B6
Great Burdon 167 D6
Great Burgh 35 A5
Great Burstead 69 D6
Great Busby 158 A4
Great Canfield 69 B5
Great Carlton 135 A4
Great Casterton 100 A2
Great Chart 38 A1
Great Chatwell 112 D1
Great Chesterford 85 C7
Great Cheverell 44 D3
Great Chishill 85 D6
Great Clacton 71 B5
Great Cliff 139 B6
Great Clifton 162 B3
Great Coates 143 C4
Great Comberton 80 C2
Great Corby 176 D2
Great Cornard 87 C4
Great Cowden 151 C5
Great Coxwell 64 D3
Great Crakehall 157 B6
Great Cransley 99 D5
Great Cressingham 103 A4
Great Crosby 136 D2
Great Cubley 113 B5
Great Dalby 115 D5
Great Denham 84 C2
Great Doddington 83 A5
Great Dunham 119 D5
Great Dunmow 69 A6
Great Durnford 31 B5
Great Easton
Essex 69 A6
Leics 99 B5
Great Eccleston 144 C4
Great Edstone 159 C6
Great Ellingham 103 B6
Great Elm 30 A1
Greater Doward 62 B1
Great Eversden 85 B5
Great Fencote 157 B6
Great Finborough 87 B6
Greatford 116 D3
Great Fransham 119 D5
Great Gaddesden 67 B5
Greatgate 113 A4
Great Gidding 100 C3
Great Givendale 149 B7
Great Glemham 88 A4
Great Glen 98 B3
Great Gonerby 116 B1
Great Gransden 85 B4
Great Green
Norf 104 C3
Suff 87 B5
Great Habton 159 D6
Great Hale 116 A4
Greatham Hants 33 B6
Hrtlpl 168 C2
W Sus 20 A3
Great Hampden 66 C3
Great Harrowden 99 D5
Great Harwood 146 D1
Great Haseley 66 C1
Great Hatfield 151 C4
Great Haywood 112 C3
Great Heath 97 C6
Great Heck 140 A3
Great Henny 87 D4
Great Hinton 44 D3
Great Hockham 103 B5
Great Holland 71 B6
Great Horkesley 87 D5
Great Hormead 68 A3
Great Horton 147 D5
Great Horwood 83 D4
Great Houghton
Northants 83 B4
S Yorks 140 C2
Great Hucklow 130 B1
Great Kelk 151 B4
Great Kimble 66 C3
Great Kingshill 66 D3
Great Langton 157 B6
Great Leighs 70 B1
Great Lever 137 C6
Great Limber 142 C3
Great Linford 83 C5
Great Livermere 103 D4
Great Longstone 130 B2
Great Lumley 167 A5
Great Lyth 94 A2
Great Malvern 79 C5
Great Maplestead 87 D4
Great Marton 144 D3
Great Massingham 119 C4
Great Melton 104 A2
Great Milton 66 C1
Great Missenden 66 C3
Great Mitton 145 D7
Great Mongeham 53 D5
Great Moulton 104 B2
Great Munden 68 A3
Great Musgrave 165 D5
Great Ness 110 D2
Great Notley 70 A1
Great Oakley
Essex 71 A5
Northants 99 C5
Great Offley 67 A6
Great Ormside 165 D5
Great Orton 175 C6
Great Ouseburn 148 A3
Great Oxendon 99 C4
Great Oxney Green 69 C6
Great Palgrave 119 D5
Great Paxton 84 A4
Great Plumpton 144 D3
Great Plumstead 121 D5
Great Ponton 116 B2
Great Preston 140 A2
Great Raveley 101 C4
Great Rissington 64 B2
Great Rollright 81 D6
Great Ryburgh 119 C6
Great Ryle 188 B3
Great Ryton 94 A2
Great Saling 69 A7
Great Salkeld 164 B3
Great Sampford 86 D2
Great Sankey 127 A5
Great Saxham 86 A3
Great Shefford 46 B1
Great Shelford 85 B6
Great Smeaton 158 A2
Great Snoring 119 B6
Great Somerford 44 A3
Great Stainton 167 C6
Great Stambridge 70 D2
Great Staughton 84 A3
Great Steeping 135 C4
Great Stonar 53 D5
Greatstone on Sea 38 C2
Great Strickland 164 C3
Great Stukeley 100 D4
Great Sturton 134 B2
Great Sutton
Ches W 126 B3
Shrops 94 C3
Great Swinburne 178 B1
Great Tew 65 A4
Great Tey 70 A2
Great Thurlkleby 158 D3
Great Thurlow 86 B2
Great Torrington 25 D5
Great Tosson 188 C3
Great Totham
Essex 70 B2

Great Totham
continued
Essex 70 B2
Great Tows 143 D4
Great Urswick. . .153 C3
Great Wakering . 51 A6
Great
Waldingfield. . . . 87 C5
Great
Walsingham . . .119 B6
Great Waltham . . .69 B6
Great Warley. . . .69 D5
Great
Washbourne. . . .80 D2
Great Weldon . . .99 C6
Great Welnetham 87 B4
Great Wenham . . .87 D6
Great
Whittington . . .178 B2
Great
Wigborough 70 B3
Great Wilbraham .86 B1
Great Wishford. . .31 B4
Great Witcombe. . .63 B5
Great Witley 79 A5
Great Wolford. . . .81 D5
Greatworth 82 C2
Great Wratting . . .86 C2
Great
Wymondley. 68 A2
Great Wyrley. . . .96 A2
Great
Wytheford. . . .111 D4
Great Yarmouth 105 A6
Great Yeldham . . .86 D3
Greave 138 A1
Greeba 152 C3
Green 125 C5
Greenbank. 284 C7
Greenburn 208 D2
Greendikes 188 A3
Green End 84 B3
Greenfield C Beds .84 D2
  Flint 126 B1
  Gtr Man 138 C2
  Highld. 239 B6
  Oxon. 66 D2
Greenford 48 A4
Greengairs. 207 C5
Greenham 46 C2
Green
  Hammerton . . .148 B3
Greenhaugh 177 A5
Greenhead. 177 C4
Greenhill Falk . .207 C6
  Kent 52 C3
  Leics. 114 D2
  London 49 A4
Greenhills 204 C3
Greenhithe 50 B2
Greenholm. 193 B5
Greenholme 155 A4
Greenhouse. . . .187 A4
Greenhow Hill. .147 A5
Greenigoe 283 G5
Greenland 280 B4
Greenlands 47 A5
Green Lane 93 B5
Greenlaw Aberds 268 D1
  Borders 197 B6
Greenlea 174 A3
Greenloaning . . .218 D3
Greenmount 137 B6
Greenmow. 285 L6
Greenock 204 A2
Greenock West. .204 A2
Greenodd. 154 C2
Green Ore 43 D4
Greenrow. 174 C4
Green St Green. . .50 C1
Greenside. 178 C3
Greensidehill . . .188 B2
Greens Norton . . .82 C3
Greenstead
  Green. 70 A2
Greensted 69 C5
Green Street 68 D1
Greenwich. 49 B6
Greet. 80 D3
Greete. 94 D3
Greetham Lincs . .134 B3
  Rutland. 116 D2

Greetland 138 A3
Gregg Hall 154 B3
Gregson Lane . . .137 A4
Greinetobht. 287 G3
Greinton. 28 B4
Gremista 285 J6
Grenaby 152 D2
Grendon Northants 83 A5
  Warks. 97 A5
Grendon
  Common 97 B5
Grendon Green. . .78 B3
Grendon
  Underwood. 66 A1
Grenofen 11 D5
Grenoside 139 D6
Greosabhagh . . .288 H2
Gresford. 126 D3
Gresham. 120 B3
Greshornish. 258 C3
Gressenhall 119 D6
Gressingham . . .145 A5
Gresty Green. . . .128 D2
Greta Bridge . . .166 D3
Gretna. 175 B6
Gretna Green . . .175 B6
Gretton Glos. 80 D3
  Northants. 99 B5
  Shrops 94 B3
Grewelthorpe . . .157 D6
Greygarth. 157 D5
Grey Green 141 C5
Greynor 57 B5
Greysouthen . . .162 B3
Greystoke. 164 B2
Greystone Angus 232 D3
  Dumfries 174 A2
Greywell 47 D5
Griais. 288 C5
Grianan. 288 D5
Gribthorpe. 149 D6
Gridley Corner . . .11 B4
Griff. 97 C6
Griffithstown. . . .61 D4
Grimbister 282 F4
Grimblethorpe . .134 A2
Grimeford
  Village 137 B5
Grimethorpe 140 C2
Griminis 286 A3
Grimister 284 D6
Grimley. 79 A6
Grimoldby 134 A3
Grimpo 110 C2
Grimsargh 145 D5
Grimsbury 82 C1
Grimsby 143 B4
Grimscote 82 B3
Grimscott 10 A3
Grimsthorpe 116 C3
Grimston E Yorks 151 D5
  Leics. 115 C4
  Norf 119 C4
  York 149 B5
Grimstone 15 B6
Grinacombe
  Moor. 11 B5
Grindale 161 D5
Grindigar 283 G6
Grindiscol 285 K6
Grindle 95 A5
Grindleford 130 B2
Grindleton 146 C1
Grindley 112 C4
Grindley Brook .111 A4
Grindlow 130 B1
Grindon
  Northumb. 198 B3
  Staffs 129 D5
Grindonmoor
  Gate 129 D5
Gringley on the
  Hill 141 D5
Grinsdale 175 C6
Grinshill 111 C4
Grinton 156 B4
Griomsidar. 288 E4
Grishipoll 223 B4
Grisling Common 36 D2
Gristhorpe 161 C4
Griston 103 B5

Gritley. 283 G6
Grittenham 44 A4
Grittleton 44 A2
Grizebeck. 153 B3
Grizedale 154 B2
Grobister 282 E7
Groby 98 A2
Groes Conwy . . .125 C5
  Neath. 40 C2
Groes-faen 41 C5
Groesffordd
  Marli. 125 B5
Groeslon Gwyn. . .107 A4
  Gwyn 123 D5
Groes-lwyd 109 D7
Grogport 202 D3
Gromford. 89 B4
Gronant 125 A5
Groombridge 36 C3
Grosmont Mon . . .61 A6
  N Yorks. 160 A2
Groton 87 C5
Groucfoot 208 C3
Grouville Jersey. 6
Grove Dorset. 15 D7
  Kent 53 C4
  Notts 132 B2
  Oxon. 65 D5
Grove Park. 49 B7
Grovesend 57 B5
Grove Vale 96 B3
Grudie 263 D5
Gruids. 272 D3
Gruinard House .261 A6
Grula 246 B2
Gruline 225 B4
Grunasound. . . .285 K5
Grundisburgh . . .88 B3
Grunsagill 146 B1
Gruting 285 J4
Grutness. 285 N6
Gt. Bridge 96 B2
Gt. Hallingbury . .69 B5
Gt. Parndon. 68 C4
Gualachulain . . .227 B6
Gualin Ho. 276 C4
Guardbridge 221 C4
Guarlford 79 C6
Guay 230 D4
Guestling Green. .23 A6
Guestling Thorn. .23 A6
Guestwick 120 C2
Guestwick
  Green. 120 C2
Guide 137 A6
Guide Post. 179 A4
Guilden Morden. .85 C4
Guilden Sutton . .127 C4
Guildford 34 B2
Guildtown 219 A6
Guilsborough 98 D3
Guilsfield 109 D7
Guilton 53 D4
Guineaford 25 B6
Guisborough . . .168 D4
Guiseley 147 C5
Guist 120 C1
Guith 282 D6
Guiting Power. . . .64 A1
Gulberwick 285 K6
Gullane 210 B1
Gulval 2 B2
Gulworthy 11 D5
Gumfreston 55 D7
Gumley 98 B3
Gummow's Shop . .4 B3
Gunby E Yorks. . .149 D6
  Lincs. 116 C2
Gundleton 33 B5
Gun Hill 22 A3
Gunn 26 B1
Gunnerside 156 B3
Gunnerton 177 B7
Gunness 141 B6
Gunnislake. 11 D5
Gunnista. 285 J7
Gunthorpe Norf. .120 B2
  Notts 115 A4
  Pboro. 100 A3
Gunville 18 C3
Gunwalloe 3 C4
Gurnard 18 B3

Gurnett. 129 B4
Gurney Slade 29 A6
Gurnos 59 E4
Gussage All
  Saints. 31 D4
Gussage St
  Michael 30 D3
Guston 39 A5
Gutcher 284 D7
Guthrie 232 C3
Guyhirn. 101 A5
Guyhirn Gull . .101 A5
Guyhirn 101 A5
Guy's Head 118 C1
Guy's Marsh 30 C2
Guyzance 189 C5
Gwaenysgor . . .125 A5
Gwalchmai. 122 C3
Gwaun-Cae-
  Gurwen 59 D4
Gwaun-Leision. . .59 D4
Gwbert 73 B4
Gweek. 3 C5
Gwehelog. 61 C5
Gwenddwr 77 C4
Gwennap. 4 D2
Gwenter 3 D5
Gwernaffield . . .126 C2
Gwernesney 61 C6
Gwernogle. 58 B2
Gwernymynydd. .126 C2
Gwersyllt 126 D3
Gwespyr 125 A6
Gwithian. 2 A3
Gwredog 123 B4
Gwyddelwern . .109 A5
Gwyddgrug 58 B1
Gwydyr Uchaf . .124 C2
Gwynfryn 126 D2
Gwystre 77 A4
Gwytherin 124 C3
Gyfelia 110 A2
Gyffin 124 B2
Gyre. 283 G4
Gyrn-goch 107 B4

H

Haffenden
  Quarter 37 B6
Hafod-Dinbych. .124 D3
Hafod-lom. 124 B3
Haggate 146 D2
Haggbeck. 176 B2
Haggerston 198 B4
Haggrister 284 F5
Hagley Hereford . .78 C3
  Worcs. 96 C2
Hagworthingham
  . . . . .134 C3
Haigh Gtr Man. . .137 C5
  S Yorks. 139 B5
Haigh Moor 139 A5
Haighton Green .145 D5
Haile 162 D3
Hailes 80 D3
Hailey Herts 68 B3
  Oxon. 65 B4
Hailsham 22 B3
Hail Weston. 84 A3
Haimer 280 B3
Hainault 69 D4
Hainford 120 D4
Hainton. 134 A1
Hairmyres 205 C6
Haisthorpe. 151 A4
Hakin. 55 D4
Halam 132 D1
Halbeath 208 B4
Halberton 27 D5
Halcro. 280 B4
Hale Gtr Man. . . .128 A2
  Halton 127 A4
  Hants 31 D5
Hale Bank 127 A4
Halebarns 128 A2
Hales Norf. 105 B4
  Staffs 111 B6
Halesfield 95 A5
Halesgate 117 C6
Halesowen 96 C2
Hales Place 52 D3
Halesworth 105 D4
Halewood. 127 A4
Halford Shrops. . .94 C2
  Warks. 81 C5
Halfpenny Furze. .56 A2
Halfpenny Green .95 B6
Halfway Carms. . .58 B3
  Carms. 59 B5
  W Berks. 46 C2
Halfway Bridge. . .34 D2
Halfway House . .110 D2
Halfway Houses . .51 B6
Halifax 138 A3
Halket 205 C4
Halkirk 280 C3
Halkyn. 126 B2
Halland 22 A2
Hallaton 99 B4
Hallatrow. 43 D5
Hallbankgate . . .176 D3
Hall Dunnerdale 153 A3
Hallen 43 A4
Hall Green W Mid .96 C4
  W Yorks 139 B6
Hall Grove 68 B2
Halliburton 197 B5
Hallin 258 C2
Halling 51 C4
Hallington Lincs. .134 A3
  Northumb. 178 B1
Halliwell 137 B6
Hall of
  Tankerness . . .283 G6
Hall of the Forest 93 C6
Halloughton 132 D1
Hallow. 79 B6
Hallrule. 187 B4
Hallsands 8 D2
Halls 210 C3
Hall's Green 68 A2
Hallthwaites 153 B2
Hallworthy 10 C2
Hallyburton
  House. 220 A2
Hallyne 195 B6
Halmer End 112 A1
Halmore 62 C2

Halmyre Mains . .195 B6
Halnaker. 20 B2
Halsall. 136 B2
Halse Northants . . .82 C2
  Som 27 C6
Halsetown 2 B3
Halsham 143 A4
Halsinger 25 B6
Halstead Essex. . . .87 D4
  Kent 50 C1
  Leics. 99 A4
Halstock. 15 A5
Haltham 134 C2
Halton Bucks. 66 B3
  Halton 127 A5
  Lancs 145 A5
  Northumb. 178 C1
  Wrex 110 B2
  W Yorks 148 D2
Halton East 147 B4
Halton Gill 156 D2
Halton Holegate 135 C4
Halton Lea Gate 176 D4
Halton West. . . .146 B2
Haltwhistle 177 C5
Halvergate 105 A5
Halwell 8 B1
Halwill 11 B5
Halwill Junction. .11 A5
Ham Devon 14 A2
  Glos 62 D2
  Highld. 280 A4
  Kent 53 D5
  London 49 B4
  Shetland. 285 K1
  Wilts. 46 C1
Hambleden 47 A5
Hambledon Hants 33 D5
  Sur. 34 C2
Hamble-le-Rice. .18 A3
Hambleton Lancs 144 C3
  N Yorks. 149 D4
Hambridge. 28 C3
Hambrook S Glos. .43 B5
  W Sus. 19 A6
Ham Common . . .30 C2
Hameringham. . .134 C3
Hamerton. 100 D3
Hametoun 285 K1
Ham Green
  Hereford 79 C5
  Kent 37 D6
  Kent 51 C5
  N Som 43 B4
  Worcs. 80 A3
Hamilton 194 A2
Hammer 34 C1
Hammerpot. 20 B3
Hammersmith. . . .49 B5
Hammerwich 96 A3
Hammerwood. . . .36 C2
Hammond Street 68 C3
Hammoon 30 D2
Hamnavoe
  Shetland. 284 E4
  Shetland. 284 E6
  Shetland. 284 F6
  Shetland. 285 K5
Hampden Park . . .22 B4
Hamperden End. .86 D1
Hampnett. 64 B1
Hampole. 140 B3
Hampreston 17 B4
Hampstead 49 A5
Hampstead
  Norreys 46 B3
Hampsthwaite . .147 B6
Hampton London . .48 C4
  Shrops 95 C5
  Worcs. 80 C3
Hampton Bishop .78 D3
Hampton Heath .110 A3
Hampton in
  Arden. 97 C5
Hampton Loade . .95 C5
Hampton Lovett . .80 A1
Hampton Lucy. . .81 B5

Hampton on the
Hill 81 A5
Hampton Poyle . .65 B6
Hamrow 119 C6
Hamsey 22 A2
Hamsey Green . . .35 A6
Hamstall
Ridware 113 D5
Hamstead IoW . . .18 B3
W Mid 96 B3
Hamstead
Marshall 46 C2
Hamsterley
Durham 166 B4
Durham 178 D3
Hamstreet 38 B2
Ham Street . . .29 B5
Hamworthy . . .16 B3
Hanbury Staffs . .113 C5
Worcs. 80 A2
Hanbury
Woodend 113 C5
Hanby 116 B3
Hanchurch 112 A2
Handbridge . . .127 C4
Handcross 35 D5
Handforth . . .128 A3
Handley 127 D4
Handsacre . . .113 D4
Handsworth
S Yorks 131 A4
W Mid 96 B3
Handy Cross . .25 C5
Hanford 112 A2
Hanging
Langford 31 B4
Hangleton . . .20 B3
Hanham 43 B5
Hankelow 111 A5
Hankerton . . .63 D5
Hankham 22 B4
Hanley 112 A2
Hanley Castle . . .79 C6
Hanley Child . . .79 A4
Hanley Swan . . .79 C6
Hanley William . . .79 A4
Hanlith 146 A3
Hanmer 110 B3
Hannah 135 B5
Hannington Hants 46 D3
Northants. 99 D5
Swindon 64 D2
Hannington Wick 64 D2
Hansel Village . .192 B3
Hanslope 83 C5
Hanthorpe . . .116 C3
Hanwell London . . .49 A4
Oxon. 82 C1
Hanwood 94 A2
Hanworth London .48 B4
Norf 120 B3
Happendon . . .194 C3
Happisburgh . . .121 B5
Happisburgh
Common 121 C5
Hapsford 127 B4
Hapton Lancs . .146 D1
Norf 104 B2
Harberton 8 B1
Harbertonford 8 B1
Harbledown 52 D3
Harborne 96 C3
Harborough
Magna 98 D1
Harbottle . . .188 C2
Harbury 81 B6
Harby Leics . . .115 B5
Notts 132 B3
Harcombe 13 B6
Harden W Mid . . .96 A3
W Yorks 147 D4
Hardenhuish . . .44 B3
Hardgate . . .245 B4
Hardham 20 A3
Hardingham . .103 A6
Hardingstone . .83 B4
Hardington . . .43 D6
Hardington
Mandeville . . .29 D5

Hardington
Marsh. 15 A5
Hardley. 18 A3
Hardley Street. 105 A4
Hardmead 83 C6
Hardrow 156 B2
Hardstoft 131 C4
Hardway Hants . . .19 A5
Som 29 B7
Hardwick Bucks . . .66 B3
Cambs 85 B5
Norf 104 C3
Norf 118 D3
Northants. 83 A5
Notts 131 B6
Oxon. 65 A6
Oxon. 65 C4
W Mid 96 B3
Hardwicke Glos . . .62 B3
Glos. 63 A5
Hereford. 77 C6
Hardy's Green . .70 A3
Hareby 134 C3
Hareden 145 B6
Harefield 67 D5
Hare Green . . .71 A4
Hare Hatch . . .47 B6
Harehills 148 D2
Harehope 188 A3
Haresceugh . .165 A4
Harescombe . .63 B4
Haresfield . . .63 B4
Hareshaw 207 D6
Hareshaw Head .177 A6
Hare Street . . .68 A3
Harewood . . .148 C2
Harewood End . . .62 A1
Harford Carms . . .58 A3
Devon. 7 B5
Hargate 104 B2
Hargatewall . . .129 B6
Hargrave Ches W 127 C4
Northants. 100 D2
Suff 86 B3
Harker. 175 B6
Harkland 284 E6
Harkstead 88 D2
Harlaston . . .113 D6
Harlaw Ho. . . .256 D2
Harlaxton . . .116 B1
Harlech 107 C5
Harlequin . . .115 B4
Harlescott . . .111 D4
Harlesden 49 A5
Harleston Devon . .8 C1
Norf 104 C3
Suff 87 B6
Harlestone 83 A4
Harle Syke . . .146 D2
Harley Shrops . . .94 A3
S Yorks 139 D6
Harleyholm . .194 C4
Harlington C Beds 84 D2
London 48 B3
S Yorks 140 C2
Harlosh 258 D2
Harlow 69 B4
Harlow Hill
Northumb. 178 C2
N Yorks 148 B1
Harlthorpe . .149 D6
Harlton 85 B5
Harman's Cross . .16 C3
Harmby. 157 C5
Harmer Green . .68 B2
Harmer Hill . . .110 C3
Harmondsworth . .48 B3
Harmston 133 C4
Harnham 178 B2
Harnhill 63 C6
Harold Hill 69 D5
Haroldston West .55 C4
Haroldswick . .284 B8
Harold Wood . . .69 D5
Harome 159 C5
Harpenden . . .67 B6
Harpford 13 B5
Harpham 150 A3
Harpley Norf . . .119 C4
Worcs. 79 A4
Harpole 82 A3
Harpsdale . . .280 C3

Harpsden 47 A5
Harpswell. 133 A4
Harpurhey . . .138 C1
Harpur Hill 129 B5
Harraby. 175 C7
Harrapool 247 B5
Harrier 285 J1
Harrietfield . .219 B4
Harrietsham . . .37 A6
Harrington Cumb 162 B2
Lincs. 134 B3
Northants. 99 C4
Harringworth . .99 B6
Harris 234 A2
Harrogate . . .148 B2
Harrold 83 B6
Harrow 49 A4
Harrowbarrow . .6 A2
Harrowden . . .84 C2
Harrowgate Hill .167 D5
Harrow on the
Hill 49 A4
Harrow Street. . .87 D5
Harrow Weald . .67 D5
Harston Cambs . . .85 B6
Leics. 115 B6
Harswell. 150 C1
Hart 168 B2
Hartburn
Northumb. 178 A2
Stockton. 168 D2
Hart Common . .137 C5
Hartest 87 B4
Hartfield. 36 C2
Hartford Cambs . .101 D4
Ches W. 127 B6
Hartfordbridge . .47 D5
Hartford End . .69 B6
Hartforth 157 A5
Harthill Ches W . .127 D5
N Lanark. 208 D2
S Yorks 131 A4
Hart Hill 67 A6
Hartington . .129 C6
Hartland. 24 C3
Hartlebury. 95 D6
Hartlepool . . .168 B3
Hartley Cumb . .155 A6
Kent 37 C5
Kent 50 C3
Northumb. 179 B5
Hartley Westpall .47 D4
Hartley Wintney .47 D5
Hartlip. 51 C5
Hartoft End . .159 B6
Harton N Yorks . .149 A6
Shrops. 94 C1
T&W. 179 C5
Hartpury 62 A3
Hartshead . . .139 A4
Hartshill. 97 B6
Hartshorne . .113 C7
Hartsop. 164 D2
Hart Station . .168 B2
Hartwell. 83 B4
Hartwood . . .194 A3
Harvieston . .206 B3
Harvington. . . .80 C3
Harvington Cross 80 C3
Harwell. 46 A2
Harwich. 88 D3
Harwood Durham 165 B6
Gtr Man 137 B6
Harwood Dale . .160 B3
Harworth. . . .140 D4
Hasbury. 96 C2
Hascombe 34 B2
Haselbech 99 D4
Haselbury
Plucknett. . . .29 D4
Haseley. 81 A5
Haselor. 80 B4
Hasfield. 63 A4
Hasguard 55 D4
Haskayne . . .136 C2
Hasketon 88 B3
Hasland 130 C3
Haslemere 34 C2
Haslingden . .137 A6
Haslingfield. . .85 B6
Haslington . .128 D2
Hassall. 128 D2

Hassall Green . .128 D2
Hassell Street . . .38 A2
Hassendean. . .186 A4
Hassingham . .105 A4
Hassocks 21 A5
Hassop 130 B2
Hastigrow . . .281 B4
Hastingleigh . . .38 A2
Hastings 23 B6
Hastingwood. . .69 C4
Hastoe 67 C4
Haswell. 167 A6
Haswell Plough .167 A6
Hatch C Beds . . .84 C3
Hants 47 D4
Wilts. 30 C3
Hatch
Beauchamp . . .28 C3
Hatch End 67 D6
Hatchet Gate . . .18 A2
Hatch Green . .28 D3
Hatching Green . .67 B6
Hatchmere . . .127 B5
Hatcliffe 143 C4
Hatfield Hereford . .78 B3
Herts. 68 C2
S Yorks 141 C4
Worcs. 80 B1
Hatfield Broad
Oak 69 B5
Hatfield Garden
Village 68 C2
Hatfield Heath . .69 B5
Hatfield Hyde . .68 B2
Hatfield Peverel .70 B1
Hatfield
Woodhouse . .141 C4
Hatford 64 D4
Hatherden . . .46 D1
Hatherleigh . . .11 A6
Hathern 114 C2
Hatherop 64 C2
Hathersage . .130 A2
Hathershaw . .138 C2
Hatherton Ches E 111 A5
Staffs. 112 D3
Hatley St George .85 B4
Hatt 6 A2
Hattingley. . . .33 B5
Hatton Aberds . .257 C5
Derbys. 113 C6
Lincs. 134 B1
Shrops. 94 B2
Warks. 81 A5
Warr. 127 A5
Hatton Castle . .256 B2
Hattoncrook . .256 D3
Hatton Heath. .127 C4
Hatton of
Fintray. 245 A5
Hauxton 85 B6
Havant 19 A6
Haven 78 B2
Haven Bank . .134 D2
Haven Side . .142 A3
Havenstreet . . .19 B4

Havercroft 140 B1
Haverfordwest
Hwlffordd. 55 C5
Haverhill. 86 C2
Haverigg 153 C2
Havering-atte-
Bower. 69 D5
Haveringland . .120 C3
Haversham . . .83 C5
Haverthwaite . .154 C2
Haverton Hill. .168 C2
Hawarden
Penarlâg. . . .126 C3
Hawcoat 153 C3
Hawen 73 B6
Hawes 156 C2
Hawes' Green . .104 B3
Hawes Side . .144 D3
Hawford 79 A6
Hawick 186 B4
Hawkchurch . . .14 A3
Hawkedon 86 B3
Hawkenbury Kent .36 C3
Kent 37 B6
Hawkeridge . . .44 D2
Hawkerland . . .13 C5
Hawkesbury
S Glos. 43 A6
Warks. 97 C6
Hawkesbury
Upton. 44 A1
Hawkes End. . . .97 C6
Hawk Green . .129 A4
Hawkhill 189 B5
Hawkhurst 37 C5
Hawkinge 39 B4
Hawkley 33 C6
Hawkridge . . .26 B3
Hawkshead . .154 B2
Hawkshead Hill .154 B2
Hawksland . .194 C3
Hawkswick . .156 D3
Hawksworth
Notts. 115 A5
W Yorks 147 C5
W Yorks 147 D6
Hawkwell 70 D2
Hawley Hants . .34 A1
Kent 50 B2
Hawling 63 A6
Hawnby. 158 C4
Haworth. 147 D4
Hawstead 87 B4
Hawthorn
Durham 168 A2
Rhondda. 41 C6
Wilts. 44 C2
Hawthorn Hill
Brack 48 B1
Lincs. 134 D2
Hawthorpe. . .116 C3
Hawton 132 D2
Haxby 149 B5
Haxey 141 C5
Haydock. 137 D4
Haydon 29 D6
Haydon Bridge . .177 C6
Haydon Wick. . .45 A5
Haye 6 A2
Hayes London . . .48 A4
London 49 C7
Hayfield Derbys .129 A5
Fife. 209 A5
Hay Green . . .118 D2
Hayhill. 182 A2
Hayhillock . . .232 D3
Hayle 2 B3
Haynes 84 C2
Haynes Church
End 84 C2
Hay-on-Wye Y Gelli
Gandryll 77 C6
Hayscastle 55 B4
Hayscastle Cross .55 B5
Hayshead . . .233 D4
Hay Street . . .68 A3
Hayton Aberdeen 245 B6
Cumb 174 D4
Cumb 176 D3
E Yorks. 149 C7
Notts. 132 A2
Hayton's Bent . .94 C3

Haytor Vale 12 D2
Haywards Heath. .35 D6
Haywood 140 B3
Haywood Oaks .131 D6
Hazelbank . . .194 B3
Hazelbury Bryan. .16 A1
Hazeley. 47 D5
Hazel Grove. .129 A4
Hazelhurst . . .138 C2
Hazelslade. . . .112 D4
Hazel Street . . .37 C4
Hazelton. 64 B1
Hazelton Walls .220 B3
Hazelwood. . . .114 A1
Hazlemere 66 D3
Hazlerigg 179 B4
Hazlewood . . .147 B4
Hazon 189 C4
Heacham 118 B3
Headbourne
Worthy 32 B3
Headbrook. . . .77 B7
Headcorn 37 B6
Headingley . . .148 D1
Headington . . .65 C6
Headlam 167 D4
Headless Cross . .80 A3
Headley Hants . .33 B7
Hants. 46 C3
Sur 35 A5
Head of Muir . .207 B6
Headon. 132 B2
Heads 194 B2
Heads Nook . .176 D2
Heage 130 D3
Healaugh
N Yorks 148 C3
N Yorks 156 B4
Heald Green . .128 A3
Heale Devon . . .26 A1
Som 29 A6
Healey Gtr Man. .138 B1
Northumb. 178 D2
N Yorks 157 C5
Healing. 143 B4
Heamoor. 2 B2
Heanish 222 C3
Heanor. 114 A2
Heanton
Punchardon . .25 B6
Heapham 132 A3
Hearthstane . .195 D6
Heasley Mill. . . .26 B2
Heast 247 C5
Heath Cardiff . . .41 D6
Derbys. 131 C4
Heath and Reach 67 A4
Heathcote. . .129 C6
Heath End Hants .46 C3
Sur 34 B1
Warks. 81 A5
Heather 114 D1
Heatherfield . .259 D4
Heathfield Devon. .12 D3
E Sus. 36 D3
Som 27 C6
Heathhall 174 A2
Heath Hayes . .112 D3
Heath Hill . . .111 D6
Heath House . .28 A4
Heathrow Airport 48 B3
Heathstock. . . .14 A2
Heathton 95 B6
Heath Town. . . .96 B2
Heatley. 128 A2
Heaton Lancs . .144 A4
Staffs. 129 C4
T&W. 179 C4
W Yorks 147 D5
Heaton Moor. .138 D1
Heaverham 36 A3
Heaviley. 129 A3
Heavitree. 13 B4
Hebburn. 179 C5
Hebden. 147 A4
Hebden Bridge. .138 A2
Hebron Anglesey 123 B4
Carms. 73 D4
Northumb. 178 A3
Heck. 184 D3
Heckfield. 47 C5
Heckfield Green 104 D2

Heckfordbridge . . 70 A3
Heckington 116 A4
Heckmondwike . 139 A5
Heddington 44 C3
Heddle 282 F4
Heddon-on-the-
  Wall 178 C3
Hedenham 104 B4
Hedge End 32 D3
Hedgerley 48 A2
Hedging 28 C3
Hedley on the
  Hill 178 D2
Hednesford 112 D3
Hedon 142 A3
Hedsor 48 A2
Hedworth 179 C5
Hegdon Hill 78 B3
Heggerscales . . . 165 D6
Heglibister 285 H5
Heighington
  Darl 167 C5
  Lincs 133 C5
Heights of Brae . 263 D7
Heights of
  Kinlochewe . . . 262 D2
Heilam 277 B5
Heiton 197 C6
Hele Devon 13 A4
  Devon 25 A6
Helensburgh . . . 215 D5
Helford 3 C5
Helford Passage . . . 3 C5
Helhoughton . . . 119 C5
Helions
  Bumpstead 86 C2
Hellaby 140 D3
Helland 10 D1
Hellesdon 120 D4
Hellidon 82 B2
Hellifield 146 B2
Hellingly 22 A3
Hellington 104 A4
Hellister 285 J5
Helm 189 D4
Helmdon 82 C2
Helmingham 88 B2
Helmington
  Row 167 B4
Helmsdale 274 C4
Helmshore 137 A6
Helmsley 159 C5
Helperby 148 A3
Helperthorpe . . . 160 D3
Helpringham . . . 116 A4
Helpston 100 A3
Helsby 127 B4
Helsey 135 B5
Helston 3 C4
Helstone 10 C1
Helton 164 C3
Helwith Bridge . 146 A2
Hemblington . . . 121 D5
Hemel
  Hempstead 67 C5
Hemingbrough . 149 D5
Hemingby 134 B2
Hemingford
  Abbots 101 C4
Hemingford
  Grey 101 D4
Hemingstone . . . 88 B2
Hemington Leics 114 C2
  Northants 100 C2
  Som 43 D6
Hemley 88 C3
Hemlington . . . 168 D3
Hemp Green . . . 89 A4
Hempholme 150 B3
Hempnall 104 B3
Hempnall Green 104 B3
Hempriggs
  House 281 D5
Hempstead Essex . 86 D2
  Medway 51 C4
  Norf 120 B3
  Norf 121 C6
Hempsted 63 B4
Hempton Norf . . 119 C6
  Oxon 82 D1
Hemsby 121 D6
Hemswell 142 D1

Hemswell Cliff . . 133 A4
Hemsworth 140 B2
Hemyock 27 D6
Henbury Bristol . . 43 B4
  Ches E 128 B3
Hendon London . . . 49 A5
  T&W 179 D6
Hendre 126 C1
Hendre-ddu . . . 124 C3
Hendreforgan . . 41 C4
Hendy 57 B5
Heneglwys 123 C4
Hen-feddau fawr 73 C5
Henfield 21 A5
Henford 11 B4
Henghurst 38 B1
Hengoed Caerph . . 41 B6
  Powys 77 B6
  Shrops 110 B1
Hengrave 87 A4
Henham 69 A5
Heniarth 93 A5
Henlade 28 C2
Henley Shrops . . 94 D3
  Som 28 B4
  Suff 88 B2
  W Sus 34 D1
Henley-in-Arden 81 A4
Henley-on-
  Thames 47 A5
Henley's Down . . . 23 A5
Henllan Ceredig . . 73 B6
  Denb 125 C5
Henllan Amgoed . 73 D4
Henllys 61 D4
Henlow 84 D3
Hennock 12 C3
Henny Street 87 D4
Henryd 124 B2
Henry's Moat . . . 55 B6
Hensall 140 A3
Henshaw 177 C5
Hensingham . . . 162 C2
Henstead 105 C5
Henstridge 30 D1
Henstridge Ash . . 29 C7
Henstridge
  Marsh 30 C1
Henton Oxon 66 C2
  Som 29 A4
Henwood 10 D3
Heogan 285 J6
Heol-las 40 B1
Heol Senni 59 C6
Heol-y-Cyw 40 C4
Hepburn 188 A3
Hepple 188 C2
Hepscott 179 A4
Heptonstall . . . 138 A2
Hepworth Suff . . . 103 D5
  W Yorks 139 C4
Herbrandston 55 D4
Hereford 78 C3
Heriot 196 A2
Hermiston 209 C4
Hermitage
  Borders 186 D4
  Dorset 15 A6
  W Berks 46 B3
  W Sus 19 A6
Hermon Anglesey 122 D3
  Carms 58 C3
  Carms 73 C6
  Pembs 73 C5
Herne 52 C3
Herne Bay 52 C3
Herner 25 C6
Hernhill 52 C2
Herodsfoot 5 A7
Heronsford . . . 180 C3
Herriard 33 A5
Herringfleet 105 B5
Herringswell . . . 102 D3
Hersden 53 C4
Hersham Corn . . . 10 A3
  Sur 48 C4
Herstmonceux . . . 22 A4
Herston 283 H5
Hertford 68 B3
Hertford Heath . . 68 B3
Hertingfordbury . . 68 B3

Hesketh Bank . . . 136 A3
Hesketh Lane . . . 145 C6
Hesket
  Newmarket . . . 163 A6
Heskin Green . . . 136 B4
Hesleden 168 B2
Hesleyside 177 A6
Heslington 149 B5
Hessay 148 B4
Hessenford 6 B2
Hessett 87 A5
Hessle 142 A2
Hest Bank 145 A4
Heston 48 B4
Hestwall 282 F3
Heswall 126 A2
Hethe 65 A6
Hethersett . . . 104 A2
Hethersgill 176 C2
Hethpool 188 A1
Hett 167 B5
Hetton 146 B3
Hetton-le-Hole . . 167 A6
Hetton Steads . . . 198 C4
Heugh 178 B2
Heugh-head 243 A6
Heveningham . . . 104 D4
Hever 36 B2
Heversham 154 C3
Hevingham 120 C3
Hewas Water 5 C4
Hewelsfield 62 C1
Hewish N Som . . 42 C3
  Som 14 A4
Heworth 149 B5
Hexham 178 C1
Hextable 50 B2
Hexton 84 D3
Hexworthy 12 D1
Hey 146 C2
Heybridge Essex . 69 D6
  Essex 70 C2
Heybridge Basin . . 70 C2
Heybrook Bay 7 C4
Heydon Cambs . . . 85 C6
  Norf 120 C3
Heydour 116 B3
Heylipol 222 C2
Heylor 284 E4
Heysham 144 A4
Heyshott 20 A1
Heyside 138 C2
Heytesbury 30 A3
Heythrop 64 A4
Heywood
  Gtr Man 138 B1
  Wilts 44 D2
Hibaldstow . . . 142 C1
Hickleton 140 C2
Hickling Norf . . . 121 C6
  Notts 115 C4
Hickling Green . . 121 C6
Hickling Heath . . 121 C6
Hickstead 35 D5
Hidcote Boyce . . . 81 C4
High Ackworth . . 140 B2
Higham Derbys . . 130 D3
  Kent 51 B4
  Lancs 146 D2
  Suff 86 A3
  Suff 87 D6
Higham Dykes . . 178 B3
Higham Ferrers . . 83 A6
Higham Gobion . . 84 D3
Higham on the
  Hill 97 B6
Highampton 11 A5
Higham Wood . . . 36 B3
High Angerton . . 178 A2
High Bankhill . . 164 A3
High Barnes . . . 179 D5
High Beach 68 D4
High Bentham . . 145 A6
High Bickington . . 25 C7
High Birkwith . . 155 D6
High Blantyre . . 194 A1
High
  Bonnybridge . . 207 C6
High Bradfield . . 139 D5
High Bray 26 B1
Highbridge
  Highld 239 D5

Highbridge continued
  Som 28 A3
Highbrook 35 C6
High Brooms 36 B3
High Bullen 25 C6
High Buston . . . 189 C5
High Callerton . . 178 B3
High Catton . . . 149 B6
Highclere 46 C2
Highcliffe 17 B6
High Cogges 65 C4
High Coniscliffe 167 D5
High Cross Hants . . 33 C6
  Herts 68 B3
High Easter 69 B6
High
  Eggborough . . . 140 A3
High Ellington . . 157 C5
Higher Ansty 16 A1
Higher Ashton . . . 12 C3
Higher Ballam . . 144 D3
Higher Bartle . . . 145 D5
Higher Boscaswell, 2 B1
Higher
  Burwardsley . . 127 D5
High Ercall 111 D4
Higher Clovelly . . . 24 C4
Higher End . . . 136 C4
Higher
  Kinnerton 126 C3
Higher
  Penwortham . . 136 A4
Higher Town
  Scilly P02 E4
Higher
  Walreddon 11 D5
Higher Walton
  Lancs 137 A4
  Warr 137 A5
Higher
  Wheelton 137 A5
Higher Whitley . . 127 A6
Higher
  Wincham 128 B1
Higher Wych 110 A3
High Etherley . . 167 C4
Highfield E Yorks 149 D6
  Gtr Man 137 C6
  N Ayrs 204 C3
  Oxon 65 A6
  S Yorks 130 A3
  T&W 178 D3
Highfields Cambs . . 85 B5
  Northumb 198 A3
High Garrett 70 A1
Highgate 49 A5
High Grange . . 167 B4
High Green Norf 104 A2
  S Yorks 139 D6
  Worcs 80 C1
High Halden 37 C6
High Halstow 51 B4
High Ham 28 B4
High Harrington 162 B3
High Hatton . . 111 C5
High Hawsker . . 160 A3
High Hesket . . . 164 A2
High Hesleden . . 168 B2
High Hoyland . . 139 B5
High Hunsley . . 150 D2
High Hurstwood . . 36 D2
High Hutton . . 149 A6
High Ireby 163 A5
High Kelling . . 120 A3
High Kilburn . . 158 D4
High Lands . . . 166 C4
Highlane Ches E . . 128 C3
  Derbys 131 A4
High Lane
  Gtr Man 129 A4
  Worcs 79 A4
High Laver 69 C5
High Legh 128 A2
Highleigh 20 C1
High Leven . . . 168 D2
Highley 95 C5
High Littleton . . . 43 D5
High Lorton . . . 163 B4

High Marishes . . 159 D7
High Marnham . . 132 B3
High Melton . . . 140 C3
High Mickley . . 178 C2
High Mindork . . 171 B5
Highmoor Cross . . 47 A5
Highmoor Hill . . 42 A3
Highnam 62 B3
Highnam Green . . 62 A3
High Newton . . 154 C3
High Newton-by-the-
  Sea 189 A5
High Nibthwaite 154 C1
High Offley . . . 112 C1
High Ongar 69 C5
High Onn 112 D2
High Roding 69 B6
High Row 163 A6
High Salvington . . 21 B4
High Sellafield . . 162 D3
High Shaw 156 B2
High Spen 178 D3
Highsted 51 C6
High Stoop . . . 166 A4
High Street Corn . . 5 B4
  Kent 37 C5
  Suff 87 C4
  Suff 89 B5
  Suff 105 D5
Highstreet Green 86 D3
High Street
  Green 87 B6
Hightae 174 A3
High Throston . . 168 B2
Hightown Ches E 128 C3
  Mers 136 C2
Hightown Green . . 87 B5
High Toynton . . 134 C2
High Trewhitt . . 188 C3
High Valleyfield 208 B3
Highway 44 B4
Highweek 12 D3
High Westwood . 178 D3
Highworth 64 D3
High Wray 154 B2
High Wych 69 B4
High Wycombe . . 66 D3
Hilborough . . . 103 A4
Hilcote 131 D4
Hilcott 45 D5
Hildenborough . . 36 B3
Hilden Park 36 B3
Hildersham 86 C1
Hilderstone . . . 112 B3
Hilderthorpe . . 151 A4
Hilfield 15 A6
Hilgay 102 B2
Hill Pembs 55 D7
  S Glos 62 D2
  W Mid 96 B4
Hillam 140 A3
Hillbeck 165 D5
Hillborough 53 C6
Hill Brow 33 C6
Hillbutts 16 A3
Hillclifflane . . . 113 A6
Hillcommon 27 C6
Hill Dale 136 B3
Hill Dyke 117 A6
Hillend 208 B4
Hill End Durham . 166 B3
  Fife 208 B3
  N Yorks 147 B4
Hillerton 12 B2
Hillesden 66 A1
Hillesley 43 A6
Hillfarance 27 C6
Hillhead Aberds . 255 C6
  Devon 8 B3
  S Ayrs 182 B3
Hill Head Hants . . 18 A4
  Northumb 178 C1
Hillhead of
  Auchentumb . . 269 D4
Hillhead of
  Cocklaw 257 B5
Hillhouse 197 A4
Hilliclay 280 B3
Hillingdon 48 A3

Hillington
  Glasgow 205 B5
  Norf 119 C4
Hillmorton 98 D2
Hillockhead
  Aberds 243 B6
  Aberds 244 A1
Hill of Beath . . 209 A4
Hill of Fearn . . 265 C4
Hill of
  Mountblairy . . 268 D1
Hill Ridware . . 113 D4
Hillside Aberds . . 245 C6
  Angus 233 B5
  Mers 136 B2
  Orkney 283 H5
  Shetland 285 G6
Hillswick 284 F4
Hill Top Durham . . 166 C2
  Hants 18 A3
  W Mid 96 B2
Hill View 16 B3
Hillway 19 C5
Hillwell 285 M5
Hilmarton 44 B4
Hilperton 44 D2
Hilsea 19 A5
Hilston 151 D5
Hilton Aberds . . 257 C4
  Cambs 85 A4
  Cumb 165 C5
  Derbys 113 B6
  Dorset 16 A1
  Durham 167 C4
  Highld 264 B3
  Shrops 95 B5
  Stockton 168 D2
Hilton of
  Cadboll 265 C4
Himbleton 80 B2
Himley 96 B1
Hincaster 154 C4
Hinckley 98 B1
Hinderclay . . . 103 D6
Hinderton 126 B3
Hinderwell . . . 169 D5
Hindford 110 B2
Hindhead 34 C1
Hindley 137 C5
Hindley Green . . 137 C5
Hindlip 80 B1
Hindolveston . . 120 C2
Hindon 30 B3
Hindringham . . 120 B1
Hingham 103 A6
Hinstock 111 C5
Hintlesham 88 C1
Hinton Hants . . . 17 B6
  Hereford 78 D1
  Northants 82 B2
  S Glos 43 B6
  Shrops 94 A2
Hinton Ampner . . 33 C4
Hinton Blewett . . 43 D4
Hinton
  Charterhouse . . 43 D6
Hinton-in-the-
  Hedges 82 D2
Hinton Martell . . 17 A4
Hinton on the
  Green 80 C3
Hinton Parva . . . 45 A6
Hinton St George 28 D4
Hinton St Mary . . 30 D1
Hinton Waldrist . . 65 D4
Hints Shrops 95 D4
  Staffs 97 A4
Hinwick 83 A6
Hinxhill 38 A2
Hinxton 85 C6
Hinxworth 84 C4
Hipperholme . . 139 A4
Hipswell 157 B5
Hirael 123 C5
Hiraeth 73 D4
Hirn 245 B4
Hirnant 109 C5

Hirst N Lanark....207 D6
 Northumb......179 A4
Hirst Courtney .140 A4
Hirwaun.........125 C6
Hirwaun........59 E6
Hiscott.........25 C6
Histon.........85 A6
Hitcham.......87 B5
Hitchin........68 A1
Hither Green....90 A4
Hittisleigh....12 B2
Hive..........149 D7
Hixon.........112 C4
Hoaden.......53 D4
Hoaldalbert....61 A5
Hoar Cross....113 C5
Hoarwithy....62 A1
Hoath.........53 C4
Hobarris.......93 D7
Hobbister....283 G4
Hobkirk......187 B4
Hobson......178 D3
Hoby.........115 D4
Hockering....120 D2
Hockerton....132 D2
Hockley........70 D2
Hockley Heath..97 D4
Hockliffe......67 A4
Hockwold cum
 Wilton......102 C3
Hockworthy....27 D5
Hoddesdon....68 C3
Hoddlesden...137 A6
Hoddomcross .175 A4
Hoddom Mains .175 A4
Hodgeston......55 E6
Hodley.......93 B5
Hodnet.......111 C5
Hodthorpe....131 B5
Hoe Hants.......33 D4
 Norf.........120 D1
Hoe Gate......33 D5
Hoff.........165 D4
Hoggard's Green .87 B4
Hoggeston.....66 A3
Hogha
 Gearraidh 287 G2
Hoghton.....137 A5
Hognaston....130 D2
Hog Patch.....34 B1
Hogsthorpe ...135 B5
Holbeach.....117 C6
Holbeach Bank .117 C6
Holbeach
 Clough......117 C6
Holbeach Drove 117 D6
Holbeach Hurn .117 C6
Holbeach St
 Johns.......117 D6
Holbeach St
 Marks.......117 B6
Holbeach St
 Matthew.....117 B7
Holbeck Notts ..131 B5
 W Yorks.......148 D1
Holbeck
 Woodhouse ..131 B5
Holberrow Green .80 B3
Holbeton......7 B5
Holborn......49 A6
Holbrook Derbys .114 A1
 Suff..........88 D2
 S Yorks......131 A4
Holburn.....198 C4
Holbury.......18 A3
Holcombe Devon .13 D4
 Som..........29 A6
Holcombe Rogus .27 D5
Holcot.......83 A4
Holden.......146 C1
Holdenby......82 A3
Holdenhurst ...17 B5
Holdgate......94 C3
Holdingham...116 A3
Holditch......14 A3
Holefield.....198 C2
Holehouses ...128 B2
Hole-in-the-
 Wall........62 A2

Holemoor.......11 A5
Holestane....183 C6
Holford.......27 A6
Holgate......149 B4
Holker......154 D2
Holkham.....119 A5
Hollacombe.....11 A4
Holland Orkney .282 B5
 Orkney.....282 E7
Holland Fen...117 A5
Holland-on-Sea..71 B6
Hollandstoun .282 B8
Hollee......175 B5
Hollesley......89 C4
Hollicombe......8 A2
Hollingbourne ..37 A6
Hollington
 Derbys.......113 B6
 E Sus.........23 A5
 Staffs.......113 B4
Hollington
 Grove......113 B6
Hollingworth..138 D3
Hollins......137 C7
Hollinsclough .129 C5
Hollins Green ..137 D5
Hollins Lane ...145 B4
Hollinwood
 Gtr Man......138 C2
 Shrops.......111 B4
Hollocombe....26 D1
Holloway......130 D3
Hollowell......98 D3
Hollow
 Meadows....130 A2
Hollybush Caerph .41 A6
 E Ayrs.......182 A1
 Worcs.......79 D5
Holly End....101 A4
Holly Grn......79 C4
Hollym......143 A5
Hollywood......96 D3
Holmbridge...139 C4
Holmbury St
 Mary........35 B4
Holmbush......5 B5
Holmcroft....112 C3
Holme Cambs....100 C3
 Cumb.......154 D4
 Notts.......132 D3
 N Yorks.......158 C2
 W Yorks.......139 C4
Holme Chapel..138 A1
Holme Green..149 C4
Holme Hale....103 A4
Holme Lacy....78 D3
Holme Marsh...78 B1
Holme next the
 Sea.........119 A4
Holme-on-Spalding-
 Moor........149 D7
Holme on the
 Wolds.......150 C2
Holme
 Pierrepont ...115 B4
Holmer.......78 C3
Holmer Green...67 D4
Holme St
 Cuthbert....174 D4
Holmes Chapel .128 C2
Holmesfield...130 B3
Holmeswood...136 B3
Holmewood....131 C4
Holme Wood...147 D5
Holmfirth....139 C4
Holmhead
 Dumfries....183 D5
 E Ayrs.......193 C5
Holmisdale...258 D1
Holmpton....143 A5
Holmrook....153 A1
Holmsgarth...285 J6
Holmwrangle ..164 A3
Holne........7 A6
Holnest......15 A6
Holsworthy....10 A4
Holsworthy
 Beacon......11 A4
Holt Dorset....17 A4
 Norf.......120 B2
 Wilts.........44 C2
 Worcs.......79 A6

Holt continued
 Wrex.......127 D4
Holtby.......149 B5
Holt End Hants...33 B5
 Worcs.......80 A3
Holt Fleet.....79 A6
Holt Heath.....79 A6
Holton Oxon.....65 C7
 Som..........29 C6
 Suff.........105 D4
Holton cum
 Beckering....133 A6
Holton Heath...16 B3
Holton le Clay .143 C4
Holton le Moor .142 D2
Holton St Mary...87 D6
Holt Park.....147 C6
Holwell Dorset...29 D7
 Herts.........84 D3
 Leics.......115 C5
 Oxon.........64 C3
Holwick......166 C2
Holworth......16 C1
Holybourne.....33 A6
Holy Cross.....96 D2
Holyhead
 Caergybi.....122 B2
Holy Island....199 B5
Holymoorside .130 C3
Holyport......48 B1
Holystone....188 C2
Holytown....207 D5
Holywell Cambs .101 D5
 Corn..........4 B2
 Dorset........15 A5
 E Sus.........22 C3
 Northumb.....179 B5
Holywell
 Treffynnon ...126 B1
Holywell Green .138 B3
Holywell Lake ...27 C6
Holywell Row ..102 D3
Holywood....184 D2
Homer.......95 A4
Homersfield...104 C3
Hom Green.....62 A1
Homington....31 C5
Honeyborough ..55 D5
Honeybourne....80 C4
Honeychurch...12 A1
Honey Hill......52 C3
Honey Street....45 C5
Honey Tye......87 D5
Honiley.......97 D5
Honing......121 C5
Honingham...120 D3
Honington Lincs .116 A2
 Suff.........103 D5
 Warks.........81 C5
Honiton.......13 A6
Honley......139 B4
Hood Green...139 C6
Hooe E Sus......23 B4
 Plym..........7 B4
Hooe Common...23 A4
Hoo Green....128 A2
Hook E Yorks....141 A5
 Hants.........47 D5
 London.......49 C4
 Pembs........55 C5
 Wilts.........45 A4
Hooke.......15 B5
Hookgate....111 B6
Hook Green Kent .37 C4
 Kent..........50 C3
Hook Norton....81 D6
Hookway......12 B3
Hookwood.....35 B5
Hoole......127 C4
Hooley.......35 A5
Hoop.........61 C7
Hoo St.Werburgh .51 B4
Hooton.......126 B3
Hooton Levitt ..140 D3
Hooton Pagnell .140 C2
Hooton Roberts .140 D2
Hope Derbys....129 A6
 Devon..........7 D5
 Highld......277 C5
 Powys........93 A6
 Shrops........94 A1
 Staffs.......129 D6

Hope Yr Hôb.....126 D3
Hope Bagot.....94 D3
Hope Bowdler...94 B2
Hope End Green..69 A5
Hope Green....129 A4
Hopeman.....266 C2
Hope Mansell...62 B2
Hopesay.......94 C1
Hope's Grn......51 A4
Hope under
 Dinmore.....78 B3
Hopley's Green...78 B1
Hopperton....148 B3
Hop Pole......117 D4
Hopstone......95 B5
Hopton Shrops ..110 C5
 Shrops.......111 C4
 Staffs.......112 C3
 Suff.........103 D5
Hopton
 Cangeford....94 C3
Hopton Castle...94 D1
Hoptonheath....94 D1
Hopton on Sea .105 A6
Hopton Wafers..95 D4
Hopwas......97 A4
Hopwood
 Gtr Man......138 C1
 Worcs........96 D3
Horam.......22 A3
Horbling......116 B4
Horbury......139 B5
Horcott.......64 C2
Horden.....168 A2
Horderley......94 C2
Hordle......17 B6
Hordley......110 B2
Horeb Carms.....57 B4
 Carms........58 C2
 Ceredig.......73 B6
Horfield......43 B5
Horham......104 D3
Horkesley Heath .70 A3
Horkstow....142 B1
Horley Oxon.....81 C7
 Sur..........35 B5
Hornblotton
 Green.......29 B5
Hornby Lancs...145 A5
 N Yorks......157 B6
 N Yorks......158 A2
Horncastle...134 C2
Hornchurch....50 A2
Horncliffe...198 B3
Horndean
 Borders.....198 B2
 Hants.........33 D6
Horndon.......11 D6
Horndon on the
 Hill..........50 A3
Horne.......35 B6
Horniehaugh...232 B2
Horning......121 D5
Horninghold....99 B5
Horninglow....113 C6
Horningsea.....85 A6
Horningsham...30 A2
Horningtoft...119 C6
Hornsby......176 D3
Hornsby Cross...37 C5
Horns Cross
 Devon........25 C4
 E Sus.........37 D6
Hornsea......151 C5
Hornsea Bridge .151 C5
Hornsey......49 A6
Hornton......81 C6
Horrabridge.....7 A4
Horringer......87 A4
Horringford....18 C4
Horsebridge
 Devon........11 D5
 Hants.........32 B2
Horse Bridge..129 D4
Horsebrook....112 D2
Horsehay......95 A4
Horseheath.....86 C2
Horsehouse...156 C4
Horsell.......34 A2
Horseman's
 Green.......110 A3
Horseway....101 C6

Horsey.......121 C6
Horsford......120 D3
Horsforth....147 D6
Horsham Worcs...79 B5
 W Sus.........35 C4
Horsham St
 Faith.......120 D4
Horsington Lincs 134 C1
 Som..........29 C7
Horsley Derbys..114 A1
 Glos..........63 D4
 Northumb.....178 C2
 Northumb.....188 D1
Horsley Cross ...71 A5
Horsleycross
 Street......71 A5
Horsleyhill....186 B4
Horsleyhope...166 A3
Horsley
 Woodhouse ..114 A1
Horsmonden....37 B4
Horspath......65 C6
Horstead....121 D4
Horsted Keynes .36 D1
Horton Bucks....67 B4
 Dorset........17 A4
 Lancs.......146 B2
 Northants.....83 B5
 S Glos........43 A6
 Shrops.......110 C3
 Som..........28 D3
 Staffs.......129 D4
 Swansea......57 D4
 Windsor.......48 B3
Horton-cum-
 Studley......65 B6
Horton Green ..110 A3
Horton Heath...32 D3
Horton in
 Ribblesdale...155 D7
Horton Kirby...50 C2
Hortonlane....110 D3
Horwich......137 B5
Horwich End...129 A5
Horwood.......25 C6
Hose.........115 C5
Hoselaw......198 C2
Hoses.......153 A3
Hosh.........218 B3
Hoswick......285 L6
Hotham......150 D1
Hothfield......38 A1
Hoton........114 C3
Houbie......284 D8
Houdston....181 B3
Hough Ches E....128 B3
 Ches E.......128 D2
Hougham......116 A1
Hough Green..127 A4
Hough-on-the-
 Hill.........116 A2
Houghton Cambs 101 D4
 Cumb.......175 C7
 Hants.........32 B2
 Pembs........55 D5
 W Sus.........20 A3
Houghton
 Conquest....84 C2
Houghton Green
 E Sus..........37 D7
 Warr.........137 D5
Houghton-le-
 Side.......167 C5
Houghton-Le-
 Spring......167 A6
Houghton on the
 Hill..........98 A3
Houghton Regis .67 A5
Houghton St
 Giles.......119 B6
Houlland
 Shetland.....284 F7
 Shetland.....285 H5
Houlsyke....159 A6
Hound.......18 A3
Hound Green....47 D5
Houndslow...197 B5
Houndwood....211 D5
Hounslow......48 B4
Hounslow Green .69 B6

Housay.......284 F8
House of Daviot .252 B3
House of
 Glenmuick ...243 C5
Housetter....284 E5
Houss......285 K5
Houston.....205 B4
Houstry......275 A5
Houton......283 G4
Hove.........21 B5
Hoveringham ..115 A4
Hoveton.....121 D5
Hovingham...159 D5
How.........176 D3
Howbrook....139 D6
How Caple.....79 D4
Howden Borders .187 A5
 E Yorks......141 A5
Howden-le-
 Wear.......167 B4
Howe Highld....281 B5
 Norf.........104 A3
 N Yorks......158 C2
Howe Bridge..137 C5
Howe Green....70 C1
Howell......116 A4
How End......84 C2
Howe of
 Teuchar....256 B2
Howe Street
 Essex........69 B6
 Essex........86 D2
Howey.......77 B4
Howgate....196 A1
How Green....36 B2
Howick......189 B5
Howle Durham...166 C3
 Telford......111 C5
Howlett End....86 D1
Howley.......14 A2
Hownam......187 A6
Hownam Mains .187 A6
Howpasley....185 B6
Howsham
 N Lincs......142 C2
 N Yorks......149 A6
Howslack....184 B3
Howtel......198 C2
Howton.......61 A6
Howtown....164 D2
Howwood....204 B3
Hoxne.......104 D2
Hoy.........283 G3
Hoylake.....126 A2
Hoyland.....139 C6
Hoylandswaine .139 C5
Hubberholme ..156 D3
Hubbert's
 Bridge......117 A5
Huby N Yorks....147 C6
 N Yorks......149 A4
Hucclecote 63 B4
Hucking......37 A6
Hucknall....114 A3
Huddersfield..139 B4
Huddington....80 B2
Hudswell....157 A5
Huggate.....150 B1
Hugglescote ..114 D2
Hughenden
 Valley.......66 D3
Hughley......94 B3
Hugh Town Scilly... 2 E4
Huish Devon....25 D6
 Wilts.........45 C5
Huish
 Champflower...27 C5
Huish Episcopi ..28 C4
Huisinis....287 C4
Hulcott......66 B3
Hulland.....113 A6
Hulland Ward ..113 A6
Hullavington ...44 A2
Hullbridge....70 D2
Hulme......138 D1
Hulme End...129 D6
Hulme Walfield .128 C3
Hulverstone....18 C2
Hulver Street..105 C5
Humber......78 B3
Humber Bridge .142 A2
Humberston ..143 C5

Humbie........210 D1
Humbleton
  E Yorks.......151 D5
  Northumb......188 A2
Humby........116 B3
Hume.........197 B6
Humshaugh....177 B7
Huna.........281 A5
Huncoat......146 D1
Huncote......98 B2
Hundalee.....187 B5
Hunderthwaite.166 C2
Hundleby.....134 C3
Hundle Houses.134 D2
Hundleton....55 D5
Hundon.......86 C3
Hundred Acres..33 D4
Hundred End..136 A3
Hundred House..77 B5
Hungarton....98 A3
Hungerford Hants 31 D5
  W Berks......46 C1
Hungerford
  Newtown.....46 B1
Hungerton....116 C1
Hungladder...258 A3
Hunmanby....161 D4
Hunmanby
  Moor........161 D5
Hunningham...81 A6
Hunny Hill...18 C3
Hunsdon......68 B4
Hunsingore...148 B3
Hunslet......148 D2
Hunsonby.....164 B3
Hunspow......280 A4
Hunstanton...118 A3
Hunstanworth..166 A2
Hunsterson...111 A5
Hunston Suff..87 A5
  W Sus........20 B1
Hunstrete.....43 C5
Hunt End.....80 A3
Hunter's Quay.203 A6
Hunthill Lodge.232 A2
Huntingdon...100 D4
Huntingfield..104 D4
Huntingford...30 B2
Huntington
  E Loth.......210 C1
  Hereford.....77 B6
  Staffs.......112 D3
  York........149 B5
Hunting-tower.219 B5
Huntley......62 B3
Huntly.......255 C6
Huntlywood...197 B5
Hunton Kent...37 B5
  N Yorks......157 B5
Hunt's Corner.103 C6
Hunt's Cross..127 A4
Huntsham.....27 C5
Huntspill....28 A3
Huntworth....28 A3
Hunwick......167 B4
Hunworth....120 B2
Hurdsfield...129 B4
Hurley Warks..97 B5
  Windsor.....47 A6
Hurlford.....193 B4
Hurliness....283 J3
Hurn.........17 B5
Hurn's End...118 A1
Hursley......32 C3
Hurst N Yorks.156 A4
  Som.........29 D4
  Wokingham...47 B5
Hurstbourne
  Priors......32 A3
Hurstbourne
  Tarrant......46 D1
Hurst Green E Sus 37 D5
  Lancs.......145 D6
Hurstpierpoint.21 A5
Hurst Wickham..37 B5
Hurstwood....146 D2
Hurtmore.....47 A6
Hurworth Place.157 A6
Hury.........166 D2
Husabost.....258 C2
Husbands
  Bosworth.....98 C3

Husborne
  Crawley......83 D6
Husthwaite...158 D4
Hutchwns.....40 D1
Huthwaite...131 D4
Huttoft......135 B5
Hutton Borders.198 A3
  Cumb.......164 C2
  Essex.......69 D6
  E Yorks.....150 B3
  Lancs.......136 A3
  N Som.......42 D2
Hutton Buscel..160 C3
Hutton Conyers.158 D2
Hutton
  Cranswick...150 B3
Hutton End...164 B2
Hutton Gate..168 D3
Hutton Henry..168 B2
Hutton-le-Hole.159 B6
Hutton Magna..166 D4
Hutton Roof
  Cumb.......155 D4
  Cumb.......163 A6
Hutton Rudby..158 A3
Hutton Sessay.158 D3
Hutton Village..168 D3
Hutton
  Wandesley...148 B4
Huxley.......127 C5
Huxter Shetland.285 G7
  Shetland.....285 H5
Huxton......211 D5
Huyton......136 D3
Hycemoor....153 B1
Hyde Glos....63 C4
  Gtr Man......138 D2
  Hants.......31 D5
Hyde Heath...67 C4
Hyde Park...140 C3
Hydestile....34 B2
Hylton Castle..179 D5
Hyndford
  Bridge......194 B4
Hynish......222 D2
Hyssington...93 B7
Hythe Hants...18 A3
  Kent........38 B3
Hythe End....48 B3
Hythie......269 D5

Ibberton.....16 A1
Ible.........130 D2
Ibsley.......17 A5
Ibstock......114 D2
Ibstone......66 D2
Ibthorpe.....46 D1
Ibworth......46 D3
Ichrachan....227 C5
Ickburgh....103 B4
Ickenham.....48 A3
Ickford......66 C1
Ickham......53 D4
Ickleford....84 D3
Icklesham....23 A6
Ickleton.....85 C6
Icklingham...102 D3
Ickwell Green..84 C3
Icomb.......64 A3
Idbury......64 B3
Iddesleigh...11 A6
Ide..........12 B3
Ideford......12 D3
Ide Hill.....36 A2
Iden.........37 D7
Iden Green Kent.37 C5
  Kent........37 C6
Idle.........147 D5
Idlicote.....81 C5
Idmiston.....31 B5
Idole........57 A4
Idridgehay...113 A6
Idrigill.....258 B3
Idstone......45 A6
Idvies.......232 D3
Iffley.......65 C6
Ifield.......35 C5
Ifold........34 C3
Iford........22 B2

Ifton Heath...110 B2
Ightfield....111 B4
Ightham......36 A3
Iken.........89 B5
Ilam........129 D6
Ilchester....29 C5
Ilderton.....188 A3
Ilford.......50 A1
Ilfracombe...25 A6
Ilkeston....114 A2
Ilkeshall St
  Andrew......105 C4
Ilkeshall St
  Lawrence....105 C4
Ilkeshall St
  Margaret....104 C4
Ilkley.......147 C5
Illey........96 C2
Illingworth...138 A3
Illogan......3 A4
Illston on the Hill.99 B4
Ilmer........66 C2
Ilmington....81 C5
Ilminster....28 D3
Ilsington....12 D2
Ilston.......57 C5
Ilton N Yorks.157 D5
  Som.........28 D3
Imachar......202 D3
Imeraval.....200 D3
Immingham...142 B3
Impington....85 A6
Ince........127 B4
Ince Blundell..136 C2
Ince in
  Makerfield...137 C4
Inchbare.....233 B4
Inchberry....266 D4
Inchbraoch...233 C5
Incheril.....262 D2
Inchgrundle..232 A2
Inchina.....261 A6
Inchinnan....205 B4
Inchkinloch..277 D6
Inchlaggan...239 B5
Inchlumpie...264 C1
Inchmore.....251 B5
Inchnacardoch
  Hotel.......240 A1
Inchnadamph..271 B5
Inch of Arnhall.233 A4
Inchree......237 C4
Inchture.....220 B2
Inchyra......219 B6
Indian Queens....4 B4
Inerval......200 D3
Ingatestone...69 D6
Ingbirchworth.139 C5
Ingestre.....112 C3
Ingham Lincs.133 A4
  Norf.......121 C5
  Suff.......103 D4
Ingham Corner.121 C5
Ingleborough..118 D1
Ingleby Derbys.114 C1
  Lincs.......132 B3
Ingleby
  Arncliffe...158 A3
Ingleby Barwick 168 D2
Ingleby
  Greenhow...159 A4
Inglemire....150 D3
Inglesbatch...43 C6
Inglesham....64 D3
Ingleton Durham.167 C4
  N Yorks.....155 D5
Inglewhite...145 C5
Ingliston....208 C4
Ingoe.......178 B2
Ingol........145 D5
Ingoldisthorpe.118 B3
Ingoldmells..135 C5
Ingoldsby....116 B3
Ingon.........81 B5
Ingram.......188 B3
Ingrow.......147 D4
Ings.........154 B3
Ingst........43 A4
Ingworth....120 C3
Inham's End..101 B4
Inkberrow....80 B3
Inkpen.......46 C1

Inkstack.....281 A4
Inn..........154 A3
Innellan.....203 A6
Innerleithen..196 C2
Innerleven...220 D3
Innermessan..170 A2
Innerwick E Loth.211 C4
  Perth.......229 D4
Innis Chonain.227 D6
Insch........256 D1
Insh.........241 B6
Inshore......276 B4
Inskip.......145 D4
Instoneville..140 B3
Instow.......25 B5
Intake......140 C3
Inver Aberds..243 C5
  Highld......265 B4
  Perth.......230 D4
Inverailort..235 B6
Inveraldie...220 A4
Inverallign..249 A5
Inverallochy..269 C5
Inveran Highld.264 A1
  Highld......264 A1
Inveraray....214 B3
Inverarish...248 C2
Inverarity...232 D2
Inverarnan...215 A6
Inverasdale..261 B5
Inverbeg....206 A1
Inverbervie..233 A6
Inverboyndie.268 C1
Inverbroom...262 B3
Invercassley..272 D2
Invercauld
  House.......243 C4
Inverchaolain.203 A5
Invercharnan..227 B6
Inverchoran..251 A4
Invercreran..227 B5
Inverdruie...242 A2
Inverebrie...257 C4
Invereck.....215 D4
Inverernan Ho..243 A6
Invereshie
  House.......241 B6
Inveresk.....209 C6
Inverey......242 D3
Inverfarigaig..251 D7
Invergarry...239 B7
Invergelder..243 C5
Invergeldie..218 B2
Invergordon..264 D3
Invergowrie..220 A3
Inverguseran..247 D6
Inverhadden..229 C5
Inverharroch..255 C4
Inverherive..216 B3
Inverie......247 E6
Inverinan....214 A2
Inverinate...249 D6
Inverkeilor..233 D4
Inverkeithing.208 B4
Inverkeithny..256 B1
Inverkip.....204 A2
Inverkirkaig..270 C3
Inverlael....262 B3
Inverlochlarig.216 C4
Inverlochy Argyll.227 D6
  Highld......237 B5
Inverlussa...213 D4
Inver Mallie..239 D5
Invermark
  Lodge......244 D1
Invermoidart..235 C5
Invermoriston.240 A2
Invernaver...278 B3
Inverneill...213 D6
Inverness....252 B2
Invernettie..257 B6
Invernoaden..215 C4
Inveroran Hotel.228 D1
Inverpolly
  Lodge......270 C3
Inverquharity.232 C2
Inverquhomery.257 B5
Inverroy.....239 D6
Inversanda...236 D3
Invershiel...238 A3
Invershin....264 A1
Inversnaid Hotel 215 B6
Inveruglie...257 B6

Inveruglas...215 B6
Inveruglass..241 B6
Inverurie....256 D2
Invervar.....229 D5
Inverythan...256 B2
Inwardleigh...11 B6
Inworth......70 B2
Iochdar......286 B3
Iping........34 D1
Ipplepen.....8 A2
Ipsden.......47 A4
Ipsley.......80 A3
Ipstones.....129 D5
Ipswich......88 C2
Irby.........126 A2
Irby in the
  Marsh......135 C4
Irby upon
  Humber.....142 C3
Irchester....83 A6
Ireby Cumb...163 A5
  Lancs.......155 D5
Ireland Orkney.283 G4
  Shetland.....285 L5
Ireland's Cross.111 A6
Ireleth......153 C3
Ireshopeburn..165 B6
Irlam........137 D6
Irnham.......116 C3
Iron Acton....43 A5
Ironbridge...95 A4
Iron Cross....80 B3
Irongray....173 A7
Ironmacannie..173 A4
Ironside.....268 D3
Ironville....131 D4
Irstead......121 C5
Irthington...176 C2
Irthlingborough.99 D6
Irton........160 C4
Irvine......192 B3
Isauld.......279 B5
Isbister Orkney..282 E3
  Orkney......282 F4
  Shetland.....284 D5
  Shetland.....285 G7
Isfield......22 A2
Isham........99 D5
Isle Abbotts..28 C3
Isle Brewers..28 C3
Isleham.....102 D2
Isle of Whithorn 171 D6
Isleornsay...247 C6
Islesburgh...284 G5
Islesteps....174 A2
Isleworth....49 B4
Isley Walton..114 C2
Islibhig....287 B4
Islington....49 A6
Islip Northants..100 D1
  Oxon.......65 B6
Istead Rise...50 C3
Isycoed.....127 D4
Itchen.......32 D3
Itchen Abbas..32 B4
Itchen Stoke..33 B4
Itchingfield...35 D4
Itchington...43 A5
Itteringham..120 B3
Itton........12 B1
Itton Common..61 D6
Ivegill......164 A2
Iver.........48 A3
Iver Heath...48 A3
Iveston.....178 D3
Ivinghoe.....67 B4
Ivinghoe Aston..67 B4
Ivington.....78 B2
Ivington Green.78 B2
Ivybridge.....7 B5
Ivy Chimneys..68 C4
Ivychurch....38 C2
Ivy Cross....30 C2
Ivy Hatch....36 A3
Iwade........51 C6
Iwerne Courtney or
  Shroton....30 D2
Iwerne Minster..30 D2
Ixworth.....103 D5
Ixworth Thorpe.103 D5

J

Jack Hill....147 B6
Jack in the Green 13 B5
Jacksdale....131 D4
Jackstown....256 C2
Jacobstow....10 B2
Jacobstowe...11 A6
Jameston.....55 E6
Jamestown
  Dumfries.....185 C6
  Highld......251 A6
  W Dunb.....206 B1
Jarrow......179 C5
Jarvis Brook...36 D3
Jasper's Green..69 A7
Java.........225 C6
Jawcraig.....207 C6
Jaywick......71 B5
Jealott's Hill...47 B6
Jedburgh.....187 A5
Jeffreyston...55 D6
Jellyhill....205 A6
Jemimaville..264 D3
Jersey Farm...67 C6
Jesmond.....179 C4
Jevington....22 B3
Jockey End....67 B5
Johnby......164 B2
John o' Groats.281 A5
John's Cross...37 D5
Johnshaven...233 B5
Johnston.....55 C5
Johnstone....205 B4
Johnstonebridge
  ....184 C3
Johnstown Carms 57 A4
  Wrex.......110 A2
Joppa Edin...209 C6
  S Ayrs......182 A2
Jordans......67 D4
Jordanthorpe..130 A3
Jump........140 C1
Jumpers Green...17 B5
Juniper Green..209 D4
Jurby East...152 B3
Jurby West...152 B3

K

Kaber.......165 D5
Kaimend.....195 B4
Kaimes......209 D5
Kalemouth...187 A6
Kames Argyll..203 A4
  Argyll......213 A6
  E Ayrs......194 D1
Kea.........4 C3
Keadby......141 B6
Keal Cotes...134 C3
Kearsley....137 C6
Kearstwick...155 C5
Kearton.....156 B3
Kearvaig.....276 A3
Keasden.....145 A7
Keckwick....127 A5
Keddington..134 A3
Kedington....86 C3
Kedleston...113 A7
Keelby......142 B3
Keele........112 A2
Keeley Green..84 C2
Keeston.....55 C5
Keevil.......44 D3
Kegworth....114 C2
Kehelland....3 A4
Keig........244 A3
Keighley....147 C4
Keil........236 B3
Keilarsbrae..208 A1
Keilhill....268 D2
Keillmore...213 D4
Keillor.....231 D6
Keillour....219 B4
Keills......201 B4
Keils.......201 B5

Keinton
 Mandeville 29 B5
Keir Mill 183 C6
Keisby 116 C3
Keiss 281 B5
Keith 267 D5
Keith Inch 257 B6
Keithock 233 B4
Kelbrook 146 C3
Kelby 116 A3
Keld Cumb 164 D3
 N Yorks 156 A2
Keldholme 159 C6
Kelfield N Lincs . . 141 C6
 N Yorks 149 D4
Kelham 132 D2
Kellan 225 B4
Kellas Angus 221 A4
 Moray 266 D2
Kellaton 8 D2
Kelleth 155 A5
Kelleythorpe 150 B2
Kelling 120 A2
Kellingley 140 A3
Kellington 140 A3
Kelloe 167 B6
Kelloholm 183 A5
Kelly 11 C4
Kelly Bray 11 D4
Kelmarsh 99 D4
Kelmscot 64 D3
Kelsale 89 A4
Kelsall 127 C5
Kelsall Hill 127 C5
Kelsick 175 C4
Kelso 197 C6
Kelstedge 130 C3
Kelstern 143 D4
Kelston 43 C6
Keltneyburn 229 D6
Kelton 174 A2
Kelty 208 A4
Kelvedon 70 B2
Kelvedon Hatch . . 69 D5
Kelvin 205 C6
Kelvinside 205 B5
Kelynack 2 B1
Kemback 220 C4
Kemberton 95 A5
Kemble 63 D5
Kemerton 80 D2
Kemeys
 Commander . . . 61 C5
Kemnay 245 A4
Kempley 62 A2
Kempsey 79 C6
Kempsford 64 D2
Kemps Green 96 D4
Kempshott 47 D4
Kempston 84 C2
Kempston
 Hardwick 84 C2
Kempton 94 C1
Kemp Town 21 B6
Kemsing 36 A3
Kemsley 51 C6
Kenardington 38 B1
Kenchester 78 C2
Kencot 64 C3
Kendal 154 B4
Kendoon 182 D4
Kendray 139 C6
Kenfig 40 C3
Kenfig Hill 40 C3
Kenilworth 97 D5
Kenknock 217 A4
Kenley London 35 A6
 Shrops 94 A3
Kenmore Highld. . . 249 A4
 Perth 230 D1
Kenn Devon 7 G6
 N Som 42 C3
Kennacley 288 H2
Kennacraig 202 B3
Kennerleigh 12 A3
Kennet 208 A2
Kennethmont . . . 255 D6
Kennett 86 A2

Kennford 13 C4
Kenninghall 103 C6
Kenninghall
 Heath 103 C6
Kennington Kent . . 38 A2
 Oxon 65 C6
Kennoway 220 D3
Kenny Hill 102 D2
Kennythorpe 149 A6
Kenovay 222 C2
Kensaleyre 259 C4
Kensington 49 B5
Kensworth 67 B5
Kensworth
 Common 67 B5
Kentallen 237 D4
Kentchurch 61 A6
Kentford 86 A3
Kentisbeare 13 A5
Kentisbury 25 A7
Kentisbury Ford . . 25 A7
Kentmere 154 A3
Kenton Devon 13 C4
 Suff 88 A2
 T&W 179 C4
Kenton
 Bankfoot 179 C4
Kentra 235 D5
Kents Bank 154 D2
Kent's Green 62 A3
Kent's Oak 32 C2
Kent Street E Sus. . 23 A5
 Kent 37 A4
 W Sus. 35 D5
Kenwick 110 B3
Kenwyn 4 C3
Keoldale 277 B4
Keppanach 237 C4
Keppoch 249 D6
Keprigan 190 D2
Kepwick 158 B3
Kerchesters 197 C6
Keresley 97 C6
Kernborough 8 C1
Kerne Bridge 62 B1
Kerris 2 C2
Kerry 93 C5
Kerrycroy 203 B6
Kerrysdale 261 C5
Kerry's Gate 78 D1
Kersall 132 C2
Kersey 87 C6
Kershopefoot 176 A2
Kersoe 80 D2
Kerswell 13 A5
Kerswell Grn. 79 C6
Kesgrave 88 C3
Kessingland 105 C6
Kessingland
 Beach 105 C6
Kessington 205 A5
Kestle 5 C4
Kestle Mill 4 B3
Keston 49 C7
Keswick Cumb . . . 163 B5
 Norf 104 A3
 Norf 121 B5
Ketley 111 D5
Ketley Bank 111 D5
Ketsby 134 B3
Kettering 99 D5
Ketteringham . . . 104 A2
Kettins 220 A2
Kettlebaston 87 B5
Kettlebridge 220 D3
Kettleburgh 88 A3
Kettlehill 220 D3
Kettleholm 174 A4
Kettleness 169 D6
Kettleshume 129 B4
Kettlesing
 Bottom 147 B6
Kettlesing Head . . 147 B6
Kettlestone 119 B6
Kettlethorpe 132 B3
Kettletoft 282 D7
Kettlewell 156 D3
Ketton 100 A1
Kew 49 B4
Kew Br. 49 B4
Kewstoke 42 C2
Kexbrough 139 C6

Kexby Lincs 132 A3
 York 149 B6
Key Green 128 C3
Keyham 98 A3
Keyhaven 18 B2
Keyingham 143 A4
Keymer 21 A6
Keynsham 43 C5
Keysoe 84 A2
Keysoe Row 84 A2
Keyston 100 D2
Keyworth 115 B4
Kibblesworth . . . 179 D4
Kibworth
 Beauchamp 98 B3
Kibworth
 Harcourt 98 B3
Kidbrooke 49 B7
Kiddemore
 Green 95 A6
Kidderminster . . . 95 D6
Kiddington 65 A5
Kidlington 65 B5
Kidmore End 47 B4
Kidsgrove 128 D3
Kidstones 156 C3
Kidwelly Cydweli . . 57 B4
Kiel Crofts 226 C4
Kielder 187 D5
Kierfield Ho. 282 F3
Kilbagie 208 B2
Kilbarchan 205 B4
Kilbeg 247 D5
Kilberry 202 B2
Kilbirnie 204 C3
Kilbride Argyll . . . 226 D3
 Argyll 226 D4
 Highld. 247 B4
Kilburn Angus. . . . 232 B1
 Derbys 114 A1
 London 49 A5
 N Yorks 158 D4
Kilby 98 B3
Kilchamaig 202 B3
Kilchattan 212 C1
Kilchattan Bay . . 203 C6
Kilchenzie 190 C2
Kilcheran 226 C3
Kilchiaran 200 B2
Kilchoan Argyll. . . 213 A5
 Highld. 234 D3
Kilchoman 200 B2
Kilchrenan 227 D5
Kilconquhar. 221 D4
Kilcot 62 A2
Kilcoy 252 A1
Kilcreggan 215 D5
Kildale 159 A5
Kildalloig 190 D3
Kildary 264 C3
Kildermorie
 Lodge 263 C7
Kildonan 191 C6
Kildonan Lodge . 274 B3
Kildonnan 234 B3
Kildrummy 244 A1
Kildwick 147 C4
Kilfinan 203 A4
Kilfinnan 239 C6
Kilgetty 56 B1
Kilgwrrwg
 Common 61 D6
Kilham E Yorks . . 150 A3
 Northumb. 198 C2
Kilkenneth 222 C2
Kilkerran 190 D3
Kilkhampton 24 D3
Killamarsh 131 A4
Killay 57 C6
Killbeg 225 B5
Killean 202 D1
Killearn 206 B3
Killen 252 A2
Killerby 167 D4
Killichonan 229 C4
Killiechonate . . . 239 D6
Killiechronan . . . 225 B4
Killiecrankie 230 B3
Killiemor 224 C3
Killiemore
 House. 224 D3
Killilan 249 C6

Killimster. 281 C5
Killin 217 A5
Killinallan. 200 A3
Killinghall 148 B1
Killington. 155 C5
Killingworth 179 B4
Killin Lodge 240 B3
Killmahumaig . . . 213 C5
Killochyett 196 B3
Killundine 225 B4
Kilmacolm 204 B3
Kilmaha 214 B2
Kilmahog 217 D6
Kilmalieu 236 D2
Kilmaluag. 259 A4
Kilmany 220 B3
Kilmarie 247 C4
Kilmarnock 193 B4
Kilmaron Castle . 220 C3
Kilmartin 213 C6
Kilmaurs. 205 D4
Kilmelford 213 A6
Kilmeny 200 B3
Kilmersdon 43 D5
Kilmeston 33 C4
Kilmichael 190 C2
Kilmichael
 Glassary 214 C1
Kilmichael of
 Inverlussa 213 D5
Kilmington Devon . 14 B2
 Wilts. 30 B1
Kilmonivaig 239 D5
Kilmorack 251 B6
Kilmore Argyll . . . 226 D3
 Highld. 247 D5
Kilmory Argyll. . . 202 A2
 Highld. 235 C4
 Highld. 246 D2
 N Ayrs 191 C5
Kilmuir Highld . . . 252 B2
 Highld. 258 A3
 Highld. 258 D2
 Highld. 264 C3
Kilmun Argyll . . . 214 A2
 Argyll 215 D4
Kilncadzow 194 B3
Kilndown 37 C5
Kilnhurst 140 D2
Kilninian 224 B2
Kilninver 226 D3
Kiln Pit Hill 178 D2
Kilnsea 143 B6
Kilnsey 146 A3
Kilnwick 150 C2
Kilnwick Percy . . 149 B7
Kiloran 212 C1
Kilpatrick 191 C5
Kilpeck 78 D2
Kilphedir 274 C3
Kilpin 141 A5
Kilpin Pike 141 A5
Kilrenny 221 D5
Kilsby 98 D2
Kilspindie 220 B2
Kilsyth. 207 C5
Kiltarlity 251 B7
Kilton Notts. 131 B5
 Som 27 A6
Kilton Thorpe . . . 169 D4
Kilvaxter 258 B3
Kilve 27 A6
Kilvington 115 A5
Kilwinning 204 D3
Kimberley Norf . . 103 A6
 Notts 114 A3
Kimberworth . . . 140 D2
Kimble Wick 66 C3
Kimblesworth . . . 167 A5
Kimbolton Cambs . 84 A2
 Hereford 78 A3
Kimcote 98 C2
Kimmeridge 16 D3
Kimmerston 198 C3
Kimpton Hants. . . 32 A1
 Herts 68 B1
Kinbrace 274 A2
Kinbuck 218 D2
Kincaple 221 C4
Kincardine Fife . . 208 B2
 Highld. 264 B2

Kincardine
 Bridge 208 B2
Kincardine
 O'Neil. 244 C2
Kinclaven 219 A6
Kincorth. 245 B6
Kincorth Ho. 265 D6
Kincraig 241 B6
Kincraigie 230 D3
Kindallachan. . . . 230 D3
Kineton Glos. 64 A1
 Warks. 81 B6
Kinfauns 219 B6
Kingairloch 236 D2
Kingarth. 203 C5
Kingcoed 61 C6
King Edward 268 D2
Kingerby. 142 D2
Kingham 64 A3
Kingholm Quay. . 174 A2
Kinghorn 209 B5
Kingie 239 B5
Kinglassie 209 A5
Kingoodie 220 B3
King's Acre 78 C2
Kingsand 6 B3
Kingsbarns 221 C5
Kingsbridge Devon . 7 C6
 Som 27 B4
King's Bromley . . 113 D5
Kingsburgh 258 C3
Kingsbury London . 49 A5
 Warks. 97 B5
Kingsbury
 Episcopi. 28 C4
King's Caple 62 A1
Kingsclere 46 D3
King's Cliffe 100 B2
Kingscote 63 D4
Kingscott 25 D6
King's Coughton . 80 B3
Kingscross 191 C6
Kingsdon 29 C5
Kingsdown 39 A5
Kingseat 208 A4
Kingsey 66 C2
Kingsfold 35 C4
Kingsford E Ayrs . 205 D4
 Worcs. 95 C6
Kingsforth 142 B2
Kingsgate 53 B5
Kingsheanton . . . 25 B6
King's Heath 96 C3
Kings Hedges . . . 85 A6
King's Hill 37 A4
Kingshouse
 Hotel. 237 D6
Kingside Hill . . . 175 C4
Kingskerswell 8 A2
Kingskettle 220 D3
Kingsland
 Anglesey 122 B2
 Hereford 78 A2
Kings Langley . . . 67 C5
Kingsley Ches W . 127 B5
 Hants 33 B6
 Staffs 112 A4
Kingsley Green . . 34 C1
Kingsley Holt. . . . 112 A4
Kingsley Park . . . 83 A4
King's Lynn 118 C3
King's Meaburn . 165 C4
King's Mills 110 A2
Kingsmuir Angus 232 D2
 Fife. 221 D5
Kings Muir 196 C1
King's Newnham . 98 D1
King's Newton . . 114 C1
Kingsnorth 38 B2
King's Norton
 Leics. 98 A3
 W Mid 96 D3
King's Nympton . 26 D1
King's Pyon 78 B2
King's Ripton . . . 101 D4
King's Somborne . 32 B2
King's Stag 30 D1
King's Stanley . . . 63 C4
King's Sutton . . . 82 D1
Kingstanding 96 B3
Kingsteignton . . . 12 D3
King Sterndale . . 129 B5

King's Thorn 78 D3
Kingsthorpe 83 A4
Kingston Cambs . . 85 B5
 Devon. 7 C5
 Dorset 16 A1
 Dorset 16 D3
 E Loth. 210 B2
 Hants 17 A5
 IoW 18 C3
 Kent 52 D3
 Moray 266 C4
Kingston
 Bagpuize 65 D5
Kingston Blount . 66 D2
Kingston by Sea . 21 B5
Kingston Deverill. 30 B2
Kingstone
 Hereford 78 D2
 Som 28 D3
 Staffs 113 C4
Kingston Gorse. . . 20 B3
Kingston Lisle . . . 45 A7
Kingston
 Maurward 15 B7
Kingston near
 Lewes. 22 B1
Kingston on
 Soar 114 C3
Kingston Russell . 15 B5
Kingston St Mary . 28 C2
Kingston
 Seymour 42 C3
Kingston Upon
 Hull. 142 A2
Kingston upon
 Thames 49 C4
Kingston Vale . . . 49 B5
Kingstown 175 C6
King's Walden . . . 67 A6
Kingswear 8 B2
Kingswells 245 B5
Kingswinford 96 C1
Kingswood Bucks . 66 B1
 Glos 62 D3
 Hereford 77 B6
 Kent 37 A6
 Powys 93 A6
 S Glos. 43 B5
 Sur 35 A5
 Warks. 97 D4
Kings Worthy 32 B3
Kingthorpe 133 B6
Kington Hereford . . 77 B6
 Worcs. 80 B2
Kington Langley . 44 B3
Kington Magna. . . 30 C1
Kington St
 Michael 44 B3
Kingussie 241 B5
Kingweston 29 B5
Kininvie Ho. 254 B4
Kinkell Bridge . . 218 C4
Kinknockie 257 B5
Kinlet 95 C5
Kinloch Fife 220 C2
 Highld. 234 A2
 Highld. 247 C5
 Highld. 271 A6
 Perth 231 D5
 Perth 231 D6
Kinlochan. 236 C2
Kinlochard 217 D4
Kinlochbeoraid. . 238 D2
Kinlochbervie. . . 276 C3
Kinlocheil 236 B3
Kinlochewe 262 D2
Kinloch Hourn . . 238 B3
Kinloch Laggan . 240 D3
Kinlochleven. . . . 237 C5
Kinloch Lodge . . 277 C6
Kinlochmoidart . 235 C6
Kinlochmorar . . . 238 C2
Kinlochmore 237 C5
Kinloch
 Rannoch 229 C5
Kinlochspelve. . . 225 D5
Kinloid 235 B5
Kinloss 265 D6
Kinmel Bay 125 A4
Kinmuck 256 E3
Kinmundy. 245 A5
Kinnadie 257 B4

Kinnaird 220 B2
Kinnaird Castle. .233 C4
Kinneff 233 A6
Kinnelhead 184 B3
Kinnell 233 C4
Kinnerley 110 C2
Kinnersley
  Hereford 78 C1
  Worcs. 79 C6
Kinnerton. 77 A6
Kinnesswood . . .219 D6
Kinninvie 166 C3
Kinnordy. 232 C1
Kinoulton. 115 B4
Kinross 219 D6
Kinrossie 219 A6
Kinsbourne
  Green. 67 B6
Kinsey Heath. . . .111 A5
Kinsham Hereford . .78 A1
  Worcs. 80 D2
Kinsley 140 B2
Kinson 17 B4
Kintbury 46 C1
Kintessack 265 D5
Kintillo 219 C6
Kintocher. 244 B2
Kinton Hereford . . .94 D2
  Shrops 110 D2
Kintore 245 A4
Kintour 201 C4
Kintra Argyll 200 D3
  Argyll 224 D2
Kintraw. 213 B6
Kinuachdrachd. .213 C5
Kinveachy 242 A2
Kinver 95 C6
Kippax. 148 D3
Kippen 207 A4
Kippford or
  Scaur 173 C6
Kirbister Orkney. .282 E7
  Orkney 283 G4
Kirbuster 282 E3
Kirby Bedon. 104 A3
Kirby Bellars 115 D5
Kirby Cane. 105 B4
Kirby Cross 71 A6
Kirby
  Grindalythe. 150 A2
Kirby Hill N Yorks 148 A2
  N Yorks. 157 A5
Kirby Knowle. . . .158 C3
Kirby-le-Soken . .71 A6
Kirby Misperton 159 D6
Kirby Muxloe. 98 A2
Kirby Row 105 B4
Kirby Sigston . . .158 B3
Kirby Underdale 149 B7
Kirby Wiske. 158 C2
Kirdford 34 D3
Kirk 281 C4
Kirkabister. 285 K6
Kirkandrews 172 D4
Kirkandrews upon
  Eden 175 C6
Kirkbampton 175 C6
Kirkbean. 174 C2
Kirk Bramwith . .140 B4
Kirkbride 175 C5
Kirkbuddo 232 D3
Kirkburn Borders 196 C1
  E Yorks. 150 B2
Kirkburton. 139 B4
Kirkby Lincs 142 D2
  Mers. 136 D3
  N Yorks. 158 A4
Kirkby Fleetham 157 B6
Kirkby Green. . . .133 D5
Kirkby In
  Ashfield. 131 C5
Kirkby-in-
  Furness 153 B3
Kirkby la
  Thorpe. 116 A4
Kirkby Lonsdale 155 D5
Kirkby Malham . .146 A2
Kirkby Mallory . . .98 A1
Kirkby
  Malzeard 157 D6
Kirkby Mills 159 C6
Kirkbymoorside .159 C5

Kirkby on Bain . .134 C2
Kirkby Overflow 148 C2
Kirkby Stephen. .155 A6
Kirkby Thore. . . .165 C4
Kirkby
  Underwood. . . .116 C3
Kirkby Wharfe. . .148 C4
Kirkcaldy 209 A5
Kirkcambeck. . . .176 C3
Kirkcarswell 173 D5
Kirkcolm. 170 A2
Kirkconnel 183 A5
Kirkconnell 174 B2
Kirkcowan 171 A5
Kirkcudbright . . .173 C4
Kirkdale 136 D2
Kirk Deighton . . .148 B2
Kirk Ella 142 A2
Kirkfieldbank . . .194 B3
Kirkgunzeon 173 B6
Kirk Hallam 114 A2
Kirkham Lancs . . .144 D4
  N Yorks. 149 A6
Kirkhamgate 139 A5
Kirk
  Hammerton. . . .148 B3
Kirkharle 178 A2
Kirkheaton
  Northumb. 178 B2
  W Yorks 139 B4
Kirkhill Angus. . . .233 B4
  Highld. 252 B1
  Midloth. 209 D5
  Moray. 254 C3
Kirkhope 186 A2
Kirkhouse 196 C2
Kirkiboll 277 C6
Kirkibost. 247 C4
Kirkinch 231 D7
Kirkinner 171 B6
Kirkintilloch 205 A6
Kirk Ireton 130 C1
Kirkland Cumb . . .162 C3
  Cumb 165 B4
  Dumfries 183 A5
  Dumfries 183 C6
Kirk Langley 113 B6
Kirkleatham. 168 C3
Kirklevington . . .158 A3
Kirkley 105 B6
Kirklington
  Notts 132 D1
  N Yorks. 157 C7
Kirklinton. 176 C2
Kirkliston 208 C4
Kirkmaiden 170 D3
Kirk Merrington 167 B5
Kirkmichael
  Perth 231 C4
  S Ayrs. 192 E3
Kirk Michael 152 B3
Kirkmuirhill 194 B2
Kirknewton
  Northumb. 198 C3
  W Loth 208 D4
Kirkney 255 C6
Kirk of Shotts . . .207 D6
Kirkoswald
  Cumb 164 A3
  S Ayrs 192 E2
Kirkpatrick
  Durham 173 A5
Kirkpatrick-
  Fleming 175 A5
Kirk Sandall. 140 C4
Kirksanton 153 B2
Kirk Smeaton . . .140 B3
Kirkstall 147 D6
Kirkstead 134 C1
Kirkstile 255 C6
Kirkstyle 281 A5
Kirkton Aberds . .256 D1
  Aberds 268 C1
  Angus 220 A4
  Angus 232 D2
  Borders 186 B4
  Dumfries 184 D2
  Fife. 220 B3
  Highld. 249 B6
  Highld. 249 D5
  Highld. 252 A3
  Highld. 265 A3

Kirkton continued
  Perth 219 C4
Kirkton of Airlie 231 C7
Kirkton of
  Auchterhouse .220 A3
Kirkton of
  Auchterless . . .256 B2
Kirkton of
  Barevan 253 B4
Kirkton of
  Bourtie. 256 D3
Kirkton of
  Collace. 219 A6
Kirkton of Craig 233 C5
Kirkton of
  Culsalmond . . .256 C1
Kirkton of
  Durris 245 C4
Kirkton of
  Glenbuchat. . .243 A6
Kirkton of
  Glenisla 231 B6
Kirkton of
  Kingoldrum . . .232 C1
Kirkton of
  Largo 220 D4
Kirkton of
  Lethendy 231 D5
Kirkton of Logie
  Buchan. 257 D4
Kirkton of
  Maryculter . . .245 C5
Kirkton of
  Menmuir 232 B3
Kirkton of
  Monikie 221 A5
Kirkton of Oyne .256 D1
Kirkton of
  Rayne. 256 D1
Kirkton of
  Skene. 245 B5
Kirkton of
  Tough. 244 A3
Kirktown 269 D5
Kirktown of
  Alvah 268 C1
Kirktown of
  Deskford 267 C6
Kirktown of
  Fetteresso. . . .245 D5
Kirktown of
  Mortlach 254 C4
Kirktown of
  Slains 257 D5
Kirktown of
  Auchterhouse .195 B4
Kirkwall 282 F5
Kirkwhelpington
  . . . . .178 A1
Kirk Yetholm . . .188 A1
Kirmington 142 B3
Kirmond le
  Mire 142 D3
Kirn 203 A6
Kirriemuir 232 C1
Kirstead Green . .104 B3
Kirtlebridge. 175 A5
Kirtleton 185 D5
Kirtling 86 B2
Kirtling Green. . . .86 B2
Kirtlington 65 B5
Kirtomy. 278 B3
Kirton Lincs. 117 B6
  Notts 132 C1
  Suff 88 D3
Kirton End 117 A5
Kirton Holme . . .117 A5
Kirton in
  Lindsey 142 D1
Kislingbury 82 B3
Kites Hardwick . .82 A1
Kittisford 27 C5
Kittle 57 D5
Kitt's Green 97 C4
Kitt's Moss 128 A3
Kittybrewster . . .245 B6
Kitwood 33 B5
Kivernoll 78 D2
Kiveton Park 131 A4

Knaith 132 A3
Knaith Park 132 A3
Knap Corner 30 C2
Knaphill 34 A2
Knapp Perth 220 A2
  Som 28 C3
Knapthorpe 132 D2
Knapton Norf . . .121 B5
  York 149 B4
Knapton Green. . .78 B2
Knapwell 85 A5
Knaresborough . .148 B2
Knarsdale. 177 D4
Knauchland 267 D6
Knaven 256 B3
Knayton 158 C3
Knebworth. 68 A2
Knedlington 141 A5
Kneesall 132 C2
Kneesworth 85 C5
Kneeton 115 A5
Knelston 57 D4
Knenhall 112 B3
Knettishall 103 C5
Knightacott 26 B1
Knightcote 81 B6
Knightley Dale . .112 C2
Knighton Devon . . .7 C4
  Leicester 98 A2
  Staffs 111 A6
  Staffs 111 C6
Knighton Tref-y-
  Clawdd 93 D6
Knightswood. . . .205 B5
Knightwick 79 B5
Knill 77 A6
Knipton 115 B6
Knitsley. 166 A4
Kniveton. 130 C2
Knock Argyll 225 C4
  Cumb 165 C4
  Moray. 267 D6
Knockally 275 B5
Knockan. 271 C5
Knockandhu 254 D3
Knockando 254 B3
Knockando Ho. .254 B3
Knockbain 252 A2
Knockbreck 258 B2
Knockbrex 172 D3
Knockdee. 280 B3
Knockdolian 180 C3
Knockenkelly . . .191 C6
Knockentiber . . .192 B3
Knockespock
  Ho. 255 D6
Knockfarrel 251 A7
Knockglass 170 B2
Knockholt 36 A2
Knockholt Pound 36 A2
Knockie Lodge . .240 A2
Knockin. 110 C2
Knockinlaw 193 B4
Knocklearn 173 A5
Knocknaha 190 D2
Knocknain 170 A1
Knockrome 201 A5
Knocksharry 152 C2
Knodishall 89 A5
Knolls Green 128 B3
Knolton. 110 B2
Knolton Bryn . . .110 B2
Knook 30 A3
Knossington 99 A5
Knott End-on-
  Sea 144 C3
Knotting 84 A2
Knotting Green. . .84 A2
Knottingley 140 A3
Knotts Cumb 164 C2
  Lancs 146 B1
Knotty Ash 136 D3
Knotty Green. . . .67 D4
Knowbury. 94 D3
Knowe. 181 D5
Knowehead 182 C4
Knowesgate 178 A1
Knowes of
  Elrick 267 D7
Knoweton 194 A2
Knowhead 269 D4
Knowle Bristol . . .43 B5

Knowle continued
  Devon. 12 A2
  Devon. 13 C5
  Devon. 25 B5
  Shrops 94 D3
  W Mid 97 D4
Knowle Green . . .145 D6
Knowle Park 147 C4
Knowl Hill 47 B6
Knowlton Dorset . .31 D4
  Kent 53 D4
Knowsley 136 D3
Knowstone. 26 C3
Knox Bridge. 37 B5
Knucklas 93 D6
Knuston 83 A6
Knutsford 128 B2
Knutton 112 A2
Knypersley 128 D3
Kuggar 3 D5
Kyleakin 247 B6
Kyle of
  Lochalsh 249 D4
Kylerhea. 247 B6
Kylesknoydart. .238 C2
Kylesku 271 A5
Kylesmorar 238 C2
Kylestrome 271 A5
Kyllachy House. .252 D3
Kynaston 110 C2
Kynnersley 111 D5
Kyre Magna 79 A4

L

Labost. 288 C3
Lacasaidh. 288 C4
Lacasdal 288 D5
Laceby 143 C4
Lacey Green 66 D3
Lach Dennis 128 B2
Lackford. 102 D3
Lacock 44 C3
Ladbroke 81 B7
Laddingford. 37 B4
Lade Bank 134 D3
Ladock 4 B3
Lady. 282 C7
Ladybank 220 C3
Ladykirk 198 B2
Ladysford. 269 C4
La Fontenelle Guern. .6
Laga. 235 D5
Lagalochan 214 A1
Lagavulin 201 D4
Lagg Argyll 201 A5
  N Ayrs 191 C5
Laggan Argyll . . .200 C2
  Highld. 235 C6
  Highld. 239 C6
  Highld. 241 C4
Lagganulva 224 B3
Laide 261 A6
Laigh Fenwick . .205 D4
Laigh Glengall . .192 D3
Laighmuir 205 D4
Laindon 50 A3
Lair 250 B2
Lairg 272 D3
Lairg Lodge 272 D3
Lairgmore 252 C1
Lairg Muir 272 D3
Laisterdyke 147 D5
Laithes 164 B2
Lake IoW 19 C4
  Wilts. 31 B5
Lakenham 104 A3
Lakenheath 102 C3
Lakesend 101 B7
Lakeside. 154 C2
Laleham 48 C3
Laleston 40 D3
Lamarsh 87 D4
Lamas 120 C4
Lambden 197 B6
Lamberhurst 37 C4
Lamberhurst
  Quarter 37 C4
Lamberton. 198 A3
Lambeth 49 B6

Lambhill 205 B5
Lambley
  Northumb. 177 D4
  Notts 115 A4
Lamborough Hill .65 C5
Lambourn 46 B1
Lambourne End . .69 D4
Lambs Green. 35 C5
Lambston 55 C5
Lamellion. 6 A3
Lamerton. 11 D5
Lamesley 179 D4
Laminess 282 D7
Lamington
  Highld. 264 C3
  S Lanark 195 C4
Lamlash 191 B6
Lamloch 182 C3
Lamonby 164 B2
Lamorna. 2 C2
Lamorran 4 C3
Lampardbrook . .88 A3
Lampeter Llanbedr
  Pont Steffan 75 D4
Lampeter Velfrey 56 A1
Lamphey. 55 D6
Lamplugh. 162 B3
Lamport 99 D4
Lamyatt. 29 B6
Lana. 10 B4
Lanark. 194 B3
Lancaster. 145 A4
Lanchester. 167 A4
Lancing. 21 B4
Landbeach. 85 A6
Landcross 25 C5
Landerberry 245 B4
Landford. 31 D6
Landford Manor . .31 C6
Landimore 57 C4
Landkey 25 B6
Landore 57 C6
Landrake 6 A2
Landscove 8 A1
Landshipping . . .55 C6
Landshipping
  Quay 55 C6
Landulph 6 A3
Landwade 86 A2
Lane. 4 A3
Laneast 10 C3
Lane End Bucks . .66 D3
  Cumb 153 A2
  Dorset 16 B2
  Hants 33 C4
  IoW 19 C5
  Lancs 146 C2
Lane Ends Lancs .146 B1
  Lancs 146 D1
  N Yorks. 146 C3
Laneham 132 B3
Lanehead
  Durham 165 A6
  Northumb. 177 A5
Lane Head
  Derbys 129 B6
  Durham 166 D4
  Gtr Man 137 D5
  W Yorks 139 C4
Lanercost. 176 C3
Laneshaw
  Bridge 146 C3
Lane Side. 137 A6
Lanfach. 41 B7
Langar. 115 B5
Langbank. 204 A3
Langbar 147 B4
Langcliffe. 146 A2
Langdale 278 D2
Langdale End . . .160 B3
Langdon. 10 C4
Langdon Beck . . .165 B6
Langdon Hills . . .50 A3
Langdyke 220 D3
Langenhoe. 71 B4
Langford C Beds . .84 C3
  Devon. 13 A5
  Essex 70 C2

Langford *continued*
Notts 132 D3
Oxon. 64 C3
Langford
Budville 27 C6
Langham Essex . . 87 C6
Norf 120 A2
Rutland. 115 D6
Suff 103 E5
Langhaugh. 195 C7
Langho 145 D7
Langholm. 185 D6
Langleeford. 188 A2
Langley Ches E. . .129 B4
Hants 18 A3
Herts 68 A2
Kent 37 A6
Northumb. 177 C6
Slough 48 B3
Warks. 81 A4
W Sus. 33 C7
Langley Burrell. . . 44 B3
Langley
Common 113 B6
Langley Heath. . . 37 A6
Langley Lower
Green. 85 D6
Langley Marsh . . 27 C5
Langley Park. . . .167 A5
Langley Street . . .105 A4
Langley Upper
Green. 85 D6
Langney 22 B4
Langold 131 A5
Langore 10 C4
Langport. 28 C4
Langrick. 117 A5
Langridge 43 C6
Langridge Ford. . .25 C6
Langrigg. 175 D4
Langrish. 33 C6
Langsett. 139 C5
Langshaw. 197 C4
Langside. 218 C2
Langskaill 282 C5
Langstone Hants . .19 A6
Newport. 61 D5
Langthorne 157 B6
Langthorpe 148 A2
Langthwaite 156 A4
Langtoft E Yorks . . .150 A3
Lincs. 116 D4
Langton Durham .167 D4
Lincs. 134 B3
Lincs. 134 C2
N Yorks. 149 A6
Langton by
Wragby 133 B6
Langton Green
Kent 36 C3
Suff 104 D2
Langton Herring. . 15 C6
Langton
Matravers 17 C4
Langtree. 25 D5
Langwathby. 164 B3
Langwell Ho. 275 B5
Langwell Lodge .271 D4
Langwith 131 C5
Langwith
Junction 131 C5
Langworth 133 B5
Lanivet 5 A5
Lanlivery. 5 B5
Lanner 4 D2
Lanreath 5 B6
Lansallos 5 B6
Lansdown. 63 A5
Lanteglos Highway 5 B6
Lanton Borders. . .187 A5
Northumb. 198 C3
Lapford. 12 A2
Laphroaig. 200 D3
La Planque Guern . . .6
Lapley. 112 D2
Lapworth 97 D4
Larachbeg 225 B5
Larbert 207 B6
Larden Green 127 D5

Largie 255 C7
Largiemore 214 D2
Largoward. 221 D4
Largs. 204 C2
Largybeg 191 C6
Largymore. 191 C6
Larkfield 204 A2
Larkhall 194 A2
Larkhill 31 A5
Larling 103 C5
Larriston 186 D4
Lartington 166 D3
Lary 243 B6
Lasham 33 A5
Lashenden 37 B6
Lassington 62 A3
Lassodie 208 A4
Lastingham 159 B6
Latcham 29 A4
Latchford Herts . . .68 A3
Warr. 127 A6
Latchingdon 70 C2
Latchley. 11 D5
Lately Common .137 D5
Lathbury. 83 C5
Latheron. 275 A5
Latheronwheel . . .275 A5
Latheronwheel
Ho. 275 A5
Lathones 221 D4
Latimer 67 D5
Latteridge 43 A5
Lattiford 29 C6
Latton. 64 D1
Latton Bush. 69 C4
Lauchintilly 245 A4
Lauder 197 B4
Laugharne 56 A3
Laughterton 132 B3
Laughton E Sus . .22 A3
Leics. 98 C3
Lincs. 116 B3
Lincs. 141 D6
Laughton
Common 131 A5
Laughton en le
Morthen. 131 A5
Launcells 10 A3
Launceston 10 C4
Launton 65 A7
Laurencekirk. 233 A5
Laurieston
Dumfries 173 B4
Falk 208 C2
Lavendon 83 B6
Lavenham 87 C5
Laverhay. 185 C4
Laversdale 176 C2
Laverstock 31 B5
Laverstoke. 32 A3
Laverton Glos. . . .80 D3
N Yorks. 157 D6
Som 44 D1
Lavister. 126 D3
Law. 194 A3
Lawers Perth 217 A5
Perth 218 B2
Lawford. 88 D1
Lawhitton. 11 C4
Lawkland 146 A1
Lawley. 95 A4
Lawnhead 112 C2
Lawrenny 55 D6
Lawshall. 87 B4
Lawton 78 B2
Laxey 152 C4
Laxfield. 104 D3
Laxfirth Shetland .285 H6
Shetland. 285 J6
Laxford Bridge . .276 D3
Laxo. 285 G6
Laxobigging 284 F6
Laxton E Yorks . . .141 A5
Northants. 99 B6
Notts 132 C2
Laycock 147 C4
Layer Breton. . . .70 B3
Layer de la Haye. .70 B3
Layer Marney 70 B3
Layham. 87 C6
Laylands Green. . .46 C1
Laytham 149 D6

Layton. 144 D3
Lazenby 168 C3
Lazonby 164 B3
Lea Derbys. 130 D3
Hereford 62 A2
Lincs. 132 A3
Shrops 94 A3
Shrops 94 C1
Wilts. 44 A3
Leabrooks 131 D4
Leac a Li 288 H2
Leachkin. 252 B2
Leadburn 196 A1
Leadenham 133 D4
Leaden Roding . . 69 B5
Leadgate Cumb . .165 A5
Durham 178 D3
T&W. 178 D3
Leadhills. 183 A6
Leafield 64 B4
Leagrave 67 A5
Leake 158 B3
Leake
Commonside . . .134 D3
Lealholm 159 A6
Lealt Argyll 213 C4
Highld. 259 B5
Lea Marston 97 B5
Leamington
Hastings 82 A1
Leamonsley. 96 A4
Leamside 167 A6
Leanaig. 252 A1
Leargybreck. 201 A5
Leasgill. 154 C3
Leasingham. 116 A3
Leasingthorne . . .167 C5
Leasowe 136 D1
Leatherhead. 35 A4
Leatherhead
Common 35 A4
Leathley. 147 C6
Leaton. 110 D3
Lea Town 145 D4
Leaveland 52 D2
Leavening. 149 A6
Leaves Green 49 C7
Leazes. 178 D3
Lebberston 161 C4
Lechlade-on-
Thames 64 D3
Leck 155 D5
Leckford. 32 B2
Leckfurin 278 C3
Leckgruinart 200 B2
Leckhampstead
Bucks 83 D4
W Berks 46 B2
Leckhampstead
Thicket. 46 B2
Leckhampton 63 B5
Leckie. 262 D2
Leckmelm 262 A3
Leckwith 41 D6
Leconfield 150 C3
Ledaig 226 C4
Ledburn 67 A4
Ledbury 79 D5
Ledcharrie 217 B5
Ledgemoor 78 B2
Ledicot 78 A2
Ledmore 271 C5
Lednagullin 278 B3
Ledsham Ches W .126 B3
W Yorks 140 A2
Ledston 140 A2
Ledston Luck. 148 D3
Ledwell 65 A5
Lee Argyll. 224 D3
Devon. 25 C6
Hants 32 D2
Lancs. 145 B5
Shrops 110 B3
Leebotten 285 L6
Leebotwood 94 B2
Lee Brockhurst. . .111 C4
Leece 153 D3
Leechpool 55 C5
Lee Clump 67 C4
Leeds Kent 37 A6
W Yorks 148 D1

Leedstown 3 B4
Leek. 129 D4
Leekbrook 129 D4
Leek Wootton 81 A5
Lee Mill. 7 B5
Leeming 157 C6
Leeming Bar 157 B6
Lee Moor 7 A4
Lee-on-the-
Solent. 19 A4
Lees Derbys. 113 B6
Gtr Man 138 C2
W Yorks 147 D4
Leeswood. 126 C2
Legbourne 134 A3
Legerwood 197 B4
Legsby 133 A6
Leicester 98 A2
Leicester Forest
East. 98 A2
Leigh Dorset 15 A6
Glos 63 A4
Gtr Man 137 C5
Kent 36 B3
Shrops 94 A1
Sur 35 B5
Wilts. 63 D6
Worcs. 79 B5
Leigh Beck. 51 A5
Leigh Common. . .30 C1
Leigh Delamere . . 44 B2
Leigh Green. 37 C7
Leigh Park 19 A6
Leigh Sinton. 79 B5
Leighswood. 96 A3
Leighterton. 63 D4
Leighton N Yorks . .157 D5
Powys 93 A6
Shrops 95 A4
Som 29 A7
Leighton
Bromswold 100 D3
Leighton Buzzard 67 A4
Leigh upon
Mendip 29 A6
Leigh Woods. 43 B4
Leinthall Earls. . . .78 A2
Leinthall Starkes. .78 A2
Leintwardine. 94 D2
Leire 98 B2
Leirinmore. 277 B5
Leiston 89 A5
Leitfie 231 D6
Leith 209 C5
Leitholm 198 B1
Lelant 2 B3
Lelley 151 D5
Lem Hill 95 D5
Lemington
Hall. 189 B4
Lempitlaw 198 C1
Lenchwick 80 C3
Lendalfoot. 180 C3
Lendrick Lodge .217 D5
Lenham. 37 A6
Lenham Heath . . .37 B7
Lennel 198 B2
Lennoxtown. 205 A6
Lenton Lincs 116 B3
Nottingham 114 B3
Lentran 252 B1
Lenwade. 120 D2
Leny Ho.. . . . . . . .217 D6
Lenzie 205 A6
Leoch 220 A3
Leochel-
Cushnie 244 A2
Leominster 78 B2
Leonard Stanley. . .63 D4
Leorin 200 D3
Lepe. 18 B3
Lephin 258 D1
Lephinchapel 214 C2
Lephinmore. 214 C2
Le Planel Guern 6
Leppington 149 A6
Lepton 139 B5
Lerryn. 5 B6
Lerwick 285 J6
Lesbury 189 B5

Le Skerne
Haughton 167 D6
Leslie Aberds 255 D6
Fife. 220 D2
Lesmahagow. 194 C3
Lesnewth 10 B2
Lessendrum. 255 B6
Lessingham. 121 C5
Lessonhall 175 C5
Leswalt 170 A2
Letchmore Heath 67 D6
Letchworth 84 D4
Letcombe
Bassett. 46 A1
Letcombe Regis . .46 A1
Letham Angus. . . .232 D3
Falk 208 B1
Fife. 220 C3
Perth 219 B5
Letham Grange. . .233 D4
Lethenty. 256 B3
Letheringham. 88 B3
Letheringsett 120 B2
Lettaford 12 C2
Lettan 282 C8
Letterewe 261 C6
Letterfearn 249 D5
Letterfinlay 239 C6
Lettermorar. 235 B6
Lettermore 224 B3
Letters 262 B3
Letterston 55 B5
Lettoch Highld 242 A3
Highld. 254 C1
Letton Hereford . . .78 C1
Hereford 94 D1
Letton Green. . . .103 A5
Letty Green 68 B2
Letwell 131 A5
Leuchars 221 B4
Leuchars Ho.. . . .266 C3
Leumrabhagh . . .288 F4
Levan. 204 A2
Levaneap 285 G6
Levedale. 112 D2
Leven E Yorks 151 C4
Fife. 220 D3
Levencorroch 191 C6
Levens. 154 C3
Levens Green 68 A3
Levenshulme. 138 D1
Levenwick 285 L6
Leverington 118 D1
Leverton 117 A7
Leverton
Highgate. 117 A7
Leverton
Lucasgate. 117 A7
Leverton
Outgate. 117 A7
Le Villocq Guern 6
Levington. 88 D3
Levisham 160 B2
Levishie 240 A2
Lew 64 C4
Lewannick 10 C3
Lewdown 11 C5
Lewes 22 A2
Leweston 55 B5
Lewisham. 49 B6
Lewiston 251 D7
Lewistown 40 C4
Lewknor 66 D2
Leworthy Devon. . .10 A4
Devon. 26 B1
Lewtrenchard 11 C5
Lexden 70 A3
Ley Aberds. 244 A2
Corn 5 A6
Leybourne 37 A4
Leyburn 157 B5
Leyfields. 97 A5
Leyhill 67 C4
Leyland. 136 A4
Leylodge 245 A4
Leys Aberds. 269 D5
Perth 220 A2
Leys Castle. 252 B2
Leysdown-on-
Sea 52 B2
Leysmill. 233 D4

Leys of Cossans .232 D1
Leysters Pole 78 A3
Leyton. 49 A6
Leytonstone. 49 A6
Lezant 10 D4
Leziate 118 D3
Lhanbryde. 266 C3
Liatrie 250 C4
Libanus 60 A1
Libberton 195 B4
Liberton 209 D5
Liceasto 288 H2
Lichfield. 96 A4
Lickey 96 D2
Lickey End. 96 D2
Lickfold 34 D2
Liddel 283 J5
Liddesdale. 236 D1
Liddington 45 A6
Lidgate 86 B3
Lidget 141 C4
Lidget Green. . . .147 D5
Lidgett 131 C6
Lidlington 84 D1
Lidstone 65 A4
Lieurary 279 B6
Liff. 220 A3
Lifton. 11 C4
Liftondown 11 C4
Lighthorne. 81 B6
Lightwater 48 C2
Lightwood. 112 A3
Lightwood Green
Ches E 111 A5
Wrex 110 A2
Lilbourne 98 D2
Lilburn Tower. . . .188 A3
Lilleshall. 111 D6
Lilley Herts 67 A6
W Berks. 46 B2
Lilliesleaf 186 A4
Lillingstone
Dayrell 83 D4
Lillingstone
Lovell 83 C4
Lillington Dorset . .29 D6
Warks. 81 A6
Lilliput 17 B4
Lilstock 27 A6
Lilyhurst 111 D6
Limbury 67 A5
Limebrook. 78 A1
Limefield 137 B7
Limekilnburn 194 A2
Limekilns 208 B3
Limerigg 207 C6
Limerstone 18 C3
Limington 29 C5
Limpenhoe 105 A4
Limpley Stoke. . . .44 C1
Limpsfield. 36 A2
Limpsfield Chart .36 A2
Linby. 131 D5
Linchmere 34 C1
Lincluden 174 A2
Lincoln 133 B4
Lincomb 79 A6
Lincombe. 7 B6
Lindal in
Furness 154 C3
Lindean 196 C3
Lindfield. 35 D6
Lindford 33 B7
Lindifferon. 220 C3
Lindley 139 B4
Lindley Green. . . .147 C6
Lindores 220 C2
Lindridge 79 A4
Lindsell. 69 A6
Lindsey 87 C5
Linford Hants 17 A5
Thurrock. 50 B3
Lingague 152 D2
Lingards Wood. . .138 B3
Lingbob 147 D4
Lingdale 169 D4
Lingen 78 A1
Lingfield. 36 B1
Lingreabhagh . . .287 F5
Lingwood. 105 A4
Linicro 258 B3

Linkenholt 46 D1
Linkhill 37 D6
Linkinhorne. 10 D4
Linklater. 283 J5
Linksness 283 G3
Linktown 209 A5
Linley 94 B1
Linley Green . . . 79 B4
Linlithgow 208 C3
Linlithgow
  Bridge 208 C2
Linshiels. 188 C1
Linsiadar 288 D3
Linsidemore 264 A1
Linslade 67 A4
Linstead Parva . 104 D4
Linstock 176 D2
Linthwaite 139 B4
Lintlaw 198 A2
Lintmill. 267 C6
Linton Borders . 187 A6
  Cambs 86 C1
  Derbys 113 D6
  Hereford 62 A2
  Kent 37 B5
  Northumb. . . . 189 D5
  N Yorks. 146 A3
  W Yorks 148 C2
Linton-on-Ouse 148 A3
Linwood Hants. . 17 A5
  Lincs. 133 A6
  Renfs 205 B4
Lionacleit. 286 B3
Lional 288 A6
Liphook 34 C1
Liscard 136 D2
Liscombe 26 B3
Liskeard 6 A1
L'Islet Guern 6
Liss 33 C6
Lissett. 151 B4
Liss Forest 33 C6
Lissington 133 A6
Lisvane 41 C6
Liswerry 42 A2
Litcham 119 D5
Litchborough . . 82 B3
Litchfield 46 D2
Lit. Hallingbury. 69 B4
Litherland 136 D2
Litlington Cambs. 85 C5
  E Sus 22 B3
Little Abington . 86 C1
Little Addington . 99 D6
Little Alne 80 A4
Little Altcar. . . 136 C2
Little Asby 155 A5
Little Assynt. . . 271 B4
Little Aston . . . 96 A3
Little Atherfield . 18 C3
Little Ayre 283 H4
Little-ayre 285 G5
Little Ayton . . . 168 D3
Little Baddow . . 70 C1
Little Badminton . 44 A2
Little Ballinluig. 230 C3
Little Bampton . 175 C5
Little Bardfield . 86 D2
Little Barford . . 84 B3
Little
  Barningham . 120 B3
Little Barrington . 64 B3
Little Barrow . . 127 C4
Little Barugh . . 159 D6
Little Bavington . 178 B1
Little Bealings. . 88 C3
Littlebeck 160 A2
Little Bedwyn . . 45 C6
Little Bentley. . 71 A5
Little
  Berkhamsted . 68 C2
Little Billing. . . 83 A5
Little Birch. . . . 78 D3
Little Blakenham . 88 C2
Little Blencow . . 164 B2
Little Bollington 128 A2
Little Bookham. 35 A4
Littleborough
  Gtr Man 138 B2
  Notts 132 A3
Littlebourne . . . 53 D4
Little Bowden . . 99 C4

Little Bradley . . . 86 B2
Little Brampton . 94 C1
Little Brechin . . 232 B3
Littlebredy. . . . 15 C5
Little Brickhill . . 83 D6
Little Brington . 82 A3
Little Bromley . 71 A4
Little
  Broughton. . . 162 A3
Little Budworth .127 C5
Little Burstead . 69 D6
Littlebury 85 D7
Littlebury Green. 85 B6
Little Bytham. . 116 D3
Little Carlton
  Lincs. 134 A3
  Notts 132 D2
Little Casterton .100 A2
Little
  Cawthorpe . . 134 A3
Little Chalfont. . 67 D4
Little Chart . . . 38 A1
Little
  Chesterford . . 85 C7
Little Cheverell. 44 D3
Little Chishill. . 85 D6
Little Clacton . 71 B5
Little Clifton . . 162 B3
Little Colp . . . 256 B2
Little Comberton .80 C2
Little Common . 23 B4
Little Compton . 81 D5
Little Cornard . . 87 D4
Little Cowarne . 79 B4
Little Coxwell . . 64 D3
Little Crakehall .157 B6
Little
  Cressingham .103 B4
Little Crosby . 136 C2
Little Dalby . .115 D5
Little Dawley . . 95 A4
Littledean 62 B2
Little Dens . . . 257 B5
Little Dewchurch 78 D3
Little Downham .101 C7
Little Driffield . 150 B3
Little Dunham . 119 D5
Little Dunkeld . 230 C3
Little Dunmow . 69 A6
Little Easton . . 69 A6
Little Eaton . . 114 A1
Little Eccleston . 144 C4
Little Ellingham .103 B6
Little End 69 C5
Little Eversden. 85 B5
Little Faringdon . 64 C3
Little Fencote . 157 B6
Little Fenton . . 148 C4
Littleferry 265 A2
Little Finborough. 87 B6
Little Fransham .119 D6
Little Gaddesden. 67 B6
Little Gidding . 100 C3
Little Glemham . 88 B4
Little Glenshee .219 A4
Little Gransden. 85 B4
Little Green . . . 29 A7
Little Grimsby .143 D5
Little Gruinard .261 B6
Little Habton . .159 D6
Little Hadham . 68 A4
Little Hale . . . 116 A4
Littleham Devon. .15 C5
  Devon. 25 C5
Little Hampden . 66 C3
Littlehampton . 20 B3
Little Harrowden .99 D5
Little Haseley . . 66 C1
Little Hatfield . 151 C4
Little Hautbois .121 C4
Little Haven . . 55 C4
Little Hay 96 A4
Little Hayfield . 129 A5
Little Haywood .112 C4
Little Heath . . . 97 C6
Littlehempston . 8 A2
Little Hereford . 78 A3
Little Horkesley . 87 D5
Little Horsted . . 22 A2
Little Horton . . 45 C4
Little Horwood . 83 D4
Littlehoughton .189 B5

Little Houghton
  Northants. . . . 83 B5
  S Yorks. 140 C2
Little Hucklow . 129 B6
Little Hulton . . 137 C6
Little Humber . .142 A3
Little Hungerford. 46 B3
Little Irchester . . 83 A6
Little Kimble. . . 66 C3
Little Kineton . . 81 B6
Little Kingshill . 66 D3
Little Langdale . 154 A2
Little Langford . 31 B4
Little Laver 69 C5
Little Leigh . . . 127 B6
Little Leighs . . . 69 B7
Little Lever . . . 137 C6
Little London
  Bucks 66 B1
  E Sus 22 A3
  Hants. 32 A2
  Hants. 47 D4
  Lincs. 117 C5
  Lincs. 118 C1
  Norf 120 C3
  Powys 92 C4
Little Longstone 130 B1
Little Lynturk. . 244 A2
Little Malvern . . 79 C5
Little Maplestead 87 D4
Little Marcle . . 79 D4
Little Marlow. . 47 A6
Little Marsden . .146 D2
Little
  Massingham. .119 C4
Little Melton . . 104 A2
Littlemill Aberds .243 C6
  E Ayrs. 182 A2
  Highld. 253 A5
  Northumb. . . . 189 B5
Little Mill 61 C5
Little Milton . . 65 C7
Little Missenden . 67 D4
Littlemoor 15 C6
Littlemore 65 C6
Little Musgrave .165 D5
Little Ness . . . 110 D3
Little Neston . 126 B2
Little Newcastle . 55 B5
Little Newsham .166 D4
Little Oakley
  Essex 71 A6
  Northants. . . . 99 C5
Little Orton . . 175 C6
Little Ouseburn .148 A3
Littleover 114 B1
Little Paxton . . 84 A3
Little Petherick. 9 D5
Little Pitlург . . 255 B5
Little Plumpton .144 D3
Little
  Plumstead. . .121 D5
Little Ponton . 116 B2
Littleport 102 C1
Little Raveley . .101 D4
Little Reedness . 141 A6
Little Ribston . 148 B2
Little Rissington . 64 B2
Little Ryburgh . 119 C6
Little Ryle . . . 188 B3
Little Salkeld . . 164 B3
Little Sampford . 86 D2
Little Sandhurst . 47 C6
Little Saxham . . 86 A3
Little Scatwell . 251 A5
Little Sessay . . 158 D3
Little Shelford . 85 B6
Little Singleton .144 D3
Little
  Skillymarno .269 D4
Little Smeaton . 140 B3
Little Snoring . 119 B6
Little Sodbury . 43 A6
Little Somborne . 32 B2
Little Somerford . 44 A3
Little Stainforth .146 A2
Little Stainton . 167 C6
Little Stanney . 127 B4
Little Staughton . 84 A3
Little Steeping . 135 C4
Little Stoke . . . 112 B3

Littlestone on
  Sea 38 C2
Little Stonham . 88 A2
Little Stretton
  Leics. 98 A3
  Shrops 94 B2
Little Strickland 164 D3
Little Stukeley. .100 D4
Little Sutton . 126 B3
Little Tew 65 A4
Little Thetford . 102 D1
Little Thirkleby .158 D3
Little Thornton . 86 B2
Little Thorpe . . 50 B3
Little Thurrock . 50 B3
Little Torboll . . 264 A3
Little Torrington . 25 D5
Little Totham . . 70 B2
Little Toux . . . 267 D6
Littletown . . . 167 A6
Little Town
  Cumb 163 C5
  Lancs 145 D6
Little Urswick . 153 C3
Little Wakering. 51 A6
Little Walden . . 86 C1
Little
  Waldingfield. . 87 C5
Little
  Walsingham . .119 B6
Little Waltham . 69 B7
Little Warley . . 69 D6
Little Weighton .150 D2
Little Weldon . . 99 C6
Little Welnetham 87 A4
Little Wenlock . 95 A4
Little Whittingham
  Green. 104 D3
Littlewick Green. 47 B6
Little Wilbraham . 86 B1
Little Wishford . 31 B4
Little Witley . . 79 A5
Little Wittenham . 65 D6
Little Wolford . . 81 D5
Littleworth
  Bedford 84 C2
  Glos 63 C4
  Oxon. 64 D4
  Staffs 112 D4
  Worcs. 80 B1
Little Wratting . 86 C2
Little Wymington 83 A6
Little Wymondley 68 A2
Little Wyrley . . 96 A3
Little Yeldham . 86 D3
Litton Derbys . 129 B6
  N Yorks. . . . 156 D3
  Som 43 D4
Litton Cheney . 15 B5
Liurbost 288 E4
Liverpool . . . 136 D2
Liverpool
  Airport 127 A4
Liversedge . . 139 A5
Liverton Devon. . 12 D3
  Redcar 169 D5
Livingston . . . 208 D3
Livingston
  Village 208 D3
Lixwm 125 B6
Lizard 3 D5
Llaingoch . . . 122 B2
Llaithddu 93 C4
Llan 91 B6
Llanaber 90 A4
Llanaelhaearn. .106 B3
Llanafan 75 A5
Llanafan-fawr. . 76 B3
Llanallgo . . . 123 B4
Llanarmon . . . 107 C4

Llanarmon Dyffryn
  Ceiriog. 109 B6
Llanarmon-yn-
  Ial 126 D1
Llanarth Ceredig . 73 A7
  Mon 61 B5
Llanarthne . . . 58 C2
Llanasa 125 A6
Llanbabo 122 B3
Llanbadarn Fawr .90 D4
Llanbadarn
  Fynydd 93 D5
Llanbadarn-y-
  Garreg 77 C5
Llanbadoc . . . 61 C5
Llanbadrig . . . 122 A3
Llanbeder. . . . 61 D5
Llanbedr Gwyn. .107 D5
  Powys 60 A4
  Powys 77 C5
Llanbedr-Dyffryn-
  Clwyd 125 D6
Llanbedrgoch . 123 B5
Llanbedrog . . 106 C3
Llanbedr-y-
  cennin 124 C2
Llanberis . . . 123 D5
Llanbethêry . . 41 E5
Llanbister. . . . 93 D5
Llanblethian . 41 D4
Llanboidy . . . 73 D5
Llanbradach . 41 B6
Llanbrynmair . 91 B6
Llancarfan . . 41 D5
Llancayo. . . . 61 C5
Llancloudy . . 61 A6
Llancynfelyn . 90 C4
Llandaff 41 D6
Llandanwg . . 107 D5
Llandarcy . . . 40 B2
Llandawke . . 56 A2
Llanddaniel Fab 123 C4
Llanddarog . . 57 A5
Llanddeiniol . . 74 A4
Llanddeiniolen .123 D5
Llandderfel . . 109 B6
Llanddeusant
  Anglesey . . . 122 B3
  Carms 59 C4
Llanddew . . . 77 D4
Llanddewi . . . 57 D4
Llanddewi-Brefi. 75 C5
Llanddewi'r Cwm 76 C4
Llanddewi
  Rhydderch . . 61 B5
Llanddewi
  Velfrey 56 A1
Llanddoged . . 124 C3
Llanddona . . 123 C5
Llanddowror . 56 A2
Llanddulas . . 125 B4
Llanddwywan .107 D5
Llanddyfnan . 123 C5
Llandefaelog
  Fach 76 D4
Llandefaelog-tre'r-
  graig. 77 E5
Llandefalle. . . . 77 D5
Llandegai . . . 123 C5
Llandegfan . . 123 C5
Llandegla . . . 126 D1
Llandegley . . . 77 A5
Llandegveth . . 61 D5
Llandegwning . 106 C2
Llandeilo . . . 58 C3
Llandeilo Graban 77 C4
Llandeilo'r Fan . 59 B5
Llandeloy . . . 55 B4
Llandenny . . . 61 C6
Llandevenick . 42 A3
Llandewednock . 3 D5
Llandewi
  Ystradenny . . 77 A5
Llandinabo . . 61 A7
Llandinam . . 92 C4
Llandissilio . . 55 B7
Llandogo . . . 62 C1
Llandough V Glam 41 D4
  V Glam 41 D6
Llandovery
  Llanymddyfri . 59 B4
Llandow 40 D4

Llandre Carms . . . 58 A3
  Ceredig 90 D4
Llandrillo 109 B5
Llandrillo-yn-
  Rhos 124 A3
Llandrindod Wells
  Llandrindod . . 77 A4
Llandrinio . . . 110 D1
Llandudno . . . 124 A2
Llandudno Junction
  Cyffordd
  Llandudno. . . 124 B2
Llandwrog . . . 107 A4
Llandybie. . . . 57 A6
Llandyfaelog . . 57 A4
Llandyfan . . . 57 A6
Llandyfriog . . . 73 B6
Llandyfrydog . . 123 B4
Llandygwydd. . 73 B5
Llandynan . . . 109 A6
Llandyrnog . . 125 C6
Llandysilio . . . 110 D1
Llandyssil 93 B5
Llandysul . . . 73 B7
Llanedeyrn . . . 41 C7
Llanedi 57 B5
Llaneglwys . . . 77 D4
Llanegryn . . . 90 B3
Llanegwad . . 58 C2
Llaneilian . . . 123 A4
Llanelian-yn-
  Rhos 124 B3
Llanelidan . . 125 D6
Llanelieu 77 D5
Llanellen . . . 61 B5
Llanelli 57 C5
Llanelltyd . . . 91 A5
Llanelly 60 B4
Llanelly Hill . . 60 B4
Llanelwedd . . 76 B4
Llanenddwyn. .107 D5
Llanengan . . 106 D2
Llanerchymedd .123 B4
Llanerfyl . . . 92 A4
Llanfachraeth. .122 B3
Llanfachreth . 108 C2
Llanfaelog . . 122 C3
Llanfaelrhys. .106 D2
Llanfaenor . . 61 B6
Llanfaes
  Anglesey . . .123 C6
  Powys 60 A2
Llanfaethlu . . 122 B3
Llanfaglan . . 123 D4
Llanfair 107 D5
Llanfair-ar-y-
  bryn 59 B5
Llanfair
  Caereinion . . 93 A5
Llanfair Clydogau 75 C5
Llanfair-Dyffryn-
  Clwyd 125 D6
Llanfairfechan . 124 B1
Llanfair
  Kilgheddin . . 61 C5
Llanfair-Nant-
  Gwyn 73 C4
Llanfairpwll-
  gwyngyll . . . 123 C5
Llanfair
  Talhaiarn. . . 125 B4
Llanfair
  Waterdine . . 93 D6
Llanfairyneubwll
  . . . . 122 C3
Llanfairynghornwy
  . . . . 122 A3
Llanfallteg . . 56 A1
Llanfaredd . . 77 B4
Llanfarian . . . 75 A4
Llanfechain . 109 C6
Llanfechan. . . 76 B3
Llanfechell. . 122 A3
Llanfendigaid . 90 B3
Llanferres . . 126 C1
Llan Ffestiniog .108 A2
Llanfflewyn . 122 B3
Llanfihangel-ar-
  arth. 58 B1

Llanfihangel-
   Crucorney......61 A5
Llanfihangel Glyn
   Myfyr...........109 A4
Llanfihangel Nant
   Bran...........59 B6
Llanfihangel-nant-
   Melan............77 B5
Llanfihangel
   Rhydithon........77 A5
Llanfihangel
   Rogiet...........42 A3
Llanfihangel Tal-y-
   llyn.............60 A3
Llanfihangel-uwch-
   Gwili.........58 C1
Llanfihangel-y-
   Creuddyn......75 A5
Llanfihangel-yn-
   Ngwynfa.....109 D5
Llanfihangel yn
   Nhowyn......122 C3
Llanfihangel-y-
   pennant
   Gwyn..........91 B4
   Gwyn.........107 B5
Llanfihangel-y-
   traethau.....107 C5
Llanfilo..........77 D5
Llanfoist.........61 B4
Llanfor..........108 B4
Llanfrechfa.....61 D5
Llanfrothen....107 B6
Llanfrynach.....60 A2
Llanfwrog
   Anglesey.....122 B3
   Denb..........125 D6
Llanfyllin.......109 D6
Llanfynydd Carms.58 C2
   Flint...........126 D2
Llanfyrnach......73 C5
Llangadfan....109 D5
Llangadog......59 C4
Llangadwaladr
   Anglesey.....122 D3
   Powys........109 B6
Llangaffo......123 D4
Llangain........56 A3
Llangammarch
   Wells.........76 C3
Llangan..........41 D4
Llangarron......62 A1
Llangasty
   Talyllyn........60 A3
Llangathen......58 C2
Llangattock......60 B4
Llangattock
   Lingoed......61 A5
Llangattock nigh
   Usk............61 C5
Llangattock-Vibon-
   Avel............61 B6
Llangedwyn....109 C6
Llangefni.......123 C4
Llangeinor......40 C4
Llangeitho......75 C5
Llangeler.......73 C6
Llangelynin......90 B3
Llangendeirne...57 A4
Llangennech....57 B5
Llangennith......57 C4
Llangenny.......60 B4
Llangernyw....124 C3
Llangian.......106 D2
Llanglydwen....73 D4
Llangoed......123 C6
Llangoedmor....73 B4
Llangollen.....109 A7
Llangolman.....55 B7
Llangors........60 A3
Llangovan......61 C6
Llangower.....108 B4
Llangranog......73 A6
Llangristiolus..123 C4
Llangrove......62 B1
Llangunllo.......93 D6
Llangunnor......57 A4
Llangurig........92 D3

Llangwm Conwy..109 A4
   Mon............61 C6
   Pembs.........55 D5
Llangwnnadl....106 C2
Llangwyfan....125 C6
Llangwyfan-isaf 122 D3
Llangwyllog....123 C4
Llangwyryfon....75 A4
Llangybi Ceredig..75 C5
   Gwyn.........107 B4
   Mon...........61 D5
Llangyfelach.....57 C6
Llangynhafal...125 D6
Llangynidr......60 B3
Llangynin......56 A3
Llangynog Carms..56 A3
   Powys........109 C5
Llangynwyd.....40 C3
Llanhamlach.....60 A2
Llanharan......41 C5
Llanharry.......41 C5
Llanhennock....61 D5
Llanhilleth......61 B6
Llanidloes.......92 C3
Llaniestyn......106 C2
Llanifyny........91 D6
Llanigon........77 D6
Llanilar.........75 A5
Llanilid.........41 C4
Llanishen Cardiff.41 C6
   Mon...........61 C5
Llanllawddog....58 C1
Llanllechid....123 D6
Llanllowell......61 D5
Llanllugan......93 A4
Llanllwch......56 A3
Llanllwchaiarn....93 B5
Llanllwni.......58 B1
Llanllyfni......107 A4
Llanmadoc......57 C4
Llanmaes......41 E4
Llanmartin......42 A3
Llanmorlais.....57 C5
Llannefydd....125 B4
Llannon.........57 B5
Llannor........106 C3
Llanon..........75 B4
Llanover.........61 C5
Llanpumsaint....73 D7
Llanreithan......55 B4
Llanrhaeadr....125 C5
Llanrhaeadr-ym-
   Mochnant....109 C6
Llanrhian.......54 A4
Llanrhidian......57 C4
Llanrhos.......124 A2
Llanrhyddlad...122 B3
Llanrhystud.....75 B4
Llanrosser......77 D6
Llanrothal......60 A2
Llanrug........123 D5
Llanrumney......41 C7
Llanrwst......124 C3
Llansadurnen....56 A2
Llansadwrn
   Anglesey.....123 C5
   Carms.........58 B3
Llansaint.......56 B3
Llansamlet......40 B1
Llansannan....125 C4
Llansannor.....41 D4
Llansantffraed
   Ceredig........75 B4
   Powys.........60 A3
Llansantffraed
   Cwmdeuddwr...76 A3
Llansantffraed-in-
   Elvel...........77 B4
Llansantffraid-ym-
   Mechain.....109 C7
Llansawel......58 B3
Llansilin......109 C7
Llansoy.........61 C6
Llanspyddid.....60 A2
Llanstadwell.....55 D5
Llansteffan.....56 A3
Llanstephan.....77 C5
Llantarnam.....61 D5
Llanteg.........56 A1
Llanthony......61 A4

Llantilio
   Crossenny.....61 B5
Llantilio
   Pertholey......61 B5
Llantood........73 B4
Llantrisant
   Anglesey.....122 B3
   Mon...........61 D5
   Rhondda.......41 C5
Llantrithyd......41 D5
Llantwit Fardre..41 C5
Llantwit Major
   Llanilltud Fawr...41 E4
Llanuwchllyn...108 B3
Llanvaches......61 D6
Llanvair Discoed .61 D6
Llanvapley......61 B5
Llanvetherine....61 B5
Llanveynoe......77 D7
Llanvihangel
   Gobion........61 C5
Llanvihangel-Ystern-
   Llewern.......61 B6
Llanwarne......61 A7
Llanwddyn....109 D5
Llanwenog......74 D3
Llanwern........42 A2
Llanwinio.......73 D5
Llanwnda Gwyn..107 A4
   Pembs.........72 C2
Llanwnnen......75 D4
Llanwnog........92 B4
Llanwrda.......59 B4
Llanwrin.........91 B5
Llanwrthwl......76 A3
Llanwrtyd......76 C2
Llanwrtyd Wells
   Llanwrtud.....76 C2
Llanwyddelan....93 A4
Llanyblodwel...110 C1
Llanybri.........56 A3
Llanybydder.....58 A2
Llanycefn.......55 B6
Llanychaer......72 C2
Llanycil.......108 B4
Llanycrwys......75 D5
Llanymawddwy...91 A7
Llanymynech...110 C1
Llanynghenedl..122 B3
Llanynys......125 C6
Llan-y-pwll....126 D3
Llanyre.........76 A4
Llanystumdwy...107 C4
Llanywern......60 A3
Llawhaden......55 C6
Llawnt.........110 B1
Llawr Dref.....106 D2
Llawryglyn......92 B3
Llay...........126 D3
Llechcynfarwy..122 B3
Llecheiddior...107 B4
Llechfaen......60 A2
Llechryd Caerph..60 C3
   Ceredig.......73 B5
Llechrydau....110 B1
Lledrod.........75 A5
Llenmerewig....93 B5
Llethrid........57 C5
Llidiad Nenog...58 B2
Llidiardau.....108 B3
Llidiart-y-parc..109 A6
Llithfaen......106 B3
Llong..........126 C2
Llowes.........77 C5
Llundain-fach...75 C4
Llwydcoed......41 A4
Llwyn..........93 C6
Llwyncelyn......74 C3
Llwyndafydd....73 A6
Llwynderw......93 A6
Llwyn-du........61 B4
Llwyndyrys....106 B3
Llwyngwril......90 B3
Llwyn-hendy....57 C5
Llwynmawr.....110 B1
Llwyn-têg.......57 B5
Llwyn-y-brain...56 A1
Llwyn-y-groes...75 C4
Llwynypia......41 B4
Llynclys.......110 C1
Llynfaes......123 C4
Llysfaen......124 B3

Llyswen.........77 D5
Llysworney......41 D4
Llys-y-frân......55 B6
Llywel...........59 B5
Loan............208 C2
Loanend........198 A3
Loanhead.......209 D5
Loans..........192 B3
Loans of Tullich 265 C4
Lobb.............25 B5
Loch a Charnain 286 B4
Loch a'
   Ghainmhich...288 E3
Lochailort......235 B6
Lochaline.......225 B5
Lochanhully....253 D5
Lochans........170 B2
Locharbriggs...184 D2
Lochawe........227 D6
Loch Baghasdail
   Lochboisdale...286 E3
Lochbuie.......225 D5
Lochcarron......249 C5
Loch Choire
   Lodge.........273 A4
Lochdhu........279 D6
Lochdochart
   House.........216 B4
Lochdon........225 C6
Lochdrum......263 C4
Lochead........202 A2
Lochearnhead...217 B5
Lochee.........220 A3
Lochend Highld...252 C1
   Highld.........281 B4
Locherben......184 C2
Loch Euphoirt..287 H3
Lochfoot.......173 A6
Lochgair.......214 C2
Lochgarthside...240 A3
Lochgelly......209 A4
Lochgilphead...214 D1
Lochgoilhead...215 B5
Loch Head......171 C5
Lochhill.......266 C3
Lochindorb
   Lodge.........253 C5
Lochinver......270 B3
Lochlane.......218 B3
Loch Loyal
   Lodge.........277 D7
Lochluichart...263 D5
Lochmaben.....184 D3
Lochmore
   Cottage.......280 D2
Lochmore
   Lodge.........271 A5
Loch nam Madadh
   Lochmaddy...287 H4
Lochore........209 A4
Lochportain....287 G4
Lochranza......203 C4
Lochs Crofts...266 C4
Loch Sgioport..286 C4
Lochside Aberds.233 B5
   Highld.........253 A4
   Highld.........274 A2
   Highld.........277 C5
Lochslin.......265 B4
Lochstack
   Lodge.........276 D3
Lochton........245 C4
Lochty Angus...232 B3
   Fife..........221 D5
Lochuisge......236 D1
Lochurr........183 D5
Lochwinnoch...204 C3
Lochwood......184 C3
Lochyside......237 B5
Lockengate.......5 A5
Lockerbie......185 D4
Lockeridge......45 C5
Lockerley.......32 C1
Locking.........42 D2
Lockinge........46 A2
Lockington
   E Yorks.......150 C2

Lockington continued
   Leics.........114 C2
Lockleywood...111 C5
Locks Heath.....18 A4
Lockton........160 B2
Lockwood......139 B4
Loddington Leics..99 A4
   Northants......99 D5
Loddiswell.......7 C6
Loddon........105 B4
Lode............86 A1
Loders..........15 B4
Lodsworth......34 D2
Lofthouse
   N Yorks.......157 D5
   W Yorks......139 A6
Loftus.........169 D5
Logan..........193 C5
Loganlea.......208 D2
Logan Mains...170 C2
Loggerheads...111 B6
Logie Angus....233 B4
   Fife..........220 B4
   Moray.........253 A6
Logiealmond
   Lodge.........219 A4
Logie Coldstone 244 B1
Logie Hill......264 C3
Logie Newton...256 C1
Logie Pert.....233 B4
Logierait......230 C3
Login...........73 D4
Lolworth........85 A5
Lonbain........248 A3
London Colney..68 C1
Londonderry...157 C7
Londonthorpe...116 B2
Londubh.......261 B5
Long Ashton.....43 B4
Longbar........204 C3
Long
   Bennington...115 A6
Longbenton....179 C4
Longborough....64 A2
Long Bredy......15 B5
Longbridge Warks 81 A5
   W Mid..........96 D3
Longbridge
   Deverill.......30 A2
Long Buckby.....82 A3
Longburton.....29 D6
Long Clawson..115 C5
Longcliffe.....130 D2
Long Common....32 D4
Long Compton
   Staffs.........112 C2
   Warks..........81 D5
Longcot........64 D3
Long Crendon...66 C1
Long Crichel....30 D3
Longcroft.....207 C5
Longden........94 A2
Long Ditton.....49 C4
Longdon Staffs..113 D4
   Worcs..........79 D6
Longdon Green..113 D4
Longdon on
   Tern.........111 D5
Longdown.......12 B3
Longdowns.......4 D2
Long Drax.....141 A4
Long
   Duckmanton..131 B4
Long Eaton....114 B2
Longfield Kent...50 C3
Longford Derbys 113 B6
   Glos...........63 A4
   London........48 B3
   Shrops.......111 B6
   Telford.......111 D6
   W Mid..........97 C6
Longfordlane...113 B6
Longforgan....220 B3
Longformacus..197 A5
Longframlington
   ....189 C4
Long Green......79 D6
Longham Dorset..17 A4
   Norf.........119 D6

Long
   Hanborough....65 B5
Longhaven......257 C6
Longhill.......269 D4
Longhirst......179 A4
Longhope Glos...62 B2
   Orkney.......283 H4
Longhorsley...189 D4
Longhoughton..189 B5
Long Itchington..81 A7
Longlane Derbys 113 B6
   W Berks........46 B2
Long Lawford....98 D1
Longlevens......63 A4
Longley.......139 C4
Longley Green...79 B5
Long Load.......29 C4
Longmanhill...268 C2
Long Marston
   Herts..........66 B3
   N Yorks.......148 B4
   Warks..........81 C4
Long Marton...165 C4
Long Melford....87 C4
Longmoor Camp..33 B6
Longmorn......266 D3
Long Newnton...63 D5
Longnewton
   Borders......187 A4
   Stockton......167 D6
Long Newton...210 D2
Longney.........62 B3
Longniddry....210 C1
Longnor Shrops..94 A2
   Staffs.........129 C5
Longparish......32 A3
Longport.......112 A2
Long Preston...146 B2
Longridge Lancs 145 D6
   Staffs.........112 D3
   W Loth.......208 D2
Longriggend...207 C6
Long Riston....151 C4
Longsdon......129 D4
Longshaw......136 C4
Longside......257 B5
Long Sight.....138 C2
Longstanton.....85 A5
Longstock.......32 B2
Longstone......56 B1
Longstowe......85 B5
Long Stratton..104 B2
Long Street.....83 C4
Long Sutton
   Hants..........33 A6
   Lincs.........118 C1
   Som...........29 C4
Longthorpe....100 B3
Long Thurlow...87 A6
Longthwaite...164 C2
Longton Lancs...136 A3
   Stoke........112 A2
Longtown Cumb..175 B6
   Hereford.......61 A5
Longview.......136 D3
Longville in the
   Dale..........94 B3
Long Whatton..114 C2
Longwick........66 C2
Long Wittenham .65 D6
Longwitton.....178 A2
Longwood.......95 A4
Longworth......65 D4
Longyester....210 D2
Lonmay........269 D5
Lonmore......258 D2
Looe............6 B1
Loose...........37 A5
Loosley Row.....66 C3
Lopcombe
   Corner........31 B6
Lopen..........28 D4
Loppington....110 C3
Lopwell..........6 A3
Lorbottle.....188 C3
Lorbottle Hall..188 C3
Lornty.........231 D5
Loscoe........114 A2
Losgaintir.....287 E5
Lossiemouth...266 B3
Lossit.........200 C1
Lostford......111 B5

Lostock Gralam . 128 B1
Lostock Green . 128 B1
Lostock Hall 136 A4
Lostock
  Junction 137 C5
Lostwithiel. 5 B6
Loth. 282 D7
Lothbeg 274 C3
Lothersdale 146 C3
Lothmore 274 C3
Loudwater 67 D4
Loughborough . . 114 D3
Loughor 57 C5
Loughton Essex . . 68 D4
  M Keynes 83 D5
  Shrops 95 C4
Lound Lincs. 116 D3
  Notts 132 A1
  Suff 105 B6
Lount 114 D1
Louth. 134 A3
Love Clough 137 A7
Lovedean 33 D5
Lover. 31 C6
Loversall. 140 D3
Loves Green 69 C6
Lovesome Hill . . . 158 B2
Loveston. 55 D6
Lovington. 29 B5
Low Ackworth. . . 140 B2
Low Barlings. . . . 133 B5
Low Bentham . . . 145 A6
Low Bradfield . . . 139 D5
Low Bradley 147 C4
Low Braithwaite 164 A2
Lowbridge
  House. 154 A4
Low Brunton 177 B7
Low Burnham . . . 141 C5
Low Burton 157 C6
Low Buston 189 C5
Lowca 162 B2
Low Catton 149 B6
Low Clanyard . . . 170 D3
Low Coniscliffe. . 167 D5
Low Crosby 176 D2
Low Dalby 160 C2
Lowdham. 115 A4
Low Dinsdale . . . 167 D6
Lowe 111 B4
Lowe Hill 129 D4
Low Ellington . . . 157 C6
Lower Aisholt . . . 28 B2
Lower Arncott. . . 65 B7
Lower Ashton 12 C3
Lower Assendon . 47 A5
Lower Badcall . . 276 D2
Lower Bartle . . . 145 D4
Lower Basildon . . 47 B4
Lower Beeding . . 35 D5
Lower
  Benefield. 100 C1
Lower
  Boddington. . . . 82 B1
Lower Brailes . . . 81 D6
Lower Breakish . 247 B5
Lower
  Broadheath. . . . 79 B6
Lower
  Bullingham. . . 78 D3
Lower Cam 62 C3
Lower Chapel . . . 76 D4
Lower Chute . . . 45 D7
Lower Cragabus 200 D3
Lower
  Crossings 129 A5
Lower
  Cumberworth. . 139 C5
Lower Cwm-
  twrch 59 D6
Lower Darwen . . 137 A5
Lower Dean 84 A2
Lower Diabaig . . 261 D4
Lower Dicker 22 A3
Lower Dinchope. . 94 C2
Lower Down 94 C1
Lower Drift 2 C2
Lower
  Dunsforth 148 A3
Lower Egleton . . . 79 C4
Lower Elkstone. . 129 D5
Lower End 67 A4

Lower Everleigh . . 45 D5
Lower
  Farringdon 33 B6
Lower Foxdale . . 152 D2
Lower Frankton . 110 B2
Lower Froyle. 33 A6
Lower Gledfield . 264 A1
Lower Green 120 B1
Lower Hacheston. 88 B4
Lower Halistra . . 258 C2
Lower Halstow . . . 51 C5
Lower Hardres . . . 52 D3
Lower
  Hawthwaite . . 153 B3
Lower Heath . . . 128 C3
Lower
  Hempriggs . . . 266 C2
Lower Hergest . . . 77 B6
Lower Heyford . . . 65 A5
Lower Higham . . . 51 B4
Lower Holbrook . . 88 D2
Lower Hordley . . 110 C2
Lower
  Horsebridge . . . 22 A3
Lower Killeyan . . 200 D2
Lower
  Kingswood 35 A5
Lower
  Kinnerton 126 C3
Lower Langford . . 42 C3
Lower Largo 220 D4
Lower Leigh 112 B4
Lower Lemington 81 D5
Lower Lenie. 251 D7
Lower Lydbrook . . 62 B1
Lower Lye 78 A2
Lower Machen . . . 42 A1
Lower Maes-
  coed. 78 D1
Lower Mayland. . . 70 C3
Lower Midway . . 113 C7
Lower Milovaig. . 258 C1
Lower Moor. 80 C2
Lower Nazeing . . . 68 C3
Lower
  Netchwood 95 B4
Lower Ollach. . . 247 A4
Lower Penarth . . . 41 D6
Lower Penn. 95 B6
Lower
  Pennington 18 B2
Lower Peover . . . 128 B2
Lower Pexhill . . . 128 B3
Lower Place 138 B2
Lower Quinton . . . 81 C4
Lower Rochford . . 79 A4
Lower Seagry 24 B4
Lower Shelton . . . 84 C1
Lower Shiplake . . 47 B5
Lower
  Shuckburgh 82 A1
Lower Slaughter . 64 A2
Lower Stanton St
  Quintin. 44 A3
Lower Stoke 51 B5
Lower Stondon . . 84 D3
Lower Stow
  Bedon. 103 B5
Lower Street
  Norf 121 B4
  Norf 121 D5
Lower Strensham 80 C2
Lower Stretton . . 127 A6
Lower Sundon . . . 67 A5
Lower Swanwick . 18 A3
Lower Swell. 64 A2
Lower Tean 112 B4
Lower Thurlton . 105 B5
Lower Tote 259 B5
Lower Town 72 C2
Lower Tysoe 81 C6
Lower Upham 32 D4
Lower Vexford . . . 27 B6
Lower Weare. 42 D3
Lower Welson 77 B6
Lower Whitley. . . 127 B6
Lower Wield 33 A5
Lower
  Winchendon . . . 66 B2
Lower
  Withington . . . 128 C3
Lower Woodend . 47 A6

Lower Woodford . 31 B5
Lower Wyche 79 C5
Lowesby 99 A4
Lowestoft. 105 B6
Loweswater. 163 B4
Low Etherley. . . . 167 C4
Low Fulney 117 C5
Low Garth 159 A6
Low Gate 177 C7
Lowgill Cumb . . . 155 B5
  Lancs 145 A6
Low Grantley. . . 157 D6
Low Habberley . . 95 D6
Low Ham 28 C4
Low Hesket 164 A2
Low
  Hesleyhurst . . 188 D3
Low Hutton 149 A6
Lowick Northants 100 C1
  Northumb. 198 C4
Lowick Bridge. . 154 C1
Lowick Green . . 154 C1
Low Laithe. 147 A5
Lowlands 61 D4
Low Leighton . . . 129 A5
Low Lorton 163 B4
Low Marishes . . 159 D7
Low Marnham. . 132 C3
Low Mill 159 B5
Low Moor Lancs. 146 C1
  W Yorks 139 A4
Lowmoor Row. . . 165 C4
Low Moorsley. . . 167 A6
Low Newton 154 C3
Low Newton-by-the-
  Sea 189 A5
Lownie Moor. . . 232 D2
Low Row Cumb. . 163 A6
  Cumb 176 C3
  N Yorks. 156 B3
Low Salchrie . . . 170 A2
Low Smerby . . . 190 C3
Lowsonford 81 A4
Lowther 164 C3
Lowthorpe 150 A3
Lowton 137 D5
Lowton
  Common 137 D5
Low Torry. 208 B3
Low Worsall . . . 158 A2
Low Wray 154 A2
Loxbeare 27 D4
Loxhill. 34 C3
Loxhore 25 B7
Loxley 81 B5
Loxton. 42 D2
Loxwood. 34 C3
Lubcroy. 271 D6
Lubenham 99 C4
Luccombe 27 A4
Luccombe
  Village 19 D4
Lucker. 199 C5
Luckett 11 D4
Luckington 44 A2
Lucklawhill 220 B4
Luckwell Bridge. . 27 B4
Lucton. 78 A2
Ludag 286 E3
Ludborough. . . . 143 D4
Ludchurch 56 A1
Luddenden 138 A3
Luddenden Foot 138 A3
Luddesdown 50 C3
Luddington
  N Lincs. 141 B6
  Warks. 81 B4
Luddington in the
  Brook 100 C3
Lude House 230 B2
Ludford Lincs . . . 134 A2
  Shrops 94 D3
Ludgershall Bucks. 66 B1
  Wilts. 45 D6
Ludgvan 2 B3
Ludham 121 D5
Ludlow 94 D3
Ludwell. 30 C3
Ludworth 167 A6
Luffincott. 10 B4

Lugar. 193 C5
Luggate Burn . . 210 C3
Lugg Green 78 A2
Luggiebank 207 C5
Lugton 205 C4
Lugwardine 78 C3
Luib 247 B4
Lulham 78 C2
Lullenden 36 B2
Lullington
  Derbys 113 D6
  Som 44 D1
Lulsgate Bottom. 43 C4
Lulsley 79 B5
Lumb. 138 A3
Lumby 148 D3
Lumloch 205 B6
Lumphanan 244 B2
Lumphinnans . . . 209 A4
Lumsdaine 211 D5
Lumsden 255 D5
Lunan 233 C4
Lunanhead 232 C2
Luncarty 219 B5
Lund E Yorks . . . 150 C2
  N Yorks. 149 D5
  Shetland 284 C7
Lunderton 269 E6
Lundie Angus . . 220 A2
  Highld. 239 A5
Lundin Links . . 220 D4
Lunga 213 B5
Lunna 284 G6
Lunning 284 G7
Lunnon 57 D5
Lunsford's Cross . 23 A5
Lunt 136 C2
Luntley 78 B1
Luppitt 13 A6
Lupset 139 B6
Lupton 155 C4
Lurgashall 34 D2
Lusby 134 C3
Luson 7 C5
Luss 206 A1
Lussagiven 213 D4
Lusta 258 C2
Lustleigh 12 C2
Luston 78 A2
Luthermuir 233 B4
Luthrie 220 C3
Luton Devon 13 D4
  Luton 67 A5
  Medway 51 C4
Lutterworth 98 C2
Lutton Devon 7 B4
  Lincs. 118 C1
  Northants. . . . 100 C3
Lutworthy. 26 D2
Luxborough. 27 B4
Luxulyan. 5 B5
Lybster 275 A6
Lydbury North. . . 94 C1
Lydcott 26 B1
Lydd 38 C2
Lydden 39 A4
Lyddington 99 B5
Lydd on Sea 38 C2
Lydeard St
  Lawrence 27 B6
Lyde Green 47 D5
Lydford 11 C7
Lydford-on-
  Fosse 29 B5
Lydgate. 138 A2
Lydham 94 B1
Lydiard Green . . . 45 A4
Lydiard Millicent . 45 A4
Lydiate 136 C2
Lydlinch 30 D1
Lydney 62 C2
Lydstep 55 E6
Lye 96 C2
Lye Green Bucks . 67 C4
  E Sus 36 C3
Lyford 65 D4
Lymbridge Green 38 A3
Lyme Regis 14 B3
Lyminge 38 A3
Lymington 18 B2
Lyminster 20 B3
Lymm 128 A1

Lymore 18 B1
Lympne. 38 B3
Lympsham 42 D2
Lympstone 13 C4
Lynchat. 241 B5
Lyndale Ho. 258 C3
Lyndhurst 18 A2
Lyndon 99 A6
Lyne. 48 C3
Lyneal 110 B3
Lyne Down 79 D4
Lyneham Oxon . . 64 A3
  Wilts. 44 B4
Lynemore 253 D6
Lynemouth. 189 D5
Lyne of
  Gorthleck 252 D1
Lyne of Skene . . 245 A4
Lyness 283 H4
Lyng Norf. 120 D2
  Som 28 C3
Lynmouth. 26 A2
Lynsted 51 C6
Lynton. 26 A2
Lyon's Gate 15 A6
Lyonshall 78 B1
Lytchett
  Matravers 16 B3
Lytchett Minster. 16 B3
Lyth 281 B4
Lytham 136 A2
Lytham St
  Anne's 136 A2
Lythe 169 D6
Lythes 283 J5

M

Mabe Burnthouse . 4 D2
Mabie 174 A2
Mablethorpe . . . 135 A5
Macclesfield . . . 129 B4
Macclesfield
  Forest. 129 B4
Macduff 268 C2
Mace Green 88 C2
Machan 41 C7
Machrihanish . . 190 C2
Machynlleth 91 B5
Machynys 57 C5
Mackerel's
  Common 34 D3
Mackworth 113 B7
Macmerry 210 C1
Madderty 219 B4
Maddiston 208 C2
Madehurst 20 A2
Madeley Staffs . 111 A6
  Telford 95 A4
Madeley Heath . 112 A1
Madeley Park . . 112 A1
Madingley 85 A5
Madley 78 D2
Madresfield 79 C6
Madron 2 B2
Maenaddwyn. . . 123 B4
Maenclochog . . . 55 B6
Maendy 41 D5
Maentwrog 107 B6
Maen-y-groes . . 73 A4
Maer 112 B1
Maerdy Conwy . 109 A5
  Rhondda. 41 B4
Maesbrook. 110 C1
Maesbury
  Marsh. 110 C2
Maesgwyn-Isaf. 109 D6
Maesgwynne . . . 73 D5
Maeshafn 126 C2
Maesllyn 73 B6
Maesmynis 76 C4
Maesteg 40 B3
Maestir 75 D4
Maes-Treylow . . 77 A6
Maesybont. 57 A5
Maesycrugiau . . . 58 A1
Maesy cwmmer . 41 B6
Maesymeillion . . 73 B7
Magdalen Laver . 69 C5

Maggieknockater
  . . . . 254 B4
Magham Down . . 22 A4
Maghull 136 C2
Magor 42 A3
Magpie Green. . . 104 D1
Maiden Bradley . 30 B2
Maidencombe. . . . 8 A3
Maidenhall 88 C2
Maidenhead 48 A1
Maiden Law. . . . 167 A4
Maiden Newton . 15 B5
Maidens 192 E2
Maidensgrave. . . 88 C3
Maiden's Green . . 48 B1
Maidenwell Corn. . 10 D2
  Lincs. 134 B3
Maiden Wells . . . 55 E5
Maidford 82 B3
Maids Moreton . . 83 D4
Maidstone 37 A5
Maidwell 99 D4
Mail 285 L6
Main 109 D6
Maindee 42 A2
Mainsforth. 167 B6
Mains of Airies . 170 A1
Mains of
  Allardice 233 A6
Mains of
  Annochie 257 B4
Mains of
  Ardestie 221 A5
Mains of Balhall 232 B3
Mains of
  Ballindarg . . . 232 C2
Mains of
  Balnakettle . . . 233 A4
Mains of
  Birness 257 C4
Mains of Burgie . 266 D1
Mains of Clunas 253 B4
Mains of Crichie 257 B4
Mains of Dalvey 254 C2
Mains of
  Dellavaird 245 D4
Mains of Drum . 245 C5
Mains of
  Edingight 267 D6
Mains of
  Fedderate 268 E3
Mains of
  Inkhorn 257 C4
Mains of Mayen . 255 B6
Mains of
  Melgund 232 C3
Mains of
  Thornton 233 A4
Mains of
  Watten 281 C4
Mainsriddle 174 C2
Mainstone 93 C6
Maisemore 63 A4
Malacleit 287 G2
Malborough. 7 D6
Malcoff 129 A5
Maldon 70 C2
Malham 146 A3
Maligar 259 B4
Malinbridge . . . 130 A3
Mallaig 235 A5
Malleny Mills . . 209 D4
Malling 217 D5
Malltraeth 123 D4
Mallwyd 91 A6
Malmesbury 44 A3
Malmsmead. 26 A2
Malpas Ches W.. 110 A3
  Corn. 4 C3
  Newport 61 D5
Malswick 62 A3
Maltby Stockton . 168 D2
  S Yorks. 140 D3
Maltby le Marsh 135 A4
Malting Green. . . 70 A3
Maltman's Hill . . 37 B7
Malton 159 D6
Malvern Link . . . 79 C5
Malvern Wells. . . 79 C5
Mamble 95 D4

Manaccan 3 C5
Manafon. 93 A5
Manar Ho. 256 D2
Manaton. 12 C2
Manby. 134 A3
Mancetter 97 B6
Manchester 138 D1
Manchester
 Airport 128 A3
Mancot 126 C3
Mandally 239 B6
Manea. 101 C6
Manfield. 167 D5
Mangaster 284 F5
Mangotsfield. . . . 43 B5
Mangurstadh. . . . 287 A5
Mankinholes . . . 138 A2
Manley 127 B5
Man-moel 41 A6
Mannal 222 C2
Mannerston . . . 208 C3
Manningford
 Bohune 45 D5
Manningford
 Bruce. 45 D5
Manningham. . . 147 D5
Mannings Heath. 35 D5
Mannington. . . . 17 A4
Manningtree . . . 88 D1
Mannofield . . . 245 B6
Manor. 50 A1
Manorbier 55 E6
Manordeilo 58 C2
Manor Estate. . 130 A3
Manorhill. 197 C5
Manorowen 72 C2
Manselfield 57 D5
Mansel Lacy . . . 78 C2
Mansell Gamage 78 C1
Mansergh 155 C5
Mansfield E Ayrs . 182 A4
 Notts 131 C5
Mansfield
 Woodhouse . . 131 C5
Mansriggs 154 C1
Manston Dorset . . 30 D2
 Kent 53 C5
 W Yorks 148 D2
Manswood. . . . 16 A3
Manthorpe Lincs 116 B2
 Lincs. 116 D3
Manton N Lincs. 142 C1
 Notts 131 B5
 Rutland. 99 A5
 Wilts. 45 C5
Manuden 69 A4
Maperton 29 C6
Maplebeck. . . 132 C2
Maple Cross . . 67 D5
Mapledurham. . 47 B4
Mapledurwell . . 47 B4
Maplehurst . . . 35 D4
Maplescombe. . 50 C2
Mapleton . . . 113 A5
Mapperley . . . 114 A2
Mapperley Park 114 A2
Mapperton. . . 15 B5
Mappleborough
 Green. 80 A3
Mappleton . . . 151 C5
Mappowder. . . 16 A1
Maraig 288 G2
Marazanvose. . 4 B3
Marazion . . . 2 B3
Marbhig . . . 288 F5
Marbury . . . 111 A4
March Cambs . 101 B6
 S Lanark. . . 184 A2
Marcham. . . 65 D5
Marchamley . 111 C4
Marchington . 113 B5
Marchington
 Woodlands . 113 C5
Marchroes. . 106 D3
Marchwiel . . 110 A2
Marchwood . . 32 D2
Marcross . . . 40 E4
Marden Hereford . . 78 C3
 Kent 37 B5

Marden continued
 T&W. 179 B5
 Wilts. 45 D4
Marden Beech . . 37 B5
Marden Thorn. . . 37 B5
Mardy 61 B5
Marefield 99 A4
Mareham le Fen 134 C2
Mareham on the
 Hill 134 C2
Marehay. 114 A1
Marehill 20 A3
Maresfield 36 D2
Marfleet 142 A3
Marford 126 D3
Margam 40 C2
Margaret Marsh . 30 D2
Margaret Roding 69 B5
Margaretting. . . 69 C6
Margate 53 B5
Margnaheglish . 191 B6
Margrove Park . 169 D4
Marham 119 D4
Marhamchurch. . 10 A3
Marholm. 100 A3
Mariandyrys . . 123 B6
Marianglas. . . 123 B5
Mariansleigh . . 26 C2
Marionburgh . . 245 B4
Marishader . . 259 B4
Marjoriebanks . 184 D3
Mark Dumfries . . 170 B3
 S Ayrs. 180 D2
 Som 28 A3
Markbeech . . 36 B2
Markby. 135 B4
Mark Causeway . 28 A3
Mark Cross E Sus. 22 A2
 E Sus 36 C3
Market Bosworth 97 A7
Market Deeping 116 E4
Market Drayton .111 B5
Market
 Harborough . . 99 C4
Markethill . . . 220 A2
Market
 Lavington . . . 44 D4
Market Overton .116 D5
Market Rasen . 133 A6
Market Stainton 134 B2
Market Warsop. 131 C5
Market
 Weighton . . . 150 C1
Market Weston. 103 D5
Markfield 114 D2
Markham 41 A6
Markham Moor. 132 B2
Markinch . . . 220 D2
Markington . . 148 A1
Marksbury . . 43 C5
Marks Tey . . 70 A3
Markyate . . . 67 B5
Marland . . . 138 B1
Marlborough. . 45 C5
Marlbrook
 Hereford . . . 78 B3
 Worcs. 96 D2
Marlcliff 80 B3
Marldon . . . 8 A2
Marlesford. . . 88 B4
Marley Green . 111 A4
Marley Hill . . 179 D4
Marley Mount . 17 B6
Marlingford . 104 A2
Mar Lodge . . 242 C3
Marloes 54 D3
Marlow Bucks . 47 A6
 Hereford . . . 94 D2
Marlow Bottom . 47 A6
Marlpit Hill . . 36 B2
Marlpool. . . . 114 A2
Marnhull. . . . 30 D1
Marnoch. . . . 267 D6
Marnock . . . 207 D5
Marple 129 A4
Marple Bridge. 129 A4
Marr 140 C3
Marrel. 274 C2
Marrick . . . 157 B4
Marrister . . . 285 G2
Marros 56 B2
Marsden T&W. . 179 C5

Marsden continued
 W Yorks 138 B3
Marsett. 156 C3
Marsh Devon. . . . 28 D2
 W Yorks 147 D4
Marshall's Heath . 67 B6
Marshalsea 14 A3
Marshalswick . . 67 C6
Marsham 120 C3
Marshaw 145 B5
Marsh Baldon . . 65 D6
Marshborough . . 53 D5
Marshbrook. . . . 94 C2
Marshchapel . . 143 D5
Marshfield
 Newport 42 A1
 S Glos. 44 B1
Marshgate 10 B2
Marsh Gibbon . . 66 A1
Marsh Green
 Devon. 13 B5
 Kent 36 B2
 Staffs 128 D3
Marshland St
 James. 101 A7
Marsh Lane . . 131 B4
Marshside . . . 136 B2
Marsh Street. . . 27 A4
Marshwood . . . 14 B3
Marske 157 A5
Marske-by-the-
 Sea 168 C4
Marston Ches W. 127 B6
 Hereford 78 B1
 Lincs. 116 A1
 Oxon. 65 C6
 Staffs 112 C3
 Staffs 112 D2
 Warks. 97 B5
 Wilts. 44 D3
Marston Doles . 82 B1
Marston Green . 97 C4
Marston Magna . 29 C5
Marston Meysey. 64 D2
Marston
 Montgomery. . 113 B5
Marston
 Moretaine . . 84 C1
Marston on
 Dove 113 C6
Marston St
 Lawrence . . . 82 C2
Marston Stannett. 78 B3
Marston Trussell . 98 C3
Marstow 62 B1
Marsworth . . . 67 B4
Marten 45 D6
Marthall 128 B3
Martham . . . 121 D6
Martin Hants. . . 31 D4
 Kent 39 A5
 Lincs. 133 D6
 Lincs. 134 C2
Martin Dales . . 134 C1
Martin Drove End 31 C4
Martinhoe . . . 26 A1
Martinhoe Cross . 26 A1
Martin
 Hussingtree . . 80 A1
Martin Mill . . 39 A5
Martinscroft . . 127 A6
Martinstown . . 15 C6
Martlesham . . 88 C3
Martlesham
 Heath 88 C3
Martletwy. . . 55 C6
Martley 79 A5
Martock . . . 29 D4
Marton Ches E . 128 C3
 E Yorks 151 D4
 Lincs. 132 A3
 Mbro 168 D3
 N Yorks. . . . 148 A3
 N Yorks. . . . 159 C6
 Shrops 93 A6
 Shrops 110 C3
 Warks. 81 A7
Marton-le-
 Moor- 158 D2
Martyr's Green . 34 A3
Martyr Worthy . 32 B4
Marwick . . . 282 E3

Marwood 25 B6
Marybank. 251 A6
Maryburgh. . . . 252 A1
Maryhill 205 B5
Marykirk. 233 B4
Marylebone . . 137 C4
Marypark 254 C2
Maryport Cumb . 162 A3
 Dumfries . . . 170 D3
Mary Tavy 11 D6
Maryton 233 C4
Marywell Aberds 244 C2
 Aberds 245 C6
 Angus. 233 D4
Masham 157 C6
Mashbury. . . . 69 B6
Masongill 155 D5
Masonhill. . . . 192 C3
Mastin Moor . 131 B4
Mastrick 245 B5
Matching 69 B5
Matching Green. 69 B5
Matching Tye . . 69 B5
Matfen 178 B2
Matfield 37 B4
Mathern 62 D1
Mathon 79 C5
Mathry 55 A4
Matlaske. . . 120 B3
Matlock . . . 130 C2
Matlock Bath. . 130 D2
Matson 63 B4
Matterdale End. 164 C1
Mattersey . . 132 A1
Mattersey
 Thorpe . . . 132 A1
Mattingley . . 47 D5
Mattishall. . 120 D2
Mattishall
 Burgh. . . . 120 D2
Mauchline . . 193 C4
Maud. 257 B4
Maugersbury . . 64 A3
Maughold . . 152 B4
Mauld 251 C6
Maulden . . . 84 D2
Maulds
 Meaburn . . 165 D4
Maunby . . . 158 C2
Maund Bryan. 78 B3
Maundown. . 27 C5
Mautby. . . . 121 D6
Mavis Enderby . 134 C3
Mawbray . . 174 D3
Mawdesley. . 136 B3
Mawdlam . . 40 C3
Mawgan . . . 3 C5
Maw Green . 128 D2
Mawla 4 C2
Mawnan . . . 3 C5
Mawnan Smith . 3 C5
Mawsley. . . 99 D5
Maxey 100 A3
Maxstoke . . 97 C5
Maxton Borders . 197 C5
 Kent 39 A5
Maxwellheugh . 197 C6
Maxworthy . . 10 B3
Mayals 57 C6
May Bank . . 112 A2
Maybole . . . 192 E3
Mayfield E Sus . 36 D3
 Midloth. . . . 209 D6
 Staffs 113 A5
 W Loth . . . 208 D2
Mayford . . . 34 A2
Mayland . . . 70 C3
Maynard's Green 22 A3
Maypole Mon . . 61 B6
 Scilly 2 E4
Maypole Green
 Essex 70 A3
 Norf 105 B5
 Suff 88 A3
Maywick . . 285 L5
Meadle . . . 66 C3
Meadowtown . 93 A7
Meaford . . 112 B2
Meal Bank . 288 D5
Mealabost
 Bhuirgh . . 288 B5

Meal Bank 154 B4
Mealsgate 175 D5
Meanwood . . . 148 D1
Mearbeck. . . . 146 A2
Meare 29 A4
Meare Green. . . 28 C3
Mears Ashby . . 83 A5
Measham 114 D1
Meath Green . . 35 B5
Meathop 154 C3
Meaux 150 D3
Medbourne . . 99 B4
Medburn . . . 178 B3
Meddon 24 D3
Meden Vale. . 131 C5
Medlam 134 D3
Medmenham. . 47 A6
Medomsley . . 178 D3
Medstead . . . 33 B5
Meerbrook. . . 129 C4
Meer End . . . 97 D5
Meers Bridge . 135 A4
Meesden . . . 85 D6
Meeth 11 A6
Meggethead . 195 D6
Meidrim . . . 73 D5
Meifod Denb. . 125 D5
 Powys . . . 109 D6
Meigle N Ayrs. . 204 B1
 Perth 231 D6
Meikle Earnock 194 A2
Meikle Ferry . 264 B3
Meikle Forter . 231 B5
Meikle Gluich . 264 B2
Meiklour . . . 219 A6
Meikle
 Pinkerton . . 211 C4
Meikle Strath . 233 A4
Meikle Tarty . 257 D4
Meikle Wartle. 256 C2
Meinciau . . . 57 A4
Meir 112 A3
Meir Heath. . 112 A3
Melbourn . . 85 C5
Melbourne
 Derbys . . . 114 C1
 E Yorks. . . . 149 C6
 S Lanark. . . 195 B5
Melbury Abbas . 30 C2
Melbury Bubb. . 15 A5
Melbury Osmond 15 A5
Melbury
 Sampford . . 15 A5
Melby 285 H3
Melchbourne . . 84 A2
Melcombe
 Bingham . . 16 A1
Melcombe Regis . 15 C6
Meldon Devon . . 11 B6
 Northumb. . . 178 A3
Meldreth . . . 85 C5
Meldrum Ho.. . 256 D3
Melfort 213 A6
Melgarve . . . 240 C2
Meliden . . . 125 A5
Melinbyrhedyn . 91 C6
Melincourt. . . 40 A3
Melin-y-coed . 124 C3
Melin-y-ddol . 93 A4
Melin-y-grug . 93 A4
Melin-y-Wig . 109 A5
Melkinthorpe . 164 C3
Melkridge . . 177 C5
Melksham . . 44 C3
Melldalloch . . 203 A4
Melling Lancs . 155 D4
 Mers. 136 C2
Melling Mount . 136 C3
Mellis 104 D2
Mellon Charles. 261 A5
Mellon Udrigle . 261 A5
Mellor Gtr Man . 129 A4
 Lancs 145 D6
Mellor Brook. . 145 D6
Mells 30 A1
Melmerby Cumb. 165 B4
 N Yorks. . . . 157 C4
 N Yorks. . . . 158 D2
Melplash . . . 15 B4
Melrose . . . 197 C4
Melsetter . . 283 J3

Melsonby 157 A5
Meltham 138 B4
Melton 88 B3
Meltonby 149 B6
Melton
 Constable . . 120 B2
Melton
 Mowbray. . . 115 D5
Melton Ross . . 142 B2
Melvaig. 261 B4
Melverley
 Green 110 D2
Melverley . . . 110 D2
Melvich 279 B4
Membury . . . 14 A2
Memsie . . . 269 C4
Memus 232 C2
Menabilly . . . 5 B5
Menai Bridge
 Porthaethwy . 123 C5
Mendham . . 104 C3
Mendlesham . 88 A2
Mendlesham
 Green 88 A1
Menheniot . . 6 A1
Mennock . . 183 B6
Menston . . . 147 C5
Menstrie . . . 207 A6
Menthorpe. . 149 D5
Mentmore . . 67 B4
Meoble . . . 238 D1
Meole Brace . 110 D3
Meols 136 D1
Meonstoke. . 33 D5
Meopham . . 50 C3
Meopham
 Station . . . 50 C3
Mepal 101 C6
Meppershall . . 84 D3
Merbach. . . 77 C7
Mere Ches E . . 128 A2
 Wilts. 30 B2
Mere Brow. . 136 B3
Mereclough. . 146 D2
Mere Grn.. . . 96 B4
Mereside . . 144 D3
Mereworth . . 37 A4
Mergie . . . 245 D4
Meriden . . . 97 C5
Merkadale . . 246 A2
Merkland
 Dumfries . . . 173 A5
 S Ayrs. . . . 181 B4
Merkland Lodge 271 B7
Merley. . . . 17 B4
Merlin's Bridge . 55 C5
Merrington . . 110 C3
Merrion . . . 55 E5
Merriott . . . 28 D4
Merrivale . . 11 D6
Merrow. . . . 34 A3
Merrymeet. . 6 A1
Mersham . . 38 B2
Merstham . . 35 A5
Merston . . . 20 B1
Merstone . . 18 C4
Merther . . . 4 C3
Merthyr. . . . 73 D6
Merthyr Cynog . 76 D3
Merthyr-Dyfan . 41 E6
Merthyr Mawr. . 40 D3
Merthyr Tydfil
 Merthyr Tudful . 60 C2
Merthyr Vale. . 41 B5
Merton Devon. . 25 D6
 London 49 B5
 Norf 103 B5
 Oxon. 65 B6
Mervinslaw . 187 B5
Meshaw . . . 26 D2
Messing . . . 70 B2
Messingham . 141 C6
Metfield . . . 104 C3
Metherell . . 6 A3
Metheringham . 133 C5
Methil 209 A6
Methlem . . 106 C1
Methley . . . 140 A1
Methlick . . 256 C3
Methven . . 219 B5
Methwold. . 102 B3
Methwold Hythe 102 B3
Mettingham. . 105 C4

Mevagissey 5 C5
Mewith Head. . . . 145 A7
Mexborough 140 C2
Mey 281 A4
Meysey Hampton 64 D2
Miabhag W Isles . 287 D5
W Isles 288 H2
Miabhig 287 A5
Michaelchurch . . . 61 A7
Michaelchurch
Escley. 77 D7
Michaelchurch on
Arrow. 77 B6
Michaelston-le-
Pit 41 D6
Michaelston-y-
Fedw. 42 A1
Michaelstow 10 D1
Michealston-super-
Ely. 41 D6
Micheldever 32 B4
Michelmersh. . . . 32 C2
Mickfield 88 A2
Micklebring. . . . 140 D3
Mickleby. 169 D6
Mickleham. 35 A4
Mickleover. 113 B7
Micklethwaite. . . 147 C5
Mickleton
Durham 166 C2
Glos 81 C4
Mickletown 140 A1
Mickle Trafford 127 C4
Mickley. 157 D6
Mickley Square . 178 C2
Mid Ardlaw 269 C4
Mid Auchinleck .204 A3
Midbea 282 C5
Mid Beltie 244 B3
Mid Calder. 208 D3
Mid Cloch
Forbie 268 D2
Mid Clyth 275 A6
Middle Assendon 47 A5
Middle Aston. . . . 65 A5
Middle Barton. . . 65 A5
Middlebie. 175 A5
Middle
Cairncake 256 B3
Middle Claydon . . 66 A2
Middle Drums . 232 C3
Middleforth
Green. 136 A4
Middleham 157 C5
Middle Handley 131 B4
Middlehope. 94 C2
Middle Littleton . 80 C3
Middle Maes-
coed 78 D1
Middlemarsh. . . . 15 A6
Middle Mill 54 B4
Middlemuir . . . 257 D4
Middle Rasen . . 133 A5
Middle Rigg. . . . 219 D5
Middlesbrough. 168 C2
Middleshaw
Cumb 155 C4
Dumfries 174 A4
Middlesmoor. . . 157 D4
Middlestone
Moor. 167 B5
Middlestown . . . 139 B5
Middlethird . . . 197 B5
Middleton
Aberds 245 A5
Argyll 222 C2
Cumb 155 C5
Derbys 130 C1
Derbys 130 D2
Essex 87 D4
Gtr Man 138 C1
Hants 32 A3
Hereford 78 A3
Lancs 144 B4
Midloth. 196 A2
Norf 118 D3
Northants. 99 C5
Northumb. 178 A2
Northumb. 199 C5
N Yorks. 147 C5
N Yorks. 159 C6

Middleton continued
Perth 219 D6
Perth 231 D5
Shrops 93 B6
Shrops 94 D3
Shrops 110 C2
Suff 89 A5
Swansea 57 D4
Warks. 97 B4
W Yorks 139 A5
Middleton
Cheney. 82 C1
Middleton
Green. 112 B3
Middleton Hall . 188 A2
Middleton-in-
Teesdale 166 C2
Middleton Moor. 89 A5
Middleton One
Row. 167 D6
Middleton-on-
Leven 158 A3
Middleton-on-
Sea 20 B2
Middleton on the
Hill 78 A3
Middleton-on-the-
Wolds 150 C2
Middleton Priors . 95 B4
Middleton
Quernham . . . 158 D2
Middleton St
George. 167 D6
Middleton
Scriven. 95 C4
Middleton
Stoney 65 A4
Middleton Tyas. 157 A6
Middletown
Cumb 162 D2
Powys 110 D2
Middle Tysoe . . 81 C6
Middle Wallop . 32 B1
Middlewich . . . 128 C1
Middle
Winterslow . . 31 B6
Middle Woodford. 31 B5
Middlewood
Green. 88 A4
Middlezoy 28 B3
Middridge 167 C5
Midfield 277 B6
Midge Hall 136 A4
Midgeholme . . . 176 D4
Midgham 46 C3
Midgley W Yorks 138 A3
W Yorks 139 B5
Midhopestones. 139 D5
Midhurst. 34 D1
Mid Lavant. . . . 20 B1
Midlem 186 A4
Mid Main 251 C6
Midmar. 244 B3
Midsomer
Norton 43 D5
Midton 204 A2
Midtown Highld. 261 B5
Highld. 277 B6
Midtown of
Buchromb. . . 254 B4
Mid Urchany . . 253 B4
Midville. 134 D3
Mid Walls 285 H4
Midway 129 A4
Mid Yell 284 D7
Migdale 264 A2
Migvie. 244 B1
Milarrochy . . . 206 A2
Milborne Port . 29 D6
Milborne St
Andrew 16 B2
Milborne Wick . 29 C6
Milbourne 178 B3
Milburn. 165 C4
Milbury Heath. . 62 D2
Milcombe. 81 D7
Milden. 87 C5
Mildenhall Suff 102 D3
Wilts. 45 C6
Milebrook 93 D7
Milebush 37 B5
Mile Cross 120 D4

Mile Elm. 44 C3
Mile End Essex . . 70 A3
Glos 62 B1
Mileham 119 D6
Mile Oak 21 B5
Milesmark 208 B3
Milfield 198 C3
Milford Derbys . . 114 A1
Devon. 24 C3
Powys 93 B4
Staffs 112 C3
Sur 34 B2
Surr 31 C5
Milford Haven Aber-
daugleddau. . . 55 D5
Milford on Sea . 18 B1
Milkwall 62 C1
Milkwell 30 C3
Milland 34 D1
Millarston 205 B4
Millbank Aberds. 257 B6
Highld. 280 B3
Mill Bank 138 A3
Millbeck 163 B5
Millbounds . . . 282 D6
Millbreck 257 B5
Millbridge 34 B1
Millbrook C Beds. 84 D2
Corn 6 B3
Soton 32 D2
Millburn 193 C4
Millcombe 8 C2
Mill Common . . 105 C5
Millcorner 37 D6
Milldale 129 D6
Millden Lodge. . 232 A3
Milldens 232 C3
Mill End Bucks . . 47 A5
Herts 85 D5
Millerhill 209 D6
Miller's Dale . . 129 B6
Miller's Green. . 130 D2
Millgreen 111 C5
Mill Green Essex . 69 C6
Norf 104 C2
Suff 87 C5
Millhalf 77 C6
Millhayes 14 A2
Millhead 154 D3
Millheugh 194 A2
Mill Hill 68 D2
Millholme. 155 B4
Millhouse Argyll. 203 A4
Cumb 163 A6
Millhousebridge
. . . . 185 D4
Millhouse
Green. 139 C5
Millhouses. . . . 130 A3
Millikenpark . . 205 B4
Millin Cross . . . 55 C5
Millington 150 B1
Mill Lane 47 D5
Millmeece 112 B2
Mill of
Kingoodie . . . 256 D3
Mill of Muiresk . 256 B1
Mill of Sterin. . 243 C6
Mill of Uras . . . 245 D5
Millom 153 B2
Millook 10 B2
Mill Place 142 C1
Millpool 10 D2
Millport 204 C1
Millquarter . . . 182 D4
Mill Side. 154 C3
Mill Street 120 D2
Millthorpe 116 B4
Millthrop 155 B5
Milltimber 245 B5
Milltown Corn . . . 5 B6
Derbys 130 C3
Devon. 25 B6
Dumfries 175 A6
Milltown of
Aberdalgie . . 219 B5
Milltown of
Auchindoun . . 255 B4
Milltown of
Edinvillie 254 B3

Milltown of
Kildrummy . . . 244 A1
Milltown of
Rothiemay. . . . 255 B6
Milltown of
Towie 244 A1
Milnathort 219 D6
Milner's Heath . 127 C4
Milngavie 205 A5
Milnrow 138 B2
Milnshaw 137 A6
Milnthorpe. . . . 154 C3
Milo 57 A5
Milson 95 D4
Milstead 37 A7
Milston 31 A5
Milton Angus . . 232 D1
Cambs 85 A6
Cumb 176 C3
Derbys 113 C7
Dumfries 171 B4
Dumfries 173 A6
Dumfries 183 D6
Highld. 251 A5
Highld. 251 C6
Highld. 252 B1
Highld. 264 C3
Highld. 281 C5
Moray. 267 C6
Notts 132 B2
N Som 42 C2
Oxon. 65 D5
Oxon. 82 D1
Pembs 55 D6
Perth 219 C4
Ptsmth 19 B5
Stirling 217 D5
Stoke 129 D4
W Dunb 205 A4
Milton Abbas . . 16 A2
Milton Abbot. . . 11 D5
Milton Bridge . 209 D5
Milton Bryan . . 83 D6
Milton Clevedon. 29 B6
Milton
Coldwells . . . 257 C4
Milton Combe . . 6 A3
Milton Damerel . 25 D4
Miltonduff . . . 266 C2
Milton End. . . . 64 C2
Milton Ernest . . 84 B2
Milton Green. . 127 C4
Miltonhill 266 C1
Milton Hill. . . . 65 D5
Miltonise 180 D3
Milton Keynes . 83 D5
Milton Keynes
Village 83 D5
Milton Lilbourne . 45 C5
Milton Malsor . 83 B4
Milton
Morenish. . . . 217 A6
Milton of
Auchinhove. . 244 B2
Milton of
Balgonie 220 D3
Milton of
Buchanan . . . 206 A2
Milton of
Campfield . . . 244 B3
Milton of
Campsie 205 A6
Milton of
Corsindae . . . 244 B3
Milton of
Cushnie 244 A2
Milton of
Dalcapon . . . 230 C3
Milton of
Edradour . . . 230 C3
Milton of
Gollanfield . . 252 A3
Milton of
Lesmore 255 D5
Milton of Logie. 244 B1
Milton of Murtle 245 B5
Milton of Noth . 255 D6
Milton of
Tullich 243 C6
Milton on Stour . 30 C1
Milton Regis . . . 51 C6

Milton under
Wychwood . . . 64 B3
Milverton Som . . 27 C6
Warks. 81 A6
Milwich 112 B3
Minard 214 C2
Minchinhampton . 63 C4
Mindrum 198 C2
Minehead. 27 A4
Minera 126 D2
Minety. 63 D6
Minffordd Gwyn. . 91 A5
Gwyn 107 C5
Gwyn 123 C5
Miningsby 134 C3
Minions 10 D3
Minishant. 192 D3
Minllyn 91 A6
Minnes 257 D4
Minngearraidh . 286 D3
Minnigaff 171 A6
Minnonie 268 C2
Minskip. 148 A2
Minstead 32 D1
Minsted 34 D1
Minster Kent. . . 51 B6
Kent 53 C5
Minsterley 94 A1
Minster Lovell. . 64 B4
Minsterworth . . 62 B3
Minterne Magna . 15 A6
Minting 134 B1
Mintlaw 257 B5
Minto 187 A4
Minton 94 B2
Minwear. 55 C6
Minworth 97 B4
Mirbister 282 E4
Mirehouse 162 C2
Mireland. 281 B5
Mirfield. 139 B5
Miserden 63 C5
Miskin. 41 C5
Misson 141 D4
Misterton Leics . . 98 C2
Notts 141 D5
Som 15 A4
Mistley 88 D2
Mitcham 49 C5
Mitcheldean . . 62 B2
Mitchell 4 B3
Mitchel Troy . . 61 B6
Mitcheltroy
Common 61 C6
Mitford 178 A3
Mithian 4 B2
Mitton 112 D2
Mixbury 82 D3
Moat 175 A7
Moats Tye 87 B6
Mobberley
Ches E 128 B2
Staffs 112 A4
Moccas 78 C1
Mochdre Conwy. 124 B3
Powys 93 C4
Mochrum 171 C5
Mockbeggar . . . 17 A5
Mockerkin . . . 162 B3
Modbury. 7 B5
Moddershall . . 112 B3
Moelfre Anglesey 123 B5
Powys 109 C6
Moffat. 184 B3
Moggerhanger . 84 C3
Moira. 113 D7
Molash 52 D2
Mol-chlach . . . 246 C3
Mold Yr
Wyddgrug. . . 126 C2
Moldgreen . . . 139 B4
Molehill Green . 69 A5
Molescroft . . . 150 C3
Molesden 178 A3
Molesworth . . . 100 D2
Moll 247 A4
Molland 26 C2
Mollington
Ches W. 126 B3
Oxon. 82 C1
Mollinsburn . . . 207 C5
Monachty. 75 B4

Monachylemore 217 C4
Monar Lodge. . . 250 B4
Monaughty 77 A6
Monboddo
House 233 A5
Mondynes 233 A5
Monevechadan . 215 B4
Monewden. 88 B3
Moneydie 219 B5
Moniaive 183 C5
Monifieth 221 A4
Monikie 221 A4
Monimail 220 C2
Monington. 72 B4
Monk Bretton . 139 C6
Monken Hadley . 68 D2
Monk Fryston . 140 A3
Monkhopton . . . 95 B4
Monkland. 78 B2
Monkleigh 25 C5
Monknash 40 D4
Monkokehampton
. . . . 11 A6
Monkseaton . . . 179 B5
Monks Eleigh . . 87 C5
Monk's Gate . . . 35 D5
Monks Heath. . 128 C3
Monk Sherborne . 47 D4
Monkshill 256 B2
Monksilver. . . . 27 B5
Monks Kirby . . 98 C1
Monk Soham. . . 88 A3
Monkspath. . . . 96 D4
Monks
Risborough. . 66 C3
Monk Street . . 69 A6
Monkswood. . . 61 C5
Monkton Devon . 14 A1
Kent 53 C4
Pembs 55 D5
S Ayrs. 192 C3
Monkton Combe . 44 C1
Monkton Deverill. 30 B2
Monkton
Farleigh. 44 C2
Monkton
Heathfield. . . 28 C2
Monkton Up
Wimborne. . . 31 D4
Monkwearmouth
. . . . 179 D5
Monkwood. . . . 33 B5
Monmouth
Trefynwy 61 B7
Monmouth Cap. . 61 A5
Monnington on
Wye. 78 C1
Monreith 171 C5
Monreith Mains . 171 C5
Montacute. . . . 29 D4
Montcoffer Ho.. 268 C1
Montford Argyll . 203 B6
Shrops 110 D3
Montford
Bridge 110 D3
Montgarrie . . . 244 A2
Montgomery
Trefaldwyn . . 93 B6
Montrave 220 D3
Montrose 233 C5
Mont Saint Guern . 6
Montsale 71 D4
Monxton 32 A2
Monyash 129 C6
Monymusk . . . 244 A3
Monzie 218 B3
Monzie Castle. . 218 B3
Moodiesburn. . 207 C4
Moonzie 220 C3
Moor Allerton . 148 D1
Moorby 134 C2
Moor Crichel. . 16 A3
Moordown . . . 17 B4
Moore 127 A5
Moorend 62 C3
Moor End
E Yorks 149 D7
York 149 B5
Moorends. . . . 141 B4

Moorgate 140 D2
Moorgreen 114 A2
Moorhall. 130 B3
Moorhampton . . 78 C1
Moorhead 147 D5
Moorhouse
Cumb 175 C6
Notts 132 C2
Moorlinch 28 B3
Moor Monkton . . 148 B4
Moor of
Granary 253 A6
Moor of
Ravenstone . . . 171 C5
Moor Row 162 C3
Moorsholm 169 D4
Moorside 138 C2
Moor Street. . . . 51 C5
Moorthorpe 140 B2
Moortown Hants . . 17 A5
IoW 18 C3
Lincs. 142 D2
Morangie 264 B3
Morar 235 A5
Morborne 100 B3
Morchard Bishop 12 A2
Morcombelake . . 14 B4
Morcott 99 A6
Morda 110 C1
Morden Dorset. . 16 B3
London 49 C5
Mordiford 78 D3
Mordon. 167 C6
More 94 B1
Morebath 27 C4
Morebattle. 187 A6
Morecambe 144 A4
Morefield 262 A3
Moreleigh 7 B6
Morenish 217 A5
Moresby 162 B2
Moresby Parks . 162 C2
Morestead 32 C4
Moreton Dorset . . 16 C2
Essex 69 C5
Mers. 136 D1
Oxon. 66 C1
Staffs 112 D1
Moreton Corbet 111 C4
Moretonhampstead
. . . . 12 C2
Moreton-in-
Marsh. 81 D5
Moreton Jeffries . 79 C4
Moreton Morrell . 81 B6
Moreton on Lugg 78 C3
Moreton Pinkney 82 C2
Moreton Say . . . 111 B5
Moreton Valence 62 C3
Morfa Carms. . . 57 A5
Carms 57 C5
Morfa Bach 56 A3
Morfa Bychan . 107 C5
Morfa Dinlle . . . 107 A4
Morfa Glas 59 E5
Morfa Nefyn . . 106 B2
Morfydd 109 A6
Morgan's Vale . . 31 C5
Moriah 75 A5
Morland 164 C3
Morley Derbys . . 114 A1
Durham 166 C4
W Yorks 139 A5
Morley Green . . 128 A3
Morley St
Botolph 104 B1
Morningside
Edin 209 C5
N Lanark 194 A3
Morningthorpe . 104 B3
Morpeth 179 A4
Morphie 233 B5
Morrey 113 D5
Morris Green . . 86 D3
Morriston. 57 C6
Morston 120 A2
Mortehoe 25 A5
Mortimer 47 C4
Mortimer's Cross 78 A2

Mortimer West
End 47 C4
Mortlake. 49 B5
Morton Cumb . . 175 C6
Derbys 131 C4
Lincs. 116 C3
Lincs. 132 C3
Lincs. 141 D6
Norf 120 D3
Notts 132 D2
S Glos. 62 D2
Shrops 110 C1
Morton Bagot . . 80 A4
Morton-on-
Swale 157 B7
Morvah 2 B2
Morval. 6 B1
Morvich Highld. . 249 D6
Highld. 273 D5
Morville 95 B4
Morville Heath . . 95 B4
Morwenstow . . 24 D3
Mosborough . . 131 A4
Moscow 205 D4
Mosedale 163 A6
Moseley W Mid. . 96 B2
W Mid 96 C3
Worcs. 79 B6
Moss Argyll . . . 222 C2
Highld. 235 D5
S Yorks 140 B3
Wrex 126 D3
Mossat 244 A1
Mossbank. 284 F6
Moss Bank 136 D4
Mossbay 162 B2
Mossblown 193 C4
Mossbrow 128 A2
Mossburnford. . 187 B5
Mossdale 173 A4
Moss Edge 144 C4
Moss End 47 B6
Mosser 163 B4
Mossfield 264 C2
Mossgiel 193 C4
Mosside 232 C2
Mossley Ches E. . 128 C3
Gtr Man 138 C2
Mossley Hill. . . 126 A3
Moss of
Barmuckity . 266 C3
Moss Pit 112 C3
Moss-side 253 A4
Moss Side 144 D3
Mosstodloch . . 266 D4
Mosston 232 D3
Mossy Lea 136 B4
Mosterton 15 A4
Moston Gtr Man . 138 C1
Shrops 111 C4
Moston Green . . 128 C2
Mostyn 125 A6
Mostyn Quay . . 125 A6
Motcombe 30 C2
Mothecombe . . 7 C5
Motherby 164 C2
Motherwell . . . 194 A2
Mottingham . . . 49 B7
Mottisfont 32 C2
Mottistone 18 C3
Mottram in
Longdendale . 138 D2
Mottram St
Andrew 128 B3
Mouilpied Guern . 6
Mouldsworth. . 127 B5
Moulin 230 C3
Moulsecoomb . . 21 B6
Moulsford 46 A3
Moulsoe 83 C6
Moulton Ches W. 127 C6
Lincs. 117 C6
Northants. . . . 83 A4
N Yorks. 157 A6
Suff 86 A2
V Glam 41 D5
Moulton Chapel 117 D5
Moulton
Eaugate . . . 117 D6
Moulton St
Mary 105 A4

Moulton Seas
End 117 C6
Mounie Castle. . 256 D2
Mount Corn. . . . 4 B2
Corn 5 A6
Highld. 253 B5
Mountain 147 D4
Mountain Ash
Aberpennar . . 41 B5
Mountain Cross 195 B6
Mountain Water . 55 B5
Mountbenger . . 196 D2
Mount Bures . . . 87 D5
Mount Canisp . . 264 C3
Mountfield. 37 D5
Mountgerald . . 264 D1
Mount Hawke . . . 4 C2
Mountjoy 4 A3
Mountnessing . . 69 D6
Mounton. 61 D7
Mount Pleasant
Ches E 128 D3
Derbys 113 D6
Derbys 114 A1
Flint 126 B2
Hants 18 B1
W Yorks 139 A5
Mountsorrel . . 114 D3
Mount Sorrel. . 31 C4
Mount Tabor . . 138 A3
Mousehole. . . . 2 C2
Mousen. 199 C5
Mouswald 174 A3
Mow Cop 128 D3
Mowhaugh. . . . 187 A7
Mowsley 98 C3
Moxley 96 B2
Moy Highld 240 D2
Highld. 252 C3
Moy Hall. 252 C3
Moy Ho. 265 D6
Moyles Court. . . 17 A5
Moylgrove 72 B4
Moy Lodge . . . 240 D2
Muasdale 202 D1
Muchalls. 245 C6
Much Birch . . . 78 D3
Much Cowarne . 79 C4
Much
Dewchurch . . 78 D2
Muchelney . . . 28 C4
Much Hadham . . 68 B4
Much Hoole. . . 136 A3
Muchlarnick . . 5 B7
Much Marcle. . . 79 D4
Muchrachd . . . 251 C4
Much Wenlock . 95 A4
Muckernich . . . 252 A1
Mucking 50 A3
Muckleford . . . 15 B6
Mucklestone . . 111 B6
Muckleton 111 C4
Muckletown . . . 255 D6
Muckley Corner. 96 A3
Muckton. 134 A3
Mudale 272 A3
Muddiford 25 B6
Mudeford 17 B5
Mudford 29 D5
Mudgley 28 A4
Mugdock 205 A5
Mugeary. 246 A3
Mugginton . . . 113 A6
Muggleswick. . 166 A3
Muie 273 D4
Muir. 242 D3
Muirden 268 D2
Muirdrum 221 A5
Muirhead Angus. 220 A3
Fife. 220 D2
N Lanark 207 D4
S Ayrs. 192 B3
Muirhouselaw. . 187 A5
Muirhouses . . . 208 B3
Muirkirk 194 D1
Muirmill 207 B5
Muir of
Fairburn . . . 251 A6
Muir of Fowlis. . 244 A2
Muir of Ord . . . 252 A1
Muir of Pert. . . 220 A4
Muirshearlich . 239 D5

Muirskie 245 C5
Muirtack. 257 C4
Muirton Highld. . 264 D3
Perth 218 C4
Perth 219 B6
Muirton Mains . 251 A6
Muirton of
Ardblair 231 D5
Muirton of
Ballochy. . . . 233 B4
Muiryfold 268 D2
Muker 156 B3
Mulbarton . . . 104 A2
Mulben 267 D4
Mulindry 200 C3
Mullardoch
House. 250 C4
Mullion 3 D4
Mullion Cove. . . 3 D4
Mumby 135 B5
Munderfield Row 79 B4
Munderfield
Stocks 79 B4
Mundesley . . . 121 B5
Mundford 103 B4
Mundham . . . 104 B4
Mundon 70 C2
Mundurno . . . 245 A6
Munerigie . . . 239 B6
Muness 284 C8
Mungasdale . . 261 A6
Mungrisdale . . 163 A6
Munlochy . . . 252 A2
Munsley 79 C4
Munslow 94 C3
Murchington . . 12 C1
Murcott 65 B6
Murkle 280 B3
Murlaggan
Highld. 238 C4
Highld. 239 D7
Murra 283 G3
Murrayfield . . 209 C5
Murrow. 101 A5
Mursley 66 A3
Murthill 232 C2
Murthly. 219 A5
Murton Cumb . . 165 C5
Durham 167 A6
Northumb. . . 198 B3
York 149 B5
Musbury 14 B2
Muscoates . . . 159 C5
Musdale 226 D4
Musselburgh . 209 C6
Muston Leics . . 115 B6
N Yorks. . . . 161 D4
Mustow Green . 95 D6
Mutehill 173 D4
Mutford 105 C5
Muthill 218 C3
Mutterton. . . . 13 A5
Muxton. 111 D6
Mybster 280 C3
Myddfai 59 C4
Myddle 110 C3
Mydroilyn. . . . 74 C3
Myerscough . . 145 D4
Mylor Bridge. . . 4 D3
Mynachlog-ddu 72 C4
Myndtown . . . 94 C1
Mynydd Bach . 75 A6
Mynydd-bach . 61 D6
Mynydd
Bodafon . . . 123 B4
Mynydd-isa . . 126 C2
Mynyddygarreg . 57 B4
Mynytho 106 C3
Myrebird 245 C4
Myrelandhorn . 281 C4
Myreside 220 B2
Myrtle Hill . . . 59 B4
Mytchett. 34 A1
Mytholm 138 A2
Mytholmroyd. . 138 A3
Myton-on-
Swale 148 A3
Mytton 110 D3

N

Naast. 261 B5
Naburn 149 C4
Nackington . . 52 D3
Nacton 88 C3
Nafferton . . . 150 B3
Na Gearrannan . 288 C2
Nailbridge . . . 62 B2
Nailsbourne. . 28 C2
Nailsea 42 B3
Nailstone . . . 97 A7
Nailsworth . . 63 D4
Nairn 253 A4
Nalderswood . 35 B5
Nancegollan . 3 B4
Nancledra . . . 2 B2
Nanhoron . . . 106 C2
Nannau 108 C2
Nannerch . . . 125 C6
Nanpantan . . 114 D3
Nanpean 5 B4
Nanstallon . . 5 A5
Nant-ddu . . . 60 B2
Nanternis . . . 73 A6
Nantgaredig . 58 C1
Nantgarw. . . 41 C6
Nant-glas . . . 76 A3
Nantglyn. . . . 125 C5
Nantgwyn. . . 92 D3
Nantlle 107 A5
Nantmawr . . 110 C1
Nantmel 76 A4
Nantmor. . . . 107 B6
Nant Peris . . 107 A6
Nant Uchaf. . 125 D5
Nantwich . . . 127 D6
Nant-y-Bai . . 59 A4
Nant-y-cafn . 59 E5
Nant-y-derry . 61 C5
Nant-y-ffin . . 58 B2
Nantyffyllon. . 40 B3
Nantyglo . . . 60 B3
Nant-y-moel. . 40 B4
Nant-y-pandy . 124 B1
Naphill 66 D3
Nappa 146 B2
Napton on the
Hill 82 A1
Narberth Arberth . 55 C7
Narborough Leics . 98 B2
Norf 119 D4
Nasareth. . . . 107 A4
Naseby 98 D3
Nash Bucks . . 83 D4
Hereford . . . 77 A7
Newport. . . . 42 A2
Shrops 95 D4
Nash Lee . . . 66 C3
Nassington . . 100 B2
Nasty 68 A3
Nateby Cumb . 155 A6
Lancs 145 C4
Natland. 154 C4
Naughton . . . 87 C6
Naunton Glos . 64 A2
Worcs. 80 D1
Naunton
Beauchamp . 80 B2
Navenby . . . 133 D4
Navestock Heath. 69 D5
Navestock Side. . 69 D5
Navidale 274 C4
Nawton 159 C5
Nayland 87 D5
Nazeing 68 C4
Neacroft . . . 17 B5
Neal's Green . 97 C6
Neap 285 H7
Near Sawrey . 154 B2
Neasham . . . 167 D6
Neath Castell-
Nedd 40 B2
Neath Abbey . 40 B2
Neatishead . . 121 C5
Nebo Anglesey 123 A4
Ceredig . . . 75 B4
Conwy 124 D3
Gwyn 107 A4
Necton 103 A4

Nedd 270 A4
Nedderton . . 179 A4
Nedging Tye . . 87 C6
Needham . . . 104 C3
Needham Market. 88 B1
Needingworth. . 101 D5
Needwood . . 113 C5
Neen Savage . . 95 D4
Neen Sollars . . 95 D4
Neenton 95 C4
Nefyn. 106 B3
Neilston . . . 205 C4
Neithirion . . 92 A3
Neithrop. . . . 82 C1
Nelly Andrews
Green. 93 A6
Nelson Caerph . . 41 B6
Lancs 146 D2
Nelson Village . 179 B4
Nemphlar . . . 194 B3
Nempnett
Thrubwell . . 43 C4
Nene Terrace . 101 A4
Nenthall . . . 165 A5
Nenthead . . . 165 A5
Nenthorn . . . 197 C5
Nerabus . . . 200 C2
Nercwys . . . 126 C2
Nerston . . . 205 C6
Nesbit 198 C3
Ness 126 B3
Nesscliffe. . . 110 D2
Neston Ches W . 126 B2
Wilts. 44 C2
Nether Alderley . 128 B3
Netheravon . . 31 A5
Nether Blainslie 197 B4
Nether Booth . 129 A6
Netherbrae . . 268 D2
Netherbrough. . 282 F4
Nether
Broughton. . 115 C4
Netherburn . . 194 B3
Nether Burrow . 155 D5
Netherbury . . 15 B4
Netherby Cumb . 175 A6
N Yorks. . . . 148 C2
Nether Cerne . . 15 B6
Nether Compton . 29 D5
Nethercote . . 82 A2
Nethercott . . 25 B5
Nether Crimond 256 D3
Nether
Dalgliesh . . 185 B5
Nether Dallachy 267 C4
Netherend . . 62 C1
Nether Exe. . . 13 A4
Netherfield . . 23 A5
Nether
Glasslaw . . 268 D3
Netherhampton . 31 C5
Nether
Handwick . . 232 D1
Nether Haugh . 140 D2
Nether Heage . 130 D3
Nether Heyford . 82 B3
Nether
Hindhope . . 187 B6
Nether
Howecleuch . 184 A3
Nether Kellet. . 145 A5
Nether
Kinmundy . . 257 B5
Nether
Langwith . . 131 B5
Netherlaw . . 173 D5
Nether Leask. . 257 C5
Nether Lenshie. 256 B1
Netherley Aberds 245 C5
Mers. 127 A4
Nethermill . . 184 D3
Nether Monynut 211 D4
Nethermuir . . 257 B4
Nether Padley . 130 B2
Nether Park . . 269 D5
Netherplace . . 205 C5
Nether
Poppleton . . 149 B4
Netherseal . . 113 D6
Nether Silton . 158 B3
Nether Stowey . 28 B1
Netherthird . . 182 A3

Netherthong 139 C4
Netherthorpe ...131 A5
Netherton Angus 232 C3
Devon.........12 D3
Hants..........46 D1
Mers..........136 C2
Northumb......188 C2
Oxon..........65 D5
Perth.........231 C5
Stirling......205 A5
W Mid.........96 C2
Worcs.........80 C2
W Yorks......139 B4
W Yorks......139 B5
Nethertown
Cumb.........162 D2
Highld.......281 A5
Nether
Urquhart 219 D6
Nether Wallop ..32 B2
Nether Wasdale 163 D4
Nether Whitacre .97 B5
Netherwitton...189 D4
Netherwood ...193 C6
Nether Worton ..82 D1
Nethy Bridge...253 D6
Netley 18 A3
Netley Marsh...32 D2
Netteswell 69 B4
Nettlebed 47 A5
Nettlebridge ...29 A6
Nettlecombe ...15 B5
Nettleden 67 B5
Nettleham 133 B5
Nettlestead 37 A4
Nettlestead
Green 37 A4
Nettlestone ...19 B5
Nettlesworth ..167 A5
Nettleton Lincs .142 C3
Wilts.........44 B2
Neuadd........58 C3
Nevendon 70 D1
Nevern 72 B3
New Abbey....174 B2
New Aberdour .268 C3
New Addington. .49 C6
Newall........147 C5
New Alresford ..33 B4
New Alyth....231 D6
Newark Orkney..282 C8
Pboro.........100 A4
Newark-on-
Trent.........132 D2
New Arley 97 C5
Newarthill 194 A2
New Ash Green. .50 C3
New Barn......50 C3
New Barnetby .142 B2
Newbarns.....153 C3
New Barton 83 A5
Newbattle 209 D6
New Bewick...188 A3
Newbiggin Cumb 153 A1
Cumb.........153 D3
Cumb.........164 A3
Cumb.........164 C2
Cumb.........165 C4
Durham.......166 C2
N Yorks.......156 B3
N Yorks.......156 C3
Newbiggin-by-the-
Sea 179 A5
Newbigging
Angus........220 A4
Angus........221 A4
S Lanark......195 B5
New-bigging...231 D6
Newbiggin-on-
Lune 155 A6
New Bilton.....98 D1
Newbold Derbys.130 B3
Leics.........114 D2
Newbold on
Avon........98 D1
Newbold on
Stour.......81 C5
Newbold Pacey. .81 B5
Newbold Verdon .98 A1
New
Bolingbroke ..134 D3

Newborough
Anglesey 123 D4
Pboro.........100 A4
Staffs........113 C5
Newbottle
Northants......82 D2
T&W.........179 D5
New Boultham .133 B4
Newbourne 88 C3
New Bradwell ..83 C5
New
Brancepeth...167 A5
Newbridge Caerph 41 B7
Ceredig........75 C4
Corn..........2 B2
Corn..........6 A2
Dumfries 174 A2
Edin..........208 C4
Hants.........32 D1
IoW..........18 C3
Pembs.........55 A5
New Bridge 110 A1
Newbridge
Green........79 D6
Newbridge-on-
Usk 61 D5
Newbridge on
Wye..........76 B4
New Brighton
Flint.........126 C2
Mers.........136 D2
New Brinsley ...131 D4
Newbrough 177 C6
New Broughton .126 D3
New
Buckenham ...104 B1
Newbuildings ...12 A2
Newburgh
Aberds........257 D4
Aberds........269 D4
Borders.......185 A6
Fife..........220 C2
Lancs.........136 B3
Newburn......178 C3
Newbury......46 C2
Newbury Park...50 A1
Newby Cumb....164 C3
Lancs.........146 C2
N Yorks.......155 D6
N Yorks.......160 B4
N Yorks.......168 D3
Newby Bridge ..154 C2
Newby East 176 D2
New Byth......268 D3
Newby West ...175 C6
Newby Wiske ..158 C2
Newcastle Mon ..61 B6
Shrops........93 C6
Newcastle Emlyn
Castell Newydd
Emlyn.........73 B6
Newcastleton or
Copshaw
Holm.........176 A2
Newcastle-under-
Lyme.........112 A2
Newcastle Upon
Tyne.........179 C4
New Catton 120 D4
Newchapel Pembs 73 C5
Powys........92 C3
Staffs........128 D3
Sur...........35 B6
New Cheriton ...33 C4
Newchurch Carms 73 C4
IoW..........19 C4
Kent..........38 B2
Lancs.........146 D2
Mon..........61 D6
Powys........77 B6
Staffs........113 C5
New Costessey .120 D4
Newcott.......14 A2
New Cowper ...174 D4
Newcraighall...209 C6
New Cross Ceredig 75 A5
London.......122 C4
New Cumnock..182 A4
New Deer......256 B3
New Delaval...179 B4
Newdigate.....35 B4
New Duston....83 A4

New Earswick...149 B5
New Edlington ..140 D3
New Elgin.....266 C3
New Ellerby...151 D4
Newell Grn.....48 B1
New Eltham....50 B1
New End......80 B3
Newenden.....37 D6
Newent.......62 A3
Newerne.......62 C2
New Farnley...147 D6
New Ferry....126 A3
Newfield Durham 167 B5
Highld........264 C3
Newford Scilly ...2 E4
Newfound.....46 D3
New Fryston ...140 A2
Newgale......54 B4
New Galloway..172 A4
Newgate.......120 A2
Newgate Street ..68 C3
New Grimsby Scilly. 2 E3
New Hainford ..120 D4
Newhall Ches E ..111 A5
Derbys.......113 C6
Newhall House .264 D2
Newhall Point...264 D3
Newham.......189 A4
Newham Hall ..189 A4
New Hartley...179 B5
Newhaven
Derbys........129 D6
Edin..........209 C5
E Sus.........22 B2
New Haw......48 C3
New Hedges ...56 B1
New Herrington 179 D5
Newhey.......138 B2
New Hinksey ...65 C6
New Holkham ..119 B5
New Holland ...142 A2
Newholm......169 D6
New Houghton
Derbys........131 C4
Norf..........119 C4
Newhouse.....207 D5
New Houses ...155 D7
New
Humberstone ..98 A3
New Hutton....155 B4
New Hythe.....37 A5
Newick........36 D2
Newingreen....38 B3
Newington Kent...38 B3
Kent..........51 C5
Kent..........53 C5
Notts.........141 D4
Oxon..........65 D7
Shrops........94 C2
New Inn Carms...58 B1
Mon..........61 C6
Pembs........55 A6
New Invention
Shrops........93 D6
W Mid.........96 A2
New Kelso.....249 B6
New Kingston ..114 C3
New Lanark....194 B3
Newland Glos....62 C1
Hull..........150 D3
N Yorks.......141 A4
Worcs.........79 C5
Newlandrig....209 D6
Newlands
Borders.......186 A4
Highld........252 B3
Moray........266 D4
Northumb......178 A1
Newland's Corner 34 B3
Newlandsmuir..205 C6
Newlands of
Geise........280 B2
Newlands of
Tynet........267 C4
Newlands Park .122 B2
New Lane.....136 B3
New Lane End...137 D5
New Leake.....135 D4
New Leeds.....269 D4
New Longton...136 A4

Newlot.......282 F6
New Luce.....170 A3
Newlyn 2 C2
Newmachar...245 A5
Newmains....194 A3
New Malden...49 C5
New Marske...168 C4
New Marton...110 B2
New Micklefield 148 D3
Newmill Borders .186 B3
Corn..........2 B2
Moray........267 D5
New Mill Aberds .245 D4
Herts.........67 B4
Wilts.........45 C5
W Yorks......139 C4
Newmill of
Inshewan.....232 B2
New Mills Ches E 128 A2
Corn..........4 B3
Derbys........129 A4
Powys........93 A4
Newmills of
Boyne........267 D6
Newmiln......219 A6
Newmilns.....193 B5
New Milton 17 B6
New Moat......55 B6
Newnham Cambs. 85 B6
Glos..........62 B2
Hants.........47 D5
Herts.........84 D4
Kent..........51 D6
Northants......82 A3
Newnham Bridge 79 A4
New Ollerton...131 C6
New Oscott 96 B3
Newpark......221 C4
New Park......148 B3
New Pitsligo ...268 D3
New Polzeath ...9 D5
Newport Devon ..25 B6
Essex.........85 D7
E Yorks.......150 D1
Highld........275 B5
IoW..........18 C4
Norf..........121 D7
Telford.......111 D6
Newport
Casnewydd....42 A2
Newport
Trefdraeth 72 C3
Newport-on-
Tay.........220 B4
Newport Pagnell .83 C5
Newpound
Common.....34 D3
Newquay......4 A3
New Quay
Ceinewydd....73 A6
New Rackheath .121 D4
New Radnor 77 A6
New Rent.....164 B2
New Ridley.....178 D2
New Road Side .146 C3
New Romney....38 C2
New Rossington 140 D4
New Row Ceredig. 75 A6
Lancs.........145 D6
N Yorks.......168 D4
New Sarum 31 B5
Newsbank....128 C3
Newseat Aberds .256 C2
Aberds........257 D5
Newsham
Northumb......179 B5
N Yorks.......158 C2
N Yorks.......166 D4
Newsholme
E Yorks.......141 A4
Lancs.........146 B2
New Silksworth .179 D5
Newsome.....139 B4
Newstead
Borders.......197 C4
Northumb......189 A4
Notts.........131 D5
New Stevenston 194 A2
New Street.....129 D5

New Street
Lane.........111 B5
New Swanage...17 C4
Newthorpe....148 D3
Newton Argyll...214 C3
Borders.......187 B2
Bridgend......40 D3
Cambs........85 C6
Cambs........118 D1
Cardiff.......42 B1
Ches W.......127 B5
Ches W.......127 C4
Ches W.......127 D5
Cumb.........153 C3
Derbys........131 D4
Dorset.......30 D1
Dorset.......16 D2
Dumfries......175 A5
Dumfries......185 C4
Gtr Man......138 D2
Hereford......78 B3
Hereford......78 D1
Highld........252 B3
Highld........264 D3
Highld........271 A5
Highld........281 D5
Lancs.........144 D4
Lancs.........145 B6
Lancs.........155 D4
Lincs.........116 B3
Moray........266 C2
Norf..........119 D5
Northants......99 C5
Northumb......178 C2
Notts.........115 A4
Perth.........218 A3
S Lanark......194 C4
S Lanark......205 B6
Staffs........112 C4
Suff..........87 C5
Swansea......57 D6
S Yorks.......140 C3
Warks........98 D2
Wilts.........31 C6
W Loth.......208 C3
Newton Abbot...12 D3
Newtonairds ...175 C4
Newton Arlosh .175 C4
Newton Aycliffe .167 C5
Newton Bewley .168 C2
Newton
Blossomville... .83 B6
Newton
Bromswold 84 A1
Newton
Burgoland......97 A6
Newton by Toft. .133 A5
Newton Ferrers ..7 C4
Newton
Flotman.....104 B3
Newtongrange .209 D6
Newton Hall ...178 C2
Newton Harcourt 98 B3
Newton Heath. .138 C1
Newton Ho.....256 D1
Newton Kyme..148 C3
Newton-le-Willows
Mers.........137 D4
N Yorks.......157 C6
Newton Longville 83 D4
Newton Mearns .205 C5
Newtonmill 233 B4
Newtonmore ...241 C5
Newton Morrell .157 A6
Newton
Mulgrave.....169 D5
Newton of
Ardtoe......235 C5
Newton of
Balcanquhal ..219 C6
Newton of
Falkland.....220 D2
Newton on
Ouse........148 B4
Newton-on-
Rawcliffe.....159 B7
Newton-on-the-
Moor........189 C4

Net–Nin 325

Newton on
Trent.........132 B3
Newton Park....203 B6
Newton
Poppleford....13 C5
Newton Purcell ..82 D3
Newton Regis ..97 A5
Newton Reigny .164 B2
Newton St Cyres..12 B3
Newton St Faith 120 C3
Newton St Loe ..43 C6
Newton St
Petrock......25 D5
Newton Solney .113 C6
Newton Stacey ..32 A3
Newton Stewart 171 A6
Newton Tony....31 A6
Newton Tracey ..25 C6
Newton under
Roseberry....168 D3
Newton upon
Derwent.....149 C6
Newton Valence. .33 B6
New Totley.....130 B3
Newtown Argyll .214 B3
Ches W.......127 B5
Corn..........3 C5
Corn..........174 D3
Cumb.........176 C3
Derbys........129 A4
Devon.........26 C2
Glos..........62 C2
Glos..........80 D2
Hants.........18 A3
Hants.........31 D6
Hants.........32 C2
Hants.........32 D4
Hants.........33 D5
Hants.........46 C2
Hereford......79 C4
Highld........240 B1
IoM..........152 D3
IoW..........18 B3
Northumb......188 A3
Northumb......188 C3
Northumb......198 C3
Poole.........17 B4
Shrops........110 B3
Staffs........129 C4
Staffs........129 C5
Wilts.........30 C3
New Town.....210 C1
Newtown Y
Drenewydd....93 B5
Newtown Linford 98 A2
Newtown St.
Boswells.....197 C4
Newtown
Unthank......98 A1
New Tredegar
Tredegar
Newydd.......41 A6
New Trows.....194 C3
Newtyle......231 D6
New Ulva.....213 D5
New Walsoken .101 A6
New Waltham ..143 C4
New
Whittington ..130 B3
New Wimpole...85 C5
New Winton....210 C5
New Yatt......65 B4
New York Lincs .134 D2
N Yorks.......147 A5
Neyland......55 D5
Niarbyl.......152 D2
Nibley........43 A5
Nibley Green...62 D3
Nibon........284 F5
Nicholashayne. .27 D6
Nicholaston 57 D5
Nidd..........148 A2
Nigg Aberdeen .245 B6
Highld........265 C4
Nigg Ferry....264 D3
Nightcott.....26 C3
Nilig.........125 D5
Nine Ashes....69 C5
Ninebanks....177 D5

Nine Mile Burn . .195 A6
Nine Wells 54 B3
Ninfield. 23 A3
Ningwood 18 C2
Nisbet 187 A5
Nisthouse Orkney 282 F4
 Shetland. 285 G7
Niton 18 D4
Nitshill 205 B5
Noak Hill 69 C5
Noblethorpe 139 C5
Nobottle 82 A3
Nocton 133 C5
Noke 65 B6
Nolton 55 C4
Nolton Haven 55 C4
No Man's Heath
 Ches W. 111 A4
 Warks. 97 A5
Nomansland
 Devon. 26 D3
 Wilts. 31 D6
Noneley 110 C3
Nonikiln 264 C2
Nonington 53 D4
Noonsbrough . .285 H4
Norbreck 144 C3
Norbridge 79 C5
Norbury Ches E . .111 A4
 Derbys 113 A5
 Shrops 94 B1
 Staffs 112 C1
Nordelph 102 A1
Norden 138 B1
Norden Heath . . .16 C3
Nordley. 95 B4
Norham 198 B3
Norley. 127 B5
Norleywood. 18 B2
Normanby
 N Lincs. 141 B6
 N Yorks. 159 C6
 Redcar 168 D3
Normanby-by-
 Spital 133 A5
Normanby by
 Stow 132 A3
Normanby le
 Wold. 142 D3
Norman Cross. . .100 B3
Normandy 34 A2
Norman's Bay 23 B4
Norman's Green. .13 A5
Normanstone . . .105 B6
Normanton
 Derby 114 B1
 Leics. 115 A6
 Lincs. 116 A2
 Notts 132 D2
 Rutland. 99 A6
 W Yorks 140 A1
Normanton le
 Heath 114 D1
Normanton on
 Soar 114 C3
Normanton-on-the-
 Wolds. 115 B4
Normanton on
 Trent. 132 C2
Normoss. 144 D3
Norney 34 B2
Norrington
 Common 44 C2
Norris Green 136 D2
Norris Hill 114 D1
Northacre 103 B5
Northallerton . . .158 B2
Northam Devon . .25 C5
 Soton 32 D3
Northampton 83 A4
North Anston. . . .131 A5
North Aston. 65 A5
Northaw 68 C2
North Baddesley . 32 D2
North
 Ballachulish . .237 C4
North Barrow 29 C6
North Barsham . .119 B6
Northbeck 116 A3

North Benfleet . . .51 A4
North Bersted 20 B2
North Berwick . .210 B2
North Boarhunt . .33 D5
Northborough. . .100 A3
Northbourne 53 D5
North Bovey 12 C2
North Bradley 44 D2
North Brentor 11 C5
North Brewham . .29 B7
Northbridge
 Street. 37 D5
North Buckland . .25 A5
North
 Burlingham. . . .121 D5
North Cadbury . . .29 C6
North Cairn 180 D1
North Carlton . . .133 B4
North Carrine . . .190 E2
North Cave. 150 D1
North Cerney 63 C6
Northchapel 34 D2
North Charford. . . 31 D5
North Charlton . .189 A4
North Cheriton . . .29 C6
Northchurch 67 C4
North Cliff 151 C5
North Cliffe 150 D1
North Clifton 132 B3
North
 Cockerington. .143 D5
North Coker. 29 D5
North Collafirth .284 E5
North Common. . . .36 D1
North Connel 226 C4
North Cornelly . . .40 C3
North Cotes 143 C5
Northcott. 10 B4
North Cove 105 C5
North Cowton . . .157 A6
North Crawley. . . .83 C6
North Cray. 50 B1
North Creake 119 B5
North Curry 28 C3
North Dalton 150 B2
North Dawn 283 G5
North Deighton .148 B2
Northdown 53 B5
North Duffield . .149 D5
Northdyke 282 E3
North Elkington .143 D4
North Elmham . .120 C1
North Elmsall . .140 B2
Northend Bath 44 C1
 Bucks. 66 D2
 Warks. 81 B6
North End Bucks . .66 A3
 Essex 69 B6
 E Yorks. 151 D5
 Hants 46 C2
 Lincs. 117 A5
 N Som 42 C3
 Ptsmth 19 A5
 Som 28 C2
 W Sus. 21 B4
Northenden. 137 D7
North Erradale . .261 B4
North Fambridge 70 D2
North Fearns. . . .248 C2
North
 Featherstone . .140 A2
North Ferriby . . .142 A1
Northfield
 Aberdeen 245 B6
 Borders 211 D6
 E Yorks. 142 A2
 W Mid 96 D3
Northfields 100 A2
Northfleet 50 B3
North
 Frodingham . . .151 B4
Northgate 117 C4
North Gluss 284 F5
North Gorley. 31 D5
North Green
 Norf 104 C3
 Suff 105 D4
North Greetwell 133 B5
North Grimston .150 A1
North Halley 283 G6
North Halling 51 C4
North Hayling 19 A6

North Hazelrigg .199 C4
North Heasley . . .26 B2
North Heath. 34 D3
North Hill Cambs 101 D6
 Corn. 10 D3
North Hinksey. . . .65 C5
North Holmwood .35 B4
Northhouse 186 C3
North Howden . .149 D6
North Huish. 7 B6
North Hykeham .133 C4
Northiam 37 D6
Northill. 84 C3
Northington. 33 B4
North Johnston . .55 C5
North Kelsey 142 C2
North Kelsey
 Moor. 142 C2
North Kessock . .252 B2
North
 Killingholme. . .142 B3
North
 Kilvington 158 C3
North Kilworth . . .98 C3
North Kirkton . . .269 D6
North Kiscadale .191 C6
North Kyme. 133 D6
North Lancing. . . .21 B4
Northlands. 134 D3
Northlea 179 D6
Northleach. 64 B2
North Lee. 66 C3
Northleigh 14 B1
North Leigh 65 B4
North Leverton with
 Habblesthorpe
 . . . . .132 A2
Northlew 11 B6
North Littleton . .80 C3
North Lopham. . .103 C6
North Luffenham 99 A6
North Marden. . . .33 D7
North Marston . .66 A2
North Middleton
 Midloth. 196 A2
 Northumb. 188 A3
North Molton . . .26 C2
Northmoor. 65 C5
Northmoor Green or
 Moorland 28 B3
North Moreton . .46 A3
Northmuir 232 C1
North Mundham. .20 B1
North Muskham 132 D2
North Newbald . .150 D2
North Newington 81 D7
North Newnton. . .45 D5
North
 Nibley 19 A6
North Nibley 62 D3
North Oakley 46 D3
North Ockendon. .50 A2
Northolt 48 A4
Northop 126 C2
Northop Hall 126 C2
North Ormesby. .168 C3
North Ormsby . . .143 D4
Northorpe Lincs . .116 D3
 Lincs. 117 B5
 Lincs. 141 B6
North
 Otterington. . . .158 C2
Northover Som. . .29 B4
 Som 29 C5
North Owersby . .142 D3
Northowram 139 A4
North Perrott 15 A4
North Petherton . 28 B2
North Petherwin .10 C3
North
 Pickenham 103 A4
North Piddle 80 B2
North Poorton . . .15 B5
Northport. 16 C3
North Port 227 D5
Northpunds 285 L6
North
 Queensferry . . .208 B4
North Radworthy .26 B2
North Rauceby . .116 A3
Northrepps 120 B4
North Reston. . . .134 A3

North Rigton 148 C1
North Rode 128 C3
North Roe 284 E5
North Runcton . .118 D3
North Sandwick .284 D7
North Scale 153 D2
North Scarle 132 C3
North Seaton. . . .179 A4
North Shian 226 B4
North Shields . . .179 C5
North Shoebury . .51 A6
North Shore. 144 D3
North Side Cumb 162 B3
 Pboro. 101 B4
North Skelton . . .169 D4
North
 Somercotes . . .143 D6
North Stainley. . .157 D6
North
 Stainmore 165 D6
North Stifford . . .50 A3
North Stoke Bath. . 43 C6
 Oxon. 47 A4
 W Sus. 20 A3
North Street
 Hants 33 B5
 Kent 52 D2
 Medway 51 B5
 W Berks 47 B4
North
 Sunderland. . . .199 C6
North Tamerton . .10 B4
North Tawton . . .12 A1
North Thoresby .143 D4
North Tidworth. . .31 A6
North Togston . .189 C5
North
 Tuddenham . . .120 D2
North Walbottle 178 C3
North Walsham . .121 B4
North Waltham . .33 A4
North
 Warnborough. . .47 D5
North Water
 Bridge 233 B4
North Watten . . .280 C4
Northway 80 D2
North Weald
 Bassett. 69 C4
North Wheatley .132 A2
North
 Whilborough . . .8 A2
Northwich 127 B6
Northwick 43 A4
North Wick 43 C4
North
 Willingham 133 A4
North Wingfield 131 C4
North Witham . . .116 C2
Northwold 102 B3
Northwood
 Derbys 130 C2
 IoW 18 B3
 Kent 53 C5
 London 67 D5
 Shrops 110 B3
Northwood
 Green 62 B3
North Woolwich . .50 B1
North Wootton
 Dorset 29 D6
 Norf 118 C3
 Som 29 A5
North Wraxall . . .44 B2
North Wroughton 45 A5
Norton E Sus. . . .22 B2
 Glos 63 A4
 Halton 127 A5
 Herts 84 D4
 IoW 18 C2
 Mon 61 B6
 Northants. 82 A3
 Powys 77 A7
 Shrops 94 A3
 Shrops 94 C2
 Shrops 95 A5
 Stockton. 168 C2
 Suff 87 A5
 S Yorks 140 B3
 Wilts. 44 A2

Norton continued
 Worcs. 80 B1
 Worcs. 80 C3
 W Sus. 20 C1
Norton Bavant . . .30 A3
Norton Bridge. . .112 B2
Norton Canes 96 A3
Norton Canon . . .78 C1
Norton Corner . .120 C2
Norton Disney. . .132 D3
Norton East. 96 A3
Norton Ferris 30 B1
Norton
 Fitzwarren 28 C1
Norton Green 18 C2
Norton
 Hawkfield 43 C4
Norton Heath 69 C6
Norton in Hales .111 B6
Norton-in-the-
 Moors. 128 D3
Norton-Juxta-
 Twycross. 97 A6
Norton-le-Clay. .158 D3
Norton Lindsey. . .81 A5
Norton
 Malreward 43 C5
Norton
 Mandeville 69 C5
Norton-on-
 Derwent. 159 D6
Norton St Philip . .43 D6
Norton sub
 Hamdon. 29 D4
Norton
 Woodseats 130 A3
Norwell. 132 C2
Norwell
 Woodhouse . . .132 C2
Norwich 104 A3
Norwick 284 B8
Norwood 131 A4
Norwood Hill. 35 B5
Norwoodside . . .101 B6
Noseley. 99 B4
Noss 285 M5
Noss Mayo 7 C4
Nosterfield. 157 C6
Nostie 249 D5
Notgrove 64 A2
Nottage 40 D3
Nottingham 114 B3
Nottington. 15 C6
Notton Wilts 44 C3
 W Yorks 139 B6
Nounsley 70 B1
Noutard's Green. .79 A5
Novar House 264 D2
Nox 110 D3
Nuffield 47 A4
Nunburnholme. .150 C1
Nuncargate 131 D5
Nuneaton 97 B6
Nuneham
 Courtenay 65 D6
Nun Hills 138 A1
Nun Monkton . .148 B4
Nunney 30 A1
Nunnington 159 D5
Nunnykirk 188 D3
Nunsthorpe 143 C4
Nunthorpe Mbro 168 D3
 York 149 B5
Nunton 31 C5
Nunwick 157 D7
Nupend 62 C3
Nursling 32 D2
Nursted 33 C6
Nutbourne W Sus . 19 A6
 W Sus. 20 A3
Nutfield 35 A6
Nuthall 114 A3
Nuthampstead . .85 D6
Nuthurst. 35 D4
Nutley E Sus. . . .36 D2
 Hants 33 A5
Nutwell 140 C4
Nybster 281 B5
Nyetimber 20 C1
Nyewood 33 C7
Nymet Rowland . .12 A2

Nymet Tracey 12 A2
Nympsfield 63 C4
Nynehead. 27 C6
Nyton. 20 B2

O

Oadby 98 A3
Oad Street 51 C5
Oakamoor 113 A4
Oakbank. 208 D3
Oak Cross. 11 B6
Oakdale 41 B6
Oake 27 C6
Oaken 95 A6
Oakenclough. . . .145 C5
Oakengates 111 D6
Oakenholt 126 B2
Oakenshaw
 Durham 167 B5
 W Yorks 139 A4
Oakerthorpe 130 D3
Oakes 139 B4
Oakfield 61 D5
Oakford Ceredig . .74 C3
 Devon. 27 C4
Oakfordbridge . . .27 C4
Oakgrove 129 C4
Oakham 99 A5
Oakhanger. 33 B6
Oakhill 29 A6
Oakhurst 36 A3
Oakington 85 A6
Oaklands Herts . . .68 B2
 Powys 76 B4
Oakle Street 62 B3
Oakley Bedford. . .84 B2
 Bucks. 66 B1
 Fife. 208 B3
 Hants 46 D3
 Oxon. 66 C2
 Poole 17 B4
 Suff 104 D2
Oakley Green 48 B2
Oakley Park 92 C3
Oakmere 127 C5
Oakridge Glos 63 C5
 Hants 47 D4
Oaks 94 A2
Oaksey 63 D5
Oaks Green 113 B5
Oakthorpe 113 D7
Oakwoodhill 35 C4
Oakworth 147 D4
Oape 272 D2
Oare Kent 52 C2
 Som 26 A3
 W Berks 46 B3
 Wilts. 45 C5
Oasby 116 B3
Oathlaw 232 C2
Oatlands 148 B2
Oban Argyll 226 D3
 Highld. 238 D2
Oborne 29 D6
Obthorpe 116 D3
Occlestone
 Green 128 C1
Occold 104 D2
Ochiltree 193 C5
Ochtermuthill . .218 C3
Ochtertyre 218 B3
Ockbrook 114 B2
Ockham 34 A3
Ockle 235 C4
Ockley. 35 C4
Ocle Pychard. . . .78 C3
Octon 150 A3
Octon Cross
 Roads. 150 A3
Odcombe 29 D5
Odd Down 43 C6
Oddendale 164 D3
Odder 133 B4
Oddingley 80 B2
Oddington Glos . . .64 A3
 Oxon. 65 B6
Odell 83 B6
Odie. 282 E7
Odiham 47 D5
Odstock 31 C5

Odstone 97 A6
Offchurch 81 A6
Offenham 80 C3
Offham E Sus 22 A1
  Kent 37 A4
  W Sus 20 B3
Offord Cluny 84 A4
Offord Darcy 84 A4
Offton 87 C6
Offwell 14 B1
Ogbourne Maizey . 45 B5
Ogbourne St
  Andrew 45 B5
Ogbourne St
  George 45 B6
Ogil 232 B2
Ogle 178 B3
Ogmore 40 D3
Ogmore-by-Sea . . 40 D3
Ogmore Vale 40 B4
Okeford
  Fitzpaine 30 D2
Okehampton 11 B6
Okehampton
  Camp 11 B6
Okraquoy 285 K6
Old 99 D4
Old Aberdeen . . . 245 B6
Old Alresford . . . 33 B4
Old Arley 97 B5
Old Basford 114 A3
Old Basing 47 D4
Oldberrow 80 A4
Old Bewick 188 A3
Old Bolingbroke 134 C3
Oldborough 12 A2
Old Bramhope . . 147 C6
Old Brampton . . 130 B3
Old Bridge of
  Tilt 230 B2
Old Bridge of
  Urr 175 B5
Old Buckenham . 103 B6
Old Burghclere . . 46 D2
Oldbury Shrops . 95 B5
  Warks 97 B6
  W Mid 96 C2
Oldbury-on-
  Severn 62 D2
Oldbury on the
  Hill 44 A2
Old Byland 159 C4
Old Cassop 167 B6
Oldcastle Bridgend 40 D4
  Mon 61 A5
Old Castleton . . 186 D4
Old Catton 120 D4
Old Clee 143 C4
Old Cleeve 27 A5
Old Clipstone . . 131 C6
Old Colwyn 124 B3
Oldcotes 131 A5
Old Coulsdon . . 35 A6
Old Crombie . . . 267 D6
Old Dailly 181 B4
Old Dalby 115 C4
Old Deer 257 B4
Old Denaby . . . 140 D2
Old Edlington . . 140 D3
Old Eldon 167 C5
Old Ellerby . . . 151 D4
Oldfallow 112 D3
Old Felixstowe . 88 D4
Oldfield 79 A6
Old Fletton . . . 100 B3
Oldford 44 D1
Old Glossop . . 138 D3
Old Goole 141 A5
Old Hall 91 D7
Oldham 138 C2
Oldhamstocks . 211 C4
Old Heath 71 A4
Old Heathfield . 36 D3
Old Hill 96 C2
Old Hunstanton 118 A3
Old Hurst 101 D4
Old Hutton . . . 155 C4
Old Kea 4 C3
Old Kilpatrick . 205 A4
Old Kinnernie . 245 B4
Old Knebworth . 68 A2

Oldland 43 B5
Old Langho 145 D7
Old Laxey 152 C4
Old Leake 135 D4
Old Malton 159 D6
Oldmeldrum . . . 256 D3
Old Micklefield . 148 D3
Old Milton 17 B6
Old Milverton . . 81 A5
Old Monkland . . 207 D5
Old Netley 18 A3
Old Philpstoun . 208 C3
Old Quarrington 167 B6
Old Radnor 77 B6
Old Rattray 269 D5
Old Rayne 256 D1
Old Romney . . . 38 C2
Oldshore Beg . . 276 C2
Oldshoremore . . 276 C3
Old Sodbury . . . 43 A6
Old Somerby . . 116 B2
Oldstead 158 C4
Old Stratford . . 83 C4
Old Thirsk 158 C3
Oldtown 255 D6
Old Town Cumb 155 C4
  Cumb 164 A2
  Northumb 188 D1
  Scilly 2 E4
Oldtown of Ord . 267 D7
Old Trafford . . . 137 D7
Old Tupton 130 C3
Old Warden . . . 84 C3
Oldway 57 D5
Oldways End . . . 26 C3
Old Weston . . . 100 D2
Oldwhat 268 D3
Old Whittington 130 B3
Old Wick 281 C5
Old Windsor . . . 48 B2
Old Wives Lees . 52 D2
Old Woking . . . 34 A3
Old Woodhall . . 134 C2
Olgrinmore . . . 280 C2
Oliver's Battery . 32 C3
Ollaberry 284 E5
Ollerton Ches E . 128 B2
  Notts 131 C6
  Shrops 111 C5
Olmarch 75 C5
Olney 83 B5
Olrig Ho. 280 B3
Olton 96 C4
Olveston 43 A5
Olwen 75 D4
Ombersley 79 A6
Ompton 132 C1
Onchan 152 D3
Onecote 129 D5
Onen 61 B6
Ongar Hill 118 C2
Ongar Street . . 78 A1
Onibury 94 D2
Onich 237 C4
Onllwyn 59 D5
Onneley 111 A6
Onslow Village . 34 B2
Onthank 205 D4
Openwoodgate . 114 A1
Opinan Highld . 261 A5
  Highld 261 C4
Orange Lane . . 198 B1
Orange Row . . . 118 C2
Orasaigh 288 F4
Orbliston 266 D4
Orbost 258 D2
Orby 135 C4
Orchard Hill . . . 25 C5
Orchard Portman 28 C2
Orcheston 31 A4
Orcop 61 A6
Orcop Hill 61 A6
Ord 247 C5
Ordhead 244 A3
Ordie 244 B1
Ordiequish . . . 266 D4
Ordsall 132 A1
Ore 23 A6
Oreton 95 C4
Orford Suff 89 C5
  Warr 137 D5
Orgreave 113 D5

Orleston 38 B1
Orleton Hereford . 78 A2
  Worcs 79 A4
Orlingbury 99 D5
Ormesby 168 D3
Ormesby St
  Margaret 121 D6
Ormesby St
  Michael 121 D6
Ormiclate
  Castle 286 C3
Ormiscaig 261 A5
Ormiston 209 D7
Ormsaigbeg . . 234 D3
Ormsaigmore . . 234 D3
Ormsary 202 A2
Ormsgill 153 C2
Ormskirk 136 C3
Orpington 50 C1
Orrell Gtr Man . 136 C4
  Mers 136 D2
Orrisdale 152 B3
Orroland 173 D5
Orsett 50 A3
Orslow 112 D2
Orston 115 A5
Orthwaite . . . 163 A5
Ortner 145 B5
Orton Cumb . . 155 A5
  Northants 99 D5
Orton
  Longueville . . 100 B3
Orton-on-the-
  Hill 97 A6
Orton
  Waterville . . 100 B3
Orwell 85 B5
Osbaldeston . . 145 D6
Osbaldwick . . 149 B5
Osbaston 110 C2
Osbournby . . . 116 B3
Oscroft 127 C5
Ose 258 D3
Osgathorpe . . 114 D2
Osgodby Lincs . 142 D2
  N Yorks 149 D5
  N Yorks 161 C4
Oskaig 248 C2
Oskamull 224 B3
Osmaston Derby 114 B1
  Derbys 113 A6
Osmington . . . 16 C1
Osmington Mills . 16 C1
Osmotherley . . 158 B3
Ospisdale . . . 264 B3
Ospringe 52 C2
Ossett 139 A5
Ossington . . . 132 C2
Ostend 70 D3
Oswaldkirk . . . 159 D5
Oswaldtwistle . 137 A6
Oswestry 110 C1
Otford 36 A3
Otham 37 A5
Othery 28 B3
Otley Suff 88 B3
  W Yorks 147 C6
Otterbourne . . 32 C3
Otterburn
  Northumb . . . 188 D1
  N Yorks 146 B2
Otterburn Camp 188 D1
Otter Ferry . . . 214 D2
Otterham 10 B2
Otterhampton . 28 A2
Ottershaw . . . 48 C3
Otterswick . . . 284 E7
Otterton 13 C5
Ottery St Mary . 13 B6
Ottinge 38 A3
Ottringham . . 143 A4
Oughterby . . . 175 C5
Oughtershaw . 156 C2
Oughterside . . 174 D4
Oughtibridge . 139 D6
Oughtrington . 128 A1
Oulston 158 D4
Oulton Cumb . 175 C5
  Norf 120 C3
  Staffs 112 B3
  Suff 105 B6
  W Yorks 139 A6

Oulton Broad . . 105 B6
Oulton Street . . 120 C3
Oundle 100 C2
Ousby 165 B4
Ousdale 275 B4
Ousden 86 B3
Ousefleet 141 A6
Ouston Durham . 179 D4
  Northumb 178 B2
Outertown . . . 282 F3
Outgate 154 B2
Outhgill 155 A6
Outlane 138 B3
Out Newton . . 143 A5
Out Rawcliffe . . 144 C4
Outwell 101 A7
Outwick 31 D5
Outwood Sur . . 35 B6
  W Yorks 139 A6
Outwoods . . . 112 D1
Ovenden 138 A3
Ovenscloss . . 196 C3
Over Cambs . . 101 D5
  Ches W 127 C6
  S Glos 43 A4
Overbister . . . 282 C7
Overbury 80 D2
Overcombe . . . 15 C6
Over Compton . 29 D5
Overgreen . . . 130 B3
Over Green . . . 97 B4
Over Haddon . . 130 C2
Over Hulton . . 137 C5
Over Kellet . . . 154 D3
Over Kiddington . 65 A5
Over Knutsford . 128 B2
Overleigh 29 B4
Overley Green . 80 B3
Over Monnow . 61 B7
Over Norton . . 64 A4
Over Peover . . 128 B2
Overpool 126 B3
Overscaig Hotel 271 B7
Overseal 113 D6
Over Silton . . . 158 B3
Oversland 52 D2
Overstone . . . 83 A5
Over Stowey . . 28 B1
Overstrand . . . 120 A4
Over Stratton . 28 D4
Over Tabley . . 128 A2
Overthorpe . . . 82 C1
Overton
  Aberdeen . . . 245 A5
  Ches W 127 B5
  Dumfries . . . 174 B2
  Hants 32 A4
  Lancs 144 B4
  N Yorks 149 B4
  Shrops 94 D3
  Swansea 57 D4
  W Yorks 139 B5
Overton Owrtyn 110 A2
Overton Bridge . 110 A2
Overtown 194 A3
Over Wallop . . 32 B1
Over Whitacre . 97 B5
Over Worton . . 65 A5
Oving Bucks . . . 66 A2
  W Sus 20 B2
Ovingdean . . . 21 B6
Ovingham . . . 178 C2
Ovington Durham 166 D4
  Essex 86 C3
  Hants 33 B4
  Norf 103 A5
  Northumb . . . 178 C2
Ower 32 D2
Owermoigne . . 16 C1
Owlbury 93 B7
Owler Bar . . . 130 B2
Owlerton 130 A3
Owl's Green . . 88 A3
Owlswick 66 C2
Owmby 142 C2
Owmby-by-
  Spital 133 A5
Owston Leics . . 99 A4
  S Yorks 140 B3
Owston Ferry . 141 C6
Owstwick . . . 151 D5

Owthorne . . . 143 A5
Owthorpe . . . 115 B4
Oxborough . . 102 A3
Oxcombe 134 B3
Oxenholme . . 154 C4
Oxenhope . . . 147 D4
Oxen Park . . . 154 C2
Oxenton 80 D2
Oxenwood . . . 45 D7
Oxford 65 C6
Oxhey 67 D6
Oxhill 81 C6
Oxley 96 A2
Oxley Green . . 70 B3
Oxley's Green . 37 D4
Oxnam 187 B2
Oxshott 48 C4
Oxspring . . . 139 C5
Oxted 36 A1
Oxton Borders . 196 A3
  Notts 131 D6
Oxwich 57 D4
Oxwick 119 C6
Oykel Bridge . 271 D6
Oyne 256 D1

P

Pabail Iarach . . 288 D6
Pabail Uarach . 288 D6
Pace Gate . . . 147 B5
Packington . . 114 D1
Padanaram . . 232 C2
Padbury 83 D4
Paddington . . 49 A5
Paddlesworth . 38 B3
Paddockhaugh . 266 D3
Paddockhole . 185 D5
Paddock Wood . 37 B4
Padfield 138 D3
Padiham 146 D1
Padog 124 D3
Padside 147 B5
Padstow 9 D5
Padworth . . . 47 C4
Page Bank . . . 167 B5
Pagham 20 C1
Paglesham
  Churchend . . 70 D3
Paglesham
  Eastend 70 D3
Paibeil 287 H2
Paible 287 E5
Paignton 8 A2
Pailton 98 C1
Painscastle . . 77 C5
Painshawfield . 178 C2
Painsthorpe . . 149 B7
Painswick . . . 63 C4
Pairc Shiaboist . 288 C3
Paisley 205 B4
Pakefield . . . 105 B6
Pakenham . . . 87 A5
Pale 109 B4
Palestine 31 A6
Paley Street . . 47 B6
Palfrey 96 B3
Palgowan . . . 181 C5
Palgrave 104 D2
Pallion 179 D5
Palmarsh 38 B3
Palnackie . . . 173 C6
Palnure 171 A6
Palterton . . . 131 C4
Pamber End . . 47 D4
Pamber Green . 47 D4
Pamber Heath . 47 C4
Pamphill 16 A3
Pampisford . . 85 C6
Pan 283 H4
Panbride . . . 221 A5
Pancrasweek . 10 A3
Pandy Gwyn . . 90 B4
  Mon 61 A5
  Powys 91 B7
  Wrex 109 B6
Pandy Tudur . 124 C3
Panfield 70 A1
Pangbourne . . 47 B4
Pannal 148 B2
Panshanger . . 68 B2

Pant 110 C1
Pant-glas Carms . 58 C2
  Gwyn 107 B4
Pant-glâs 91 C5
Pant-glas . . . 110 B1
Pantgwyn Carms . 58 C2
  Ceredig 73 B5
Pant-lasau . . . 57 C6
Pant Mawr . . . 91 D6
Panton 134 B1
Pant-teg 58 C1
Pantperthog . . 91 B5
Pant-y-Caws . . 73 D4
Pant-y-dŵr . . 93 D4
Pant-y-ffridd . 93 A5
Pantyffynnon . 57 A6
Pantymwyn . . 126 C1
Pant-yr-awel . 40 C4
Pant-y-Wacco . 125 B6
Panxworth . . 121 D5
Papcastle . . . 163 A4
Papigoe 281 C5
Papil 285 K5
Papley 283 H5
Papple 210 C2
Papplewick . . 131 D5
Papworth
  Everard 85 A4
Papworth St
  Agnes 85 A4
Par 5 B5
Parbold 136 B3
Parbrook Som . 29 B5
  W Sus 34 D3
Parc 108 B3
Parc-Seymour . 61 D6
Parcllyn 73 A5
Parc-y-rhôs . . 75 D4
Pardshaw . . . 162 B3
Parham 88 A4
Park 183 C7
Park Corner Oxon 47 A4
  Windsor 47 A6
Parkend 62 C2
Park End Mbro . 168 D3
  Northumb . . . 177 B6
Parkeston . . . 88 D3
Parkgate Ches W 126 B2
  Dumfries . . . 184 D3
  Kent 37 C6
  Sur 35 B5
Park Gate . . . 18 A4
Parkham 25 C4
Parkham Ash . . 25 C4
Park Hill Notts . 132 D1
  N Yorks 148 A2
Parkhill Ho. . . 245 A5
Parkhouse . . . 61 C6
Parkhouse
  Green 131 C4
Parkhurst . . . 18 B3
Parkmill 57 D5
Parkneuk . . . 233 A5
Parkstone . . . 17 B4
Park Street . . 35 C4
Parley Cross . . 17 B4
Parracombe . . 26 A1
Parrog 72 C3
Parsley Hay . . 129 C6
Parsonage Green 69 C7
Parsonby . . . 163 A4
Parson Cross . 139 D6
Parson Drove . 101 A5
Parson's Heath . 71 A4
Partick 205 B5
Partington . . 137 D6
Partney 135 C4
Parton Cumb . 162 B2
  Dumfries . . . 173 A4
  Glos 63 A4
Partridge Green . 21 A4
Parwich 130 D1
Passenham . . 83 D4
Paston 121 C5
Patchacott . . 11 B5
Patcham . . . 21 B6
Patching . . . 20 B3
Patchole . . . 25 A7
Patchway . . . 43 A4

Pateley Bridge 147 A5
Paternoster
  Heath 70 B3
Pathe 28 B3
Pathhead Aberds 233 B5
  E Ayrs 182 A4
  Fife 209 A5
  Midloth 209 D6
Path of Condie 219 C5
Pathstruie 219 C5
Patna 182 A2
Patney 45 D4
Patrick 152 C2
Patrick
  Brompton 157 B6
Patrington 143 A5
Patrixbourne 52 D3
Patterdale 164 D1
Pattingham 95 B6
Pattishall 82 B3
Pattiswick Green 70 A2
Patton Bridge 155 B4
Paul 2 C2
Paulerspury 83 C4
Paull 142 A3
Paulton 43 D5
Pavenham 84 B1
Pawlett 28 A3
Pawston 198 C2
Paxford 81 D4
Paxton 198 A3
Payhembury 13 A5
Paythorne 146 B2
Peacehaven 22 B2
Peak Dale 129 B5
Peak Forest 129 B6
Peakirk 100 A3
Pearsie 232 C1
Peasedown St
  John 43 D6
Peasemore 46 B2
Peasenhall 89 A4
Pease Pottage 35 C5
Peaslake 34 B3
Peasley Cross 136 D4
Peasmarsh 37 D6
Peaston 210 D1
Peastonbank 210 D1
Peathill 269 C4
Peat Inn 221 D4
Peatling Magna 98 B2
Peatling Parva 98 C2
Peaton 94 C3
Peats Corner 88 A2
Pebmarsh 87 D4
Pebworth 80 C4
Pecket Well 138 A2
Peckforton 127 D5
Peckham 49 B6
Peckleton 98 A1
Pedlinge 38 B3
Pedmore 96 C2
Pedwell 28 B4
Peebles 196 B1
Peel 152 C2
Peel Common 19 A4
Peel Park 205 C6
Peening Quarter . .37 D6
Pegsdon 84 D3
Pegswood 179 A4
Pegwell 53 C5
Peinchorran 247 A4
Peinlich 259 C4
Pelaw 179 C4
Pelcomb Bridge . .55 C5
Pelcomb Cross 55 C5
Peldon 70 B3
Pellon 138 A3
Pelsall 96 A3
Pelton 179 D4
Pelutho 174 D4
Pelynt 5 B7
Pemberton 137 C4
Pembrey 57 B4
Pembridge 78 B1
Pembroke
  Penfro 55 D5
Pembroke Dock Doc
  Penfro 55 D5

Pembury 36 B4
Penallt 61 B7
Penally 55 E7
Penalt 62 A1
Penare 5 C4
Penarth 41 D6
Pen-bont
  Rhydybeddau . . .91 D4
Penbryn 73 A4
Pencader 58 B1
Pencaenewydd . . .107 B4
Pencaitland 210 D1
Pencarnisiog 122 C3
Pencarreg 75 D4
Pencelli 60 A2
Pen-clawdd 57 C5
Pencoed 41 C4
Pencombe 78 B3
Pencoyd 61 A7
Pencraig Hereford 62 A1
  Powys 109 C5
Pendeen 2 B1
Penderyn 59 E6
Pendine 56 B2
Pendlebury 137 C6
Pendleton 146 D1
Pendock 79 D5
Pendoggett 9 D6
Pendomer 29 D5
Pendoylan 41 D5
Pendre 40 C4
Penegoes 91 B5
Pen-ffordd 55 B6
Pengam 41 B6
Penge 49 B6
Pengenffordd 77 D5
Pengorffwysfa . . .123 A4
Pengover Green 5 C7
Pen-groes-oped .61 C5
Penhale Corn 3 D4
  Corn 4 B4
Penhallow 4 D2
Penhill 45 A5
Penhow 61 D6
Penhurst 23 A4
Peniarth 90 B4
Penicuik 209 D5
Peniel Carms 58 C1
  Denb 125 C5
Penifiler 259 D4
Peninver 190 C3
Penisarwaun 123 D5
Penistone 139 C5
Penjerrick 4 D2
Penketh 127 A5
Penkill 181 B4
Penkridge 112 D3
Penley 110 B3
Penllergaer 57 C6
Penllyn 41 D4
Pen-llyn 122 B3
Pen-lon 123 D4
Penmachno 124 D2
Penmaen 57 D5
Penmaenan 124 B2
Penmaenmawr . .124 B2
Penmaenpool 91 A4
Penmark 41 E5
Penmarth 4 D2
Penmon 123 B6
Penmore Mill 224 A3
Penmorfa Ceredig 73 A6
  Gwyn 107 B5
Penmynydd 123 C5
Penn Bucks 67 D4
  W Mid 96 B1
Pennal 91 B5
Pennan 268 C2
Pennant Ceredig . . .75 B4
  Denb 109 B5
  Denb 125 D5
  Powys 91 C6
Pennant
  Melangell 109 C5
Pennar 55 D5
Pennard 57 D5
Pennerley 94 B1
Pennington
  Cumb 153 C3
  Gtr Man 137 D5
  Hants 18 B2
Penn Street 67 D4

Penny Bridge . . .154 C2
Pennycross 225 D4
Pennygate 121 C5
Pennygown 225 B4
Pennymoor 26 D3
Pennywell 179 D5
Penparc Ceredig . . .73 B5
  Pembs 55 A4
Penparcau 90 D3
Penperlleni 61 C5
Penpillick 5 B5
Penpol 4 D3
Penpoll 5 B6
Penpont
  Dumfries 183 C6
  Powys 59 C6
Penrherber 73 C5
Penrhiwceiber 41 B5
Penrhiw goch 57 A5
Penrhiw-llan 73 B6
Penrhiw-pâl 73 B6
Penrhos 106 C3
Penrhôs 61 B6
Penros 59 D4
Penrhosfeilw 122 B2
Penrhyn Bay 124 A3
Penrhyn-coch 90 D4
Penrhyndeudraeth
  . . . . .107 C6
Penrhynside 124 A3
Penrice 57 D4
Penrith 164 B3
Penrose 9 D4
Penruddock 164 C2
Penryn 4 D2
Pensarn Carms 57 A4
  Conwy 125 B4
Pen-sarn Gwyn . .107 B4
  Gwyn 107 C5
Pensax 79 A5
Pensby 126 A2
Penselwood 30 B1
Pensford 43 C5
Penshaw 179 D5
Penshurst 36 B3
Pensilva 6 A1
Penston 210 C1
Pentewan 5 C5
Pentir 123 D5
Pentire 4 A2
Pentlow 87 C4
Pentney 119 D4
Penton Mewsey . . .32 A2
Pentraeth 123 C5
Pentre Carms 57 A5
  Powys 93 B4
  Powys 93 C4
  Rhondda 41 B4
  Shrops 110 D2
  Wrex 109 B6
  Wrex 110 A1
Pentrebach
  M Tydf 41 A5
  Swansea 57 B6
Pentre-bâch 75 D4
Pentre-bach 59 B6
Pentrebeirdd 109 D6
Pentre Berw 123 C4
Pentre-bont 124 D2
Pentrecagal 73 B6
Pentre-celyn
  Denb 125 D6
  Powys 91 B6
Pentre-chwyth . . .57 C6
Pentre-cwrt 73 C6
Pentre Dolau-
  Honddu 76 C3
Pentredwr 109 A6
Pentre-dwr 40 B1
Pentrefelin Carms . .58 C2
  Ceredig 75 D5
  Conwy 124 B3
  Gwyn 107 C5
Pentrefoelas 124 D3
Pentre-galar 73 C4
Pentregat 73 A6
Pentre-Gwenlais 57 A6
Pentre
  Gwynfryn 107 D5
Pentre Halkyn . . .126 B2
Pentreheyling 93 B6
Pentre-Isaf 124 C3

Pentre
  Llanrhaeadr . . .125 C5
Pentre-llwyn-
  ll yd 76 B3
Pentre-llyn 75 A5
Pentre-llyn
  cymmer 125 D4
Pentre Meyrick . . .41 D4
Pentre-poeth 42 A1
Pentre'r Felin . . .124 C3
Pentre'r-felin 59 B6
Pentre-rhew 75 C5
Pentre-tafarn-y-
  fedw 124 C3
Pentre-ty-gwyn . .59 B5
Pentrich 130 D3
Pentridge 31 D4
Pen-twyn 61 C7
Pentyrch 41 C6
Penuchadre 40 D3
Penuwch 75 B4
Penwithick 5 B5
Penwyllt 59 D5
Penybanc 57 A6
Pen-y-banc 58 C3
Penybont 77 A5
Pen-y-bont
  Carms 73 D6
  Gwyn 91 B5
  Gwyn 107 D6
  Powys 109 C7
Penybontfawr . . .109 C5
Pen-y-bryn Gwyn .91 A4
  Pembs 73 B4
Penycae 110 A1
Pen-y-cae 59 D5
Pen-y-cae-mawr 61 D6
Pen-y-cefn 125 B6
Pen-y-clawdd 61 C6
Pen-y-coedcae . . .41 C5
Penycwm 54 B4
Pen-y-fai 40 C3
Penyffordd 126 C3
Penyffridd 107 A5
Pen-y-garn Carms 58 B2
  Ceredig 90 D4
Penygarnedd 109 C6
Pen-y-garnedd .123 C5
Pen-y-gop 108 A4
Penygraig 41 B4
Pen-y-graig 106 C1
Penygroes Gwyn .107 A4
  Pembs 73 C4
Pen-y-groes 57 A5
Pen-y-groeslon 106 C2
Pen-y-Gwryd
  Hotel 107 A6
Penyrheol 41 C6
Pen-yr-heol 61 B6
Pen-yr-
  Heolgerrig 60 C2
Penysarn 123 A4
Pen-y-stryt 126 D1
Penywaun 41 A4
Penzance 2 B2
Peopleton 80 B2
Peover Heath 128 B2
Peper Harow 34 B2
Perceton 204 D3
Percie 244 C2
Percyhorner 269 C4
Periton 27 A4
Perivale 49 A4
Perkinsville 179 D4
Perlethorpe 131 B6
Perranarworthal . .4 D2
Perranporth 4 B2
Perranuthnoe 2 C3
Perranzabuloe 4 B2
Perry Barr 96 B3
Perry Green Herts. 68 B4
Perryfoot 129 A6
Perry Street 50 B3
Pershall 112 B2
Pershore 80 C2
Pert 233 B4
Pertenhall 84 A2
Perth 219 B6
Perthy 110 B2
Perton 95 B6
Pertwood 30 B2

Peterborough 100 B3
Peterburn 261 B4
Peterchurch 78 D1
Peterculter 245 B5
Peterhead 257 B6
Peterlee 168 A2
Petersfield 33 C6
Peter's Green 67 B6
Peters Marland . . .25 D5
Peterstone
  Wentlooge 42 A1
Peterston super-
  Ely 41 D5
Peterstow 62 A1
Peter Tavy 11 D6
Petertown 283 G4
Petham 52 D3
Petrockstow 11 A6
Pett 23 A6
Pettaugh 88 B2
Petteridge 37 B4
Pettinain 195 B4
Pettistree 88 B3
Petton Devon 27 C5
  Shrops 110 C3
Petts Wood 50 C1
Petty 256 C2
Pettycur 209 B5
Pettymuick 257 D4
Petworth 34 D2
Pevensey 22 B4
Pevensey Bay 23 B4
Pewsey 45 C5
Philham 24 C3
Philiphaugh 186 A3
Phillack 2 B3
Philleigh 4 D3
Philpstoun 208 C3
Phocle Green 62 A2
Phoenix Green 47 D5
Pica 162 B3
Piccotts End 67 C5
Pickering 159 C6
Picket Piece 32 A2
Picket Post 17 A5
Pickhill 158 C2
Picklescott 94 B2
Pickletillem 220 B4
Pickmere 128 B1
Pickney 28 C1
Pickstock 111 C6
Pickwell Devon . . .25 A5
  Leics 115 D5
Pickworth Lincs. .116 B3
  Rutland 116 D2
Picton Ches W . . .127 B4
  Flint 125 A6
  N Yorks 158 A3
Piddinghoe 22 B2
Piddington
  Northants. 83 B5
  Oxon 66 B1
Piddlehinton 15 B7
Piddletrenthide . .15 B7
Pidley 101 D5
Piercebridge 167 D5
Pierowall 282 C5
Pigdon 178 A3
Pikehall 130 D1
Pilgrims Hatch . . .69 D5
Pilham 141 D6
Pill 43 B4
Pillaton 6 A2
Pillerton Hersey . .81 C6
Pillerton Priors. . . .81 C5
Pilleth 77 A6
Pilley Hants. 18 B2
  S Yorks 139 C6
Pilling 144 C4
Pilling Lane 144 C4
Pillowell 62 C2
Pillwell 30 D1
Pilning 43 A4
Pilsbury 129 C6
Pilsdon 14 B4
Pilsgate 100 A2
Pilsley Derbys. 130 B2
  Derbys 131 C4
Pilton Devon 25 B6
  Northants 100 C2
  Rutland 99 A6
  Som 29 A5

Pilton Green 57 D4
Pimperne 16 A3
Pinchbeck 117 C5
Pinchbeck Bars .117 C4
Pinchbeck West 117 C5
Pincheon Green 141 B4
Pinehurst 45 A5
Pinfold 136 B2
Pinged 57 B4
Pinhoe 13 B4
Pinkneys Grn. 47 A6
Pinley 97 D6
Pin Mill 88 D3
Pinminnoch 180 B3
Pinmore 181 B4
Pinmore Mains. . .181 B4
Pinner 48 A4
Pinvin 80 C2
Pinwherry 180 C3
Pinxton 131 D4
Pipe and Lyde 78 C3
Pipe Gate 111 A6
Piperhill 253 A4
Piper's Pool 10 C3
Pipewell 99 C5
Pippacott 25 B6
Pipton 77 D5
Pirbright 34 A2
Pirnmill 202 D3
Pirton Herts. 84 D3
  Worcs. 80 C1
Pisgah Ceredig 75 A5
  Stirling 218 D2
Pishill 47 A5
Pistyll 106 B3
Pitagowan 230 B2
Pitblae 269 C4
Pitcairngreen 219 B5
Pitcalnie 265 C4
Pitcaple 256 D2
Pitchcombe 63 C4
Pitchcott 66 A2
Pitchford 94 A3
Pitch Green 66 C2
Pitch Place 34 A2
Pitcombe 29 B6
Pitcorthie 221 D5
Pitcox 210 C3
Pitcur 220 A2
Pitfichie 244 A3
Pitforthie 233 A6
Pitgrudy 264 A3
Pitkennedy 232 C3
Pitkevy 220 D2
Pitkierie 221 D5
Pitlessie 220 D3
Pitlochry 230 C3
Pitmachie 256 D1
Pitmain 241 B5
Pitmedden 256 D3
Pitminster 28 D2
Pitmuies 232 D3
Pitmunie 244 A3
Pitney 29 C4
Pitscottie 220 C4
Pitsea 51 A4
Pitsford 83 A4
Pitsmoor 130 A3
Pitstone 67 B4
Pitstone Green . . .67 B4
Pittendreich 266 C2
Pittentrail 273 D5
Pittenweem. 221 D5
Pittington 167 A6
Pittodrie 256 D1
Pitton 31 B6
Pittswood 36 B4
Pittulie 269 C4
Pityme 9 D5
Pity Me 167 A5
Pityoulish 242 A2
Pixey Green 104 D3
Pixley 79 D4
Place Newton 160 D2
Plaidy 268 D2
Plains 207 D5
Plaish 94 B3
Plaistow 34 C3
Plaitford 32 D1
Plank Lane 137 D5
Plas-canol 90 A3

Plas Gogerddan . . 90 D4
Plas Llwyngwern . 91 B5
Plas Nantyr 109 B6
Plastow Green 46 C3
Plas-yn-Cefn . . . 125 B5
Platt 36 A4
Platt Bridge 137 C5
Platts Common . . 139 C6
Plawsworth 167 A5
Plaxtol 36 A4
Playden 37 D7
Playford 88 C3
Play Hatch 47 B5
Playing Place 4 C3
Playley Green 79 D5
Plealey 94 A2
Plean 207 B6
Pleasington 137 A5
Pleasley 131 C5
Pleckgate 145 D6
Plenmeller 177 C5
Pleshey 69 B6
Plockton 249 D5
Plocrapol 288 H2
Ploughfield 78 C1
Plowden 94 C1
Ploxgreen 94 A1
Pluckley 38 A1
Pluckley Thorne . . 37 B7
Plumbland 163 A4
Plumley 128 B3
Plumpton Cumb . 164 B2
    E Sus 21 A6
Plumpton Green . . 21 A6
Plumpton Head . 164 B3
Plumstead London. 50 B1
    Norf 120 B3
Plumtree 115 B4
Plungar 115 B5
Plush 15 A7
Plwmp 73 A6
Plymouth 6 B3
Plympton 7 B4
Plymstock 7 B4
Plymtree 13 A5
Pockley 159 C5
Pocklington 149 C7
Pode Hole 117 C5
Podimore 29 C5
Podington 83 A6
Podmore 112 B1
Point Clear 71 B4
Pointon 116 B4
Pokesdown 17 B5
Pol a Charra 286 E3
Polbae 181 D4
Polbain 270 C2
Polbathic 6 B2
Polbeth 208 D3
Polchar 242 B1
Polebrook 100 C2
Pole Elm 79 C6
Polegate 22 B3
Poles 264 A3
Polesworth 97 A5
Polgigga 2 C1
Polglass 270 D3
Polgooth 5 B4
Poling 20 B3
Polkerris 5 B5
Polla 277 C4
Pollington 140 B4
Polloch 236 C1
Pollok 205 B5
Pollokshields 5 C4
Polmassick 5 C4
Polmont 208 C2
Polnessan 182 A2
Polnish 235 B6
Polperro 5 B7
Polruan 5 B6
Polsham 29 A5
Polstead 87 D5
Poltalloch 213 C6
Poltimore 13 B4
Polton 209 D5
Polwarth 197 A6
Polyphant 10 C3
Polzeath 9 D5
Ponders End 68 D3
Pondtail 34 A1

Ponsanooth 4 D2
Ponsworthy 12 D2
Pont Aber 59 C4
Pont Aber-
    Geirw 108 C2
Pontamman 57 A6
Pontantwn 57 A4
Pontardawe 40 A2
Pontarddulais . . . 57 B5
Pont-ar-gothi 58 C2
Pont ar Hydfer . . . 59 C5
Pont-ar-llechau . . 59 C4
Pontarsais 58 C1
Pontblyddyn . . . 126 C2
Pontbren Araeth . 58 C3
Pontbren Llwyd . 59 E6
Pont Cwm
    Pydew 109 B5
Pont Cyfyng . . . 124 D2
Pont Cysyllte . . . 110 A1
Pont Dolydd
    Prysor 108 B2
Pontefract 140 A2
Ponteland 178 B3
Ponterwyd 91 D5
Pontesbury 94 A1
Pontfadog 110 B1
Pontfaen 55 A6
Pont-faen 76 D3
Pont Fronwydd . 108 C3
Pont-gareg 72 B4
Pontgarreg 73 A6
Pont-Henri 57 B4
Ponthir 61 D5
Ponthirwaun 73 B5
Pontllanfraith . . . 41 B6
Pontlliw 57 B6
Pont-Llogel 109 D5
Pontllyfni 107 A4
Pontlottyn 60 C3
Pontneddfechan . 59 E6
Pontnewydd 61 D4
Pont Pen-y-
    benglog 123 D6
Pontrhydfendigaid
    . . . . 75 B6
Pont Rhyd-
    goch 124 C1
Pont-Rhyd-sarn 108 C3
Pont Rhyd-y-cyff 40 C3
Pontrhydyfen . . . 40 B2
Pont-rhyd-y-
    groes 75 A6
Pontrilas 61 A5
Pontrobert 109 D6
Pont-rug 123 D5
Ponts Green 23 A4
Pontshill 62 A2
Pont-siân 74 D3
Pontsticill 60 B2
Pontwgan 124 B2
Pontyates 57 B4
Pontyberem 57 A5
Pontyclun 41 C5
Pontycymer 40 B4
Pontyglasier 72 C4
Pont-y-gwaith . . . 41 B5
Pont-y-pant . . . 124 D2
Pont y Pennant . 108 C4
Pontypool Pont-Y-
    Pŵl 61 C4
Pontypridd 41 C5
Pont yr Afon-
    Gam 108 A2
Pont-y-rhafod . . . 55 B5
Pontywaun 41 B7
Pooksgreen 32 D2
Pool Corn 3 A4
    W Yorks 147 C6
Poole 17 B4
Poole Keynes . . . 63 D5
Poolend 129 D4
Poolewe 261 B5
Pooley Bridge . . 164 C2
Poolfold 128 D3
Poolhill 62 A3
Pool o'
    Muckhart . . . 219 D5
Pool Quay 110 D1
Poolsbrook 131 B4
Pootings 36 B2
Pope Hill 55 C5

Popeswood 47 C6
Popham 33 A4
Poplar 49 A6
Popley 47 D4
Porchester 114 A3
Porchfield 18 B3
Porin 251 A5
Poringland 104 A3
Porkellis 3 B4
Porlock 26 A3
Porlock Weir 26 A3
Portachoillan . . . 202 C2
Port Ann 214 D2
Port Appin 226 B4
Port Arthur 285 K5
Port Askaig 201 B4
Portavadie 203 B4
Port Bannatyne . 203 B5
Portbury 43 B4
Port Carlisle 175 B5
Port Charlotte . . 200 C1
Portchester 19 A5
Portclair 240 A2
Port Clarence . . . 168 C2
Port Driseach . . . 203 A4
Port Ellen 200 D3
Port
    Elphinstone . . 256 E2
Portencalzie 180 D2
Portencross 204 D1
Port Erin 152 E1
Port Erroll 257 C5
Portesham 15 C6
Portessie 267 C5
Port e Vullen . . . 152 B4
Port-Eynon 57 D4
Portfield Gate . . . 55 C5
Portgate 11 C5
Port Gaverne 9 C6
Port Glasgow . . . 204 A3
Portgordon 267 C4
Portgower 274 C4
Porth Corn 4 A3
    Rhondda 41 B5
Porthallow Corn . . 3 C5
    Corn 6 B1
Porthcawl 40 D3
Porthcothan 9 D4
Porthcurno 2 C1
Port Henderson . 261 C4
Porthgain 54 A4
Porthill 110 D3
Porthkerry 41 E5
Porthleven 3 C4
Porthllechog . . . 123 A4
Porthmadog . . . 107 C5
Porthmeor 2 B2
Porth Navas 3 C5
Portholland 5 C4
Porthoustock 3 C6
Porthpean 5 B5
Porthtowan 3 A4
Porthyrhyd Carms 57 A5
    Carms 59 B4
Porth-y-waen . . . 110 C1
Portincaple 215 C5
Portington 149 D6
Portinnisherrich
    . . . . 214 A2
Portinscale 163 B5
Port Isaac 9 C5
Portishead 42 B3
Portkil 215 D5
Portknockie 267 C5
Port Lamont 203 A5
Portlethen 245 C6
Portling 173 C6
Port Lion 55 D5
Portloe 4 D4
Port Logan 170 C2
Portmahomack . . 265 B5
Portmeirion 107 C5
Portmellon 5 C5
Port Mholair . . . 288 D6
Port Mor 234 C3
Portmore 18 B2
Port Mulgrave . . 169 D5
Portnacroish . . . 226 B4
Portnahaven . . . 200 C1
Portnalong 246 A2
Portnaluchaig . . 235 B5
Portnancon 277 B5

Port Nan
    Giùran 288 D6
Port nan Long . . 287 G3
Portnellan 216 B4
Port Nis 288 A6
Portobello 209 C6
Port of
    Menteith 217 D5
Porton 31 B5
Portpatrick 170 B2
Port Quin 9 C5
Port Ramsay . . . 226 B3
Portreath 3 A4
Portree 259 D4
Port St Mary . . . 152 E2
Portscatho 4 D3
Portsea 19 A5
Portskerra 279 B4
Portskewett 43 A4
Portslade 21 B5
Portslade-by-
    Sea 21 B5
Portsmouth 19 A5
    W Yorks 138 A2
Portsonachan . . 227 D5
Portsoy 267 C6
Port Sunlight . . . 126 A3
Portswood 32 D3
Port Talbot 40 B2
Porttanachy 267 C4
Port Tennant 57 C6
Portuairk 234 D3
Portway Hereford . . 78 D2
    Worcs 96 D3
Port Wemyss . . . 200 C1
Port William . . . 171 C5
Portwrinkle 6 B2
Poslingford 86 C3
Postbridge 12 D1
Postcombe 66 D2
Postling 38 B3
Postwick 104 A3
Potholm 185 D6
Potsgrove 67 A4
Potten End 67 C5
Potter
    Brompton . . . 160 D3
Potterhanworth . 133 C5
Potterhanworth
    Booths 133 C5
Potter Heigham . 121 D6
Potterne 44 D3
Potterne Wick . . . 44 D4
Potternewton . . . 148 D2
Potters Bar 68 C2
Potter's Cross . . . 95 C6
Potterspury 83 C4
Potter Street 69 C4
Potterton Aberds 245 A6
    W Yorks 148 D3
Potto 158 A3
Potton 84 C4
Pott Row 119 C4
Pott Shrigley . . . 129 B4
Poughill Corn . . . 10 A3
    Devon 12 A3
Poulshot 44 D3
Poulton Glos 64 C2
    Mers. 136 D2
Poulton-le-
    Fylde 144 D3
Pound Bank 95 D5
Poundfield 36 C3
Pound Green
    E Sus 36 D3
    IoW 18 C2
    Worcs 95 D5
Pound Hill 35 C5
Poundland 180 C3
Poundon 66 A1
Poundsgate 12 D2
Poundstock 10 B3
Powburn 188 B3
Powderham 13 C4
Powerstock 15 B5
Powfoot 174 B4
Powick 79 B6
Powmill 208 A3
Poxwell 16 C1
Poyle 48 B3
Poynings 21 A5

Poyntington 29 D6
Poynton 129 A4
Poynton Green . . 111 D4
Poystreet Green . . 87 B5
Praa Sands 2 C3
Pratt's Bottom . . . 50 C1
Praze 2 B3
Praze-an-Beeble. . 3 B4
Predannack
    Wollas 3 D4
Prees 111 B4
Preesall 144 C3
Prees Green 111 B4
Preesgweene . . . 110 B1
Prees Heath 111 B4
Prees Higher
    Heath 111 B4
Prees Lower
    Heath 111 B4
Prenderguest . . . 198 A3
Prendwick 188 B3
Prengwyn 73 B7
Prenteg 107 B5
Prenton 126 A3
Prescot 136 D3
Prescott 110 C3
Pressen 198 C2
Prestatyn 125 A5
Prestbury Ches E 129 B4
    Glos 63 A5
Presteigne
    Llanandras . . . 77 A7
Presthope 94 B3
Prestleigh 29 A6
Preston Borders . 198 A1
    Brighton 21 B6
    Devon. 12 D3
    Dorset 15 C7
    E Loth 210 C2
    E Yorks 151 D4
    Glos 63 C6
    Glos 79 D4
    Herts 68 A1
    Kent 52 C2
    Kent 53 C4
    Lancs 136 A4
    Northumb . . . 189 A4
    Rutland 99 A5
    Shrops 111 D4
    Wilts 44 B4
    Wilts 45 B6
Preston Bagot . . . 81 A4
Preston Bissett . . 66 A1
Preston Bowyer . . 27 C6
Preston
    Brockhurst . . 111 C4
Preston Brook . . 127 A5
Preston
    Candover 33 A5
Preston Capes . . 82 B2
Preston
    Crowmarsh . . 65 D7
Preston
    Gubbals 110 D3
Prestonmill 174 C2
Preston on Stour 81 C5
Preston on the
    Hill 127 A5
Preston on Wye . 78 C1
Prestonpans . . . 209 C6
Preston
    Plucknett 29 D5
Preston St Mary . 87 B5
Preston-under-
    Scar 157 B4
Preston upon the
    Weald Moors . 111 D5
Preston Wynne . . 78 C3
Prestwich 137 C7
Prestwick
    Northumb. . . . 178 B3
    S Ayrs 192 C3
Prestwood 66 C3
Price Town 40 B4
Prickwillow 102 C1
Priddy 43 D4
Priesthaugh 186 C3
Priest Hutton . . . 154 D4
Priest Weston . . . 93 B6
Primethorpe 98 B2
Primrose Green . 120 D2
Primrosehill 67 C5

Primrose Valley . 161 D5
Princes Gate 56 A1
Princes
    Risborough. . . 66 C3
Princethorpe 97 D7
Princetown
    Caerph 60 B3
    Devon. 11 D6
Prion 125 C5
Prior Muir 221 C5
Prior Park 198 A3
Priors Frome 78 D3
Priors Hardwick . 82 B1
Priorslee 111 D6
Priors Marston . . 82 B1
Priory Wood 77 C6
Priston 43 C5
Pristow Green . . 104 C2
Prittlewell 51 A5
Privett 33 C5
Prixford 25 B6
Probus 4 C3
Proncy 264 A3
Prospect 174 D4
Prudhoe 178 C2
Ptarmigan
    Lodge 215 B6
Pubil 228 D3
Puckeridge 68 A3
Puckington 28 D3
Pucklechurch . . . 43 B5
Pucknall 32 C2
Puckrup 80 D1
Puddinglake . . . 128 C2
Puddington
    Ches W. 126 B3
    Devon. 26 D3
Puddledock 103 B6
Puddletown. 16 B1
Pudleston 78 B3
Pudsey 147 D6
Pulborough 20 A3
Puleston 111 C6
Pulford 126 D3
Pulham 15 A7
Pulham Market . 104 C2
Pulham St Mary . 104 C3
Pulloxhill 84 D2
Pumpherston . . . 208 D3
Pumsaint 58 A3
Puncheston 55 B6
Puncknowle 15 C5
Punnett's Town . . 36 D4
Purbrook 19 A5
Purewell 17 B5
Puriton 28 A3
Purleigh 70 C2
Purley London . . . 49 C6
    W Berks 47 B4
Purlogue 93 D6
Purls Bridge . . . 101 C6
Purse Caundle . . 29 D6
Purslow 94 C1
Purston Jaglin . . 140 B2
Purton Glos 62 C2
    Glos 62 C2
    Wilts 45 A4
Purton Stoke . . . 64 D1
Pury End 83 C4
Pusey 65 D4
Putley 79 D4
Putney 49 B5
Putsborough 25 A5
Puttenham Herts . 66 B3
    Sur. 34 B2
Puxton 42 C3
Pwll 57 B4
Pwllcrochan 55 D5
Pwll-glas 125 D5
Pwllgloyw 76 D4
Pwllheli 106 C3
Pwllmeyric 61 D7
Pwll-trap 56 A2
Pwll-y-glaw 40 B2
Pyecombe 21 A5
Pye Corner 42 A2
Pye Green 112 D3
Pyewipe 143 B4

Pyle 18 D3
Pyle Y Pîl 40 C3
Pylle 29 B6
Pymoor 101 C6
Pyrford 34 A3
Pyrton 66 D1
Pytchley 99 D5
Pyworthy 10 A4

Q

Quabbs 93 C6
Quadring 117 B5
Quainton 66 B2
Quarley 31 A6
Quarndon 114 A1
Quarrier's
 Homes 204 B3
Quarrington 116 A3
Quarrington Hill 167 B6
Quarry Bank 96 C2
Quarryford 210 D2
Quarryhill 264 B3
Quarrywood 266 C2
Quarter 194 A2
Quatford 95 B5
Quatt 95 C5
Quebec 167 A4
Quedgeley 63 B4
Queen Adelaide .102 C1
Queenborough 51 B6
Queen Camel 29 C5
Queen Charlton . . .43 C5
Queen Dart 26 D3
Queenhill 79 D6
Queen Oak 30 B1
Queensbury 147 D5
Queensferry
 Edin 208 C4
 Flint 126 C3
Queen's Head 110 C2
Queen's Park
 Bedford 84 C2
 Northants 83 A4
Queenstown 144 D4
Queen Street Kent 37 B4
 Wilts 44 A4
Queenzieburn 207 C4
Quemerford 44 C4
Quendale 285 M5
Quendon 85 D7
Queniborough 115 D4
Quenington 64 C2
Quernmore 145 B5
Quethiock 6 A2
Quholm 282 F3
Quicks Green 46 B3
Quidenham 103 C6
Quidhampton
 Hants 46 D3
 Wilts 31 B5
Quilquox 257 C4
Quina Brook 111 B4
Quindry 283 H5
Quinton Northants . 83 B4
 W Mid 96 C2
Quintrell Downs . . . 4 A3
Quixhill 113 A5
Quoditch 11 B5
Quoig 218 B3
Quorndon 114 D3
Quothquan 195 C4
Quoyloo 282 E3
Quoyness 283 G3
Quoys Shetland . . .284 B8
 Shetland 285 G6

R

Raasay Ho 248 C2
Rabbit's Cross 37 B5
Raby 126 B3
Rachan Mill 195 C6
Rachub 123 D6
Rackenford 26 D3
Rackham 20 A3
Rackheath 121 D4

Racks 174 A3
Rackwick Orkney 282 C5
 Orkney 283 H3
Radbourne 113 B6
Radcliffe Gtr Man 137 C6
 Northumb 189 C5
Radcliffe on
 Trent 115 B4
Radclive 82 D3
Radcot 64 D3
Raddery 252 A3
Radernie 221 D4
Radford Semele . .81 A6
Radipole 15 C6
Radlett 67 D6
Radley 65 D6
Radmanthwaite .131 C5
Radmore Green .127 D5
Radnage 66 D2
Radstock 43 D5
Radstone 82 C2
Radway 81 C6
Radway Green . . .128 D2
Radwell Bedford . .84 B2
 Herts 84 D4
Radwinter 86 D2
Radyr 41 C6
Rafford 253 A6
Ragdale 115 D4
Raglan 61 C6
Ragnall 132 B3
Rahane 215 D5
Rainford 136 C3
Rainford
 Junction 136 C3
Rainham London . .50 A2
 Medway 51 C5
Rainhill 136 D3
Rainhill Stoops . .136 D3
Rainow 129 B4
Rainton 158 D2
Rainworth 131 D5
Raisbeck 155 A5
Raise 165 A5
Rait 220 B2
Raithby Lincs 134 A3
 Lincs 134 C3
Rake 33 C7
Rakewood 138 B2
Ram 75 D4
Ramasaig 258 D1
Rame Corn 4 D2
 Corn 6 C3
Rameldry Mill
 Bank 220 D3
Ram Lane 38 A1
Ramnageo 284 C8
Rampisham 15 A5
Rampside 153 D3
Rampton Cambs . . .85 A6
 Notts 132 B2
Ramsbottom 137 B6
Ramsbury 45 B6
Ramscraigs 275 B5
Ramsdean 33 C6
Ramsdell 46 D3
Ramsden 65 B4
Ramsden
 Bellhouse 69 D7
Ramsden Heath . . .69 D7
Ramsey Cambs . . .101 C4
 Essex 88 D3
 IoM 152 B4
Ramseycleuch . .185 A5
Ramsey Forty
 Foot 101 C5
Ramsey Heights 101 C4
Ramsey Island . . .70 C3
Ramsey
 Mereside 101 C4
Ramsey St
 Mary's 101 C4
Ramsgate 53 C5
Ramsgill 157 D5
Ramshorn 113 A4
Ramsnest
 Common 34 C2
Ranais 288 E5
Ranby Lincs 134 B2
 Notts 131 A6
Rand 133 B6

Randwick 63 C4
Ranfurly 204 B3
Rangag 280 D3
Rangemore 113 C5
Rangeworthy 43 A5
Rankinston 182 A2
Ranmoor 130 A3
Ranmore
 Common 35 A4
Rannerdale 163 C4
Rannoch
 Station 228 C3
Ranochan 238 D2
Ranskill 131 A6
Ranton 112 C2
Ranworth 121 D5
Raploch 207 A5
Rapness 282 C6
Rascal Moor 149 D7
Rascarrel 173 D5
Rashiereive 257 D4
Raskelf 158 D3
Rassau 60 B3
Rastrick 139 A4
Ratagan 238 A3
Ratby 98 A2
Ratcliffe Culey . . .97 B6
Ratcliffe on
 Soar 114 C2
Ratcliffe on the
 Wreake 115 D4
Rathen 269 C5
Rathillet 220 B3
Rathmell 146 B2
Ratho 208 C4
Ratho Station 208 C4
Rathven 267 C5
Ratley 81 C6
Ratlinghope 94 B2
Rattar 281 A4
Ratten Row 144 C4
Rattery 7 A6
Rattlesden 87 B5
Rattray 231 D5
Raughton Head .164 A1
Raunds 100 D1
Ravenfield 140 D2
Ravenglass 153 A1
Raveningham 105 B4
Ravenscar 160 A3
Ravenscraig 204 A2
Ravensdale 152 B3
Ravensden 84 B2
Ravenseat 156 A2
Ravenshead 131 D5
Ravensmoor 127 D6
Ravensthorpe
 Northants 98 D3
 W Yorks 139 A5
Ravenstone
 Leics 114 D2
 M Keynes 83 B5
Ravenstonedale 155 A6
Ravenstown 154 D2
Ravenstruther . . .194 B4
Ravensworth 157 A5
Raw 160 A3
Rawcliffe E Yorks 141 A4
 York 149 B4
Rawcliffe
 Bridge 141 A4
Rawdon 147 D6
Rawmarsh 140 D2
Rawreth 70 D1
Rawridge 14 A2
Rawtenstall 137 A7
Raxton 256 C3
Raydon 87 D6
Raylees 188 D2
Rayleigh 70 D2
Rayne 70 A1
Rayners Lane 48 A4
Raynes Park 49 C5
Reach 86 A1
Read 146 D1
Reading 47 B5
Reading Street . . .37 C7
Reagill 165 D4
Rearquhar 264 A3
Rearsby 115 D4
Reaster 281 B4
Reawick 285 J5

Reay 279 B5
Rechullin 249 A5
Reculver 53 C4
Redberth 55 D6
Redbourn 67 B6
Redbourne 142 D1
Redbrook Mon 62 B1
 Wrex 111 A4
Redburn Highld . . .253 B5
 Highld 264 D1
 Northumb 177 C5
Redcar 168 C4
Redcastle Angus .233 C4
 Highld 252 B1
Redcliff Bay 42 B3
Red Dial 175 D5
Redding 208 C2
Reddingmuirhead
 . . . . .208 C2
Reddish 138 D1
Redditch 80 A3
Rede 87 B4
Redenhall 104 C3
Redesdale
 Camp 187 D7
Redesmouth 177 A6
Redford Aberds . .233 A5
 Angus 232 D3
 Durham 166 B3
Redfordgreen 185 A6
Redgorton 219 B5
Redgrave 103 D6
Redhill Aberds . . .245 B4
 Aberds 256 C1
 N Som 42 C3
 Sur 35 A5
Red Hill 79 B6
Redhouse 202 B3
Redhouses 200 B3
Red Houses Jersey . . 6
Redisham 105 C5
Redland Bristol . . .43 B4
 Orkney 282 E4
Redlingfield 104 D2
Red Lodge 102 D2
Redlynch Som 29 B7
 Wilts 31 C6
Redmarley
 D'Abitot 79 D5
Redmarshall 167 C6
Redmile 115 B5
Redmire 156 B4
Redmoor 5 A5
Rednal 110 C2
Redpath 197 C4
Redpoint 261 D4
Red Rail 62 A1
Red Rock 137 C4
Red Roses 56 A2
Red Row 189 D5
Redruth 3 A4
Red Street 128 D3
Redvales 137 C7
Red Wharf Bay .123 B5
Redwick Newport . .42 A3
 S Glos 43 A4
Redworth 167 C5
Reed 85 D5
Reedham 105 A5
Reedness 141 A5
Reeds Beck 134 C2
Reepham Lincs . . .133 B5
 Norf 120 C2
Reeth 156 B4
Regaby 152 B4
Regoul 253 A4
Reiff 270 C2
Reigate 35 A5
Reighton 161 D5
Reighton Gap . . .161 D5
Reinigeadal 288 G3
Reiss 281 C5
Rejerrah 4 B2
Releath 3 B4
Relubbus 2 B4
Relugas 253 B5
Remenham 47 A5
Remenham Hill . .47 A5
Remony 229 D6
Rempstone 114 C3
Rendcomb 63 C6
Rendham 88 A4

Rendlesham 88 B4
Renfrew 205 B5
Renhold 84 B2
Renishaw 131 B4
Rennington 189 B5
Renton 206 C1
Renwick 164 A3
Repps 121 D6
Repton 113 C7
Reraig 249 D5
Rescobie 232 C3
Resipole 235 D6
Resolis 264 D2
Resolven 40 A3
Reston 211 D5
Reswallie 232 C3
Retew 4 B4
Retford 132 A2
Rettendon 70 D1
Rettendon Place . 70 D1
Revesby 134 C2
Revesby Bridge .134 C3
Rewe 13 B4
Rew Street 18 B3
Reydon 105 D5
Reydon Smear . .105 D5
Reymerston 103 A6
Reynalton 55 D6
Reynoldston 57 C4
Rezare 11 D4
Rhandirmwyn . . .59 A4
Rhayader Rhaeadr
 Gwy 76 A3
Rhedyn 106 C2
Rhemore 225 A4
Rhencullen 152 B3
Rhes-y-cae 126 B1
Rhewl Denb 109 A6
 Denb 125 C6
Rhian 272 C3
Rhicarn 270 B3
Rhiconich 276 C3
Rhiculen 264 C2
Rhidorroch Ho. .262 A3
Rhifail 278 D3
Rhigos 59 E6
Rhilochan 273 D5
Rhiroy 262 B3
Rhiw 106 D2
Rhiwbina 41 C6
Rhiwbryfdir 107 B6
Rhiwderin 42 A1
Rhiwlas Gwyn . . .108 B4
 Gwyn 123 D5
 Powys 109 B6
Rhodes 138 C1
Rhodesia 131 B5
Rhodes Minnis . . .38 A3
Rhodiad 54 B3
Rhondda 41 B4
Rhonehouse or
 Kelton Hill 173 C5
Rhoose Y Rhws 41 E5
Rhôs Carms 73 C6
 Neath 40 A2
Rhosaman 59 D4
Rhosbeirio 122 A3
Rhoscefnhir 123 C5
Rhoscolyn 122 C2
Rhoscrowther 55 D5
Rhosesmor 126 C2
Rhos-fawr 106 C3
Rhosgadfan 107 A5
Rhosgoch 123 B4
Rhos-goch 77 C5
Rhos-hill 73 B4
Rhoshirwaun 106 D1
Rhoslan 107 B4
Rhoslefain 90 B3
Rhosllanerchrugog
 . . . . .110 A1
Rhosmaen 58 C3
Rhosmeirch 123 C4
Rhosneigr 122 C3
Rhosnesni 126 D3
Rhos-on-Sea 124 A3
Rhosrobin 126 D3
Rhossili 57 D4
Rhosson 54 B2
Rhostryfan 107 A4
Rhostyllen 110 A2

Rhosybol 123 B4
Rhos-y-brithdir 109 C6
Rhos-y-garth 75 A5
Rhos-y-gwaliau 108 B4
Rhos-y-llan 106 C2
Rhos-y-Madoc . .110 A2
Rhos-y-meirch . . .77 A6
Rhu Argyll 202 B3
 Argyll 215 D5
Rhuallt 125 B5
Rhuddall Heath .127 C5
Rhuddlan Ceredig . 58 A2
 Denb 125 B5
Rhue 262 A2
Rhulen 77 B5
Rhunahaorine . . .202 D2
Rhyd Gwyn 107 B6
 Powys 92 A3
Rhydaргeаeu 58 C1
Rhydcymerau 58 B2
Rhydd 79 C6
Rhyd-Ddu 107 A5
Rhydding 40 B2
Rhydfudr 75 B4
Rhydlewis 73 B6
Rhydlios 106 C1
Rhydlydan 124 D3
Rhyd-moel-ddu . .93 D4
Rhydness 77 C5
Rhydowen 74 D3
Rhyd-Rosser 75 B4
Rhydspence 77 C6
Rhydtalog 126 D2
Rhyd-uchaf 108 B4
Rhyd-wen 91 A5
Rhydwyn 122 B3
Rhyd-y-clafdy . .106 C3
Rhydycroesau . .110 B1
Rhydyfelin Ceredig 75 A4
 Rhondda 41 C5
Rhyd-y-fro 59 E4
Rhyd-y-gwin 57 B6
Rhydymain 108 C2
Rhyd-y-meirch . . .61 C5
Rhyd-y-
 meudwy 125 D6
Rhydymwyn 126 C2
Rhyd-y-pandy 57 B6
Rhyd-yr-onen 90 B4
Rhyd-y-sarn 107 B6
Rhyl Y Rhyl 125 A5
Rhymney Rhymni . 60 C3
Rhynd Fife 221 B4
 Perth 219 B6
Rhynie Aberds . . .255 D5
 Highld 265 C4
Ribbesford 95 D5
Ribblehead 155 D6
Ribbleton 145 D5
Ribchester 145 D6
Ribigill 277 C6
Riby 142 C3
Riby Cross
 Roads 142 C3
Riccall 149 D5
Riccarton 193 B4
Richards Castle . .78 A2
Richings Park 48 B3
Richmond London .49 B4
 N Yorks 157 A5
Rickarton 245 D5
Rickinghall 103 D6
Rickleton 179 D4
Rickling 85 D6
Ridge Lane 97 B5
Ridgeway Cross . . .79 C5
Ridgewell 86 C3
Ridgewood 22 A2
Ridgmont 84 D1
Rickmansworth . . .67 D5
Riddings Cumb . . .175 A7
 Derbys 131 D4
Riddlecombe 25 D7
Riddlesden 147 C4
Riddrie 205 B6
Ridge Dorset 16 C3
 Hants 32 D2
 Wilts 30 B3
Ridgebourne 77 A4
Ridge Green 35 B6
Ridgehill 43 C4
Riding Mill 178 C2

Ridleywood 127 D4
Ridlington Norf . . 121 B5
Rutland. 99 A5
Ridsdale 177 A7
Riechip 231 D4
Riemore 230 D4
Rienachait 270 A3
Rievaulx 159 C4
Rift House 168 B2
Rigg 175 B5
Riggend 207 C5
Rigsby 135 B4
Rigside 194 C3
Riley Green 137 A5
Rileyhill 113 D5
Rilla Mill 10 D3
Rillington 160 D2
Rimington 146 C2
Rimpton 29 C6
Rimswell 143 A5
Rinaston 55 B5
Ringasta 285 M5
Ringford 173 C4
Ringinglow 130 A2
Ringland 120 D3
Ringles Cross . . . 36 D2
Ringmer 22 A2
Ringmore 7 C5
Ringorm 254 B3
Ring's End 101 A5
Ringsfield 105 C5
Ringsfield
  Corner 105 C5
Ringshall Herts . . 67 B4
  Suff 87 B6
Ringshall Stocks . 87 B6
Ringstead Norf. . 119 A4
  Northants. 100 D1
Ringwood 17 A5
Ringwould 39 A5
Rinmore 243 A7
Rinnigill 283 H4
Rinsey 2 C3
Riof 288 D2
Ripe 22 A3
Ripley Derbys . . . 130 D3
  Hants 17 B5
  N Yorks. 148 A1
  Sur 34 A3
Riplingham 150 D2
Ripon 157 D7
Rippingale 116 C3
Ripple Kent 39 A5
  Worcs. 79 D6
Ripponden 138 B3
Rireavach. 262 A2
Risabus 200 D3
Risbury 78 B3
Risby 86 A3
Risca Rhisga 60 D4
Rise 151 C4
Riseden 36 C4
Risegate 117 C5
Riseholme 133 B4
Riseley Bedford . . 84 A2
  Wokingham 47 C5
Rishangles 88 A2
Rishton 146 D1
Rishworth 138 B3
Rising Bridge . . . 137 A6
Risley Derbys . . . 114 B2
  Warr. 137 D5
Risplith 147 A6
Rispond 277 B5
Rivar 45 C7
Rivenhall End . . . 70 B2
River Bank 86 A1
Riverhead. 36 A3
Rivington 137 B5
Roachill 26 C3
Roade 83 B4
Road Green 104 B3
Roadhead. 176 B3
Roadmeetings . . 194 B3
Roadside 280 B3
Roadside of
  Catterline 233 A6
Roadside of
  Kinneff. 233 A6
Roadwater 27 B5
Roag 258 D2
Roa Island 153 D3

Roath. 41 D6
Roberton
  Borders 186 B3
  S Lanark. 194 D4
Robertsbridge. . . 37 D5
Roberttown 139 A4
Robeston Cross . . 55 D4
Robeston
  Wathen 55 C6
Robin Hood 139 A6
Robin Hood's
  Bay 160 A3
Roborough Devon . . 7 A4
  Devon. 25 D6
Roby 136 D3
Roby Mill 136 C4
Rocester. 113 B5
Roch 55 B4
Rochdale 138 B1
Roche 5 A4
Rochester
  Medway 51 C4
  Northumb. 188 D1
Rochford 70 D2
Roch Gate 55 B4
Rock Corn 9 D5
  Northumb. 189 A5
  Worcs. 95 D5
  W Sus. 21 A4
Rockbeare 13 B5
Rockbourne. 31 D5
Rockcliffe Cumb 175 B6
  Dumfries 173 C6
Rock Ferry 126 A3
Rockfield Highld . 265 B5
  Mon 61 B6
Rockford 17 A5
Rockhampton . . 62 D2
Rockingham 99 B5
Rockland All
  Saints 103 B5
Rockland St
  Mary 104 A4
Rockland St
  Peter 103 B5
Rockley. 45 B5
Rockwell End . . . 47 A5
Rockwell Green . 27 C6
Rodborough 63 C4
Rodbourne
  Swindon 45 A5
  Wilts. 44 A3
Rodbourne
  Cheney. 45 A5
Rodd 77 A7
Roddam 188 A3
Rodden 15 C6
Rode 44 D2
Rodeheath 128 C3
Rode Heath 128 D3
Roden 111 D4
Rodhuish 27 B5
Rodington 111 D4
Rodley Glos. 62 B3
  W Yorks 147 D6
Rodmarton 63 D5
Rodmell 22 B2
Rodmersham . . . 51 C6
Rodney Stoke . . . 42 D3
Rodsley 113 A6
Rodway. 28 B2
Rodwell 15 D5
Roecliffe. 148 A2
Roe Green 85 D5
Roehampton . . . 49 B5
Roesound. 284 G5
Roffey 35 C4
Rogart 273 D5
Rogart Station . . 273 D5
Rogate 33 C7
Rogerstone 42 A1
Roghadal 287 F5
Rogiet 42 A3
Rogue's Alley . . . 101 A5
Roke 66 D1
Roker 179 D6
Rollesby 121 D6
Rolleston Leics. . . 99 A4
  Notts 132 D2
Rolleston-on-
  Dove 113 C6
Rolston 151 C5

Rolvenden 37 C6
Rolvenden Layne 37 C6
Romaldkirk 166 C2
Romanby 158 B2
Romannobridge 195 B6
Romansleigh . . . 26 C2
Romford 50 A2
Romiley 138 D2
Romsey. 32 C2
Romsey Town . . . 85 B6
Romsley Shrops . 95 C5
  Worcs. 96 D2
Ronague 152 D2
Rookhope 166 A2
Rookley 18 C4
Rooks Bridge . . . 42 D2
Roos 151 D5
Roosebeck 153 D3
Rootham's Green. 84 B3
Rootpark 195 A4
Ropley. 33 B5
Ropley Dean 33 B5
Ropsley. 116 B2
Rora. 269 D5
Rorandle 244 A3
Rorrington. 93 A7
Roscroggan 3 A4
Rose 4 B2
Roseacre Kent . . . 37 A5
  Lancs 144 D4
Rose Ash 26 C2
Rosebank 194 B3
Rosebrough. 189 A4
Rosebush. 55 B6
Rosecare 10 B2
Rosedale Abbey 159 B6
Roseden 188 A3
Rosefield 253 A4
Rose Green 20 C2
Rose Grove 146 D2
Rosehall 272 D2
Rosehaugh
  Mains 252 A2
Rosehearty 269 C4
Rosehill 111 B5
Rose Hill E Sus. . . 22 A2
  Lancs 146 D2
  Suff 88 C2
Roseisle 266 C2
Roselands 22 B4
Rosemarket. 55 D5
Rosemarkie. 252 A3
Rosemary Lane . . 27 D6
Rosemount 231 D5
Rosenannon 5 A4
Rosewell. 209 D5
Roseworth 168 C2
Roseworthy 3 B4
Rosgill. 164 D3
Roshven 235 C6
Roskhill 258 D2
Roskill House . . . 252 A2
Rosley. 175 D6
Roslin 209 D5
Rosliston 113 D6
Rosneath 215 D5
Ross Dumfries . . 172 D4
  Northumb. 199 C5
  Perth 218 B2
Rossett 126 D3
Rossett Green . . 148 B2
Rossie Ochill . . . 219 C5
Rossie Priory. . . 220 A2
Rossington. 140 D4
Rosskeen 264 D2
Rossland. 205 A4
Ross-on-Wye . . . 62 A2
Roster 281 E4
Rostherne 128 A2
Rosthwaite. 163 C5
Roston 113 A5
Rosyth 208 B4
Rothbury 188 C3
Rotherby 115 D4
Rotherfield 36 D3
Rotherfield Greys 47 A5
Rotherfield
  Peppard. 47 A5
Rotherham. 140 D2
Rothersthorpe . . 83 B4
Rotherwick 47 D5
Rothes 254 B3

Rothesay 203 B5
Rothiebrisbane. . 256 C2
Rothienorman. . . 256 C2
Rothiesholm . . . 282 E7
Rothley Leics . . . 114 D3
  Northumb. 178 A2
Rothley Shield
  East. 188 D3
Rothmaise 256 C1
Rothwell Lincs . . 142 D3
  Northants. 99 C5
  W Yorks 139 A6
Rothwell Haigh. 139 A6
Rotsea. 150 B3
Rottal 232 B1
Rotten End. 89 A4
Rottingdean 21 B6
Rottington. 162 C2
Roud 18 C4
Rougham Norf . . 119 C5
  Suff 87 A5
Rougham Green. . 87 A5
Roughburn 240 D1
Rough Close . . . 112 B3
Rough Common . 52 D3
Roughlee 146 C2
Roughley 96 B4
Roughsike 176 B3
Roughton Lincs . 134 C2
  Norf 120 B4
  Shrops 95 B5
Roughton Moor 134 C2
Roundhay. 148 D2
Roundstonefoot 185 B4
Roundstreet
  Common 34 D3
Roundway. 44 C4
Rousdon 14 B2
Rous Lench 80 B3
Routenburn 204 B1
Routh 150 C3
Row Corn. 10 D1
  Cumb 154 C3
Rowanburn 175 A7
Rowardennan . . 206 A1
Rowde. 44 C3
Rowen 124 B2
Rowfoot 177 C4
Row Heath 71 B5
Rowhedge 71 A4
Rowhook 35 C4
Rowington 81 A5
Rowland 130 B2
Rowlands Castle. 33 D6
Rowlands Gill . . 178 D3
Rowledge. 33 A7
Rowlestone 61 A5
Rowley E Yorks . . 150 D2
  Shrops 93 A7
Rowley Hill 139 B4
Rowley Regis . . . 96 C2
Rowly 34 B3
Rowney Green . . 96 D3
Rownhams. 32 D2
Rowrah 162 C3
Rowsham 66 B3
Rowsley 130 C2
Rowstock. 46 A2
Rowston 133 D5
Rowton Ches W . 127 C4
  Shrops 110 D2
  Telford 111 D5
Roxby N Lincs . . 141 B7
  N Yorks. 169 D5
Roxton 84 B3
Roxwell. 69 C6
Royal Leamington
  Spa 81 A6
Royal Oak Darl . . 167 C5
  Lancs 136 C3
Royal Tunbridge
  Wells 36 C3
Royal Wootton
  Bassett. 45 A4
Roybridge 239 D6
Roydhouse. 139 B5
Roydon Essex . . . 68 C4
  Norf 104 C1
  Norf 119 C4
Roydon Hamlet. . 68 C4
Royston Herts . . 85 C5

Royston continued
  S Yorks 139 B6
Royton 138 C2
Rozel Jersey 6
Ruabon
  Rhiwabon 110 A2
Ruaig. 222 C3
Ruan Lanihorne . . 4 C3
Ruan Minor 3 D5
Ruarach 249 D6
Ruardean 62 B2
Ruardean
  Woodside 62 B2
Rubery 96 D2
Ruckcroft 164 A3
Ruckhall 78 D2
Ruckinge 38 B2
Ruckland 134 B3
Ruckley. 94 A3
Rudbaxton 55 B5
Rudby 158 A3
Ruddington 114 B3
Rudford 62 A3
Rudge Shrops . . . 95 B6
  Som 44 D2
Rudgeway 43 A5
Rudgwick 34 C3
Rudhall. 62 A2
Rudheath 128 B1
Rudley Green . . . 70 C2
Rudry. 41 C6
Rudston 150 A3
Rudyard 129 D4
Rufford 136 B3
Rufforth 148 B4
Rugby 98 D2
Rugeley 112 D4
Ruglen 181 A4
Ruilick. 251 B7
Ruishton. 28 C2
Ruisigearraidh . . 287 F4
Ruislip. 48 A3
Ruislip Common. 48 A3
Rumbling
  Bridge 208 A3
Rumburgh 104 C4
Rumford 9 D4
Rumney 41 D7
Runcorn 127 A5
Runcton 20 B1
Runcton Holme . 102 A2
Rundlestone . . . 11 D6
Runfold. 34 B1
Runhall 103 A6
Runham Norf . . . 105 A6
  Norf 121 D6
Runnington 27 C6
Runsell Green. . . 70 C1
Runswick Bay . . 169 D6
Runwell 70 D1
Ruscombe 47 B5
Rush-head. 256 B3
Rushall Hereford . 79 D4
  Norf 104 C2
  Wilts. 45 D5
  W Mid 96 A3
Rushbrooke 87 A4
Rushbury 94 B3
Rushden Herts . . 85 D5
  Northants. 83 A6
Rushenden 51 B6
Rushford 103 C5
Rush Green 50 A2
Rush-head. 256 B3
Rushlake Green . 22 A4
Rushmere 105 C5
Rushmere St
  Andrew 88 C3
Rushmoor 34 B1
Rushock 96 D1
Rusholme 138 D1
Rushton Ches W . 127 C5
  Northants. 99 C5
  Shrops 95 A4
Rushton
  Spencer 129 C4
Rushwick 79 B6
Rushyford 167 C5
Ruskie 217 D6
Ruskington 133 D5
Rusland 154 C2
Rusper 35 C5
Ruspidge 62 B2

Russell's Water . 47 A5
Russel's Green . 104 D3
Rusthall 36 C3
Rustington. 20 B3
Ruston 160 C3
Ruston Parva. . . 150 A3
Ruswarp. 160 A2
Rutherford. 197 C5
Rutherglen 205 B6
Ruthernbridge . . . 5 A5
Ruthin Rhuthun . 125 D6
Ruthrieston . . . 245 B6
Ruthven Aberds . 255 B6
  Angus. 231 D6
  Highld. 241 C5
  Highld. 253 C4
Ruthven House . 231 D7
Ruthvoes 4 A4
Ruthwell 174 B3
Ryton-Xl-
  Towns 110 C2
Ryal 178 B2
Ryal Fold 137 A5
Ryall 14 B4
Ryarsh. 37 A4
Rydal 154 A2
Ryde 19 B4
Rye. 37 D7
Ryecroft Gate . . 129 C4
Rye Foreign. . . . 37 D6
Rye Harbour . . . 38 D1
Ryehill. 143 A4
Rye Park. 68 B3
Rye Street 79 D5
Ryhall 116 D3
Ryhill. 140 B1
Ryhope 179 D6
Rylstone 146 B3
Ryme Intrinseca. 29 D5
Ryther 149 D4
Ryton Glos. 79 D5
  N Yorks. 159 D6
  Shrops 95 A5
  T&W. 178 C3
Ryton-on-
  Dunsmore 97 D6

S

Sabden 146 D1
Sacombe 68 B3
Sacriston 167 A5
Sadberge 167 D6
Saddell 190 B3
Saddington 98 B3
Saddle Bow . . . 118 D3
Saddlescombe . . 21 A5
Sadgill. 154 A3
Saffron Walden . 86 D1
Sageston 55 D6
Saham Hills . . . 103 A5
Saham Toney . . 103 A5
Saighdinis 287 H3
Saighton. 127 C4
St Abbs 211 D6
St Agnes Corn . . . 4 B2
  Scilly 2 F3
St Albans 67 C6
St Allen. 4 B3
St Andrews 221 C5
St Andrew's
  Major 41 D6
St Anne Ald. 7
St Annes 136 A2
St Ann's 184 C3
St Ann's Chapel
  Corn 11 D5
  Devon. 7 C5
St Anthony-in-
  Meneage 3 C5
St Anthony's Hill. 22 B4
St Arvans 61 D7
St Asaph
  Llanelwy 125 B5
St Athan 41 E5
St Aubin Jersey . . . 6
St Austell 5 B5
St Bees 162 C2

St Blazey 5 B5
St Brelade *Jersey* ... 6
St Breock 9 D5
St Breward 10 D1
St Briavels 62 C1
St Bride's 54 C4
St Brides Major .. 40 D3
St Brides
  Netherwent 42 A3
St Brides super
  Ely 41 D5
St Brides
  Wentlooge 42 A1
St Budeaux 6 B3
Saintbury 80 D4
St Buryan 2 C2
St Catherine 44 B1
St Catherine's .. 215 B4
St Clears *Sanclêr* .. 56 A2
St Cleer........... 6 A1
St Clement........ 4 C3
St Clements *Jersey* ... 6
St Clether......... 6 A1
St Colmac 203 B5
St Columb Major .. 4 A4
St Columb Minor .. 4 A3
St Columb Road .. 4 B4
St Combs 269 C5
St Cross South
  Elmham 104 C3
St Cyrus 233 B5
St David's 218 B4
St David's
  Tyddewi 54 B3
St Day 4 C2
St Dennis 4 B4
St Devereux 78 D2
St Dogmaels 73 B4
St Dogwells 55 B5
St Dominick 6 A3
St Donat's 40 E4
St Edith's 44 C3
St Endellion..... 9 D5
St Enoder 4 B3
St Erme 4 B3
St Erney 6 B2
St Erth.......... 2 B3
St Ervan 9 D4
St Eval 4 A3
St Ewe 5 C4
St Fagans 41 D6
St Fergus 269 D5
St Fillans 217 B6
St Florence 55 D6
St Genny's 10 B2
St George 125 B4
St George's 41 D5
St Germans 6 B2
St Giles 133 B4
St Giles in the
  Wood 25 D6
St Giles on the
  Hth......... 11 B4
St Harmon 92 D3
St Helena 97 A5
St Helen
  Auckland 167 C4
St Helens *IoW* ... 19 C5
  Mers........... 136 D4
St Helen's 23 A6
St Helier *Jersey* 6
  London 49 C5
St Hilary *Corn.*... 2 B3
  V Glam 41 D5
Saint Hill 36 C1
St Illtyd...... 41 A7
St Ippollytts... 68 A1
St Ishmael's.... 54 D4
St Issey 9 D5
St Ive 6 A2
St Ives *Cambs* ... 101 D5
  Corn......... 2 A3
  Dorset 17 A5
St James South
  Elmham 104 C4
St Jidgey 9 E5
St John 6 B3
St John's *IoM*.... 152 C2
  Jersey 6

St John's *continued*
  Sur..............34 A2
  Worcs.......... 79 B6
St John's
  Chapel 166 B1
St John's Fen
  End 118 D2
St John's
  Highway......118 D2
St John's Town of
  Dalry........182 D4
St Judes 152 B3
St Just.......... 2 B1
St Just in
  Roseland 4 D3
St Katherine's.. 256 C2
St Keverne 3 C5
St Kew 9 D6
St Kew Highway .. 9 D6
St Keyne........ 6 A1
St Lawrence *Corn* .. 5 A5
  Essex 70 C3
  IoW 18 D4
St Leonards
  Dorset 17 A5
  E Sus 23 B5
St Leonard's ... 67 C4
Saint Leonards .. 205 C6
St Levan 2 C1
St Lythans 41 D6
St Mabyn 9 D6
St Madoes 219 B6
St Margarets .. 68 B3
St Margaret's .. 78 D1
St Margaret's at
  Cliffe.......... 39 C5
St Margaret South
  Elmham 104 C4
St Mark's 152 D2
St Martin 6 B3
St Martins *Corn* ... 3 C5
  Perth 219 A6
St Martin's *Jersey* ... 6
  Shrops 110 B2
St Mary Bourne .. 46 D2
St Mary Church .. 41 D5
St Mary Cray .. 50 C1
St Mary Hill 41 D4
St Mary Hoo .. 51 B5
St Mary in the
  Marsh......... 38 C2
St Mary's *Jersey* 6
  Orkney 283 G5
St Mary's Bay .. 38 C2
St Maughans .. 61 B6
St Mawes 4 D3
St Mawgan 4 A3
St Mellion 6 A2
St Mellons 42 A1
St Merryn 9 D4
St Mewan 5 B4
St Michael
  Caerhays...... 5 C4
St Michael
  Penkevil........ 4 C3
St Michaels ... 78 A3
St Michael's 37 C6
St Michael's on
  Wyre......145 C4
St Michael South
  Elmham 104 C4
St Minver 9 D5
St Monans ... 221 D5
St Neot 5 A6
St Neots 84 A3
St Newlyn East .. 4 B3
St Nicholas *Pembs* 72 C1
  V Glam 41 D5
St Nicholas at
  Wade 53 C4
St Ninians ... 207 A5
St Osyth 71 B5
St Osyth Heath .. 71 B5
St Ouens *Jersey* 6
St Owens Cross .. 62 A1
St Paul's Cray .. 50 C1
St Paul's Walden .. 68 A1
St Peter Port *Guern* .. 6
St Peter's *Jersey* 6
  Kent 53 C5
St Petrox 55 E5
St Pinnock 5 A7

St Quivox 192 C3
St Ruan 3 D5
St Sampson *Guern*..... 6
St Stephen....... 4 B4
St Stephens *Corn* .. 6 B3
  Herts 67 C5
St Stephen's .. 10 C4
St Teath 9 C6
St Thomas 13 B4
St Tudy 9 D6
St Twynnells .. 55 E5
St Veep.......... 5 B6
St Vigeans 233 D4
St Wenn 5 A4
St Weonards .. 61 A6
Salcombe 7 D6
Salcombe Regis .. 13 C6
Salcott 70 B3
Sale 137 D6
Sale Green 80 B2
Salehurst 37 D5
Salem *Carms* .. 58 C3
  Ceredig 91 D4
Salen *Argyll*.... 225 B4
  Highld......... 235 D5
Salesbury 145 D6
Salford *C Beds* .. 83 D6
  Gtr Man 137 D7
  Oxon......... 64 A3
Salford Priors .. 80 B3
Salfords 35 B5
Salhouse 121 D5
Saline 208 A3
Salisbury 31 C5
Sallachan 236 C3
Sallachy *Highld* .. 249 C6
  Highld......... 272 D3
Salle 120 C3
Salmonby 134 B3
Salmond's Muir .. 221 A5
Salperton 64 A1
Salph End...... 84 B2
Salsburgh.... 207 D6
Salt 112 C3
Saltaire...... 147 D5
Saltash 6 B3
Saltburn...... 264 D3
Saltburn-by-the-
  Sea 169 C4
Saltby 115 C6
Saltcoats *Cumb* .. 153 A1
  N Ayrs 204 D2
Saltdean...... 22 B1
Salt End 142 A3
Salter 145 A6
Salterforth .. 146 C2
Salterswall... 127 C6
Saltfleet 143 D6
Saltfleetby All
  Saints.......143 D6
Saltfleetby St
  Clements.....143 D6
Saltfleetby St
  Peter 135 A4
Salton 159 D6
Saltwick 178 B3
Saltwood 38 B3
Salum 222 C3
Salvington .. 21 B4
Salwarpe 80 A1
Salwayash ... 15 B4
Sambourne .. 80 A3
Sambrook ... 111 C6
Samhla 287 H2
Samlesbury .. 145 D5
Samlesbury
  Bottoms.......137 A5
Sampford
  Arundel 27 D6
Sampford Brett .. 27 A5
Sampford
  Courtenay 12 A1
Sampford
  Peverell........ 27 D5
Sampford Spiney 11 B7
Samuelston ...210 C1

Sanachan 249 B5
Sanaigmore.... 200 A2
Sancreed 2 C2
Sancton 150 D2
Sand *Highld*...... 261 A6
  Shetland...... 285 J5
Sandaig 247 D6
Sandale 175 D5
Sandal Magna .. 139 B6
Sandbach 128 C2
Sandbank 215 D4
Sandbanks 17 C4
Sandend 267 C6
Sanderstead 49 C6
Sandfields 63 A5
Sandford *Cumb* .. 165 D5
  Devon......... 12 A3
  Dorset 16 C3
  IoW 18 C4
  N Som 42 D3
  Shrops 111 A4
  S Lanark..... 194 B2
Sandfordhill .. 257 B6
Sandford on
  Thames 65 C6
Sandford Orcas .. 29 C6
Sandford St
  Martin 65 A5
Sandgate 38 B3
Sandgreen 172 C3
Sandhaven.... 269 C4
Sandhead 170 C2
Sandhills 34 C2
Sandhoe 178 C1
Sand Hole 149 D7
Sandholme
  E Yorks......150 D1
  Lincs........ 117 B6
Sandhurst *Brack* .. 47 C6
  Glos 63 A4
  Kent 37 D5
Sandhurst Cross .. 37 D5
Sandhutton .. 158 C2
Sandiacre.... 114 B2
Sandilands *Lincs* 135 A5
  S Lanark..... 194 C3
Sandiway 127 B6
Sandleheath .. 31 D5
Sandling...... 37 A5
Sandlow Green .. 128 C2
Sandness 285 H3
Sandon *Essex*.... 70 C1
  Herts 85 D5
  Staffs 112 B3
Sandown 19 C4
Sandplace 6 B1
Sandridge *Herts* .. 67 B6
  Wilts........... 44 C3
Sandringham .. 118 C3
Sandsend 169 D6
Sandside Ho... 279 B5
Sandsound .. 285 J5
Sandtoft 141 C5
Sandway 37 A6
Sandwell 96 C3
Sandwich 53 D5
Sandwick *Cumb* .. 164 D2
  Orkney 283 J5
  Shetland...... 285 L6
Sandwith 162 C2
Sandy *Carms*.... 57 B4
  C Beds 84 C3
Sandy Bank .. 134 D2
Sandycroft .. 126 C3
Sandyford
  Dumfries 185 C5
  Stoke 128 D3
Sandygate 152 B3
Sandy Haven .. 55 D4
Sandyhills 173 C6
Sandylands .. 144 A4
Sandy Lane *Wilts*.. 44 C3
  Wrex 110 A2
Sandypark 12 C2
Sandysike 175 B6
Sangobeg 277 B5
Sangomore .. 277 B5
Sanna 234 D3
Sanndabhaig
  W Isles 286 B4
  W Isles 288 D5

Sannox 203 D5
Sanquhar 183 B5
Santon 142 B1
Santon Bridge.. 163 D4
Santon
  Downham 103 C4
Sapcote 98 B1
Sapey Common .. 79 A5
Sapiston 103 D5
Sapley........ 100 D4
Sapperton *Glos* .. 63 C5
  Lincs......... 116 B3
Saracen's Head .117 C6
Sarclet 281 D5
Sardis 57 B5
Sarn *Bridgend* 40 C4
  Powys 93 B6
Sarnau *Carms*.... 56 A3
  Ceredig 73 A6
  Gwyn 109 B4
  Powys 76 D4
  Powys 110 D1
Sarn Bach 106 D3
Sarnesfield 78 B1
Sarn Meyllteyrn .106 C2
Saron *Carms*.... 57 A6
  Carms 73 C6
  Denb.......... 125 C5
  Gwyn 107 A4
  Gwyn 123 D5
Sarratt 67 D5
Sarre 53 C4
Sarsden 64 A3
Sarsgrum 277 B4
Satley 166 A4
Satron 156 B3
Satterleigh...... 26 C1
Satterthwaite .. 154 B2
Satwell 47 A5
Sauchen 244 A3
Saucher 219 A6
Sauchie 208 A1
Sauchieburn .. 233 B4
Saughall 126 B3
Saughtree 187 D4
Saul 62 C3
Saundby 132 A2
Saundersfoot .. 56 B1
Saunderton .. 66 C2
Saunton 25 B5
Sausthorpe .. 134 C3
Saval 272 D3
Savary 225 B5
Savile Park .. 138 A3
Sawbridge 82 A2
Sawbridgeworth . 69 B4
Sawdon...... 160 C3
Sawley *Derbys* .. 114 B2
  Lancs........ 146 C1
  N Yorks...... 147 A6
Sawston 85 C6
Sawtry 100 C3
Saxby *Leics* .. 115 D6
  Lincs........ 133 A5
Saxby All Saints .142 B1
Saxelbye 115 C5
Saxham Street .. 88 A1
Saxilby 132 B3
Saxlingham
  Green 104 B3
Saxlingham
  Nethergate .. 104 B3
Saxlingham
  Thorpe......104 B3
Saxmundham .. 89 A4
Saxondale 115 B4
Saxon Street .. 86 B2
Saxtead...... 88 A3
Saxtead Green .. 88 A3
Saxthorpe 120 B3
Saxton 148 D3
Sayers Common .. 21 A5
Scackleton 159 D5
Scadabhagh .. 288 H2
Scaftworth .. 141 D4
Scagglethorpe .. 160 B2
Scaitcliffe 137 A6
Scalasaig 212 C1
Scalby *E Yorks* .141 A6
  N Yorks...... 160 B4
Scaldwell...... 99 D4

Scaleby........ 176 C2
Scaleby Hill .. 176 C2
Scale Houses .. 164 A3
Scales *Cumb* 153 C3
  Cumb 163 B6
  Lancs........ 145 D4
Scalford 115 C5
Scaling 169 D5
Scallastle 225 C5
Scalloway 285 K6
Scalpay...... 288 H3
Scalpay Ho... 247 B5
Scalpsie 203 C5
Scamadale .. 235 A6
Scamblesby .. 134 B2
Scamodale .. 236 B2
Scampston .. 160 D2
Scampton .. 133 B4
Scapa 283 G5
Scapegoat Hill .138 B3
Scar........ 282 C7
Scarborough .. 160 C4
Scarcliffe 131 C4
Scarcroft 148 C2
Scarcroft Hill .. 148 C2
Scardroy.... 250 A4
Scarff 284 E4
Scarfskerry .. 281 A4
Scargill...... 166 D3
Scarinish 222 C3
Scarisbrick .. 136 B2
Scarning 119 D6
Scarrington .. 115 A5
Scartho 143 C4
Scarwell 282 E3
Scatness 285 M5
Scatraig 252 C3
Scawby 142 C1
Scawsby 140 C3
Scawton 158 C4
Scayne's Hill ... 35 D6
Scethrog 60 A3
Scholar Green .. 128 D3
Scholes *W Yorks* .139 A4
  W Yorks...... 139 C4
  W Yorks...... 148 D2
School Green .. 127 C6
Scleddau 55 A5
Scofton...... 131 A6
Scole...... 104 D2
Scolpaig 287 G2
Scone 219 B6
Sconser 247 A4
Scoonie 220 D3
Scoor........ 224 E3
Scopwick 133 D5
Scoraig 262 A2
Scorborough .. 150 C3
Scorrier 4 C2
Scorton *Lancs* .. 145 C5
  N Yorks...... 157 A6
Sco Ruston .. 121 C4
Scotbheinn .. 286 A4
Scotby........ 176 D2
Scotch Corner .. 157 A6
Scotforth 145 B4
Scothern 133 B5
Scotland Gate.. 179 A4
Scotlandwell .. 219 D6
Scotsburn 264 C3
Scotscalder
  Station......280 C2
Scotscraig .. 220 B4
Scots' Gap .. 178 A2
Scotston *Aberds*.. 233 A5
  Perth 230 D3
Scotstoun .. 205 B5
Scotstown .. 236 C2
Scotswood .. 178 C3
Scottas 247 D6
Scotter 141 C6
Scotterthorpe .. 141 C6
Scottlethorpe .. 116 C3
Scotton *Lincs* .. 141 D6
  N Yorks...... 148 B2
  N Yorks...... 157 B5
Scottow 121 C4
Scoughall .. 210 B3
Scoulag 203 C6
Scoulton .. 103 A5
Scourie 276 D2
Scourie More .. 276 D2

Scousburgh.... 285 M5
Scrabster...... 280 B2
Scrafield....... 134 C3
Scrainwood.... 188 C2
Scrane End 117 A6
Scraptoft 98 A3
Scratby........ 121 D7
Scrayingham... 149 A6
Scredington ... 116 A3
Scremby....... 135 C4
Scremerston.. 198 B4
Screveton..... 115 A5
Scrivelsby 134 C2
Scriven....... 148 B2
Scrooby....... 141 D4
Scropton 113 B5
Scrub Hill..... 134 D2
Scruton....... 157 B6
Sculcoates.... 150 D3
Sculthorpe.... 119 B5
Scunthorpe.... 141 B6
Scurlage...... 57 D4
Seaborough.... 14 A4
Seacombe..... 136 D2
Seacroft Lincs .. 135 C5
  W Yorks...... 148 D2
Seadyke 117 B6
Seafield S Ayrs.. 192 C3
  W Loth....... 208 D3
Seaford....... 22 C2
Seaforth...... 136 D2
Seagrave...... 115 D4
Seaham....... 168 A2
Seahouses 199 C6
Seal......... 36 A3
Sealand...... 126 C3
Seale........ 34 B1
Seamer N Yorks .. 160 C4
  N Yorks...... 168 D2
Sea Palling... 121 C6
Searby....... 142 C2
Seasalter..... 52 C2
Seascale..... 162 D3
Seathorne.... 135 C5
Seathwaite
  Cumb......153 A3
  Cumb......163 C5
Seatoller..... 163 C5
Seaton Corn... 6 B2
  Cumb......162 A3
  Devon....... 14 B2
  Durham..... 179 D5
  E Yorks.... 151 C4
  Northumb... 179 B5
  Rutland..... 99 B6
Seaton Burn... 179 B4
Seaton Carew.. 168 C3
Seaton Delaval. 179 B5
Seaton Ross... 149 C6
Seaton Sluice.. 179 B5
Seatown Aberds. 267 C6
  Dorset....... 14 B4
Seave Green... 159 A4
Seaview..... 19 B5
Seaville...... 175 C4
Seavington St
  Mary........ 28 D3
Seavington St
  Michael..... 28 D4
Sebergham... 164 A1
Seckington ... 97 A5
Second Coast.. 261 A6
Sedbergh 155 B5
Sedbury...... 62 D1
Sedbusk..... 156 B2
Sedgeberrow... 80 D3
Sedgebrook... 115 B6
Sedgefield.... 167 C6
Sedgeford.... 119 B4
Sedgehill 30 C2
Sedgley...... 96 B2
Sedgwick.... 154 C4
Sedlescombe.. 23 A5
Sedlescombe
  Street...... 23 A5
Seend........ 44 C3
Seend Cleeve.. 44 C3
Seer Green.... 67 D4
Seething..... 104 B4
Sefton....... 136 C2
Seghill...... 179 B4

Seifton........ 94 C2
Seighford...... 112 C2
Seilebost..... 287 E5
Seion........ 123 D5
Seisdon...... 95 B6
Seisiadar 288 D6
Selattyn...... 110 B1
Selborne...... 33 B6
Selby........ 149 D5
Selham....... 34 D2
Selhurst...... 49 C6
Selkirk....... 186 A3
Sellack...... 62 A1
Sellafirth.....284 D7
Sellibister....282 C8
Sellindge 38 B2
Sellindge Lees.. 38 B3
Selling....... 52 D2
Sells Green.... 44 C3
Selly Oak..... 96 C3
Selmeston.... 22 B3
Selsdon...... 49 C6
Selsey....... 20 C1
Selsfield
  Common..... 35 C6
Selsted...... 39 A4
Selston...... 131 D4
Selworthy.... 27 A4
Semblister....285 H5
Semer....... 87 C5
Semington.... 44 C2
Semley...... 30 C2
Send........ 34 A3
Send Marsh... 34 A3
Senghenydd... 41 B6
Sennen...... 2 C1
Sennen Cove... 2 C1
Sennybridge Pont
Senni........ 59 C6
Serlby....... 131 A6
Sessay...... 158 D3
Setchey...... 118 D3
Setley....... 18 A2
Setter Shetland... 284 E6
  Shetland....285 H5
  Shetland.... 285 J7
Settiscarth....282 F4
Settle....... 146 A2
Settrington... 160 D2
Sevenhampton. 63 A6
Seven Kings... 50 A1
Sevenoaks.... 36 A3
Sevenoaks Weald 36 A3
Seven Sisters.. 59 E5
Severn Beach.. 43 A4
Severnhampton 64 D3
Severn Stoke... 79 C6
Sevington.... 38 A2
Sewards End... 86 D1
Sewardstone... 68 D3
Sewardstonebury 68 D3
Sewerby..... 151 A4
Seworgan..... 4 D2
Sewstern..... 116 C1
Sezincote..... 81 D4
Sgarasta Mhor . 287 E5
Sgiogarstaigh . 288 A6
Shabbington... 66 C1
Shackerstone... 97 A6
Shackleford.... 34 B2
Shade....... 138 A2
Shadforth.... 167 A6
Shadingfield... 105 C5
Shadoxhurst... 38 B1
Shadsworth... 137 A6
Shadwell Norf.. 103 C5
  W Yorks..... 148 D2
Shaftesbury... 30 C2
Shafton...... 140 B1
Shalbourne... 45 C7
Shalcombe.... 18 C2
Shalden..... 33 A5
Shaldon..... 13 C4
Shalfleet..... 18 C3
Shalford Essex.. 42 B3
  Sur........ 34 B3
Shalford Green.. 69 A7
Shallowford.... 26 A2
Shalmsford
  Street...... 52 D2
Shalstone..... 82 D3
Shamley Green.. 34 B3

Shandon......215 D5
Shandwick....265 C4
Shangton 99 B4
Shankhouse.... 179 B4
Shanklin...... 19 C4
Shanquhar.... 255 C6
Shanzie...... 231 C6
Shap......... 164 D3
Shapwick Dorset.. 16 A3
  Som........ 28 B4
Shardlow..... 114 B2
Shareshill..... 96 A2
Sharlston..... 140 B1
Sharlston
  Common.... 140 B1
Sharnbrook.... 84 B1
Sharnford.... 98 B1
Sharoe Green.. 145 D5
Sharow...... 158 D2
Sharpenhoe.... 84 D2
Sharperton ... 188 C2
Sharpness.... 62 C2
Sharp Street... 121 C5
Sharpthorne... 35 C6
Sharrington... 120 B2
Shatterford.... 95 C5
Shaugh Prior... 7 A4
Shavington... 128 D2
Shaw Gtr Man.. 138 C2
  W Berks..... 46 C2
  Wilts....... 44 C2
Shawbury.... 111 C4
Shawdon Hall .. 188 B3
Shawell...... 98 C2
Shawford..... 32 C3
Shawforth.... 138 A1
Shaw Green... 136 B4
Shawhead.... 173 A6
Shawhill..... 175 B5
Shaw Mills.... 147 A6
Shawton..... 194 B1
Shawtonhill... 194 B1
Shear Cross.... 30 A2
Shearington... 174 B3
Shearsby..... 98 B3
Shebbear..... 11 A5
Shebdon..... 111 C6
Shebster..... 279 B6
Sheddens.... 205 C5
Shedfield.... 33 D4
Sheen...... 129 C6
Sheepscar.... 148 D2
Sheepscombe... 63 B4
Sheepstor.... 7 A4
Sheepwash... 11 A5
Sheepway.... 42 B3
Sheepy Magna.. 97 A6
Sheepy Parva.. 97 A6
Sheering..... 69 B5
Sheerness.... 51 B6
Sheet....... 33 C6
Sheffield.... 130 A3
Sheffield Bottom 47 C4
Sheffield Green. 36 D2
Shefford..... 84 D3
Shefford
  Woodlands.. 46 B1
Sheigra...... 276 B2
Sheinton..... 95 A4
Shelderton.... 94 D2
Sheldon Derbys. 129 C6
  Devon...... 13 A6
  W Mid...... 97 C4
Sheldwich.... 52 D2
Shelf....... 139 A4
Shelfanger.... 104 C2
Shelfield Warks.. 80 A4
  W Mid...... 96 A3
Shelford..... 115 A4
Shellacres.... 198 B2
Shelley Essex.. 69 C5
  Suff........ 87 D6
  W Yorks..... 139 B5
Shellingford... 64 D4
Shellow Bowells. 69 C6
Shelsley
  Beauchamp.. 79 A5
Shelsley Walsh.. 79 A5
Shelthorpe.... 114 D3
Shelton Bedford.. 84 A2
  Norf....... 104 B3
  Notts...... 115 A5

Shelton continued
  Shrops.....110 D3
Shelton Green.. 104 B3
Shelve....... 94 B1
Shelwick..... 78 C3
Shenfield.... 69 D6
Shenington... 81 C6
Shenley..... 68 C1
Shenley Brook
  End......... 83 D5
Shenleybury... 68 C1
Shenley Church
  End......... 83 D5
Shenmore.... 78 D1
Shennanton... 171 A5
Shenstone Staffs. 96 A4
  Worcs...... 95 D6
Shenton..... 97 A6
Shenval Highld.. 251 D6
  Moray...... 254 D3
Shepeau Stow.. 117 D6
Shephall..... 68 A2
Shepherd's
  Green...... 47 A5
Shepherd's Port 118 B3
Shepherdswell.. 39 A4
Shepley..... 139 C4
Shepperdine... 62 D2
Shepperton... 48 C3
Shepreth..... 85 C5
Shepshed.... 114 D2
Shepton
  Beauchamp... 28 D4
Shepton Mallet.. 29 A6
Shepton
  Montague... 29 B6
Shepway..... 37 A5
Sheraton..... 168 B2
Sherborne Dorset 29 D6
  Glos...... 64 B2
Sherborne St
  John....... 47 D4
Sherbourne... 81 A5
Sherburn
  Durham.... 167 A6
  N Yorks.... 160 D3
Sherburn in
  Elmet...... 148 D3
Shere....... 34 B3
Shereford.... 119 C5
Sherfield English 32 C1
Sherfield on
  Loddon..... 47 D4
Sherford..... 8 C1
Sheriffhales... 111 D6
Sheriff Hutton.. 149 A5
Sheringham... 120 A3
Sherington... 83 C5
Shernal Green.. 80 A2
Shernborne... 119 B4
Sherrington... 30 B3
Sherston..... 44 A2
Sherwood Green. 25 C6
Shettleston... 205 B6
Shevington... 136 C4
Shevington
  Moor...... 136 B4
Shevington Vale 136 C4
Sheviock..... 6 B2
Shide....... 18 C3
Shiel Bridge... 238 A3
Shieldaig Highld.. 249 A5
  Highld...... 261 C5
Shieldhill
  Dumfries....184 D3
  Falk....... 208 C1
  S Lanark.... 195 B5
Shielfoot..... 235 D5
Shielhill Angus.. 232 C2
  Involyd..... 204 A2
Shifford..... 65 C4
Shifnal...... 95 A5
Shilbottle.... 189 C4
Shildon..... 167 C5
Shillingford Devon 27 C4
  Oxon...... 65 D6
Shillingford St
  George..... 13 C4
Shillingstone... 30 D2
Shillington... 84 D3
Shillmoor.... 188 C1

Shilton Oxon..... 64 C3
  Warks....... 97 C7
Shilvington... 178 A3
Shimpling Norf.. 104 C2
  Suff........ 87 B4
Shimpling Street. 87 B4
Shincliffe.... 167 A5
Shiney Row... 179 D5
Shinfield.... 47 C5
Shingham.... 102 A3
Shingle Street.. 89 C4
Shinner's Bridge. 8 A1
Shinness.....272 C3
Shipbourne... 36 A3
Shipdham.... 103 A5
Shipham..... 42 D3
Shiphay..... 8 A2
Shiplake..... 47 B5
Shipley Derbys. 114 A2
  Northumb... 189 B4
  Shrops..... 95 B6
  W Sus...... 35 D4
  W Yorks.... 147 D5
Shipley Shiels.. 187 D6
Shipmeadow.. 105 C4
Shippea Hill
  Sta........ 102 C2
Shippon..... 65 D5
Shipston-on-
  Stour...... 81 C5
Shipton Glos.. 63 B6
  N Yorks.... 149 B4
  Shrops..... 94 B3
Shipton Bellinger 31 A6
Shipton Gorge.. 15 B4
Shipton Green... 19 A7
Shipton Moyne.. 44 A2
Shipton on
  Cherwell.... 65 B5
Shipton Solers.. 63 B6
Shiptonthorpe . 150 C1
Shipton-under-
  Wychwood.. 64 B3
Shirburn..... 66 D1
Shirdley Hill... 136 B2
Shirebrook.... 131 C5
Shiregreen... 139 D6
Shirehampton.. 43 B4
Shiremoor.... 179 B5
Shirenewton... 61 D6
Shireoaks.... 131 A5
Shirkoak..... 38 B1
Shirland.... 130 D3
Shirley Derbys. 113 A6
  London..... 49 C6
  Soton...... 32 D3
  W Mid...... 96 D4
Shirl Heath... 78 B2
Shirrell Heath.. 33 D4
Shirwell..... 25 B6
Shirwell Cross.. 25 B6
Shiskine.... 191 C5
Shobdon.... 78 A2
Shobnall.... 113 C6
Shobrooke... 12 A3
Shoby...... 115 D4
Shocklach.... 110 A3
Shoeburyness.. 51 A6
Sholden.... 53 D5
Sholing..... 32 D3
Shoot Hill... 110 D3
Shop Corn... 9 D4
  Corn...... 24 D3
Shop Corner.. 88 D3
Shoreditch... 49 A6
Shoreham.... 50 C2
Shoreham-By-
  Sea........ 21 B5
Shore Mill... 264 D3
Shoresdean.. 198 B3
Shoreswood.. 198 B3
Shoreton.... 264 D2
Shorncote... 63 D6
Shorne..... 50 B3
Shortacombe.. 11 C6
Shortgate.... 22 A2
Short Heath... 96 A2
Shortlanesend. 4 C3
Shortlees.... 193 B4
Shortstown... 84 C2
Shorwell.... 18 C3
Shoscombe... 43 D6

Shotatton.... 110 C2
Shotesham... 104 B3
Shotgate..... 70 D1
Shotley..... 88 D3
Shotley Bridge. 178 D2
Shotleyfield... 178 D2
Shotley Gate.. 88 D3
Shottenden... 52 D2
Shottermill... 34 C1
Shottery..... 81 B4
Shotteswell... 81 C7
Shottisham... 88 C4
Shottle..... 113 A7
Shottlegate... 113 A7
Shotton Durham.. 168 B2
  Flint....... 126 C3
  Northumb... 198 C2
Shotton Colliery 167 A6
Shotts...... 207 D6
Shotwick.... 126 B3
Shouldham... 102 A2
Shouldham
  Thorpe..... 102 A2
Shoulton.... 79 B6
Shover's Green.. 37 C4
Shrawardine... 110 D3
Shrawley.... 79 A6
Shrewley
  Common... 81 A5
Shrewsbury... 110 D3
Shrewton.... 31 A4
Shripney.... 20 B2
Shrivenham... 45 A6
Shropham... 103 B5
Shrub End... 70 A3
Shucknall.... 78 C3
Shudy Camps.. 86 C2
Shulishadermor 259 D4
Shurdington... 63 B5
Shurlock Row... 47 B6
Shurrery.....279 C6
Shurrery Lodge.279 C6
Shurton..... 28 A2
Shustoke.... 97 B5
Shute Devon... 12 A3
  Devon...... 14 B2
Shutford.... 81 C6
Shuthonger... 80 D1
Shutlanger... 83 B4
Shuttington... 97 A5
Shuttlewood... 131 B4
Siabost bho
  Dheas.....288 C3
Siabost bho
  Thuath.....288 C3
Siadar......288 B4
Siadar Iarach.288 B4
Siadar Uarach.288 B4
Sibbaldbie...185 D4
Sibbertoft.... 98 C3
Sibdon Carwood .94 C2
Sibford Ferris.. 81 D6
Sibford Gower... 81 D6
Sible Hedingham 86 D3
Sibsey...... 134 D3
Sibson Cambs.. 100 B2
  Leics...... 97 A6
Sibthorpe.... 115 A5
Sibton...... 89 A4
Sibton Green.. 105 D4
Sicklesmere.. 87 A4
Sicklinghall.. 148 C2
Sid........ 13 C6
Sidbury Devon.. 13 B6
  Shrops..... 95 C4
Sidcot...... 42 D3
Sidcup...... 50 B1
Siddick..... 162 A3
Siddington
  Ches E..... 128 B3
  Glos....... 63 D6
Sidemoor.... 96 D2
Sidestrand.. 121 B4
Sidford..... 13 B6
Sidlesham... 20 C1
Sidley...... 23 B5
Sidlow...... 35 B5
Sidmouth... 13 C6
Sigford..... 12 D2

Sigglesthorne 151 C4
Sighthill 209 C4
Sigingstone 41 D4
Signet 64 B3
Silchester. 47 C4
Sildinis 288 F3
Sileby 114 D3
Silecroft 153 B2
Silfield 104 B2
Silian 75 C4
Silkstone 139 C5
Silkstone
 Common 139 C5
Silk Willoughby . 116 A3
Silloth 174 C4
Sills 188 C1
Sillyearn 267 D6
Siloh 59 B4
Silpho 160 B3
Silsden 147 C4
Silsoe 84 D2
Silverburn 209 D5
Silverdale Lancs. . 154 D3
 Staffs 112 A2
Silver End. 70 B2
Silvergate 120 C3
Silverhill 23 A5
Silverley's
 Green 104 D3
Silverstone 82 C3
Silverton. 13 A4
Silvington. 95 D4
Silwick 285 J4
Simmondley 138 D3
Simonburn. 177 B6
Simonsbath 26 B2
Simonstone 146 D1
Simprim 198 B2
Simpson 83 D5
Simpson Cross 55 C4
Sinclair's Hill 198 A2
Sinclairston 182 A2
Sinderby 158 C2
Sinderhope 177 D6
Sindlesham 47 C5
Singdean 187 C4
Singleborough 83 D4
Singleton Lancs. . . 144 D3
 W Sus. 20 A1
Singlewell 50 B3
Sinkhurst Green . . 37 B6
Sinnahard 244 A1
Sinnington. 159 C6
Sinton Green 79 A6
Sipson 48 B3
Sirhowy 60 B3
Sisland 104 B4
Sissinghurst 37 C5
Sisterpath 197 B6
Siston 43 B5
Sithney 3 C4
Sittingbourne 51 C5
Six Ashes 95 C5
Sixhills 133 A6
Six Hills 115 C4
Six Mile Bottom . 86 B1
Sixpenny
 Handley 30 D3
Sizewell 89 A5
Skail 278 D3
Skaill Orkney. 282 D5
 Orkney 282 F3
 Orkney 283 G6
Skares. 182 A3
Skateraw 211 C4
Skaw 284 G7
Skeabost 259 D4
Skeabrae 282 E3
Skeeby 157 A6
Skeffington 99 A4
Skeffling 143 B5
Skegby 131 C4
Skegness 135 C5
Skelberry 285 M5
Skelbo 264 A3
Skelbrooke 140 B3
Skeldyke 117 B6
Skellingthorpe . . 133 B4
Skellister 285 H6

Skellow 140 B3
Skelmanthorpe. . 139 B5
Skelmersdale 136 C3
Skelmonae. 256 C3
Skelmorlie. 204 B1
Skelmuir. 257 B4
Skelpick 278 C3
Skelton Cumb. . . . 164 B2
 E Yorks. 141 A5
 N Yorks. 157 A4
 Redcar 169 D4
 York 149 B4
Skelton-on-Ure 148 A2
Skelwick. 282 C5
Skelwith Bridge 154 A2
Skendleby 135 C4
Skene Ho. 245 B4
Skenfrith 61 A6
Skerne 150 B3
Skeroblingarry . . 190 C3
Skerray 278 B2
Skerton 145 A4
Sketchley 98 B1
Sketty 57 C6
Skewen 40 B2
Skewsby 159 D5
Skeyton 120 C4
Skiag Bridge 271 B5
Skibo Castle 264 B3
Skidbrooke 143 D6
Skidbrooke North
 End 143 D6
Skidby. 150 D3
Skilgate 27 C4
Skillington. 116 C1
Skinburness 174 C4
Skinflats 208 B2
Skinidin 258 D2
Skinnet 277 B6
Skinningrove. . . . 169 C5
Skipness. 202 C3
Skippool 144 C3
Skipsea. 151 B4
Skipsea Brough . 151 B4
Skipton 146 B3
Skipton-on-
 Swale 158 D2
Skipwith 149 D5
Skirbeck 117 A6
Skirbeck
 Quarter 117 A6
Skirlaugh 151 D4
Skirling 195 C5
Skirmett 47 A5
Skirpenbeck 149 B6
Skirwith 165 B4
Skirza 281 B5
Skulamus 247 B5
Skullomie. 277 B7
Skyborry Green . 93 D6
Skye of Curr 253 D5
Skyreholme 147 A4
Slackhall 129 A5
Slackhead 267 C5
Slad 63 C4
Slade Devon 25 A6
 Pembs 55 C5
Slade Green. 50 B2
Slaggyford 177 D4
Slaidburn 145 B7
Slaithwaite 138 B3
Slaley 178 D1
Slamannan. 207 C4
Slapton Bucks. . . . 67 A4
 Devon. 8 C2
 Northants. 82 C3
Slatepit Dale 130 C3
Slattocks 138 C1
Slaugham 35 D5
Slaughterford . . . 44 B2
Slawston 99 B4
Sleaford Hants. . . 33 B7
 Lincs. 116 A3
Sleagill 164 D3
Sleapford 111 D5
Sledge Green 79 D6
Sledmere 150 A2
Sleightholme . . . 166 D2
Sleights 160 A2
Slepe 16 B3
Slickly 281 B4
Sliddery 191 C5

Sligachan Hotel . 246 B3
Slimbridge. 62 C3
Slindon Staffs. . . . 112 B2
 W Sus. 20 B2
Slinfold. 35 C4
Sling 123 D6
Slingsby 159 D5
Slioch 255 C6
Slip End C Beds . . 67 B5
 Herts 85 D4
Slipton 99 D6
Slitting Mill 112 D4
Slochd. 253 D4
Slockavullin. . . . 213 C6
Sloley 121 C4
Slochty. 135 B4
Slough 48 B2
Slough Green 35 D5
Sluggan 253 D4
Slumbay 249 C5
Slyfield 34 A2
Slyne 145 A4
Smailholm 197 C5
Smallbridge 138 B2
Smallburgh 121 C5
Smallburn
 Aberds 257 B5
 E Ayrs. 194 D1
Small Dole 21 A5
Smalley. 114 A2
Smallfield 35 B6
Small Hythe 37 C6
Smallridge. 14 A3
Smannell 32 A2
Smardale 155 A6
Smarden. 37 B6
Smarden Bell 37 B6
Smeatharpe. 28 D1
Smeeth 38 B2
Smeeton
 Westerby. 98 B3
Smercleit 286 E3
Smerral 275 A5
Smethwick. 96 C3
Smirisary 235 C5
Smisby 114 D1
Smithfield 176 C2
Smith Green 145 B4
Smithincott. 27 D5
Smith's Green. . . . 69 A5
Smithstown 261 C4
Smithton 252 B3
Smithy Green . . . 128 B2
Smockington. . . . 98 C1
Smoogro 283 G4
Smythe's Green . . 70 B3
Snaigow House .231 D4
Snailbeach. 94 A1
Snailwell 86 A2
Snainton. 160 C3
Snaith 140 A4
Snape N Yorks . . . 157 C6
 Suff 89 B4
Snape Green 136 B2
Snarestone 97 A6
Snarford 133 A5
Snargate 38 C1
Snave 38 C2
Snead 93 B7
Sneath
 Common 104 C2
Sneaton 160 A2
Sneatonthorpe . . 160 A3
Snelland 133 A5
Snelston 113 A5
Snettisham 118 B3
Sniseabhal 286 C3
Snitter 188 C3
Snitterby 142 D1
Snitterfield 81 B5
Snitton 94 D3
Snodhill 77 C7
Snodland 51 C3
Snowden Hill. . . . 139 C5
Snowdown. 53 D4
Snowshill 80 D3
Snydale 140 B2
Soar Anglesey . . . 122 C3
 Carms 58 C3
 Devon. 7 D6
Soar-y-Mynydd . 76 B1
Soberton 33 D5

Soberton Heath . . 33 D5
Sockbridge 164 C3
Sockburn 158 A2
Soham. 102 D1
Soham Cotes. . . . 102 D1
Solas 287 G3
Soldon Cross. 24 D4
Soldridge. 33 B5
Sole Street Kent . . 38 A2
 Kent 50 C3
Solihull 97 D4
Sollers Dilwyn. . . 78 B2
Sollers Hope 79 D4
Sollom 136 B3
Solva 54 B3
Somerby Leics . . 115 D5
 Lincs. 142 C2
Somercotes. 131 D4
Somerford 17 B5
Somerford
 Keynes. 63 D6
Somerley 19 B7
Somerleyton . . . 105 B5
Somersal
 Herbert 113 B5
Somersby. 134 B3
Somersham
 Cambs 101 D5
 Suff 88 C1
Somerton Oxon . . 65 A5
 Som 29 C4
Sompting 21 B4
Sonning 47 B5
Sonning
 Common 47 A5
Sonning Eye 47 B5
Sontley 110 A2
Sopley 17 B5
Sopwell 67 C6
Sopworth 44 A2
Sorbie 171 C6
Sordale 280 B3
Sorisdale 223 A5
Sorn. 193 C5
Sornhill. 193 B5
Sortat 281 B4
Sotby. 134 B2
Sots Hole 133 C6
Sotterley 105 C5
Soudley 111 C6
Soughton 126 C2
Soulbury. 66 A3
Soulby 165 D5
Souldern 82 D2
Souldrop 84 A1
Sound Ches E . . . 111 A5
 Shetland. 285 H5
 Shetland. 285 J6
Sound Heath . . . 111 A5
Soundwell 43 B5
Sourhope 188 A1
Sourin 282 D5
Sourton 11 B6
Soutergate 153 B3
South Acre. 119 D5
Southall 48 A4
South Allington . . 8 D1
South Alloa 208 A1
Southam Glos. . . . 63 A5
 Warks. 81 A7
South
 Ambersham 34 D2
Southampton 32 D3
South Anston . . . 131 A5
South Ascot 48 C2
South
 Ballachulish . . 237 D4
South Balloch . . 181 B5
South Bank 168 C3
South Barrow . . . 29 C6
South Beach 106 C3
South Benfleet . . 51 A4
South Bersted . . . 20 B2
Southborough . . . 36 B3
Southbourne
 Bmouth. 17 B5
 W Sus. 19 A6
South Brent 7 A5
South Brewham . 29 B7
South
 Broomhill 189 D5
Southburgh 103 A5

South
 Burlingham. . . 105 A4
Southburn 150 B2
South Cadbury . . 29 C6
South Cairn 170 A1
South Carlton . . 133 B4
South Cave 150 D2
South Cerney . . . 63 D6
South Chard 14 A3
South Charlton . 189 A4
South Cheriton. . 29 C6
Southchurch 51 A6
South Cliffe 150 D1
South Clifton. . . 132 B3
South
 Cockerington . . 134 A3
South Cornelly . . 40 C3
Southcott. 45 D5
Southcourt 66 B3
South Cove 105 C5
South Creagan . . 227 B4
South Creake . . . 119 B5
South Croxton . . 115 D4
South Croydon . . 49 C6
South Dalton . . . 150 C2
South Darenth . . 50 C2
Southdean 187 C5
South Duffield . . 149 D5
Southease 22 B2
South Elkington 134 A2
South Elmsall . . 140 B2
Southend Argyll. 190 E2
 W Berks. 46 B3
 Wilts. 45 B5
South End Bucks . 66 A3
 Cumb 153 D3
 N Lincs. 142 A3
Southend-on-
 Sea 51 A5
Southernden 37 B6
Southerndown . . 40 D3
Southerness 174 C2
South Erradale . 261 C4
Southery. 102 B2
South
 Fambridge 70 D2
South Fawley . . . 46 A1
South Ferriby . . 142 A1
Southfield 179 B4
Southfleet 50 B3
South Garth . . . 284 D7
South Garvan . . 236 B3
Southgate Ceredig 75 A4
 London 68 D2
 Norf 120 C3
 Swansea 57 D5
South Glendale . 286 E3
South Godstone . 35 B6
South Gorley . . . 31 D5
South Green
 Essex 69 D6
 Kent 51 C5
South-haa 284 E5
South Ham. 47 D4
South Hanningfield . . 70 D1
South Harting . . 33 D6
South Hatfield . . 68 C2
South Hayling . . 19 B6
South Hazelrigg 199 C4
South Heath . . . 67 C4
South Heighton . 22 B2
South Hetton . . 167 A6
South Hiendley . 140 B1
South Hill 10 D4
South Hinksey . . 65 C6
South Hole 24 C3
South Holme . . . 159 D5
South Holmwood 35 B4
South Hornchurch . . 50 A2
South Hykeham . 133 C4
South Hylton . . 179 D5
Southill 84 C3
South Kelsey . . . 142 D2
South Kessock . 252 B2
South Killingholme . . 142 B3
South Kilvington 158 C3
South Kilworth . 98 C3
South Kirkby . . . 140 B2

South Kirkton . . . 245 B4
South Kiscadale . 191 C6
South Kyme. 117 A4
South Lancing. . . . 21 B4
Southleigh 14 B2
South Leigh. 65 C4
South Leverton . 132 A2
South Littleton . . 80 C3
South Lopham . . 103 C6
South Luffenham 99 A6
South Malling . . . 22 A2
South Marston . . 45 A5
South
 Middleton. . . . 188 A2
South Milford . . 148 D3
South Millbrex . 256 B3
South Milton . . . 7 C6
South Mimms . . 68 C2
Southminster . . . 70 D3
South Molton . . 26 C2
Southmoor 65 D4
South Moreton . 46 A3
South Mundham . 20 B1
South Muskham 132 D2
South Newbald . 150 D2
South Newington 81 D7
South Newton . . 31 B4
South
 Normanton . . 131 D4
South Norwood . 49 C6
South Nutfield . . 35 B6
South Ockendon . 50 A2
Southoe 84 A3
Southolt 88 A2
South Ormsby . . 134 B3
Southorpe 100 A2
South
 Otterington . . . 158 C2
South Owersby . 142 D2
Southowram . . . 139 A4
South Oxhey . . . 67 D6
South Perrott . . 15 A4
South Petherton . 28 D4
South Petherwin . 10 C4
South
 Pickenham . . . 103 A4
South Pool 7 C6
Southport. 136 B2
South Port 227 D5
Southpunds . . . 285 L6
South Radworthy . 26 B2
South Rauceby . 116 A3
South Raynham 119 C5
Southrepps . . . 121 B4
South Reston . . 135 A4
Southrey. 133 C6
Southrop 64 C2
Southrope 33 A5
South Runcton . 102 A2
South Scarle . . . 132 C3
Southsea 19 B5
South Shian. . . . 226 B4
South Shields . . 179 C5
South Shore . . . 144 D3
South
 Somercotes . . 143 D6
South Stainley . 148 A2
South
 Stainmore. . . 165 D6
South Stifford . . 50 B3
Southstoke 43 C6
South Stoke Oxon 46 A3
 W Sus. 20 B3
South Street
 E Sus. 22 A1
 Kent 52 C3
 Kent 52 D2
 London 36 A2
South Tawton . . 12 B1
South Thoresby 135 B4
South Tidworth . 31 A6
Southtown Norf. 105 A6
 Orkney 283 H5
South Town . . . 33 B5
South View 47 D4
Southwaite 164 A2
South Walsham .121 D5
Southwark. 49 B6
South
 Warnborough. . 33 A6
Southwater 35 D4

Southwater
  Street........35 D4
Southway........29 A5
South Weald.....69 D5
Southwell Dorset..15 D6
  Notts........132 D1
South Weston....66 D2
South Wheatley
  Corn.........10 B3
  Notts........132 A2
South
  Whiteness....285 J5
Southwick Hants..19 A5
  Northants....100 B2
  T&W.........179 D5
  Wilts.........44 D2
  W Sus........21 B5
South Widcombe 43 D4
South Wigston..98 B2
South
  Willingham...134 A1
South Wingfield 130 D3
South Witham..116 D2
Southwold....105 D6
South Wonston..32 B3
Southwood Norf.105 A4
  Som..........29 B5
South Woodham
  Ferrers.......70 D2
South Wootton..118 C3
South Wraxall....44 C2
South Zeal......12 B1
Soval Lodge....288 E4
Sowber Gate....158 C2
Sowerby N Yorks.158 C3
  W Yorks......138 A3
Sowerby Bridge 138 A3
Sowerby Row...164 B1
Sowood.......138 B3
Sowton.........13 B4
Soyal.........264 A1
Spacey Houses..148 B2
Spa Common...121 B4
Spadeadam
  Farm........176 B3
Spalding......117 C5
Spaldington....149 D6
Spaldwick....100 D3
Spalford......132 C3
Spanby.......116 B3
Sparham......120 D2
Spark Bridge..154 C2
Sparkford......29 C6
Sparkhill.......96 C3
Sparkwell.......7 B4
Sparrow Green..119 D6
Sparrowpit....129 A5
Sparsholt Hants..32 B3
  Oxon.........46 A1
Spartylea....165 A6
Spaunton....159 C6
Spaxton........28 B2
Spean Bridge..239 D6
Spear Hill......21 A4
Speen Bucks....66 D3
  W Berks......46 C2
Speeton......161 D5
Speke........127 A4
Speldhurst.....36 B3
Spellbrook......69 B4
Spelsbury......64 A4
Spelter.........40 B3
Spencers Wood...47 C5
Spennithorne..157 C5
Spennymoor...167 B5
Spetchley......50 D4
Spetisbury......16 A3
Spexhall.....105 C4
Spey Bay......267 C4
Speybridge...253 D6
Speyview....254 B3
Spilsby.......135 C4
Spindlestone...199 C5
Spinkhill.....131 B4
Spinningdale...64 A4
Spirthill.......44 B3
Spital Hill....140 D4
Spital in the
  Street.......133 A4
Spithurst......22 A2
Spittal Dumfries.171 B5
  E Loth.......210 C1

Spittal continued
  Highld.......280 C3
  Northumb....198 A4
  Pembs........55 B5
  Stirling......206 B3
Spittalfield....231 D5
Spittal of
  Glenmuick....243 D6
Spittal of
  Glenshee....231 A5
Spixworth....120 D4
Splayne's Green..36 D2
Spofforth....148 B2
Spondon......114 B2
Spon End......97 D6
Spon Green...126 C2
Spooner Row...104 B1
Sporle.......119 D5
Spott........210 C3
Spratton.......99 D4
Spreakley......34 B1
Spreyton......12 B1
Spridlington...133 A5
Springburn....205 B6
Springfield
  Dumfries....175 B6
  Essex.........69 C7
  Fife.........220 C3
  Moray.......253 A6
  W Mid........96 C3
Springhill......96 A2
Springholm...173 B6
Springkell...175 A5
Springside....192 B3
Springthorpe..132 A3
Spring Vale...139 C5
Spring Valley..152 D3
Springwell....179 D4
Sproatley....151 D4
Sproston Green 128 C2
Sprotbrough...140 C3
Sproughton....88 C2
Sprouston....197 C6
Sprowston....120 D4
Sproxton Leics..115 C6
  N Yorks......159 C5
Spurstow.....127 D5
Spynie........266 C3
Squires Gate..144 D3
Srannda......287 F5
Sronphadruig
  Lodge......229 A6
St. Abb's Haven .211 D6
Stableford Shrops..95 B5
  Staffs.......112 B2
Stacey Bank...139 D5
Stackhouse....146 A2
Stackpole......55 E5
Staddiscombe...7 B4
Staddlethorpe..141 A6
Stadhampton..65 D7
Stadhlaigearraidh
  ....286 C3
Staffield.....164 A3
Staffin......259 B4
Stafford......112 C3
Stagsden......84 C1
Stainburn Cumb.162 B3
  N Yorks......147 C6
Stainby......116 C2
Staincross...139 B6
Staindrop....166 C4
Staines-upon-
  Thames......48 B3
Stainfield Lincs..116 C3
  Lincs........133 B6
Stainforth
  N Yorks.....146 A2
  S Yorks......140 B4
Staining.....144 D3
Stainland....138 B3
Stainsacre...160 A3
Stainsby.....131 C4
Stainton Cumb..154 C4
  Cumb........164 C2
  Durham......166 D3
  Mbro........168 D2
  N Yorks......157 B5
  S Yorks......140 D3
Stainton by
  Langworth...133 B5
Staintondale..160 B3

Stainton le Vale .142 D3
Stainton with
  Adgarley.....153 C3
Stair Cumb....163 B5
  E Ayrs.......193 C4
Stairhaven...171 B4
Staithes.....169 D5
Stakeford....179 A4
Stake Pool...144 C4
Stalbridge.....30 D1
Stalbridge
  Weston........29 D7
Stalham......121 C5
Stalham Green..121 C5
Stalisfield Green .51 D6
Stallingborough 142 B3
Stalling Busk..156 C3
Stalmine.....144 C3
Stalybridge...138 D2
Stambourne...86 D3
Stambourne
  Green........86 D3
Stamford......100 A2
Stamford Bridge
  Ches W......127 C4
  E Yorks......149 B6
Stamfordham..178 B2
Stanah.......163 C6
Stanborough..68 B2
Stanbridge C Beds 67 A4
  Dorset........17 A4
Stanbrook......79 C6
Stanbury.....147 D5
Stand Gtr Man...137 C6
  N Lanark.....207 D5
Standburn....208 C2
Standeford.....96 A2
Standen........37 B6
Standford......33 B7
Standingstone .162 A3
Standish.....137 B4
Standlake......65 C4
Standon Hants..32 C3
  Herts.........68 A3
  Staffs......112 B2
Stane.......194 A3
Stanfield.....119 C6
Stanford C Beds..84 C3
  Kent..........38 B3
Stanford Bishop..79 B4
Stanford Bridge..79 A5
Stanford Dingley .46 B3
Stanford in the
  Vale.........64 D4
Stanford-le-
  Hope.........50 A3
Stanford on Avon 98 D2
Stanford on
  Soar........114 C3
Stanford on
  Teme........79 A5
Stanford Rivers .69 C5
Stanfree.....131 B4
Stanghow....169 D4
Stanground..100 B4
Stanhoe.....119 B5
Stanhope
  Borders.....195 D6
  Durham......166 B2
Stanion.......99 C6
Stanley Derbys..114 A2
  Durham......178 D3
  Lancs.......136 C3
  Perth.......219 A6
  Staffs......129 D4
  W Yorks.....139 A6
Stanley
  Common.....114 A2
Stanley Gate..136 C3
Stanley Hill....79 C4
Stanlow.....127 B4
Stanmer......21 B6
Stanmore Hants..32 C3
  London.......67 D6
  W Berks.......46 B2
Stannergate..220 A4
Stanningley..147 D6
Stannington
  Northumb....179 B4
  S Yorks......130 A3
Stansbatch....78 A1
Stansfield.....86 B3

Stanstead......87 C4
Stanstead
  Abbotts......68 B3
Stansted......50 C3
Stansted Airport..69 A5
Stansted
  Mountfitchet..69 A5
Stanton Glos....80 D3
  Mon..........61 A5
  Northumb....178 A3
  Staffs.......113 A5
  Suff.........103 D5
Stanton by
  Bridge......114 C1
Stanton-by-
  Dale........114 B2
Stanton Drew..43 C4
Stanton
  Fitzwarren....64 D2
Stanton Harcourt 65 C5
Stanton Hill...131 C4
Stanton in Peak .130 C2
Stanton Lacy...94 D2
Stanton Long...94 B3
Stanton-on-the-
  Wolds......115 B4
Stanton Prior...43 C5
Stanton St
  Bernard.......45 C4
Stanton St John ..65 C6
Stanton St
  Quintin.......44 B3
Stanton Street...87 A5
Stanton under
  Bardon......114 D2
Stanton upon Hine
  Heath.......111 C4
Stanton Wick...43 C5
Stanwardine in the
  Fields.......110 C3
Stanwardine in the
  Wood.......110 C3
Stanway Essex...70 A3
  Glos.........80 D3
Stanway Green .104 D3
Stanwell......48 B3
Stanwell Moor..48 B3
Stanwick....100 D1
Stanwick-St-
  John.......167 D4
Stanwix.....175 C7
Staoinebrig...286 C3
Stape.......159 B6
Stapehill......17 A4
Stapeley.....111 A5
Stapenhill....113 C6
Staple Kent....53 D4
  Som..........27 A6
Staple Cross....37 D5
Staplefield.....35 D5
Staple Fitzpaine .28 D2
Stapleford Cambs .85 B6
  Herts.........68 B3
  Leics........115 D6
  Lincs.......132 D3
  Notts.......114 B2
  Wilts........31 B4
Stapleford
  Abbotts......69 D5
Stapleford
  Tawney.......69 D5
Staplegrove...28 C2
Staplehay......28 C2
Staplehurst....37 B5
Staplers.......18 C4
Stapleton Bristol ..43 B5
  Cumb.......176 B3
  Hereford.....78 A1
  Leics.........98 B1
  N Yorks......167 D5
  Shrops.......94 A2
  Som..........29 C4
Stapley.......28 D1
Staploe.......84 A3
Staplow.......79 C4
Star Fife.....220 D3
  Pembs.......73 C5
  Som..........42 D3
Stara.......282 E3
Starbeck....148 B2
Starbotton..156 D3

Starcross.......13 C4
Stareton.......97 D6
Starkholmes...130 D3
Starlings Green ..85 D6
Starston......104 C3
Startforth....166 D3
Startley.......44 A3
Stathe.........28 C3
Stathern.....115 B5
Station Town...168 B2
Staughton Green 84 A3
Staughton
  Highway.......84 A3
Staunton Glos....62 A3
  Glos.........62 B1
Staunton in the
  Vale.......115 A6
Staunton on
  Arrow........78 A1
Staunton on Wye 78 C1
Staveley Cumb..154 B3
  Cumb.......154 C2
  Derbys......131 B4
  N Yorks......148 A2
Staverton Devon ..8 A1
  Glos.........63 A4
  Northants....82 A2
  Wilts.........44 C1
Staverton Bridge .63 A4
Stawell.......28 B3
Staxigoe.....281 C5
Staxton......160 D4
Staylittle......91 C6
Staynall.....144 C3
Staythorpe..132 D2
St. Boswells...197 C4
Stean.......157 D4
Stearsby.....159 D5
Steart........28 A2
Stebbing......69 A6
Stebbing Green ..69 A6
Stedham......34 D1
Steele Road...186 D4
Steen's Bridge ..78 B3
Steep.........33 C6
Steeple Dorset...16 C3
  Essex.........70 C3
Steeple Ashton..44 D3
Steeple Aston..65 A5
Steeple Barton..65 A5
Steeple
  Bumpstead....86 C2
Steeple Claydon..66 A1
Steeple Gidding 100 C3
Steeple Langford .31 B4
Steeple Morden..85 C4
Steep Marsh....33 C6
Steeton.....147 C4
Stein.........258 C2
Steinmanhill..256 B2
Stelling Minnis..38 A3
Stemster......280 B3
Stemster Ho....280 B3
Stenalees......5 B5
Stenhousemuir 207 B6
Stenigot.....134 A2
Stenness.....284 F4
Stenscholl...259 B4
Stenso.......282 E4
Stenson......114 C1
Stenton E Loth..210 C3
  Fife.........209 A5
Stenwith.....115 B6
Stepaside......56 B1
Stepping Hill..129 A4
Steppingley....84 D2
Stepps.......205 B6
Sterndale Moor .129 C6
Sternfield.....89 A4
Sterridge......25 A6
Stert.........44 D4
Stetchworth....86 B2
Stevenage....68 A2
Stevenston...204 D2
Steventon Hants..32 A4
  Oxon.........65 D5
Stevington....84 B1
Stewartby......84 C2
Stewarton Argyll .190 D2
  E Ayrs.......205 D4
Stewkley......66 A3
Stewton......134 A3

Steyne Cross....19 C5
Steyning.......21 A4
Steynton.......55 D5
Stibb.........24 D3
Stibbard.....120 C1
Stibb Cross....25 D5
Stibb Green....45 C6
Stibbington...100 B2
Stichill.....197 C6
Sticker........5 B4
Stickford....134 D3
Sticklepath....12 B1
Stickney.....134 D3
Stiffkey.....119 A6
Stifford's Bridge .79 C5
Stillingfleet...149 C4
Stillington
  N Yorks......149 A4
  Stockton.....167 C6
Stilton......100 C3
Stinchcombe....62 D3
Stinsford......15 B7
Stirchley......95 A5
Stirkoke Ho....281 C5
Stirling Aberds ..257 B6
  Stirling......207 A5
Stisted........70 A1
Stithians.......4 D2
Stittenham...264 C2
Stivichall......97 D6
Stixwould....134 C1
St. Margaret's
  Hope.......283 H5
Stoak........127 B4
Stobieside....193 B6
Stobo.......195 C6
Stoborough....16 C3
Stoborough
  Green........16 C3
Stobshiel....210 D1
Stobswood...189 D5
Stock.........69 D6
Stockbridge....32 B2
Stockbury.....51 C5
Stockcross....46 C2
Stockdalewath .164 A1
Stockerston....99 B5
Stock Green....80 B2
Stockheath....19 A6
Stockiemuir..206 B3
Stockingford....97 B6
Stocking Pelham 69 A4
Stockland....14 A2
Stockland Bristol 28 A2
Stockleigh
  English......12 A3
Stockleigh
  Pomeroy.....12 A3
Stockley......44 C4
Stocklinch....28 D3
Stockport....138 D1
Stocksbridge..139 D5
Stocksfield...178 C2
Stockton Hereford 78 A3
  Norf........105 B4
  Shrops.......93 A6
  Shrops.......95 B5
  Warks........82 A1
  Wilts.........30 B3
Stockton Heath .127 A6
Stockton-on-
  Tees.......168 D2
Stockton on
  Teme........79 A5
Stockton on the
  Forest......149 B5
Stock Wood....80 B3
Stodmarsh....53 C4
Stody.......120 B2
Stoer.......270 B3
Stoford Som....29 D5
  Wilts.........31 B4
Stogumber....27 B5
Stogursey......28 A2
Stoke Devon....24 C3
  Hants........19 A6
  Hants........46 D2
  Medway......51 B5
  Suff.........88 C2

Stoke Abbott......15 A4
Stoke Albany......99 C5
Stoke Ash......104 D2
Stoke Bardolph .115 A4
Stoke Bliss......79 A4
Stoke Bruerne ...83 C4
Stoke by Clare ..86 C3
Stoke-by-
Nayland........87 D5
Stoke Canon 13 B4
Stoke Charity 32 B3
Stoke Climsland..11 D4
Stoke D'Abernon 35 A4
Stoke Doyle.....100 C2
Stoke Dry........99 B5
Stoke Farthing ...31 C4
Stoke Ferry 102 B3
Stoke Fleming 8 C2
Stokeford........16 C2
Stoke Gabriel 8 B2
Stoke Gifford ...43 B5
Stoke Golding ...97 B6
Stoke Goldington 83 C5
Stoke Green 48 A2
Stokeham......132 B2
Stoke Hammond .66 A3
Stoke Heath.....111 C5
Stoke Holy
Cross........104 A3
Stokeinteignhead
............13 D4
Stoke Lacy......79 C4
Stoke Lyne......65 A6
Stoke Mandeville 66 B3
Stokenchurch ...66 D2
Stoke Newington 49 A6
Stokenham 8 C2
Stoke on Tern...111 C5
Stoke Orchard ..63 A5
Stoke Poges 48 A2
Stoke Prior
Hereford.......78 B3
Worcs.........80 A2
Stoke Rivers ...26 B1
Stoke Rochford .116 C2
Stoke Row......47 A4
Stoke St Gregory 28 C3
Stoke St Mary ...28 D2
Stoke St Michael .29 A6
Stoke St
Milborough.....94 C2
Stokesay.........94 C2
Stokesby.......121 D6
Stokesley......158 A4
Stoke sub
Hamdon........29 D4
Stoke Talmage ...66 D1
Stoke Trister 30 C1
Stoke Wake.....16 A1
Stolford........28 A2
Stondon Massey..69 C5
Stone Bucks 66 B2
Glos..........62 D2
Kent..........38 C1
Kent..........50 B2
Staffs........112 B3
S Yorks.......131 A5
Worcs.........95 D6
Stone Allerton ..42 D3
Ston Easton....43 D5
Stone Bridge
Corner.......101 A4
Stonebroom....131 D4
Stone Chair 139 A4
Stone Cross E Sus. 22 B4
Kent..........53 D5
Stone-edge
Batch........42 B3
Stoneferry......151 D4
Stonefield.....194 A1
Stonegate E Sus...37 D4
N Yorks......159 A6
Stonegrave....159 D6
Stonehaugh....177 B5
Stonehaven....245 D6
Stonehouse Glos..63 C4
Northumb......177 D4
S Lanark.....194 B2

Stone House 155 C6
Stoneleigh......97 D6
Stonely........84 A3
Stoner Hill......33 C6
Stonesby......115 C6
Stonesfield 65 B4
Stone's Green ...71 A5
Stone Street Kent .36 A3
Suff..........87 D5
Suff.........105 C4
Stonethwaite ...163 C5
Stoneybreck ...285 R4
Stoneyburn 208 D2
Stoney Cross 31 D6
Stoneygate
Aberds........257 C5
Leicester 98 A3
Stoneyhills......70 D3
Stoneykirk 170 B2
Stoney
Middleton....130 B2
Stoney Stanton...98 B1
Stoney Stoke....29 B7
Stoney Stratton ..29 B7
Stoney Stretton ..94 A1
Stoneywood
Aberdeen.....245 A5
Falk..........207 B5
Stonganess 284 C7
Stonham Aspal ..88 B2
Stonnall 96 A3
Stonor..........47 A5
Stonton Wyville ..99 B4
Stony Cross 79 C5
Stony Stratford...27 D4
Stoodleigh......27 D4
Stopes........130 A2
Stopham........20 A3
Stopsley........67 A6
Stores Corner ...89 C4
Storeton.......126 A3
Stornoway.....288 D5
Storridge.......79 C5
Storrington 20 A3
Storrs.........154 B2
Storth.........154 C3
Storwood......149 C6
Stotfield......266 B3
Stotfold........84 D4
Stottesdon 95 C4
Stoughton Leics...98 A3
Sur...........34 A2
W Sus..........33 D7
Stoul.........235 A6
Stoulton.......80 C2
Stourbridge....96 C2
Stourpaine......16 A2
Stourport on
Severn........95 D6
Stour Provost ...30 C1
Stour Row 30 C2
Stourton Staffs...95 C6
Warks........81 D5
Wilts.........30 B1
Stourton
Caundle........29 D7
Stove Orkney...282 D7
Shetland.....285 L6
Stoven.........105 C5
Stow Borders ..196 B3
Lincs........116 B3
Lincs........132 A3
Stow Bardolph .102 A2
Stow Bedon ...103 B5
Stowbridge 102 A2
Stow cum Quy...85 A7
Stowe.........93 D7
Stowe-by-
Chartley......112 C4
Stowe Green 62 C1
Stowell........29 C6
Stowford 11 C5
Stowlangtoft ...87 A5
Stow Longa ...100 D3
Stow Maries 70 D2
Stowmarket.....87 B6
Stow-on-the-
Wold........64 A2
Stowting.......38 A3
Stowupland.....87 B6
Straad.........203 B5

Strachan........244 C3
Stradbroke 104 D3
Stradishall......86 B3
Stradsett......102 A2
Stragglethorpe .133 D4
Straid........180 B3
Straith........183 D6
Straiton Edin ...209 D5
S Ayrs........181 A5
Straloch Aberds..256 D3
Perth.........230 B4
Stramshall 113 B4
Strang........152 D3
Stranraer......170 A2
Stratfield
Mortimer......47 C4
Stratfield Saye ...47 C4
Stratfield Turgis..47 C4
Stratford.......49 A6
Stratford St
Andrew........89 A4
Stratford St Mary 87 D6
Stratford Sub
Castle......31 B5
Stratford Tony ...31 C4
Stratford-upon-
Avon.........81 B4
Strath Highld...261 C4
Highld........281 C4
Strathan Highld .238 C3
Highld........270 B3
Highld........277 B6
Strathaven.....194 B2
Strathblane 205 A5
Strathcanaird ..271 D4
Strathcarron ...249 B6
Strathcoil.....225 C5
Strathdon......243 A6
Strathellie 269 C5
Strathkinness ..221 C4
Strathmashie
House.......240 C3
Strathmiglo 220 C2
Strathmore
Lodge........280 D3
Strathpeffer ...251 A6
Strathrannoch ..263 C5
Strathtay......230 C3
Strathvaich
Lodge.......263 C5
Strathwhillan ..191 B6
Strathy........279 B4
Strathyre......217 C5
Stratton Corn 10 A3
Dorset........15 B6
Glos..........63 C6
Stratton Audley ..65 A7
Stratton on the
Fosse........43 D5
Stratton St
Margaret......45 A5
Stratton St
Michael.....104 B3
Stratton
Strawless 120 C4
Stravithie.....221 C5
Streat.........21 A6
Streatham......49 B6
Streatley C Beds...67 A5
W Berks.......46 A3
Strensall.....149 A5
Stretcholt......28 A2
Strete..........8 C2
Stretford......137 D7
Strethall.......85 D6
Stretham......101 D7
Strettington 20 B1
Stretton Ches W..127 D4

Stretton continued
Derbys.......130 C3
Rutland.......116 D2
Staffs........112 D2
Staffs........113 C6
Warr..........127 A6
Stretton
Grandison 79 C4
Stretton-on-
Dunsmore 97 D7
Stretton-on-
Fosse........81 D5
Stretton Sugwas .78 C2
Stretton under
Fosse........98 C1
Stretton
Westwood.....94 B3
Strichen......269 D4
Strines.......129 A4
Stringston 28 A1
Strixton.......83 A6
Stroat..........62 D1
Stromeferry....249 C5
Stromemore ...249 C5
Stromness....283 G3
Stronaba......239 D6
Stronachlachar..216 C4
Stronchreggan ..237 B4
Stronchrubie...271 C5
Strone Argyll...215 D4
Highld.......239 D5
Highld.......252 D1
Invclyd......204 A2
Stronmilchan ..227 D6
Strontian......236 C2
Strood.......115 A4
Strood Green Sur .35 B5
W Sus.........34 D3
W Sus.........35 C4
Stroud Glos.....63 C4
Hants........33 C6
Stroud Green ...70 D2
Stroxton......116 B2
Struan Highld ..246 A2
Perth.........230 B2
Strubby.......135 A4
Strumpshaw ..104 A4
Strutherhill ...194 B2
Struy.........251 C5
Stryt-issa.....110 A1
Stuartfield 257 B4
Stubbington 19 A4
Stubbins......137 B6
Stubbs Cross ...38 B1
Stubbs Green ..105 B4
Stubb's Green .104 B3
Stubhampton ...30 D3
Stub Place 153 A1
Stubton......115 A6
Stuckgowan ...215 B6
Stuckton.......31 D5
Stud Grn........48 B1
Studham........67 B5
Studland.......17 C4
Studley Warks ...80 A3
Wilts.........44 B3
Studley Roger ..157 D6
Stuntney......102 D1
Sturbridge 112 B2
Sturmer........86 C2
Sturminster
Marshall.....16 A3
Sturminster
Newton.......30 D1
Sturry.........52 C3
Sturton.......142 C1
Sturton by Stow 132 A3
Sturton le
Steeple......132 A2
Stuston......104 D2
Stutton N Yorks .148 C3
Suff..........88 D2
Styal.........128 A3
Styrrup.......140 D4
Suainebost....288 A6
Suardail......288 D5
Succoth Aberds .255 C5
Argyll.......215 B5
Suckley........79 B5
Suckquoy.....283 J5
Sudborough 99 C6

Sudbourne......89 B5
Sudbrook Lincs .116 A2
Mon..........43 A4
Sudbrooke....133 B5
Sudbury Derbys .113 B5
London........49 A4
Suff..........87 C4
Suddie.......252 A2
Sudgrove.......63 C5
Suffield Norf...120 B4
N Yorks......160 B3
Sugnall.......112 B1
Sugwas Pool ...78 C2
Suladale......258 C3
Sulaisiadar...288 D6
Sulby.........152 B3
Sulgrave.......82 C2
Sulham........47 B4
Sulhamstead....47 C4
Sulland......282 C6
Sullington 20 A3
Sullom.......284 F5
Sullom Voe Oil
Terminal.....284 F5
Sully..........41 E6
Sumburgh.....285 N6
Summer Bridge .147 A6
Summercourt 4 B3
Summerfield ...119 B4
Summergangs ..151 D4
Summer-house .167 D5
Summerleaze ...42 A3
Summersdale ...20 B1
Summerseat ...137 B6
Summertown ...65 C6
Summit.......138 C2
Sunbury-on-
Thames......48 C4
Sundaywell ...183 D6
Sunderland
Argyll.......200 B2
Cumb........163 A4
T&W.........179 D5
Sunderland
Bridge.......167 B5
Sundhope.....196 D2
Sundon Park ...67 A5
Sundridge 36 A2
Sunipol.......224 A2
Sunk Island ...143 B4
Sunningdale 48 C2
Sunninghill 48 C2
Sunningwell ...65 C5
Sunniside
Durham......166 B4
T&W.........179 D4
Sunnyhurst ...137 A5
Sunnylaw 207 A5
Sunnyside 36 C1
Sunton........45 D6
Surbiton.......49 C4
Surby.........152 D2
Surfleet......117 C5
Surfleet Seas
End.........117 C5
Surlingham ...104 A4
Sustead......120 B3
Susworth.....141 C6
Sutcombe 24 D4
Suton........104 B1
Sutors of
Cromarty.....265 C4
Sutterby.....134 B3
Sutterton.....117 B5
Sutton Cambs...101 D6
C Beds........84 C4
Kent..........39 A5
London.......49 C5
Mers.........136 D4
Norf.........121 C5
Notts........115 B5
Notts........132 A1
N Yorks......140 A2
Oxon.........65 C5
Pboro........100 B2
Shrops.......95 C5
Shrops.......111 B5
Som...........29 B6
Staffs.......111 C6
Suff..........88 C4
Sur...........34 B4
S Yorks......140 B3
W Sus.........20 A2

Sutton at Hone ...50 B2
Sutton Bassett ...99 B4
Sutton Benger ..44 B3
Sutton
Bonington.....114 C3
Sutton Bridge ..118 C1
Sutton Cheney ...97 A7
Sutton Coldfield..96 B4
Sutton Courtenay 65 D6
Sutton Crosses .118 C1
Sutton Grange .157 D6
Sutton Green...34 A3
Sutton
Howgrave....157 D7
Sutton In
Ashfield.....131 D4
Sutton-in-
Craven......147 C4
Sutton Ings ...151 D4
Sutton in the
Elms.........98 B2
Sutton Lane
Ends.......129 B4
Sutton Leach...136 D4
Sutton Maddock..95 A5
Sutton Mallet ...28 B3
Sutton
Mandeville 30 C3
Sutton Manor ..136 D4
Sutton Montis ...29 C6
Sutton on Hull .151 D4
Sutton on Sea...135 A5
Sutton-on-the-
Forest.......149 A4
Sutton on the
Hill........113 B6
Sutton on Trent .132 C2
Sutton St
Edmund.....117 D6
Sutton St
James.......117 D6
Sutton St
Nicholas 78 C3
Sutton
Scarsdale 131 C4
Sutton Scotney ..32 B3
Sutton under
Brailes......81 D6
Sutton-under-White-
stonecliffe....158 C3
Sutton upon
Derwent.....149 C6
Sutton Valence ..37 B6
Sutton Veny 30 A2
Sutton Waldron ..30 D2
Sutton Weaver .127 B5
Sutton Wick....43 D4
Swaby........134 B3
Swadlincote ...113 D7
Swaffham......103 A4
Swaffham
Bulbeck......86 A1
Swaffham Prior .86 A1
Swafield......121 B4
Swainby......158 A3
Swainshill.......78 C2
Swainsthorpe ..104 A3
Swainswick.....43 C6
Swalcliffe......81 D6
Swalecliffe.....52 C3
Swallow......142 C3
Swallowcliffe ...30 C3
Swallowfield ...47 C5
Swallownest...131 A4
Swallows Cross .69 D6
Swanage........17 D4
Swanbister ...283 G4
Swanbourne ...66 A3
Swan Green
Ches W........128 B2
Suff.........104 D3
Swanland......142 A1
Swanley........50 C2
Swanley Village .50 C2
Swanmore.......33 D4
Swannington
Leics........114 D2
Norf.........120 D3
Swanscombe.....50 B3
Swansea
Abertawe......57 C6
Swanton Abbott 121 C4

Swanton
   Morley 120 D2
Swanton Novers 120 B2
Swanton Street .. 37 A6
Swanwick
   Derbys 131 D4
   Hants 18 A4
Swarby 116 A3
Swardeston 104 A3
Swarister 284 E7
Swarkestone 114 C1
Swarland 189 C4
Swarland Estate 189 C4
Swarthmoor 153 C3
Swathwick 130 C3
Swaton 116 B4
Swavesey 85 A5
Sway 18 B1
Swayfield 116 C2
Swaythling 32 D3
Sweet Green ...79 A4
Sweetham 12 B3
Sweethouse......5 A5
Sweffling 88 A4
Swepstone 114 D1
Swerford 81 D6
Swettenham ...128 C3
Swetton 157 D5
Swffryd 60 D4
Swiftsden 37 D5
Swilland 88 B2
Swillington ...148 D2
Swimbridge 25 C7
Swimbridge
   Newland 25 B7
Swinbrook 64 B3
Swinderby 132 C3
Swindon Glos. ..63 A5
   Staffs 95 B6
   Swindon 45 A5
Swine 151 D4
Swinefleet 141 A5
Swineshead
   Bedford 84 A2
   Lincs 117 A5
Swineshead
   Bridge 117 A5
Swiney 275 A6
Swinford Leics ..98 D2
   Oxon 65 C5
Swingate 114 A3
Swingfield
   Minnis 39 A4
Swingfield Street 39 A4
Swinhoe 189 A5
Swinhope 143 D4
Swining 284 G6
Swinithwaite ..156 C4
Swinnow Moor .147 D6
Swinscoe 113 A5
Swinside Hall .187 B6
Swinstead 116 C3
Swinton Borders .198 B2
   Gtr Man 137 C6
   N Yorks 157 D6
   N Yorks 159 D6
   S Yorks 140 D2
Swintonmill ...198 B2
Swithland 114 D3
Swordale 264 D1
Swordland 238 C1
Swordly 278 B3
Sworton Heath .128 A1
Swydd-ffynnon . 75 B5
Swynnerton ...112 B2
Swyre 15 C5
Sychtyn 92 A3
Syde 63 B5
Sydenham London . 49 B6
   Oxon 66 C2
Sydenham
   Damerel.......11 D5
Syderstone 119 B5
Sydling St
   Nicholas 16 B5
Sydmonton 46 D2
Syerston 115 A5
Syke 138 B1
Sykehouse 140 B4
Sykes 145 B6
Syleham 104 D3
Sylen 57 B5

Symbister.......285 G7
Symington
   S Ayrs. 192 B3
   S Lanark. 195 C4
Symondsbury 14 B4
Symonds Yat....62 B1
Synod Inn......73 A7
Syre 278 D2
Syreford 63 A6
Syresham 82 C3
Syston Leics ...115 D4
   Lincs. 116 A2
Sytchampton....79 A6
Sywell 83 A5

T

Taagan 262 D2
Tàbost. 288 A6
Tabost 288 F4
Tackley 65 A5
Tacleit. 288 D2
Tacolneston ...104 B2
Tadcaster......148 C3
Taddington ...129 B6
Taddiport 25 D5
Tadley 47 C4
Tadlow 85 C4
Tadmarton 81 D6
Tadworth 35 A5
Tafarnau-bach ...60 B3
Tafarn-y-gelyn .126 C1
Taff's Well......41 C6
Tafolwern 91 B6
Tai 124 C2
Taibach 40 C2
Tai-bach 109 C6
Taigh a
   Ghearraidh ...287 G2
Tai-mawr 109 A4
Tain Highld ...264 B3
   Highld. 280 B4
Tainant 110 A1
Tainlon 107 A4
Tairbeart
   Tarbert. 288 G2
Tai'r-Bull 60 A1
Tairgwaith 59 D4
Tai-Ucha 125 D5
Takeley 69 A5
Takeley Street ...69 A5
Talachddu 77 D4
Talacre 125 A6
Talardd 108 C3
Talaton 13 B5
Talbenny 54 C4
Talbot Green ...41 C5
Talbot Village ..17 B4
Tale 13 A5
Talerddig 92 A3
Talgarreg 74 C3
Talgarth 77 D5
Talisker 246 A2
Talke 128 D3
Talkin 176 D3
Talladale 261 C6
Talla Linnfoots .195 D6
Tallarn Green ..110 A3
Tallentire 163 A4
Talley 58 B3
Tallington 100 A2
Talmine 277 B6
Talog 73 D6
Talsarn 59 C4
Tal-sarn 75 C4
Talsarnau 107 C6
Talskiddy 4 A4
Talwrn Anglesey .123 C4
   Wrex 110 A1
Tal-y-bont
   Ceredig 91 D4
   Conwy 124 C2
   Gwyn 107 D5
   Gwyn 123 C6
Talybont-on-Usk 60 A3
Tal-y-cafn 124 B2
Talygarn 41 C5
Talyllyn 60 A3
Tal-y-llyn.....107 A4
Tal-y-wain 61 C4

Tal-y-wern 91 B6
Tame Bridge 158 A4
Tamerton Foliot ...6 A3
Tamworth 97 A5
Tandem 139 B4
Tanden 37 C7
Tandridge 35 A6
Tanerdy 73 D7
Tanfield 178 D3
Tanfield Lea ..178 D3
Tangasdal 286 G2
Tangiers 55 C5
Tangley 46 D1
Tanglwst 73 C6
Tangmere 20 B2
Tangwick 284 F4
Tan Hinon 91 D6
Tankersley 139 C6
Tankerton 52 C3
Tan-lan Conwy ..124 C2
   Gwyn 107 B6
Tannach 281 D5
Tannachie 245 D4
Tannadice 232 C2
Tannington 88 A3
Tansley 130 D3
Tansley Knoll ..130 C3
Tansor 100 B2
Tantobie 178 D3
Tanton 168 D3
Tanworth-in-
   Arden 96 D4
Tan-y-bwlch ...107 B6
Tan-y-fron 125 C4
Tan-y-graig
   Anglesey 123 C5
   Gwyn 106 C3
Tanygrisiau ...107 B6
Tan-y-groes 73 B5
Tan-y-pistyll..109 C5
Tan-yr-allt ...107 A4
Tanyrhydiau ...75 B6
Taobh a
   Chaolais.....286 E3
Taobh a'
   Ghlinne 288 F4
Taobh a Thuath Loch
   Aineort.......286 D3
Taobh a Tuath Loch
   Baghas-
   dail 286 D3
Taobh Tuath ...287 F4
Taplow 48 A2
Tapton 130 B3
Tarbat Ho. 264 C3
Tarbert Argyll ..202 B3
   Argyll 202 C1
   Argyll 213 D4
Tarbet Argyll ..215 B6
   Highld.........238 C1
   Highld.........276 D2
Tarbock Green .127 A4
Tarbolton 193 C4
Tarbrax 195 A5
Tardebigge 80 A3
Tarfside 232 A2
Tarland 244 B1
Tarleton 136 A3
Tarlogie 264 B3
Tarlscough 136 B3
Tarlton 63 D5
Tarnbrook 145 B5
Tarporley 127 C5
Tarr 27 B6
Tarrant Crawford 16 A3
Tarrant Gunville..30 D3
Tarrant Hinton ..30 D3
Tarrant
   Keyneston 16 A3
Tarrant
   Launceston.....16 A3
Tarrant Monkton .16 A3
Tarrant Rawston .16 A3
Tarrant Rushton .16 A3
Tarrel 265 B4
Tarring Neville ..22 B2
Tarrington 79 C4
Tarsappie 219 B6
Tarskavaig 247 C4
Tarves 256 C3
Tarvie Highld...251 A6
   Perth 230 B4

Tarvin 127 C4
Tasburgh 104 B3
Tasley 95 B4
Taston 65 A4
Tatenhill......113 C6
Tathall End 83 C5
Tatham 145 A6
Tathwell 134 A3
Tatling End 48 A3
Tatsfield 36 A2
Tattenhall 127 D4
Tattenhoe 83 D5
Tatterford 119 C5
Tattersett 119 B5
Tattershall ...134 D2
Tattershall
   Bridge 134 D1
Tattershall
   Thorpe 134 D2
Tattingstone ...88 D2
Tatworth 14 A3
Taunton 28 C2
Taverham 120 D3
Tavernspite 56 A1
Tavistock 11 D5
Taw Green 12 B1
Tawstock 25 C6
Taxal 129 B5
Tay Bridge 220 B4
Tayinloan 202 D1
Taymouth
   Castle 230 D1
Taynish 213 D5
Taynton Glos ...62 A3
   Oxon. 64 B3
Taynuilt 227 C5
Tayport 221 B4
Tayvallich 213 D5
Tealby 142 D3
Tealing 220 A4
Teangue 247 D5
Teanna
   Mhachair.....287 H2
Tebay 155 A5
Tebworth 67 A4
Tedburn St Mary ..12 B3
Teddington Glos ..80 D2
   London 49 B4
Tedstone
   Delamere 79 B4
Tedstone Wafre ..79 B4
Teeton 98 D3
Teffont Evias ...30 B3
Teffont Magna ...30 B3
Tegryn 73 C5
Teigh 115 D6
Teigncombe 12 C1
Teigngrace 12 D3
Teignmouth.....13 D4
Telford 95 A4
Telham 23 A5
Tellisford 44 D2
Telscombe 22 B2
Telscombe Cliffs .22 B1
Templand 184 D3
Temple Corn....10 D2
   Glasgow 205 B5
   Midloth. 196 A2
Temple Balsall ..97 D5
Temple Bar Carms 57 A5
   Ceredig 75 C4
Temple Cloud ...43 D5
Temple Combe ..29 C7
Temple Ewell ...39 A4
Temple Grafton ..80 B4
Temple Guiting ..64 A1
Templehall 209 A5
Temple
   Herdewyke 81 B6
Temple Hirst ..140 A4
Temple
   Normanton ...131 C4
Temple
   Sowerby 165 C4
Templeton Devon .26 D3
   Pembs 55 C7
Templeton
   Bridge 26 D3
Templetown 178 D3
Tempsford 84 B3
Tenbury Wells...78 A3

Tenby Dinbych-y-
   Pysgod 56 B1
Tendring 71 A5
Tendring Green .71 A5
Ten Mile Bank...102 B2
Tenston 282 F3
Tenterden 37 C6
Terling 70 B1
Ternhill 111 B5
Terregles Banks .174 A2
Terrick 66 C3
Terrington 159 D5
Terrington St
   Clement........118 D2
Terrington St
   John 118 D2
Teston 37 A5
Testwood 32 D2
Tetbury 63 D4
Tetbury Upton...63 D4
Tetchill 110 B2
Tetcott 10 B4
Tetford 134 B3
Tetney 143 C5
Tetney Lock....143 C5
Tetsworth 66 C1
Tettenhall 96 B1
Teuchan 257 C5
Teversal 131 C4
Teversham 85 B6
Teviothead....186 C3
Tewel 245 D5
Tewin 68 B2
Tewkesbury.....80 D1
Teynham 51 C6
Thackthwaite ..163 B4
Thainston 233 A4
Thakeham 21 A4
Thame 66 C2
Thames Ditton ..49 C4
Thames Haven ..51 A4
Thamesmead ...50 A1
Thanington 52 D3
Thankerton ...195 C4
Tharston 104 B2
Thatcham 46 C3
Thatto Heath...136 D4
Thaxted 86 D2
The Aird 259 C4
Theakston 157 C7
Thealby 141 B6
Theale Som.....29 A4
   W Berks 47 B4
The Arms 103 B4
Thearne 150 D3
The Bage 77 C6
The Balloch ...218 C3
The Barony 282 E3
Theberton 89 A5
The Bog 94 B1
The Bourne 33 A7
The Braes 247 A4
The Broad 78 A2
The Butts 30 A1
The Camp Glos ..63 C5
   Herts 67 C6
The Chequer ...110 A3
The City 66 D2
The Common 31 B6
The Craigs 263 A6
The Cronk 152 B3
Theddingworth .98 C3
Theddlethorpe All
   Saints 135 A4
Theddlethorpe St
   Helen 135 A4
The Dell 105 B5
The Den 204 C3
The Eals 177 A5
The Eaves 62 C2
The Flatt 176 B3
The Four Alls ..111 B5
The Garths 284 B8
The Green Cumb .153 B2
   Wilts. 30 B2
The Grove 174 A2
The Hall 284 D8
The Haven 34 C3
The Heath Norf .120 C3
   Suff 88 D2
The Hill 153 B2
The Howe Cumb. .154 C3

The Howe continued
   IoM 152 E1
The Hundred 78 A3
Thelbridge
   Barton 26 D2
The Lee. 67 C4
The Lhen 152 A3
Thelnetham ...103 D6
Thelveton 104 C2
Thelwall 127 A6
The Marsh Powys .93 B7
   Wilts. 45 A4
Themelthorpe...120 C2
The Middles ...179 D4
The Moor 37 D5
The Mumbles Y
   Mwmbwls......57 D6
The Murray 205 C6
The Neuk 245 C4
Thenford 82 C2
The Oval 43 C6
The Pole of
   Itlaw 268 D1
The Quarry......62 D3
Therfield 85 D5
The Rhos 55 C6
The Rock 95 A4
The Ryde 68 C2
The Sands 34 B1
The Stocks 37 D7
Thetford Lincs ..116 D4
   Norf 103 C4
The Throat 47 C6
The Vauld 78 C3
The Wyke 95 A5
Theydon Bois ..68 D4
Thickwood 44 B2
Thimbleby Lincs .134 C2
   N Yorks. 158 B3
Thingwall 126 A2
Thirdpart 204 D1
Thirlby 158 C3
Thirlestane ...197 B4
Thirn 157 C6
Thirsk 158 C3
Thirtleby 151 D4
Thistleton Lancs .144 D4
   Rutland. 116 D2
Thistley Green ..102 D2
Thixendale 150 A1
Thockrington ..178 B1
Tholomas Drove 101 A5
Tholthorpe 148 A3
Thomas Chapel ..55 D7
Thomas Close...164 A2
Thomastown ...255 C6
Thompson 103 B5
Thomshill 266 D3
Thong 50 B3
Thongsbridge .139 C4
Thoralby 156 C4
Thoresway 142 D3
Thorganby Lincs .143 C4
   N Yorks. 149 C5
Thorgill 159 B6
Thorington ...105 D5
Thorington
   Street 87 D6
Thorlby 146 B3
Thorley 69 B4
Thorley Street
   Herts 69 B4
   IoW 18 C2
Thormanby 158 D3
Thornaby-on-
   Tees 168 D2
Thornage 120 B2
Thornborough
   Bucks 83 D4
   N Yorks. 157 D6
Thornbury Devon. 11 A5
   Hereford 79 B4
   S Glos. 62 D2
   W Yorks. 147 D5
Thornby 98 D3
Thorncliffe ...129 D5
Thorncombe
   Dorset 14 A3
   Dorset 16 A2

Thorncombe Street. 34 B3
Thorncote Green 84 C3
Thorncross 18 C3
Thorndon 88 A2
Thorndon Cross . . 11 B6
Thorne 141 B4
Thorner 148 C2
Thorne St Margaret 27 C5
Thorney Notts . . . 132 B3
Pboro 101 A4
Thorney Crofts . 143 A4
Thorney Green . . . 87 A6
Thorney Hill. 17 B5
Thorney Toll 101 A5
Thornfalcon. 28 C2
Thornford 29 D6
Thorngumbald . . 143 A4
Thornham 119 A4
Thornham Magna 104 D2
Thornham Parva 104 D2
Thornhaugh. 100 A2
Thornhill Cardiff . . 41 C6
Cumb 162 D3
Derbys 130 A1
Dumfries 183 C6
Soton 32 D3
Stirling 207 A4
W Yorks 139 B5
Thornhill Edge . . 139 B5
Thornhill Lees. . . 139 B5
Thornholme 151 A4
Thornley Durham 166 B4
Durham 167 B6
Thornliebank . . . 205 C5
Thorns 86 B3
Thornsett 129 A5
Thorns Green . . 128 A2
Thornthwaite Cumb 163 B5
N Yorks. 147 B5
Thornton Angus. 232 D1
Bucks 83 D4
E Yorks 149 C6
Fife. 209 A5
Lancs 144 C3
Leics. 98 A1
Lincs. 134 C2
Mbro 168 D2
Mers. 136 C2
Northumb. 198 B3
Pembs 55 D5
W Yorks 147 D5
Thornton Curtis 142 B2
Thorntonhall. . . 205 C5
Thornton Heath . 49 C6
Thornton Hough 126 A3
Thornton in Craven 146 C3
Thornton-le-Beans 158 B2
Thornton-le-Clay 149 A5
Thornton-le-Dale 160 C2
Thornton le Moor 142 D2
Thornton-le-Moor. 158 C2
Thornton-le-Moors 127 B4
Thornton-le-Street 158 C3
Thorntonloch . . . 211 C4
Thorntonpark . . 198 B3
Thornton Rust. . 156 C2
Thornton Steward 157 C5
Thornton Watlass 157 C6
Thornwood Common 69 C4
Thornydykes . . . 197 B5
Thoroton 115 A5
Thorp Arch 148 C3

Thorpe Derbys . . . 129 D6
E Yorks 150 C2
Lincs. 135 A4
Norf 105 B5
Notts 115 A5
N Yorks. 147 A4
Sur 48 C3
Thorpe Abbotts 104 D2
Thorpe Acre . . . 114 C3
Thorpe Arnold . . 115 C5
Thorpe Audlin. . 111 B6
Thorpe Bassett. 160 D2
Thorpe Bay 51 A6
Thorpe by Water . 99 B5
Thorpe Common . 88 D3
Thorpe Constantine . . . 97 A5
Thorpe Culvert . . 135 C4
Thorpe End 121 D4
Thorpe Fendykes. 135 C4
Thorpe Green Essex 71 A5
Suff 87 B5
Thorpe Hesley . . 140 D1
Thorpe in Balne 140 B3
Thorpe in the Fallows 133 A4
Thorpe Langton . . 99 B4
Thorpe Larches .167 C6
Thorpe-le-Soken 71 A5
Thorpe le Street. 150 C1
Thorpe Malsor . . 99 D5
Thorpe Mandeville 82 C2
Thorpe Market . . 120 B4
Thorpe Marriot. 120 D3
Thorpe Morieux . 87 B5
Thorpeness 89 B5
Thorpe on the Hill 133 C4
Thorpe St Andrew 104 A3
Thorpe St Peter .135 C4
Thorpe Salvin . . 131 A5
Thorpe Satchville 115 D5
Thorpe Thewles 168 C2
Thorpe Tilney . . 133 D6
Thorpe Underwood. . . . 148 B3
Thorpe Waterville . . 100 C2
Thorpe Willoughby. . 149 D4
Thorrington. 71 A4
Thorverton. 13 A4
Thrandeston . . . 104 D2
Thrapston 100 D1
Thrashbush 207 D5
Threapland Cumb 163 A4
N Yorks. 146 A3
Threapwood Ches W. 110 A3
Staffs 112 A4
Three Ashes 61 A7
Three Bridges. . . 35 C5
Three Burrows . . . 4 C2
Three Chimneys . 37 C6
Three Cocks 77 D5
Three Crosses . . 57 C5
Three Cups Corner 36 D4
Threehammer Common 121 D6
Three Holes . . . 101 A7
Threekingham . 116 B3
Three Leg Cross . 37 C4
Three Legged Cross 17 A4
Threemile Cross . 47 C5
Threemilestone . . 4 C2
Threemiletown. 208 C3
Three Oaks 23 A6
Threlkeld 163 B6
Threshfield 146 A3
Thrigby 121 D6
Thringarth 166 C2
Thringstone . . . 114 D2
Thrintoft 157 B7

Thriplow. 85 C6
Throckenholt . . 101 A5
Throcking 85 D5
Throckley. 178 C3
Throckmorton . . 80 C2
Throphill 178 A3
Thropton 188 C3
Throsk. 207 A6
Throwleigh 12 B1
Throwley 52 D1
Thrumpton 114 B3
Thrumster 281 D5
Thrunton 188 B3
Thrupp Glos 63 C4
Oxon. 65 B5
Thrushelton 11 C5
Thrussington. . . 115 D4
Thruxton Hants . . 32 A1
Hereford 78 D2
Thrybergh 140 D2
Thulston 114 B2
Thundergay . . . 202 D3
Thundersley. 51 A4
Thundridge 68 B3
Thurcaston 114 D3
Thurcroft 131 A4
Thurgarton Norf . 120 B3
Notts 115 A4
Thurgoland 139 C5
Thurlaston Leics . 98 B2
Warks. 98 D1
Thurlbear. 28 C2
Thurlby Lincs . . . 116 D4
Lincs. 133 C4
Thurleigh 84 B2
Thurlestone 7 C5
Thurloxton. 28 B2
Thurlstone 139 C5
Thurlton 105 B5
Thurlwood 128 D3
Thurmaston 98 A3
Thurnby 98 A3
Thurne 121 D6
Thurnham Kent . . 37 A6
Lancs 145 B4
Thurning Norf . . 120 C2
Northants. . . . 100 C2
Thurnscoe 140 C2
Thurnscoe East. 140 C2
Thursby 175 C6
Thursford 120 B1
Thursley. 34 C2
Thurso 280 B3
Thurso East . . . 280 B3
Thurstaston . . . 126 A2
Thurston. 87 A5
Thurstonfield . . 175 C6
Thurstonland . . 139 B4
Thurton 104 A4
Thurvaston 113 B6
Thuxton 103 A6
Thwaite N Yorks. 156 B2
Suff 88 A2
Thwaites. 147 C4
Thwaite St Mary 104 B4
Thwaites Brow . 147 C4
Thwing 160 D4
Tibbermore . . . 219 B5
Tibberton Glos. . . 62 A3
Telford 111 C5
Worcs. 80 B2
Tibenham 104 C2
Tibshelf 131 C4
Tibthorpe 150 B2
Ticehurst 37 C4
Tichborne 33 B4
Tickencote 100 A1
Tickenham 42 B3
Tickhill 140 D3
Ticklerton 94 B2
Ticknall 114 C1
Tickton 150 C3
Tidcombe 45 D6
Tiddington Oxon . 66 C1
Warks. 81 B5
Tidebrook 36 C4
Tideford 6 B2
Tideford Cross . . . 6 A2
Tidenham 62 D1
Tideswell 129 B6
Tidmarsh 47 B4
Tidmington 81 D5

Tidpit. 31 D4
Tidworth 31 A6
Tiers Cross. 55 C5
Tiffield 82 B3
Tifty 256 B2
Tigerton 232 B3
Tigh-na-Blair . . 218 C2
Tighnabruaich . 203 A4
Tighnafiline. . . . 261 B5
Tigley 7 A6
Tilbrook 84 A2
Tilbury 50 B3
Tilbury Juxta Clare. 86 C3
Tile Cross. 97 C4
Tile Hill. 97 D5
Tilehurst 47 B4
Tilford. 34 B1
Tilgate 35 C5
Tilgate Forest Row. 35 C5
Tillathrowie. . . . 255 C5
Tilley 111 C4
Tillicoultry 208 A2
Tillingham 70 C3
Tillington Hereford 78 C2
W Sus. 34 D2
Tillington Common 78 C2
Tillyarblet 232 B3
Tillybirloch . . . 244 B3
Tillycorthie . . . 257 D4
Tillydrine 244 C3
Tillyfour 244 A3
Tillyfourie 244 A3
Tillygarmond. . 244 C3
Tillygreig 256 D3
Tillykerrie 256 D3
Tilmanstone 53 D5
Tilney All Saints 118 D2
Tilney High End .118 D2
Tilney St Lawrence 118 D2
Tilshead 31 A4
Tilstock 111 B4
Tilston 127 D4
Tilstone Fearnall 127 C5
Tilsworth 67 A4
Tilton on the Hill . 99 A4
Timberland . . . 133 D6
Timbersbrook. . 128 C3
Timberscombe . . 27 A4
Timble. 147 B5
Timperley. 128 A2
Timsbury Bath . . 43 D5
Hants 32 C2
Timsgearraidh . 287 A5
Timworth Green. 87 A4
Tincleton 16 B1
Tindale 176 D4
Tingewick 82 D3
Tingley 139 A5
Tingrith 84 D2
Tingwall 282 E4
Tinhay 11 C4
Tinshill 147 D6
Tinsley 140 D2
Tintagel 9 C6
Tintern Parva . . . 62 C1
Tintinhull 29 D5
Tintwistle 138 D3
Tinwald 184 D3
Tinwell 100 A2
Tipperty 257 D4
Tipsend 101 B7
Tipton 96 B2
Tipton St John . . 13 B5
Tiptree 70 B2
Tirabad 59 A5
Tiraghoil 224 D2
Tirley 63 A4
Tirphil 41 A6
Tirril 164 C3
Tir-y-dail 57 A6
Tisbury 30 C3
Tisman's Common 34 C3
Tissington 130 D1
Titchberry 24 C3
Titchfield 18 A4

Titchmarsh 100 D2
Titchwell 119 A4
Tithby 115 B4
Titley. 78 A1
Titlington 189 B4
Titsey 36 A2
Tittensor 112 B2
Tittleshall. 119 C5
Tiverton Ches W. 127 C5
Devon. 27 D4
Tivetshall St Margaret 104 C2
Tivetshall St Mary 104 C2
Tividale. 96 B2
Tivy Dale 139 C5
Tixall 112 C3
Tixover 99 A6
Toab Orkney . . . 283 G6
Shetland. . . . 285 M5
Toadmoor 130 D3
Tobermory 225 A4
Toberonochy . . 213 B5
Tobha Mor. . . . 286 C3
Tobhtarol. 288 D2
Tobson 288 D2
Tocher 256 C1
Tockenham 44 B4
Tockenham Wick 44 A4
Tockholes 137 A5
Tockington 43 A5
Tockwith 148 B3
Todber 30 C2
Todding 94 D2
Toddington C Beds 67 A5
Glos 80 D3
Todenham 81 D5
Todhills 175 B6
Todlachie 244 A3
Todmorden . . . 138 A2
Todrig 186 B3
Todwick 131 A4
Toft Cambs 85 B5
Lincs. 116 D3
Toft Hill Durham. 167 C4
Lincs. 134 C2
Toft Monks . . . 105 B5
Toft next Newton 133 A5
Toftrees 119 C5
Tofts 281 B5
Toftwood 120 D1
Togston 189 C5
Tokavaig. 247 C5
Tokers Green . . . 47 B5
Tolastadh a Chaolais. 288 D2
Tolastadh bho Thuath 288 C6
Toll Bar. 140 C3
Tollard Royal. . . . 30 D3
Toll Bar 140 C3
Tollbar End 97 D6
Toll End 96 B2
Toller Fratrum . . 15 B5
Toller Porcorum . 15 B5
Tollerton Notts . 115 B4
N Yorks. 148 A4
Tollesbury 70 B3
Tolleshunt D'Arcy 70 B3
Tolleshunt Major . 70 B3
Toll of Birness . 257 C5
Tolm 288 D5
Tolpuddle 16 B1
Tolvah 241 C6
Tolworth 49 C4
Tomatin 253 D4
Tombreck 252 C2
Tomchrasky . . 239 A6
Tomdoun 239 B5
Tomich Highld . . 251 D5
Highld. 264 C2
Tomich House. . 252 B1
Tomintoul Aberds 242 C4
Moray. 243 A4
Tomnaven 255 C5
Tomnavoulin . . 254 D3
Tonbridge 36 B3
Tondu 40 C3
Tonfanau 90 B3

Tong Shrops 95 A5
W Yorks 147 D6
Tonge 114 C2
Tongham 34 B1
Tongland 173 C4
Tong Norton . . . 95 A5
Tongue 277 C6
Tongue End . . . 117 D4
Tongwynlais . . . 41 C6
Tonna 40 B2
Ton-Pentre 41 B4
Tonwell 68 B3
Tonypandy 41 B4
Tonyrefail 41 C5
Toot Baldon 65 C6
Toothill 32 D2
Toot Hill 69 C5
Topcliffe. 158 D3
Topcroft 104 B3
Topcroft Street. 104 B3
Top of Hebers . . 138 C1
Toppesfield 86 D3
Toppings 137 B6
Topsham 13 C4
Torbay. 8 B3
Torbeg 191 C5
Torboll Farm. . . 264 A3
Torbrex 207 A5
Torbryan 8 A2
Torcross 8 C2
Tore 252 A2
Torinturk 202 B3
Torksey 132 B3
Torlum 286 A3
Torlundy 237 B5
Tormarton 43 B6
Tormisdale 200 C1
Tormitchell . . . 181 B4
Tormore 191 B4
Tornagrain. . . . 252 B3
Tornahaish . . . 243 B5
Tornaveen 244 B3
Torness. 252 D1
Toronto 167 B4
Torpenhow 163 A5
Torphichen . . . 208 C2
Torphins. 244 B3
Torpoint 6 B3
Torquay 8 A3
Torquhan. 196 B3
Torran Argyll. . . . 214 B1
Highld. 248 B2
Torrance 205 A6
Torrans. 224 D3
Torranyard. . . . 204 D3
Torre 8 A2
Torridon 249 A6
Torridon Ho. . . . 249 A5
Torrin 247 B4
Torrisdale 278 B2
Torrisdale-Square 190 B3
Torrish 274 C2
Torrisholme . . . 145 A4
Torroble. 272 D3
Torry Aberdeen. . 245 B6
Torryburn. 208 B3
Torterston 257 B5
Torthorwald . . . 174 A3
Tortington. 20 B3
Tortworth. 62 D3
Torvaig 259 D4
Torver 154 B1
Torwood. 207 B6
Torworth 131 A6
Tosberry 24 C3
Toscaig. 249 C4
Toseland 84 A4
Tosside. 146 B1
Tostock 87 A5
Totaig Highld . . 249 D5
Highld. 258 C2
Tote 259 D4
Totegan 279 B4
Tothill 135 A4
Totland 18 C2
Totnes. 8 A2
Toton. 114 B3
Totronald 223 B4
Totscore 258 B3

Tottenham.......68 D3
Tottenhill.......118 D3
Tottenhill Row ..118 D3
Totteridge.......68 D2
Totternhoe 67 A4
Tottington....137 B6
Totton..........32 D2
Touchen End....48 B1
Tournaig......261 B5
Toux..........269 D4
Tovil..........37 A5
Toward......203 B6
Towcester......82 C3
Towednack......2 B2
Tower End......118 D3
Towersey......66 C2
Towie Aberds ...244 A1
  Aberds.......268 C3
Towiemore 255 B4
Tow Law......166 B4
Townend 205 A4
Town End Cambs 101 B6
  Cumb.........154 C3
Towngate......116 D4
Townhead Cumb.164 B3
  Dumfries.....173 D4
  S Ayrs.......181 A4
  S Yorks......139 C4
Townhead of
  Greenlaw....173 B5
Townhill......208 B4
Town Row 36 C3
Townsend Bucks ..66 C2
  Herts.........67 C6
Townshend 2 B3
Town Yetholm ..187 A7
Towthorpe 149 B5
Towton........148 D3
Towyn 125 B4
Toxteth........126 A3
Toynton All
  Saints.......134 C3
Toynton Fen
  Side.........134 C3
Toynton St
  Peter.......135 C4
Toy's Hill 36 A2
Trabboch 193 C4
Traboe 3 C5
Tradespark
  Highld.......253 A4
  Orkney......283 G5
Trafford Park ..137 D6
Trallong 59 C6
Tranent......209 C7
Tranmere 126 A3
Trantlebeg....279 C4
Trantlemore ..279 C4
Tranwell......178 A3
Trapp 57 A6
Traprain 210 C2
Traquair 196 C2
Trawden......146 D3
Trawsfynydd ..108 B2
Trealaw 41 B5
Treales......144 D4
Trearddur 122 C2
Treaslane....258 C3
Trebanog 41 B5
Trebanos 40 A2
Trebartha......10 D3
Trebarwith......9 C6
Trebetherick 9 D5
Treborough 27 B5
Trebudannon 4 A3
Trebullett......10 D4
Treburley......10 D4
Trebyan 5 A5
Trecastle 59 C5
Trecenydd 41 C6
Trecwn......55 A5
Trecynon......41 A4
Tredavoe 2 C2
Treddiog 55 B4
Tredegar......60 C3
Tredington Glos ..63 A5
  Warks.......81 C5
Tredinnick......9 D5
Tredomen......77 D5
Tredunnock....61 D5
Tredustan......77 D5
Treen..........2 C1

Treeton........131 A4
Trefasser......72 C1
Trefdraeth....123 C4
Trefecca........77 D5
Trefechan......90 D3
Trefeglwys 92 B3
Trefenter......75 B5
Treffgarne 55 B5
Treffynnon....54 B4
Trefgarn Owen ..55 B4
Trefil..........60 B3
Trefilan......75 C4
Trefin........54 A4
Treflach......110 C1
Trefnanney ..109 D7
Trefnant......125 B5
Trefonen......110 C1
Trefor Anglesey ..122 B3
  Gwyn.......106 B3
Treforest......41 C5
Trefriw......124 C2
Tregadillett 10 C3
Tregaian......123 C4
Tregare........61 B6
Tregaron......75 C5
Tregarth......123 D6
Tregeare 10 C3
Tregeiriog 109 B6
Tregele......122 A3
Tre-Gibbon 60 C1
Tregidden 3 C5
Treglemais 54 B4
Tregole......10 B2
Tregonetha......5 A4
Tregony........4 C4
Tregoss........5 A4
Tregoyd........77 D6
Tregroes......73 B7
Tregurrian......4 A3
Tregynon......93 B4
Trehafod......41 B5
Treharris......41 B5
Treherbert......40 B4
Trekenner......10 D4
Treknow........9 C6
Trelan..........3 D5
Trelash........4 B3
Trelassick......4 B3
Trelawnyd 125 B5
Trelech........73 C5
Treleddyd-fawr ..54 B3
Trelewis......41 B6
Treligga........9 C6
Trelights......9 D5
Trelill..........9 D6
Trelissick......4 D3
Trellech........61 C7
Trelleck Grange ..61 C6
Trelogan......125 A6
Trelystan......93 A6
Tremadog 107 B5
Tremail......10 C2
Tremain......73 B5
Tremaine 10 C3
Tremar 6 A1
Trematon........6 B3
Tremeirchion ..125 B5
Trenance 4 A3
Trenarren 5 C5
Trench......111 D5
Treneglos......10 C3
Trenewan 5 B6
Trent..........29 D5
Trentham 112 A2
Trentishoe 26 A1
Trent Vale 112 A2
Treoes..........41 B5
Treorchy Treorci ..41 B4
Tre'r-ddôl......91 C4
Trerulefoot 6 B2
Tresaith......73 A5
Tresawle........4 C3
Trescott......95 B6
Trescowe........2 C3
Tresham......62 D3
Tresillian......4 C3
Tresinwen 72 B1
Treskinnick
  Cross......10 B3
Tresmeer......10 C3
Tresparrett....10 B2
Tresparrett Posts. 10 B2

Tressait........230 B2
Tresta Shetland...284 D8
  Shetland.....285 H5
Treswell......132 B2
Tre-Taliesin 91 C4
Trethosa........4 B4
Trethurgy......5 B5
Tretio........54 B3
Tretower......60 A3
Treuddyn....126 D2
Trevalga......10 C1
Trevalyn......126 D3
Trevanson......9 D5
Trevarren......4 A4
Trevarrian......4 A3
Trevarrick......5 C4
Trevaughan....56 A1
Tre-vaughan....73 D7
Treveighan......9 D6
Trevellas........4 B2
Treverva........4 D2
Trevethin......61 C4
Trevigro........6 A2
Treviscoe......4 B4
Trevone........9 D4
Trewarmett......9 C6
Trewassa......10 C2
Trewellard......2 B1
Trewen........10 C3
Trewennack 3 C4
Trewern......110 D1
Trewethern......9 D6
Trewidland 6 B1
Trewint Corn ..10 B2
  Corn.........10 C3
Trewithian......4 D3
Trewoofe........2 C2
Trewoon........5 B4
Treworga........4 C3
Treworlas......4 D3
Tre-wyn......61 A5
Treyarnon......9 D4
Treyford W Sus ..20 A1
  W Sus........33 D7
Trezaise........5 B4
Ty'r-felin-isaf..132 C2
Triangle......138 A3
Triffleton......55 B5
Trimdon......167 B6
Trimdon
  Colliery....167 B6
Trimdon Grange 167 B6
Trimingham ..121 B4
Trimley Lower
  Street........88 D3
Trimley St Martin 88 D3
Trimley St Mary ..88 D3
Trimley........95 D5
Trimsaran......57 B4
Trimstone......25 A5
Trinafour 229 B6
Trinant........41 A7
Tring..........67 B4
Tring Wharf 67 B4
Trinity Angus ..233 B4
  Jersey........P06
Trisant........75 A6
Trislaig......237 B4
Trispen........4 B3
Tritlington ..189 D5
Trochry......230 D3
Trodigal......190 C2
Troed-rhiwdalar 76 B3
Troedyraur 73 B6
Troedyrhiw 41 A5
Tromode......152 D3
Trondavoe 284 F5
Troon Corn 3 B4
  S Ayrs......192 B3
Trosaraidh....286 E3
Trossachs Hotel 217 D5
Troston......103 D4
Trottiscliffe 50 C3
Trotton........34 D1
Troutbeck Cumb.154 A3
  Cumb......164 C1
Troutbeck
  Bridge......154 A3
Trowbridge....44 D2
Trowell......114 B2
Trow Green 62 C1

Trowle Common .44 D2
Trowley Bottom ..67 B5
Trows........197 C5
Trowse Newton .104 A3
Trudoxhill 30 A1
Trull..........28 C2
Trumaisgear-
  raidh.......287 G3
Trumpan......258 B2
Trumpet........79 D4
Trumpington....85 B6
Trunch........121 B4
Trunnah......144 C3
Truro..........4 C3
Trusham......12 C3
Trusley......113 B6
Trusthorpe....135 A5
Trysull..........95 B6
Tubney........65 D5
Tuckenhay 8 B2
Tuckhill........95 C5
Tuckingmill 3 A4
Tuddenham St
  Martin......88 C2
Tudeley........36 B4
Tudhoe......167 B5
Tudorville......62 A1
Tudweiliog ..106 C2
Tuesley........34 B2
Tuffley........63 B4
Tufton Hants 32 A3
  Pembs........55 B6
Tugby..........99 A4
Tugford........94 C3
Tullibardine ..218 C4
Tullibody....207 A6
Tullich Argyll ..214 A3
Tullich Muir...264 C3
Tulliemet....230 C3
Tulloch Aberds...233 A5
  Aberds......256 C3
  Perth......219 B5
Tulloch Castle..264 D1
Tullochgorm ..214 C2
Tulloes......232 D3
Tullybannocher 218 B2
Tullybelton ..219 A5
Tullyfergus ..231 D6
Tullymurdoch ..231 C5
Tullynessle ..244 A2
Tumble........57 A5
Tumby
  Woodside ..134 D2
Tummel Bridge .229 C6
Tunga........288 D5
Tunstall E Yorks .151 D6
  Kent..........51 C5
  Lancs......155 D5
  Norf........105 A5
  N Yorks......157 B6
  Stoke.......128 D3
  Suff..........89 B4
  T&W........179 D5
Tunstead Derbys .129 B6
  Gtr Man......138 C3
  Norf........121 C4
Tunworth 33 A5
Tupsley........78 C3
Tupton......130 C3
Turgis Green ..47 D4
Turin........232 C3
Turkdean 64 B2
Tur Langton ..99 B4
Turleigh......44 C2
Turn..........137 B7
Turnastone......78 D1
Turnberry....192 E2
Turnditch......113 A6
Turners Hill 35 C6
Turners Puddle ..16 B2
Turnford........68 C3
Turnhouse....209 C4
Turnworth 16 A2
Turriff......268 D2
Turton Bottoms .137 B6
Turves......101 B5
Turvey........83 B6
Turville........66 D2
Turville Heath ..66 D2
Turweston......82 D3

Tushielaw 185 A6
Tutbury......113 C6
Tutnall........96 D2
Tutshill........62 D1
Tuttington ..120 C4
Tutts Clump 46 B3
Tuxford......132 B2
Twatt Orkney...282 E3
  Shetland.....285 H5
Tweedmouth ..198 A3
Tweedsmuir ..195 D5
Twelve Heads 4 C2
Twemlow Green 128 C2
Twenty......117 C4
Twerton........43 C6
Twickenham 49 B4
Twigworth......63 A4
Twineham 21 A5
Twinhoe........43 D6
Twinstead......87 D4
Twinstead Green .87 D4
Twiss Green ..137 D5
Twiston......146 C2
Twitchen Devon ..26 B2
  Shrops......94 D1
Two Bridges 11 D7
Two Dales 130 C2
Two Mills 126 B3
Twycross......97 A6
Twyford Bucks ..66 A1
  Derbys......114 C1
  Hants........32 C3
  Leics........115 D5
  Lincs........116 C2
  Norf........120 C2
  Wokingham 47 B5
Twyford
  Common 78 D3
Twynholm 173 C4
Twyning........80 D1
Twyning Green ..80 D2
Twynllanan 59 C4
Twynmynydd 57 A6
Twyn-y-Sheriff ..61 C6
Twywell........99 D6
Tyberton........78 D1
Tyburn........96 B4
Tycroes........57 A6
Tycrwyn......109 D6
Tydd Gote 118 D1
Tydd St Giles...118 D1
Tydd St Mary...118 D1
Tyddewi Tyddyn-mawr..107 B5
Ty-draw......124 D3
Tye Green Essex ..69 C4
  Essex.........70 A1
  Essex.........86 D1
Ty-hen Carms...73 D6
  Gwyn......106 C1
Tyldesley....137 C5
Tyler Hill......52 C3
Tylers Green 67 D4
Tylorstown 41 B5
Tylwch........92 C3
Ty-mawr......123 B4
Ty-mawr Cwm..108 A4
Ty-nant Conwy ..109 A4
  Gwyn......108 C2
Tyncelyn......75 B5
Tyndrum......216 A3
Tyneham........16 C2
Tynehead......196 A2
Tynemouth ..179 C5
Tyne Tunnel ..179 C5
Tynewydd......40 B4
Tyningham ..210 C3
Tynron......183 C6
Tyn-y-celyn ..109 B6
Tyn-y-coed ..110 C1
Tyn-y-fedwen ..109 B6
Tyn-y-ffridd ..109 B6
Tynygongl 123 B5
Tynygraig......75 B5
Ty-nygraig......84 B4
Tyn-y-groes ..124 B2
Ty'n-y-maes ..123 D6
Tyn-y-pwll....123 B4
Ty'n-yr-eithin ..75 B5
Tyrie........269 C4
Tyringham......83 C5

Tythecott 25 D5
Tythegston......40 D3
Tytherington
  Ches E......129 B4
  S Glos.........43 A5
  Som..........30 A1
  Wilts..........30 A3
Tytherleigh 14 A3
Ty-uchaf....109 C5
Tywardreath 5 B5
Tywyn Conwy ..124 B2
  Gwyn........90 B3

U

Uachdar......286 A3
Uags........249 C4
Ubbeston Green 104 D4
Ubley..........43 D4
Uckerby......157 A6
Uckfield........36 D2
Uckington 63 A5
Uddingston ..207 D4
Uddington ..194 C3
Udimore........23 A6
Udny Green ..256 D3
Udny Station ..257 D4
Udston......194 A1
Udstonhead....194 B2
Uffcott........45 B5
Uffculme......27 D5
Uffington Lincs ..100 A2
  Oxon..........45 A7
  Shrops......111 D4
Ufford Pboro....100 A2
  Suff..........88 B3
Ufton..........81 A6
Ufton Nervet ..47 C4
Ugadale......190 C3
Ugborough 7 B5
Uggeshall....105 C5
Ugglebarnby ..160 A2
Ughill......139 D5
Ugley..........69 A5
Ugley Green 69 A5
Ugthorpe....169 D5
Uidh........286 G2
Uig Argyll......215 D4
  Highld......258 B3
  Highld......258 C1
Uigen......287 A5
Uigshader 259 D4
Uisken......224 E2
Ulbster......281 D5
Ulceby Lincs....135 B4
  N Lincs......142 B3
Ulceby Skitter..142 B3
Ulcombe........37 B6
Uldale......163 A5
Uley..........62 D3
Ulgham......189 D5
Ullapool......262 A3
Ullenhall......80 A4
Ullenwood......63 A5
Ulleskelf......148 C4
Ullesthorpe 98 C2
Ulley..........131 A4
Ullingswick 78 C3
Ullinish......246 A2
Ullock......162 B3
Ulnes Walton ..136 B4
Ulpha........153 A2
Ulrome......151 B4
Ulsta........284 E6
Ulva House 224 C3
Ulverston 154 D1
Ulwell..........17 C4
Umberleigh 25 C7
Unapool......271 A5
Unasary......286 D3
Underbarrow ..154 B3
Undercliffe ..147 D5
Underhoull....284 C7
Underriver 36 A3
Underwood 131 D4
Undy..........42 A3
Unifirth......285 H4
Union Cottage..245 C5

Union Mills 152 D3
Union Street 37 C5
Unstone 130 B3
Unstone Green . .130 B3
Unthank Cumb . .164 B2
Cumb 165 A4
Unthank End 164 B2
Upavon 45 D5
Up Cerne 15 A6
Upchurch 51 C5
Upcott 78 B1
Upend 86 B2
Up Exe 13 A4
Upgate 120 D3
Uphall 208 C3
Uphall Station . . .208 C3
Upham Devon 12 A3
Hants 32 C4
Uphampton 79 A6
Up Hatherley 63 A5
Uphill 42 D2
Up Holland 136 C4
Uplawmoor 205 C4
Upleadon 62 A3
Upleatham 168 D4
Uplees 52 C1
Uploders 15 B5
Uplowman 27 D5
Uplyme 14 B3
Up Marden 33 D6
Upminster 50 A2
Up Nately 47 D4
Upnor 51 B4
Upottery 14 A2
Upper Affcot 94 C2
Upper
  Ardchronie 264 B2
Upper Arley 95 C5
Upper Arncott . . .65 B7
Upper Astrop 82 D2
Upper Badcall . . .276 D2
Upper Basildon . . .46 B3
Upper Beeding . . .21 A4
Upper Benefield 100 C1
Upper Bighouse 279 C4
Upper
  Boddington 82 B1
Upper Borth 90 D4
Upper Boyndlie .269 C4
Upper Brailes 81 D6
Upper Breakish .247 B5
Upper Breinton . .78 C2
Upper
  Broadheath. . . .79 B6
Upper
  Broughton 115 C4
Upper
  Bucklebury 46 C3
Upper
  Burnhaugh . . .245 C5
Upperby 175 C7
Upper Caldecote . 84 C3
Upper Catesby . . .82 B2
Upper Chapel 76 C4
Upper Church
  Village 41 C5
Upper Chute 45 D6
Upper Clatford . . .32 A2
Upper Clynnog . .107 B4
Upper
  Cumberworth. .139 C5
Upper Cwmbran. .61 D4
Upper Cwm-
  twrch 59 D4
Upper Dallachy. .267 C4
Upper Dean 84 A2
Upper Denby 139 C5
Upper Denton . . .176 C4
Upper Derraid . . .253 D6
Upper Dicker 22 B3
Upper
  Dovercourt 88 D3
Upper Druimfin .225 A4
Upper
  Dunsforth 148 A3
Upper Eathie 264 D2
Upper Elkstone. .129 D5
Upper End 129 B5

Upper
  Farringdon 33 B6
Upper Framilode . 62 B3
Upper
  Glenfintaig . . .239 D6
Upper Gornal 96 B2
Upper
  Gravenhurst . . .84 D3
Upper Green Mon . 61 B5
  W Berks. 46 C1
Upper Grove
  Common 262 A1
Upper Hackney. .130 C2
Upper Hale 34 B1
Upper Halistra . .258 C2
Upper Halling 50 C3
Upper
  Hambleton 99 A5
Upper Hardres
  Court 52 D3
Upper Hartfield . .36 C2
Upper Haugh. . . .140 D2
Upper Heath 94 C3
Upper
  Hellesdon 120 D4
Upper Helmsley .149 B5
Upper Hergest . . .77 B6
Upper Heyford
  Northants. 82 B3
  Oxon. 65 A5
Upper Hill 78 B2
Upper Hopton . .139 B4
Upper
  Horsebridge. . . .22 A3
Upper Hulme. . . .129 C5
Upper Inglesham 64 D3
Upper
  Inverbrough . .253 C4
Upper Killay 57 C5
Upper
  Knockando . . .254 B2
Upper Lambourn .45 A7
Upper Leigh. 112 B4
Upper Lenie. 251 D7
Upper Lochton . .244 C3
Upper Longdon .113 D4
Upper Lybster . . .275 A6
Upper Lydbrook . 62 B2
Upper Maes-
  coed 78 D1
Upper Midway . .113 C6
Uppermill. 138 C2
Upper Milovaig .258 D1
Upper Minety 63 D6
Upper Mitton 95 D6
Upper North
  Dean. 66 D3
Upper Obney 219 A5
Upper Ollach 247 A4
Upper Padley . . .130 B2
Upper Pollicott . .66 B2
Upper
  Poppleton 149 B4
Upper Quinton . . .81 C4
Upper Ratley 32 C2
Upper Rissington 64 B3
Upper Rochford . .79 A4
Upper Sandaig . .238 A1
Upper Sanday . . .283 G6
Upper Sapey 79 A4
Upper
  Saxondale 115 B4
Upper Seagry 44 A3
Upper Shelton . . .84 C1
Upper
  Sheringham . .120 A3
Upper
  Skelmorlie 204 B2
Upper Slaughter . 64 A2
Upper Soudley . . .62 B2
Uppersound. 285 J6
Upper Stondon . .84 D3
Upper Stowe 82 B3
Upper Stratton . . .45 A5
Upper Street
  Hants 31 D5
  Norf 121 D5
  Norf 121 D5
  Suff 88 D2
Upper Strensham 80 D2
Upper Sundon . . .67 A5
Upper Swell. 64 A2

Upper Tean 112 B4
Upperthong 139 C4
Upperthorpe 141 C5
Upper Tillyrie . . .219 D6
Upperton 34 D2
Upper Tooting . . .49 B5
Upper Tote 259 C5
Uppertown
  Derbys 130 C4
  Highld. 281 A5
  Orkney 283 H5
Upper Town. 43 C4
Upper
  Treverward 93 D6
Upper Tysoe 81 C6
Upper Upham 45 B6
Upper
  Wardington 82 C1
Upper Weald 83 D4
Upper Weedon . . .82 B3
Upper Wield 33 B5
Upper
  Winchendon. . . .66 B2
Upper Witton 96 B3
Upper Woodend 244 A3
Upper Woodford . 31 B5
Upper Wootton . . .46 D3
Upper Wyche 79 C5
Uppingham 99 B5
Uppington 95 A4
Upsall 158 C3
Upshire. 68 C4
Up Somborne 32 B2
Upstreet 53 C4
Up Sydling 15 A6
Upthorpe 103 D5
Upton Cambs 100 D3
  Ches W. 127 C4
  Corn. 10 A3
  Dorset 16 B3
  Dorset 16 C1
  Hants 32 D2
  Hants 46 D1
  Leics. 97 B6
  Lincs. 132 A3
  Mers. 126 A2
  Norf 121 D5
  Northants 83 A4
  Notts 132 B2
  Notts 132 D2
  Oxon. 46 A3
  Pboro 100 A3
  Slough 48 B2
  Som 27 C4
  W Yorks 140 B2
Upton Bishop 62 A2
Upton Cheyney . .43 C5
Upton Cressett . .95 B4
Upton Cross. 10 D3
Upton Grey 33 A5
Upton Hellions . .12 A3
Upton Lovell 30 A3
Upton Magna 111 D4
Upton Noble 29 B7
Upton Pyne 13 B4
Upton St
  Leonard's 63 B4
Upton
  Scudamore 30 A2
Upton Snodsbury. 80 B2
Upton upon
  Severn 79 C6
Upton Warren 80 A2
Upwaltham 20 A2
Upware. 102 D1
Upwell. 101 A6
Upwey. 15 C6
Upwood 101 C4
Uradale 285 K6
Urafirth. 284 F5
Urchfont 44 D4
Urdimarsh 78 C3
Ure. 284 F4
Ure Bank 157 D7
Urgha 288 H2
Urishay Common 77 D7
Urlay Nook 167 D6
Urmston 137 D6
Urpeth. 179 D4
Urquhart Highld . .252 A1
  Moray. 266 C3
Urra 159 A4

Urray. 251 A7
Ushaw Moor 167 A5
Usk Brynbuga. . . .61 C5
Usselby. 142 D2
Usworth 179 D5
Utkinton 127 C5
Utley 147 C4
Uton. 12 B3
Utterby 143 D5
Uttoxeter 113 B4
Uwchmynydd . . .106 D1
Uxbridge 48 A3
Uyeasound. 284 C7
Uzmaston. 55 C5

V

Valley 122 C2
Valleyfield 173 C4
Valley Truckle. . . .10 C1
Valsgarth 284 B8
Valtos 259 B5
Van 92 C3
Vange 51 A4
Varteg 61 C4
Vatten 258 D2
Vaul 222 C3
Vaynor 60 B2
Veensgarth 285 J6
Velindre 77 D5
Vellow. 27 B5
Veness 282 E6
Venn Green 25 D4
Vennington 94 A1
Venn Ottery 13 B5
Venny Tedburn . . .12 B3
Ventnor 19 D4
Vernham Dean . . .46 D1
Vernham Street . .46 D1
Vernolds
  Common 94 C2
Verwood 17 A4
Veryan 4 D4
Vicarage. 14 C2
Vickerstown 153 D2
Victoria Corn 5 A4
  S Yorks 139 C4
Vidlin. 284 G6
Viewpark 207 D5
Vigo Village. 50 C3
Vinehall Street . . .37 D5
Vine's Cross 22 A3
Viney Hill 62 C2
Virginia Water . . .48 C2
Virginstow 11 B4
Vobster. 29 A7
Voe Shetland 284 E5
  Shetland. 285 G6
Vowchurch 78 D1
Voxter. 284 F5
Voy. 282 F3

W

Wackerfield. 167 C4
Wacton 104 B2
Wadbister. 285 J6
Wadborough. 80 C2
Waddesdon 66 B2
Waddingham 142 D1
Waddington
  Lancs 146 C1
  Lincs. 133 C4
Wadebridge. 9 D5
Wadeford 28 D3
Wadenhoe 100 C2
Wadesmill 68 B3
Wadhurst 36 C4
Wadshelf 130 B3
Wadsley 139 D6
Wadworth 140 D3
Waen Denb 125 C4
  Denb. 125 C6
Waen Fach. 109 D7
Waen
  Goleugoed 125 B5
Wag 274 B4
Wainfleet All
  Saints 135 D4

Wainfleet Bank. .135 D4
Wainfleet St
  Mary. 135 D5
Wainfleet Tofts. .135 D4
Wainhouse
  Corner 10 B2
Wainscott. 51 B4
Wainstalls 138 A3
Waitby. 155 A6
Waithe 143 C4
Wakefield. 139 A6
Wake Lady
  Green 159 B5
Wakerley 99 B6
Wakes Colne. 70 A2
Walberswick 105 D5
Walberton 20 B2
Walbottle 178 C3
Walcot Lincs 116 B3
  N Lincs 141 A6
  Shrops 94 C1
  Swindon 45 A5
  Telford 111 D4
Walcote Leics. . . .98 C2
  Warks. 80 B4
Walcot Green . . .104 C2
Walcott Lincs . . .133 D6
  Norf 121 B5
Walden 156 C4
Walden Head . . .156 C3
Walden Stubbs . .140 B3
Waldersey 101 A6
Walderslade 51 C4
Walderton 33 D6
Walditch 15 B4
Waldley 113 B5
Waldridge 179 D4
Waldringfield
  Heath 88 C3
Waldron 22 A3
Wales 131 A4
Walesby Lincs. . .142 D3
  Notts 132 B1
Walford Hereford. .62 A1
  Hereford 94 D1
  Shrops 110 C3
Walford Heath . .110 D3
Walgherton 111 A5
Walgrave 99 D5
Walhampton 18 B2
Walkden 137 C6
Walker 179 C4
Walker Barn 129 B4
Walkerburn 196 C2
Walker Fold. 145 C6
Walkeringham . .141 D5
Walkerith 141 D5
Walkern 68 A3
Walker's Green. . .78 C3
Walkerville 157 B6
Walkford 17 B6
Walkhampton 7 A4
Walkington 150 D2
Walkley 130 A3
Walk Mill 146 D2
Wall Northumb . .177 C7
  Staffs 96 A4
Wallaceton 183 D6
Wallacetown
  S Ayrs. 181 A4
  S Ayrs. 192 C3
Wallasey 136 D2
Wall Bank. 94 B3
Wallcrouch 37 C4
Wall Heath 96 C1
Wallingford 47 A4
Wallington Hants . 19 A4
  Herts 85 D4
  London 49 C5
Wallis 55 B6
Walliswood 35 C4
Walls 285 J4
Wallsend 179 C4
Wallston 41 D6
Wall under
  Heywood 94 B3
Wallyford 209 C6
Walmer. 53 D5
Walmer Bridge. .136 A3
Walmersley 137 B7

Walmley 96 B4
Walpole 105 D4
Walpole Cross
  Keys 118 D2
Walpole
  Highway. 118 D2
Walpole Marsh. .118 D1
Walpole St
  Andrew 118 D2
Walpole St
  Peter 118 D2
Walsall 96 B3
Walsall Wood 96 A3
Walsden 138 A2
Walsgrave on
  Sowe 97 C6
Walsham le
  Willows 103 D5
Walshaw. 137 B6
Walshford 148 B3
Walsoken 118 D1
Walston 195 B5
Walsworth 84 D4
Walters Ash. 66 D3
Walterston. 41 D5
Walterstone 61 A5
Waltham Kent . . .38 A3
  NE Lincs 143 C4
Waltham Abbey . .68 C3
Waltham Chase . . 33 D4
Waltham Cross. . .68 C3
Waltham on the
  Wolds 115 C6
Waltham St
  Lawrence 47 B6
Walthamstow 49 A6
Walton Cumb . . .176 C3
  Derbys 130 C3
  Leics. 98 C2
  Mers. 136 D2
  M Keynes 83 D5
  Pboro 100 A3
  Powys 77 B6
  Som 29 B4
  Staffs 112 B2
  Suff 88 D3
  Telford 111 D4
  Warks. 81 B5
  W Yorks 139 B6
  W Yorks 148 C3
Walton Cardiff . .80 D2
Walton East. 55 B6
Walton-in-
  Gordano 42 B3
Walton-le-Dale .137 A4
Walton-on-
  Thames 48 C4
Walton on the Hill
  Staffs 112 C3
  Sur. 35 A5
Walton-on-the-
  Naze 71 A6
Walton on the
  Wolds 114 D3
Walton-on-
  Trent 113 D6
Walton West 55 C4
Walwen 126 B2
Walwick 177 B7
Walworth 167 D5
Walworth Gate . .167 C5
Walwyn's Castle . 55 C4
Wambrook 14 A2
Wanborough Sur. . 34 B2
  Swindon 45 A6
Wandsworth 49 B5
Wangford 105 D5
Wanlockhead . . .183 A6
Wansford E Yorks 150 B3
  Pboro 100 B2
Wanstead 49 A7
Wanstrow 29 A7
Wanswell 62 C2
Wantage. 46 A1
Wapley 43 B6
Wappenbury 81 A6
Wappenham 82 C3
Warbleton 22 A4
Warblington 19 A6
Warborough 65 D6
Warboys 101 C5
Warbreck 144 D3

Warbstow........10 B3
Warburton......128 A2
Warcop.........165 D5
Warden Kent ... 52 B2
Northumb.....177 C7
Ward End.......96 C4
Ward Green.....87 A6
Wardhill......282 E7
Wardington.....82 C1
Wardlaw.......185 A5
Wardle Ches E .127 D6
Gtr Man 138 B2
Wardley 99 A5
Wardlow.......130 B1
Wardy Hill 101 C6
Ware Herts 68 B3
Kent 53 C4
Wareham........16 C3
Warehorne......38 B1
Warenford....189 A4
Waren Mill...199 C5
Warenton....199 C5
Wareside.......68 B3
Waresley Cambs ..84 B4
Worcs.........95 D6
Warfield.......48 B1
Warfleet........8 B2
Wargrave......47 B5
Warham.......119 A6
Warhill.......138 D2
Wark Northumb...177 B6
Northumb.....198 C2
Warkleigh......26 C1
Warkton........99 D5
Warkworth
Northants.......82 C1
Northumb.....189 C5
Warlaby......158 B2
Warland......138 A2
Warleggan......5 A6
Warlingham 35 A6
Warmfield....140 A1
Warmingham ..128 C2
Warmington
Northants......100 B2
Warks..........81 C7
Warminster....30 A2
Warmlake......37 A6
Warmley.......43 B5
Warmley Tower ..43 B5
Warmonds Hill ..83 A6
Warmsworth...140 C3
Warmwell......16 C1
Warndon.......80 B1
Warnford.......33 C5
Warnham.......35 C4
Warninglid.....35 D5
Warren Ches E .128 B3
Pembs.........55 E5
Warren Heath...88 C3
Warren Row 47 A6
Warren Street...51 D6
Warrington
M Keynes......83 B5
Warr..........127 A6
Warsash........18 A3
Warslow......129 D5
Warter.........52 D4
Warthermarske.157 D6
Warthill......149 B5
Wartling.......23 B4
Wartnaby......115 C5
Warton Lancs ..136 A3
Lancs.........154 D3
Northumb.....188 C3
Warks..........97 A5
Warwick........81 A5
Warwick Bridge 176 D2
Warwick on
Eden.........176 D2
Wasbister.....282 D4
Wasdale Head..163 D4
Washaway 5 A5
Washbourne 8 B1
Wash Common...46 C2
Washfold......157 A4
Washford.......27 A5
Washford Pyne..26 D3
Washingborough
............133 B5

Washington
T&W..........179 D5
W Sus..........21 A4
Wasing........46 C3
Waskerley.....166 A3
Wasperton.....81 B5
Wasps Nest....133 C5
Wass.........159 D4
Watchet........27 A5
Watchfield Oxon ..64 D3
Som...........28 A3
Watchgate.....154 B4
Watchhill.....175 D4
Watcombe.......8 A3
Watendlath....163 C5
Water Devon.....12 C2
Lancs.........138 A1
Waterbeach.....85 A6
Waterbeck.....175 A5
Waterden.....119 B5
Water End
E Yorks.......149 D6
Herts..........67 B5
Herts..........68 C2
Waterfall.....129 D5
Waterfoot E Renf 205 C5
Lancs.........138 A1
Waterford Hants ..18 B2
Herts..........68 B3
Waterhead Cumb 154 A2
Dumfries......185 C4
Waterheads....196 A1
Waterhouses
Durham.......167 A4
Staffs........129 D5
Wateringbury ...37 A4
Waterloo
Gtr Man 138 C2
Highld........247 B5
Mers..........136 D2
N Lanark......194 A3
Norf..........120 D4
Perth.........219 A5
Poole..........17 B4
Shrops........111 B4
Waterloo Port..123 D4
Waterlooville ...19 A5
Watermeetings..184 A2
Watermillock..164 C2
Water Newton..100 B3
Water Orton....97 B4
Waterperry 66 C1
Waterrow.......27 C5
Watersfield....20 A3
Waterside
Aberds.......257 D5
Blackburn....137 A6
Cumb.........175 D5
E Ayrs.......182 B2
E Ayrs.......205 D4
E Dunb.......207 C4
E Renf.......205 C5
Water's Nook ...137 C5
Waterstock 66 C1
Waterston......55 D5
Water Stratford .82 D3
Waters Upton ..111 D5
Water Yeat.....154 C1
Watford Herts ...67 D6
Northants......82 A3
Watford Gap ...96 A4
Wath N Yorks ..147 A5
N Yorks.......157 D7
N Yorks.......159 D5
Wath Brow....162 C3
Wath upon
Dearne.......140 C2
Watley's End....43 A5
Watlington Norf..118 D3
Oxon...........66 D1
Watnall.......114 A3
Watten........280 C4
Wattisfield...103 D6
Wattisham......87 B6
Wattlesborough
Heath........110 D2
Watton E Yorks..150 B3
Norf..........103 A5
Watton at Stone .68 B3
Wattston......207 C5
Wattstown......41 B5
Wauchan......238 D3

Waulkmill
Lodge........283 G4
Waun...........91 B6
Waunarlwydd ...57 C6
Waunclunda 58 B3
Waunfawr 107 A5
Waungron.......57 B5
Waunlwyd......60 C3
Waun-y-clyn....57 B4
Wavendon......83 D6
Waverbridge...175 D5
Waverton
Ches W.......127 C4
Cumb.........175 D5
Wavertree....126 A3
Wawne........150 D3
Waxham......121 C6
Waxholme.....143 A5
Way...........53 C5
Wayfield.......51 C4
Wayford........14 A4
Waymills.....111 A4
Wayne Green ...61 B6
Way Village 26 D3
Weachyburn ...268 D1
Weald..........64 C4
Wealdstone.....49 A4
Weardley.....148 C1
Weare..........42 D3
Weare Giffard...25 C5
Wearhead.....165 B6
Weasdale.....155 A5
Weasenham All
Saints........119 C5
Weasenham St
Peter........119 C5
Weatherhill....35 B6
Weaverham....127 B6
Weaverthorpe..160 D3
Webheath......80 A3
Wedderlairs...256 C3
Wedderlie....197 A5
Weddington....97 B6
Wedhampton....45 D4
Wedmore.......28 A4
Wednesbury....96 B2
Wednesfield ...96 A2
Weedon........66 B3
Weedon Bec....82 B3
Weedon Lois...82 C3
Weeford.......96 A4
Week...........26 D2
Weeke..........32 B3
Weekley........99 C5
Week St Mary...10 B3
Weel..........150 D3
Weeley.........71 A5
Weeley Heath...71 A5
Weem.........230 D2
Weeping Cross..112 C3
Weethley Gate...80 B3
Weeting......102 C3
Weeton E Yorks .143 A5
Lancs.........144 D3
N Yorks.......148 C1
Weetwood Hall..188 A3
Weir..........138 A1
Weir Quay.......6 A3
Welborne.....120 E2
Welbourn.....133 D4
Welburn N Yorks .149 A6
N Yorks.......159 C5
Welbury......158 A2
Welby.........116 B3
Welches Dam...101 C6
Welcombe......24 D3
Weld Bank....137 B4
Weldon.......189 D4
Welford Northants 98 C3
W Berks.......46 B2
Welford-on-
Avon..........81 B4
Welham Leics ...99 B4
Notts.........132 A2
Welham Green ...68 C2
Well Hants 33 A6
Lincs.........135 B4
N Yorks.......157 C6
Welland........79 C5
Wellbank.....221 A4
Welldale......175 B4
Well End.......48 A1

Wellesbourne ...81 B5
Well Heads 147 D4
Well Hill 50 C1
Welling........50 B1
Wellingborough..83 A5
Wellingham....119 C5
Wellingore....133 D4
Wellington Cumb 162 D3
Hereford......78 C2
Som...........27 C6
Telford.......111 D5
Wellington Heath 79 C5
Wellington Hill..148 D2
Wellow Bath....43 D6
IoW...........18 C2
Notts.........131 C6
Wellpond Green..68 A4
Wells..........29 A5
Wellsborough...97 A6
Wells Green...128 D1
Wells-Next-The-
Sea..........119 A6
Wellswood 8 A3
Well Town......13 A4
Wellwood.....208 B3
Welney........102 B1
Welshampton..110 B3
Welsh Bicknor...62 B1
Welsh End....111 B4
Welsh Frankton .110 B2
Welsh Hook.....55 B5
Welsh Newton...61 B6
Welshpool Y
Trallwng......93 A6
Welsh St Donats.41 D5
Welton Cumb ...164 A1
E Yorks.......142 A1
Lincs.........133 B5
Northants......82 A2
Welton Hill....133 A5
Welton le
Marsh........135 C4
Welton le Wold..134 A2
Welwick......143 A5
Welwyn........68 B2
Welwyn Garden
City..........68 B2
Wem..........111 C4
Wembdon......28 B2
Wembley.......49 A4
Wembury 7 C4
Wemworthy....12 A1
Wemyss Bay ...204 B1
Wenallt Ceredig..75 A5
Gwyn.........109 A4
Wendens Ambo ..85 D7
Wendlebury....65 B6
Wendling.....119 D6
Wendover......66 C3
Wendron 3 B4
Wendy.........85 C5
Wenfordbridge...10 D1
Wenhaston....105 D5
Wennington
Cambs........100 D4
Lancs.........155 D5
London........50 A2
Wensley Derbys .130 C2
N Yorks.......157 C4
Wentbridge...140 B2
Wentnor.......94 B1
Wentworth
Cambs........101 D6
S Yorks.......140 D1
Wenvoe........41 D6
Weobley.......78 B2
Weobley Marsh ..78 B2
Wereham......102 A2
Wergs.........95 A6
Wern Powys ...109 D4
Powys........110 D1
Wernffrwd.....57 C5
Wernyrheolydd...61 B5
Werrington Corn .10 C4
Pboro........100 A3
Staffs........112 A3
Wervin.......127 B4
Wesham.......144 D4
Wessington...130 D3
Westacott......25 B6
West Acre....119 D4
West Adderbury..82 D1

West Allerdean..198 B3
West Alvington ..7 C6
West Amesbury ..31 A5
West Anstey 26 C3
West Ashby....134 B2
West Ashling...19 A7
West Ashton....44 D2
West Auckland..167 C4
West Ayton....160 C3
West
Bagborough....27 B6
West Barkwith .133 A6
West Barnby ...169 D6
West Barns....210 C3
West Barsham ..119 B6
West Bay.......15 B4
West Beckham ..120 B3
West Bedfont...48 B3
West Benhar...208 D1
Westbere.......52 C3
West Bergholt...70 A3
West Bexington .15 C5
West Bilney...119 D4
West
Blatchington ..21 B5
Westborough ..115 A6
Westbourne
Bmouth........17 B4
Suff...........88 C2
West Bowling..147 D5
West Bradford..146 C1
West Bradley...29 B5
West Bretton..139 B5
West Bridgford.114 B3
West Bromwich ..96 B3
Westbrook......46 B2
West Buckland
Devon..........26 B1
Som...........28 C1
West Burrafirth.285 H4
West Burton
N Yorks.......156 C4
W Sus..........20 A2
Westbury Bucks ..82 D3
Shrops........94 A1
Wilts..........44 D2
Westbury Leigh ..44 D2
Westbury-on-
Severn........62 B3
Westbury on
Trym..........43 B4
Westbury-sub-
Mendip........29 A5
West
Butterwick ...141 C6
Westby.......144 D3
West Byfleet...48 C3
West Caister...121 D7
West Calder...208 D3
West Camel....29 C5
West Challow...46 A1
West
Chelborough ...15 A5
West
Chevington...189 D5
West Chiltington .20 A3
West Chiltington
Common......20 A3
West Chinnock...29 D4
West Chisenbury .45 D5
West Clandon...34 A3
West Cliffe.....39 A5
West Clyne....274 D2
West Clyth....275 A6
West Coker.....29 D5
Westcombe.....29 B6
West Compton
Dorset........15 B5
Som...........29 A5
Westcote......64 A3
Westcott Bucks ..66 B2
Devon.........13 A5
Sur...........35 B4
Westcott Barton .65 A5
West Cowick..141 A4
West Cranmore..29 A6
West Cross.....57 D6
West Cullery..245 B4
West Curry.....10 B3

West
Curthwaite ...175 D6
West Darlochan 190 C2
Westdean.......22 C3
West Dean Wilts .31 C6
W Sus..........20 A1
West Deeping..100 A3
Westdene.......21 B5
West Derby....136 D2
West Dereham..102 A2
West Didsbury.138 D1
West Ditchburn.189 A4
West Down.....25 A6
West Drayton
London........48 B3
Notts.........132 B2
West Ella.....142 A2
West End Bedford .84 B1
E Yorks.......150 D2
E Yorks.......151 D4
Hants..........32 D3
Lancs.........137 A6
Norf..........103 A5
Norf..........121 D7
N Som..........42 C3
N Yorks.......147 B5
Oxon...........65 C5
S Lanark......195 B4
Suff..........105 C5
Sur...........48 C2
S Yorks.......141 C4
Wilts..........30 C3
Wilts..........44 B3
W Sus..........21 A5
West End Green..47 C4
Wester
Aberchalder ..252 D1
Wester
Balgedie......219 D6
Wester
Culbeuchly ...268 C1
Westerdale
Highld........280 C3
N Yorks.......159 A5
Wester
Dechmont....208 D3
Wester Denoon .232 D1
Westerfield
Shetland......285 H5
Suff...........88 C2
Wester Fintray .245 A5
Westergate.....20 B2
Wester
Gruinards....263 A7
Westerham......36 A2
Westerhope...178 C3
Wester Lealty..264 C2
Westerleigh....43 B6
Wester Milton .253 A5
Wester
Newburn.....220 D4
Wester Quarff .285 K6
Wester Skeld...285 J4
Westerton Angus 233 C4
Durham.......167 B5
W Sus..........20 B1
Westerwick...285 J4
West Farleigh...37 A5
West Felton...110 C2
West Fenton...210 B1
West Ferry....221 A4
Westfield Cumb..162 B2
E Sus..........23 A6
Hereford......79 C5
Highld........279 B6
N Lanark......207 C5
Norf..........103 A5
W Loth.......208 C2
Westfields.....15 A7
Westfields of
Rattray......231 D5
West Firle.....22 B2
Westgate
Durham.......166 B2
N Lincs.......141 C5
Norf..........119 A5
Norf..........119 A6
Westgate on Sea .53 B5
West Ginge....46 A2

West Grafton.....45 C6
West Green.....47 D5
West
  Greenskares...268 C2
West Grimstead.31 C6
West Grinstead...35 D4
West Haddlesey 140 A3
West Haddon...98 D3
West Hagbourne.46 A3
West Hagley....96 C2
Westhall Aberds..256 D1
Suff...........105 C5
West Hall.....176 C3
West Hallam.....114 A2
West Halton.....141 A7
Westham Dorset..15 D6
E Sus..........22 B4
Som...........28 A4
West Ham......49 A7
Westhampnett..20 B1
West Handley..130 B3
West Hanney....65 D5
West
  Hanningfield...70 D1
West Hardwick..140 B2
West Harnham..31 C5
West Harptree..43 D4
West Hatch....28 C2
Westhay......28 A4
Westhead......136 C3
West Head....102 A1
West Heath
  Ches E......128 C3
  Hants........34 A1
  Hants........46 D3
West Helmsdale 274 C4
West Hendred....46 A2
West Heslerton..160 D3
Westhide......78 C3
Westhill Aberds .245 B5
  Highld........252 B3
West Hill Devon...13 B5
  E Yorks......151 A4
  N Som........42 B3
West Hoathly....35 C6
West Holme....16 C2
Westhope
  Hereford......78 B2
  Shrops........94 C2
West Horndon...50 A3
Westhorpe Lincs .117 B5
  Suff.........87 A6
West Horrington.29 A5
West Horsley....34 A3
West Horton...198 C4
West Hougham..39 A4
Westhoughton...137 C5
West Houlland..285 H4
Westhouse.....155 D5
West-houses...131 D4
Westhumble...35 A4
West
  Huntington...149 B5
West Hythe....38 B3
West Ilsley.....46 A2
Westing......284 C7
West Itchenor...19 A6
West Keal.....134 C3
West Kennett...45 C5
West Kilbride..204 D2
West Kingsdown .50 C2
West Kington...44 B2
West
  Kinharrachie..257 C4
West Kirby.....126 A2
West Knapton..160 D2
West Knighton..16 C1
West Knoyle....30 B2
West Kyloe....199 B4
Westlake.......7 B5
West Lambrook.28 D4
West Langdon...39 A5
West Langwell.273 D4
West Lavington
  Wilts.........44 D4
  W Sus........34 D1
West Layton...157 A5
West Lea.....168 A2
West Leake....114 C3

West
  Learmouth....198 C2
Westleigh Devon.25 C5
  Devon........27 D5
  Gtr Man.....137 C5
West Leigh......12 A1
Westleton.....89 A5
West Lexham..119 D5
  Suff.........87 A4
Westley
  Waterless....86 B2
West Lilling....149 A5
Westlington....66 B2
West Linton...175 B6
West Linton...195 A6
West Liss.....33 C6
West Littleton..43 B6
West Luccombe.26 A3
West Lulworth..16 C2
West Lutton...150 A2
West Lydford....29 B5
West Lyng....28 C3
West Lynn....118 C3
West Malling....37 A4
West Malvern...79 C5
West Marden...33 D6
West Marina...23 B5
West Markham.132 B2
Westmarsh....53 C4
West Marsh....143 B4
West Marton...146 B2
West Meon....146 B2
West Mersea...71 B4
Westmeston....21 A6
Westmill......68 A3
West Milton...175 B6
Westminster....49 B6
West Minster...51 B6
West Molesey...48 C4
West Monkton..28 C2
West Moors....17 A4
West Morriston .197 B5
Westmuir....232 C1
West Muir....232 B3
Westness....282 E4
West Ness....159 D5
West Newham...178 B2
Westnewton
  Cumb.......174 D4
  Northumb...198 C3
West Newton
  E Yorks......151 D4
  Norf........118 C3
West Norwood..49 B6
Westoe......179 C5
West Ogwell....12 D3
Weston Bath....43 C6
  Ches E......128 D2
  Devon........13 C6
  Dorset......15 D6
  Halton......127 A5
  Hants........33 C6
  Herts.........85 D4
  Lincs........117 C5
  Northants......82 C2
  Notts.......132 C2
  N Yorks......147 C5
  Shrops........94 B3
  Shrops......111 C4
  Staffs......112 C5
  W Berks......46 B1
Weston Beggard.78 C3
Westonbirt.....44 A2
Weston by
  Welland......99 B4
Weston Colville .86 B2
Westoncommon 110 C3
Weston Coyney.112 A3
Weston Favell...83 A4
Weston Green
  Cambs.......86 B2
  Norf........120 D3
Weston Heath..111 D5
Weston Hills....117 C5
Westoning.....84 D2
Weston-in-
  Gordano.....42 B3
Weston Jones..111 C6
Weston
  Longville....120 D3

Weston
  Lullingfields...110 C3
Weston-on-the-
  Green.......65 B6
Weston-on-
  Trent.......114 C2
Weston Patrick..33 A5
Weston Rhyn...110 B1
Weston-Sub-
  Edge.......80 C4
Weston-super-
  Mare.......42 C2
Weston Turville.66 B3
Weston under
  Lizard.......112 D2
Weston under
  Penyard....62 A2
Weston under
  Wetherley....81 A6
Weston Underwood
  Derbys......113 A6
  M Keynes....83 B5
Westonzoyland..28 B3
West Orchard...30 D2
West Overton...45 C5
Westow.......149 A6
West Park....168 B2
West Parley....17 B4
West Peckham..36 A4
West Pelton....179 D4
West Pennard...29 B5
West Pentire....4 A2
West Perry....84 A3
Westport Argyll ..27 A6
  Som.........28 D3
West Putford...25 D4
West
  Quantoxhead...27 A6
West Rainton...167 A6
West Rasen....133 A5
West Raynham..119 C5
West Retford...132 A1
Westrigg......208 D2
West Rounton..158 A3
West Row....102 D2
West Rudham..119 C5
West Runton...120 A3
Westruther....197 B5
Westry.......101 B5
West Saltoun...210 D1
West Sandwick.284 E6
West Scrafton..157 C4
West Sleekburn.179 A4
West Somerton .121 D6
West Stafford....16 C1
West Stockwith.141 D5
West Stoke....20 B1
West
  Stonesdale..156 A2
West Stoughton.28 A4
West Stour....30 C1
West Stourmouth 53 C4
West Stow.....103 D4
West Stowell....45 C5
West Strathan..277 B6
West Stratton...32 A4
West Street....37 A7
West Tanfield..157 D6
West Taphouse...5 A6
West Tarbert..202 B3
West Thorney...19 A6
West Thurrock..50 B3
West Tilbury....50 B3
West Tisted....33 C5
West Tofts Norf..103 B4
  Perth.......219 A6
West
  Torrington...133 A6
West Town Hants .19 B6
  N Som........42 C3
West Tytherley..32 C1
West Tytherton..44 B3
Westville.....114 A3
West Walton...118 D1
West Walton
  Highway.....118 D1
Westward.....175 D5
Westward Ho!...25 C5
Westwell Kent...38 A1
  Oxon........64 C3
Westwell Leacon.38 A1

West Wellow....32 D1
West Wemyss..209 A6
Westwick Cambs..85 A6
  Durham......166 D3
  Norf........121 C4
West Wick....42 C2
West Wickham
  Cambs......86 C2
  London......49 C6
West
  Williamston...55 D6
West
  Willoughby...116 A2
West Winch...118 D3
West Winterslow.31 B6
West Wittering...19 B6
West Witton...157 C4
Westwood Devon.13 B5
  Wilts.........44 D2
West Woodburn 177 A6
West Woodhay..46 C1
West Woodlands .30 A1
Westwoodside...141 D5
West Worldham.33 B6
West Worlington.26 D2
West Worthing..21 B4
West Wratting..86 B2
West Wycombe..66 D3
West Wylam...178 C3
West Yell.....284 E6
Wetheral.....176 D2
Wetherby.....148 C3
Wetherden.....87 A6
Wetheringsett..88 A2
Wethersfield...86 D3
Wethersta....284 G5
Wetherup Street.88 A2
Wetley Rocks..112 A3
Wettenhall....127 C6
Wetton.......129 D6
Wetwang....150 B2
Wetwood.....111 B6
Wexcombe.....45 D6
Wexham Street..48 A2
Weybourne....120 A3
Weybread....104 C3
Weybridge....48 C3
Weycroft.....14 B3
Weydale.....280 B3
Weyhill......32 A2
Weymouth.....15 D6
Whaddon Bucks..83 D5
  Cambs.......85 C5
  Glos.........63 B4
  Wilts.........31 C5
Whale.......164 C3
Whaley......131 B5
Whaley Bridge..129 A5
Whaley Thorns.131 B5
Whaligoe....281 D5
Whalley.....146 D1
Whalton.....178 A3
Wham.......146 A1
Whaplode.....117 C6
Whaplode
  Drove......117 D6
Whaplode St
  Catherine...117 C6
Wharfe......146 A1
Wharles.....144 D4
Wharncliffe
  Side.......139 D5
Wharram le
  Street......150 A1
Wharton.....127 C6
Wharton Green.127 C6
Whashton.....157 A5
Whatcombe....16 A2
Whatcote.....81 C6
Whatfield.....87 C6
Whatley Som....14 A3
  Som.........30 A1
Whatlington...35 A5
Whatstandwell.130 D3
Whatton.....115 B5
Whauphill....171 C6
Whaw.......156 A3
Wheatacre....105 B5
Wheatcroft...130 D3
Wheathampstead 68 B1
Wheathill.....95 C4
Wheatley Devon.13 B4

Hants........33 A6
  Oxon.........65 C6
  S Yorks......140 C3
  W Yorks......138 A3
Wheatley Hill..167 B6
Wheaton Aston.112 D2
Wheddon Cross..27 B4
Wheedlemont...255 D5
Wheelerstreet...34 B2
Wheelock....128 D2
Wheelock
  Heath......128 D2
Wheelton....137 A5
Wheen......232 A1
Wheldrake....149 C5
Whelford.....64 D2
Whelpley Hill...67 C4
Whempstead...68 A3
Whenby......149 A5
Whepstead....87 B4
Wherstead....88 C2
Wherwell.....32 A2
Wheston.....129 B6
Whetsted....37 B4
Whetstone....98 B2
Whicham.....153 B2
Whichford.....81 D6
Whickham....179 C4
Whiddon Down...12 B1
Whigstreet...232 D2
Whilton......82 A3
Whimble.....11 A4
Whimple.....13 B5
Whimpwell
  Green......121 C5
Whinburgh...103 A6
Whinnieliggate..173 C5
Whinnyfold...257 C5
Whippingham..18 B4
Whipsnade....67 B5
Whipton.....13 B4
Whirlow.....130 A3
Whisby.....133 C4
Whissendine..115 D6
Whissonsett...119 C6
Whistlefield
  Argyll......215 C4
  Argyll......215 C5
Whistley
  Green......47 B5
Whiston Mers..136 D3
  Northants......83 A5
  Staffs......112 A4
  Staffs......112 D2
  S Yorks......131 A4
Whitbeck....153 B2
Whitbourne....79 B5
Whitburn T&W..179 C6
  W Loth......208 D2
Whitburn
  Colliery....179 C6
Whitby Ches W .126 B3
  N Yorks......169 D6
Whitbyheath..126 B3
Whitchurch
  Bath........43 C5
  Bucks.......66 A2
  Cardiff......41 C6
  Devon........11 D5
  Hants........32 A3
  Hereford......62 B1
  Oxon.........47 B4
  Pembs.......54 B3
  Shrops.....111 A4
Whitchurch
  Canonicorum..14 B3
Whitchurch Hill..47 B4
Whitcombe....15 C7
Whitcott Keysett.93 C6
Whiteacre....254 B3
Whiteacre Heath.97 B5
Whitebridge..240 A2
Whitebrook....62 C1
Whiteburn...197 B4
Whitecairn...171 B4
Whitecairns..245 A6
Whitecastle...195 B5
Whitechapel..145 C5
Whitecleat...283 G6
White Coppice .137 B5
Whitecraig....209 C6
Whitecroft....62 C2

Whitecross Corn...9 D5
  Falk........208 C1
  Staffs......112 C2
Whiteface....264 B3
Whitefarland..202 D3
Whitefaulds...192 E2
Whitefield
  Gtr Man.....137 C7
  Perth.......219 A6
Whiteford....256 D2
Whitegate....127 C6
Whitehall
  Blackburn....137 A5
  W Sus........35 D4
Whitehall
  Village....282 E7
Whitehaven..162 C2
Whitehill......33 B6
Whitehills
  Aberds......268 C1
  S Lanark.....205 C6
Whitehough..129 A5
Whitehouse
  Aberds......244 A3
  Argyll......202 B3
Whiteinch...205 B5
Whitekirk....210 B2
White Lackington 15 B7
White Ladies
  Aston........80 B2
Whitelaw....205 D6
Whiteleas....179 C5
Whiteley Bank..19 C4
Whiteley Green .129 B4
Whiteley Village..48 C3
White Lund....144 A4
Whitemans
  Green......35 D6
White Mill.....58 C1
Whitemire....253 A5
Whitemoor.....5 B4
Whitemore...128 C3
Whitenap.....32 C2
White Ness...285 J5
White Notley...70 B1
Whiteoak Green..64 B4
Whiteparish....31 C6
White Pit....134 B3
White Post...131 D6
Whiterashes..256 D3
White Rocks...61 A6
White Roding...69 B5
Whiterow....281 D5
Whiteshill.....63 C4
Whiteside
  Northumb....177 C5
  W Loth......208 D2
Whitesmith....22 A3
Whitestaunton..28 D2
Whitestone Devon.12 B3
  Devon........25 A5
  Warks........97 C6
Whitestones..268 D3
Whitestreet
  Green......87 D5
Whitewall
  Corner.....159 D6
Whiteway Glos...63 B5
  Glos.........63 C4
Whitewell
  Aberds......269 C4
  Lancs......145 C6
Whitewell
  Bottom.....138 A1
Whiteworks...11 D7
Whitfield Kent...39 A5
  Northants......82 D3
  Northumb....177 D5
  S Glos........62 D2
Whitford Devon...14 B2
  Flint.......125 B6
Whitgift.....141 A6
Whitgreave....112 C2
Whithorn.....171 C6
Whiting Bay..191 C6
Whitkirk.....148 D2
Whitland......56 A1
Whitletts....192 C3
Whitley N Yorks .140 A3
  Reading......47 B5
  Wilts.........44 C2

Whitley Bay 179 B5
Whitley Chapel . . 178 D1
Whitley Lower . . 139 B5
Whitley Row 36 A2
Whitlock's End . . . 96 D4
Whitminster 62 C3
Whitmore 112 A2
Whitnage 27 D5
Whitnash 81 A6
Whitney-on-Wye 77 C6
Whitrigg Cumb . . 163 A5
Cumb 175 C5
Whitsbury 31 D5
Whitsome 198 A2
Whitson 42 A2
Whitstable 52 C3
Whitstone 10 B3
Whittingham 188 B3
Whittingslow 94 C2
Whittington Glos . 63 A6
Lancs 155 D5
Norf 102 B3
Shrops 110 B2
Staffs 95 C6
Staffs 97 A4
Worcs 80 B1
Whittlebury 82 C3
Whittle-le-
Woods 137 A4
Whittlesey 101 B4
Whittlesford 85 C6
Whittlestone
Head 137 B6
Whitton Borders . 187 A6
N Lincs 141 A7
Northumb 188 C3
Powys 77 A6
Shrops 94 D3
Stockton 167 C6
Suff 88 C2
Whittonditch 45 B6
Whittonstall 178 D2
Whitway 46 D2
Whitwell Derbys . 131 B5
Herts 68 A1
IoW 18 D4
N Yorks 157 B6
Rutland 99 A6
Whitwell-on-the-
Hill 149 A6
Whitwell Street . 120 C3
Whitwick 114 D2
Whitwood 140 A2
Whitworth 138 B1
Whixall 111 B4
Whixley 148 B3
Whoberley 97 D6
Whorlton
Durham 166 D4
N Yorks 158 A3
Whygate 177 B5
Whyle 78 A3
Whyteleafe 35 A6
Wibdon 62 D1
Wibsey 147 D5
Wibtoft 98 C1
Wichenford 79 A5
Wichling 37 A7
Wick Bmouth 17 B5
Devon 13 A6
Highld 281 C5
S Glos 43 B6
Shetland 285 K6
V Glam 40 D4
Wilts 31 C5
Worcs 80 C2
W Sus 20 B3
Wicken Cambs . . 102 D1
Northants 83 D4
Wicken Bonhunt . 85 D6
Wickenby 133 A5
Wicken Green
Village 119 B5
Wickersley 140 D2
Wickford 70 D1
Wickham Hants . . 33 D4
W Berks 46 B1
Wickham
Bishops 70 B2
Wickhambreaux . . 53 D4
Wickhambrook . . 86 B3
Wickhamford 80 C3

Wickham Market . 88 B4
Wickhampton . . . 105 A5
Wickham St Paul 87 D4
Wickham Skeith . 88 A1
Wickham Street
Suff 86 B3
Suff 88 A1
Wick Hill 47 C5
Wicklewood 104 A1
Wickmere 120 B3
Wick St
Lawrence 42 C2
Wickwar 43 A6
Widdington 86 D1
Widdrington . . . 189 D5
Widdrington
Station 189 D5
Widecombe in the
Moor 12 D2
Widegates 6 B1
Widemouth Bay . 10 A3
Wide Open 179 B4
Widewall 283 H5
Widford Essex . . . 69 C6
Herts 68 B4
Widham 45 A4
Widmer End 66 D3
Widmerpool 115 C4
Widnes 127 A5
Wigan 137 C4
Wiggaton 13 B6
Wiggenhall St
Germans 118 D2
Wiggenhall St Mary
Magdalen 118 D2
Wiggenhall St Mary
the Virgin 118 D2
Wigginton Herts . 67 B4
Oxon 81 D6
Staffs 97 A5
York 149 B4
Wigglesworth . . 146 B2
Wiggonby 175 C5
Wiggonholt 20 A3
Wighill 148 C3
Wighton 119 B6
Wigley 32 D2
Wigmore Hereford 78 A2
Medway 51 C5
Wigsley 132 B3
Wigsthorpe 100 C2
Wigston 98 B3
Wigthorpe 131 A5
Wigtoft 117 B5
Wigton 175 D5
Wigtown 171 B6
Wigtwizzle 139 D5
Wike 148 C2
Wike Well End . . 141 B4
Wilbarston 99 C5
Wilberfoss 149 B6
Wilberlee 138 B3
Wilburton 101 D6
Wilby Norf 103 C6
Northants 83 A5
Suff 104 D3
Wilcot 45 C5
Wilcott 110 D2
Wilcrick 42 A3
Wilday Green . . . 130 B3
Wildboarclough 129 C4
Wilden Bedford . . 84 B2
Worcs 95 D6
Wildhern 46 D1
Wildhill 68 C2
Wildmoor 96 D2
Wildsworth 141 D6
Wilford 114 B3
Wilkesley 111 A5
Wilkhaven 265 B5
Wilkieston 208 D4
Willand 27 D5
Willaston Ches E 128 D1
Ches W 126 B3
Willen 83 C5
Willenhall W Mid . 96 B2
W Mid 97 D6
Willerby E Yorks . 150 D3
N Yorks 160 D4
Willersey 80 D4
Willersley 77 C7
Willesborough . . . 38 A2

Willesborough
Lees 38 A2
Willesden 49 A5
Willett 27 B6
Willey Shrops . . . 95 B4
Warks 98 C1
Willey Green 34 A2
Williamscot 82 C1
Willian 84 D4
Willingale 69 C5
Willingdon 22 B3
Willingham by
Stow 132 A3
Willingham
Corner 127 C5
Willisham Tye . . . 87 B6
Willitoft 149 D6
Williton 27 A5
Willoughbridge . 111 A6
Willoughby Lincs 135 B4
Warks 82 A2
Willoughby-on-the-
Wolds 115 C4
Willoughby
Waterleys 98 B2
Willoughton . . . 142 D1
Willows Grn 69 B7
Willsbridge 43 B5
Willsworthy 11 C6
Wilmcote 81 B4
Wilmington Devon 14 B2
E Sus 22 B3
Kent 50 B2
Wilminstone 11 D5
Wilmslow 128 A3
Wilnecote 97 A5
Wilpshire 145 D6
Wilsden 147 D4
Wilsford Lincs . . 116 A3
Wilts 31 B5
Wilts 45 D5
Wilsill 147 A5
Wilsley Pound . . . 37 C5
Wilsom 33 B6
Wilson 114 C2
Wilsontown 195 A4
Wilstead 84 C2
Wilsthorpe 116 D3
Wilstone 67 B4
Wilton Borders . 186 B3
Cumb 162 C3
N Yorks 160 C4
Redcar 168 D3
Wilts 31 B4
Wilts 45 C6
Wimbish 86 D1
Wimbish Green . . 86 D2
Wimblebury 112 D4
Wimbledon 49 B5
Wimblington . . . 101 B6
Wimborne
Minster 17 B4
Wimborne St
Giles 31 D4
Wimbotsham . . . 102 A2
Wimpson 32 D2
Wimpstone 81 C5
Wincanton 29 C7
Wincham 128 B1
Winchburgh . . . 208 C3
Winchcombe 63 A6
Winchelsea 23 A7
Winchelsea
Beach 23 A7
Winchester 32 C3
Winchet Hill 37 B5
Winchfield 47 D5
Winchmore Hill
Bucks 67 D4
London 68 D3
Wincle 129 C4
Wincobank 140 D1
Windermere 154 B3
Winderton 81 C6
Windhill 252 B1
Windhouse 284 D6

Windlehurst . . . 129 A4
Windlesham 48 C2
Windley 113 A7
Windmill Hill
E Sus 22 A4
Som 28 D3
Windrush 64 B2
Windsor N Lincs . 141 B5
Windsor 48 B2
Windsoredge 63 C4
Windygates 220 D3
Windyknowe . . . 208 D2
Windywalls 197 C6
Wineham 35 D5
Winestead 143 A4
Winewall 146 C3
Winfarthing 104 C2
Winford IoW 19 C4
N Som 43 C4
Winforton 77 C6
Winfrith
Newburgh 16 C2
Wing Bucks 66 A3
Rutland 99 A5
Wingate 168 B2
Wingates
Gtr Man 137 C5
Northumb 189 D4
Wingerworth . . 130 C3
Wingfield C Beds . 67 A4
Suff 104 D3
Wingham 53 D4
Wingmore 38 A3
Wingrave 66 B3
Winkburn 132 D2
Winkfield 48 B2
Winkfield Row . . 48 B1
Winkhill 129 D5
Winklebury 47 D4
Winkleigh 12 A1
Winksley 157 D6
Winkton 17 B5
Winlaton 178 C3
Winless 281 C5
Winmarleigh . . . 145 C4
Winnal 78 D2
Winnall 32 C3
Winnersh 47 B5
Winscales 162 B3
Winscombe 42 D3
Winsford Ches W 127 C6
Som 27 B4
Winsham 14 A3
Winshill 113 C6
Winskill 164 B3
Winslade 33 A5
Winsley 44 C2
Winslow 66 A2
Winson 64 C1
Winson Grn 96 C3
Winsor 32 D2
Winster Cumb . . 154 B3
Derbys 130 C2
Winston Durham . 166 D4
Suff 88 A2
Winstone 63 C5
Winston Green . . 88 A2
Winswell 25 D5
Winterborne
Clenston 16 A2
Winterborne
Herringston . . 15 C6
Winterborne
Houghton 16 A2
Winterborne
Kingston 16 B2
Winterborne
Monkton 15 C6
Winterborne
Stickland 16 A2
Winterborne
Whitechurch . . 16 A2
Winterborne
Zelston 16 B2
Winterbourne
S Glos 43 A5
W Berks 46 B2
Winterbourne
Abbas 15 B6
Winterbourne
Bassett 45 B5

Winterbourne
Dauntsey 31 B5
Winterbourne
Down 43 B5
Winterbourne
Earls 31 B5
Winterbourne
Gunner 31 B5
Winterbourne
Monkton 45 B5
Winterbourne
Steepleton . . . 15 C6
Winterbourne
Stoke 31 A4
Winterburn 146 B3
Winter Gardens . 51 A4
Winteringham . . 17 A4
Winterley 128 D2
Wintersett 140 B1
Wintershill 32 D4
Winterton 142 B1
Winterton-on-
Sea 121 D6
Winthorpe Lincs 135 C5
Notts 132 D3
Winton Bmouth . . 17 B4
Cumb 165 D5
N Yorks 158 B3
Wintringham . . . 160 D2
Winwick Cambs . 100 C3
Northants 98 D3
Warr 137 D5
Wirksworth 130 D2
Wirswall 111 A4
Wisbech 101 A6
Wisbech St
Mary 101 A6
Wisborough
Green 34 D3
Wiseton 132 A2
Wishaw N Lanark 194 A2
Warks 97 B4
Wisley 34 A3
Wispington 134 B2
Wissenden 37 B7
Wissett 105 D4
Wistanstow 94 C2
Wistanswick . . . 111 C5
Wistaston 128 D1
Wistaston
Green 128 D1
Wiston Pembs . . . 55 C6
S Lanark 195 C4
W Sus 21 A4
Wistow Cambs . . 101 C4
N Yorks 149 D4
Wiswell 146 D1
Witcham 101 C6
Witchampton . . . 16 A3
Witchford 101 D7
Witham 70 B2
Witham Friary . . . 30 A1
Witham on the
Hill 116 D3
Withcall 134 A2
Withdean 21 B6
Witherenden Hill 36 D4
Witheridge 26 D3
Witherley 97 B6
Withern 135 A4
Withernsea 143 A5
Withernwick . . . 151 C4
Withersdale
Street 104 C3
Withersfield 86 C2
Witherslack 154 C3
Withiel 5 A4
Withiel Florey . . 27 B4
Withington Glos . 63 B6
Gtr Man 138 D1
Hereford 78 C3
Shrops 111 D4
Staffs 112 B4
Withington
Green 128 B3
Withleigh 27 D4
Withnell 137 A5
Withybrook 98 C1
Withycombe 27 A5

Withycombe
Raleigh 13 C5
Withyham 36 C2
Withypool 26 B3
Witley 34 C2
Witnesham 88 B2
Witney 65 B4
Wittering 100 A3
Wittersham 37 D6
Witton Angus . . 232 A3
Worcs 80 A1
Witton Bridge . . 121 B5
Witton Gilbert . . 167 A5
Witton-le-Wear 166 B4
Witton Park 167 B4
Wiveliscombe . . . 27 C5
Wivelrod 33 B5
Wivelsfield 35 D6
Wivelsfield
Green 35 D6
Wivenhoe 71 A4
Wivenhoe Cross . 71 A4
Wiveton 120 A2
Wix 71 A5
Wixford 80 B3
Wixhill 111 C4
Wixoe 86 C3
Woburn 83 D6
Woburn Sands . . 83 D6
Wokefield Park . . 47 C4
Woking 34 A3
Wokingham 47 C6
Wolborough 12 D3
Woldingham 35 A6
Wold Newton
E Yorks 160 D4
NE Lincs 143 D4
Wolfclyde 195 C5
Wolferton 118 C3
Wolfhill 219 A6
Wolf's Castle . . . 55 B5
Wolfsdale 55 B5
Woll 186 A3
Wollaston
Northants 83 A6
Shrops 110 D2
Wollaton 114 B3
Wollerton 111 B5
Wollescote 96 C2
Wolsingham . . . 166 B3
Wolstanton 112 A2
Wolston 97 D7
Wolvercote 65 C5
Wolverhampton . 96 B2
Wolverley Shrops 110 B3
Worcs 95 D6
Wolverton Hants . 46 D3
M Keynes 83 C5
Warks 81 A5
Wolverton
Common 46 D3
Wolvesnewton . . 61 D6
Wolvey 98 C1
Wolviston 168 C2
Wombleton 159 C5
Wombourne 95 B6
Wombwell 140 C1
Womenswold . . . 53 D4
Womersley 140 B3
Wonastow 61 B6
Wonersh 34 B3
Wonson 12 C1
Wonston 32 B3
Wooburn 48 A2
Wooburn Green . 48 A2
Woodacott 11 A4
Woodale 156 D4
Woodbank 190 D2
Woodbastwick . . 121 D5
Woodbeck 132 B2
Woodborough
Notts 115 A4
Wilts 45 D5
Woodbridge
Dorset 29 D7
Suff 88 C3
Woodbury 13 C5
Woodbury
Salterton 13 C5

Woodchester 63 C4
Woodchurch Kent. 38 B1
Mers..........126 A2
Woodcombe 27 A4
Woodcote 47 A4
Woodcott.......46 D2
Woodcroft 62 D1
Woodcutts 30 D3
Wood Dalling ..120 C2
Woodditton 86 B2
Woodeaton 65 B6
Woodend Cumb ..153 A2
Northants.....82 C3
W Sus........19 A7
Wood End Herts ..68 A3
Warks.........96 D4
Warks.........97 B5
Wood Enderby ..134 C2
Woodend Green..82 C3
Woodfalls.....31 C5
Woodfield Oxon...65 A6
S Ayrs.......192 C3
Wood Field 35 A4
Woodford Corn ..24 D3
Devon.........8 B1
Glos..........62 D2
Gtr Man......128 A3
London........68 D4
Northants.....99 D6
Woodford Bridge 68 D4
Woodford Halse..82 B2
Woodgate Norf ..120 D2
W Mid........96 C2
Worcs........80 A2
W Sus........20 B2
Woodgreen 31 D5
Wood Green 68 D3
Woodhall Herts ..68 B2
Invclyd......204 A3
N Yorks......156 B3
Woodhall Spa..134 C1
Woodham 48 C3
Woodham
Ferrers......70 D1
Woodham
Mortimer.....70 C2
Woodham Walter 70 C2
Woodhaven ...220 B4
Wood Hayes ...96 A2
Woodhead 256 C2
Woodhey 137 B6
Woodhill......95 C5
Woodhorn 179 A4
Woodhouse
Leics..........114 D3
N Lincs......141 C5
S Yorks......131 A4
W Yorks......140 A1
W Yorks......148 D1
Woodhouse
Eaves........114 D3
Woodhouselee..209 D5
Woodhouselees 175 A6
Woodhouse
Park 128 A3
Woodhouses...113 D5
Woodhurst....101 D5
Woodingdean ..21 B6
Woodkirk 139 A5
Woodland
Devon.........8 A1
Durham 166 C3
Woodlands
Aberds.......245 C4
Dorset.......17 A4
Hants........32 D2
Highld.......264 D1
N Yorks......148 B2
S Yorks......140 C3
Woodlands Park.47 B6
Woodlands St
Mary 46 B1
Wood Lanes ...129 A4
Woodleigh 7 C6
Woodlesford...139 A6

Woodley Gtr Man 138 D2
Wokingham 47 B5
Woodmancote
Glos..........62 D3
Glos..........63 A5
Glos..........63 C6
W Sus........19 A6
W Sus........21 A5
Woodmancott...33 A4
Woodmansey ..150 D3
Woodmansterne .35 A5
Woodminton ...31 C4
Woodnesborough
...............53 D5
Woodnewton ..100 B2
Wood Norton ..120 C2
Woodplumpton .145 D5
Woodrising ...103 A5
Woodseaves
Shrops.......111 B5
Staffs........112 C1
Woodsend 45 B6
Woodsetts ...131 A5
Woodsford.....16 B1
Wood's Green ...36 C4
Woodside
Aberdeen 245 B6
Aberds 257 B5
Brack 48 B2
Fife.........220 D4
Hants........18 B2
Herts........68 C2
Perth 220 A2
Woodside of
Arbeadie 245 C4
Woodstock Oxon .65 B5
Pembs 55 B6
Wood Street
Norf.........121 C5
Sur..........34 A2
Woodthorpe
Derbys......131 B4
Leics........114 D3
Lincs........135 A4
York........149 C4
Woodton 104 B3
Woodtown Devon .25 C5
Devon.........25 C5
Woodvale.....136 B2
Woodville....113 D7
Woodyates.....31 D4
Woofferton ...78 A3
Wookey 29 A5
Wookey Hole...29 A5
Wool 16 C2
Woolacombe ...25 A5
Woolage Green .39 A4
Woolaston 62 D1
Woolavington ..28 A3
Woolbeding....34 D1
Wooldale 139 C4
Wooler 188 A2
Woolfardisworthy
Devon........12 A3
Devon........24 C4
Woolfords
Cottages 195 A5
Woolhampton...46 C3
Woolhope 79 D4
Woolhope
Cockshoot....79 D4
Woolland 16 A1
Woollaton 25 D5
Woolley Bath ...43 C6
Cambs........100 D3
Corn..........24 D3
Derbys.......130 C3
W Yorks......139 B6
Woolmer Green 80 A2
Woolmer Green ..68 B2
Woolpit.......87 A5
Woolscott 82 A1
Woolsington ..178 C3
Woolstanwood .128 D1
Woolstaston ..94 B2
Woolsthorpe
Lincs........115 B6
Lincs........116 C2

Woolston Devon....7 C6
Shrops.......94 C2
Shrops.......110 C2
Soton........32 D3
Warr........127 A6
Woolstone
M Keynes 83 D5
Oxon.........45 A6
Woolton 127 A4
Woolton Hill ...46 C2
Woolverstone ..88 D2
Woolverton ...44 D1
Woolwich.....50 B1
Woolwich Ferry .50 B1
Woonton 78 B1
Wooperton ...188 A3
Woore........111 A6
Wootten Green.104 D3
Wootton Bedford ..84 C2
Hants........17 B6
Hereford 78 B1
Kent..........39 A4
N Lincs......142 B2
Northants.....83 B4
Oxon.........65 B5
Oxon.........65 C5
Shrops.......94 D2
Shrops.......110 C2
Staffs........112 C2
Staffs........113 A5
Wootton Bridge ..18 B4
Wootton
Common 18 B4
Wootton
Courtenay 27 A4
Wootton
Fitzpaine 14 B3
Wootton Rivers..45 C5
Wootton St
Lawrence 45 C5
Wootton Wawen .81 A4
Worcester 79 B6
Worcester Park ..49 C5
Wordsley 96 C1
Worfield......95 B5
Work 282 F5
Workington ..162 B2
Worksop......131 B5
Worlaby 142 B2
World's End....46 B2
Worle 42 C2
Worleston ...127 D6
Worlingham ..105 C5
Worlington ...102 D2
Worlingworth..88 A3
Wormald Green .148 A2
Wormbridge ...78 D2
Wormegay 118 D3
Wormelow Tump 78 D2
Wormhill 129 B6
Wormingford ..87 D5
Worminghall ..66 C1
Wormington ...80 D3
Worminster ...29 A5
Wormit 220 B3
Wormleighton .82 B1
Wormley Herts...68 C3
Sur..........34 C2
Wormley West
End 68 C3
Wormshill 37 A6
Wormsley 78 C2
Worplesdon...34 A2
Worrall 139 D6
Worsbrough ..139 C6
Worsbrough
Common 139 C6
Worsley 137 C6
Worstead 121 C5
Worsthorne ..146 D2
Worston 146 C1
Worswell 7 C4
Worth Kent 53 D5
W Sus........35 C6
Wortham 104 D1
Worthen 94 A1
Worthenbury..110 A2
Worthing Norf ..120 D1
W Sus........21 B4

Worthington 114 C2
Worth Matravers .16 D3
Worting.......47 D4
Wortley S Yorks .139 D6
W Yorks......147 D6
Worton N Yorks ..156 B3
Wilts.........44 D3
Wortwell 104 C3
Wotherton 93 A6
Wotter........7 A4
Wotton 35 B4
Wotton-under-
Edge 62 D3
Wotton
Underwood....66 B1
Woughton on the
Green 83 D5
Wouldham 51 C4
Wrabness 88 D2
Wrafton 25 B5
Wragby Lincs ..133 B6
W Yorks......140 B2
Wragholme ..143 D5
Wramplingham .104 A2
Wrangbrook ..140 B2
Wrangham ...256 C1
Wrangle 135 D4
Wrangle Bank..135 D4
Wrangle
Lowgate.....135 D4
Wrangway 27 D6
Wrantage 28 C3
Wrawby 142 C2
Wraxall Dorset ..15 A5
N Som........42 B3
Som..........29 B6
Wray 145 A6
Wraysbury 48 B3
Wrayton 155 D5
Wrea Green...144 D3
Wreay Cumb ..164 A2
Cumb........164 C2
Wrecclesham ..34 B1
Wrekenton ...179 D4
Wrelton 159 C6
Wrenbury 111 A4
Wrench Green ..160 C3
Wreningham ..104 B2
Wrentham ...105 C5
Wrenthorpe...139 A6
Wressle E Yorks .149 D6
N Lincs......142 C1
Wrestlingworth .85 C4
Wretham 103 C5
Wretton 102 B2
Wrexham
Wrecsam....126 D3
Wrexham Industrial
Estate.......110 A2
Wribbenhall ...95 D5
Wrightington
Bar 136 B4
Wrinehill 111 A6
Wrington 42 C3
Writhlington ..43 D6
Writtle 69 C6
Wrockwardine .111 D5
Wroot 141 C5
Wrotham 36 A4
Wrotham Heath .36 A4
Wroughton ...45 A5
Wroxall IoW ...19 D4
Warks.........97 D5
Wroxeter 94 A3
Wroxham 121 D5
Wroxton......81 C7
Wyaston 113 A5
Wyberton 117 A6
Wyboston 84 B3
Wybunbury ..111 A6
Wychbold.....80 A2
Wych Cross ...36 C2
Wyck........33 B6
Wyck Rissington .64 A2
Wycoller 146 D3
Wycomb......115 C5
Wycombe Marsh .66 D3
Wyddial 85 D5

Wye 38 A2
Wyesham 61 B7
Wyfordby 115 D5
Wyke Dorset ...30 C1
Shrops.......95 A4
Sur..........34 A2
W Yorks......139 A4
Wykeham
N Yorks......159 D7
N Yorks......160 C3
Wyken 97 C6
Wyke Regis ...15 D6
Wykey 110 C2
Wylam 178 C3
Wylde Green ...96 B4
Wyllie 41 B6
Wylye 31 B4
Wymering 19 A5
Wymeswold ..115 C4
Wymington ...83 A6
Wymondham
Leics........115 D6
Norf.........104 A2
Wyndham 40 B4
Wynford Eagle ..15 B5
Wyng........283 H4
Wynyard Village 168 C2
Wyre Piddle....80 C2
Wysall 115 C4
Wythall 96 D3
Wytham 65 C5
Wythburn 163 C6
Wythenshawe..128 A3
Wythop Mill...163 B4
Wyton.......101 D4
Wyverstone ...87 A6
Wyverstone
Street........87 A6
Wyville 116 C1
Wyvis Lodge ..263 C6

Y

Yaddlethorpe ..141 C6
Yafford......18 C3
Yafforth.....158 B2
Yalding 37 A4
Yanworth 63 B6
Yapham......149 B6
Yapton......20 B2
Yarburgh 143 D5
Yarcombe 14 A2
Yard.........27 B5
Yardley 96 C4
Yardley Gobion..83 C4
Yardley Hastings 83 B5
Yardro.......77 B6
Yarkhill......79 C4
Yarlet.......112 C3
Yarlington 29 C6
Yarlside 153 D3
Yarm........168 D2
Yarmouth 18 C2
Yarnbrook 44 D2
Yarnfield 112 B2
Yarnscombe ...25 C6
Yarnton......65 B5
Yarpole.......78 A2
Yarrow 196 D2
Yarrow Feus ..196 D2
Yarsop.......78 C2
Yarwell......100 B2
Yate.........43 A6
Yateley 47 C6
Yatesbury 45 B4
Yattendon 46 B3
Yatton Hereford ..78 A2
N Som........42 C3
Yatton Keynell ..44 B2
Yaverland 19 C5
Yaxham......120 D2
Yaxley Cambs ..100 B3
Suff.........104 D2

Yealand
Redmayne....154 D4
Yealmpton.......7 B4
Yearby 168 C4
Yearsley 159 D4
Yeaton......110 D3
Yeaveley.....113 A5
Yedingham ...160 D2
Yeldon 84 A2
Yelford 65 C4
Yelland 25 B5
Yelling 85 A4
Yelvertoft 98 D2
Yelverton Devon ...7 A4
Norf.........104 A3
Yenston 29 C7
Yeoford 12 B2
Yeolmbridge....10 C4
Yeo Mill 26 C3
Yeovil 29 D5
Yeovil Marsh....29 D5
Yeovilton 29 C5
Yerbeston 55 D6
Yesnaby 282 F3
Yetlington ...188 C3
Yetminster ...29 D5
Yettington 13 C5
Yetts o'
Muckhart....219 D5
Y Felinheli ..123 D5
Y Ffôr 106 C3
Y-Ffrith 125 A5
Yieldshields...194 A3
Yiewsley 48 A3
Ynysboeth ...41 B5
Ynysddu 41 B6
Ynysgyfflog ...90 A4
Ynyshir 41 B5
Ynyslas 90 C4
Ynys-meudwy...59 E4
Ynystawe 40 A1
Ynysybwl 41 B5
Yockenthwaite ..156 D3
Yockleton.....110 D2
Yokefleet 141 A6
Yoker 205 B5
Yonder Bognie ..255 B6
York.........149 B4
Yorkletts 52 C2
Yorkley 62 C2
York Town 47 C5
Yorton.......111 C4
Youlgreave ...130 C2
Youlstone.....24 D3
Youlthorpe ...149 B6
Youlton......148 A3
Young's End ...70 B1
Young Wood ..133 B6
Yoxall.......113 D5
Yoxford......89 A4
Ysbyty-Cynfyn ..75 A6
Ysbyty Ifan...108 A3
Ysbyty Ystwyth..75 A6
Ysceifiog 125 B6
Yspitty.......57 C5
Ystalyfera....59 E4
Ystrad........41 B4
Ystrad Aeron ..75 C4
Ystradfellte...59 D6
Ystradffin....76 C1
Ystradgynlais..59 D4
Ystradmeurig...75 B6
Ystrad-mynach..41 B6
Ystradowen
Carms.......59 D4
V Glam.......41 D5
Ystumtuen....75 A6
Ythanbank....257 C4
Ythanwells...256 C1
Ythsie.......256 C3

Z

Zeal
Monachorum..12 A2
Zeals 30 B1
Zelah........4 B3
Zennor........2 B2